Priests, Prelates and People

NICHOLAS ATKIN AND FRANK TALLETT

PRIESTS, PRELATES AND PEOPLE
A History of European Catholicism since 1750

OXFORD
UNIVERSITY PRESS

2003

For Ben, Charlotte, Florence and Harriet

OXFORD
UNIVERSITY PRESS

Oxford New York
Auckland Bangkok Buenos Aires Cape Town Chennai
Dar es Salaam Delhi Hong Kong Istanbul Karachi Kolkata
Kuala Lumpur Madrid Melbourne Mexico City Mumbai Nairobi
Sao Paulo Shanghai Taipei Tokyo Toronto

Published by Oxford University Press, Inc.
198 Madison Avenue, New York, New York 10016
www.oup.com

First published by I.B.Tauris & Co. Ltd in the United Kingdom

Oxford is a registered trademark of Oxford University Press

Library of Congress Cataloging-in-Publication Data

Atkin, Nicholas.
Priests, prelates, and people : a history of European Catholicism
since 1750 / Nicholas Atkin and Frank Tallett.
    p. cm.
Includes bibliographical references and index.
ISBN 0-19-521987-2 (alk. paper)
1. Catholic Church—Europe—History. 2. Europe—Church history. I.
Tallett, Frank. II. Title.
BX1490.A85 2003
282'.4'0903—dc21   2003011856

1 3 5 7 9 8 6 4 2

Printed in Great Britain
on acid-free paper

Contents

Preface

The idea for this book arose out of our shared interest in European religious history, which had already led us to edit three volumes of essays. These were mainly concerned with France and Britain and raised a number of historical issues which we wished to explore on a broader canvas. We were also attracted to, and have enjoyed, the process of joint authorship. This has often led to questions about the mechanics of writing: whether one of us has had primary responsibility for the authorship of a particular chapter or section. In practice, it has been a genuinely collaborative effort, each sentence being a shared endeavour.

The opportunity to write this volume stemmed from an invitation from Dr Lester Crook of I.B.Tauris, and we are grateful to him and his staff for seeing the book through to completion. A book such as this could only be a collaborative effort, and the two of us have pooled our respective knowledge and research into religious history. We are, though, grateful to those numerous scholars who have written in such learned fashion and often so engagingly about European Catholicism. The enterprise owes much to their findings. We of course remain responsible for any errors of fact and of interpretation.

To have reflected the full weight of scholarship on which the book is based would have turned the text into a briar of footnotes and have added to a manuscript which is already long. We therefore made a conscious decision to cite only direct quotations, excepting papal encyclicals which can easily be found elsewhere, and to highlight those works which made an especial contribution to our own understanding. The works in particular of Hubert Jedin, John McManners, William Callahan, Owen Chadwick, Eamonn Duffy, Martin Conway, Tom Buchanan, Maurice Larkin, Frances Lannon, John Cornwell, René Rémond, Gérard Cholvy, Yves-Marie Hilaire, Hugh Mcleod, James McMillan and Mary Vincent, to name but a few, have been great sources of inspiration. As French specialists, the approaches we have adopted mirror those pioneered by Gabriel Le Bras, Fernand Boulard and Jean Delumeau, and continued by Ralph Gibson, among others, whose untimely death has proved a great loss to the academic community.

We would like to thank particular colleagues from within the School of History at the University of Reading. Brian Kemp saved us from our schoolboy Latin when it came to deciphering the nuances of papal encyclicals. David Laven provided numerous Italian and Austrian examples, both geographical areas which are under-researched, and also read through some of the earlier chapters. Michael Biddiss read the whole manuscript and saved us from a number of silly errors, as well as acting as a stimulating and challenging respondent to our ideas. Benjamin Arnold likewise went through the entire manuscript and his encyclopaedic knowledge helped us to clarify many of the links and themes running through the history of Catholicism in the medieval and modern periods. From outside the School of History, Christopher Durston of Saint Mary's College, University of Surrey, proved immensely helpful with textual advice together with interpretative suggestions. We were also assisted by the expertise of Silvo Lennart, Brian Murphy, Tomasz Schramm and Krzysztof Marchlewicz of the University of Poznan; the two latter scholars provided several suggestions for reading in the case of Eastern Europe.

Finally, we should thank our long-suffering families who have patiently borne the gestation of this volume and whose support has been unflagging.

Nicholas Atkin and
Frank Tallett

Abbreviations

ACJB	Association Catholique de la Jeunesse Belge
ACJF	Association Catholique de la Jeunesse Française
ACP	Acçãon do Católico Português
ACW	Algemeen Christelijk Wekersverbon
AF	Action Française
ALP	Action Libérale Populaire
AP	Acción Popular
AP	Alianze Popular
BUF	British Union of Fascists
BVP	Bayerische Volkspartei
CADC	Centro Academica da Democraçia Cristão
CCP	Centro Católico Portuguesa
CDA	Christen Democratisch Appel
CDU	Christliche Demokratische Union
CEDA	Confederación Española de Derechas Autónomas
CFTC	Confédération Française des Travailleurs Chrétiens
CGD	Christliche Gewerkvereine Deutschlands
CIVIC	Council for Investigation of Vatican Influence and Censorship
CNCA	Confederación Nacional Católico-Agraria
CNI	Centro Nazionale Italiano
CPC	Centrums-Parlaments-Correspondenz
CSG	Catholic Social Guild
CSU	Christliche Soziale Union
CWL	Catholic Women's League
CWSS	Catholic Women's Suffrage Society
DC	Democrazia Cristiana
DGB	Deutscher Gewerkschraftsbund
DNVP	Deutschnationale Volkspartei
ETA	Euskadi Ta Askatasuna
EVSS	European Values System Study
FDP	Freie Demokratische Partei
FNC	Fédération Nationale Catholique
HKP	Hrvatski Katolicki Pokret
HOAC	Hermandades Obreras de Acción Católica
HSLS	Hlinka Slovenská L'Udová Stranka

HSS	Hrvatska Seljacka Stranka
IRA	Irish Republican Army
JAC	Jeunesse Agricole Chrétienne
JEC	Jeunesse Etudiante Chrétienne
JOC	Jeunesse Ouvrière Chrétienne
JR	Jeune République
KPD	Kommunistiche Partei Deutschland
KRO	Katholieke Radio Omroep
KVK	Katholieke Vlaamse Kamergroeup
KVV	Katholicke Vlaamse Volkspartij
LOC	Ligue Ouvrière Chrétienne
MOC	Mouvement Ouvrier Chrétien
MP	Moçidade Portuguesa
MPF	Mouvement Populaire des Familles
MRP	Mouvement Républicain Populaire
NCCTU	National Confederation of Catholic Trade Unionists
NEF	Nouvelles Equipes Françaises
NICRA	Northern Ireland Civil Rights Association
NSB	Nationaal Socialistische Beweging
NSDAP	Nationalsozialistische Deutsche Arbeitpartei
OCIC	Office Catholique Internationale du Cinéma
PDP	Parti Démocrate Populaire
PNV	Partido Nacionalista Vaco
POB	Parti Ouvrier Belge
PPI	Partito Popolare Italiano
PSC/CVP	Parti Social Chrétien
PSP	Peoples' Social Party
PU	Partido Unica
RKSP	Rooms Katholieke Staats Partij
SPD	Sozialdemokratische Partei Deutschlands
SS	Schutzstaffel
UCB	Union Catholique Belge
UCD	Union de Centro Democrático
UDB	Union Démocrate Belge
UHRO	Ustase-Hrvatska Revolucionarna Organizaciga
UN	Uniaco Nacional
UN	Unione Nazionale
UP	Unión Patriótica
VNV	Vlaams Nationaal Verbund
VOJ	Vanguardias Obreras Juveniles
VOS	Vanguardias Obreras Sociales

Introduction

AS befits an institution whose name means literally 'universal', the Catholic Church has exerted a formidable influence upon all aspects of European life and endeavour from the Christianisation of the Roman Empire in the fourth century onwards. Whether it has truly been 'universal' remains questionable. It has always struggled against internal faction, apostasy, heresy and schism. The separation of Rome and Constantinople produced a Roman Catholicism which was soon at odds with the Orthodox version of Christianity subsisting in the Byzantine Empire. The rise of Islam mounted a further challenge, sweeping through former imperial possessions in Syria, North Africa and Spain. The Great Schism of the fourteenth century, which saw two and at one point three rival claimants to the see of Peter, augured a disintegration of the Catholic world, as did the emergence of serious forms of late-medieval heresy typified by the Cathars, Waldensians and Hussites. Notwithstanding these trials, the notion evolved that the eleventh to the thirteenth centuries witnessed the emergence of a 'golden age of Christianity' founded upon a Christendom united in its Catholicism.

Whether the medieval world truly merited such plaudits must be seriously open to doubt, particularly after the work of scholars such as Jean Delumeau and Emmanuel Le Roy Ladurie, who emphasised the superficiality or non-existence of a great deal of supposed Catholic belief and practice, particularly at the popular level.[1] Less controversy surrounds the impact of the Protestant Reformation of the sixteenth century which undeniably split Christian Europe. Many, including Catholics, have since interpreted this event as the start of a long period of retrenchment and decline, the first, and by no means the most serious, of a series of shocks with which the Church has had to contend. As the Catholic apologist Henri Daniel-Rops has remarked: 'By ousting religious authority in favour of individual judgement, the Reformers involuntarily undermined the bases of faith and prepared the ground for irreligion.'[2] To the Reformation may be added the Scientific Revolution, the Enlightenment, the French Revolution, the emergence of industrial society, the scientific and the intellectual discoveries of the late nineteenth century, the experiences and aftermath of two world wars, the rise of political extremism and the seismic cultural shifts of the 1960s. Fractured by these successive upheavals, the Catholic Church in Europe can no longer be spoken of as all-embracing, even if it ever had been.

It would, however, be a mistake to believe that in the modern period Catholicism has become marginalised, irrelevant or redundant, and that there

I

has been an irreversible and linear process towards secularisation. According to the *European Values Systems Study* (EVSS) of 1982, 54 per cent of West Europeans continued to profess allegiance to Catholicism. Although more recent statistics suggest that there has been further slippage, religious belief still gives shape, structure and a sense of purpose to the lives of millions of people; the Church, especially under the pontificate of John Paul II, does not hesitate to pronounce on a whole range of issues, from nuclear disarmament to matters of individual conscience, even if its message has not been popular, or indeed heeded; and the international nature of the faith has lent it a status largely unmatched by any other ideology. It could be plausibly argued that Catholicism was significant in the collapse of Eastern-bloc communism, a competing but materialistic ideology which had always prided itself on its universality and innate appeal.

Because of its manifest influence, its enduring qualities and claims to universality, there has been no shortage of historians, theologians and analysts who have attempted to write on European Catholicism. The range of writing displays a bewildering variety of approaches and concerns.[3] Some are works of apology or polemic. Some are accounts of institutional structures, notably the papacy and the great Vatican Councils of 1870 and 1962–65. Some place Church–state relations at their heart. Some are concerned with the leading personalities, whether they be popes, theologians, saints, or humble, albeit exceptional, individuals, such as the Curé d'Ars. Some have attempted to penetrate the life of the 'ordinary Catholic', either deploying a quantitative approach which measures attendance at weekly mass, the take-up of vocations and the number of confraternities, congregations and orders, or adopting a qualitative analysis in order to uncover what Catholicism really meant as a lived-out faith. Some have chosen instead to interrogate the faith from the standpoint of its enemies, whether these were revolutionary dechristianisers, anti-clerical peasants, positivist philosophers or atheist ideologues. Some have tackled the impact of Catholicism on the non-European world. Some have concentrated on key events in the life of the Church, most depressingly the Vatican's response to the Holocaust. Few are those who have attempted to embrace all the many diverse characteristics contained within European Catholicism. When this has been attempted, it has usually, and understandably, been undertaken as a team enterprise, an acknowledgement of the diversity, complexity and eclecticism of the subject.

The present study may, then, be considered a rash endeavour, for it seeks to provide a history of European Catholicism since the mid-eighteenth century to the present in its multifarious guises. The rationale for so doing is that it fills a gaping hole in the Anglophone scholarship. Older works, even including the magisterial series edited by Hubert Jedin, by definition do not include the late twentieth century, and several of these venerable texts privilege theology and the institutional history of the Church at the expense of its membership.[4] The aim of the present volume is to reincorporate the rank-and-file, to balance coverage of institutional matters with politics and society, and to elucidate in some measure the changing nature of the faith itself. This accounts for the

long perspective adopted here, for it is only when the history of Catholicism
is surveyed from a high vantage point that the truly significant changes in
topography can be delineated and mapped. It is only with the historian's
privileged gift of hindsight that the fortunes of the Church, whether priest,
prelate or people, can be discerned. Even then, it is probably too early to
judge the full impact of the monumental changes inaugurated by the Second
Vatican Council. After all, the after-effects of that other turning point in the
history of modern Catholicism, the Council of Trent (1545–63), did not fully
make themselves felt until the late seventeenth and eighteenth centuries.

It is with the eighteenth century that this book commences as by that
stage a form of Catholicism, most appropriately labelled as Tridentine, had
evolved which set the tone for the Church's interaction with the modern
world. The subsequent shape of the book adopts distinct episodes in the
narrative of Catholic life – revolution (1789–1815), restoration (1815–50),
retuning (1815–1914), reaction (1914–45) and revision (1945–2002) – highlighting and blending themes which illustrate both continuity and change.
Among these topics may be cited the oscillating fortunes of the papacy, the
shift from a Europe of established churches to one of state neutrality in the
matter of religion, the lives of both regular and secular clergy, Catholic
relations with the political world, gender dichotomies within the faith, the
nature and extent of practice and belief, and the impact of local circumstances
upon a religion that made claims to universality. Of necessity, some areas are
privileged at the expense of others. There is less concern with theology as a
distinct discipline than with the ways in which it affected the operations of
the Church and its adherents. Restricted attention is also given to the relationship between Catholicism and artistic endeavour, mainly because this demands
a particular expertise. The emphasis has also been on Europe, rather than its
involvement with the wider world, for instance the life of missionaries and
inter-faith dialogue. And within Europe, the authors have shunned that
emphasis upon France as the model for religious life which pervades so much
existing scholarship, a bias which naturally reflects the sheer scale of research
carried out on this one country, though some particular attention has been
given to the events of the revolution of 1789 since this was a watershed for
Catholicism not just in France but in Europe more generally. Attention has
also been paid to areas of Catholic life often overlooked in many histories
such as the fortunes of the Catholics of the Eastern Rite who acknowledge
the supremacy of Rome while retaining a distinctive liturgical identity.*

If there is any single overarching theme which dominates the particulars

---

* In many older histories, these Catholics are referred to as 'Uniates', a term that has
carried pejorative overtones ever since the Union of Brest-Litovsk of 1596 which brought
together the Ruthenian and Roman Catholic Churches. The more neutral expression
'Catholics of the Eastern Rite' is preferred here to refer to those former Greek Orthodox
Church members who were in communion with, and accepted the jurisdiction of Rome,
while continuing to enjoy a distinctive liturgy, ritual and canon law. Apart from the
Ruthenians, the most significant groups are the Copts, Maronites and Melchites, as well as
the Malabar Church of India.

in this book it is the resilience of Catholicism – its ability to interact with a society which has undergone changes far more profound, intense and rapid than anything witnessed in the medieval and early modern periods. This might offer some comfort to a religion which feels itself besieged at the present, but so much of this loyalty and adaptability has emanated from the laity and rank-and-file clergy as opposed to the hierarchy, or at least the Vatican. This might seem to be a weighted conclusion, particularly in the eyes of those who believe that John Paul II has provided a much needed discipline and sense of direction to the faith, but the authors have genuinely attempted throughout to steer away from polemic and emotive engagement with the issues. Neither is a Catholic, though whether this is a help or a hindrance is for the reader to decide. Yet both remain sympathetic to the genuineness of transcendental beliefs and would not seek to portray religion and religious disputes mainly as the outcome of economic, cultural or political tensions, nor to relegate religion to the second rank as a causal explanation. In this way, we do not share what Ferenc Fehér has termed the 'general ennui' with religion which characterises the writings of so many reared in an increasingly secular and technological world.[5] However flawed, this then is an attempt to write an up-to-date history of European Catholicism in its many guises, and with its many strengths and failings.

CHAPTER ONE

Catholicism in Retrenchment:
the Eighteenth Century

TO seize hold of eighteenth-century Catholicism is no easy matter. It lies uncomfortably between the heroic age of the Counter-Reformation with its living saints, its overseas expansion, the flowering of baroque piety and the rebuttal of the Protestant challenge, and the maelstrom of the revolutionary attack upon religion which began in France during the 1790s but which was exported to the rest of Europe on the bayonets of the French armies. In so far as it attracts attention, it is usually considered as an aspect of the period dominated by the Enlightenment, and consequently the religious identity of eighteenth-century Catholicism has been rendered indistinct. That an identity does exist should not be doubted. It is best understood as a continuation of the Catholic/Counter-Reformation of the preceding two hundred years. In particular, initiatives taken at the Council of Trent (1545–63) came fully to fruition only after 1700, producing the best trained and professional clergy that the Church had ever known. The religious life, as displayed by the women's orders especially, manifested an unprecedented variety, vigour and commitment to social purpose. Arguably, the quality of lay religiosity had never been higher.

Yet all was not well, and it is hard to resist the impression that Catholicism was almost everywhere in retrenchment. Overseas, the Church's missionary activity made little new progress: it had been decisively rebutted in Japan in the early seventeenth century and was in retreat in eighteenth-century China. Within Europe itself, a high-water mark had been reached in the reconversion of lands which had fallen to the Protestants. The elites in society had apparently lost sympathy with a baroque faith that was going out of fashion. Even the most pious states were nibbling away at the Church's autonomy and privileges. While the Church retained enormous wealth, it proved incapable of moving reform beyond the vision of the Council of Trent. At the root of much of this was a flawed papacy which failed to provide a coherent sense of purpose. The Church thus struggled to meet the challenges of the age, especially in the intellectual sphere. Yet if the 'lethargical mystique of popular conformity', as John McManners has so elegantly termed it, lulled the Church into a false sense of security, such conformity was none the less the bedrock on which all else rested.[1]

The Religious Geography of Europe

In 1448, Andreas Walperger, a Benedictine monk from Salzburg, painted a map of the world. His concept of Europe had less to do with physical geography than with religion. Europe was Christendom, its cities coloured in red to distinguish them from the surrounding unbelievers who inhabited much of the rest of the earth. Crude though the depiction may have been, there was a substantial truth behind Walperger's portrayal of Europe as essentially Christian and Catholic, despite the long-standing rift between Orthodox and Latin Churches and the presence of pockets of Judaism and Islam. Yet, one hundred years later, the fragile unity of Christendom had been shattered by the effects of the Protestant Reformation. For some, Europe still remained a synonym for Christendom, but Catholicism could no longer claim to be universal, a paradox given the spread of its missionaries in the New World. Although the tide of Protestantism would ebb and flow, pushed back in no small measure by the success of the Catholic Reformation, by the early eighteenth century the religious contours of Europe had become delineated and would endure until the present. Universality had given way to plurality.*

What, then, were the points of the religious compass around 1750? The lodestone of Catholicism pointed southwards. An arc of Catholic territories extended from the Iberian peninsula, where Spain was the Counter-Reformation state *par excellence*, with 'more habits than men', through France into the Italian lands, reaching up to include seven of the nineteen Swiss cantons, the Austrian Netherlands, elements of the Holy Roman Empire including Bavaria to the south and the assorted Rhenish polities to the west, the patrimonial possessions of the Habsburg rulers (Styria, Carinthia, Carniola, Tyrol, Silesia, Moravia, Upper and Lower Austria and the kingdom of Bohemia), as well as Croatia, Slavonia and Hungary, the home of a significant Calvinist minority which enjoyed limited freedoms granted when Catholicism was made the state religion in 1731, to end in Poland, the self-termed 'Catholic bastion', where Protestant and Orthodox minorities rubbed shoulders with the Catholic majority.

Protestantism had firmly established itself in northern and western Europe, yet even here Catholicism retained substantial enclaves. Though there were few Catholics to be found in the Scandinavian kingdoms, in the United Provinces they constituted a significant minority, enjoying effective religious

---

* The terms 'Catholic' and 'Counter-Reformation' are both unsatisfactory in describing early modern Catholicism. 'Counter' suggests that it was merely a reaction to the Protestant threat whereas, in fact, its roots were more complex. The term 'Catholic' lends insufficient weight to the way in which the Church did respond to the threat from Protestantism, and implies that the Church was in greater need of reform in the sixteenth century than at any previous time. This was simply not the case. Today, historians cannot satisfactorily agree on an appropriate label, though the terms 'Catholic Restoration' and the more neutral 'early modern Catholicism' have been proposed. Rather than get bogged down with this debate, this book has chosen to use the more traditional terms, acknowledging that they carry an interpretative baggage of which the reader should be aware.

toleration in spite of the existence of fitfully enforced punitive legislation. There were around 200,000 Catholics in Holland in 1750, 20,000 of whom were congregated in Amsterdam, though numbers were in decline as the century closed. Likewise, substantial pockets of Catholics were to be found in parts of the British Isles. In Ireland, they constituted the overwhelming majority of the population. There were perhaps five Catholics for every Protestant, despite the fact that over 4 million converted between 1703 and 1788 in order to avoid institutional discrimination. In Calvinist Scotland and Anglican England, Catholicism retained the characteristics of what one author has referred to as a 'fortress faith', largely built on the support of European refugees and Irish immigrants.[2] There were approximately 80,000 communicant Catholics in England in 1770. Middle- and lower-class Catholics tended to be concentrated in the urban centres of the north; in the south, the faith was based around the leadership of gentry houses. Wales was dominated by 'Church and Chapel', the Anglican and Nonconformist communities which reflected deeper social cleavages. Still more complex was the situation in the German territories. Not only were these lands the birthplace of Protestantism, the decentralised nature of German statehood positively encouraged the intermingling of religion and politics. Many rulers, both Catholic and Protestant, used confessionalisation to promote local integrity and independence from the empire's hierarchy as well as a means to acquire ecclesiastical wealth and enhance their social control. The early successes of the Reformation had put virtually the whole of north Germany, Bohemia, the Palatinate, Württemberg and a majority of the Imperial Cities in the hands of the Reformed religion. Yet, as a result of a militant Counter-Reformation, allied with dynastic princely interests, the Catholic Church regained much ground. Over fifty princes converted to Catholicism after 1600, and by the mid-eighteenth century an elaborate mosaic of religious affinities had given way to a clearer north–south divide and a greater degree of internal homogeneity. Catholics in northern Germany were chiefly confined to the western Rhineland (their numbers in Cleves accounted for 60 per cent and in Lingen for 97 per cent) and Silesia, which Prussia acquired in 1740.

Turning to eastern Europe, three distinct religious spheres can be discerned. While Islam had retreated from the high-water mark of its conquests after the siege of Vienna in 1683, it still retained control over Serbia, Greece, Albania, Bulgaria and the Romanian provinces though the Habsburgs clung on to Transylvania. Little effort was made to convert the indigenous populations who remained loyal to Greek Orthodoxy rather than to Rome, though Islam did find an overwhelming number of converts in Bosnia and Albania, for example. In the second sphere, the Russian territories, the population was similarly Christian, but here the Russian, rather than the Greek Orthodox Church, held sway. Given that Moscow perceived itself after the fall of Constantinople in 1453 as the 'Third Rome', there was a profound mistrust of Roman Catholics, most of whom were immigrants of German, Italian, French or Polish extraction and whose numbers were tiny. When, in 1685, the Jesuits opened a house in Moscow, it was shut down four years later by Peter the Great, although it was the Jesuits again who in the 1740s attempted to reimport their faith. Far more numerous were the Catholics of the Eastern Rite. In the eyes of Rome, these groups were important as they symbolised the universality of Catholicism, and constituted a possible means of reuniting East and West. In the eyes of the Tsars, they were objects of suspicion, and were mercilessly persecuted, notably by Catherine the Great (1762–96) whose reign cost them 8 million faithful in converts and emigrants. In the remaining sphere, Poland-Lithuania, where over half the population was Catholic, it is calculated that there were an additional 4 million or so Catholics of the Eastern Rite, their numbers swollen by conversions from the Greek Orthodox faith, the result of aggressive Catholic proselytising and the weak organisation of Orthodoxy. Adding to the religious plurality of Poland were its 200–300,000 *Dissidentes de Religione* – the Lutherans, Calvinists and numerous sectaries – mainly to be found in the west and in Polish Prussia, together with substantial Jewish minorities who had sought refuge from persecution in western Europe, always excepting the United Provinces. (As historians have observed, their concentration in the east would lay the foundations of a later tragedy which the Catholic Church would do little to prevent.) Under the three partitions (1772, 1793, 1795), the Polish state was swallowed up by its neighbours, Russia, Prussia and Austria, and the Catholic Church was significantly weakened, although the faith would continue to unite a majority of Poles and provide a sense of national identity.

If, by the eighteenth century, Catholic universalist pretensions no longer accorded with reality, the Church had nevertheless recovered its poise after the devastating blow of the Protestant Reformation. Geographically it had entrenched itself firmly in the south of Europe, won back hinterlands in northern and western territories and, through its link with the Eastern Rite churches, retained a sizeable presence east of the Elbe, where we should not of course forget Poland. Additionally, it had established successful missions in the newly discovered overseas territories, most notably South America, Africa, the Philippines and South-East Asia. Geographically reconstituted, the Church in the eighteenth century nevertheless had to confront a further dilemma: the burgeoning power of the state. What, then, of its relationships with the ruling elites?

Established Churches and Erastianism

A full appreciation of Church–state relations in the eighteenth century requires a recognition that contemporaries did not draw a clear distinction between religion and politics. Temporal and spiritual authority overlapped. Rulers occupied their thrones as a result of divine will. God's judgment on heretics and wrong-doers would operate in the here-and-now as well as in the hereafter, and would not be restricted to individuals but would extend to the whole community, thus potentially endangering the stability of the realm. Moreover, the presence of a dissident religious minority within the kingdom invited outside intervention from co-religionaries. Citizenship, social order and religion thus went hand-in-hand. For these reasons, 'established' churches had been put in place by the eighteenth century, in both Protestant and Catholic Europe, which reflected the symbiotic nature of Church–state relations. 'Where would we be if there were no state religion and submission to the Church?' asked the Empress Maria Theresa rhetorically. 'Toleration and indifference are the most certain means of destroying the accepted order.'[3]

The existence of an established Church conferred mutual benefits to both sides. First, the state protected the doctrinal exclusivity of Catholicism: for example, only active members of the established Church were allowed to participate in public affairs; it enjoyed a monopoly of public worship; actions such as heresy and apostasy were criminal offences, as were elements of the Christian code such as blasphemy and adultery; and attendance at mass was compulsory, at least on certain dates of the year. Some German ordinances even indicated that essential activities, such as feeding livestock, must be done so as not to interfere with church services. Second, the state guaranteed the Church its income, either by directly funding its ministers or, more usually, by enforcing payment of the tithe, a nominal 10 per cent of agricultural production. And, finally, the Church was accorded some representation in the machinery of the state. Merely to take one instance, in the hereditary lands of the Habsburgs churchmen sat of right in the local estates and abbots were entitled to belong to the financial commissions of the Diets; and, overall, the prelates comprised one-third of the civil bureaucracy.

The benefits to the Church from this arrangement were obvious; the benefits to the state were no less significant. The Church preached submission to the temporal authority, a significant role at a time when the pulpit remained probably the most effective means of mass communication. In the later words of Robert Browning:

> Above, behold the archbishop's most fatherly of rebukes,
> And below with his crown and lion, some little new law of the duke's.

Additionally, the collection of information and the dissemination of news and princely propaganda fell in large part to churchmen who substituted for the lack of a civil bureaucracy. It was said of eighteenth-century seminarists that they were prepared not so much to administer the sacraments, as to administer the provinces. And the Church was left to manage the charitable and, above all, the educational work which would otherwise have fallen on an under-manned, under-resourced and unwilling secular administration, or would not have been performed at all. It was surely no coincidence that subversive notions which undermined the established political and social order flourished best in those regions where the clerical grip on education was weakened.

While Church and state may have been 'joined at the hip', the trend in the eighteenth century was undoubtedly towards greater state tutelage of the Church, a process known as Erastianism. The term derived from the Swiss theologian Thomas Erastus (1524–83) who argued that civil authorities ought to exercise jurisdiction in ecclesiatical matters. The motor for this development was two-fold. On the one hand, princes were eager to curtail papal influence in their dominions, a strategy in which they generally had the backing of their clergy, though at the same time rulers were not averse to invoking papal authority as a means of disciplining the local Church when it suited their purposes. On the other hand, princes steadily encroached upon the autonomy of native Churches in respect of appointments, control of wealth and the extent of clerical jurisdiction. Yet if the state was gaining the ascendancy over the Church, the balance of power was not everywhere the same. As we shall see, at one end of the spectrum stood the Iberian peninsula, where the state had always enjoyed superiority. In the disparate patrimonies of the Habsburgs, the rulers had more ground to make up, but achieved considerable progress by the 1780s. The picture was more chequered in respect of the German and Italian lands, yet here too secular authority made substantial inroads. France, Switzerland and Poland were at opposite ends of the spectrum to the Iberian peninsula in that the Church retained appreciable independence, though for very different reasons.[4]

Within Spain, the Bourbon rulers who inherited the throne in 1700 were no less concerned than their Habsburg predecessors to maintain the symbiotic relationship between Church and state, but went further in freeing themselves from papal authority. In 1709, Bishop Francisco de Solís suggested that the king was 'obliged to protect his kingdom and churches from the slavery of the Roman Curia'.[5] To this end, a series of concordats (1717, 1732 and 1753) was forced upon an unwilling papacy, giving the Spanish crown the right of appointment to around 12,000 benefices and leaving the Holy See control of a mere fifty-two. Charles III (1759–88) further prohibited the proclamation of papal bulls without royal assent. He curbed the autonomy of the In-quisition, something not too difficult to achieve since it had been initially established as a royal council, although it did enjoy a brief renaissance when it was needed to guard against the contamination of the French Revolution. Additionally, the religious orders were subject to increasing royal scrutiny; the Jesuits and the Hospital Order of San Antonio were expelled, for example, and explicitly Spanish congregations were set up, enabling the crown to meddle more directly. The readiness of the reforming ministers of Charles III to intervene in the running of the Church stemmed partly from the fact that the clergy were viewed as royal bureaucrats with a role in the modernisation of the state; they were 'the philosopher's stone which will enrich towns and villages and make them happy'.[6] The financial pressures of continuous war between 1793 and 1812 led to further state controls, notably an appropriation of Church wealth which had disastrous consequences for the charitable work hitherto performed by the orders. The paradox was that the monarchy sought to fortify itself as a Catholic power at a time when Spain's international standing was on the wane.

The relative ease with which the crown asserted its authority over both Church and papacy during the eighteenth century owed much to the singular facts of Spanish history. With the conclusion of the *reconquista* which eventu-ated in the fall of the Moorish kingdom of Granada in 1492, the Spanish crown had established itself as the foremost defender of the Catholic cause.

Subsequently the crown took the initiative in expelling Moors, Jews and Protestants from the Iberian peninsula; Spanish armies spearheaded the Counter-Reformation within Europe; and, overseas, the *conquistadores* carried Catholicism into the New World. Both Church and papacy grudgingly acquiesced in the extension of temporal authority which royal leadership of the Catholic cause entailed, thankful for the triumphs which it produced. Paradoxically, the growth of royal authority over clerical affairs was further facilitated by the clerical Inquisition, established during the *reconquista* to safeguard Spain's religious and, above all, racial purity. Its writ theoretically ran everywhere although it was most effective within Castile. It contributed importantly to ensuring that an Hispanic-style Catholicism was central to a burgeoning sense of Spanish self-awareness.

Similarly, in neighbouring Portugal, which re-established a native dynasty in 1640, the balance between throne and altar had always been tilted in favour of the former, thus facilitating an extension of royal authority in the eighteenth century. Under John V (1706–50), the crown purchased from the papacy the right to create various ecclesiastical offices, which included transforming the court chapel into a patriarchate whose holder was always a cardinal and a member of the royal family; and, in 1740, the monarchy assumed the patronage of all dioceses and abbeys. The Marquis de Pombal, the energetic First Minister of the feckless Joseph I (1750–77), further asserted royal authority over the Church after 1751, reducing the Church's immunity from taxation, suppressing the Jesuits and sequestering their lands in 1759, as well as temporarily severing the link between the Portuguese bishops and Rome. He also took closer control of the Inquisition which had been fundamental to maintaining Portugal's religious purity. From its initial campaign against the Jews (85 per cent of its victims between 1540 and 1732 were Jewish), in the eighteenth century it turned to the indoctrination of the masses, now assisted by diocesan visitations whereby bishops and their delegates kept a close watch on local behaviour. As in Spain, Catholicism helped to forge a sense of national self-awareness.

If, in Spain and Portugal, the state had always been the dominant partner, the same could not be said of the Austrian lands, at least at the start of the eighteenth century. There were hesitant initiatives under Leopold I (1657–1705) to restrict papal authority, notably in the special case of Hungary in 1701, where the crown claimed rights of 'apostolic kingship', but it was, above all, under Maria Theresa (1740–80) and her son, Joseph II (co-regent 1768–80, sole ruler 1780–90) that the state gained the upper hand. The Empress concluded concordats with the Pope in respect of Naples and Sardinia in 1741, and unilaterally abrogated papal authority in her Austrian lands. This left the way open for a redrawing of diocesan and parish boundaries, taxation of the clergy and royal appointment to ecclesiastical positions. In Austrian Lombardy, renowned for its piety and clericalism, a *Giunta Economale* was instituted in 1767 to oversee clerical affairs which, among other things, halved the number of monastic houses and reduced their income by two-thirds. Joseph's policies impacted even more harshly upon the Church. In 1781, bishops were made to swear an oath of loyalty to the crown; papal correspondence with churchmen had to be vetted by the government; six specially created seminaries were set up to train parish clergy; and marriage became a civil contract. Perhaps most famously, Joseph's Edict on Idle Institutions, one of over six thousand ordinances relating to religious matters, suppressed the contemplative monastic orders, more than halving the number of monks in Habsburg lands, in the Emperor's own words, 'shaven-headed creatures whom the common people worship on bended knee'.[7] The sheer volume of legislation on ecclesiastical affairs led Frederick the Great of Prussia to refer to him as 'My friend the Sacristan'; he referred less flatteringly to the Empress Maria Theresa as the 'apostolic hag'.[8]

The Habsburg rulers were driven, above all, by two distinct but interrelated concerns. The first was the need to re-establish Catholicism as the dominant faith in their lands. While the southern Netherlands and the Tyrol had remained firmly within the Catholic fold, Bohemia, Moravia and Silesia, for example, had succumbed to Protestantism in the sixteenth and seventeenth centuries. There was also a need to reinvigorate the Catholic faith in the two-thirds of Hungary which had been won back from the Ottoman Empire by 1711. A good example of the measures taken to strengthen the Church in its proselytising mission was the establishment in 1733 of a General Fund to pay the salaries of parish clergy in Hungary. Prelates were initially asked to make voluntary donations, but in 1769 Maria Theresa obliged them to pay one-tenth of the income of their benefice; and when Joseph abolished the monasteries he transferred some of their wealth to clerical salaries. In the same way, he allocated revenues from the Jesuits and other orders to the payment of the parish clergy in Bohemia, in 1783 setting their annual stipend at 400 florins. The Habsburgs' second objective was to produce a more powerful and streamlined military state. This was especially important in the aftermath of Austria's defeat in the Seven Years War (1756–63) which had left the monarchy with a crippling debt of more than 280 million florins and the prospect of further conflict with Prussia. The Habsburgs had, of course, traditionally used the Church as a tool of state-building, Catholicism providing some degree of cultural uniformity in their heterogeneous lands. Joseph and his mother were no different from their predecessors in this respect, but by the late eighteenth century the emphasis had shifted. Joseph, in particular, recognised the potential of Catholicism as a powerful instrument both of social control and of modernisation, and his reforms were directed, in part, to ensuring that he controlled its pastoral and teaching activities. For example, the clergy produced by his new seminaries were to act as models of social utility in their parishes. He also recognised that the Church could be a bar to economic progress and the growth of state efficiency, and he was prepared for radical reforms to correct this. Hence his dissolution of 'unproductive' religious orders and the seizure of lands which fell under the dead hand of the Church. It comes as small surprise that the General Fund not only supplemented the meagre salaries of clerics, but also enhanced the crown's war chest.

Josephinian ecclesiastical reform thus went hand-in-hand with other institutional changes aimed at augmenting power at the centre and improving bureaucratic effectiveness at the periphery. Yet Joseph's subordination of the Church was perceived by many, including laymen, as an attack upon the institution and religion more generally, not least because he meddled in matters of liturgy and doctrine. This, together with hostility to his other state-building policies, contributed to the general unrest besetting his lands at the time of his death and the consequent reversal or abandonment of several of these measures by Leopold II (1790–92). Joseph might have done much to subordinate ecclesiastical privilege, but the extent of his achievement was never as great as he would have wished.

As Grand Duke, Leopold had already instituted a series of coherent and incremental changes in Tuscany, working principally through Scipione de Ricci, the Bishop of Pistoia and Prato, as well as through Jansenist clerics, to make the Church more effective at all levels. Papal jurisdiction and taxation were abrogated, parish and diocesan boundaries were redrawn, the regular orders were called to account, greater authority was given to synods of lower clergy, the Church's judicial powers were reformed after 1771, and there were serious efforts to raise the level of popular piety by eradicating superstitious practices. Such initiatives were not always popular. When the authorities proposed to demolish an altar dedicated to the Girdle of the Virgin Mary in 1787, a riot ensued. Leopold was undoubtedly motivated by a genuine belief in Enlightenment principles. Elsewhere in the peninsula, rulers and their ministers may not have shared his convictions, though they often professed attachment to them, but similar initiatives were everywhere adopted, though their precise nature and content varied from region to region. In Piedmont, limits were imposed on clerical legal immunities, the Inquisition was effectively squashed and Rome had to accept that vacant sees would be administered by the crown. Bernardo Tannucci, the Principal Minister in Naples between 1754 and 1776, adopted a series of anti-clerical policies including the expulsion of the Jesuits and the adoption of civil marriage. His counterpart in Sardinia, Giovani Battista Bogino, was more concerned with reform, outlawing the accumulation of multiple benefices in the hands of a single prelate, creating diocesan seminaries, limiting ecclesiastical privileges and establishing permanent vicars in parishes. The Viceroy in Sicily, Caracciolo, closed some monasteries, reduced the number of feast days, and even legislated on the amount clerics could spend on sweetmeats, though he left ecclesiastical censorship untouched. Some of the most draconian measures were adopted in the Republic of Venice, including its hinterlands of Brescia, Bergamo, Cremona and the al di la del Mincio. Driven by the influential patrician Tron, the Republic, which had always insisted upon a remarkable independence from Rome, introduced extensive ecclesiastical changes in the 1760s, including some of the most radical measures undertaken by any European state against the monasteries and convents.

To summarise the condition of Church–state relations within Germany is no easy matter, given the variety of polities comprising the empire. On one level, there were the sixty-five ecclesiastical territories ruled by archbishops, bishops, abbots and priors in whose lands the identification of Church with state was, by definition, total. Yet even here, the elected rulers were not averse to asserting their authority against that of Rome, and a series of disputes with the papacy arose over the role of the nuncios, over the refusal of Rome to recognise episcopal elections and over the control of monasteries, for example. The preoccupation of the emperors with Austrian matters after 1648 left the episcopacy to fight its battles with Rome without whole-hearted imperial support and, in any event, the emperors feared that episcopal independence from Rome might mean greater autonomy from Vienna. The most extreme statement of episcopal independence from Rome came in the document known as the Punctuation of Ems produced by the archbishops of Mainz, Cologne, Trier and Salzburg in 1786. Not all bishops were prepared openly to subscribe to this, fearing an extension of the powers of the metropolitans, those archbishops or primates who enjoyed authority over a collection of dioceses known as a province, as well as being responsible for the administration of their own particular diocese. Nevertheless, bishops and archbishops were united in rejecting papal interference. In practice, the elective nature of the ecclesiastical rulers meant that they all too often eschewed longer-term reform of the state in favour of immediate enrichment for themselves and their relatives. This meant that the ecclesiastical territories had a not unjustified reputation for inefficiency and corruption which allowed secularisation to emerge as an issue by the 1780s.

Of the Catholic dynastic states, easily the most important was Bavaria. Here, the attempts by Max III Joseph (1745–77) to solve his perennial financial difficulties, by tapping the extensive and tax-exempt land holdings of the Church and the monasteries, had only limited success against vested clerical interests. His successor, Karl Theodor (1777–99), was more interested in exchanging Bavaria for the Austrian Netherlands, and consequently bothered little with matters of internal state development, especially after his efforts to control the local bishops ended in failure. Most bizarre of all the states were the Palatinate and Saxony, whose ruling dynasties had converted to Catholicism, but whose populations remained overwhelmingly loyal to the Protestant confession. In the former, a legacy of Louis XIV's intervention in the 1680s was a Catholic ruler who, assisted by the Jesuits, sought by every means to undermine the formidable Protestant presence, a tragic policy that resulted in outright persecution and upheaval without ever denting the substantial Calvinist and Lutheran majority. In Saxony, the Catholic rulers, while offering support to their co-religionaries, nevertheless adopted a more conciliatory approach in recognition both of their political feebleness and the strength of the official Lutheran Church which retained the allegiance of a majority of their subjects.

The same impulse to encroach upon papal authority and clerical independence which has been noted in Spain and the Habsburg lands was further apparent in France, but here the impulse was most effectively resisted. The motives behind the state's claims were the same as elsewhere: a desire for greater efficiency and a need for more revenue, particularly acute during the prolonged reign of Louis XIV. It was he who, in 1682, used a council of French prelates to propound the Gallican Articles which sought to restrict the admittedly limited influence of Rome. Yet a mere ten years later these had been reversed. The eighteenth century constituted a catalogue of failed attempts on the part of the crown to assert its dominance over clerical matters. Proposals to subject the clergy to taxation in 1710 (the *dixième*), 1725–26 and 1749–51 (the *vingtième*), were unsuccessful; suggestions in 1787 that the clergy divest itself of some of its seigneurial and hunting rights in order to assist the government financially merely encountered assertions of financial immunity. Almost unbelievably, at a time when royal debts stood at 5 billion *livres*, the crown received less from the Church than it did from the royal lotteries. A Commission on the Regulars, set up in 1766 to reform the monasteries, partly in response to state prompting, achieved meagre results and merely served to demonstrate that, left to its own devices, the Church would never reform itself.

Why was the Church in France apparently so immune from state intervention? The Church's separate corporate identity was predicated, above all, on its financial autonomy. This had originated in the sixteenth century when, in return for some limited financial payments to the crown, the Church had gained the formal right to tax exemption and had established a body, the General Assembly of the Clergy, which subsequently evolved as a puissant defender of ecclesiastical privileges and immunities. No other established Church in Europe was as well organised as that in France. Meeting formally every five years, the Assembly negotiated a lump-sum payment to the crown, the so-called 'free gift' (the very name underscored the voluntary nature of the payment); it headed a system of clerical taxation which was wholly independent of the crown; and it, or its permanent officials, did not hesitate to defend clerical privilege, whether this was the right of a priest in some far-flung parish not to have his servant conscripted into the militia, or of a cardinal to exercise precedence over a peer of the realm. At the same time, the Church contrived to become an indispensable part of the matrix of government finance, without surrendering any of its fiscal autonomy. It not only contributed lump-sum payments to the crown's war chest, but also used its superior ability to mobilise credit to raise loans which were passed on to the cash-strapped monarchy. Fiscally indispensable, the French Church was immune from royal subversion.

Within Switzerland, too, the Church enjoyed autonomy from Rome, a result of its particular historical circumstances. The civic authorities had already established a large measure of *de facto* control over religious life even before the Reformation, helped by the fact that there was no Swiss diocese and by their location on the outskirts of the 'foreign' dioceses of Lausanne and Constance, both of which had feeble incumbent bishops. This autonomy was subsequently reinforced during the Counter-Reformation of the sixteenth and seventeenth centuries and the Enlightenment of the eighteenth. Catholic cities supervised clerical appointments and the dispersal of ecclesiastical revenues, for example, just as effectively as did their counterparts in Protestant cantons. Although there was conflict between Protestants and Catholics in 1712, it was not in the interest of the ruling elites of either denomination to let this get out of hand, and a series of compromises were made which permitted Catholics and Protestants to live cheek-by-jowl in reasonable harmony.

It remains to consider Poland. Here, the Church's autonomy was a product of the weakness of the central apparatus of the state rather than a result of the Church's inherent strength, though this was considerable. The elective monarchy exercised little real power, which lay in the hands of the *Sejm* or Diet, dominated by the nobility and the Catholic bishops (prelates of the Eastern Rite had no entitlement to seats). Even within the Diet there existed what may be labelled a balance of weakness since any member could individually block all legislation in that session by invoking the infamous *liberum veto* which prevented the emergence of cohesive policy. In these circumstances, the Church was rarely challenged and was, by and large, left to manage its own affairs. Because of the haphazard nature of the Polish kingdom, rather it was the Church which was able to impose something of its will on the civil bureaucracy. For instance, it was the Archbishop of Gniezno, the Polish Primate, who served as regent in periods of *interregnum*, and who arguably constituted the single most important figure in the realm after the sovereign.

From Spain to Poland, from Naples to the Rhineland, the trend towards 'established' or national Churches was thus maintained. At the same time, the extent to which the state was able to exert an ascendancy over the Church clearly varied, and owed much to local circumstances. Everywhere, there was one chief loser – the papacy – which found its room for manoeuvre in the local ecclesiastical matters circumscribed. The reasons for the loss of papal influence relate not just to the internal evolution of Church–state relationships, but to wider matters to which we must now turn.

The Latin Theocracy

The papacy was unique in Europe in that it was the only true theocracy. As a temporal ruler the Pope exercised absolute authority over the Papal States, comprising Emilia, Romagna, the Marches, Umbria and Latium and, additionally, had a more limited jurisdiction over Avignon and the Venaissin in the south of France, and the enclaves of Pontecorvo and Benevento in the Kingdom of Naples. The reasons for the Pope's claim to both spiritual and secular authority at this level were essentially two-fold. First, it stemmed from the doctrine of the Petrine Commission whereby the popes, as purported heirs of St Peter, exercised the powers which had originally been given to Peter by Christ. The key biblical texts were Matthew 16:13–23, where Christ declared to Peter: 'I will give you the keys to the kingdom of heaven, and whatever you bind on earth shall also be bound in heaven'; and Christ's thrice-repeated injunction to Peter, in John 21:15–17, to 'Feed my lambs, feed my sheep'. Second, the Latin theocracy was predicated upon the widely-held belief that papal responsibilities to the wider Church could be exercised only if the Pope enjoyed territorial independence. In the Middle Ages, these dual aspects of papal authority had come under challenge: from the Conciliarists who urged that authority lay with the national and supra-national councils of the

Church which were superior to the Pope in matters of faith and government; and from the undue influence exercised by secular rulers over the person of the Pope during the period of the Avignon Captivity (1309–77) and the Great Western Schism (1378–1417). The papacy circumvented the challenge from the Conciliarists, but at the expense of devolving a large measure of authority over clerical appointments, jurisdiction and taxation to the civil powers, resulting in the formation of nationally orchestrated or Gallican churches. It was but a short step from these to the creation of 'established' churches alluded to earlier.*

The Protestant Reformation opened a further phase in the shaping of Rome's authority. Not only did the Pope lose his claim to be head of a united Christendom, he also became ever more dependent upon his co-religionaries among the crowned heads of Europe to reimpose Catholicism, princes who were all too ready to exploit the Reformation as a means to further their autonomy. The paradox was that at the same time as papal temporal power was on the wane, Rome's authority within the Church was enhanced. Under the energetic leadership of Pius IV (1559–65), the Council of Trent was guided to a successful conclusion. Theological markers were laid down which clearly delineated the boundaries between Catholicism and the Reformed religions; a series of reforming decrees laid the basis for a long-term revival of Catholicism; and the papacy emerged as the arbiter of theological matters. A lavish building and cultural programme helped to reassert the dignity of Rome and its place at the centre of Catholicism. Much of this foreshadowed developments in the nineteenth century when Rome, stripped finally of any effective temporal authority, sought to compensate by asserting its moral and theological leadership.

The enhancement of papal authority in the sixteenth and seventeenth centuries did not survive into the eighteenth as Rome struggled to meet the challenges posed by a new intellectual climate. The anti-clericalism of the Enlightenment is commonly credited with this process but, in fact, developments within Catholic thinking were far more harmful. The whole issue of authority within the Church – whence it derived, who held it and how it was to be exercised – did not go away, and was raised again by two controversies: that over the Jansenists and that concerning Febronianism.

There was a strong irony in the case of the Jansenists. They had originated as a small, recondite group, distinguished by their particular doctrine of grace and theology derived from the writings of the Bishop of Ypres, Cornelius Jansen (1585–1638), who died from a disease contracted by inhaling the dust of old books. They incurred the frequent charge of imitating the Protestant

---

* The distinction between 'Gallican' and 'established' churches is a fine one. The former emerged during the late Middle Ages and, although the phrase refers to the French Church, it applies to most of Europe. A Gallican Church possessed certain characteristics: it was one which governed itself without reference to Rome, even though it accepted that the papacy had a primacy of honour. An 'established Church' shared this trait, but was distinguished by its symbiotic relationship with the state, though in practice the distinction becomes a largely abstract one.

doctrine of predestination, thus prompting the quip that a Jansenist was merely a Calvinist who said mass. Imbued with a sense of their own rectitude, the Jansenists were initially confident of Rome's support and adopted a pro-papal or Ultramontane posture (literally 'over the mountains', an allusion to Rome's far-reaching influence). Their illusions were finally shattered when Louis XIV, who erroneously believed them to be republicans, pressured Clement XI into issuing a definitive condemnation through the bull *Unigenitus* (1713). The Jansenists responded by reinventing themselves as a political faction opposed to despotism in all its forms, whether papal, episcopal or royal. This allowed them to draw support from secular quarters, most notably the French *parlements*, the superior courts of appeal which also exercised a representative function. The Jansenists further broadened their appeal by singling out for attack the Jesuits, an order already suspect for its wealth, excessive influence and loyalty to Rome. Yet once the Jansenists had triumphed over their enemies, they lost a focus for their energies. The strict puritanism and rigorous lifestyle of Jansenism's clerical supporters only hastened the movement's decline, alienating rather than attracting popular support.

If Jansenism was most developed within France, and enjoyed pockets of strength in Tuscany and parts of the Habsburg Empire, there were other intellectual challenges to papal authority. These are often labelled Jansenist, though their emphasis could be significantly different. For instance, in 1700 Bernard van Espen, a dry jurist at the University of Louvain, produced his *Jus Ecclesiasticum Universum*, followed thirteen years later by the *Tractatus*. In these, he revisited conciliar notions, privileging the role of bishops and the state against that of the papacy. Similar ideas were propagated in German lands by Hugo von Schönborn and Kaspar Barthel, two leading theologians, but their most distinguished advocate was Mgr de Hontheim, the co-adjutor or parallel Archbishop of Trier, a keen student of John Locke who had been trained at Louvain and who wrote under the pseudonym Justinus Febronius. In 1763, he published *De statu praesenti Ecclesiae*, which argued that the popes had no mandate to intervene at the expense of the episcopacy since the bishops had an authority as heirs to the twelve apostles which was on a par with that of the Pope as heir to St Peter. By diminishing the primacy of Rome in such a manner, Febronius aspired to a reconciliation between Catholics and Protestants. Many Protestants welcomed his attacks on the papacy though they were less keen on his plans for reconciliation. Nor were Catholic bishops eager for such a *rapprochement*, though they were attracted to his ideas because of a natural irritation with Roman interference. So too were Erastian rulers, who used his ideas as a stick with which to beat the Jesuits, the most prominent defenders of papal authority. Significantly, the monarchs of Spain, Portugal and the Habsburg lands defied a papal condemnation of Febronius (1769), and insisted that his works be used in universities. Febronian influences can be detected, too, in the policies of Joseph II. He forbade the reading of *Unigenitus* and in 1782 rebuffed Pope Pius VI when he travelled to Vienna in the hope of curtailing the Emperor's zeal for religious reform. Kaunitz, Joseph's minister, deliberately slighted the Pope by shaking Pius VI's hand rather than kissing it. Four years later, the attempts by Karl Theodor of Bavaria to bring his bishops to heel by the appointment of a papal nuncio resulted in a joint protest from the three clerical electors and the Archbishop of Salzburg which again drew on Febronian precepts. The resulting Punctuation of Ems (1786), even though it did not receive the direct support of the German episcopacy, was nevertheless the most extreme statement of anti-papalism and went further than anything Febronius had ever advocated.

Intellectual arguments over the perimeters and nature of papal power were, in practice, less damaging than the inchoate manner in which Rome dealt with them. Whereas in the sixteenth century Rome had at least established boundaries between Catholicism and Protestantism, in the eighteenth it singularly failed to impose its authority upon theological disputes within the Catholic world. *Unigenitus* in particular opened the papacy to ridicule. Jansenism was condemned not by reference to the work of Cornelius Jansen, but to that of the respected Oratorian author, Pasquier Quesnel (1634–1719), whose *Réflexions Morales sur le Nouveau Testament*, published in 1672, was reputed to contain the offending doctrines. Only one member of the commission set up to investigate the *Réflexions* spoke French and could thus understand the original text; the translation of Quesnel's work they used was flawed; Quesnel himself was not allowed to appear; and certain of the condemned extracts not only contradicted Jansen's arguments but transpired to be quotes from scripture. As an exercise in dishonesty, *Unigenitus* could hardly have been bettered. The Theology Faculty of Caen voiced a widespread sentiment when it mocked papal claims to doctrinal infallibility as 'frivolous'.[9] Overall, *Unigenitus* served only to sustain the appeal of Jansenism and, in some instances, added to its allure. The Republic of Venice and the Kingdom of Sardinia, traditionally hostile to Rome, became bastions of Jansenist dissent, and in Holland a schismatic church was formed which rejected the authority of Rome. Likewise, denunciations of van Espen and of Febronius were all too often ignored, thus revealing the weakness of Rome and the unwillingness of Catholics to accept its primacy in matters of faith.

In a similarly maladroit fashion, the papacy mishandled what is commonly referred to as the 'Chinese rites controversy', although this matter has generally received less attention, played out, as it was, a long way from Europe. The clash of cultures inherent in much overseas missionary activity was revealed with particular clarity here in China where the Virgin and the Crucifixion were puzzling and off-putting to the sophisticated indigenous civilisation. Notably, the question arose as to how far Catholicism should accommodate local customs. For their part, the Jesuit missionaries, pioneered by the remarkable Matteo Ricci (1552–1610), had successfully sought a *modus vivendi* with native habits as the best way of evangelisation, until their efforts were halted when Clement XI (1700–21) first condemned the use of Chinese rites, a prohibition subsequently confirmed by Benedict XIV (1740–58) in 1742 and 1744. In vain did the Jesuits protest that a respect for ancestors, practised by the Chinese, was different from ancestor worship. The Chinese authorities were outraged, the activities of the missionaries were restricted, and there were few converts among the literati–official elites of Chinese society. The globalisation of Catholicism had suffered a serious reverse.

The truth was that the sloppiness evidenced above was as much a symptom as a cause of the papacy's declining influence. This decline was hastened by Rome's inability to look beyond its interests as a secular princedom. The papal court was categorised by backstairs intrigue and parochialism. The Pasquino, a dilapidated classical statue situated in the heart of Rome, on which people posted so-called *pasquinades*, essentially witty epigrams, was constantly plastered with stories about high-ranking churchmen. The court's worldliness was actively encouraged by the cardinals who comprised the Curia. It suited their purposes that popes should be worthy as individuals, but enfeebled politically. At elections, factions within the Curia accordingly put forward a suitably pliant candidate, always in league with secular rulers who shared this interest in electing an acquiescent pontiff. The Spanish Foreign Minister, Grimaldi, wrote an *aide-mémoire* for the ambassador in Rome, ranking the cardinals of the conclave as 'very good', 'good', 'doubtful', 'indifferent', 'bad' and 'very bad' according to their dependability.[10]

This meant that the eighteenth century witnessed the elevation of a series of unassuming men. It was frequently remarked of Clement XI that he would always have been esteemed worthy of the papacy if he had never obtained it. After his death in 1721, illness and old age became almost prerequisites for papal office. His successor, the sixty-six-year-old Innocent XIII (1721–24) had already resigned from his diocese on grounds of ill-health before his accession. Benedict XIII (1724–30) was seventy-five on attaining office and enfeebled. Apparently, when asked a question his typical response was, 'Do it yourself!'[11] His successor, Clement XII (1730–40), was seventy-eight, and remained blind and bed-ridden for most of his pontificate. To be fair, individual popes were generally well meaning, and some possessed fine qualities, including wit and charm. The most outstanding was Benedict XIV (1740–58). His assemblage of a great library and authorship of the classic text on canonisation, the *De Servorum Deio beatificatione et beatorum canonizatione*, established his claim as a great scholar and he had considerable political acumen and moral judgement. Clement XIII (1758–69) was an unremarkable figure who lacked the vigour of his namesake, Clement XIV (1769–74), a keen horseman who had to be dissuaded from riding after taking too many tumbles, and a practical joker whose japes, in the words of E. E. Y. Hales, were 'unsuitable for any sexagenarian, let alone a pope'.[12] His successor, Pius VI (1775–99), was not without merit, proffering plans for the overhaul of the Papal States, but was vain and self-absorbed, and concentrated on secondary issues. He became especially agitated, for example, over the white horse which the King of Naples was supposed to present annually to the Pope in token of his fealty. Crucially, all the popes lacked energy, drive and leadership. Far too often, they proved defensive, rejecting reasonable initiatives for reform of the monasteries and liturgy, for example, and adhering to positions which were outmoded, a foretaste of developments in the nineteenth century.

The experience of the nineteenth century suggests that, in any case, the papacy could have done little to assert its position on the international stage. Even Benedict XIV, whose political skills, tact and shrewdness made him easily the most able of the eighteenth-century popes, was unable to rekindle Rome's authority. The problem lay in the fact the Papal States were similar to other interstitial political units in that they were incapable of standing up to the military heavyweights who disposed of much greater resources. In order to compete, successive popes, from the sixteenth century onwards, had centralised authority within their dominions and increased revenues, for example through the sale of office. This produced some success, creating an elaborate bureaucracy which was among the most sophisticated in Europe. Nevertheless, corruption and family influence were integral to the system. Nepotism was outlawed by Innocent XII in 1692, but continued to be practised, particularly by Pius VI who constructed an enormous palace at Rome for his nephew, Luigi. Pluralism and simony continued unchecked. Bizarrely, the popes were afraid to implement Tridentine reforms which would have outlawed such practices, fearing that to do so would undermine their temporal authority. So it was that the Papal States were viewed as among the most inefficient and backward on the Continent. Luther's disillusion with Rome dated from his dispiriting visit there in 1510; Metternich, a natural supporter of hierarchical and patriarchal rule, was equally scandalised three centuries later by the appalling governance of the Papal States and by the impoverishment of its peasantry which provided a constant invitation to revolt. As Roger Aubert has remarked, 'Temporal power, which was demanded from the world as an irreducible prerequisite for the independence of the papacy, had in reality become an additional cause of the weakness of this institution.'[13]

Given this enfeeblement, Rome's territories were vulnerable to outside influence. They no longer provided the freedom and independence necessary if the Pope was to look to his wider responsibilities within the Catholic world. They became the plaything of the diplomacy of the courts of Vienna, Paris and Madrid, which did not hesitate to send in their troops when it suited them. Significantly, military occupation of the Papal States in the eighteenth century produced none of the outcry which had greeted the sack of Rome by Charles V's unpaid mercenary troops in 1527, though to be fair there was none of the uncontrolled violence of the sixteenth-century soldiery. Otherwise, rulers' consciences might have been stirred. Whatever the case, it increasingly suited secular rulers to deny Rome a say in international affairs; that way matters could be dealt with more speedily by reference to power politics. It is telling that the popes were denied an effective seat at all peace settlements from Westphalia in 1648, through Utrecht in 1713, Aix-la-Chapelle in 1748 to Vienna in 1814–15, although Consalvi's skill as a diplomat compensated for the lack of a formal voice at the latter.

Preoccupied with Italian politics, constantly engaged in backstairs intrigue, undermined by the Curia, economically enfeebled, unable to stand up to the emerging great powers, and theologically discredited, the papacy in the eighteenth century acted as little more than a referee rather than as a judge in both international and domestic affairs. More and more, the popes were perceived,

and treated, as petty temporal princes rather than the fountainhead of Christendom. One sardonic tract doing the rounds in late-eighteenth-century France,
Pape en chemise, quipped: 'Christendom will be happier when the Pope is reduced
to the status of plain abbé de St Pierre.'[14] It would take the arrogance and
intransigence of Pius IX (1846–78) to restore something of Rome's theological
credibility, at a time when its temporal power was once again under threat.

The Sociology of the Church: the Secular Clergy

Making sense of the sociology of the eighteenth-century Church is no easy
matter. One possible way to broach the topic is to draw an initial distinction
between the 'secular' clergy, that is those clerics who lived in the world and
who frequently had responsibility for the cure of souls, and the 'regular'
clergy, monks and nuns who were bound by specific religious vows and
generally formed communities; though, as we shall see, the differences between
the two groups were not always clear. Common to both were issues concerned
with structure, numbers, social origin, wealth, function and calibre.

Structure was of utmost importance to the seculars, reflecting the hierarchical nature of the Church. Such hierarchy was based on an interpretation
of Christ's legacy which devolved power to St Peter, the apostles and
the disciples, and through them to their heirs, the papacy, the prelacy and the
priesthood. Although, as we have seen, it was not always accepted that
the articulation of the Church into different units implied a superiority of
one over the other, a pyramidal conception of authority had emerged which
corresponded with the priveliged world of the *ancien régime*, which still divided
society into three estates, of which the clergy was the first. Although this
division no longer reflected reality, to challenge the top-down nature of office
within the Church was to question the basis on which society was built.

The hierarchy of personnel within the Church corresponded very broadly
with a territorial and administrative framework although, on the ground,
numerous exceptions and peculiarities existed. At the top of the tree were
the cardinals, all of whom were appointed by the Pope, though some were
nominated by secular rulers. Their functions were to advise His Holiness,
administer the Church when there was a papal vacancy and to elect a new
pontiff. Some, predominantly Italians, rarely left Rome and comprised the
Curia. This latter body had been divided since 1588 into fifteen separate
congregations, six of which were concerned with administration of the Papal
States and nine with oversight of the papacy's spiritual concerns, including
the *Index* (list of prohibited books) and the regulation of the bishops. Other
cardinals rarely visited Rome and remained in their native lands, occasionally
combining service to the Church with service to the state, as in the case of
Cardinal Fleury (1653–1743) who acted as First Minister to Louis XV (1715–
74), a practice the Council of Trent had outlawed with only limited effect.

The archbishops, who might incidentally also be cardinals, had responsibility
for their own sees, as well as more limited control over a number of suffragan
dioceses. The limits of ecclesiastical jurisdiction did not always accord closely

with geopolitical boundaries. So it was that part of Inner Austria fell under the Archbishop of Salzburg and other parts to the Patriarch of Aquileia in the Republic of Venice, while Madrid, capital of a vast overseas empire, did not even enjoy diocesan status. Archbishops and bishops reigned supreme within their dioceses, giving both spiritual and administrative direction to the see. In these tasks, they were frequently hindered by the canons of the collegiate and cathedral churches, who became increasingly obstructive as the scope of their duties was reduced. More significant as props to the bishop's authority were the deans who acted as his eyes and ears in the outlying districts of the diocese. Last, but arguably most important, were the parish clergy who had care of souls. Their role had been heightened as a matter of deliberate policy by the Counter-Reformation which sought to channel popular religion within the parish.

In terms of numbers, up to 2 per cent of the population of Continental Europe in the eighteenth century laid claim to clerical status of some kind. This probably marks a decrease when compared to earlier periods both in absolute terms and as a proportion of the population; and, indeed, numbers continued to drop generally after 1700. Table 1.1, which has been culled from a variety of sources, gives some indication of the number of secular clerics within the major Catholic states, though the figures should be regarded as approximate.

TABLE 1.1 Secular clergy in the major Catholic states

Country	Year	Number	Population (millions)	% of population
France	1790	88,000	25	0.352
Hungary	1787	13,263	7	0.2
Naples	1780	48,174	5	0.96
Poland	1772–3	10,000	5–6	0.2
		(Clergy of the Latin Rite)	(Latin Catholics)	
Portugal	1789	18,000	2.5	0.72
Spain	1800	57,488	10.5	0.54

These raw figures mask a number of important variables. First, it must be stressed that not all seculars had charge of a parish. In Spain, for example, only about one-third of the ordained clergy served in this way; while in France there were 39,000 *curés* and 20,500 *vicaires* who had direct responsibility for the cure of souls, yet there were some 28,500 priests who served as canons, chaplains, hospital *aumôniers*, Lenten preachers and so on. In both Austria and Poland, it was not uncommon for regulars, most notably the Jesuits and the Capuchins, to undertake parish duties: the religious life of Vienna in this regard would have collapsed without Jesuit assistance. Second, the regional distribution of the parish clergy was all too frequently uneven. Again, to take the Spanish example, the towns were much better catered for than the country-side, and there was a greater density of parish clergy per head of population in the north than in the south. The average number of parishioners per priest was around 500 nationally, but whereas the dioceses in the north and the Mediterranean littoral fell close to or bettered this figure, the average in the south was significantly higher. Thus the ratio was 1:153 in Alava, 1:170 in León and 1:441 in Aragon, but reached 1:1,115 in Córdoba and 1:1,721 in Murcia. In France, the regional disparities were not as pronounced yet, even here, the areas of Provence, the Massif Central, the Vendée and western Brittany, with their relatively high levels of parish clergy, stood in marked contrast to Languedoc, Champagne and the central and south-western provinces. In Portugal, around three-quarters of the seculars lacked a permanent benefice but many parishes, especially in the impoverished Serra in the south, had insufficient funds to attract an incumbent. As we shall see, this imbalance between relatively clericalised and under-staffed regions prefigured nineteenth-century geographical patterns of religious piety and dechristianisation.

In terms of social make-up, two observations need to be made about the episcopacy. First, bishops were generally youthful on appointment. They moved seamlessly from ordination or university graduation to a canonry, before attaining a bishopric, usually by their mid-twenties; for example, Prince Clement Wenceslaus became Bishop of Freising and Regensburg at the age of twenty-two. Few managed the record of the eight-year-old son of Philip V whose father installed him as Archbishop of Toledo in 1735. Bishops frequently went on to exercise political office alongside their episcopal duties. Second, the highest echelons of the Church were dominated almost every-where by the aristocracy. In France, for example, only two non-noble bishops were appointed between the years 1774 and 1790, and a small handful of aristocratic families monopolised the most lucrative sees: the Rohans at Stras-bourg, the Rochefoucaulds at Rouen and the Talleyrands at Reims. Spain is usually held up as an exception to the principle of aristocratic domination, and since advancement depended heavily upon training and education it was indeed possible for men of humble origins to rise to the highest positions. In practice, however, it was the nobility, albeit the lesser aristocracy, who tended to dominate. Rather, the exceptions to the rule were located in the German lands, the Papal States and the Kingdom of Naples. In the former, leading Catholic dynasties such as the Schönborns and Wittelsbachs, and elements from the Imperial Knights, exercised a stranglehold over the Prince Bishoprics of Mainz, Cologne and Trier, as well as the smaller dioceses such as Würzburg and Salzburg. However, as they were not always members of the episcopal order, they were unable to fulfil all of their episcopal duties and, accordingly, had recourse to subordinates, known as 'suffragan bishops'. Manifesting an impressive devotion to their obligations, which belies the traditional picture of a corrupt aristocratic German Church, these suffragans, who were peculiar to the Holy Roman Empire, were principally drawn from the middling ranks of society: in the period 1600–1800, none of the ten suffragans of Speyer or the seven suffragans of Basle stemmed from the nobility. In the Italian peninsula and off-shore islands, the Papal States were unusual in that the number of noble bishops in some sixty-five dioceses declined from 40 per cent to around 30 per cent during the course of the century. Only around one-third of the occupants of the 131 sees in the Kingdom of Naples were of noble extraction although, admittedly, in Piedmont, Sardinia and Venice the trend was quite the opposite.

The canonries of the collegiate and cathedral chapters were similarly havens for the nobility. In Germany, the quarterings of nobility required before entry to a canonry had been increased during the seventeenth century, although there was some subsequent relaxation of the rules in Cologne, Liège, Brixen and Chur, for example, which permitted entry to the well-to-do non-noble. Everywhere, the aristocracy was under-represented among the ranks of the parish clergy. Of over 800 priests who were ordained in the huge archdiocese of Besançon after 1734, fewer than two dozen were titled. A similar picture can be perceived in Poland. The remuneration of the parish priest was, in general, too low to attract nobles who found more lucrative and congenial opportunities in the fields of the military, royal bureaucracies and estate management. Crudely speaking, priests were drawn from the middling ranks of society, and were overwhelmingly urban in origin. This bias derived largely from the fact that educational opportunities were more pronounced in towns, which possessed schools and monasteries, vital instruments in clerical education. The wealth qualification which was imposed, either explicitly or implicitly, upon aspirants to the priesthood also emphasised the urban basis of clerical recruitment. Although the sons of better-off peasants provided recruits, especially in France and Portugal, the very poor were everywhere excluded.

Both contemporaries and historians have encountered inordinate difficulties in assessing the wealth of the Church. In terms of corporate status, there is no doubt that it enjoyed enormous fiscal privilege. By the early eighteenth century, the Church may well have possessed one-sixteenth of the land in Bohemia, two-thirds in the Kingdom of Naples, about one-third in Lombardy, almost a half of the Papal States, perhaps just over a tenth of France, approaching two-fifths of Austria and nearly half of Bavaria. Land-ownership was low in Poland, at under one-tenth of all territory in 1772. This was due to the Amortisation Decree of 1635 which had prohibited the transfer of land to the clergy in order to prevent the emergence of a powerful rival to the land-owning nobility who, in 1772, owned some two-fifths of Polish soil. Elsewhere in Europe, clerical ownership of land may have declined in the last quarter of the century, as the estates belonging to the suppressed Jesuit order were sequestrated and monarchs dispossessed clerical institutions, but in comparison to other sections of society the Church was still a formidable player in real estate. Its properties were widespread in the countryside, but they were most noticeable in the towns where it possessed some of the choicest urban locations.

In addition to land, the Church drew its wealth from other sources: tithes, rents on property, bequests, and payments for the performance of marriage and burial services (surplice fees) as well as other religious offices. In Portugal, a long-standing colonial power, the Church was actively involved in overseas trade. Such corporate wealth was, in turn, protected in some measure by tax exemptions although these were being steadily eroded by cash-starved monarchs driven, above all, by the never-ending need to finance war. In Austria, Venice, Spain and Portugal, legislation was passed to prevent land coming into *mortmain*, that is falling under the dead hand of the Church and thereby enjoying fiscal immunity. In Spain, after 1793, the involvement in conflict with France led the crown to force clerics to contribute to state loans on a massive scale.

These above observations, however, tell us little about the distribution of wealth among the secular clergy where inequalities were enormous. Some bishops were richer than others, depending on the size of their dioceses, but none was poor. One of the most frequently quoted examples is that of the Prince-Bishop of Strasbourg who enjoyed an annual revenue of around one million *livres*, though less than half of this was ever declared for taxation purposes. The Archbishop of Toledo had an annual income of 3 million *reales*. On another level, there was the Bishop of Embrun who had a relatively meagre income of 30,200 *livres*, and the Bishops of Valladolid and Tudela who had to get by on under 100,000 *reales* though none was by any means destitute. The parish clergy, by contrast, could not marshal these levels of remuneration anywhere in Catholic Europe. In 1768, the minimum income for a *curé* in France was set at 500 *livres*, raised in 1786 to 700 *livres*. In the Austrian lands, Joseph II looked to increase the basic minimum to 400 *florins* per annum, hardly a princely sum. Somewhere between these disparities of wealth distribution stood the canons. Their salaries varied, but none was worse off than the parish clergy and some were considerably richer. So it was that the members of the canonry of St Bertrand de Comminges commanded between 800 and 5,000 *livres* annually.

Ecclesiastical wealth ensured that the functions of the secular clergy were not merely spiritual, but also economic in nature. Everywhere the Church was intimately involved in the economic life of a region, both as a consumer – the cathedral of Seville required 24,195 litres of wine, 10,040 litres of oil and 11,500 kilos of wax annually, for example – and as a major employer. Peasants and urban workers were dependent on ecclesiastical institutions for their livelihood, whether it was the 50,000 labourers who constructed the monastic palace of Mafra close to Lisbon, the hundreds of peasants who toiled on the estates of the Archbishop of Seville, the 237 musicians, vergers and other employees of the cathedral at Toledo, the wig- and robe-makers of Lyon who dressed the clergy in their finery, or the candle-makers of Angers who supplied the cathedral. The Church was also a formidable patron of the arts, providing employment for painters, sculptors and artisans of all kinds. The Counter-Reformation witnessed a (re)fashioning of church architecture in the baroque style, sometimes on a huge scale, which extended into the eighteenth century. The exalted status of the altar, the use of elaborate side chapels and windows, the symbolic meaning attaching to much decoration, was all designed to contrast with the starkness of Reformed churches and to revitalise Catholic worship. For the poor and the destitute who constituted a significant proportion of early modern society, the Church was the first port of call. The Archbishop and chapter of Seville were reckoned to have sustained 20,000 peasants in the hunger-year of 1709. Alongside these dramatic interludes was the more routine but no less significant help on offer. Well-to-do clerics made substantial bequests in their wills for the relief of poverty, and parish clergy usually ear-marked part of their income for poor relief. Research in Naples and France suggests that the clergy were also significant as providers of loans, often at low or negligible rates of interest. In Franche-Comté, the clergy were second only to lawyers in this regard. Loans came in the form of a few *sous* from the *curé*, unsecured except by a verbal promise of repayment, or as notarised loans, perhaps disguised as a 'sale' to circumvent the Church's ban on usury. The chronological pattern of lending, with many debts contracted in March–May and a second smaller peak coming in October–November, suggests that they were taken out to meet the twin low points in the peasants' fiscal year: in the spring to cope with the difficulties of provisioning and to purchase seed for planting; in the autumn to meet the demands of the tax collector. These 'soft' loans, small though the sums may have been, were of real importance in tiding parishioners over seasonal hard times and helped to prevent the irreversible slide from poverty into destitution.

The political role of the prelates at the highest levels of government has already been touched upon, but it should also be remembered that the parish formed the basic administrative building block of *ancien régime* societies. Clerics helped enumerate tax registers, kept lists of births, marriages and deaths, propagated royal decrees, provided basic demographic information and were used by governments as sources of advice on issues as various as crop management and veterinary care, all critical matters at a time when bureaucrats were overworked and governments were expanding their range of administrative concerns. More important, from his parishioners' point of view, was the role of the parish priest in finding and vetting marriage partners. Even anti-clerical critics of the Church appreciated these social and utilitarian functions of the lower clergy.

Much more contentious was the part played by the Church in the administration and enforcement of law. Ecclesiastical courts were common throughout Catholic Europe, but the scope of their jurisdiction was severely circumscribed by comparison to earlier centuries, being limited to matters such as sexual and marriage offences. The readiness of royal courts to accept writs – the *recurso de fuerza* or the *appellatio ab abusu* – from plaintiffs alleging that ecclesiastical judges had exceeded their authority, and to hear such cases themselves, meant that the area of Church jurisdiction was continually being eroded. Royal courts still looked to clerics for assistance in enforcing the law, however. In general, priests were expected to preach obedience to government edicts. They were occasionally asked to assist the law courts by issuing a monitory, effectively a kind of subpoena which threatened wrong-doers or reluctant witnesses with excommunication if they did not appear in court or cooperate with the police. Clerics displayed some reluctance to wield this rusty weapon, however, recognising that it was no longer effective and might invite ridicule. There were instances in France of priests being jeered at and stoned in the pulpit as they sought to read out the monitory. Most significant was the role accorded the Church in censorship. In France, this duty fell upon the Sorbonne (technically the Faculty of Theology of the University of Paris), alongside the government and courts. Additionally, the papacy issued the *Index*, a list of prohibited books begun in 1557, and abolished only in 1966, supplemented by locally-produced rosters. The effectiveness of censorship varied considerably. In the relatively closed societies of Spain and Portugal, where enforcement was in the hands of the quasi-independent Inquisition, and in Austria, where it fell to the Jesuits until the intervention of the Archbishop of Vienna in 1759, censorship could be severe; in Italy and in France, it proved less easy to prohibit the influx of salacious and subversive material from the Netherlands, the publishing heart of Europe, and the authorities were, in any event, divided as to what should receive a *nihil obstat* as a bill of health. As the century wore on, the nature of works placed on the *Index* shifted significantly to include a greater number of secular texts, an indication of the Church's ongoing battle against Enlightenment ideas.

The one book to which the secular clergy regularly turned was the catechism. The educational role of the Church will be examined in more detail in the case of the regulars, who were at the forefront of instruction, but the parish priest was a significant player in the administration of the catechism which was regarded as the most effective way of bringing the people to piety, a view that remained more or less unchallenged until the twentieth century. In 1861, Pius IX reiterated the importance of catechetical instruction as the key to religious indoctrination in the bull *Divini illius redemptoris*, a view that would be repeated by Pius XI in 1929. In many parts of Europe, Sunday mass would be followed by a catechism class in which children would be introduced to the basics of Catholic dogma through a question-and-answer technique. This could prove an extremely tedious business, as much depended on learning by rote; and the catechisms deployed were often dated. In the 1850s Mgr Dupanloup, the energetic Archbishop of Orléans, deplored the fact that many French parishes were still using catechisms dating back to the seventeenth century, while the Spanish Church continued to rely largely on the texts of Gaspar Astete (1599) and Jerónimo Ripalda (1618) until the mid-nineteenth century.

Although the eighteenth-century clergy was the butt of much Enlightenment sarcasm, in truth the quality of the seculars had never been better. The vices of non-residence, concubinage, pluralism and simony had been largely eradicated from the episcopacy, though it had proved more difficult to wrest control of benefices from the monarchy and the aristocracy, who valued these as placements for younger sons. To be sure, there were not many great theologians and scholars among their ranks, and the saintly Bishop of Marseille, Mgr Belzunce, who personally ministered to the city's plague victims in 1720, and whose example was invoked by the unfortunate priest struggling against disease and doubt in Camus' 1948 novel, *La Peste*, stands out by virtue of his unusual spirituality and compassion. But, taken as a group, the prelates of the eighteenth century were distinguished by their pastoral dedication and administrative efficiency. The Spanish bishops have equally been commended as models of charitable giving, assiduous in their promotion of public works, keen to ameliorate the lot of the poor and attentive to the well-being of their dioceses. Even the contemporary Protestant cleric Joseph Townsend noted that their piety and zeal 'can never be sufficiently admired'.[15]

At the bottom rung of the ecclesiastical ladder, the parish clergy was also undergoing a renaissance in the eighteenth century, though there still was a considerable degree of national texturing. Parts of Spain and the Kingdom of Naples remained notable black spots, for example. One official in the Spanish diocese of Mondoñedo bemoaned priests who parroted the Latin mass 'without understanding what they were saying'.[16] The quality of the clergy was determined by several variables. In part, it depended on the calibre of the bishops. It was not possible to have good parish priests unless an example was set from above. The Council of Trent had strengthened the authority of the prelates in their dioceses, making it possible for them, at least in theory, to exclude unworthy candidates from the priesthood and to insist upon clerical attendance at educational retreats and synods. Of even greater significance in the improvement of the parish clergy was the establishment of diocesan seminaries. These had also been ordered by the Council of Trent, but in practice there was a considerable time-lag in turning legislation into reality, so that many foundations dated from the late seventeenth, or even eighteenth, century. The intention behind Trent's reform decrees had been to create a parish clergy which was clearly distinct from, and capable of serving as a model for, the laity.

The availability of a seminary education, together with effective episcopal tutelage, ensured that France could boast the best-trained clerics in Catholic Europe by the mid-eighteenth century. Here, the *curé* was distinguished from the laity by his lifestyle (he no longer drank to excess, gambled, went hunting or played cards); by his sexual mores (a truly celibate clergy had emerged which no longer maintained mistresses and was careful to employ female servants only if they were over the canonical age of fifty); by his dress (wigs and bright stockings were out and the *soutane* was in); and was set apart by his education and culture. There was an increased stress upon his unique role in conducting certain religious rituals, including baptism and extreme unction. And even in death he was separated from the majority of his parishioners since he enjoyed the privilege of being buried inside the parish church whereas they were confined to the cemetery. Not for nothing has the French priest been described as an *être séparé*.[17]

The same could not be said of his counterpart in Spain. Bishops made commendable efforts to improve matters, but seminary education was less satisfactory than north of the Pyrenees. To be sure, seventeen new seminaries were founded, largely thanks to the efforts of the pious Charles III (1759–

88), bringing the total to forty-five by 1800, and their direction was taken out of the hands of the cathedral chapters which had used them chiefly as recruiting grounds for clerical lackeys and altar-servers rather than as vehicles for education. Nevertheless, they were small-scale and poorly administered. Theology was neglected or badly taught. This was due to the fact that heresy had effectively been eradicated, without recourse to civil war, leading to a belief that theological study was not essential, and might even be harmful, to good spiritual guidance. A system of competitive examinations, *los concursos de curatos*, was placed on a national basis by royal order in 1784 but proved only partially effective in raising the quality of clerical appointees. Although some of the criticisms directed at the parish clergy in respect of their ignorance and worldly ways were exaggerated, a better-trained priesthood would not emerge until the nineteenth century, significantly after the founding of new training schools. The problem was that state bureaucrats had made much greater progress during the same period, and often appeared more up-to-date. Herein lay the roots of a nineteenth-century anti-clericalism, which would not be restricted to Spain.

In the Holy Roman Empire, early initiatives aimed at founding seminaries in the sixteenth century were interrupted by the Thirty Years' War (1618–48). The very first seminary, set up at Eichstätt in 1564, was razed to the ground by Swedish troops seventy years later and was not reopened until 1710. A similar fate befell seminaries at Breslau, Salzburg, Basle and elsewhere. Recovery was slow because of a lack of funds. The chronic indebtedness of the German territories in the aftermath of the Thirty Years' War, and subsequent conflicts with the Turks, meant that clerical initiatives on seminaries often foundered due to a cash shortage. The issue of money was not unique to Germany. The Church may have been corporately wealthy, but its wealth was fragmented among its members and there was no mechanism for mobilising resources when they were required; accordingly, the establishment, funding and upkeep of seminaries relied on the generosity of individual donors. This problem with finance was especially acute in Poland where the Church was not as wealthy as in the German territories. War and plague at the start of the eighteenth century merely exacerbated the difficulties. It was to the credit of the Polish Church that thirty-four seminaries existed in 1772, most of them founded before 1750.

Whatever the improvements in the quality of the parish clergy during the eighteenth century, many priests remained hampered in the performance of their pastoral duties by the inadequacies of the parish structure. It frequently proved difficult to redesignate parishes, originally set up in the Middle Ages, to take account of subsequent demographic and other changes. Within the walls of Vienna, there were only three parishes, each crammed with a burgeoning population. A further problem in the parish structure was the inequality of endowments. It proved difficult to attract priests, especially of good calibre, to those parishes where the funds were inadequate to support a decent living. In Spain, there was a correlation between complaints about the ignorance and low morals of the clergy and regions where resources were slim. Often when these parishes fell vacant, it was well-nigh impossible to tempt suitable priests to take them over. The 1797 census revealed vacancies in nearly 3,000 parishes in impoverished Galicia, Extremadura and Soria. In 1800, three towns complained to the Council of Castile that they had lacked a priest for over twenty years because there was no income to support one.

Final observations concern the geography of the secular clergy. Throughout this discussion, it has been apparent that the wealth, numbers, charitable and educational resources were concentrated in towns, this at a time when the majority of lay people, perhaps as much as 95 per cent in some areas, lived in the countryside. This proved a weakness in that the seculars were not always able to direct their manpower and resources to where they were most needed. Lying alongside this town–country fissure, there was a further division to be perceived between those regions which might broadly be termed 'clericalised' and those which were not. In the former, the parish clergy were relatively numerous; they played a leading role in the direction of religious and social practices and were generally appreciated by the laity. In the latter, the clergy were relatively sparse, and there was a good deal of resistance to their claims to both spiritual and social precedence. The key factor in creating a clericalised laity was not so much the total number of clerics, including canons and regulars who would be concentrated in the towns, but the visibility and existence of parish clergy in the rural communities. Broadly speaking, there was a correlation between areas of clericalisation and religious fervour on the one hand and non-clericalisation and dechristianisation on the other, a dichotomy which was to become increasingly apparent during the nineteenth century. Spain and France are two excellent examples of this trend. As was noted above, in Spain the proportion of priests with the cure of souls was much higher in the pious north and lower per head of population in the southern dechristianised areas such as Córdoba, Murcia and Seville. In France, the rural density of the parish clergy was at its greatest in the deeply pious west compared to much of the indifferent Paris basin and provinces of the south-west.

The Sociology of the Church: the Regulars

Almost everyone in the eighteenth century, in particular the critics of the Church, insisted that there was an imbalance between the secular and the regular clergy, with far too many of the latter and too few of the former, especially at parish level. The Iberian peninsula was singled out as being a 'monks' paradise'. And in certain cities the proportion of regulars was high. So it was that in Padua in 1790, even after the radical Tron reforms, 6.5 per cent of the population was made up of monks and nuns. In truth, there were far fewer regulars than contemporaries imagined, even in purportedly clerical areas, as Table 1.2 shows.

Counting the regulars is fraught with difficulty, not least because the definition of who was, and was not, a monk or nun had never been more difficult. Crudely speaking, there appears to have been a reduction of the overall numbers of regulars in the eighteenth century, but an increase in the

TABLE 1.2 Regular clergy in France and the Iberian peninsula

Country	Year	Number Men	Number Women	Total	Population (millions)	% of population
France	1790	26,000	55,000	81,000	25	0.32
Portugal	1765	30,772	11,428	42,200	2.5	1.7
Spain	1797	53,098	24,471	77,569	10.5	0.73

diversity of those grouped under this loose heading, a vivid testimony to the strength and vitality of early modern Catholicism. The older religious orders such as the Benedictines, Carthusians and Cistercians, together with the Augustinian canons, continued to be defined by the fact that members swore solemn vows, lived in closed communities, their prime activity was prayer and meditation, and each house was largely autonomous, although it belonged to a larger religious family whose rules it followed. The thirteenth century had witnessed the foundation of a number of mendicant orders, most obviously the Franciscans and Dominicans, who circulated within the secular community. The sixteenth and seventeenth centuries saw a further expansion in the type and variety of the orders, including some such as the Sulpicians and Lazarists who were actually congregations of secular priests living under religious vows. The Jesuits, founded by St Ignatius Loyola in 1534, had the objective of undertaking missionary work within both Protestant Europe and newly-discovered 'pagan' territories overseas. Some female orders, including the Ursulines, Visitandines and Sisters of Our Lady of Charity, were established precisely with the aim of performing a function within the wider community, for example education, care of the sick and rehabilitation of 'fallen women'. All of these succumbed to the hostility of the Church's male hierarchy which objected to the uncontrolled presence of large numbers of women circulating freely in the community; ultimately, they had to accept claustration (enclosure in a nunnery) and the veil. By the late seventeenth and early eighteenth centuries, however, females were managing to free themselves of these restraints and a number of associations, properly called congregations, were set up. Their members made simple promises which might be renewed annually and which had no legal status; they lived an active and peripatetic existence within the community; they did not adopt the veil; and they were independent of any religious rule, falling under the control only of the local bishop. At the other end of the spectrum to the regular orders proper were the confraternities, pious associations of lay people, both men and women, who might give themselves full time to good works. While statistics are unreliable, it appears that confraternities and congregations were on the march in the eighteenth century. Certainly they were in the nineteenth.

Like the seculars, the regular orders were corporately wealthy, but the riches were unequally divided. Top of the pile were the older established orders whose very longevity had permitted them to accumulate substantial bequests of land, property and money. In Lower Austria, the Benedictine, Cistercian and Augustinian establishments had considerable land-holdings, the abbey of Göttweig alone owning well over a hundred seigneuries. In Poland, where as we have seen the Church was not especially wealthy, the most venerable orders, introduced between the eleventh and thirteenth centuries, dominated land-holding in the dioceses of Cracow and Gniezno. Least well endowed were those orders and congregations established in the early modern period, the exception being the Jesuits. All too often, the houses of these relative new-comers had been set up as a result of a bequest from a single generous benefactor, whose legacy did not meet running costs and did not permit the renovation of buildings as they began to fall into disrepair. Particularly un-happy was the situation of women's orders and congregations. Since they were not priests, they could not conduct masses and were thereby debarred from receiving any endowments from those wishing to have mass said on their own behalf and on behalf of relatives after death. This was the more unfortunate in that, by and large, it was the newer orders that were responding to social needs, and were most highly esteemed by the laity. Even so, this did not altogether stop the obloquy attached by Enlightenment thinkers to the contemplative orders being extended to these relative newcomers.

The functions of the religious were extraordinarily varied. The older orders maintained a commitment to a life of prayer and contemplation; those founded in the sixteenth and seventeenth centuries were much more involved in social activity. So it was that the Capuchin friars produced preachers of enormous talent and popularity in eighteenth-century Spain, organising missions in over a hundred villages in the archdiocese of Toledo in 1769–70 alone. The most gifted, Fray Diego, so inflamed his audience with a sermon against comedies that his listeners tore down the local theatre at Antequera. Other orders, such as the Brothers of St John of God, were more generally concerned with the care of the poor. Proselytising and educative missions were staged with great success by the Montfortains in the west of France. In Poland, there were 9,000 priests among the regular clergy, almost as many as the seculars, without whom the cure of souls in the parishes would have gone neglected. The women's orders and congregations undertook a variety of activities which can be subsumed under short headings: working in hospitals and providing medicines; running houses for orphans, aged poor and former prostitutes; setting up soup kitchens at times of harvest failure; organising creche-type services for working mothers; teaching industrial skills such as lace-making to young girls; and maintaining sheltered accommodation for genteel widowed geriatrics. Above all, the regulars taught. The Jesuits, Dominicans, Oratorians, Ursulines and Piarists (in eastern Europe) concentrated their efforts upon the education of the sons and daughters of the well-to-do, and also had extensive involvement in the training of priests within seminaries. The instruction of the popular classes was more patchy and was carried out, with varying degrees of efficiency, by a number of different agencies: parish schools, whose masters were notionally supervised by the local priest; dame schools, which were little more than child-care services; charity schools, which were highly dependent on local initiatives; the homeplace, where an informal schooling was provided at the mother's knee; and the limited number of schools run by religious orders, most famously the Brothers of the Christian Schools founded by Jean-Baptiste de la Salle at Reims in 1682. The Brothers distinguished themselves by imposing a discipline and harshness which exceeded even that of the Jesuit colleges.

The most successful of the orders were undoubtedly the Jesuits. They established themselves at the forefront of lay education, they dominated the seminaries, they were prominent in missionary activity in the Old and the New World, they provided confessors to Catholic princely families throughout Europe, their wealth was enormous, they had extensive commercial interests, their internal administration was second to none, and they enjoyed a particularly favourable status with the papacy to whom they swore a fourth vow of fidelity, after those of poverty, chastity and obedience. They proved uniquely successful at adapting Tridentine Catholicism to the needs and desires of the laity, encouraging the use of frequent communion, employing theatrical gestures in their missions and sermons, adapting Church ritual and practice to suit local customs, and encouraging the spread of wayside shrines and crosses and saints' statues. In 1719, a Jesuit mission not far from Augsburg was able to establish a following for St Francis Xavier when prayers for rain produced a veritable downpour.

Success was their undoing. Other orders were jealous of their dominance: there was widespread envy of their riches; there was suspicion of their influence upon monarchs; and a distaste among Gallicans for their Ultramontane tendencies. Jansenists were opposed to the supposedly lax Jesuit approach to religious belief and practice, wholly counter to their own rigorous and demanding position. Yet the Jansenists were shrewd in expanding the basis of their own support by targeting a group who were universally unpopular. From the 1750s, the Jesuits came under repeated attack. The precise reasons varied from country to country. In Portugal, their support for the Indians in South America and their commercial ventures put them at odds with the crown's interests, and in 1759 they were expelled on a trumped-up charge of intended regicide. In France, the *parlements*, which had always defended Gallican interests and were often sympathetic to Jansenism, took advantage of a legal case concerning the economic affairs of the Jesuits in the trade of Martinique to question more generally the order's rules, Ultramontane sympathies and theology. The attempted assassination of the King by a former pupil of the Jesuits was merely grist to their mill. Against a background of popular, institutional and court hostility (Madame de Pompadour, Louis XV's mistress, disliked them), the Jesuits were ousted in 1764.

Spain was the next country from which they were banished, in 1767. Here the reformist faction within the court of Charles III feared that members of the order were abusing their privileged position as educators of the nobility to pursue their own sectarian interests. Aranda, the chief minister, exploited food riots in Madrid to persuade his monarch that the Jesuits were even plotting regicide, another allegation without substance. Naples (1767), Parma (1768) and Malta (1768), under pressure from the Bourbon rulers, rapidly followed suit. Pressure ultimately fell on the papacy to take decisive action. Clement XIII (1758–69) resisted this, eliciting the comment from Louis' minister Choiseul that 'the Pope's an idiot'.[18] His successor Clement XIV (1769–74), who had been elected precisely because he was thought to be malleable on the subject, was finally obliged to dissolve the whole order in 1773, the text of the decree of abolition, *Dominus ac redemptor noster*, having been composed for him by the Spanish ambassador. Papal suppression of the Jesuits prompted Maria Theresa to abolish the order in Habsburg lands that same year and to use their confiscated lands and properties to initiate a state-sponsored elementary school system. They had been on the back foot well before this date, their role in education and censorship being circumscribed and their places in the University at Prague taken by Augustinians and Dominicans.

The suppression of the Jesuits was an unmitigated disaster for Catholicism. At a stroke, it laid bare the papacy's weakness in the face of princely bullying. The Church had lost its most successful educators, its most effective missionaries and its most innovative thinkers. The papacy abandoned a body of men dedicated to its service. 'I have cut off my right hand,' complained Clement XIV, who thereafter abandoned an earlier habit of kissing the feet of a statue of Christ lest these were poisoned by the order.[19] The demise of the Jesuits left the Church poorly positioned to tackle the intellectual challenges of the century. Paradoxically, in France the sale of Jesuit libraries led to widespread access to Enlightenment books which the fathers had purchased in order to know better their enemies.

Belief and Practice

It has long been agreed by historians of the eighteenth century that the intellectual atmosphere of the period, usually encapsulated in the term the 'Enlightenment', was hostile to religion in general and to revealed religion in particular. Catholic writers especially have regarded this as the start of the rot: Daniel-Rops remarks that before 1748, intellectuals had been 'cautious'; thereafter the 'enemies of Christianity threw off their mask'.[20] There is some truth in this observation, though, as we shall see, it is far from the whole story.

Analysis is rendered difficult because interpretations of the Enlightenment have varied. Once thought of as a monolithic movement, it is increasingly regarded as a more nebulous phenomenon which must be understood within specific regional, class and gender contexts. The Enlightenment certainly did not espouse any clear set of doctrines or prescriptions. Rather, it is best viewed as an intellectual tendency which embodied a set of approaches or attitudes. Notably, it privileged the use of reason as a tool of inquiry; it held that ultimately everything was knowable through the use of reason, while in practice using reason not as a means of elucidating *a priori*, providentially underpinned truths but as a way of investigating the hitherto uncharted verities of the empirical world; it questioned the validity of all human institutions, whatever their pedigree, and accepted them only in so far as they were demonstrably useful; and it incorporated a faith in man's capacity to improve his condition through his own efforts. The intellectual roots of the movement went back to the Scientific Revolution of the two preceding centuries, and it also drew upon the European experience of contact with non-Europeans in the overseas discoveries.

In what ways, then, was Catholicism challenged? To begin with, the astronomical discoveries of the Scientific Revolution had shattered the long-held Aristotelian view of the universe which held that the planets moved around a central, stationary earth and that the heavenly spheres and the earth were different in nature and subject to separate laws. By 1700 this interpretation was no longer viable, yet the Church had done itself great damage, in the short term, by refusing to acknowledge this, and by persecuting as heretics those who maintained such views. In the longer term, the Scientific Revolution proffered an alternative basis for knowledge to that espoused by the Church, one which was founded upon empirical observation and inductive reasoning in the case of the natural sciences and the deductive reasoning of the mathematical sciences as opposed to one founded upon revelation and faith. The greatest of the scientists, Isaac Newton, whose *Mathematical Principles of Natural Philosophy* was published in 1687, portrayed an ordered universe run by divinely-ordained mathematical laws in which God routinely intervened. The Newtonian universe offered proof of the existence of a Creator-God (the argument from design), yet it could also be argued that it proved the remoteness of God; once the mechanical cosmos was set in motion He took no further part in its functioning or in the lives of its inhabitants. A parallel view of Providence, likewise derived from Newtonian physics, was of a God who was constrained by the natural laws which He Himself had created, and who was able to intervene in earthly matters only through natural causes. In this world-view, there was no longer any room for the miraculous, the supernatural and the magical, leading to what has been termed the 'disenchantment of the world'.[21] It is easy to see how all this resulted in an often fuzzy deism. The 'natural religion' of the deists presupposed that there was a Creator-God, and that certain religious ideas might be present in all men from birth. But God was stripped of any redemptive role in man's history, the divinity of Christ was jettisoned along with original sin, and revealed religion become an anachronism.

Like the Scientific Revolution, the discovery of overseas lands and their non-Christian peoples also served to change the grounds of religious debate. Why had God chosen to leave the heathen outside of His scheme for human redemption? What was the value of the religions practised in non-European cultures? An obvious response to both questions was that all religions were merely human constructs, thus throwing doubt on the unique nature of Christianity and in particular upon its claim to be founded upon divine revelation. Put bluntly, Catholicism did not have a monopoly of truth; truth was relative, not absolute. Montesquieu's literary device contained in the *Persian*

Letters (1721), of having a body of imaginary Persian visitors travel to Paris and comment from their perspective on what they found, was part of a novel mode of discourse reflecting the new relativism. Moreover, the tendency to regard religion as a human institution had the effect of shifting debate from issues of theology to questions of social utility and the role of religion as a cement holding together the social order. Religion thus lost its independent status, and became something that could be assimilated into a wider corpus of knowledge. The Enlightenment's confidence that everything could be understood, through the process of description, reduced knowledge to the assemblage of information, a method seen most obviously in Diderot and D'Alembert's *Encyclopédie*, the first volume of which appeared in 1751. Such an approach was not wholly original, witness the efforts of Thomas Aquinas in his *Summa Theologica*, and Guicciardini in his *Histories*. What was striking about the Enlightenment approach was that its methodology potentially broke down the link between knowledge and wisdom, and divorced truth from ethics in a way that had not been the case earlier.

The possibilities of human advancement manifested by some non-European civilisations accorded well with the Enlightenment's optimistic view of human nature and stood at odds with the Church's doctrine of original sin, the Fall and redemption. John Locke, in his *Essay Concerning Human Understanding* (1690), argued that every individual was potentially perfectible since, at birth, man was a *tabula rasa*, his ideas deriving from sense impressions of the environment, the origins of what is termed 'sensualism'. Education was, therefore, crucial in moulding man's development. Rousseau's recipe for education, encapsulated in *Emile* (1762), explored these themes further by ensuring that his hero's first (and, for some time, sole) book should be Daniel Defoe's *Robinson Crusoe*. A few *philosophes* took these reductionist theories to their logical conclusion and argued that man was merely a collection of atoms, without a soul, reacting to sensory impulses. This materialist and atheistic approach, best exemplified in La Mettrie's *L'Homme Machine* (1747) and d'Holbach's *Système de la Nature* (1770), constituted a further intellectual challenge to the Church. Explicit atheism was entirely novel, and it should be stressed that it won few converts other than the *curé* Meslier and Helvétius; the majority of enlightened thinkers leaned towards deism and balked at the rigid dogma of atheist thought.

The critical spirit which pervaded Enlightenment thought found an easy target in the institutions of the Church, even if the abuses of the clergy were caricatured and parodied to an excessive degree, notably in Diderot's *The Nun* (1760) and Voltaire's *Candide* (1759). The excessive wealth of the Church drew particular fire, as did the lifestyle of canons, abbots and others who enjoyed a disproportionate share of the Church's riches without fulfilling any useful social role. The *philosophes* were less scathing about parish priests. Significantly, they regarded them as functionaries with important responsibility for the promotion of happiness and welfare, but they had little regard for the priest's sacramental functions. It was the religious orders which attracted the most obloquy. Their usefulness was questioned on several grounds. Their celibacy was viewed as a drain on the state's resources, as an unnatural state of being and as a standing temptation to indulge in bizarre sexual practices. Their devotion to prayer and contemplation was seen as wasteful when they might have been more productively occupied. The fact that a number of the older houses contained few inhabitants who nevertheless enjoyed extensive rents, tithes and other income was a standing scandal. In France and Austria, commissions were set up to close down and amalgamate smaller houses, but the limited results merely served to demonstrate that the Church could never put its own house in order and would have to be coerced.

The corollary of Enlightenment scepticism towards Catholicism was an assumption that all religions were of equal worth, and that no single cult should be privileged above others. Diderot and other *philosophes* deplored the manner in which Catholic states especially attempted to constrain men's freedom of belief. 'Violence will make a man a hypocrite if he is weak,' proclaimed the *Encyclopédie*, 'a martyr if he is courageous.'[22] A number of Protestant states had led the way in granting a *de facto* toleration. In Germany, the Augsburg Settlement of 1555 had established the principle of *cuius regio, eius religio*, whereby the prince determined the religion of his subjects, yet it, and the Treaty of Westphalia in 1648, had called upon rulers to adopt tolera-tion as a pragmatic policy. In the event, rulers were conscious that any real measure of toleration would affect their relationship with established churches and the very basis of divine-right kingship. So it was that toleration, when it was granted, bestowed only the limited right to practise religion in private; nowhere would it allow a full measure of civic rights. Moreover, toleration derived more from economic expediency and pragmatic concern for stability than from conviction. In Prussia, the Great Elector welcomed large numbers of Huguenots driven from France by the Revocation of the Edict of Nantes in 1685, and in the United Provinces the diversity of faiths necessitated a religious accommodation. In Britain, the Toleration Act of 1689 allowed religious freedom only to Protestant dissenters, and Catholics laboured under heavy legal discrimination throughout the eighteenth century, albeit fitfully enforced. The Archbishop of York noted that the government policy towards Catholics was one of 'tacit connivance ... in the private exercise of their religion'.[23] The Relief Acts of 1778 and 1791 brought some measure of relaxation by allowing Catholics to build chapels in private houses, for example. Yet they remained subject to double-assessment of the land tax; although this was revised in 1794, they continued to be taxed more highly than their Protestant neighbours. In Ireland, where Catholics were the overwhelming majority, they suffered greater repression though, as Marianne Elliott and others have commented, this was less intense than subsequently claimed.[24] The object of such discrimination was, however, less in doubt: to ensure that Catholics could not deploy either their superior numbers, or wealth and office, to exercise social or political influence.

Within Catholic Europe, Protestants fared little better. This was especially true in most parts of Italy and the Iberian peninsula, though numbers here were slight as they were just across the Alps. This did not stop the Archbishop of Salzburg forcibly expelling Protestants over the age of twelve from his lands in 1731, giving them only eight days' notice. Ironically, their movement across Germany inspired a proselytising fervour among many of their co-religionaries. When toleration did come, it was usually imposed by the ruler in the teeth of opposition from the clerical establishment. It was in these circumstances that Joseph II extended freedoms to Protestants and to Jews in 1781. It was in France that liberty of conscience was slowest to arrive. This was paradoxical given that France was at the forefront of enlightened ideas on religion and was where Voltaire used the Calas affair – the case of the unfortunate Protestant, Jean Calas, who in 1762 was broken on the wheel for allegedly killing his son in order to prevent his conversion to Catholicism – to highlight the iniquities of religious intolerance. The essentially humane but cautious Louis XVI was reluctant to act hastily and it took a crisis in the neighbouring Netherlands leading to an influx of Protestant refugees to force the government's hand. An Edict Concerning Those Who Do Not Profess the Catholic Religion gave some minimal relief to France's 700,000 Protestants; despite its title it did not extend to Jews. It allowed freedom of conscience to Protestants, recognised the validity of their marriages and permitted the inheritance of property, but there was no acceptance of their right to enter the professions or public office, no legalisation of Protestant schools, and the Catholic Church maintained a monopoly of public worship. Full civic and religious equality would not come until the revolution.

Given the diffuse nature of the movement, it is small wonder that the Enlightenment's campaign for the establishment of religious toleration should have made such slow progress. Enlightenment concerns were undoubtedly manifold, and it is a nineteenth-century misconception to see religion as constituting the dominant element. The French *philosophes* were exceptional in their anti-clerical and anti-religious preoccupations. In Scotland, the key issue was that of economics; the German *Aufklärer* were busy with cameralist concerns, including the creation of a *Polizeistaat*, an early experiment in welfarism; Italian *illuminati* were engrossed in questions of law and economics, especially money supply. Nor should the threat to revealed religion from science be exaggerated. The very term 'science' dates from the 1830s; in the eighteenth century, the term deployed was 'natural philosophy' and, as such, God still played a formidable role in the study of the world which He had created and which embodied His characteristics and purposes. Again, there is the problem of the diffusion of ideas. The *philosophes* themselves, while concerned with self-improvement and education, were none the less anxious lest their opinions should fall among the popular classes where they would inevitably be misconstrued and bastardised, and constitute a source of social unrest. As Voltaire himself reflected to Frederick the Great: 'Your majesty will do the human race an eternal service in extirpating this infamous super-stition [Christianity], I do not say among the rabble, who are not worthy of being enlightened and who are apt for every yoke; I say among the well-bred, among those who wish to think.'[25] In another famous observation, he declared: 'I want my lawyer, my tailor, my servants, even my wife to believe in God, and I think I shall then be robbed and cuckolded less often.'[26] Dostoyevsky's nineteenth-century question – If God does not exist then is everything permitted? – was one which eighteenth-century intellectuals and others obsessed with the need to preserve social order had already anticipated.[27]

In one sense, of course, the *philosophes* need not have worried since the publication and circulation of their works was largely confined to a literate and leisured elite, although there was such a thing as a 'low enlightenment' which revolved around the publishing opportunities offered by cheap newspapers, pamphlets and novels. Often salacious in tone, this material helped to undermine respect for the Church and other authorities. For example, Mercier's *2440* pointed to a future society which had successfully dispensed with the clergy, while the anonymous *Thérèse la Philosophe* recounted the sexual adventures of a courtesan with, among others, various ecclesiastics. On the other hand, this literature of the 'low enlightenment' was counter-balanced by the so-called *bibliothèque bleu*, circulating in France and named after the blue paper on which it was printed and which was also used to wrap sugar loaves. This material, comprising chap books, pamphlets and almanacs, remained religious in its focus, retailing stories of saints, miracles and fabulous tales, the very stuff of which Voltaire and others would have disapproved.

It should also be stressed that there was a Catholic Enlightenment, part of a more general Counter-Enlightenment as Isaiah Berlin termed it, which sought to grapple with the Church's critics.[28] In part, this derived from an elaboration of Counter-Reformation values, hence the greater emphasis on the training of priests; it also reflected a retreat from a lavish baroque piety to a simpler expression of belief more in accord with the sentiments of the age; and, most importantly, it drew on the new scientific discoveries to demonstrate that there was no necessary dichotomy between reason and faith. The Catholic Enlightenment strove for a religion which melded together the metaphysical and the natural. The Jesuits successfully reworked Cartesian rationalism, and the ideas of Gottfried Leibniz were taken up and applied by Catholic theologians including the Augustinian, Eusebius Amort (1692–1775) and Ulrich Weiss (1713–63). The appeal of a 'rational religion' was undoubtedly its universalism. It would win converts without the need for persecution, which could prove counter-productive; and it would pave the way towards a reunification of Christendom. This was an old idea which had been intermittently discussed in the sixteenth and seventeenth centuries and which was given a new lease of life by the Catholic Enlightenment's emphasis on a forgiving humanity. While inter-Church unity was widely bruited within Germany (where the Catholic Enlightenment was notably strong, especially in the field of education), in Italy the idea was given prominence by Ludovico Antonio Muratori (1672–1750), the standard-bearer of Catholic enlightened thought. As well as writing on Church history and publishing sources for the history of Italy, in 1740 he proposed to the papacy a series of progressive reforms which included the reduction in the number of saints' days, the removal of redundant orders and a shift away from lavish displays of practice, designed in part to assist the reunification of Catholic and Protestant churches. Benedict

XIV (1740–58) was greatly attracted to the idea of the reunification of Christendom, but he had serious doubts about Muratori's reforms, which were destined to remain on the drawing board. In any case, it is highly doubtful whether the dream of inter-Church cooperation could ever be achieved as religious prejudices and divides were as entrenched as ever.

Overall, the impact of the Catholic Enlightenment should not be exaggerated. It was watered down by two factors. The first was that Catholic intellectuals seemed generally to be on the back foot, preoccupied with theological matters such as the Jansenist controversy, responding to events and criticism rather than initiating change, always in the wake of their more famous secular counterparts, and unable to adapt in the manner of Protestant theologians who appeared better able to absorb and assimilate new ways of thinking. As Benedict XIV complained: 'Today there are people who are notable for capacity and learning, but they waste too much of their time in irrelevant matters or in unpardonable disputes among themselves, when it should be their sole aim to resist and destroy atheism and materialism.'[29] Second, the Catholic Enlightenment was just as elitist, if not more so, than the Enlightenment more generally. Although its ideas were taken up within Catholic university circles, its wider resonance was less profound. One good example of this is the case of Alfonso de'Liguori (1696–1787) who founded the Redemptorist Order in 1732 and whose book *Visits to the Holy Sacrament and the Blessed Virgin for Every Day*, published in 1745, made communion more readily available to ordinary people. Yet the work of this outstanding moral theologian only achieved any real degree of popularity in the nineteenth century when his book was reprinted in France over a hundred times.

While the ideas of Catholic theologians and enlightened writers generally are easily available to the historian through their printed works, it is much more difficult to assess their impact upon both elites and the popular classes. Even more problematic is to establish the quintessential religious beliefs of the age. In part, this is because, at a popular level, the historian is dealing with a section of society that left no written records of its own volition; ordinary people were written about, but they did not record their thoughts themselves. Indeed, some would argue that the extent to which religious belief was interiorised must for ever remain hidden, and that one can make statements about religious life only in terms of its gregarious conformity. Despite this, there have been significant attempts to measure both the quantity and quality of religious beliefs in the eighteenth century which make an imaginative use of eclectic sources, including folklore, pastoral visitations, wills, records of church courts, inquisitorial depositions and civil registers, though it must be admitted that, forty years after Gabriel Le Bras's call 'to seek out the Christian wherever', our knowledge remains patchy.[30] Certain generalisations may at least be ventured. Among the elites, it appears that there may have been some fall in religious belief, evidenced by the declining use of religious phrases and bequests in wills, perhaps as a result of Enlightenment influences. More generally, there is material suggesting a decrease in the number of communicants at Easter mass, though since this attendance was a legal obligation, and the numbers who failed to attend were very small, the significance of this is not altogether clear. In France, brewers, inn-keepers and boatmen were conspicuous in their non-attendance. Other evidence for a drop in religiosity, based upon increasing illegitimacy rates, a fall-off in membership of confraternities and the rising number of publications on secular topics, is likewise ambiguous. For instance, rising illegitimacy levels may have reflected worsening economic conditions which led couples to put off marriage, with a concomitant rise in the number of pre-marital conceptions. The decline in membership of confraternities is especially difficult to plot and may have reflected altered socio-economic conditions, not a change in religiosity. And the total number of religious publications remained stable and may even have grown, although the proportion of the printed word devoted to religion fell overall.

Indications of regional variation in belief and practice are more solid. Crudely speaking, towns had lower levels of religious observance than the countryside, offering anonymity and greater opportunities to wriggle out of services. For example, in 1780s Madrid there was a particularly brisk sale of the certificates required by the ecclesiastical authorities from those who wished to avoid the obligation of Easter communion, much of the trade incidentally being managed by the town's prostitutes. Additionally, there were regional pockets of laxity in areas such as the Paris basin and Spanish Galicia. A fondness for the Marian cult was particularly pronounced in parts of Germany, southern Italy and the Iberian peninsula. Popular religiosity in the north of Italy was clerically centred and focused upon the parish and its attendant sodalities. By contrast, in the south it retained a concern with local saints and their cults at the expense of parish observance, and was closely linked to family and village networks and sociability patterns. The laity was so outside of clerical tutelage that a local observer, Carlo Antonio Broggia, was led to remark in 1746: 'There is no people more ignorant and barbaric than our own.'[31] Ireland, too, continued to manifest an essentially pre-Tridentine variant of Catholicism, similar to that found in the south of Italy. The parish church was not at the apex of religious life, which was characterised by the plethora of superstitious practices and boisterous festivals; some of these, such as the patterns (communal visits to the local holy well) and wakes, were unique to the country.

There is also a suggestion of gender bias in eighteenth-century Catholicism. Women were more generous in their bequests than men; female orders and congregations were growing more rapidly than their male counterparts; and there are hints of higher levels of female attendance at mass, perhaps because women lacked the alternative outlets for sociability available to men. The magisterial study by Michel Vovelle, based on thousands of Provençal wills, demonstrated that women called more frequently upon the intercession of saintly figures than men, they were more generous in their charitable giving and made greater use of masses for the repose of the soul.[32] A subsequent study of testators in Paris conducted by Pierre Chaunu suggests that the demand for requiem masses fell among both sexes in the eighteenth century, but that the fall was least marked among women.[33] Thus, 76.5 per cent of women made such requests in the period 1750–1800, compared to 86.5 per cent in the previous fifty years. This was a slight fall, especially by contrast with the men. Only 53.5 per cent of male testators requested masses in the period 1750–1800, compared to 75 per cent in the first half of the century. This gender dichotomy, if it deserves so grandiose a title before 1800, would become more discernible during the nineteenth century.

Despite some slippage, commitment overall in Catholic countries remained high, evidenced not just by high levels of attendance at Sunday mass but by the popularity of the Devotion of the Sacred Heart which gained an especial following in Spain where it was propagated by Fathers Cardaveraz, de Hoyos, Pedro de Calatayud and Juan de Loyola. Its members, both clerical and lay, dedicated themselves to good works, monthly communion and confession, and the performance of pilgrimages. This impressive level of piety should not surprise us for, at a popular level, Catholicism was well attuned to people's needs and emotions. Unlike Protestantism, it proffered a number of mechanisms whereby the believer might affect not just his or her own chances of salvation in the world to come, but the chances of others as well. Just as important as the concern with the hereafter was the concern with the here-and-now. Catholicism was syncretic in that it drew on a variety of pre-Christian and folkloric traditions, incorporating these into its own systems. In a world seen by the peasant as essentially capricious, where disease, dearth and harvest failure were commonplace and occurred apparently at random, Catholicism offered a wide range of remedies designed to alleviate misfortune. A Marian girdle placed on a woman's stomach countered the pain of childbirth; clerical benedictions helped to ensure the fertility of the fields and the marriage bed; exorcisms protected the crops from vermin. Holy water that had touched the head of St Gregory Ostiense was used in Andalucia to ward off locusts and ants. There was widespread use of scapulas, ribbons, *Agnus Dei* (wax medallions imprinted with a paschal lamb), rosaries and *brevi* (a small purse into which a prayer or holy object was sewn) as means of avoiding injury, ill-fortune and promoting healing. Significantly, in a compilation of diocesan rituals put together in the Holy Roman Empire in 1777, over three-quarters of the formulae were concerned with material well-being and protection from harm. Saints' cults remained immensely popular, but they were the time-honoured (and sometimes mythical) healing, miracle-working and prophylactic saints, rather than the newer saints of the Catholic Reformation. Tellingly, the cult of St Ignatius, founder of the Jesuits, made no headway in Brittany, a region otherwise given over to holy places, statues and groves. Where it was success-fully introduced, as in Bavaria, Lorraine and Alsace, it was because the saint was given a healing role. Water blessed on his feast day could be used to relieve the pains of pregnancy. And significantly, there was massive popular support in southern Italy for the canonisation of Gerardo Mailla, a member of the Redemptorist order, whose immensely practical attributes included an ability to drive vermin from the fields with the sign of the cross, cure sick animals, relieve the pains of pregnancy and ward off the plague.

Studies of the activities of the numerous missions organised by religious orders and congregations in the eighteenth century confirm this impression of a Church that was in many respects accommodating of popular needs and foibles. The missions' styles varied. All missioners (the term they themselves used) concentrated on the fear of death and the wrath of God. However, the Jesuits specialised in relatively short, theatrical enterprises characterised by the use of blazing torches, skulls and with an emphasis on the penitential. By contrast, the Lazarists' missions were calmer and stressed catechetical teaching. The Redemptorists combined elements of both approaches. Yet none sought to impose an elite religion upon the people, instead offering a message which was straightforward, direct and uncomplicated. They made great use of processions, religious dramas, public confessions, the miraculous and forms of devotion in which an element of the carnivalesque was ubiquitous. As the Rule of the Lazarists counselled: 'Be very popular; that is, adapt yourself to the people's capabilities.'[34]

This is not to say that the Church did not seek to channel and control popular religiosity while at the same time coming to an accommodation with popular needs and fears. Particularly in the aftermath of the Reformation, it attempted to direct popular religiosity through the parish, insisted on the need for confession, and it sought to remove a number of abuses from religious practice, stung into action not least of all by Protestant charges that it condoned magic and superstition. Two hundred years later it was still endeavouring to make progress in this direction. For example, the ringing of church bells as a means of warding off bad weather was prohibited in some dioceses, and the authorities in the archdiocese of Toledo stopped the practice at Torrijos whereby a halter that had been used to lead a bull into mass on the feast of St Gil was subsequently taken to the local hospital for its miraculous curative properties. The missioners also sought to replace scandalous celebrations which were overwhelmingly bawdy, such as May Day and St John's Eve, with processions, religious dramas and exercises of piety.

Progress in the reform of popular religion was none the less slow, especially in Ireland which remained on the periphery of Catholic Europe and which was largely untouched by the changes introduced at Trent. A belief in fairies and magical people was still prevalent; holy wells were sought out for their curative properties; the last rites were held to be a passport to heaven; and the unreformed clergy frequently encouraged and participated in these practices, for instance through the so-called stations whereby the sacraments were administered in private houses. Not until the Irish 'devotional revolution' of the nineteenth century was there a serious attempt to raise the qualitative level of observance and religious knowledge.[35]

However, throughout Europe it would be anachronistic to draw too many distinctions between religion and superstition, differences which make sense in the twenty-first century but which do not properly apply to the eighteenth. Then, the use of holy objects as repositories of supernatural power or the utilisation of a sentence of exorcism as a prophylactic against pests at harvest time was not regarded as magic but as a quite proper means of introducing the supernatural force of Providence into the natural world. More importantly, it might be argued that the Church was increasingly intolerant of a series of social sins such as dancing, excess drinking and immoral sexual behaviour. In attempting to crack down on these, by curbing the number of feast days and by putting processions and lay associations under clerical tutelage, the Church may unwittingly have alienated the rank-and-file believers and helped bring about some fall-off in religious observance. A similar effect may also have resulted from the increased stress placed by Jansenist parish clergy on the internal religious life. Their emphasis on internal contrition stood in contrast to popular attitudes which privileged the external aspects of religious practice.

Everywhere, the social element to the practice of popular Catholicism was critical. Mass was an opportunity for the exchange of gossip, to learn the latest news and meet members of the opposite sex. Religious processions provided an occasion for the visible display of the town and village hierarchy, as well as a chance to show wealth. Feast days, in particular, were a chance for popular carnival well exemplified in the musical bands and *papier-maché* figures characteristic of Spanish celebrations. The church building itself was the community's identifying monument, one of the few constructions to be paid for by all members of the parish. Yet, if Catholicism retained an enormous strength, particularly at the popular level, this did not preclude the emergence of popular anti-clericalism such as that found in the Midi where it coexisted alongside deep piety. Anti-clericalism and religious fervour were not mutually exclusive. Popular anti-clericalism stemmed not so much from ideological reasoning, as in the case of the *philosophes*, but from practical resentments. The payment of the tithe, the hostility to grasping monastic landlords, the alleged use of the confessional to extract sexual secrets, and general antagonism towards the clergy as authority-figures all combined to produce the phenomenon. As we shall see, in the nineteenth century popular anti-clericalism would become a more forceful presence, facilitated by a growing professionalisation of society which cost the priest something of his status and exclusivity, and nourished by novel secular ideologies which proved far more destructive than the Enlightenment. Anti-clericalism would thus acquire a measure of respectability.

Conclusion: Catholicism in Rupture

Throughout this chapter, eighteenth-century Catholicism has been presented as being in retrenchment. Rome's spiritual authority and international status were at a low ebb. Within Catholic states, almost everywhere secular rulers enjoyed a supremacy over their established churches. Both secular and regular clergy were undergoing a crisis of recruitment. Protestantism was entrenched in northern Europe and reunification of Christendom appeared as distant a prospect as at any previous time. Religious vitality was sapped by the philosophical currents of the age which called into question all manner of traditional beliefs. And, at a popular level, the Church seemed to have lost its touch as baroque piety relinquished its grip upon the imagination. Alongside other eighteenth-century institutions, the Church was frequently caught out because of its inability to cope with new problems, thanks to its propensity to cling to habits of thought and modes of action characteristic of earlier society. Yet it would be a mistake to underestimate the dominance of Catholicism in what remained a profoundly religious age and to assume, as did the likes of Joseph de Maistre, that the challenges of the eighteenth century were responsible for the upheavals that lay just around the corner. In the 1790s, Catholicism was to face the most determined challenge since the Reformation, a challenge whose reverberations would shape the face of Catholicism for the nineteenth century and beyond. To this day, it remains questionable whether Catholicism has grappled with the issues that originated in the France of the revolution, and which spread to the rest of Europe.

CHAPTER TWO

Catholicism in Revolution:
1789–1815

IN 1789 France slid into a revolution which could have been avoided, but whose consequences were inescapable. This was a revolution like no other. The issues that it addressed were universal in nature and respected no national boundaries. The revolution was to change for ever the nature of politics and the place of the individual within society. For Catholicism, too, the revolution was a watershed. The link between religion and the state was not broken, but the preconception that the state was sympathetic towards a particular religion was. To be sure, this precedent had been set in the American Constitution of 1787–88, but outside the American context it had not fully registered. As the French Revolution inaugurated a new basis for social organisation, substituting citizens for subjects, it also ruptured the centuries-old belief that membership of the state was dependent upon affiliation to a particular denomination. It was no longer necessary to be a believer in a particular faith, or indeed to have any faith at all, in order to be a member of the new French state. Religious opinions were placed on the same level as any other ideology. Scarcely less significant was the fact that the revolution affected the leading European Catholic state. In no other country were there so many Catholics; in no other country was the Church so well organised and autonomous; in no other country had the Catholic Reformation made such headway; in no other state were there so many monastic houses. Moreover, no other country was so central, both geographically and culturally, to Europe. In short, the reverberations of the revolution in France were bound to be felt well beyond the Alps and the Pyrenees, and they were to echo throughout the modern age. For much of the nineteenth century, and indeed the twentieth, the Church, not just in France, struggled to contend with the changes wrought by the revolutionary and Napoleonic epoch.

The Rupture, 1787–90

Throughout the eighteenth century, the French Church took a not wholly undeserved pride in its fiscal competence. It was thus ironic that it was the profligacy of the state which ultimately set in train a course of events that destroyed the edifice of the old regime, including the Church. From 1786, faced with a debt of over 5 billion *livres*, the government unsuccessfully put forward a series of reforms. Driven by the impending threat of bankruptcy, Louis XVI finally gambled upon calling a meeting of the Estates General, the principal representative institution of the French kingdom which had been in mothballs since 1614, hoping for a substantial grant of taxation in return for some limited overhaul of the state apparatus. The elections to the Estates General, which were accompanied by the submission of lists of grievances from each of the three orders of society, the *cahiers de doléances*, raised expectations that the forthcoming assembly, which met in May 1789 at the royal palace of Versailles, would deliver a wholesale regeneration of French society and institutions. The crown's failure to satisfy these hopes, and its inept handling of the Estates General, led to a loss of royal control and a disintegration of the old regime monarchy. The financial crisis had become a constitutional one. The popular uprising in Paris on 14 July, fuelled both by economic distress and the fear of royal troops encircling Paris, which led to the fall of the Bastille, forestalled the King's attempt to reassert his absolutism through a military *coup*. These developments allowed the deputies at Versailles to assume power, and to embark upon a legislative programme far more ambitious than anything previously contemplated, aiming at nothing less than complete national regeneration.

There was no inevitability either to the outbreak of the revolution, or to its course. Just as in 1787, when the full extent of the royal debts had been exposed, nobody had foreseen the direction in which events were to move, likewise in 1789 no one could have perceived how matters were to unfold. At each stage, the revolution could conceivably have followed a different course yet, at each juncture, it became ever more radical. It should also be stressed that, at the time, the heterogeneous participants in the revolutionary turmoil were not always aware of the full significance of their actions, which were being driven by three interrelated impulses: their insistence upon the nation as the source of sovereignty; the influence of Enlightenment ideas; and the overwhelming imperative to reorganise state finances, all of which directly impinged upon the Church.

The question which most rapidly came to the fore was that of sovereignty. After the deputies assembled at Versailles in May, they had to decide whether to vote by head or by order; underlying this was the issue of whether they represented the sectional interest of each of the three orders or that of the nation as a whole. The Third Estate insisted upon the latter, and was joined by a number of *curés* from the clerical deputies, frustrated by the myopic vision of the bishops, together with a smattering of nobles, angered by the exclusivity of their peers. The deadlock was finally broken on 27 June when Louis XVI capitulated and ordered the rump of clerical and noble deputies to join with the Third Estate, who ten days previously had significantly adopted the mantle of 'National Assembly', thus implying that they spoke for the sovereign nation. This marked the end of the clergy as a separate order within society, leaving the Church in an exposed position, less able to mobilise its corporate strength to influence affairs.

A further turning point for the Church came with the proclamation of the

Declaration of the Rights of Man and the Citizen of 26 August 1789. Intended as a statement of first principles to underpin the task of national renewal, and drawing heavily on the writings of John Locke and Jean-Jacques Rousseau, this document has often been interpreted as *the* defining moment in the secularisation of France and, for arch-conservatives typified by Joseph de Maistre, it was an essentially anti-religious statement. This latter standpoint is misleading. That the deputies were not hostile to religion is evidenced by the invocation of the 'Supreme Being' in the preamble, a term which had regularly been used by devout Catholics throughout the eighteenth century, and by the reference to the rights of man as being 'sacred'. There is no doubt, however, that this revolutionary document fundamentally altered the place of Catholicism in French society and politics.

To begin with, the Declaration effectively ended the traditional relationship between Church and state. In future, the Church was no longer to enjoy separate corporate status with concomitant privileges. Article 3 declared, 'no body nor any individual may exercise any authority which does not derive explicitly from the sovereign nation'.[1] The Church's advantaged position was dealt a further blow by the insistence that Catholicism should be treated as one faith among many. Article 10 stated, 'no one must be troubled on account of his opinions, even his religious beliefs'. The insertion of the word 'even' might suggest to us today a grudging acknowledgement of toleration; instead, as René Rémond suggests, it should be viewed in its proper eighteenth-century context, reflecting a long-held notion that Catholicism did not possess a monopoly of the truth.[2] Effectively, the Roman faith had been placed on a par with other religious beliefs. Membership of civil society was no longer coupled with religious conformity, thus bringing to a close the confessional state. Full toleration of other denominations was, as a result, not long in coming. A pre-revolutionary edict of November 1787 had already given limited concessions to Protestants; full civic rights were conferred in December 1789. Emancipation for France's 40,000 Jews took longer, but in September 1791 they too became fully-fledged citizens. Like Catholics, Jews and Protestants were expected to be Frenchmen first and believers second; none should aspire to comprise a distinct corporation.

The concept of national sovereignty lent the Declaration coherence and posed yet further challenges to Catholicism. Locating sovereignty in the people rather than in the monarch, the deputies were not prepared to brook any restraints upon their legislative competence. All institutions derived authority from the nation and, implicitly, existed to perform such functions as the state required. As Armand-Gaston Camus, a specialist in canon law, pointed out in 1790: 'The Church is part of the state. The state is not part of the Church.'[3] It was but a short step from this position to treating the Church as a department of government, just like any other. The language used by many deputies during the debate on the Declaration, and on religious matters more generally, was revealing. The clergy were referred to as 'public officials', 'officials of morality', 'officials of instruction', who, in the words of Robespierre, were charged 'with responsibilities over public happiness'.[4] Such a perception accorded well with the Enlightenment approach which had emphasised the social and utilitarian role of ecclesiastics, especially the parish priests, at the expense of their sacerdotal functions.

Not surprisingly, it was the regulars, traditional targets of anti-clerical abuse, who were the first to be affected by this outlook, as well as by the anti-corporatist sentiments of the Assembly. In October 1789, this body voted to prohibit the taking of monastic vows, and in February of the following year existing vows were abolished; monks and nuns were given the choice of leaving their orders, with a state pension, or being regrouped into a smaller number of houses to live out their days. Only those orders involved in charitable and educational work were exempt, although the time would come when they too were subject to discriminatory legislation.

The doctrine of national sovereignty adumbrated in the Declaration also implied a new concept of belonging. The day after the Declaration's proclamation, the Assembly rejected a motion which would have made Catholicism the state religion. When a similar proposal was put forward by the Carthusian Dom Gerle, on 13 April 1790, he was persuaded to drop it before a vote could be taken on the grounds that it would engender hostilities between Catholics and Protestants. Instead, the Assembly agreed upon a motion that the subject of religion was too 'majestic' a matter for legislation, and that its attachment to religion was anyway beyond question. This was a fudge which satisfied nobody. The logic of the Assembly's actions was inescapable. Once the state had uncoupled religious belief and membership of civil society, and accepted the equality and plurality of faiths, there was no way in which Catholicism could be allowed to reassert its primacy. What this meant, of course, was that Catholicism had ceased to be a badge of national identity, at least in France. Increasingly, citizenship was the mark of belonging to a nation. The way was thus opened for the emergence of a modern nationalism which would ask questions of Catholicism's allegiance throughout the nineteenth century: Rome or the state?

The discussion of Dom Gerle's motion had been tumultuous, but this was as nothing compared to the passions aroused by the Assembly's most significant piece of legislation in respect of the Church, the Civil Constitution of the Clergy, which was voted on 12 July 1790 and reluctantly approved by the King at the end of the following month. This measure was part of the Constituent Assembly's wider package of reforms which impinged upon every aspect of France's institutions and society. As one of the elements of the old regime which had been most criticised for its internal inequalities, wealth and selfish behaviour, there was no question of the Church remaining untouched by reforms which were designed to facilitate efficiency and the general happiness of the people. The deputies wanted a streamlined Church more closely aligned with their own utilitarian views of religion. In this way, they moved yet closer towards making the Church a department of state.

Yet if the desire to bring the Church within the general ambit of reform made legislation inevitable at some point, the overwhelming pressures for change remained financial. On the momentous night of 4 August 1789, the deputies, impelled both by the rising tide of disorder in the countryside and by a wave of altruistic enthusiasm, had agreed to abolish feudal privileges of all kinds, including the Church tax, the tithe. This deprived the clergy of its major source of income. Moreover, the debts inherited from the monarchy had not gone away, and Necker's gloomy reports did nothing to underplay the seriousness of the situation. Groping for some means to offset the crisis, the deputies fixed envious eyes upon the riches of the Church. Although they exaggerated the extent of these, some erroneously believing that ecclesiastics possessed one-third of the land of France, there was no doubt that the Church was wealthy and that corporate privilege had allowed it to evade its fair share of the fiscal burden under the old regime. Accordingly, in November 1789, the deputies voted to put ecclesiastical property, up to a value of 400 million *livres*, at 'the disposal of the nation'.[5] This vague wording, and the implication that only monastic properties would be affected, was designed to reassure clerics. But as the economic crisis deepened week by week, and as the Assembly issued increasing quantities of paper money, the *assignats*, backed by the clerical lands, the deputies were obliged to go further and ordered a wholesale confiscation of Church property which was to be sold off. In coming to this decision, the deputies were no doubt alive to the loyalty to the revolution which would be engendered by creating a constituency composed of buyers of ecclesiastical property. Deprived of tithes and landed wealth, the clergy would henceforth be economically dependent upon the state, and this inevitably necessitated some reorganisation of the Church to make it as 'cost-effective' as possible.

An Ecclesiastical Committee was established to produce proposals. When a first, and moderate, draft was produced, this was foolishly blocked by the two bishops on the committee, leading an increasingly frustrated Assembly to pack the body with more radical deputies. The document produced in May 1790 went much further than anyone had initially envisaged. The episcopate was reduced from 136 to 83, with one bishop per department. Parish boundaries were to be rationalised. The anomaly of the Avignon enclave was effectively ended by the stipulation that no foreign ecclesiastic should have jurisdiction over the French clergy. All ecclesiastical offices, except those with cure of souls, were abolished, thus paring down the clergy to bishops, parish priests and curates. Clerical salaries were to be paid by the state, and were readjusted significantly downwards in the case of the prelates. Most controversially, the clergy would in future be elected to their positions by the same colleges of laymen – including non-Catholics – who voted upon all government officials; and bishops would merely notify the Pope of their election rather than seek canonical institution from His Holiness.

The proposals in the Civil Constitution were a pot-pourri of Gallican, Jansenist, Enlightenment and revolutionary precepts. The Gallicanism was reflected in the autonomy given to bishops in relation to Rome and priests in relation to bishops, and in state responsibility for ecclesiastical affairs. The Jansenism was to be perceived in the desire to strip the Church of the accretions of centuries and to return it to its apostolic purity. The Enlightenment shone through in the desire for rationality and order in the Church's structures, and the wish to make religion fulfil a social function. The revolutionary ideology was contained in the application of the principle of national sovereignty which necessarily entailed the election of clerics. To be sure, Jansenists had advocated elections in the past, but the franchise would have been restricted to fellow ecclesiastics.

Despite the uncongeniality of much of the document to many of the clergy, there was a willingness, even on the part of the episcopacy, to co-operate. The Archbishop of Aix, Mgr Boisgelin, spoke for most when he lucidly explained that the Church understood the need for reform, but it could not accept the competence of the Assembly to legislate on its own. Although he made no reference to the specifics of the proposed Civil Constitution, it is clear he had in mind the redrawing of ecclesiastical boundaries and the election of clerics as areas touching upon the Church's spiritual, rather than its purely temporal, affairs. For the former in particular to be altered, the Church must be consulted. He therefore proposed the summoning of either regional or national councils which would allow the Church to confer its blessing. Significantly, he made little reference to an appeal to the Pope, a reflection of the enduring Gallican outlook of the French clergy. He was whistling in the wind. For the Assembly to have consented to such councils would have been an acknowledgement of the Church's corporate status and an affront to the sovereignty of the nation.

Once this course of action had been rejected, the bishops (with the exception of Talleyrand, the Bishop of Autun, and Gobel, the future Archbishop of Paris), together with most of the clergy, withdrew from debates in the Assembly. The deputies tacitly left it to Cardinal de Bernis, the French ambassador to Rome, to secure papal approval, refusing to approach Pius VI openly. While deploring the Civil Constitution, the Pope was unwilling to condemn it publicly, fearing a schism of the French Church, and therefore temporised by referring the matter to a committee of cardinals which deliberated for eight months. But if Rome hoped that the Assembly, in the interim, would water down the proposals, it was to be sorely disappointed. The Civil Constitution was voted through on 12 July 1790 and sanctioned by a reluctant Louis on 24 August; it was an action he regretted until the end of his days. Unwilling to brook any further delay, which was holding up the sale of ecclesiastical lands, believing that most clerics would in any case accept the new Church order, and unaware that Pius VI was implacably opposed to the proposed changes, the deputies decided to force the issue and, on 27 November, decreed that all ecclesiastics should swear an oath accepting the Civil Constitution or lose their positions.

This was to be the first serious breach between the revolution and the Church. Although by the end of 1790 the clergy had been driven to a position of intransigence, up to this point there had at least been an attempt to maintain a consensus. It is only with the benefit of hindsight that the rupture between Catholicism and the revolution may be seen as inevitable. At issue was a clash between two different perceptions of the nature and relationship of Church and state. The deputies from the Third Estate, and many of the nobility, were not anti-religious, but they were unsympathetic to the revealed religion of the Catholic Church and came to articulate a deistic approach which emphasised man's capacity for self-improvement. They fully accepted the need for a cult of some kind as a means of maintaining the social order and providing a moral code for those too ignorant to develop one of their own. Jacques Dinochau, the deputy-cum-journalist, was unusually frank when he stated: 'Religion is the first foundation of the social order; it is the cornerstone of the edifice ... It would be most unfortunate if the common people did not believe in God; if one's valets, one's business agents, one's tradesmen, and one's workers did not believe in God.'[6] Nevertheless, the deputies resented the autonomy of the Church, and the developing ideology of national sovereignty merely increased their determination to limit ecclesiastical independence. Against this perception was a view elaborated by most, though by no means all, of the clergy, which emphasised the hierarchical nature of religion, the corporatist structure of the Church and its independence in matters of faith. Ecclesiastics generally were just as willing to be good citizens under the revolution as they had been good subjects under the King. What they were not prepared to accept was state encroachment on the spiritual capacity of the Church.

Catholicism and Counter-revolution

While there were a handful of people, most famously the King's brothers, the Counts of Artois and Provence, who refused to countenance any form of change from the outset, a majority of men and women appear to have welcomed the revolutionary events of 1789 with some degree of enthusiasm. As changes occurred, and the reforms of the Constituent Assembly were nothing if not extensive, hostility to the revolution began to manifest itself. Peasants were disappointed at the failure to abolish seigneurialism in its entirety, and disliked the intrusiveness of new bureaucratic systems. Municipalities, and a handful of large cities, griped at the administrative reorganisation which privileged some at the expense of others. Old regime office-holders balked at the loss of jobs and income, and it was the lesser nobility, whose titles alone distinguished them from the Third Estate, who were most concerned at the disappearance of aristocratic status. In the big cities there was increasing disquiet over the revolutionary government's failure to make available adequate and cheap supplies of bread, a counterpart to which was the resentment of parts of rural France which regarded the revolution as an urban phenomenon. All this added to a growing town–country divide; yet if there was increasing hostility and some lawlessness there was no counter-revolution. Discontent was inchoate, not least of all because Louis, although detesting so much of what was happening, refused to present himself as a figurehead around whom opposition could coalesce. Into this *mélange* of dissatisfaction entered those clergy who were aggrieved at the prospect of swearing an oath which was, in their eyes, tantamount to a surrender of ecclesiastical authority. Religion was about to make counter-revolution respectable and provide it with a conscience.

The King sanctioned the decree imposing the oath on the clergy on 26 December 1790, and the oath-taking ceremonies, conducted in front of municipal authorities, began the following month. Timothy Tackett's magisterial study has illuminated the patterns that emerged.[7] Overall, 60 per cent of the *curés*, 51 per cent of the *vicaires* and 7 of the 136 old-regime bishops took the oath, but these statistics mask considerable regional variations. For instance, 96 per cent of the clergy in the department of the Var became jurors whereas less than 10 per cent followed suit in the Bas-Rhin. Variables such as age, income, seminary training and social origins have some part to play in explaining the patterns of acceptance and rejection of the oath. Above all, Tackett argues, the clerical response is best understood by reference to the two models of priesthood in existence before 1789. On the one hand, there was the Tridentine clergy, obedient, hierarchical and highly trained, who saw themselves as masters of the laity and who stressed the importance of the Church as an autonomous institution. Such men tended to reject the pledge. On the other was the model of the 'citizen-priest' who regarded himself as part of the people and privileged his social role as promoter of public welfare and happiness. Clerics of this type opted for compliance. Additionally, there is a significant correlation between the map of oath-taking and that of religious practice under the old regime, with the non-jurors predominating in those regions of relative piety, and the jurors being located in areas of relative dechristianisation. Thus oath-taking was concentrated in the Paris basin, the Dauphin, Provence and the sizeable range of central departments, whereas refractory priests were most commonly found in Brittany, Normandy, Languedoc and Gascony. And it may be noted that there is a significant correlation between patterns of oath-taking and patterns of religious practice in both the nineteenth and twentieth centuries. It seems likely that, in reaching a decision, the clergy were not swayed by lay attitudes; however, the Tridentine non-jurors were supported by their parishioners because they were generally found in districts that had accepted a clericalised model of religion in which ecclesiastics were recognised as separate and dominant. Conversely, in those localities where citizen-priests were found, religion was regarded by both laity and clergy as a matter of general concern over which the state enjoyed authority.

While the Civil Constitution had succeeded in establishing a body of clerics who were financially dependent on the state and supposedly supportive of the revolution, it also created a wide range of powerful enemies who would foment the forces of counter-revolution. On 13 April 1791, Pius VI issued the encyclical *Charitas quae* condemning the Civil Constitution as heretical, schismatic and subversive. Once thought to have produced a rash of clerical retractions, this papal intervention probably swayed few. Without waiting for Rome, a number of refractories had already denounced the revolutionary document and began a campaign to undermine the oath-takers. A series of unseemly incidents occurred as non-jurors ostentatiously held services at the same time as the constitutional priests, refused to hand over the keys to the presbytery, hid the chalices, condemned the sale of Church property and proclaimed that the sacerdotal offices of a constitutional were null and void. Most of the *ancien régime* bishops joined the burgeoning number of nobles who had taken refuge abroad, whence they bombarded their flocks with pastoral homilies against the revolution. In parts of France, the laity rallied to the refractories, the catalyst for disorder frequently being the attempt to oust the local non-juror and to replace him with a constitutional, the 'intruder' as he was typically and significantly referred to. Even at this stage, women were conspicuous in their attempts to defend the old religion. In the eyes of such laity, these oath-takers were unworthy to hold office, a view repeated in traditional historiography which has all too frequently portrayed them as renegade monks, opportunists and clerical herbivores; in truth, the constitutionals were often well motivated, spiritually able and high-minded, the best-known example being the abbé Grégoire.

Taken overall, the business of oath-taking had been a defining moment. More than anything else, it ended the revolutionary consensus which had been present in 1789. It is sometimes interpreted as offering the 'ordinary' people of France a chance to express an opinion on the changes introduced thus far. By choosing whether to accept a juror or to support a refractory priest, people could manifest their feelings about revolutionary reforms more generally. Though this may have been the case, the oath is best seen as a seminal event in its own right which served to shape longer-term attitudes towards the revolution. Parishioners were genuinely concerned with the retention or loss of their priest, and these concerns dictated the attitude they displayed towards the issue of the oath.

It was no less a watershed for the clergy. The oath had created a body of refractories whose loyalty to the revolution was, by definition, suspect. Additionally, it had prompted a substantial number of clerics, including most of the old regime bishops, to join the emigration, and to campaign against the revolution from abroad. They were nearly joined by the King who, on 21 June 1791, attempted to flee France, only to be halted at Varennes and returned to Paris in disgrace. All along Louis had been deeply disquieted by the religious policies of the Assembly and had done his best to thwart measures against the refractories. In the declaration he left behind when quitting the capital, among complaints about the trimming of the civil list and the upkeep of the royal stables, were more substantive grievances about the Civil Constitution. The incident at Easter, when the King was prevented from taking mass from a non-juror at Saint Cloud, probably precipitated the decision to flee. The cause of the King and that of religion were thus conflated.

In the event, after the flight to Varennes the crown had little choice but to agree to a new political constitution, which provided for a limited monarchy and the election of a new chamber, the Legislative Assembly, which supposedly would become the platform on which the revolution could be consolidated. This was an entirely fresh body since a self-denying ordinance prevented the deputies from the Constituent Assembly standing for election. The candidates who put themselves forward tended to be local administrators from the new revolutionary bureaucracy, men who had often seen at first hand the obstructionism of the refractories. Few clerics stood in the campaign to assuage this underlying antipathy towards non-jurors. Unsurprisingly, the Legislative Assembly pursued increasingly draconian religious policies. Refractories were deprived of their pensions, were forbidden from wearing clerical dress, were declared to be 'suspect', and became targets for both official and unofficial hostility. The onset of war served only to consolidate the refractories as hate figures.

War and Dechristianisation

On 20 April 1792 France declared war on Austria, a decision which was the product of domestic politics: those on the left saw it as a means of flushing out and cleansing France of the revolution's enemies; those on the right regarded it as an opportunity to reassert royal control through foreign assistance. Subsequently extended to include the rest of Europe, the conflict endured until 1815, driven initially by revolutionary zeal and latterly by Napoleon's insatiable appetite for conquest.

The war revolutionised the revolution. In 1792–93, the French suffered a series of reverses along their northern frontier, coupled with the treason of their leading general, Dumouriez. Internal counter-revolution, centred upon the Vendée, was reignited. Additionally, a complex admixture of local rivalries, hatred of Paris, and social dissatisfaction produced so-called Federalist revolts in key urban centres. The very survival of the revolution was at stake. In response, the Convention, which succeeded the Legislative Assembly as the governing body of France in September 1792, moved towards the establishment of a republic, executing the King in January 1793, and introduced the form of government known as the Terror, a process facilitated by the predominance of militant politicians who had cut their teeth in the 'rough-and-tumbril' of previous assemblies and local administration. Political life in the new Assembly was dominated by factional infighting, virtually incomprehensible to the outsider, which resulted in the triumph of a hard-left grouping known as the Montagnards.

The blame for the setbacks, both at home and abroad, was attributed to counter-revolutionary conspirators: nobles, hoarders, paid agents of the British and, above all, the refractories. In September 1792, prompted by fears that Paris was about to be overrun by foreign troops, mobs invaded the prisons of the capital, killing some 1,400 people, including 300 clergymen and three bishops. The previous month, on the 26th, a decree had ordered the deportation of refractory clergy; and after July 1793 any non-juror who had disobeyed the injunction faced either the death penalty or deportation to Guyana, the so-called 'dry guillotine'. By the autumn of 1793, over 30,000 clerics had fled the country and those who remained on metropolitan soil led a hunted and fugitive existence. In the words of Albitte, a *représentant en mission*, they were 'sacerdotal vermin' to be ruthlessly exterminated.[8] It is estimated that some 16,000 people perished in the Terror, of whom nearly 1,000 were clergy, though these figures take no account of the numbers who died in prison, or were executed without trial, or were killed in the military campaigns in the Vendée and elsewhere.

As a corollary to this assault on the non-jurors, there was an attack on the Constitutional Church and Catholicism in general. This offensive is commonly referred to as the dechristianising campaign, though this term imputes a specious homogeneity to an episode which lacked central direction and which was characterised by enormous regional texturing both in its incidence and in its effects. It is best understood as a series of local campaigns originating in the provinces. The instigators and overseers were the *représentants en mission*, delegates sent out by the Convention. The best-known included Joseph Fouché in the Nièvre, Claude Javogues in the Loire, André Dumont at Abbeville and Rochefort and Châteauneuf-Randon in the Massif Central. There were other, albeit lesser-known, dechristianisers among the 150 or so representatives, such as Bô in the Lot, Bassal in Franche-Comté and his successor Lejeune, who invented the portable and collapsible *guillotine de table*. Local militants, drawn from the political clubs, were the shock troops of these campaigns, occasionally assisted by the so-called revolutionary armies comprising working-class townsmen.

Dechristianisation involved a number of elements, although its particular characteristics in any given area were determined above all by the proclivities of the representative. Crudely speaking, we may distinguish between two aspects in the campaigns, although it should be stressed that the dividing line was often very blurred. First, there were those 'negative' activities which aimed at nothing less than the destruction of the fabric, personnel and faith of Catholicism. Bells, crosses and statues were removed from churches, which were then shut down. Revolutionary 'trees of liberty' replaced wayside shrines and crosses. All forms of public worship were prohibited. Street and village signs were altered to remove any religious connotation, babies were given sound revolutionary or classical names such as Lycurgus or Brutus, and adults underwent debaptism ceremonies. The Constitutional Church itself, a creation of the revolution, was now destroyed. Its clergy were obliged to abdicate their priestly functions, sometimes undergoing humiliating public renunciations of their office. Occasionally they were obliged to marry; it was surely a backhanded compliment to the success of the Counter-Reformation Church, in making celibacy a defining characteristic of the clergy, that marriage was taken as the ultimate proof of their rejection of clerical status.

The second, and purportedly positive, aspect of dechristianisation involved the provision of ideological substitutes for Catholicism. On 5 October 1793 the Convention adopted the republican calendar in place of the Gregorian one: the birth of the Republic on 22 September 1792, not that of Christ, was designated year I; the *décadi* replaced Sunday as the day of rest; henceforth, revolutionary festivals, not saints' days, both marked the passage of time and provided public holidays. Months in the new calendar were named after the climate or the agricultural cycle (thus Thermidor was the hot month and Vendémiaire the wine harvest) and the days were named after fruits, flowers and animals. The historian Richard Cobb delighted in pointing out that Hébert and his cronies were guillotined on the day of tulips. The theme of Nature also occupied a prominent place in the twin revolutionary cults of Reason and of the Supreme Being. The ceremonies marking the cult of Reason were remarkably eclectic: they comprised the celebration of revolutionary martyrs such as Marat; the 'deification' of Liberty, Truth, Equality, Victory and Nature; and the propagation of every kind of materialist, deist and atheist philosophy. For the first time in the eighteenth century, atheism acquired some measure of respectability: at Nevers, Fouché had the entrance to the cemetery inscribed with the bleak phrase, 'Death is an Eternal Sleep'. Nevertheless, it should be stressed that the revolutionaries, for the most part, were deists; and a number of celebrations of Reason had included reference to the Supreme Being well before 7 May 1794 when Robespierre sponsored the decree establishing this cult. The edict set out its creed and litany. These comprised a belief in a deity who punished vice and rewarded virtue and a regular cycle of festivals to be held on the *décadi*. The cult was inaugurated at Paris on 8 June at a great festival choreographed by Jacques-Louis David. Robespierre, the cult's architect and master of ceremonies for the day, carried sheaths of wheat and flowers and processed through ranks of young girls in white-lawn dresses before setting light to a *papier-maché* effigy of atheism from which emerged a rather blackened statue of Wisdom.

How may the origins and functions of decristianisation be explained? As we have already noted, the war was fundamental to its genesis. This had been initiated with the intention of exposing traitors. As the military situation went from bad to worse, counter-revolutionaries were discovered everywhere, more often than not among the ranks of the non-jurors. It is not difficult to see why these non-jurors should have fallen under suspicion. Their loyalty had been suspect from the moment they rejected the oath to the Civil Constitution; their links with the *émigrés* and the inflammatory actions and speeches of some of their number had clearly established them as traitors. There was also a general feeling that the enemies of the state should pay for its defence, which helps to explain the early attacks on church properties. As the representative Bassal commented: 'It is time to assure the Republic that indemnity which it has the right to claim from those who have dealt it the most grievous blows.'[9] Stripping churches of anything which could be channelled into the war effort and turning them into warehouses provided a first blooding for many militants, and once this threshold had been crossed it was easy to move on to a more systematic iconoclasm.

It was, however, the constitutional clergy who were the pre-eminent victims of the rising tide of paranoia. Once again, the internal uprisings and military setbacks were calamitous for them. The Constitutional Church had been established as a revolutionary instrument, designed to inculcate loyalty to the new regime, to propagate its values and to wean the peasants away from their attachment to counter-revolution. This the constitutional clergy had signally failed to do. Moreover, the constitutional clergy were tainted by their association with the political faction known as the Girondins who had been toppled during the internecine fighting in the Convention by the all-conquering Montagnards. They had failed the regime and were now regarded as a fifth column. What the state had created, it would now destroy by removing all support for the Church and forcing its clergy to abdicate. The peremptory treatment of both refractory and constitutional clergy set a precedent which would be imitated by anti-clerical governments throughout Europe in the nineteenth century; it created visceral folk memories among the peasantry; and it left an enduring legacy of mistrust between Catholics and anti-clericals.

From an attack on the priest, it was a short step to an attack upon the faith itself. Increasingly, Catholicism had come to be regarded as the ideology of fanatics who fought indiscriminately for the return of throne and altar. It was a tool used by reactionary elements to dupe the peasantry, an alien and corrosive creed which stood in opposition to the true interests of the French nation. Catholicism therefore had to be destroyed if the revolution was to survive. Yet the revolutionaries feared that if there was no substitute for a discredited Catholicism, the people would drift into idleness, disorder or worse. Like the *philosophes*, the leaders of the revolution regarded some form of cult as essential to social stability. Moreover, as Marie de la Révellière-Lépaux opined, when a false cult was overthrown, it was necessary to replace it so that, phoenix-like, it could not rise from its own ashes. Hence the need for the establishment of the revolutionary cults of Reason and the Supreme Being. As well as serving as substitutes for Catholicism, the cults were also intended to educate and transform men so that they understood the nature of the revolutionary changes and were morally worthy of the new institutions which had been created for their benefit. Although nineteenth-century Catholic historiography all too often portrayed the dechristianising episode as 'the product of the deepest villainy' (the abbé Barruel), even 'Satan at work in humanity' (Père Félix),[10] in truth the revolutionaries were, for the most part, deeply virtuous men concerned to create a new moral order. As Robespierre, the architect of the cult of the Supreme Being, remarked: 'It is not an empty word that makes a republic, it is the character of its citizens.'[11] Thuriot, the experienced *représentant en mission*, echoed this thought: 'All religions are but conventions. Legislators make them to suit the people they govern. It is the moral order of the republic, of the revolution, that we must now preach, that will make us a people of brothers, a people of *philosophes*.'[12]

In addition to educating and regenerating the citizenry morally, the cults had a further function. The declaration of a Republic on 22 September 1792, the execution of the King the following January, and the dechristianisation campaign marked a final and total rejection of both monarchical and ecclesiastical authority, the twin underpinnings of the *ancien régime*. Yet the revolutionaries were both elated about what they had achieved and anxious about the future. While they aggressively asserted the values of the new regime, they also searched for new sources of authority to legitimate and guarantee the durability of the revolution's achievements. Accordingly, in their festivals, speeches, propaganda and art, the revolutionaries drew upon symbols which carried an implication of the eternal, of permanence, of solidity, of unchangeability. Many of these were drawn from antiquity. The revolutionary cults also made use of Nature. Here was an immutable force, constantly regenerative, a source of new beginnings, and something which was ordered, since it was governed by the laws of the universe. Reason was additionally deployed; ever since the Enlightenment it had been posited as a more reliable guide to truth than faith. And, finally, the Cult of the Supreme Being brought back the truly transcendental as the foundation for the moral truths which so exercised the revolutionaries. If in 1789 they had attempted to nationalise the Church in the service of the revolution, in 1794 the revolutionaries attempted the same thing with God.

Measuring the impact of dechristianisation is no easy matter, not least of all because it was regionally varied. Towns suffered more than the countryside, because the agents of dechristianisation, the members of the clubs and the committees of surveillance, were urban-based. The presence of a 'revolutionary army', or the lack of it, also affected the operation of the campaign. Above all, the attitude of the local representative was paramount in determining the intensity and the character of the local campaign. He alone had the authority to set dechristianisation in motion; he alone could alter the power structures within a department so as to bring to prominence local priest-haters; he alone determined the nature of the campaign, often importing into a department ideas and techniques used elsewhere. The most fervent dechristianisers – Joseph Fouché, André Dumont and Collot d'Herbois – linked their religious policy to a wider programme of social egalitarianism. This involved comforting the afflicted by afflicting the comfortable by, for example, redistributing the property of the well-to-do among the poor. Conversely, those territories least affected were overseen by more moderate representatives for whom dechristianisation was not a priority. Thus, the Var and the neighbouring Alpes-Maritimes in the south-east corner of France were placed under the tutelage of Saliccti, Moltedo and Augustin Robespierre, Maximilien's younger brother. Here, dechristianisation was limited to the appropriation of church plate and the removal of religious symbols from public view.

Many facets of dechristianisation were superficial in impact. The revolutionary cults failed to grasp the public imagination and did not survive the execution of Robespierre in July 1794. Not only were they resisted in acts of protest against an unpopular regime, they fulfilled none of the essential thaumaturgic and therapeutic functions of popular Catholicism. Cold and abstract, they brought no magic to assuage the pains and perils of everyday life, no consolation to provide solace in the hour of death. The revolutionary calendar continued to enjoy official observance until 1806, but was widely ignored by the popular classes despite attempts to fine those who worked on the *décadi* and who continued to treat Sunday as a day of rest. Good republican names, such as Fraternity, Endive and Brother Coriander, were adopted by only a few; the case of Beauvais, where more than half the children born in the Year II were given revolutionary names, was wholly atypical.

The most dramatic impact of dechristianisation was on the Constitutional Church. Threatened with death, imprisonment and the loss of income, around

20,000 constitutional priests abdicated and tendered their letters of ordination. An unknown number simply ceased their religious offices, and between 6,000 and 9,000 married. Additionally, all but a handful of France's 40,000 or so churches were closed by Easter 1794, and many were sold off, demolished or put to use as warehouses or factories. The disappearance of large numbers of priests and the ending of regular public worship necessarily disrupted the practice of Catholicism. A generation of children thus came of age without having any form of clerical instruction. Many who lost the habit of routine religious observance during the revolution never regained it, and also lost something of their respect for the office of priest. During the eighteenth century, political infighting within the Church had largely been confined to the upper echelons, whereas the *curé* himself stood outside this wrangling. In the 1790s he could not avoid it, and the clergy revealed itself to be hopelessly divided and just as sectarian as the politicians. This devaluation of the priest-hood was to have a lasting impact upon public perceptions. Here was but one reason why the Church could never hope to re-establish the institutional power it had enjoyed under the *ancien régime*.

Catholicism was not fatally wounded by dechristianisation, yet its practice was qualitatively altered. In the short term, there was a 'privatisation' of religion. Religious observance and instruction could no longer be paraded in the public sphere, but were instead restricted to the home. In the longer term, the elimination of the priesthood made room for much greater lay activity in religious matters, a phenomenon that was especially marked in the aftermath of dechristianisation when the laity took it upon themselves to reopen churches and to hold services, and even to conduct masses at which laymen officiated. This was something with which the Church would have to come to terms, just as it had to accept the reappearance and proliferation of popular forms of practice which, in the early part of the eighteenth century, it had tried to suppress or control. Festivals, the ringing of church bells to ward off bad weather and the cult of saints re-emerged with a fervour. As the republican newspaper *L'Observateur* commented in 1800: 'The follies of the carnival have reappeared with the mass. They have perhaps never started so early nor been so noisy ... How is it possible to reconcile this attachment of some people to pagan institutions with their apparent zeal for a religion which has always outlawed them.'[13]

The final and unexpected impact of dechristianisation was to emphasise the gender dimorphism of religion which had been dimly apparent in the eighteenth century, and which was to become even more marked in the nineteenth. As we have seen, before 1789 women were more likely than men to make bequests to religious institutions; they were more regular attenders at mass; and the women's orders and congregations displayed an impressive vitality which contrasted markedly with that of their male counterparts. It will be further recalled that these developments owed much to what may be termed 'alternative sociability'; Catholicism provided women with opportunities for social discourse and with outlets for their energies and talents that were otherwise denied them in a patriarchal society. The revolution exacerbated this trend, offering opportunities for men in the army and the political process, for example, but shutting women out. Religion was one domain they could make their own. Women were, quite literally, at the forefront of the resistance to the introduction of the *intru*; they defended calvaries, shrines and churches against the attacks of the dechristianisers; they took the lead in the aftermath of dechristianisation in re-establishing and reopening churches; and, in the enforced absence of the priest, they usurped the role of religious instruction. In a ceremony at Le Puy the drink-sodden representative Albitte tried to force the local *béates*, the term applied to particularly pious lay women, to swear a civic oath. In an act of collective defiance, they lifted their skirts and bared their backsides to express their contempt. In this defiance of revolutionary authority, women drew upon the role they had traditionally adopted during the *ancien régime* when they had frequently been at the forefront of bread riots, capitalising upon the fact that revolutionary officials, like their pre-1789 counterparts, adopted a lenient attitude to their displays of public disorder, which were blamed upon the hysterical and illogical qualities of the feminine mind. 'We are only women,' cried the females of Toucy in 1795 as they broke open the church doors, 'they don't do anything to women.'[14] In the nineteenth century, this gender stereotyping would became further entrenched. In the minds of the anti-clericals and republicans, both in France and elsewhere, the supposed intellectual and emotional frailties of women would always make them susceptible to clerical influence and a belief in superstition.

Such developments could not have been foreseen in 1789 when all the deputies had attempted to do was to remove the most obvious abuses from the Church and to bind it together with the state in a manner not that dissimilar from the old regime. As the revolution gathered momentum, and particularly as it became radicalised under the influence of the war, religion became the most divisive of issues. Far from underpinning the new regime, it provided a rallying point for the revolution's enemies. In the eyes of many Catholics, the revolution was above all an attack upon them and their beliefs. These sentiments would not disappear. As one woman who attended a mass held at Paris in August 1989 to atone for the crimes of two hundred years earlier, put it: 'We ... have explained (to our children) what their teachers never tell them: that the revolution was directed above all against Catholics.'[15] In the 1790s, this was a sentiment espoused by co-religionaries outside France's frontiers. It is to the impact of the revolution abroad that we must now turn.

The Revolution Abroad

Until 1793, the rest of Europe watched events in France with a mixture of glee and horror: glee that the most powerful military state in western Europe was reduced to a cypher, allowing the other great powers a latitude in their foreign policy which permitted the assault on Austria's Belgian domain (hereafter referred to simply as Belgium) and the partition of Poland; horror at the atrocities perpetrated in the name of the revolution and the overthrow of the monarchical principles of government. Up to this point, the only direct contact between the rest of Europe and France was in providing homes for the exiled clergy. Of 30–40,000 non-jurors who fled abroad, some 5,000 went to Rome, 6–8,000 to Spain, and perhaps 10,000 to Protestant Britain, an influx that was to have significant effects on the standing of the Catholic minority there, as we shall see. It was as the tide of war began to turn, and the French armies enjoyed successes in the field, that Europe experienced, at first hand, the impact of the revolutionary reforms. By 1799, certain of the French conquests had been incorporated into the French state as departments: Savoy and Nice (1796); Belgium (1795); Geneva and Mulhouse in Alsace (1798); and parts of the left bank of the Rhine. The remainder of the Rhineland was captured but never formally integrated into the French nation. Additionally, several satellite republics were established: the Batavian Republic (1795–1801), formerly the United Provinces; the Cisalpine Republic (1797–99 and 1800–02), previously Lombardy, the Duchy of Modena and eventually sections of the dismembered Venetian Republic; the Helvetian Republic (1798–1803), hitherto the Swiss Confederacy; the Ligurian Republic (1797–1805), previously Genoa; the short-lived Parthenopean or Neapolitan Republic (1799), created out of the Kingdom of Naples; and the Roman Republic (1798–99), centred upon the Holy City.

It might be thought that the French revolutionary armies would have imposed wholesale the anti-religious policies applied in the homeland. Yet this was far from the case. In practice, the picture was far more chequered and depended on several variables: the proximity to France; the attitude of the indigenous population; the fervour of the local army commander; the existing religious balance; and the previous geopolitical arrangements. Broadly speaking, Belgium and the Rhineland witnessed violent anti-Catholic policies whereas elsewhere change was more moderate and accommodating.

Initially, Belgium was leniently treated, the occupiers not wishing to stir up resentment among an Ultramontane population which, when confronted with the reforms of Joseph II, had already shown a proclivity for militant behaviour. Matters changed in the summer of 1794, when there was a brief period of dechristianisation, coinciding with events in France. The following year, Jews and Protestants received full equality and Church and state were separated. It was not, though, until 1797 that the French vigorously pursued an anti-Catholic campaign, largely because of supposed clerical involvement in a peasant uprising in the Ardennes provoked by the imposition of conscription in the area. The government response was to order the immediate deportation of over 7,000 priests who refused to swear an oath of hatred against royalty, one of two anti-royal declarations imposed on the French clergy in 1795 and 1797. Religious orders, seminaries and the Catholic University of Louvain were closed, and the wearing of clerical garb prohibited. Up to 1,000 priests were arrested; many of the remainder went underground, protected by a sympathetic population. Although they continued to conduct a clandestine ministry, and although a substantial body of clerics remained in Belgium, the experience of the three years between 1797 and 1800 was sufficiently disruptive of clerically-led religious life as to encourage the emergence of individualistic forms of lay piety, just as had happened in France. Lay persons buried the dead, baptised children, led prayers and so-called white or blind masses were held, at which a layman rather than a priest officiated.

In the Rhineland, religious policy likewise fluctuated. To begin with, the Catholic clergy were harshly treated because of their refusal to countenance union with France, but the arrival in 1797 of General Hoche, who had seen at first hand in the Vendée the effects of anti-religious legislation upon a fervent population, marked the advent of a period of moderation. Although police measures remained in place, the exercise of religion was permitted within churches, clerics continued to be salaried by the state, monasteries were allowed to stay open and the structures of the Church were more or less firm, despite the earlier abolition of ecclesiastical principalities. The General's death shortly after taking charge and the opposition to French rule from a number of ecclesiastical *émigrés*, who based themselves on the right bank of the Rhine, inaugurated a return to more draconian measures, and numerous priests and monks were driven underground.

Unlike in Belgium and the Rhineland, across the border in the Batavian Republic, formerly the United Provinces, Catholics were in the minority and had suffered discrimination at the hand of the ruling Protestant elites. Small wonder that many of them, including the clergy, rallied to the Patriot Party which overthrew the existing regime with French assistance in 1795. Their reward came immediately. The constitution of the new republic provided Catholics with full civic and religious rights and freedoms, and the over-whelming majority of the clergy happily swore the oath of eternal hatred of the old regime which was demanded of them. Catholicism flourished under the new order. Three seminaries and dozens of new churches were opened; and there was, ironically, no shortage of priests thanks to all those clerics who had sought refuge in Holland in order to avoid persecution in Belgium and the Rhineland. This new-found confidence in the direction of their own affairs led many Catholics to question whether they were not better off free from the authority of Rome, an issue which for the time being remained unresolved thanks largely to the fact that the papacy was preoccupied with fending off French aggression in Italy.

The situation in Switzerland was not altogether dissimilar in that Catholics were a minority of the population. Under the *ancien régime* they had formed the majority in only seven of the cantons, where they dominated both the religious and political life. The formation of the Helvetian Republic in 1798 provided the Swiss with a single central government, though the cantons were retained. While those Catholics who lived in Protestant cantons benefited from the introduction of religious freedom, in areas where they had previously held sway their influence was dramatically reduced. This, together with the introduction of legislation abolishing tithes and canon law and nationalising some monastic lands, created a degree of discontent which led to armed rebellion, albeit on a small scale. The potentially divisive issue of religion had been contained under the *ancien régime*, but it had now come to the fore. Four draft constitutions failed before 1803, and Napoleon would get no closer to resolving the problem, even though he reverted to a looser federal structure. As we shall see, a compromise was reached in 1815, in part by restoring the *status quo ante* of 1798, but religion remained a combustible element, sparking to life in the 1840s when the seven Catholic cantons formed the Sonderbund to defend their religious identity.

Within Italy, French religious policy was moderate on the whole. This resulted from the pragmatism of the young general Napoleon Bonaparte, whose brilliance as a strategist was equalled by his sensitivities as a politician. He was aware that, on the one hand, the French invaders had been welcomed by many, including priests and officials, who were glad to see an end to Austrian and papal interference. On the other, he was conscious of the depth of popular religious feeling and was keen not to antagonise this, particularly since Italy was a milch cow expected to contribute substantially to the funding of the war. So it was that in the Cispadane Republic (made up of the Duchy of Modena and the former papal provinces of Romagna and Emilia), Bonaparte initially consented to Catholicism becoming the established religion, even though this flew in the face of French revolutionary principles, because he was eager to mobilise popular support. This provision was subsequently overturned when the territory was absorbed into the Cisalpine Republic, where Jacobin administrators were keen to prosecute a range of anti-clerical measures including the abolition of the regulars and compulsory civil marriages, though they failed in their attempts to nationalise all Church lands. The separation of Church and state, which was characteristic of the Cisalpine Republic, was repeated in the Neapolitan Republic. Of all these complex arrangements, it was the constitution of the Ligurian Republic, formerly Genoa, which was most indulgent towards Catholicism. For a minority of Catholics – a rainbow coalition of Jansenists, reformers, crypto-Jacobins and others known as Catholic Democrats – French rule had briefly suggested the possibility of a renewed and revitalised faith, independent of Rome, with the Church stripped of the accretions of the past. But their hopes were dashed, partly by their failure to secure popular support, and finally by Bonaparte's political settlement with the papacy after 1801.

The impact of the French revolutionary changes upon Rome and the papacy will be discussed later, but some mention must be made here of Britain and Ireland, regions which never witnessed the invasion of French troops, but which were nevertheless affected by the turmoil on the Continent. Within England, changes were already afoot before 1789, particularly with respect to the social contours of Catholicism which had begun to alter quite markedly in the last decades of the eighteenth century and which would continue to do so down to the mid-nineteenth century. Despite the collapse of the Jesuits, the enthusiastic missionary activities of the 400 or so priests operating in England produced a burgeoning number of converts, many of whom were found in areas traditionally short of Catholics such as south-east Lancashire and the East Riding of Yorkshire, as well as in the industrial towns of northern England. At the same time, the domination of English Catholicism by landed families such as the Norfolks began to diminish. These trends agitated the Protestant popular classes, among whom Catholicism was identified with treason, loyalty to a foreign power, superstition, trickery and despotic government. The Gordon Riots of 1780 were a manifestation of these prejudices, which were still evident over three decades later. Cardinal Consalvi, Cardinal-Secretary of State, on a visit to England in 1814, thought it prudent to wear lay attire rather than his purple to avoid the risk of being assaulted in the street. Nevertheless, among the educated elites at least, there was a growing willingness to countenance the removal of the disabilities under which Catholics had laboured since the Glorious Revolution of 1688. In-difference, deism, and a belief in the values of toleration, together with a decline in the fear of popery, all contributed to this sentiment. The attitudes and actions of Catholics, who were anxious to play down theological divisions and to stress the common bonds which united all Christians, further facilitated this process. As the pre-eminent Catholic preacher James Archer argued, polemic and controversy should be eschewed in favour of the promotion of intra-denominational Christian precepts. Moreover, Catholics were deferential and accommodating, anxious above all to join the political nation not to destroy it, even if this meant making substantial concessions. All this eventu-ated in the passage of a Relief Act in 1778 which gave Catholics access to the armed forces, allowed them to run schools and to transmit property, and ended some penal legislation against priests. In truth, the Act did little more than legalise existing practices.

The impact of the events in France undoubtedly helped to resolve lingering doubts about the loyalty of Catholics. They, along with other dissenting groups in England, rallied forcefully to the support of the crown and the nation in the common struggle against the tyranny of the revolution which had merci-lessly persecuted the French Church and clergy. No longer was it so easy to accuse them of disloyalty and allegiance to a foreign cause. The arrival of over 5,500 or so French clergy, 700 of whom were encamped at the royal estates in Winchester, together with some 150,000 lay French exiles of all types, provided an additional fillip to the Catholic cause. As Kirsty Carpenter has suggested, there was a real fear among English Catholics that the osten-tatious piety of these continental arrivals would disfigure traditional patterns of practice and attract unwanted attention.[16] Such anxieties proved unjustified, as the *émigrés* adapted well. Collections were even organised within Protestant churches for the relief of those who were destitute. For some, England became a permanent home. It is calculated that over 1,000 clerics stayed on after the Concordat was published in France in 1802. Such *émigrés* were instrumental in refounding suppressed houses, notably that of Douai, along-side new colleges at Ushaw and Oscott, which contributed to a revitalisation of ecclesiastical life. Their life was made easier by the Second Catholic Relief Act of 1791 which removed almost all restraints on religious practice, save that mass was not permitted in buildings with a bell or steeple, and regulars were not allowed to wear their habits in public. Although Catholics were admitted to the professions, greater civic and religious freedoms would not be granted until 1829 and subsequently.

The impact of the revolutionary events in Ireland was more complex. Here, Catholics comprised the overwhelming majority of the population, of whom 95 per cent were peasants. Land-ownership among this group had fallen from 14 per cent to 5 per cent between 1700 and 1770. Lacking social or economic security, they were further denied a meaningful role in the political process, since even propertied Catholics could not vote or sit in parliament. The Irish parliament itself was Protestant, but possessed limited legislative powers and fell under the sway of London because of its venality. As for the executive, this was almost exclusively English. There also existed an Anglican Church which had shown no inclination to proselytise among Catholics, and was chiefly concerned with fending off the threat of Protestant dissent. With so many ingredients for resentment, it was surprising that Ireland was generally calm throughout the eighteenth century. Admittedly, there were agrarian disturbances from the 1760s onwards which sprang from the attempts by Protestants, under demographic pressure, to evict Catholics from their land-holdings in Ulster. There was a sectarian edge to these protests as Catholic Defender groups were formed to resist aggression, but in essence these were economic not religious in inspiration. Dissatisfaction was contained essentially because the Catholics lacked political leadership, many peasants remained unaffected by the penal legislation, and well-to-do Catholics were able to prosper both as land-owners and as merchants during the course of the eighteenth century. The latter's ambition was to secure equality via con-stitutional means, not to overthrow the existing political order by conflict, and certainly not to separate themselves from the British state since their livelihoods much depended on trade with England and its American colonies. London, in turn, valued the contribution of Ireland, both for the food it supplied and for the recruits it provided for the British armies, and it was this symbiosis which led the British government to encourage Catholics to pursue demands for equality through constitutional means.

Events in France radicalised the Irish situation. Inspired by the liberal spirit of the revolution in its early stages, Protestant dissenters and Catholics, who both laboured under penal legislation, became more vocal. Initially it was Protestant Nonconformists in Ulster, congregated together in the Society of United Irishmen (1791) led by Wolfe Tone, who campaigned for equal rights for all men irrespective of their religion. Catholics also lent support to this campaign, and soon joined the United Irishmen in large numbers. This involvement convinced the ruling Protestant elite that the Catholic Church at all levels – Rome, bishops and priests – was the principal element in the agitation. To be sure, the lower clergy, drawn from the ranks of the peasantry, living and working among their flocks, were sympathetic towards the distress of ordinary people. So too were the bishops. Yet the hierarchy was also extremely wary. Trained in continental seminaries, prelates had seen at first hand how easily popular protest could get out of control, and knew only too well that the Church was incapable of harnessing it. They were further aware of the innately conservative position of Pius VI and had no wish to upset Rome, which had its own difficulties fending off French intervention. So it was that their pronouncements, which expressed sympathy for the misery of the common people while deploring the resort to popular violence, all too often appeared equivocal. Ironically, this lent further credence to Protestant fears that they were conniving at revolution.

Various limited concessions were offered by the English government but these only succeeded in exacerbating sectarian tensions: the Protestant elite feared that it marked the end of their political and social dominance; Catholics were disappointed by the inadequacy of the proposed changes. In the course of the 1790s, rural rioting and terrorism became commonplace with Catholics and Protestants divided into rival gangs, notably the Defenders and the Peep o' Day Boys, who drew on a tradition of agrarian violence. Catholics, who by now had effectively colonised the United Irishmen, were driven increasingly towards a republican and nationalist stance, and enlisted the support of the French who sent troops in both 1796 and 1798. This marked a change in the fundamental nature of Irish patriotism. Hitherto it had been Protestant or interdenominational in character; after the 1790s, it was to have a Catholic hue, although complete separation from the British state was not an option to be explored, at least for the moment.

The threat of French involvement, together with full Catholic emancipation, so frightened the Protestant Ascendancy that a backlash ensued, with the revival of Orange lodges and the use of troops on a wide-scale basis. When, in 1798, the United Irishmen believed their only hope was a full-scale insurrection, this was brutally crushed at the cost of some 12,000 lives. Worried at the prospect of further rebellions by both Catholics and Protestant dissenters, aided by more sizeable French support, and troubled by what the intransigence of an unreconstructed ruling elite might lead to, the government in London moved towards a policy of direct rule from Westminister which culminated in the Act of Union, passed in 1800 and to take effect from 1 January 1801. William Pitt, as Prime Minister and architect of the union, had regarded Catholic emancipation as integral to a settlement of the Irish Question, with an oath of loyalty to the crown a prerequisite of membership of the political nation. However, this strategy foundered upon the stubbornness of George III, the 'rock above water' as Wilberforce termed him, who refused to contemplate such a radical solution.[17] As a result, emancipation did not form part of the Act of Union, and Pitt's resignation removed from government its chief proponent. The issue would not disappear from the political agenda. The addition of 4 million Irish meant that one-quarter of the population of Britain was now Catholic, and their constitutional disabilities could not be permanently ignored.

After 1801, Catholic emancipation could not be divorced from the Irish Question. This linkage was unwelcome to many English Catholics, who preferred to continue a long-standing policy of quietist assimilation into the political order. Such an approach stood in marked contrast to that of most Irish Catholics, though not at first the bishops, for whom emancipation had come to be seen as a means to the establishment of a new political and social order. Additionally, suspicion of the purportedly unreformed and backward nature of Irish Catholicism, 'a strange assemblage of strong faith and much superstition', as Sir James Throckmorton put it in 1806, remained common among the English gentry in particular.[18] The alleged superstition of Irish Catholicism contrasted with the thoughtful and refined character of the faith in England. There was also concern that something of the autonomy long enjoyed by English Catholicism might be lost through the Act of Union, given the long-standing, albeit erroneous prejudice concerning the suscept-ibility of the Irish to the whims of Rome. Nevertheless, it was inevitable that the papacy would cease to regard Britain as a lost cause, now that one in four of its population was Catholic. For the moment, however, Rome had plenty of problems closer to home.

Rome and Revolution: the Last Pope?

Rome was not well placed to meet the challenges posed by the French Revolution. The inherent weaknesses which had been largely concealed during the eighteenth century were to be brutally exposed in the 1790s. Economically backward, lacking a powerful army, intellectually enfeebled, and incapable of proffering strong leadership, Rome was not helped by the fact that it also became a refuge for French *émigrés* who presented the elderly and infirm Pius VI with a blinkered and lop-sided view of the world. The papacy thus found itself responding to events rather than controlling them, to such an extent that many observers believed that the very office of pontiff would not survive into the nineteenth century.

From the outset, papal policy was marked by dithering and misjudgement. The lack of protest when, in 1789–90, the French abolished annates and proposed the Civil Constitution of the Clergy led to a belief among revolu-tionaries that Pius VI would eventually legitimate the new order, especially since the Avignon enclave gave them a bargaining counter, and disinclined them to listen to the concerns of the French clergy. As we have seen, papal reticence derived from a fear of provoking the French Church into schism, although this was precisely what eventuated with the formation of the con-stitutional clergy. A further error of judgement was made over the French declaration of war in 1792. Cardinal Maury, a French non-juring priest, was dispatched to the Diet at Frankfurt to drum up support for the allied war effort. 'The pope has need', declared Maury, 'of [the princes'] swords to sharpen his pen.'[19] Such statements convinced the revolutionaries that the papacy was hopelessly counter-revolutionary. So too did Pius's reaction to the execution of Louis XVI. The Pope denounced the act as one of murder and bemoaned the treatment of Catholics in France. In the meantime, little was done to curb the popular excesses against French representatives in the Eternal City which led to the death of the French legate, Basseville. Paradoxically, by placing himself firmly in the camp of counter-revolution, Pius VI was storing up problems for himself, since he lacked the military and financial wherewithal to resist French aggression under the inspired generalship of the young Napoleon Bonaparte which in 1796 resulted in the annexation of Lombardy and the most prosperous sections of the Papal States, Ravenna and Bologna.

With the Directory pressing for Napoleon to take Rome and declare it a republic, and with the papacy only too aware of the proximity of French troops, an armistice was agreed on 20 June 1796, the terms of which imposed a tribute of 21 million *scudi*, the handing over of 100 works of art, 500 manuscripts from the papal collections and the exclusive access of French ships to Roman ports. Pius VI also issued instructions to French Catholics to remain loyal to their government and to recognise the Republic, but the Directory wanted more: a reversal of his earlier condemnations of revolutionary religious legislation, in particular the Civil Constitution, which it was hoped would draw the sting from the uprisings in the Vendée. Pius balked at this and, in September, he ended the armistice and began to form a citizens' militia to defend Rome. Napoleon's response further highlighted the military weakness and poor diplomatic judgement of the papacy. His forces simply occupied the remainder of the Papal States. While Rome itself was spared, at least for the moment, churches elsewhere were plundered, and the Marian statue at Loreto was despatched to the museum of Egyptian antiquities at Paris. The terrified Pius hastened to sign a peace at Tolentino in February 1797, which doubled French fiscal exactions, and he renounced papal possessions in Avignon, the Venaissin, Bologna, Ferrara and the Romagna, the first time a pope had signed away part of his temporal patrimony.

Tolentino did not resolve matters. Having just quashed royalist and Catholic electoral gains in the elections of 1797, the more anti-clerical elements of the Directory, including La Révellière-Lépeaux, Barras and Reubell, wanted to see nothing less than the disappearance of the papacy as an institution. General Haller, the French Commissioner to Rome, declared: 'This Babylon, gorged with the spoils of the universe, must feed us and pay our debts.'[20] Taking their cue from such sentiments, a group of Jacobin sympathisers in Rome tried to plant several trees of liberty, leading to rioting and the accidental death of the young French General Duphot, who had been betrothed to Napoleon's sister. Personal affront now entered the picture as Napoleon's troops entered Rome on 15 February 1798, twenty-three years to the day after Pius's coronation. The Vatican palace was ransacked, booty was seized, a republic was declared and a popular uprising brutally suppressed. Partly at the instigation of La Révellière-Lépeaux, who wished to destroy the spiritual and temporal power of the papacy and replace this with a deistic cult, a pagan altar was erected in St Peter's Square. The terminally-ill Pius, who was now eighty-one years of age, begged to be allowed to die in Rome, but he was placed instead under house arrest in Siena, where he was effectively unable to perform any of his duties. 'A man can die anywhere,' sneered General Berthier.[21] Fearing that Pius might become a focal point for resistance to French rule, in March 1799 he was bundled into a carriage and taken off across the unforgiving terrain of the Alps to France, even though he was now almost paralysed. He died at Valence on 29 August 1799. Humiliation accompanied him to the end. He was buried by a schismatic constitutional priest, and the local prefect recorded his death thus: 'Citizen Braschi, exercising the profession of pontiff'.

Although Rome had been ill-placed to influence international affairs at the close of the eighteenth century, Pius had been a weak, timid and egotistical pope whose misfortune had been to live in a turbulent era which demanded clear judgement and leadership, something which he was incapable of providing. As has been frequently noted, the manner of Pius's death did more for the standing of the papacy than any of his actions in life, turning him into a martyr. It remained to be seen, however, whether his successor Pius VII would be able to resurrect the fortunes of the papacy in the face of the seemingly unstoppable onslaught of Napoleon's armies.

Napoleon and Religion

The young general who came to power as First Consul in the *coup* of Brumaire, 9 November 1799, and who had himself proclaimed Emperor in 1804, was a man of seeming contradictions. He claimed to embody the principles of 1789, used the rhetoric of revolution, and indeed could not have enjoyed such a meteoric career without the opportunities offered by the collapse of the *ancien régime*. But in truth, he operated less on the basis of principle than of pragmatism, drawing indiscriminately on an eclectic mix of ideas and practices, choosing whatever worked best. This was to be perceived in all areas of Napoleonic rule, whether it be his land settlement, the creation of a new nobility, the overhaul of finances, the restructuring of government, or the introduction of a new legal code. It was no less apparent in the domain of religion. Personally, Napoleon had little need for spiritual nourishment and his scrutiny of Enlightenment texts, as well as his personal experience, had left him profoundly sceptical of the claims of revealed religion. Speaking with Bertrand, when in exile on St Helena in 1816, he argued that there was no historical proof of the existence of Christ while acknowledging that 'Mohammed, on the other hand, was a conqueror and a sovereign, and his existence is incontestable.'[22] However, his personal doubts about the truth of religion did not blind him to its power as an instrument of public policy. The revolts in the Vendée had proved the dangers of affronting people's religious beliefs; and, as a natural disciplinarian, the mob frenzy of the Paris crowd had confirmed his view of what might happen when society's rules broke down. While in Italy, he had been impressed by the influence of the clergy, and preferred to control rather than to fight them. He thus had a lively awareness of the utility of religion as a social cement: 'You believe that man can be man without God ... man without God, I have seen him at work since 1793. That man, one does not rule him, one shoots him: I have had enough of that type of man.'[23]

In practice, Napoleon was prepared to embrace any religion which suited his purpose. He was to boast that he had quelled the uprising in the Vendée by becoming a Catholic; that he had successfully won over the Egyptians by thinking of embracing Islam; and that he had secured the acceptance of popular opinion in Italy by becoming Ultramontane. He would have rebuilt the Temple of Solomon had he been the ruler of the Jews; in 1806 he did indeed restore the grand Sanhedrin of the Jews. Yet Catholicism he valued above all. Deism was dismissed for its want of moral certainty; Freemasonry he mocked for its bizarre rituals and its secrecy; Protestantism he distrusted because it lacked the organisational structure and hierarchy which was integral to Catholicism. On 5 June 1800 he informed the clergy at Milan, 'The Catholic religion is the only religion that can make a stable community happy and establish the foundations of good government', adding that, 'the faith was like an anchor which alone could save France from the storm'.[24]

Ever the pragmatist, on coming to power in 1799 Napoleon had three objectives apropos his religious policy. The first was to secure an accommodation with the Church so as to siphon off the energies of the revolt in the Vendée. The second was to use Catholicism to legitimate his regime. As a soldier, with a strong sense of military discipline, he was always uneasy with the fact that he had illegally usurped power, and he constantly sought means to underpin his regime. This was to be done by an appeal to a popular mandate in the form of plebiscites and the retention of parliaments, together with the re-creation of a nobility. Ecclesiastical approval would also be useful in this regard and would play well with the strongly Catholic areas of his burgeoning empire, notably Belgium and the Rhineland, and would undermine the claim of his European enemies, particularly Austria, that they were the upholders of the Catholic religion. Finally, he looked for a definitive religious settlement which would delineate the role, social standing and influence of the Church so that it served as a bulwark of stability, and functioned more or less as a department of state.

Napoleon moved swiftly to effect a *rapprochement* with the Church. In the Vendée, he allowed the open practice of Catholicism under the leadership of clerics who were obliged only to take an oath of fidelity to the constitution. He further ordered the body of Pius VI, which still lay unburied at Valence, to be interred with full funerary honours. This eased the way to the start of negotiations with the newly elected pope, Pius VII (1800–23), the former Benedictine monk, Barnabà Chiaramonte. 'Tell the pope', Napoleon declared, 'I want to make him a gift of 30,000,000 Frenchmen.'[25] For his part the novice pontiff, who as Bishop of Imola had preached the infamous 'Jacobin' sermon at Christmas 1797 urging an acceptance of the legitimacy of the revolutionary government, was eager to end ten years of schism and to begin his reign with a reconciliation between the Church and France, still viewed as the most prestigious Catholic country in Europe. Such a settlement could only redound to the prestige of the papacy itself, enabling it to reassert its primacy within the Church and affirm its independence of the secular powers. It was clear, however, which side was operating from a position of strength. Napoleon's decisive victory in 1800 over the Austrians at Marengo re-established French control over Italy, once again casting a doubt over the future autonomy of the Papal States in which Pius VII was tentatively introducing reform.

In the ensuing negotiations, which lasted a long eight months, both sides proved exceedingly obdurate, although it was Napoleon who was the more bloody-minded. The document which was finally signed at 2 a.m. on 16 July

1801 was both brief and apparently reasonable. The preamble acknowledged Catholicism as 'the religion of the great majority of the French people',[26] a wording which did not altogether please the Curia which had initially demanded that Catholicism should be the 'dominant' faith. Article 1 permitted the free and open practice of Catholicism, albeit in a way that did not disturb public order; Articles 2 and 3 foresaw the reorganisation of dioceses after consultation between Paris and Rome and the consequent resignation of bishops where necessary; Articles 4 and 5 placed the nomination of prelates in the hands of the First Consul, canonical institution being subsequently conferred by the Pope; Articles 6, 7 and 8 obliged bishops and priests to swear an oath of fidelity to the government and to recite prayers for the salvation of the consuls and republic; Articles 9 to 12 dealt with the internal organisation of the Church; Article 13 asserted the inviolability of the lands seized from the Church during the revolution; Article 14 made a vague promise of a 'suitable salary' to clerics to be paid by the state, while Article 15 allowed endowments to the Church; and the catch-all Article 16 conferred upon the First Consul the same rights as had been enjoyed by the *ancien régime* monarchy over the Church, without specifying what these entailed. A final article accepted that, in the event of a non-Catholic assuming the position of First Consul, the Concordat would be renegotiated.

Whereas the terms of the above agreement appeared reasonable and balanced, the longer Napoleon pondered them the less he liked them, concerned that they did not sufficiently strengthen the state's hand over the Church. He was also aware of the need to deflect criticism from anti-clericals who opposed any agreement with the Church – for this reason the Concordat was referred to as the Convention de Messidor – and he was wary of the growth of any kind of opposition at a time when his hold on power was still tenuous. The Constitution of Year X (1802), which effectively cemented his dictatorship by making him First Consul for life, still lay in the future. Napoleon therefore unilaterally added seventy-seven Organic Articles to the Concordat. Ostensibly these dealt with the policing arrangements referred to in Article 1, but in practice they went much further. Government approbation was required before papal pronunciations could be published, councils convoked, new parishes established and private chapels set up. A uniform catechism was introduced, church weddings could not precede the civil ceremony, cathedral chapters were reduced to merely ceremonial function and the powers of papal delegates were severely circumscribed. Any breach of the articles was treated as a criminal offence and was referred to the Council of State, the keystone of Napoleonic government. Additionally, clerical salaries were specified: a mere 15,000 francs per annum for an archbishop, of whom there were to be ten; 10,000 francs for each bishop, who numbered sixty in total; and 1,000 to 1,500 francs for the 3,000 or so parish priests. Although it was not specifically referred to in the Organic Articles, the creation of a Ministry of Cults in 1801 reinforced a drive towards government oversight of ecclesiastical matters.

It is commonly argued that the Concordat, together with the Organic Articles, was a victory for Napoleon and marked the end of ecclesiastical independence of the state. To be sure, clerical freedoms had been severely circumscribed, Catholicism was recognised only as one religion among others, and the Church had acknowledged something of the legitimacy of the revolution by accepting its successor, the Consulate. Nevertheless, the Church also made significant gains. In the first place, the Napoleonic settlement was founded on the basis of an agreement between Church and state, and was not the result of a government *diktat*, thus implicitly recognising the authority of the Holy See and its ability to concede privileges to the state. In this way, Rome preserved something of its authority, just as it had done by the negotiation of concordats in the early modern period and as it would do again in the nineteenth century. Additionally, the papacy rescued from schism the most important national church in Europe while strengthening its claim to intervene in its affairs. This was to be perceived most clearly with respect to the position of the bishops who comprised two groups, the *ancien régime* prelates appointed by the King and the constitutional bishops who had survived the revolutionary onslaughts under the courageous leadership of Henri Grégoire. To reconcile the two groups was impossible and the only way forwards was to start afresh. Forty-eight prelates agreed to resign, but thirty-seven (mainly *ancien régime* bishops) refused, and continued to exist as the so-called *petite église* which ultimately came to naught, although in some regions this minor schism persisted until the Second Vatican Council. Their sees were declared vacant by Pius VII and the episcopacy was renewed under the terms of the Concordat. Such an exercise of Roman authority over the Gallican Church would have been impossible before 1789 and marked a new stage in the relationship between papacy and Church in France, and helped to lay the foundations for a developing Ultramontanism within the French clergy.

To sign the Concordat was one thing, but to reconstruct the Church in France was quite another. The task was made easier by the generally high quality of the new bishops. Well educated and conciliatory, they approached their jobs with commendable fairness and assiduity, overcoming the administrative difficulties of having to govern new dioceses which had been put together with reference to both the pre- and post-1789 situations. Even though a majority of the newly appointed bishops were refractories, they lacked that collegiate sense which had characterised the old regime episcopacy, not least because the Napoleonic Church no longer had a body equivalent to the pre-revolutionary General Assembly of the Clergy which had provided a corporate sense of identity, but merely a series of ranks and offices through which orders were barked.

More troubling were the shortage and quality of the parish clergy. Well over 3,000 of those who had resigned their office, apostatised or married during the 1790s now sought reconciliation with the Church and presented themselves for scrutiny before the legation led by Cardinal Caprara, who had been appointed to handle this sensitive task. Former refractories also presented themselves for service, and they dominated the ranks of the Napoleonic Church, often making life difficult for the constitutional clerics. But even when such recruits were taken into account, there were insufficient clerics of the right kind available. Many were aged, temperamentally unsuited to the demands of parish life and wholly unqualified for the cure of souls: former regulars, *émigrés*, ex-canons and prebendaries. By 1808, almost 10,500 parishes, over 20 per cent of the total, remained vacant. Some areas of France, particularly the Vendée where counter-revolution and repression had been most intense, were especially short of clergy: barely half the *ancien régime* clergy were eligible for office in 1801 and nearly one-third of these would die within the decade. The department of the Var was obliged to depend upon Italian priests until the 1820s. Poor career prospects and low salaries did little to entice new ordinands. In the period 1801 to 1815, there were only 6,000 recruits, the same number as had come forward in the year 1789 alone. Small wonder that the average age of priests was high and rising: over one-third were in their sixties in 1809. The seminary system, which had been one of the highlights of the French Church in the eighteenth century, was unable to furnish the replacements needed, even though seminarians were excused military service until 1809. There was also a shortage of teachers, buildings and income, for no provision was made to fund the seminaries. Clerical recruitment was increasingly from the ranks of the peasantry, and herein lay the roots of the anti-urban and anti-liberal attitudes which characterised the nineteenth-century lower clergy. Additionally, the Concordat had enormously strengthened the authority of bishops within their dioceses. The majority of priests had no security of tenure, but served at the bishop's pleasure. So it was that the Richerist dream of the eighteenth-century lower clergy of a synodal and democratic Church, which had initially led some ecclesiastics to favour the revolution, had been stymied.* Priests discovered themselves looking increasingly to Rome as a counter-balance to episcopal despotism; paradoxically, the bishops themselves looked to the Eternal City as a counter-weight to the despotism of the state. One of the unlooked-for products of the Napoleonic religious settlement was thus the emergence of a strong Ultramontane sentiment among all levels of the French clergy.

If Napoleon had anticipated that the Concordatory Church would be a faithful servant of his regime, he was to be disappointed. To be sure, the Church preached compliance with the conscription laws. It also accepted the Imperial Catechism of 1806, significantly drawn up by the Ministry of Cults, albeit with serious reservations with respect to Article 7. This threatened with damnation all those who refused adherence to 'Napoleon I, our emperor, love, respect, obedience, loyalty, military service ... because God ... has made him the agent of His power and His image upon earth'.[27] The Feast of the Assumption of 15 August was followed by the feast of St Napoleon, an early Christian martyr whose pedigree always remained distinctly dubious. Yet the

---

* Edmond Richer, a syndic of the Sorbonne in the seventeenth century, had argued that councils of the Church were superior to the papacy and that the spiritual authority of parish priests, as heirs to the seventy-two disciples, was on a par with that of the bishops. In the eighteenth century, his viewpoint was adopted by many parish priests in France who opposed 'episcopal despotism', wanted a greater voice in Church affairs and who sought a more equal division of the Church's wealth.

Church could not be stopped from going its own way, at least in some spheres. Prefects in the dioceses of Aix, Bayeux, Bordeaux, Nancy and Rennes turned a blind eye when constitutional clergy were illegally forced to swear humiliating recantations. Prefects further ignored the reconsecration ceremonies for those churches which had been supposedly sullied by constitutional uses as well as the collective rebaptism and remarriage ceremonies undertaken by those who had had recourse to the services of the constitutional clergy. More seriously, some bishops presided over open-air festivals even though these contravened police regulations over public assembly. After 1809, when Napoleon treated Pius VII in much the same way as the Directory had handled Pius VI, the prelates became ever more outspoken in their criticisms of his government, and privately longed for the restoration of the Bourbons.

The Concordat made no mention of the regular orders, and the revolutionary legislation suppressing them was not rescinded. While Napoleon had some admiration for the military organisation of the Jesuits, he was deeply mistrustful of all male orders, believing them to be useless 'unprofitable creatures', subversive and inherently disloyal because of their outside allegiance. Moreover, the male regulars fell beyond the control of the bishop whose authority in respect of the secular clergy the Concordat had done much to strengthen. In practice, some limited restoration of the male congregations took place. Those allowed to function were concerned primarily with the provision of elementary education and public welfare, more or less free of charge, thereby not imposing financial burdens on the state. Such orders included the Brothers of the Christian Schools and the Ignorantins. Tolerance was also extended to those orders, such as the Lazarists and the Fathers of the Holy Spirit, which were instrumental in propagating French culture and *esprit* abroad. Conveniently out of the way, those orders based in the mountainous terrain linking France with Italy and Spain were allowed to survive, providing convenient stop-overs for travellers, thanks in part to the generosity the canons of St Bernard had displayed to Napoleon himself on his way to the battle of Marengo.

Much greater indulgence was displayed towards the female religious who were regarded as less of a political threat and who, above all, were engaged in utilitarian social functions. In some instances, they were even given official encouragement and blessing. Once again, it was those *congréganistes* concerned with education, care of the sick and poor relief that benefited most. These included the Daughters of Charity, who were permitted to return in 1800, and the Sisters of Mercy who, in 1805, were put under the protection of Napoleon's mother. A number of new congregations, stimulated by official toleration, also sprang up. These were mainly local in influence, and were devoted to philanthropic activities, notably the education of girls, a reflection of Napoleon's own misogynistic attitudes which viewed women as deeply inferior to men and incapable of rational thought. So it was that the Sacred Heart Society was founded in Paris in 1800, the Sisters of Charity of Jesus and Mary at Ghent in 1806, the Sisters of Notre Dame at Amiens in 1804 and the Daughters of the Holy Cross at Poitiers in 1807. Concerned at the proliferation of local initiatives, Napoleon attempted to enforce some over-arching authority upon the congregations in 1807 but, in the event, he had to be content with setting out common guidelines for their operation. Without this window of opportunity, it is inconceivable that the startling growth of the women's orders in the nineteenth century could have got under way.

Something of the nature of nineteenth-century popular religious practice in France was also to be shaped by the revolutionary and Napoleonic experience. In the first instance, there was a growing laicisation of religion. Under the Directory, the Church had been restored at the initiative of the laity, who reopened religious buildings, refurbished wayside shrines and even held services, including masses, with a lay person officiating. Freed from the tutelage of the clergy, lay people became accustomed to taking the lead in religious practices, a trend which could not be easily reversed. In the aftermath of the schism of the French Church, priests no longer commanded the same respect and had been shown wanting in several regards, not always able to offer guidance and leadership. Suggestions after 1814 that tithes might be re-established were met with absolute hostility and there was reluctance to provide financial support for the returning *curés*. The parish priest of Rognon in eastern France complained that, 'certain people say that they do very well without their *curés*'.[28] In a related development, one may point to the resurgence of popular religious practices which the eighteenth-century clergy had sought to control or stamp out altogether, but which were now reinstituted by a laity liberated from clerical supervision. The cult of the saints, the establishment of wayside crosses and shrines, night-time pilgrimages and processions, the use of benedictions, all made a comeback. Finally, and perhaps most significantly in the long term, there was a noticeable feminisation of religion which built upon the leading role of women in the defence of the faith during the high point of dechristianisation in particular, and reinforced an eighteenth-century trend towards a gender dichotomy in religious matters. In part, this reflected women's search for areas of empowerment, since they were effectively excluded from so many spheres of public life under the revolution, as they had been in the pre-1789 period. It also emerged out of a 'dearth, disease, devotion' syndrome. Bearing the brunt of the economic privations which were intense, especially for the poorest elements of society in the 1790s when the harvests were seriously disrupted, women sought consolation in religion.

In ways unlooked for, the Church in France regrouped and laid the parameters for religious life in the nineteenth century. No less significant were the effects of the Napoleonic regime on religious life in the rest of Europe.

Napoleon and Europe

An accident of geography ensured that it was the Catholic states of Europe which were principally affected by the Napoleonic conquests since they lay adjacent to the French frontiers and, with the important exception of Spain where Napoleon's hegemony was never complete, were the first areas of

Europe to be occupied by French forces. It has been noted that Belgium, early on, bore the brunt of occupation. It will further be recalled that revolutionary legislation was applied in its full vigour from 1794, and the imposition of a Napoleonic regime brought some easing of the situation. Diocesan boundaries were redrawn, the Concordat of 1801 was put into effect and the free practice of Catholicism permitted. The fact that none of the constitutional bishops was put into a position of responsibility additionally eased matters. It would be a mistake, however, to believe that the religious situation in Belgium was reconciled. A *petite église*, linked to that in France, persisted; seminarists resented the obligatory teaching of Gallican precepts; the parish clergy havered when told to advocate obedience to the conscription laws, fearing the wrath of their parishioners; Napoleon's occupation of the Papal States in 1809 aroused some animosity; and there was little enthusiasm for Bonapartist propaganda in the shape of the Imperial Catechism.

The Napoleonic impact upon Germany was yet more considerable. By the end of 1794, the revolutionary armies had reversed their earlier defeats and had overrun the Rhineland. The defeat of the Second Coalition and the resulting Treaty of Lunéville in 1801 produced further French gains and, in 1806, Napoleon united his German satellite states into the Confederation of the Rhine, ending the thousand-year-old Reich. Lands on the left bank of the Rhine were annexed to France and here French religious policy held sway. The properties of the Church were expropriated, monastic orders were closed, and the terms of the Concordat of 1801 were applied. The ecclesiastical principalities, which had combined secular and spiritual power in the person of a prelate, were secularised. Moreover, since lay princes who had lost land were compensated by the acquisition of ecclesiastical properties on the right bank of the river, ecclesiastical power disintegrated here as well. The Imperial Recess of 1803 declared that the sovereignty of the ecclesiastical rulers was now at an end. Only one prince-bishop remained, Dalberg, the client of Napoleon, who was made primate of all Germany with his see at Regensburg.

The wholesale reorganisation of the ecclesiastical structures of the Holy Roman Empire had implications which went far beyond the ending of the medieval prince-bishoprics. The Holy Roman Emperor lost his special role as protector of Catholicism. The privileged constitutional position of the Roman faith, shored up by the presence of numerous ecclesiastical principalities which enjoyed separate representation at the Diet and the existence of three prince-bishops who sat in the electoral college, was ended. Accordingly, the faith was increasingly at the behest of the secular authorities who were keen to subvert the independent position of the Church. In Württemberg and Baden, for example, the Church was placed under the control of a single ministry, regular orders were dissolved and their lands sequestrated, diocesan and parish boundaries were redrawn and the lower clergy, salaried by the state, took on the characteristics of a civil bureaucracy. Only three Catholic universities – Freiburg, Münster and Würzburg – remained, and theology faculties were instead established inside state establishments. Many Catholics now found themselves under Protestant rule. As it happened, such princes were in some respects more benign than their Catholic counterparts, as they were eager to demonstrate their even-handedness in matters of faith. Nevertheless, Catholics were not free of discrimination, and in Prussia they were treated as second-class citizens. Although unperceived at the time, the turmoil of the Napoleonic era had laid the foundations for the emergence of Prussia as the leading German state, something which was to have deleterious consequences for Catholicism both inside and outside the German lands. Paradoxically, the same upheavals contributed to a growth of Ultramontanism. The death of the ecclesiastical principalities saw off some of the most intransigent and independent advocates of Febronianism; and there was an increasing tendency for the state-dominated churches to look to Rome as a counter-weight.

The effects of the Napoleonic interlude upon Spain were multiform and, in some respects, conflicting. Even before the arrival of French troops, in 1798 Charles IV (1788–1808) and his favourite Manuel de Godoy had confiscated the lands of some religious houses, forced the sale of some charitable properties and obliged the Church to contribute to a state loan. One effect of the state's aggressive regalism was to widen the division between the upper clergy, who proved best capable of defending their wealth, and the lower clergy, who in practice bore the brunt of the state's financial demands and accordingly became increasingly impoverished. A second result was to heighten tensions between traditionalists in the Spanish Church who believed in the unyielding maintenance of its institutions and privileges, and the reformers who recognised the need to adjust its organisation and methods if Catholicism was to survive the new exigencies. The process of state encroachment on the Church was furthered when Napoleon pushed aside the new King, Ferdinand VII, and put his brother on the throne in June 1808. Joseph moved quickly to close the monasteries and sequestrate Church property. These measures were bitterly resented by the monks themselves, the 'beastly friars' as Napoleon called them, and were likewise resisted by the peasantry who united in defence of the Catholic faith against the invading French 'infidels'. Significantly, however, when a national Cortes emerged at the head of a liberated Spain in the period 1810–13, no real attempt was made to restore the Church to its former ascendancy. Dominated by a liberal elite, the Cortes meeting at Cadiz did indeed recognise Catholicism as the national religion, and St Teresa of Avila was made co-patron alongside St James, but the closure of monasteries and the expropriation of Church lands continued, the papal nuncio was expelled when he protested, and in 1813 the Inquisition was suppressed. The following year, the Bourbon Ferdinand VII was again put on the throne and many looked for a wholesale return to the old regime. The new King restored the Inquisition, permitted the re-establishment of the Jesuits, and reopened monasteries. Yet there were limits to Ferdinand's indulgence. Only a small proportion of former Church properties were restored and there was no attempt to create a theocracy. In this sphere at least, Ferdinand pursued policies almost identical to those of the eighteenth-century Spanish rulers, appointing over sixty bishops. If Catholicism had been confirmed as the badge of identity in Spain, nevertheless the Church paid a price, for it had relinquished much of its autonomy to the state. Moreover, most clerics were now hostile to any liberal reform of politics or society, convinced that this was 'a rebellion against God and human society', as the newspaper *El Catolico* would put it in 1840; a pattern had been established that would endure until the twentieth century.[29]

Whereas Napoleonic hegemony in Spain was never complete, Bonaparte enjoyed more success in bringing the Italian states into his empire. Religious policy was broadly in line with that pursued in France, although Napoleon, perhaps wary of upsetting clerical and popular susceptibilities, allowed the Church greater freedoms. Michael Broers has pointed out that the Emperor was keen to refashion the Church so that it operated as a servant of the state and to employ the clergy in the role of 'a sort of moral gendarmerie', as one contemporary put it.[30] At the same time, he could not ignore the wealth of the Church, and his need to exploit this grew as the fiscal demands upon his empire became ever more pressing. Towards the end of his regime, this led him to adopt a more combative policy apropos the Church which alienated many clerics who, up to this moment, had been surprisingly quiescent, not least because they had a sneaking sympathy with some of the Bonapartist reforms, although it should be stressed that regional variations in this respect were pronounced. Moreover, many of the French administrators developed a contempt for the local culture and religion, contrasting this unfavourably with their own advanced views. As one of them, Degerando, noted:

> Religion as it is understood by Enlightened men and felt by virtuous men, as it generally exists in France – that is as the product of a reasoned and reasonable conviction, whose main aim is to improve morals – is scarcely even perceived to exist by the Romans ... Relics, indulgences, the Forty Hours, the rosary, the little medals are what interests them; reading the scriptures would be a profanity; and whoever should discourse to a Roman of these august and simple truths, the existence of the author of all things, would be suspected of heresy, if not of atheism.[31]

These themes in French attitudes towards, and treatment of, Catholicism are perhaps best illustrated in the case of the former Cisalpine Republic, reorganised as the Italian Republic in 1802, and further restructured in 1805 when these territories became the Kingdom of Italy which also incorporated Lombardy, Venetia and Romagna, a former papal territory, and not the last of Rome's possessions to become a part of this entity. Here, the Concordat of 1803 was closely modelled on that of 1801, but, for example, allowed the retention of Church lands, gave clerics jurisdiction over marriages, provided for subsidies towards the seminaries and even permitted the existence of cathedral chapters. Above all, Catholicism was recognised as the religion of the state. After 1805, matters took a turn for the worse, and Napoleon was inclined to deal more brusquely with the clergy as his relations with the papacy deteriorated. The introduction of the French Civil Code, legalising divorce, was badly received, as was the introduction of the Imperial Catechism in 1807, although a question mark must remain over whether this was widely deployed, especially in remote mountainous areas. Entry into religious orders was at first tightly regulated, then the orders were banned and their properties sequestrated. A decree of April 1810 removed from Lombardy and Venetia almost all of the 800 or so monasteries and convents which had existed in 1796. In Venice, the extensive lands belonging to the lay confraternities were also taken over. Paradoxically, as in France, a small number of new orders, principally concerned with educational and charitable functions, were established with state blessing. This might have contributed to a nineteenth-century revival of the regulars and congregations, but in 1814 the secular clergy was in a sorry state. Priests might have welcomed state salaries and the redrawing of parishes, but there was a real crisis of recruitment, as elsewhere in Europe, and the clergy had lost something of its grip over lay religiosity. In 1809, the Bishop of Vercelli bemoaned the fact that a third of the faithful no longer attended Easter communion.

Across on the western seaboard of Italy, Bonaparte likewise tightened his grip – Piedmont, Genoa, Tuscany, and eventually Rome in 1808 becoming a part of France itself, divided into departments and governed directly from Paris, although Rome was accorded the status of the 'second city'. All these territories became subject to the French Concordat of 1801, as well as the Civil Code. While there was a wooing of the secular clergy, there was a fierce onslaught on the regulars culminating in their dissolution in 1808. As in the Kingdom of Italy, the Church might have emerged in a fitter and leaner state, at least in regard to its organisation, but again it was short of personnel and had lost something of its status within society.

Matters turned out rather differently in the Kingdom of Naples where Napoleon's brother, Joseph, succeeded the Bourbon King Ferdinand in 1805. Joseph immediately embarked upon radical reform of the Church, which until then had been largely cocooned from the turmoil of the revolutionary and Napoleonic decades, beginning with the destruction of monasteries and priories, almost all of which had been dissolved by 1809. Well over a thousand monasteries were sold off, and in 1815 the clergy possessed less than 13 per cent of national property compared to over 25 per cent in 1800. A concordat was promised but foundered on the refusal of Pius VII to countenance a sizeable reduction in the number of dioceses from an astonishing 131 – almost as many as in *ancien régime* France which had five times the population – to a more sensible fifty. In this traditionally 'priest-ridden' area, Joseph had wanted to cut the numbers of seculars and reorganise parishes along more rational lines, but only limited progress was made as he left to become King of Spain in 1808. His successor, General Murat, was preoccupied with military matters. Bizarrely, although the impact of the French was less severe in religious affairs in the Kingdom of Naples than in the north of the peninsula, popular hostility tended to be greater, reflecting the relative backwardness of southern Italy.

Events in Italy naturally rebounded on the papacy whose relationship with Napoleon deteriorated steadily after 1801. Pius VII had suppressed his deep misgivings about the Concordat in the interests of restoring France to the bosom of the faith, yet several points of conflict remained, particularly on the part of Napoleon. The Pope's refusal to annul the marriage of Jérôme,

Napoleon's brother, to an American Protestant, was a particular grievance to the French ruler, a man who set tremendous store on family loyalties. When, in 1804, the Pope travelled to Paris, against the advice of the Curia, for the coronation of Napoleon as Emperor, Bonaparte was deeply irritated by the fervour with which the pontiff was greeted. Many people who had undergone marriage and baptism during the time of the Constitutional Church pressed forward to receive absolution and a fresh blessing from the pontiff. The coronation ceremony itself was to increase the hostility between the two men. The Pope refused to go ahead with the occasion until Napoleon and Josephine went through a Christian rite of marriage, something which was conducted the day before the crowning itself. In Notre Dame, Napoleon would not allow Pius to place the crown on his head, lifting it himself from the altar. The newly-anointed monarch went through with this ritual, which was deeply irritating to him, only because he appreciated and needed the legitimacy that papal confirmation bestowed. As he himself complained: 'Nobody thought of the pope when he was in Rome. My coronation and appearance in Paris made him important.'[32]

It was, though, the situation in Italy that occasioned the most serious breach between Paris and Rome. Pius was more angered than the clergy in the peninsula by Napoleonic religious policy there, resenting the break-up of dioceses and the imposition of the Concordats of 1801 and 1803. Above all, it was the attempt by Napoleon to incorporate the Pope and the Papal States into the French Empire that most rankled. A steady drip of papal possessions found themselves in French hands: Romagna (1801); the port of Ancona (1805); and the Kingdom of Naples (1806), a papal fiefdom. Continuing papal refusal to close ports to the allies, an action which Pius declared would be tantamount to an act of war, and Napoleon's confidence after the stunning defeat of the Austrians at Austerlitz, thus removing the last significant defender of the Catholic cause, opened the way for the French occupation of Rome itself in January 1808.

When, in July of that year, Pius refused to abdicate his temporal sovereignty, he was taken north to Savona where he was held in isolation. Meanwhile, the remaining papal possessions were annexed to France; Pius responded by excommunicating 'the robbers of Peter's patrimony', although he carefully avoided mentioning Napoleon by name. Tempers flared again when Pius refused to acknowledge Napoleon's divorce and remarriage to an Austrian princess, Marie-Louise, and would not grant canonical institution to any of the clergy nominated by Napoleon to vacant sees. These were becoming numerous throughout Europe as aged prelates died off. To circumvent this growing problem, Napoleon summoned a Council of the Imperial Bishops in Paris at which eighty-five agreed, after much cajoling, to permit institution by an archbishop in lieu of papal conferment. Those cardinals and bishops who dared defy this were dispersed to provincial towns and a number exiled to Corsica. Exasperated by papal intransigence and worried lest the Pope was liberated by the heretical English, whose frigates lay off the coast of Italy, in June 1812 Napoleon ordered that Pius be brought to Fontainebleau. Troubled by a serious urinary infection, the Pope had to stop every ten minutes on the arduous twelve-day journey to relieve himself. He arrived 'more dead than alive', having been given the last sacraments.[33] Napoleon was not there to meet him, having embarked on his disastrous Russian adventure. The Emperor returned, his army decimated, but certain enough of himself to bully and physically assault Pius, who was eventually forced to sign a humiliating concordat. According to the terms of this, the Pope would no longer possess any temporal power; the location of the pontiff's seat would be decided later, although Napoleon clearly had Paris in mind; and papal authority over the appointment of bishops was severely curtailed. Napoleon ordered the proclamation of the Concordat throughout the empire, to the particular dismay of the so-called 'black cardinals', those who had snubbed the command to attend the Emperor's marriage to Marie-Louise and who had remained a symbol of ecclesiastical intransigence. Pius later repudiated the Concordat, but the letter he sent to Napoleon was suppressed by the Emperor. The brutal treatment of Pius would enhance further the status of the office of pontiff, in much the same way as had the 'martyrdom' of Pius VI. Yet, ultimately, the survival of the papacy depended upon the victory of the allied powers. In April 1814, Napoleon abdicated, returning from a brief exile only to be decisively defeated in June 1815 at Waterloo, the irony being that the head of the Catholic Church owed his salvation to a military coalition, only one of whose members was a co-religionary.

Conclusion: Revolution in Retrospect

The revolutionary and Napoleonic decades constituted the most momentous epoch for Catholicism since the religious upheavals of the sixteenth century. No country within Europe was unaffected, yet it was France which underwent the most traumatic impact. On the European stage, it could no longer claim to be the most Catholic of nations. The mantle of Catholic leadership had fallen upon Austria, even though few at the time perceived this clearly; even fewer recognised how ill-placed the Habsburgs were to discharge this responsibility in the nineteenth century when the international balance of power increasingly favoured the Protestant states, Prussia on the Continent and Britain overseas. Internally, once again, it was France that was most severely dislocated, though many of the changes that occurred there may be perceived elsewhere, albeit in a less pronounced fashion. The physical structures of the Church had been overturned, quite literally in some instances. Secularisation had been advanced in several senses: through the devaluation of the clergy; through the destruction of churches; through the depletion in the numbers of priests; and through the disruption in the habits of regular practice. A laicisation of religion had also taken place, with a reassertion of popular devotional practices, including the cult of the saints, the formation of pilgrimages as well as the first emergence of lay activists who would reach their fullest prominence under the Restoration. In the realm of ideas, materialist ideologies had gained a foothold and respectability, even if they had not always mustered a widespread following. More serious for Catholicism, in the long term, was the emergence of new ideologies, most notably liberalism and nationalism which, despite being in their infancy, promised a stormy adolescence. Catholicism would take refuge in the embrace of reaction, conservatism and Romanticism, rejecting all things modern and storing up problems for later in the century when progressive elements within the Church struggled to come to terms with the contemporary world.

In the sphere of Church–state relations, it was now the latter which very clearly had the upper hand. In this area, the revolution merely exacerbated existing trends and even the most pious of rulers was not going to relinquish easily his oversight of clerical matters. National churches looked to the papacy as a counter-weight to the influence of the state, thus giving rise to an Ultramontanism which further emphasised the conservative nature of the faith. Rome itself had been exceedingly fortunate to survive. There had been more than one moment when contemporary observers believed that they were witnessing the death of an institution. Yet survive it had. In the short term, its status had been revived by the sufferings endured by both Pius VI and Pius VII, although these might quickly have been overlooked had it not been for a more significant longer-term development. The Napoleonic wars had made the existence of the Papal States a concern of international diplomacy and had demonstrated that pontifical authority was reliant upon the survival of temporal sovereignty. Buttressed by diplomatic support, and lapping up Ultramontane sentiments to the full, the Pope now had a voice that was listened to in a way which had not been the case in the eighteenth century. What had remained the same was the underlying weakness of Rome. When it suited the interests of the great powers to ignore papal injunctions, they did so. This disregard would become ever more blatant in the late nineteenth century when nation-states were consolidated, most awkwardly within Italy itself; yet, for the first half of the nineteenth century, Rome enjoyed something of a honeymoon as a conservative mood enveloped the Continent.

CHAPTER THREE

Catholicism Restored
1815—50

WITH the collapse of the Napoleonic Empire in 1814 and 1815, Europe breathed a collective sigh of relief, and hastened to put behind it two-and-a-half decades of turmoil and innovation. This sentiment was felt as much by the Catholic Church as by the ruling houses. Yet the work of restoration in religious matters, as much as in political and social affairs, was not going to be straightforward. Too many things had changed for the clock to be turned back to 1789, even though the leaders of the Church desired this. Wherever the French armies had trampled, the material goods of the Church had been devastated, its structures had been uprooted, its personnel decimated, its intellectual and theological foundations had been undermined and habits of popular conformity had been irrevocably altered.

A good deal of the work of restoration would depend on the new geo-political context that emerged out of the revolutionary and Napoleonic wars; and in several respects the omens were not good. It will be recalled that only one Catholic country was among the coalition that defeated Bonaparte. The international balance of power was fundamentally different in 1815 to that pertaining in 1789. Catholic Spain was no longer counted among the great powers; France, the pre-eminent Catholic country of the eighteenth century, had been weakened by unrelenting warfare and had ceased to be at the cutting edge of the faith. However misguidedly, it was now viewed as the cradle of liberal and revolutionary sentiments. And Catholic Poland had been wiped off the map. Notwithstanding Catholic Austria, whose eventual wane in the face of Hohenzollern *realpolitik* was far from clear at the time of the Vienna Congress, the dominant powers were henceforward Protestant Britain and Prussia, and Orthodox Russia. Nor should it be overlooked that across the Atlantic the United States of America, Protestant in outlook albeit purportedly neutral in matters of religion, was beginning to flex its muscles.

It was to the credit of the Church that it was able to overcome this unfavourable climate and reassert its presence. Its problem was that it had so much ground to make up in terms of rebuilding institutions, opening seminaries and recruiting personnel that this was always going to be an uphill struggle, although one bright spot would be the growth of the congregations and confraternities. The Church could also draw comfort from the widespread and continuing popular attachment to Catholicism, even though this meant that it had to accommodate some elements of lay practice and involvement which would have been unacceptable in the preceding century. Ideologically, too, the Church recovered some of its intellectual authority, helped by the vogue for a romanticist view of the past and the concomitant rejection of the cold rationalism which had characterised the eighteenth century and the French Revolution. This, however, was at the cost of associating itself closely with the cause of conservatism and led to a series of compromises with secular authority. It was also at the cost of failing to nurture any of those differing responses to the revolutionary decades, most conveniently grouped under the portmanteau heading of liberal Catholicism, which sought to arrive at some constructive accommodation with this heritage. Because of this, the Church was badly placed to respond to the revolutionary upheavals of 1848, themselves a reflection of underlying social, political, economic and ideological trends which would come increasingly to the fore as the century progressed.

A New Religious Geography of Europe

A full appreciation of the position of the Catholic Church in the first half of the nineteenth century demands a recognition not just of the preponderance of Protestant states among the great powers, but also of the fact that the religious configuration was very different within Europe itself thanks to the geopolitical rearrangements made at the Congress of Vienna of 1814–15. This great conference, whose purpose was to draw a line under the revolutionary upheavals, has all too frequently been characterised as an orgy of reaction which overlooked the rights of peoples and ignored liberal principles. Prince Metternich, the Chancellor of the Austrian Empire, has subsequently come to personify all that was backward-looking about this settlement. In truth, Metternich was very much a man of the eighteenth-century Enlightenment and, like most of the other representatives at Vienna, the exception being the erratic Alexander I of Russia, had a pragmatic concern with the achievement of international stability. Together, they sought to place a *cordon sanitaire* around France while at the same time satiating the interests of the great powers. So it was that the Vienna peace-makers restored to power legitimate rulers only when it served their wider purpose; otherwise, they shuffled the peoples of Europe with little regard for their national, never mind religious, affiliations.

Nowhere were the underlying concerns of the Vienna diplomats more clearly manifested than with respect to the territorial settlement in Italy which, unlike other aspects of the treaty, was not displeasing to the papacy. Rome was fortunate to be represented at the Congress by the astute Cardinal Consalvi rather than Pius VII himself who was in too much of a hurry to reclaim his forfeited lands. Consalvi, who enjoyed a diet of pink champagne and oysters, though he was eventually forced to renounce this in favour of boiled eggs, was pivotal to the conduct of papal policy in the aftermath of Napoleon's fall. Not only did he discourage the Pope from travelling to Vienna but he also used what few cards he had at his disposal to good effect, particularly in countering Austrian influence in the peninsula. He played up the courageous resistance of Pius and his predecessor to Napoleon; he exploited rulers' long-standing faith in throne and altar as bulwarks of social stability; he deftly manipulated the Tsar's mystic fervour for the injection of Christian principles into international politics; he capitalised on the determination of the French and Piedmontese not to let Austria have a completely free hand in the peninsula; he pointed to the need for the Pope's territorial independence if he was to exercise his spiritual authority; and he quickly seized upon Metternich's abandonment of Joachim Murat, who was King of Naples and Sicily until May 1815, to assert the claims of a friendly Bourbon prince. So it was that the Pope secured the repossession of almost all of his former territories, including Rome and its surrounding lands, the Legations and the Marches of Ancona, Emilia and Romagna. Elsewhere Piedmont-Sardinia was declared an independent state under the house of Savoy; the newly-founded Kingdom of the Two Sicilies was handed back to the Bourbons; Lombardy and Venetia became an integral part of the Austrian Empire; and scions of the Habsburg dynasty were put in charge of the duchies of Tuscany, Parma and Modena. As a result, Austrian power was greatest in northern Italy where it was most useful in countering possible French incursions into the peninsula. Given this framework, there was no need to restore Avignon and the Venaissin to the papacy and, in any event, it remains questionable whether the French negotiator at Vienna, Prince Talleyrand, the former *ancien régime* and concordatory bishop, would have permitted this. Keeping France happy by not turning it into a disaffected power, which in effect meant imposing a lenient settlement upon it, was in any case far more important to the peace-makers than responding to Rome's demands. None of the negotiators at Vienna at this stage contemplated even a partial unification of the Italian peninsula, but when this did eventually appear on the agenda, the existence of the Papal States would be a significant stumbling block to its achievement.

The Pope was far less happy about the settlement elsewhere, notably in Germany. Significantly, there was no thought of resurrecting the Holy Roman Empire, itself a political expression of a certain type of medieval Catholicism. The reconstitution of the ecclesiastical principalities, such as the prince-bishoprics of Cologne, Mainz and Trier, did not even enter the equation – indeed, Mainz, formerly the premier see of the Holy Roman Empire, became a mere suffragan of the newly-created archdiocese of Freiburg-im-Breisgau – thus spelling the end of a 1,000-year-old Catholic tradition. Consalvi made some mild protest at this but, in truth, both he and the Pope were not altogether unhappy to see the eradication of territories which had previously been bastions of anti-papal resistance, though the smaller ecclesiastical units which replaced them did not prove as amenable to Rome's direction as might have been wished. Nor did the new overarching administrative structure for Germany bode well for future papal influence. The Napoleonic Confederation of the Rhine was supplanted by a loose confederation of thirty-five principalities and four free cities, with a Diet at Frankfurt, again a construct designed to dissuade the French from future foreign adventures. Although Austria dominated the new set-up, Prussia did well out of the German settlement acquiring, among other lands, northern Saxony, whose population was predominantly Protestant, and a large chunk of the west bank of the Rhine and Westphalia, whose peoples were overwhelmingly Catholic. What this meant, of course, was that large sections of the Pope's flock were now under a Protestant king, a situation repeated elsewhere in the confederation. Although it was not perceived at the time, Prussia's new Catholic territorial acquisitions would subsequently provide a large part of the industrial resources upon which the Protestant Hohenzollerns would build a dominance over the German lands.

The other parts of the Vienna settlement which deeply irritated Rome were those which placed sizeable Catholic populations under non-Catholic rulers. Belgium (formerly the Austrian Netherlands), despite having a strongly developed sense of self-identity, was united with the Dutch to form the United Kingdom of the Netherlands under the rule of the Protestant William I. The objectives were partly economic – Belgian agricultural interests were sup- posedly complementary to Dutch maritime trade – but the strategic value of having a single buffer state between France and Germany weighed most heavily with the peace-makers. The arrangement meant that out of a total population of 6 million, 4 million were Catholic, yet were under the rule of a Protestant prince. Moreover, the key offices in the new state were monopolised by Protestant Dutchmen. As we shall see, religious grievances would play a significant part in the Belgian revolt of 1830. They would also intrude into the troubled affairs of the Swiss Confederation. Switzerland had been revived in 1815, and for the first time all Swiss lands fell under the control of Swiss dioceses rather than belonging to foreign bishops. Paradoxically, this heightened tensions between Catholics and Protestants which had been easier to contain under the old regime. The growing disaffection of the seven Catholic cantons would eventually lead to a short civil war in 1845. As for Poland, the 'inter- national vandalism', as Norman Davies has termed it, which had characterised its treatment in the eighteenth century continued at Vienna in 1815.[1] After some troublesome negotiations, the former lands of Poland remained divided between Austria, Prussia and Russia, which again meant that the predominantly Catholic population was left under the rule of two non-Catholic princes. The same kind of emboldened diplomacy did not, however, extend to the Otto- mans, in whose lands several million Christians, including 500,000 Catholics of the Eastern Rite, continued to live. Their deteriorating situation had been revealed in a papal inquiry, but the diplomats at Vienna were adamant in refusing entreaties from the Pope to act upon this.

The territorial settlements arrived at in 1815 would endure largely unchanged until the 1860s, revealing in uncompromising fashion that the affairs of Europe were now dominated by five great powers: Austria, Britain, Russia, Prussia and France. In this scenario, the position of the Pope as an international power-broker was minimal; and religious issues played little part in the figurings of the diplomats. To be sure, in the supposed 'Congress System' which emerged out of Vienna, there was the Holy Alliance of 1815 between Austria, Prussia and Russia in which their respective rulers agreed to behave as 'members of one and the same Christian nation'. However, after the conferences of Troppau and Laibach in 1820 and 1821 respectively, it was obvious that this 'high-sounding nothing', as Metternich accurately termed it, was little more than a pretext for the three signatories, most importantly Austria, to interfere in the internal affairs of other states whenever this suited them. In any event, the Pope could hardly have signed up to an agreement in which a Protestant and an Orthodox ruler claimed to belong to the same Christian family. Thus excluded, Rome concentrated upon more immediate matters, correlating ecclesiastical structures with the refashioned state boundaries and making arrangements with the rulers, both old and new, who governed in 1815.

The Age of Concordats?

Just as the great powers were convening in 1814 to discuss the redrawing of the map of Europe, the Pope established a new Congregation for Extra-ordinary Ecclesiastical Affairs, whose membership, thanks in part to the absence of Consalvi in Vienna, comprised the so-called *zelanti*, the die-hard cardinals and theologians determined to restore the Church to its pre-1789 position. It was this body that mulled over the proposals for numerous concordats although, in practice, the actual negotiating of these arrangements was often conducted by Consalvi himself. The *zelanti* themselves were un-prepared to conduct the diplomacy, believing that it was the duty of secular rulers to accept papal precepts. It was fortunate for Rome that Consalvi's diplomacy prevailed in the immediate post-Vienna period though this did not prevent conservatives within the Curia from securing his fall in 1823 following the advent of the new pope, Leo XII (1823–29).

Given the territorial remapping of Europe, Consalvi appreciated that some new legal and administrative framework was a necessity in Church–state relations. It was hoped that such arrangements would also permit Rome to circumscribe secular interference in religious matters. Papal mistrust of govern-ment intervention was even greater in the aftermath of the revolution than it had been before 1789, and a formal accord was believed to be one way of putting limits to this. It was further recognised that Rome had to secure the cooperation of secular princes in the rebuilding of the Church. However, while it was acknowledged that some cooperation with the secular authorities was needed, it was Consalvi's intention that new Church–state relationships embodied in the concordats would enhance Rome's supra-national authority. The very fact that Rome had seen fit to delegate authority to the state by means of a concordat was in itself a statement that the pontiff was the source of authority. In this way, Rome drew upon the precedent of the fifteenth century when the Conciliarist movement had been outflanked through the signing of concordatory agreements. Where perhaps the papacy and Consalvi acted for slightly different motives was in concluding arrangements within Italy itself. Here, the pontiff behaved more as a temporal ruler seeking to use the concordat as a tool of diplomatic rather than religious policy, a reflection of his desire to safeguard his territories and remain on good terms with his neighbours. What was not fully appreciated, even by the pragmatic Consalvi, was the extent to which the world had changed since the fifteenth century. The nature and orbit of state responsibilities were much greater than in the past and would continue to expand phenomenally. In the event, fewer concordats were actually signed than were negotiated; and where they were agreed, governments frequently interpreted the terms to their own advantage in the most elastic fashion possible.

The list of concordats and other less formal agreements may be summarised as follows: Bavaria and Sardinia in 1817; Naples and the Kingdom of Poland in 1818, although in the case of the latter this was essentially an agreement to reorganise the dioceses; a settlement with Prussia and the Lower Rhine provinces in 1821; Hanover in 1824; Belgium in 1827; Switzerland in 1828 and again in 1845; the Kingdom of the Two Sicilies in 1834. In the case of Prussia, the Protestant Hohenzollerns were keen for a settlement so as to ensure the loyalty of the Rhinelanders and to prevent Polish Catholics in their lands from coming under the jurisdiction of the diocese of Warsaw which was, of course, indirectly under the control of the Russians. Additionally, with respect to several of the German Protestant states, several bulls of circumscription were issued which embodied the results of Consalvi's negotiations and had the force of a treaty. There were to be seventeen further concordats signed between 1847 and 1862, including one with Austria in 1855 and eleven with former Spanish colonies or Spain itself.

The details of the concordats varied from country to country, but there was a consistency in their essential elements. Perhaps surprisingly, the Church did better out of these arrangements than might have been anticipated. The state agreed, for instance, to act against religious dissidence. In Bavaria, the government promised to suppress books that conflicted with Catholic theology and to act against blasphemers. In Naples, heresy, polygamy and sacrilege now became offences to be prosecuted in the secular courts, though this may be regarded less as a concession to the Church than as an unwelcome continuation of the eighteenth-century trend whereby ecclesiastical jurisdiction was being whittled away. Additionally, the Church retained such lands as remained in its possession, the re-establishment of seminaries was permitted and some religious houses were even allowed to reopen. Yet everywhere the balance of power rested very firmly with the state. Governments resisted clerical blandishments to restore sequestrated Church properties. Some degree of religious toleration was further enforced by rulers. Moreover, the Church's lack of endowments meant that it would, in future, be state-funded, at least in part. The state in return demanded control over the appointment of bishops, not just because it paid their salaries but because governments valued them as instruments of social control. Such clerical appointments had once been mediated through the cathedral chapters, with secular governments and the papacy vying for control of the canons. It will be recalled that in the eighteenth century, the electoral authority of the canonries was already being chipped away; henceforward, it became increasingly rare for chapters to have any say in a bishop's appointment, and in several places the chapters were not even restored. In Switzerland, a typically complex procedure was established which gave cathedral chapters substantial nominal powers to elect bishops while in practice giving the secular authorities almost total control of the process, one which continues to this day. As Jonathan Steinberg observes, 'there is no episcopal electoral procedure anywhere in the Catholic world which affords the secular, democratic state such an influence on the choice of a bishop'.[2] Elsewhere in Europe the concordatory arrangements meant that by 1829 no fewer than 555 of 646 bishops had been appointed by the state. The figures for state-appointed bishops by country, cited by Eamon Duffy, are as follows: 113 in the Two Sicilies; eighty-six in France; eighty-two in Habsburg Germany; sixty-seven in Sardinia and the Italian duchies; sixty-one in Spain and its possessions; twenty-four in Portugal; and nine in Bavaria. The Pope appointed to only ninety-four bishoprics, twenty-four in his capacity as pontiff, seventy *qua* sovereign of the Papal States.[3]

Rome was especially disappointed by the failure to revise the Napoleonic settlement in France and to secure any kind of concordat with Austria. In the former, where it was claimed by Chateaubriand that 'the throne of Saint Louis without the religion of Saint Louis is an absurd concept', the restored Bourbon Louis XVIII pledged to resurrect Catholicism to its former status, and entertained Pius VII's proposals for the cancellation of the Organic Articles. Negotiations for a concordat in 1817 were, however, stymied by the plethora of conflicting interests: the desire of Rome to avoid a revival of Gallicanism; the unbending stance of the so-called Ultras, a hard-right grouping of notables and clerics who were determined on revenge for 1789 and who wanted not just a restoration but an expansion of French clerical power; the determination of the King to retain state independence of episcopal controls; and the opposition of liberals in the Chamber to any policy that smacked of clericalism. The upshot was that the Concordat of 1801 remained in force. At least some consolation could be drawn from the fact that, in institutional terms, Church–state relations under the restored Bourbons were more harmonious than during the last years of the old regime. The Ultras succeeded in recovering some limited state compensation for appropriated lands; the short-lived White Terror of 1815–16 saw the rounding up and incarceration of several thousand former Jacobin and Napoleonic anti-clericals; the Pantheon in Paris, taken over as a shrine for revolutionary heroes during the 1790s, was restored to the Church, and the remains of Voltaire and Rousseau expelled; government included several high-ranking clerics such as Mgr Frayssinous, Minister for Ecclesiastical Affairs; lay Catholic ministers such as Joseph Villèle, who claimed to have been visited on the eve of the 1830 revolution by the Virgin Mary, were also prominent; a rigid Sacrilege Law providing the most bizarre of punishments was introduced in 1825 though never enforced; and there followed the traditional crowning at Reims of Charles X who counted 'cards, hunting and the Church' among his favourite pastimes in place of the traditional Bourbon pursuits of 'cards, hunting and women'. The paradox is that it was during the so-called 'liberal' July Monarchy of Louis-Philippe (1830–48), when Church–state relations were considerably relaxed, and government was dominated by the Protestant minister François Guizot, that French Catholicism underwent its most significant revival, both intellectually and on the ground, as it gradually recovered from the traumatic upheavals of the revolutionary and Napoleonic epochs. The question of a concordat would not resurface until the Second Empire.

In the Habsburg Empire, the omens for a concordat had seemed good in the aftermath of the Congress of Vienna. In the first instance, Austria was unwilling to bully the Pope lest he became pro-French; fear of French incursions into the Italian peninsula was a perennial preoccupation of Austrian foreign policy. Additionally, the Emperor Francis II (1792–1835), who made a special visit to Rome in 1817, and Metternich, Chief Minister after 1809, vaunted Catholicism as the most effective means of reining in the spread of liberal ideas and of maintaining the hierarchical and patriarchal nature of society. Yet, much to Rome's disappointment, neither man was prepared to relinquish the Josephinian tradition of a state-controlled Church with all the possibilities this provided in the governance of a disparate empire. Nor were Francis's other close advisers prepared to see any weakening of state centralisation. There was even opposition to a concordat from the Austrian episcopacy, which was overwhelmingly Josephinian in outlook in the sense that it favoured autonomy from Rome and cooperation with the state. So it was that negotiations for a concordat came to naught. While there were some token concessions to the Church, especially in the period after 1830 when Metternich personally felt closer to Catholicism, the religious settlement was largely a continuation of the eighteenth-century situation. It was not until the aftermath of the 1848 revolutions, when the Church had proved its loyalty and when the imperial family came increasingly under the influence of the future Cardinal Rauscher that a concordat was entered into in 1855.

If, in the immediate post-Vienna period, the papacy had failed to secure concordats in France and Austria, it took comfort in the knowledge that the governments there remained kindly disposed towards Catholicism as a faith even though the secular rulers were not always favourable to the Church as an institution. That Rome had been able to conclude concordats elsewhere was in itself a substantial achievement given the parlous position of Pius VII up to 1812, the uncompromising stance of the *zelanti* and the undeniable growth of state power. Yet there was no hiding the fact that secular authority had usually come out on top in the course of Consalvi's negotiations, and the remainder of the century would generally witness the unassailable march of state power. The concordats thus illustrated both Rome's grasp of reality and its lack of political clairvoyance. In the meantime, however, the more pressing concern was the fate of those millions of its flock who were under the rule of non-Catholics.

Catholics under Non-Catholic Rule

If the many Church–state settlements concluded in the years immediately after the Congress of Vienna accorded some limited degree of toleration to those Protestants and other religious minorities living in a Catholic state, Rome was distressed at the significant proportion of Catholics who now laboured under 'heretic' rulers, Protestant or Orthodox. Such was the lot of those Catholics who, as a result of the territorial reshuffling of 1814–15, now found themselves living in the Kingdom of the United Netherlands, in Prussia or in a still partitioned Poland. It will be recalled that 4 out of 6 million inhabitants of the United Netherlands were Catholic. In Prussia, there were 4 million Catholics, constituting around two-fifths of the population of 10.3 million. Three million Polish Catholics were under Orthodox Russian government. In other non-Catholic countries, the plight of 'dissident' Catholics was of longer standing. In the Ottoman Empire the status of its 500,000 Catholics was a perennial issue; in the Protestant British Isles, Ireland's 4.5 million Catholics had been incorporated into the overall population as a result of the Act of Union of 1801; and in Switzerland there resided 750,000 Catholics out of an approximate population of 2.3 million. What should be stressed, at this point, is that Catholicism still remained the majority religion in Europe, its 100 million adherents outnumbering all other faiths combined. In the wider world, on the other hand – and despite sustained missionary activity – the situation was reversed. It has been calculated that in the South Americas five-sixths of the 18 million or so indigenous peoples were no more than titular Christians. In North America, Catholics comprised a mere 350,000 souls. On the African continent, and in China and Japan, Catholic conversions were minimal and in East Asia, more generally, only pockets of Catholics subsisted, notably in the Philippines.

Crudely speaking, it will be seen that in Belgium and Ireland Catholics were to make headway in reasserting religious and civil liberties; in Prussia and Switzerland they would enjoy more mixed fortunes; further east, in Poland, Russia and the Ottoman territories, they continued to labour under debilitating restrictions. What is striking about the response of Catholics in non-Catholic states to their situation is that they would frequently deploy new methods of mobilisation, in particular mass agitation, techniques which paradoxically owed something to the experience of the French Revolution and which hitherto would have been anathema to the papacy and the episcopacy in the countries in question. Paradoxically, Catholics were joined in their struggles by some odd bedfellows, in that they occasionally attracted support from liberals. The latter valued individual religious rights alongside economic and social ones while often having little personal faith themselves and manifesting a high degree of anti-clericalism. The other irony is that Catholics in non-Catholic countries became increasingly Ultramontane as they sought to assert their presence and independence, while also valuing their religion as a badge of identity. Under the old regime, Catholicism had been a necessary condition of membership of the Catholic state. After 1789, those Catholics who found themselves in non-Catholic countries deployed their faith as a means of securing their separate identity within the wider body of citizens. It is small wonder that, when fully-fledged nationalism emerged in the second third of the nineteenth century, the Catholic response would be ambivalent.

In the United Kingdom of the Netherlands, Catholics were at least able to extend their freedoms, though their eventual situation was not wholly satisfactory to all shades of opinion. Given the fact that a predominantly Catholic south and an overwhelmingly Protestant north had emerged as a result of the revolt against Spanish rule in the sixteenth century, tying the two together in 1814–15 to provide a safeguard against French encroachment in northern Europe was always likely to be an unhappy arrangement. So it proved. William I, the new constitutional monarch, was not especially inimical to Catholics, but ruled in a high-handed manner and did not make life easy for his Catholic subjects. They paid more tax than their Protestant counterparts; in 1825, they were obliged to contribute to the maintenance of Protestant state schools; their own schools and seminaries, save for those narrowly concerned with the preparation of ordinands, were closed; and Catholics were actively discriminated against in the tenure of public office. All this was especially galling to a Catholic clergy whose long-established Ultramontane sentiments had not been diminished by the revolution, and who fed off the writings of Félicité de Lamennais, the French Catholic priest and writer who, at this stage of his career, espoused a rigidly conservative construct in which the Church would occupy a favoured position within the state. To circumscribe the autonomy of the Catholic Church in the Netherlands, the King attempted in 1827 to negotiate a concordat which would allow him to control future episcopal elections. The move backfired, facilitating a bizarre alliance between the clerical and liberal factions within the body politic which was encouraged by the young and impatient deputy, Baron de Gerlache. Notwithstanding the fierce anti-clericalism of the liberals, they colluded in this arrangement as both sides valued individual rights which would guarantee such things as a free press, educational autonomy, an accountable government and an end to discrimination, whether religious or otherwise. Together, they founded in July 1828 the so-called Union, a loose parliamentary alliance which had its own ministry in mind.

There matters might have remained had it not been for the economic downturn of 1827–28, flagrant government incompetence and the example of the revolutionary events of July 1830 in France. These factors produced the Belgian revolution of the same year. Belgium now severed its attachment to Holland, independence being secured on 4 October. The Catholic clergy deplored this display of popular disorder, and Catholics more generally were divided on how best to proceed with regard to a new constitutional framework. A significant number had followed Lamennais in his recent switch to a liberal outlook which envisaged a 'free Church in a free state', whereas others looked for a return to an established Church on the *ancien régime* model. This latter group, together with the papacy, was deeply concerned by the provisions of the constitution of February 1831 which established the Protestant Leopold of Saxe-Coburg-Gotha as King. While he converted to Rome – if Paris was worth a mass to Henry IV, then so was Brussels to Leopold – anxiety remained that the Belgian Church would become too independent in spirit. The constitutional concessions granted to Catholics were indeed considerable and subsequently proved an inspiration to liberal Catholics throughout Europe. Catholicism was acknowledged as the dominant religion of the state, freedom of association was granted to regular orders, and the Church continued to enjoy state funding. Ecclesiastical appointments were specifically exempted from secular interference, and papal pronouncements were similarly free of governmental control.

Despite these generous provisions, Catholics, both liberal and conservative, would not find life straightforward in the newly-independent state. On the one hand, the papacy in its encyclicals *Mirari vos* (1832) and *Singulari nos* (1834) condemned the liberal outlook articulated by Lamennais and, implicitly, the Belgian constitution which reflected it. This came as an especially bitter blow to the Catholic Primate of Belgium, Engelbert Sterckx, who had played a major part in the drafting of the constitution, and it troubled the consciences of many Catholic deputies in the Union, some of whom temporarily withdrew from political life. On the other hand, Leopold I pressed for the subordination of ecclesiastical matters to government control. The Union meanwhile persisted, Catholics gaining important educational privileges in a law of 1842 which provided for clerical encroachment in state elementary schools and the compulsory teaching of religious instruction. Yet, ultimately, the anti-clerical impulses of the liberals could not be restrained, and in 1847 they broke away to impose their line. Catholics would intermittently win elections, but it was not until the 1880s that they had a stable majority in the Chamber, by which time liberal Catholicism had interlarded with social Catholicism.

Those Catholics left in post-1830 Holland again found themselves in a minority and, as in 1815, had the task of reconstructing their Church. That Dutch Catholicism was to undergo something of a renaissance in the second third of the nineteenth century may be credited to four factors. First, the accession of William II in 1840 brought to the throne a monarch who believed Catholicism to be a bulwark against revolution, and he moved quickly to lift restrictions against the religious orders, thus facilitating a rapid rise in the number of female religious in particular. Second, Holland was favoured with a series of intellectual clerics, formed at the seminary of Warmond, notably Van Vree and Broere, who reinvigorated religious life, reminding the clergy of their pastoral duties and revalorating the liturgy. Third, the influence of the liberal Lamennais still resonated and even had an appeal in those traditionally reserved areas where Catholic business interests, concentrated in Utrecht, Amsterdam and Rotterdam, appreciated the benefits of occupying public office. Finally, this Catholic liberalism helped shape the constitution of 1848 which, to the disappointment of conservative Calvinists, provided for the equality of religions, a relaxation of legislation against the religious orders, and the right of individual denominations to regulate their own affairs.

Although the Vienna settlement enforced no territorial changes on the United Kingdom, the inclusion of Ireland through the Act of Union of 1801, partly in response to the government's worries about the threat of revolt, had left unresolved the issue of emancipation, both for English and Irish Catholics, 5 million of whom were now British citizens. Legislation to admit Catholics fully to all civil rights was frequently tabled in the Westminster Parliament after 1815, only to founder on a wide range of familiar obstacles: the continuing opposition of George III down to his death in 1820; the havering of Lord Liverpool's administration; the intransigence of High Church Anglicans; anxiety about the security implications of emancipation for Canada where 200,000 French-speaking Catholics lived under British rule; and, above all, widescale popular prejudice. Significantly, many of the petitions opposing reform came from cities such as Manchester, Liverpool and Glasgow, where low-paid immigrant Irish Catholics had undercut the local labour force. Even dissenters, including the Wesleyan Methodists, who themselves suffered from discrimination, had strong reservations about extending full civil liberties to Catholics, sharing the common view that they were an alien influence subject to a foreign power. Paradoxically, English Catholics also had doubts about the inclusion of Irish Catholics, seeing them as the cat's paw of Rome and as harbingers of a backward and regressive faith. They preferred a gradualist, assimilationist approach, the value of which was illustrated in 1817 when Catholics were permitted to accept commissions as officers in the army. Indeed, had it been a question of merely enfranchising English Catholics, then this would probably have happened in either 1823 or 1824 when both Peel and Liverpool supported bills to this effect.

Despite opposition, some further concessions appeared likely during the 1820s and 1830s, for there had been a shift of opinion in favour of emancipa-tion, at least among the elites and particularly in parliament. The contribution of Catholics on the battlefield during the recent conflicts had also helped to lay to rest the bogey of suspect loyalty, and there was an awareness that Britain, as a great imperial power, did not need the repressive 'security' measures which had been deemed appropriate in the seventeenth century. Yet it was Irish pressure that was critical, making emancipation inevitable and determining its timing. Within Ireland, a new generation of clerics was reinvigorating Catholicism and deploying innovative propaganda techniques. A number of these had been trained at the Royal Catholic College of Maynooth fifteen miles from Dublin, founded in 1795 and ironically funded by government money. Indicative of their new militancy were the newspaper campaigns in the *Chronicle* orchestrated by John England, the director of the seminary at Cork, and the publications of Hierophilus, the pseudonym of John McHale, the Professor of Dogmatics at Maynooth. Of overwhelming importance, however, was the contribution of the 'uncrowned king of Ireland', the lawyer and demagogue, Daniel O'Connell. His achievement was to put together a coalition of Irish Catholics of all kinds – bishops, priests, gentry, tenants, labourers, journalists and merchants – organised into the Catholic Association. Hitherto the preserve of the middle classes who alone could afford the annual subscription of 20 shillings, this became the basis of a national organisation with the introduction of the penny-a-month subscription. After initial hesitation, the Church rallied behind the Association's crusade which united all Catholics, whatever their other differences, against the Protestant ascendancy, and which proved capable of organising 'simultaneous parish meetings in two thirds of Ireland's 2,500

Catholic parishes'.[4] Such support guaranteed, if there had been any doubt beforehand, that emancipation was predominantly an Irish issue, and wholly transformed the terms of the debate.

The repeal of the Test and Corporation Acts in 1828, which lifted restrictions on dissenters including Catholics, presaged wider Catholic reform, something which was acknowledged by the House of Commons itself. In July of that year, the underlying strength of O'Connell's support was demonstrated when he won the parliamentary seat for County Clare even though he was not allowed to take this up at Westminster. To more farsighted politicians, the embarrassing spectacle arose of a future general election in Ireland returning numerous Catholic MPs, none of whom could sit in parliament, thus making a mockery of the constitution. Moreover, by September, O'Connell was making threatening noises about rebellion, convincing Wellington, the Prime Minister, that emancipation had to be conceded if Ireland was to remain governable. For Wellington, as for Peel, emancipation was a political, not a religious, issue. So it was that, in April 1829, a bill was passed which permitted Catholics to occupy all offices of state bar those of Lord Chancellor, the Lord Keeper and the Lord Lieutenant of Ireland. Entrusted with near-comprehensive civil freedoms, Catholics were enfranchised, though in Ireland the qualification was raised from a 40-shilling freehold to £10. Recruitment of monks from among the British population was prohibited, Catholics were required to swear an oath denying the authority of the Pope to depose monarchs or to exercise temporal and civil jurisdiction in the United Kingdom, and no formal place was accorded to the institution of the Catholic Church, Wellington judging it expedient to avoid the inevitable tensions that would have occurred had a Catholic Church been put under the auspices of a Protestant state.

The significance of emancipation in altering the political and religious character of the United Kingdom should not be underestimated. A parliamentary oligarchy, acting in defiance of the wishes of the nation and the King, had weakened the Anglican character of the state which had underpinned the constitutional settlement since 1688–89. Moreover, in doing this it had not imposed any of those restraints upon the Catholic Church, including a concordat, state funding of the clergy, government veto of episcopal appointments, which Catholic states elsewhere in Europe had hastened to put into place, even though such measures had been actively discussed after 1800. In 1850, the Catholic Church in the United Kingdom, inspired by the Oxford Movement (see below), restored a diocesan hierarchy without significant opposition from the state. Religious pluralism was now an acknowledged fact.

Ireland, even more than Belgium, was an inspiration for liberal Catholics in Europe. Nowhere else had the Catholic Church placed itself so firmly behind a mass movement and campaigned so successfully for religious liberties. Yet the truth was that emancipation promised more than it could deliver. Some of the restrictions imposed under the Act, such as the injunction to Catholic priests not to wear ecclesiastical dress in public, were irksome, but many Catholics had also linked religious freedom with economic betterment. This was particularly true of those Irish immigrants to England, around

450,000 in 1840, who worked in menial, urban occupations and whose earning capacity was limited. Emancipation offered nothing to them, nor to their cousins on the Irish mainland who largely subsisted on agriculture, and who did not meet the franchise property qualification. There was disappointment, too, for O'Connell who had hoped that the 1829 legislation would ultimately lead to a dissolution of the Union of 1801, something which even the liberal Whig administration, busy implementing reform in all walks of life, was not prepared to contemplate.

Despite their disappointment at what had been achieved, Catholics in Ireland had undoubtedly made significant progress towards the acquisition of complete religious and civil, if not social, freedoms. The same could not be said of their co-religionaries under Protestant princes in the German Confederation, most obviously those Polish and Rhenish Catholics who now found themselves a part of the recently enlarged Prussia. Two-fifths of its population were henceforth Catholic, half of whom were Polish. Hitherto, the Hohenzollerns maintained the Protestant hegemony while permitting confessional pluralism, largely as a way of attracting much-needed immigrants to this underpopulated region and to inculcate a certain measure of loyalty among its religiously diverse subjects. While the law of 1793 had secured state supervision of ecclesiastical affairs, it had, in theory at least, permitted freedom of conscience and liberty of worship. The acquisition of large and regionally concentrated numbers of Catholics in frontier areas, both east and west, strained this policy of confessional pluralism, as did the enforced unification of the Lutheran, Reformed Lutheran and Calvinist churches in 1817. The fact that the Rhineland contained a Protestant minority, a lingering admiration for certain French institutions, an Ultramontane clergy, and was a bastion of liberal sentiment, all added further to government anxieties. In this situation the Hohenzollerns judged it prudent to retain the Napoleonic Concordat and Organic Articles, while curbing any ostentatious displays of Catholic piety. Yet, as Michael Rowe succinctly notes: 'What was acceptable from the Catholic French was unacceptable from the Protestant Prussians.'[5] The fudged settlement with the papacy in 1821, in which church provinces were restructured and ambiguous arrangements made for the appointment of prelates, pleased no one. The first significant rumblings of discontent emanated from Joseph Görres, a Catholic from Mainz, whose newspaper, *Der Katholik*, railed at the Protestant monopoly of civil positions in the bureaucracy.

Battle was truly joined in 1825, when an order from the Prussian cabinet extended to the Rhenish provinces the stipulation that, in the case of marriages of mixed religion, the children should be instructed in the faith of the father. Despite papal attempts to pour oil on troubled waters, the issue boiled over in 1837 when the uncompromising Bishop of Cologne, Clemens von Droste-Vischering, who had earlier ejected the Protestant faculty from the University of Bonn, announced that Tridentine policy would be scrupulously observed: children of a mixed marriage would be brought up in the Catholic faith. For his pains, he was promptly arrested, provoking an outcry among the lower clergy and the laity in particular who correctly perceived the measure as an instrument of Protestant, state aggrandisement which threatened both the future existence of the Catholic faith and their separate identity within the Prussian polity. The matter was defused by the accession of King Frederick William IV in 1840. He believed in a single Church made up of different denominations, but saw the usefulness of the Rhenish clergy and nobility as a counter-balance to liberalism in the region. His intervention ensured that the matter blew over, and in 1841 he backtracked over the marriage issue and conceded several additional freedoms to the Church. In this climate, German Catholicism was to undergo a renaissance in the 1840s, and at the same time there emerged a fledgling 'Catholic Party', the forerunner of the Zentrum or Centre Party that took shape in the 1850s and which was to flourish in the German Empire. One symbol of this renewed sense of Catholic, national purpose, was that from the 1840s Cologne Cathedral, which had stood half-finished for five centuries, was rebuilt using the original thirteenth-century plans.

In neighbouring Switzerland, the Vienna settlement had restored the old cantonal structure in the guise of a federal system, albeit looser than its eighteenth-century predecessor. This structure did not please radical and liberal opinion, which sought a more centralised as well as a more democratic construct reminiscent of the French-inspired Helvetian Republic of 1798. Although the details of political policy divided liberals and radicals, they were at least at one in their anti-clericalism. In 1834, they had militated in an abortive attempt to assert state control over the Church, a project swiftly denounced by the Catholic cantons and the Pope. When, in 1841, radical forces took over the canton of Aargau, they indulged in the dissolution of local monasteries, prompting the Catholic cantons of Lucerne, Uri, Schwyz, Unterwalden, Zug, Fribourg, and Valais to form a defensive alliance known as the Sonderbund. Supported by a mere fifth of the population of the country, this armed league proved no match for the federal Diet, which ordered its dissolution together with that of the Jesuits. Federal troops rapidly dispersed the Sonderbund's forces in a short-lived and virtually bloodless conflict which Bismarck slightingly described as a 'hare shoot'. No assistance was forthcoming to the Sonderbund from the great powers despite Metternich's keenness to intervene, thanks largely to Anglo-French diplomacy and the onset of the 1848 revolutions. A revised constitution, drafted by the radicals and approved by a plebiscite in 1848, provided a greater degree of central authority, excluded the Jesuits and closed monasteries in several cantons. The Swiss Catholics, bruised and resentful, retreated into an isolationist and insular faith which was both Ultramontane and conservative.

Catholics in Poland had yet more reason to feel resentment. Their country had in 1815 been partitioned yet again between Prussia, Austria and Russia. So-called Congress Poland had both a constitution and a parliament known as the *Sejm* in which the social elites predominated. But, in truth, it was the Russian Tsar Alexander I who exercised real authority in his capacity as king. Up to a point, Catholics could be relatively sanguine about their prospects. Alexander regarded himself as a Christian prince, he was eager to draw the other Christian princes of Europe together, he valued the papacy as a bulwark against revolution and he moved rapidly to restore diplomatic relations with the Papal States. Such high-minded ideals, however, did little to dilute his Muscovite autocracy and extravagant Byzantine notions of the ruler as God's representative on earth. Rarely troubling even to inform Rome, he took a series of steps to assert control over both the Eastern and Latin Rite Churches; diocesan boundaries were fixed to suit Russian interests, clerics were strictly supervised, the theological training of the clergy at the University of Warsaw was high-handedly altered, and a swathe of monasteries and other religious houses were closed. Far distant from Moscow, and eager to appease an arch-enemy of revolution, the Pope barely protested against these measures which intensified when Nicholas I came to the throne in 1825. Utterly uncompromising in his autocracy and Orthodoxy, he expected total obedience from his subjects and refused to countenance the expression of any minority belief. Moreover, he regarded the Polish Catholics as an Austrian fifth column. So it was that punitive measures were taken against individual clerics, the Primate of Poland was unceremoniously deposed in favour of a government nonentity, episcopal sees were allowed to fall vacant for years at a time, synods were suppressed, and marriage was placed under the civil authority thus facilitating divorce even for Catholics.

In November 1830, liberal elements within the *Sejm*, nationalist army officers from the Patriotic Society, and clerics from all sections of the Catholic Church headed a rebellion, announcing the following year that the throne was vacant. The insurrection was brutally suppressed and Polish national institutions, including the *Sejm*, army and universities were eradicated. The Catholic Church fared little better. The laity were bullied into converting to Orthodoxy, clerical freedom of movement was strictly circumscribed, prominent ecclesiastics were replaced by 'good Russians' and the see of Warsaw was kept vacant (save for a mere eight years) in the period 1827–83. The Eastern Rite Catholics were simply integrated into the Russian Orthodox Church, protesters being exiled to Siberia. The revolt came at a time of revolution elsewhere, in France, Belgium and some German states, and the Pope, Gregory XVI (1831–46), had no hesitation in issuing an encyclical condemning the rebels who 'under the cloak of religion have set themselves against the legitimate power of princes'. A subsequent encyclical bemoaned the maltreatment of Catholics, but was simply ignored, as were further papal protests. Those brave clerics who dared to raise their voices in opposition were quickly whisked away, and it was not until the 1840s that there was a cessation in the persecution of Polish Catholics. Papal condemnation of the uprising in 1830 led a few radical democrats to reject links with Catholicism, and Adam Mickiewicz, the Polish poet, subsequently denounced 'Rome and official Catholicism'.[6] Yet if there was disillusion with Rome the overall experience of partition and persecution undoubtedly helped to cement Catholicism as a key element of Poland's identity and struggle for survival. Indeed, the notion of Poland as a bastion of Catholicism owed much to the invention of a tradition in the nineteenth century as part of the ongoing struggle for the survival of a Polish identity.

Within Russia itself, the Slavophile tendencies of Nicholas I and his un-yielding desire to unite his country around the one true Orthodox faith ensured that Catholics suffered more than their co-religionaries in Poland. Russian persecution took two forms. To begin with, the Eastern Rite Catholics, prominent especially in the Ukraine, were compelled to amalgamate with the Russian Orthodox Church as a result of a sustained crusade which endured from 1827 to 1839. Second, Catholic institutions came under official dis-crimination and tutelage. Parish priests were kept among the poorest in Europe, schools were placed in the hands of the Orthodox clergy, monasteries and convents were continually under threat, almost two-thirds being closed in 1832 alone. Whenever an episcopal see became vacant, it was left empty or filled with a Russian appointee who generally lacked the requisite training and pastoral skills.

This miserable saga was repeated in the Ottoman Empire whose European provinces included Macedonia, Thrace, Bosnia, Serbia, Albania, Bulgaria, Moldavia, Wallachia and Greece. Overwhelmingly Islamic in its religious complexion, 10 million people or around one-third of the empire's population none the less adhered to some form of the Christian rite, and of these approximately 10 per cent were Catholic. A fitfully repressive power, in the 1820s the Ottomans once more embarked on a systematic persecution of Christians, impelled by fears of great-power encroachment into the straits and Balkan states, and by the successful Greek uprising of 1821 to 1829 which had been underwritten by Orthodox Russia. Attempts to restore diocesan structures to Catholic areas of the Ottoman Empire, in Albania, Bosnia-Herzegovina and Moldavia, where in any case Muslims comprised a majority, encountered fierce resistance from the Turks. In Constantinople itself, Catholic estab-lishments and missions, generally manned by French and Italian religious, were in precipitate decline. Some measure of recovery was provided by indefatigable missionary orders in the 1840s, who were especially active in the Holy Places of Palestine. As we shall see in the next chapter, the unfortunate consequence of their activities was to provide the European powers with a pretext to enter that 'most unnecessary of wars', the Crimean conflict.

The militancy which Catholics in non-Catholic states had to deploy in asserting their claims to religious and individual rights presaged new forms of confessional action. Yet, as we have seen, their cause was ill-served by the papacy which remained steadfastly committed to the repression of popular unrest. Indeed, the overriding impression given by the Catholic Church in the first half of the nineteenth century was that it was a conservative, even reactionary, institution. As with most generalisations, there is some measure of truth in this observation, but beneath the surface it is possible to see that European Catholicism was awash with many different political currents.

Reaction in Theory and Practice

To understand why Catholicism in the first half of the nineteenth century has been so closely associated with reaction and conservatism it is necessary to look no further than the internal policies pursued by the two polities which in 1815 could claim to be the most devout, the Papal States and Spain, though neither carried much weight in the new international balance of power. At the same time, the intellectual currents of Catholic thought reflected the general backlash against the rationalism and modernism that was the French Revolution. This backlash would find expression in the eclectic movement known as Romanticism, and would be characterised in part by a renaissance of religious studies and by an appreciation of Catholicism as an aesthetic force. Ultramontanism was another facet of the Catholic response to the new age. What should not be forgotten, however, is that these conservative trends sat uneasily alongside a liberal Catholicism, whose chief proponent, Lamennais, had once been the high-priest of Ultramontanism.

Reaction in Practice: Rome and Madrid

The reactionary impulses of the Holy See could barely be contained on the death, on 20 July 1823, of Pius VII, whose demise could be prevented neither by the twenty-five bottles of *tokay* sent to him by the Austrian Emperor nor by the adjustable bed despatched by Louis XVIII. His passing gave the *zelanti* their opportunity to put forward a man in their own image and one who would rid them of the troublesome Consalvi. Their initial choice, Severoli, proved too extreme even for Metternich who had his own candidate in mind. Nevertheless, the compromise candidate, Cardinal della Genga, who took the name Leo XII (1823–29), was hardly a moderate. Sixty-three years old, in a frail condition, and suffering from excruciating piles, the pope-elect protested to his cardinals that they were electing a corpse, though in view of the Curia's long-standing reservations about installing sprightly men who were likely to live for a long time, this was hardly a novelty. Apart from a penchant for practising his marksmanship on birds in the Vatican gardens, he was respected for his piety and simplicity, which was just as well practised. Leo XII was an innately conservative man, out of tune with the moderate and prudent policies of Consalvi whom he quickly dismissed; this was sweet revenge, for Consalvi had sacked della Genga in 1814 for incompetence in the handling of negotiations over Avignon. After a disastrous opening to his conduct of foreign policy which saw Leo XII chastise Louis XVIII for failing to offer adequate support to the clergy, he pursued a more temperate line, extending the concordatory policy of his predecessor and siding with the Holy Alliance powers, an alignment that earned him the soubriquet 'the pontiff of the *ancien régime*'.

While he may have displayed some appreciation of Church government, Leo XII had no aptitude as a temporal ruler and the Papal States remained as badly governed as before. As Cardinal Giuseppe Sala outlined in reports of 1798 and 1815, the problems lay in the confusion of 'the sacral and the profane', the adherence to the notion that 'things have always been done in this way', a bias against change so as 'not to make things worse' and the forgotten 'art of understanding men'.[7] Sala's remedy was to separate temporal from ecclesiastical power, including ending the practice of 'abbatism' whereby secular bureaucrats wore clerical garb. Such a vision was beyond Leo XII whose domestic policies soon degenerated into a 'grotesque caricature of tyranny'.[8] Imprisonment was ordered for those caught playing games on Sundays or feast days; a similar punishment befell those men who walked too closely behind women, the latter being forbidden to wear tight-fitting dresses; the waltz was banned as provocative; works of art featuring nudes were removed from public view; encores and ovations were banned in the theatre lest they provided an opportunity for seditious comment and for the same reason actors were not allowed to ad lib; press censorship, which was already rigorous, was strengthened still further; police visits to brothels were discontinued in case this lent a legitimacy to the prostitutes' activities, though one result was a rapid rise in venereal disease; most unpopular of all was the closure of bars in Rome so that alcohol could be purchased only at grilles in the street – a procedure that led to unprecedented levels of drunkenness. However, one myth about Leo XII ought to be put to rest: that he denounced vaccination against smallpox, a measure introduced by Consalvi. In truth he left this optional, although some priests refused to condone the practice, regarding it as an unnatural interference with Nature, in some ways a harbinger of twentieth-century Catholic attitudes towards contraception and abortion. The ugliest features of Leo XII's rule over the Papal States were his treatment of the Jews who were herded into a ghetto and forced to listen to sermons every Sunday, and his appointment of Cardinals Ravorolla and Palotta as Rome's representatives in the Legations which led to further draconian police measures, including the introduction of martial law, the practice of delation or informing on one's neighbours and the summary execution of bandits. When Palotta was forced to resign, after only a month in office, local *banditti* paid for a service of thanksgiving.

Leo XII's successor, the sixty-seven-year old Pius VIII (1829–30), has been described as 'a confirmed valetudinarian',[9] who suffered from herpes of the neck which meant that his head was continually bowed. Politically he was more in the mould of Consalvi, yet his short twenty-month rule was marked by the restatement of conservative policies for he was confronted with social upheaval both in the Papal States, where the political associations of the Carbonari were increasingly active, and elsewhere in Europe where there was revolution in France, Belgium, Poland and a handful of the German states. As we have seen, Pius did not hesitate to condemn this unrest despite the fact that in Poland and Belgium Catholics had actively participated in the uprisings and looked likely to benefit from an extension of religious freedoms if they were successful.

If Pius VIII had been pushed into a conservative outlook by the uprisings of 1830, Gregory XVI (1831–46) was profoundly cautious by nature and deeply obscurantist by inclination. Blessed with a longer than usual span in office, his principal medical ailment was a bright red clown's nose, the product of snuff-taking which eventually caused a tumour of the face. Trained as a theologian in the ascetic Camaldolese Order, he knew little of the outside world, speaking only Latin and Italian. Shrewd observers had been able to gauge the intellectual baggage of the new Pope from his 1799 book, *The Triumph of the Holy See*, which denounced Josephinianism and advanced the belief that the Church was a monarchy, independent of the civil power, whose head was infallible in matters of faith. Small wonder, therefore, that there was little immediate change in the governance of the Papal States, even though these were plunged into rebellion within three weeks of his taking office. In both 1831 and 1832 the Austrians were forced to come to his assistance, even though this unsettled the French who were fearful of Metternich's dominance throughout the Italian peninsula. To allay such fears, the Austrian Chancellor convoked the five great powers at a conference in May 1831 which subsequently recommended sweeping reforms of the papal territories, including the appointment of more laymen, the creation of a consultative assembly and public oversight of financial affairs. Such reforms would have undercut Gregory XVI's absolutist powers and he announced that he would accept exile before conceding. Although not a worldly man, he knew full well that he needed to do little in the way of reform as the Austrians could always be relied upon to bail him out.

So it was that reform initiatives came to naught and the Pope continued with the repressive and retrograde policies of his predecessors; prudish and oppressive measures remained the norm. These did little to alleviate the suffering of the Roman peasantry, among the poorest in Europe, who also had to contend with a series of natural disasters including earthquakes. Gregory XVI's earlier refusal to adopt public health measures exacerbated these destructive events; his carrying of a picture of the Madonna did nothing to ward off their onset. His hostility to any modern innovation extended to the steamboats and the railways; industrialisation, of which Gregory knew nothing, was not for the Papal States. 'Chemins de fer' equalled 'Chemins d'enfer', he quipped.[10] He preferred instead to glorify the past, building a series of museums and art galleries and promoting the cult of the saints and the foundation of new orders and congregations in a manner reminiscent of his sixteenth-century predecessors. The spirit of his pontificate was encapsulated in his denunciations of Lamennais and of Italian nationalism as expressed through the phenomenon known as neo-Guelfism, both of which will be addressed later, and in his encyclical *Mirari vos* of 1832. This, in many senses, foreshadowed the infamous *Syllabus of Errors* of Pius IX in its condemnation of modern political and social developments and its refusal to acknowledge that the Church stood in need of any real reform. Change was to be welcomed only whenever it strengthened the authority of the Curia. His handling of European affairs was maladroit, to say the least. He failed to offer support to Polish and Belgian Catholics in their hour of need; he was unhappy at proposed clerical reform in Austria in 1835 because it still smacked of Josephinianism, although ultimately it was the death of Francis II which stymied this; he mishandled the marriage issue in Prussia, as we have already seen; he chose badly in the Spanish marriages dispute of the 1830s, merely alienating the court at Madrid; and he did not dare to stand up to the Russian

Tsar who was busily circumventing Catholic rights. His only real success was overseas in India and Latin America where he condemned slavery and Portuguese misrule, and was instrumental in the promotion of missionary activity and the establishment of new diocesan structures. As a result, the papacy took a decisive lead in the creation and organisation of the Church in the New World; within Europe, he had merely highlighted Rome's defects and obscurantism.

If the Pope, heading the only theocracy in Europe, had clearly associated Rome with illiberalism through his incompetent governance within Italy, the restored Bourbons in Spain would further enhance Catholicism's reputation for reaction by taking the Church with them in their regressive and retrograde policies. The overriding legacy of the Napoleonic intervention in Spain was decades of political instability and, at each crisis, the Church was firmly placed in the camp of counter-revolution, its views expressed most eloquently by Bishop Rafael de Vélez of Ceuta, whose *Throne and Altar* of 1818 was a trenchant defence of the sacral state. It will be recalled that immediately upon his restoration in 1814, Ferdinand VII lost no time in overturning all the liberal reforms passed by the Cortes of Cadiz, annulling the constitution of 1812 and persecuting its proponents. He also put back the religious clock, reintroducing the Inquisition and the Jesuits, for example, and reopening closed monasteries. Although he is sometimes regarded as an arch-clerical, as we have seen, he had no intention whatsoever of allowing the Church to become independent of crown control: he was as regalist as any of his eighteenth-century predecessors. Nevertheless, a majority of ecclesiastics were happy to back his regime, which appeared vastly preferable to the liberal administration of 1812, and some joined enthusiastically in a campaign against any kind of modernism, epitomised most vividly by the unyielding Father Ferrer who, at the head of an unruly mob and with brazier and dustbin in hand, ransacked the houses of liberals in a search for seditious literature. Ferdinand's incompetence, and in particular his neglect of the army, led to a coup in 1820, which put the liberals back into power for three years. They not only forced Ferdinand to restore the constitution of 1812, but had their revenge on the Church. Although they regarded it as hopelessly hidebound and an obstacle to change, the liberals concentrated their attacks upon ecclesiastical wealth, dissolving nearly half the monasteries, quashing tithes and expropriating ecclesiastical lands. But in January 1823 a French army under the Duke of Angoulême marched into Spain and restored the absolutism of Ferdinand, acting under the auspices of the great powers who had met at the Congress of Verona the previous year and with full papal blessing.

A second period of reaction ensued, the so-called 'ominous decade',[11] in which some of the most regressive elements from within the Church played a prominent role, notably the Nuncio, Giustiniani. The death of Ferdinand in 1833 without a male heir plunged Spain into a long-running, albeit sporadic, civil war in which the religious were a particular target of the anti-clericals. The fundamental issue concerned the succession, yet the contending parties (though the term imputes a specious unity to the fractious elements involved) took up pro- and anti-clerical positions, not least of all because churchmen generally allied themselves with the cause of one of the contenders, the conservative Charles, Ferdinand's brother. The results of this conflict were significant for Catholicism. The Church was yet again identified with political reaction, and the already existing breach within Spanish society between a conservative, clericalised peasantry and a liberal, anti-clerical middle class was strengthened. Charles ultimately lost the war, but clerical unwillingness to accept the validity of his rival, Isabella, confirmed for many that the Church was incapable of living with a liberal regime. The violence of the wars, in which some bishops and numbers of monks were killed, ecclesiastical property was damaged or simply appropriated to balance the budget, worsened the condition of the Church and delayed still further much-needed reform. Over half the sees were vacant by 1846. Moribund and hopelessly regressive, the low reputation of the Church in Spain was not undeserved.

Reaction in Theory: Romanticism and Ultramontanism

Although the Spanish Church, with its medieval institutions, mystical ways and hankering after the past, might have presented a regressive image to the rest of Europe, Catholic thinkers were not discouraged by this practical example of reaction, and frequently looked to the Middle Ages as a source of inspiration and emulation. In so doing, they were in union with the intellectual climate of Romanticism which dominated artistic and academic life in the first third of the nineteenth century. Like most intellectual movements, Romanticism was an extremely eclectic phenomenon. Its origins were rooted in the close of the eighteenth century, especially the writings of Goethe, which had taken issue with the rationalism of the *philosophes*; it was also geographically diverse, and was not especially associated with any one country, although during its final stages, in the 1830s, it was linked specifically with Paris-based artists such as Victor Hugo, Eugène Delacroix and Frédéric Chopin. It was thus a movement that encompassed a broad spectrum of human artistic endeavour, including music, the plastic arts, literature, theology, scholasticism and history. Herein lay a common characteristic of Romanticism: an appeal to the aesthetic and spiritual as a source of inspiration to deal with the problems of the modern world. As such, it was not exclusively religious and, in some of its manifestations, notably the writings of Shelley and Byron, it was distinctly anti-clerical and critical of Christianity. Nevertheless, after the attacks of the French Revolution which had dismissed Catholicism as an outmoded and obscurantist creed, it is small wonder that Catholics should have seized upon an opportunity to reassert the spiritual and cultural authority of their faith.

Crudely speaking, there were two dimensions to Catholic Romantic endeavour – the theological and the mystical – although some writers were to combine the two. The first was located in the religious and academic revival that took place in the immediate aftermath of the Napoleonic wars. Its leading acolytes were Friedrich Schlegel (1772–1829), a Lutheran convert who taught religious history in Vienna; Georg Hermes (1775–1831), a professor at Bonn University who combined his teaching with priestly zeal; Johann Michael Sailer, Professor of Pastoral Theology at Landshut who viewed the Church as a living organic body of believers rather than as a legal institution; the dominating figures of the Tübingen school (Johann Sebastian Drey, Johann Baptist Herscher and Johann Adam Möhler) who stressed the living, and by implication mutable, traditions of the Christian faith; Louis Bautain (1796–1867), a French priest; and Antonio Rosmini (1797–1855), an outstanding Italian philosopher. What these disparate figures had in common was their resort to the past, especially the Christian fathers and the scholastics of the Middle Ages, as a fount of inspiration. In their different ways, they shifted the emphasis of theology away from a Kantian insistence upon the demonstrability of truth towards the triad of faith, spirituality and mysticism as the key to appreciating the divine. In this respect, they were to be accused of fideism, that is a denial of man's rational capacity to understand God and his world. Unquestionably, they rejected the Enlightenment's insistence on the values of individualism, stressing instead the organic nature of human society and of the Church, hence their fondness for the Middle Ages.

In its mystical guise, the Catholic variants of Romanticism embodied a rejection of the rationalistic currents of the eighteenth century, together with the disorder and social egalitarianism of the revolution. Small wonder, then, that its most articulate exponents were chiefly French, either by birth or adoption, and significantly all were laymen: François René Vicomte de Châteaubriand (1768–1848); Louis Gabriel Ambroise Vicomte de Bonald (1754–1840); and Joseph de Maistre (1754–1821), originally a Sardinian nobleman. Having lost his family as a result of the revolution, and mindful of an appeal from his sister to embrace the religion of his childhood, Châteaubriand repented of his early rakish lifestyle and, in 1801, published *Le Génie du christianisme*. This passionate and powerful rebuttal of eighteenth-century rationalism appeared at exactly the right moment, coming as it did in the wake of Napoleon's reversal of the worst excesses of revolutionary secularism. In highly emotive language, it appealed to mankind's emotions as the well-spring of religious sentiment and championed the aesthetic value of Catholicism as the greatest inspirational source of European culture since the classics. De Bonald was similar in his scathing attacks on the *philosophes*, notably through his *Pensées diverses* of 1818. Herein, he outlined his corporatist and hierarchical vision of society, to which religion was fundamental. Disputing man's ability to arrive at the truth through the deployment of reason, he argued in favour of divine revelation as the original source of authority, and of the need for tradition – the writings of the early Fathers and established institutions – as the underpinning of all social and political structures. As he himself declared, religion was once thought of as something a man needed; now, he argued, it was something that society needed. Put simply, de Bonald was concerned with the social necessity of religion, rather than with the truth of its assertions. A similar approach was displayed by de Maistre in his caustic and occasionally conflicting writings, although he attached less importance to the teachings of

Augustine and Aquinas, concerning himself instead with the broad sweep of history in which he discerned the hand of God and certain providential verities. Above all, he argued, strong government was needed if man was to be saved from the vices of his own nature. Tradition proved that the proper form of government was monarchical. To prevent abuse of royal authority, he looked to the papacy as the arbiter of all sovereigns. His work *Le Pape* (1819), expounding this theory, had a wide circulation and gave some measure of intellectual support and substance to the growing Ultramontanism of the early nineteenth century.

The other leading apostle of Ultramontanism was, of course, Lamennais (1782–1854). A latecomer to Catholicism, he had all the zeal of a convert, albeit one whose career was punctuated by bouts of self-doubt and depression. Ordained a priest in 1816, he was correctly described by Leo XII as 'a fanatic who had talent and good faith, but a perfectionist who, if allowed, would convulse the world'.[12] Despite his rather gaunt appearance, he possessed great charisma and built a loyal and enthusiastic following among young priests and sacristans. He expounded his views in a series of works – notably *Les Réflexions sur l'église en France* (1808), the *Essai sur l'indifférence* (1817), his *Défense de l'essai* (1818) and *La Religion considérée dans ses rapports avec l'ordre politique* (1826) – in which he pointed to the social utility of Catholicism and the truth of its dogmas, the need for a reform of the Church and, in particular, of the French bishops whom he called 'tonsured lackeys'. 'They are men who have no desire to act but give them a kick in the appropriate place and you find they have moved a hundred paces,' he wrote.[13] Most importantly, he initially advocated the authority of the papacy which was both absolute and infallible. In 1828, he established in his native Brittany a new religious order, the Brothers of Christian Instruction, whose purpose was to serve as the shock troops of Rome.

Lamennais was to reconsider his position in 1830, at the time of the liberal revolutions in France, Belgium and Poland. Although he never discounted the unerring authority of the Pope in theological matters, he discounted him with regard to temporal affairs. He further re-evaluated the relationship between throne and altar. Hitherto he had championed a close alliance between the two but, thinking about the disappointing outcomes of the 1830 uprisings, objected that, 'the Church is being suffocated beneath the weight of the fetters which the temporal power has put upon it'.[14] To promote the separation of throne and altar, he founded the newspaper *L'Avenir* in 1830 which campaigned under the slogan 'A free Church in a free state', and which enjoyed a wide circulation among younger French clergy and their counterparts in Belgium, at one point selling over 2,000 copies daily. For Lamennais, monarchical government had run its course; the Church must now espouse the ideals of freedom and democracy enshrined in the revolution of 1789. Alongside *L'Avenir*, Lamennais also spoke of a 'Catholic Action', that is an attempt to energise the faith and make it more accessible to the popular classes, especially those urban workers who seemed to have been abandoned by a Church which could not keep pace with industrialisation. It was the fate of these unfortunates that formed the basis of his *Le Drapeau Blanc* of 1828, reckoned by many to be the first stirrings of social Catholicism in France. Not surprisingly, Lamennais encountered hostility from the French episcopacy, yet he unwisely chose to appeal directly to the papacy which had been impressed by his earlier espousal of Ultramontanism. Mistrustful of Lamennais' flirtation with populism, blind to the social changes that were beginning to affect northern Europe, affronted by the suggestion that the Church was in need of restoration and regeneration, and frightened by the democratic implications of liberalism, Gregory XVI condemned all that Lamennais had now come to represent. He did so through the encyclicals *Mirari vos* of 1832 and *Singulari nos* of 1834, the latter being one of the rare occasions when Rome has explicitly denounced the thought of an individual. Such intransigence was instrumental in bringing about Lamennais' eventual apostasy.

Although the encyclicals were accepted by many in the *L'Avenir* circle, they could not stem the beginnings of both a liberal and social Catholicism, which at this stage were largely conflated and whose torch was carried by the Dominican priest Henri Lacordaire and the nobleman Charles de Montalambert. What these two men had in common was an insistence that the laity should play a far more active role in the day-to-day running of the Church; the establishment of religious freedoms, especially educational ones, by statute; a regeneration of religious life; the embracing of democratic ideals by the papacy; and the active involvement of Catholics in the political life of the nation through petitions, newspapers and elections. Such an approach was inimical not just to the papacy but to most of the ecclesiastical hierarchy. Thus the Archbishop of Rouen advised that laymen's 'best course is to pray while the bishops make requests'.[15] On the other hand, the Primate of Belgium, Archbishop Sterckx of Malines, who had played a key role in securing Belgian independence, endorsed the views of Montalambert and refused to publish *Singulari nos*.

As the example of Archbishop Sterckx suggests, Catholic liberalism was heavily influenced by the national context within which it operated. Nowhere was this more true than in Italy itself. Here, the fractured nature of the political settlement of 1815 had given rise to nationalist stirrings of manifold kinds, expressed for example through the secret societies of the Carbonari of the 1820s, and most eloquently in Mazzini's *Young Italy* movement. Having witnessed at first hand the failure of secret societies to force change in Italy during the attempted *coups* of 1830 in the Habsburg duchies of Parma, Modena and Bologna, Mazzini looked to the creation of a mass movement in which the people would express their will through violence, although he would never achieve more than minority support. Interestingly both a deist and a republican, Mazzini regarded the papacy, and the clergy to a lesser extent, as obstacles to the unification of Italy. Not all Italian nationalists agreed on this latter point, most significantly the so-called neo-Guelfs. Represented by writers such as Alessandro Manzoni, Cesare Cantù, Cesare Balbo, Nicolò Tommaseo and most notably the priests Vincenzo Gioberti and the Abbé Rosmini, this intellectual and vaguely Romanticist phenomenon looked back to the thirteenth century when a Guelf party had sought to defend the papacy from imperial pretensions. They now looked to the Pope as a focus for unification, presiding over a confederation of Italian constitutional rulers, underpinned by the military strength of the Kingdom of Piedmont-Sardinia, the strongest of the Italian states. They would probably not have regarded themselves as liberal Catholics; though, like their counterparts in France and Belgium, they had reform of the Church high on their agenda and sought an accommodation with progressive political regimes. Never a coordinated movement, lacking any real sense of how to achieve their objectives and without much popular backing, they were easily picked off by the unremitting Gregory XVI. He commissioned the arch-reactionary Catholic polemicist Jacques Crétineau-Joly to write a pejorative account of secret societies in which they were placed alongside a long line of freemasons, *philosophes*, Jacobins and others whose conspiracies had brought about the French Revolution and which now threat-ened the stability of the post-Napoleonic order.

The examples of the neo-Guelfs and the *L'Avenir* circle illustrate both the eclecticism and the fragility of liberal Catholicism during this period. By contrast, the reactionary tone of Catholicism was well established in both theory and practice. The scene was thus set for internecine struggles within the nineteenth-century Church. Whereas in the preceding century, differences of approach to theological, social and political issues had been largely con-tained, the trauma of the revolutionary decades not only threw up new issues but brought them into sharper focus. The arrival of new ideologies, the changing social and economic environment, the growing participation of the people in politics, the burgeoning power of the state – these were matters that simply could not be ignored by Catholics. They demanded a response and, in this process, it was almost inevitable that the Church would begin to lose its coherence and its grip over the enthusiasms of the rank-and-file.

A Religious Revival?

Alongside the restoration of Catholic institutions and the Church's response to the post-revolutionary world, Europe witnessed a revival of religious fervour, something common to Catholicism and Protestantism. In part, this renaissance resulted from underground religious practice that had subsisted during the 1790s and 1800s, and which now blossomed in the daylight. It was also facilitated by the concordatory regimes and the erection of new clerical structures, especially the role accorded to the Church in schooling. It may further have owed something to the vogue for Romanticism, or at least the enthusiasm for a more affective and emotive faith. Nor should the role of individual clerics, notably the Curé d'Ars in the Dombes, Giuseppe Benaglio from Bergamo and John Henry Newman in England be overlooked. The manifestations of this revival were disparate. They are to be perceived in the resurgence of religious orders and congregations, the growing number of communicants at Sunday mass and Easter, the re-emergence of popular forms of worship including pilgrimages and the cult of the saints, and the conspicuous involvement of women. What should not be forgotten, however, is that the forces of secularisation – the legacy of 1789, new ideologies, socio-economic change and a demographic revolution – were also on the march, and ultimately it would prove difficult to resist these.

Maybe the most salient characteristic of this religious revival was the return of those venerable orders, which had found the preceding twenty years distinctly uncomfortable, together with the emergence of new orders, congregations and confraternities which underwent impressive recruitment until the final decades of the nineteenth century. The Jesuits made the most impressive comeback. Suppressed in 1773, they were refounded by Pius VII in 1814 and spread rapidly both geographically and in numbers, something which did not altogether please either liberal Catholics or Jansenists. It has been calculated that there were some 22,000 Jesuits in Europe at the time of their order's suppression; and some 800 at the moment of their re-establishment. This figure more than doubled within five years. By 1830, they numbered over 2,000, and nearly 5,000 in 1848. The Jesuits never again exercised the dominance over the Church's missionary and educational activities which they had enjoyed in the eighteenth century, though they were significant none the less, founding new missions in Bengal, the USA, South America and North Africa. Around one-fifth of the membership was engaged in such overseas activity by mid-century. Their comeback, however, reignited old jealousies and their enemies portrayed them as elitist, overly independent and precocious, with dangerous political ideas. They were expelled once again from Spain and Portugal in 1834, from Switzerland in 1847, and from Naples, Piedmont-Sardinia and the Papal States in the 1840s. It was to be during the strong conservative backlash which followed the revolutions of 1848 that the Jesuits recovered most strongly.

A number of older orders, including the Benedictines, Dominicans, Capuchins and Trappists also re-emerged, though they were frequently constrained to abandon a life given over wholly to prayer and contemplation, and to undertake more socially useful functions. Nor were they entitled to properties sequestered during the revolutionary decades. The Dominicans concentrated their existence in Italy and reopened eighty of their 500 friaries by the 1820s. Within France, the order was refounded by the Abbé Lacordaire in 1850. The Franciscans, riven by internal disputes, were less successful in reasserting their presence: a province was set up in Belgium in 1844 and one in France in 1850. Whereas they had 25,000 brothers in 1773, by the mid-nineteenth century they numbered a mere 1,500.

Among female religious, the Clarissas, the Benedictines, the Carmelites and the Ursulines also recovered part of their membership. In spite of the execution of sixteen Carmelite nuns from Compiègne in 1794, the women's orders had enjoyed something of a charmed existence during the revolutionary epoch, thanks to the fact that they were more actively engaged in the provision of charity and welfare, burdens that governments were reluctant to shoulder. They were also thought to be less politically dangerous than their male counterparts; it was always easier to dismiss the protests of women as hysterical ramblings. Already in 1814, more than 14,000 nuns were operating in France. Here, a new order of the Sacred Heart set up in six cities under the energetic leadership of Sophie Barat in 1815 had expanded to include around forty houses by 1830. Within Spain, numbers were reinvigorated by the 1817 papal relaxation on the rules of claustration. By 1868, it is calculated that there were approximately 20,000 female religious, roughly the same figure as a hundred years earlier.

Despite these successes, the overall membership of the regulars never recovered to pre-1789 levels. Much more striking was the activity of the congregations, both new and old, in which women figured prominently. Among the older of these, the regeneration of the Filles de la Charité was most spectacular, boasting some 9,000 members by the last third of the nineteenth century in France. Emulating their example were the Sisters of Mercy, originally established in Münster in 1808, who quickly established a foothold in a majority of the German states. Another new German order, that of the Poor Teaching Sisters of Our Lady (1833), was soon active in no fewer than thirteen European states. Other congregations, local in repute and activity, blossomed. Not to be outdone, new male congregations were also on the scene, notably the Christian Brothers, started in Ireland in 1802 and 1820, who quickly established a grip on schooling there. The Picpus Fathers, created in France in 1800/1817, were especially active in preaching and missionary work, as were the Oblates of Mary Immaculate, founded by Charles Mazenod in 1816, who pursued their missionary activities beyond Europe into Canada, Mexico, Australia and Ceylon.

In this great flowering of religious associations, it became increasingly difficult, even for contemporaries, to draw a clear distinction between regular orders, that is those who swore solemn vows and tended to pursue a closed and sedentary existence, and congregations, whose members made simple promises, or no formal commitments at all, and pursued a more mobile lifestyle given over to socially useful activity. A good example was that of the Marists, founded in 1824 at Lyon, who included both priests and lay brothers among their membership, and whose activities were not restricted to education. At the close of the century, however, the distinctions between orders and congregations would prove of little concern to those anti-clerical jurists and politicians in France and elsewhere who regulated their existence through association laws aimed above all at controlling and limiting the activities of their members.

Alongside the reappearance of the religious orders and the impressive growth of congregations, especially female ones, the post-Napoleonic period further witnessed the evolution of confraternities. Essentially, these were pious associations of lay males and females, usually organised around the parish or a trade or a profession, occasionally led by a cleric, which devoted themselves to godly and charitable works. For example, they ensured a good turn-out at the funeral of one of their members, they might provide some limited form of financial assistance in case of need, they oversaw the upkeep of cemeteries, they fostered an interest in the rosary, and they played a conspicuous part in organising local religious festivals. A small number continued to concern themselves with the welfare of galley slaves.

There is some evidence that the confraternities were in decline during the eighteenth century as religious tastes changed, though this is hard to measure statistically: for every confraternity that disappeared another would take its place. It is known, however, that Joseph II disapproved of them, a reflection of his general disdain for parasitical religious associations which were an economic drain. Unquestionably, under the revolution and Napoleon con-fraternities suffered a marked decline. Within France, they were proscribed in 1797; their funds were sequestered; and the general climate was not conducive to the kind of ostentatious displays of piety in which some of them indulged. Conscription, at least within France, also cut a swathe through the male membership. Slowly but surely, confraternities made a comeback in the Res-toration period. In 1817, the Austrian government largely reversed Joseph's restrictive legislation. The most famous to reappear was that of the Most Holy Sacrament, known in Italy as the Santissima, but which was found throughout Europe. The male confraternities of penitents also made a revival, particularly in southern Europe, where they had always been strongest, much to the chagrin of the clergy who distrusted their independence and dis-approved of their activities which often seemed to sacrifice religious discipline in pursuit of profane pastimes, including dancing and drinking. In 1837, Bishop Thibault of Montpellier described them as 'purely and simply scum'.[16] Faced with overt clerical hostility and with increased alternative possibilities for sociability opening up for men, notably politics and drinking clubs, the re-emergence of confraternities of penitents was short-lived. They were replaced by associations over which the clergy exercised a greater measure of control and, more often than not, they comprised women. Such bodies were repres-ented by such associations as the Blessed Sacrament, the Rosary and the Scapula.

How do we explain this revival of religious orders, congregations and confraternities, and in particular their overwhelmingly female membership? The explanations must perforce be speculative, although historians have been extremely imaginative in their use of sources: obituaries of individuals, wills, notarial acts establishing the institution, prefectoral reports and the occasional biography, although it is questionable whether these accounts of particular spiritual athletes are typical of the membership as a whole. Some recent advances in psychological theory have also contributed to an understanding of motivation. It seems clear that many adherents were impelled by a genuine sense of piety and vocation, although we should also recognise that a mixture of imperatives may well have been involved. Testimony to their devotion was the diligence with which they performed an arduous range of duties and good works. To explain why women were especially drawn to the religious life, we can point to five additional impulses, but it should be stressed that these were specific to congregations rather than confraternities. First, member-ship offered women the chance of a career and an adventurous lifestyle, opportunities that were by and large denied them in the secular world. As

Frances Lannon says of Spain: 'They chose to teach, or preach, or nurse, as well as to pray.'[17] Second, for the especially pious, to enter into such a community was an opportunity to take a stand against a corrupt and un-regenerate world; unlike men, who could enter politics or take up positions of social notability, they had no possibility otherwise of reforming it. Third, the religious life promised care in their old age, and the possibility of a 'good death'. Fourth, it may have provided an escape from the very real dangers associated with childbirth, which killed many mothers, and from the sexual demands made by men of women and which were regarded as the norm within marriage. Finally, it has been speculated that latent and overt lesbianism may have drawn some to an all-female environment, though plainly the male orders offered a matching version of same-sex intimacy.

In respect of confraternities, cognate arguments have been developed. To begin with, these bodies provided occasions for sociability that were not available to women in a male-dominated environment. 'It's not piety that binds them to the confraternity', observed one priest, 'but the desire to have the church all decked out with flowers for their wedding, and to please the *curé* rather than to please God.'[18] Moreover, there have been suggestions that the confraternities offered opportunities for the practice of a particularly saccharine and emotive faith which, it is alleged, had a peculiar fascination for women. Conversely, men shunned the confraternities as being clerically dom-inated and offering little in the way of their own spiritual needs.

The growth of congregations and confraternities in the post-Napoleonic period were vibrant green shoots of recovery. Similar indications of a renais-sance are more difficult to discern among the seculars, though it must be admitted that this remains an under-researched area. Impressionistic evidence suggests that there existed real problems in recruitment. A whole generation of ordinands had been lost and an older generation of priests had died out. The situation was especially bad in Italy. On average, only six priests were ordained annually in the diocese of Treviso, nowhere near enough to replace the average of twenty-two clerics who died each year. Moreover, the semin-aries to train replacements, even if they had been forthcoming, were in disarray. It is known that the seminary at Ferrara possessed 114 students in 1814. In 1829, it housed a mere twenty-five. In the city of Rome itself, it was easier to recruit monks and nuns whose numbers rose dramatically, than it was to encourage seminarists. There were 465 seminarists in 1814, the figure reducing by 1823. In Lombardy-Venetia, the theology faculty at the University of Padua, closed by Napoleon, was reopened in a desperate attempt to furnish the region with priests.

Within France, the heartland of the revolution and the dechristianising campaign, the toll upon the clergy had been most dramatic. Not only had levels of ordination plummeted to an all-time low, but many clergy had been driven from the ministry, and those who remained were for the most part aged, infirm and inactive. In the pre-1789 period, self-perpetuating clerical dynasties had existed: an uncle would resign his benefice in favour of a nephew, ensuring himself a pension and his relative a place in the Church.

The refiguring of the parish structure and the introduction of a new system of appointment dealt a body blow to this method of recruitment which may have been nepotistic but which secured a supply of *curés*. As a trenchant analysis in 1839 by the two clerical Allignol brothers, *De l'état actuel du clergé*, pointed out, the concordat lay at the root of the problem. This allotted only one parish to a canton and relegated all other parishes to auxiliary status and their priests to the rank of assistant. This meant that most priests could never aspire to the status and security of *curé* of a parish, thus rendering the clerical profession much less appealing than previously. It is small wonder that the French Church would rely increasingly on the priest espying a particularly promising and pious child within the classroom and the catechism lessons and encouraging him and his family, even before first communion, to think about a vocation. Such methods, repeated in Spain, coupled with the very real need to fill empty parishes in the immediate post-Napoleonic period, did lead to a resurgence of numbers at least in such especially devout areas as Le Mans, Quimper and Vannes, for instance, yet this did not survive the July Monarchy (1830–48). Between 1830 and 1845, annual ordinations fell by more than half from 2,357 to 1,095. For the remainder of the century, overall totals were more or less satisfactory, but the distribution was skewed and, as we shall see, rapidly urbanising and industrialising districts were left uncatered for. In the Iberian peninsula, too, the distribution of the clergy was remarkably skewed although, overall, there was probably a surfeit of recruits. The dioceses with the highest number of seminarians were in the pious north, while those with the worst showing were, with the significant exception of Valencia, in the south.

To determine the social origins of the priesthood in the post-Napoleonic period is an almost impossible task, although certain broad generalisations may be hazarded. With the exception of Lombardy-Venetia and some other regions of the Habsburg Empire, where impoverished nobles entered the ranks of the parish clergy, the clerical career held few attractions for the aristocracy, a trend which we have already observed in the eighteenth century. Nor did priests emanate from the better-off classes. The law, medicine, universities, state service, journalism and business, in short the increasingly professional and complex social world of the nineteenth century, offered better opportunities for enrichment and status. On the other hand, the very poorest in society still discovered their way into the clergy barred. They encountered ecclesiastical prejudice – the Bishop of Valence remarked that they did not 'usually possess either generosity of heart or elevation of spirit, or anything that constitutes the high moral tone so important in our holy calling' – and, in any event, did not possess the financial wherewithal to see themselves through the seminary system.[19] So it was that the priesthood derived from the middling ranks of society, both artisan and peasant. This had always been true in Spain and Portugal. It was further the case in the large archdiocese of Vienna, remodelled under Joseph II: around one-third of the parish clergy came from predominantly rural backgrounds in Bohemia and Moravia, and the majority had fathers who were skilled artisans and better-off peasants. The phenomenon was most marked in France. It will be recalled that there, the eighteenth-century priest had been very much an *être séparé*, distinct in his education, dress, lifestyle and culture, and was often drawn from the better-off peasants and the literate and leisured classes. In the nineteenth century there was a definite shift in emphasis in that recruitment came increasingly from those levels of society that were not well off. Although urban centres continued to provide a disproportionate number of recruits, increasingly the clergy were drawn from the countryside, this at a time when industrialisation and urbanisation were starting to establish a foothold in the 1830s. Between 1820 and 1914, well over 80 per cent of the parish clergy in the diocese of Besançon were originally rural inhabitants.

In view of the collapse of the seminary system, and the difficulties of re-establishing it, and given the fact that most clergy originated from humble backgrounds, it is difficult to avoid the conclusion that the parish clergy during this period were not well educated and closely resembled the caricature drawn by Rainer, the brother of Francis II. In 1817, he noted: 'The clergy of this province [Veneto] are in a piteous state both from the point of view of learning and education; they have sunk to the level of a mass of uneducated men, drawn from the most vulgar classes ... who are not in a position either to preach or to put forward Christian teaching so that the whole population has fallen into complete ignorance of religion.'[20] The condition of the lower clergy was also qualitatively different from the eighteenth century when they had been 'popes in their own parish'. They were now generally paid by the state and subject to a greater extent to the whims of the local bishop, who bothered little with their material welfare, and did not hesitate to move priests from one parish to another. Because of the decline of the cathedral chapters and the implementation of concordats, bishops themselves were frequently nominated by governments who had an eye on their administrative prowess rather than their pastoral skills, and who did not pay much regard to the local origins of the nominee.

Yet, while not necessarily well educated, even in theology, in many senses this clergy was more closely attuned to the rhythms, aspirations and concerns of their parishioners than had been the case previously. They were just as able to fulfil their sacerdotal offices and had a greater sympathy for popular religion. The principal example of this must surely be the Curé d'Ars, Jean-Marie-Baptiste Vianney (1786–1859) who in 1818 was charged with a benighted parish in marshland close to Lyon. The son of a particularly devout peasant family, he had few social graces, was uncomfortable in the presence of women, even his mother (like his inspiration Liguori), and shunned intellectual pursuits. His sermons were simply a regurgitation of extracts from two or three clerical manuals. The *curé* none the less effected an extraordinary transformation in the life of his parish, securing full attendance of both men and women at mass and confession, stamping out 'sinful' practices such as dancing and working on Sundays, while promoting pilgrimages and Marianism. Such was his reputation and the pulling power of the miraculous cures reported in Ars, that the parish became a pilgrimage centre even during his lifetime, attracting over 60,000 visitors annually. Quite why this humble priest was able to transform the religious life of his parish is not clear. He certainly tapped a rich vein of popular piety in his promotion of the cult of the saints: nearly every household in the surrounding neighbourhood possessed a plaster saint by the end of his life. It was possibly his technique in the confessional that was the key to his success. He increasingly adopted a more tolerant approach, reflecting the views of the eighteenth-century writer Alfonso de'Liguori (see above), and he received hundreds of letters from people far and wide seeking his advice on spiritual and moral problems. In this way, he served as a type of 'agony aunt' for the laity and a model for the parish clergy, most of whom showed a similar devotion to their pastoral duties, though not all were as successful in emulating his popularity.

The fact that Liguori himself was beatified in 1816 and canonised in 1839 was an indicator that the approach of this eighteenth-century priest to moral theology was gaining ground. The heartland of his influence was France, where his writings enjoyed the influential patronage of Gousset, the Archbishop of Reims, but it spread well beyond this country. His teachings, encapsulated in short, easy-to-read handbooks of instruction, were widely translated into German, Polish, Latin and French, and were of course already available in his native Italian. Historians have since encapsulated the approach of Liguori when speaking of the transition from a 'God of fear' to a 'God of love'. Liguorism is generally associated with a more tolerant attitude towards absolution and confession. Prior to 1789, many clergy, and not just Jansenists, were accused of adopting a rigorist position and refusing to absolve penitents of their sins until they had demonstrated contrition and completed the required atonement which was often onerous. The nineteenth-century clergy appear to have been less insistent in the confessional, though this is an area that must remain speculative given the secrecy which perforce surrounds it. Even so, there is evidence that parish priests took a more understanding attitude towards usury, sexual peccadillos, the use of *coitus interruptus* as a means of contraception and the acquisition of former Church properties. Similarly, there were signs of a shift in emphasis in the missions organised by the Redemptorists and Lazarists. There were fewer hell-fire sermons replete with references to the eternal punishments reserved for the impenitent and, instead, a greater insistence upon Providential forgiveness and the tenderness of Marian love.

Yet to ascribe this change in emphasis wholly to the teachings of Liguori would be to exaggerate his influence. The theology of the newly-formed Sisters of the Sacred Heart also emphasised the forgiveness of God, for example, though this was a legacy of the teaching of François de Sales and Jean Eudes rather than of Liguori. At parish level, the new approach probably reflected the altered socio-economic background of the clergy who were perhaps less intellectual and more sympathetic to their parishioners than their eighteenth-century predecessors. And it marked a recognition on the part of the Church that adjustments were needed if it was to retain the loyalty of its adherents in the aftermath of the revolutionary and Napoleonic decades. As a consequence, the Church demonstrated a more accommodating attitude to popular practices. With the slackening of clerical tutelage brought about by the momentous events of the 1790s and 1800s, forms of religious observance such as the cult of the saints, pilgrimages and the use of therapeutic rites had resurfaced, as already noted in earlier chapters. While continuing to deplore the resurgence of gross and superstitious elements in everyday religion, the clergy none the less recognised that it was better to tolerate these things, and put them under clerical control wherever possible, an acknowledgement that practice of this kind was better than no practice at all. It needs also to be recognised that many elements of superstition, present in the eighteenth century, persisted into the nineteenth. Peasants still prayed to the moon, crossed themselves to ward off harm and used holy water to cure sick cattle. A belief in vampires, often later caricatured in Hammer horror films, persisted in the remote areas of central and eastern Europe, although the popular imagination pictured the vampire as stocky and rosy-cheeked rather than as the gaunt and pallid celluloid image of Christopher Lee. It was reported that in Serbia, as late as the 1830s, villagers lopped off the arms and legs of those dead bodies which still retained some flexibility, nailing them to the coffins with stakes, lest they became part of the undead.

The one region in which the Church did not indulge popular practice to the same extent was Ireland. This was principally because the country had never undergone any Tridentine reforms of note and popular religiosity remained of the grossest kind, riddled with abuses, superstition and pagan practices. The nineteenth century witnessed what Emmett Larkin has not improperly termed a 'devotional revolution' which succeeded in transforming the nature of Irish Catholicism so that it caught up with the developments that had overtaken the remainder of Europe.[21] A trained and disciplined parish clergy was gradually put into place, capable of offering a relatively high level of instruction, and raising the quality of belief, and the Church gained control of education and social activities. The reasons for this devotional revolution lay partially in the Catholic response to what has been termed a 'Second Reformation' in Ireland, the attempt by militant Protestants to evangelise, notably through missionary societies. The Catholic revival further stemmed from the energetic zeal of Paul Cullen who, as Archbishop of Armagh (1849–52) and of Dublin (1852–78), was the effective head of the Church. He established a number of Italian devotions, and other features such as benedictions, novenas, a devotion to the Sacred Heart and the exposition of the Blessed Sacrament, together with other exterior ceremonies of religion which he noted to be 'very neglected'. Additionally, new religious orders were introduced, including the Redemptorists and the Sisters of Mercy. Significant though Cullen's work was, it should also be noted there had been some faint indication of Catholic reform in the late eighteenth century, suggesting that this was not entirely a response to Protestant militancy.

Despite developments in Ireland, the Catholicism of the social elites was of a very different type. It, too, underwent something of a revival, the most dramatic example being the so-called Oxford Movement in England. This was an intellectual trend within an elite of the Church of England, and included figures such as Keble, Pusey, John Henry Newman (1801–90), Henry Edward Manning (1809–92), and William Ward, all academics at Oxford University. In contrast to earlier prominent English converts, notably Kenelm Digby, George Spencer and Augustus Pugin, these men were not attracted to Catholicism because of romantic revivalist notions about the Church of the Middle Ages, and not all of them would cross the Rubicon by converting. Manning and Newman were the most prominent of those who did, both ultimately becoming cardinals. It is commonly argued that their decision was prompted by the widespread abuses within the Church of England, although recent scholarship has emphasised that the Anglican communion was, in many respects, in good heart and in good order.[22] It was more that they rebelled against the liberal trends within Anglican theology and the latitudinarianism found in the Church of England. They hit upon a more congenial home within the Church of Rome which had never compromised on the doctrine of apostolic succession and whose revitalised Ultramontanism provided a further attraction.

Though at one level rarefied spiritual athletes, they sought to combine this with a concern for the spiritual and material welfare of ordinary men and women. Manning, for example, worked extensively in the slums of London's East End. There was considerable rejoicing elsewhere in Europe at their conversion, masses being said in France, Belgium, the German lands and Rome. Inevitably, this publicity incited anti-papal feeling within the body of English Protestantism, as did the European 'Crusade of Prayer', launched by Catholics in 1838 in a bid to secure the conversion of England as part of a wider movement of religious regeneration within Christendom. It was Disraeli who put this revival into context when he quipped that 'he would only begin to worry when he heard that grocers were becoming converts'.[23] A more significant effect of the Oxford Movement was the division it injected into English Catholicism. Many 'old' Catholics, who were already disturbed by the wide-scale Irish immigration, were suspicious of the papalism and sincerity of the new converts, and found their proselytising fervour distasteful.

A final indicator of the revitalisation of Catholic intellectual life was the establishment of a distinctive Catholic press, comprising both journals, published weekly or monthly, and daily newspapers: the *Université Catholique* (1836), *Le Correspondant* (1843) and *L'Univers* (1833) in France; *De Katholik* (1842) and *De Tijd* (1845) in Belgium; the *Dublin Review* (1836), *The Tablet* (1840) and *The Lamp* (1846) in Britain; *La Sociedad* and *La Civilizacion* in 1830 in Spain; and *Der Katholik* (1821) and the *Historisch-Politische Blätter* in the German lands. The growth of a Catholic press, which built upon the success of eighteenth-century publications such as the Jansenist *Nouvelles Ecclésiastiques*, signified that something had been learned about the techniques of persuasion from the revolutionary decades. Such publications permitted a greater interaction between practising theologians and laymen, and brought issues of doctrine, pastoral care and Church politics into the public arena. As the century wore on, this press would be crucial in the development of new forms of Catholic action, but its influence should not be exaggerated. Circulation was limited in comparison to the secular press; it tended to be concentrated in the provinces as opposed to the capital cities; and, with some notable exceptions, it was not characterised by the intellectual quality of its writing.

Whatever the successes of Catholicism in the post-1815 period, there were limits to its revival. It is, of course, undeniable that the Church made good some of the institutional damage that had been perpetrated during the French Revolution. It was also true that Catholicism remained a formidable and significant presence in the daily lives of the popular classes. Indeed, the trend towards a laicisation of religion, and the enhanced participation of women, was a powerful testimony to the indigenous strength of the faith. The problem was that the Church needed more time than was available so that elements of recovery could be nurtured and given the opportunity to take deep root. Obsessed with recovering from the trauma of the revolutionary and Napoleonic decades by securing a return to a position as close as possible to that of the old regime, the Church, with the exception of some liberal Catholics such as Lamennais, failed to perceive that several of the trends initiated or highlighted by 1789 – popular participation in politics, the emergence of new ideologies such as liberalism, nationalism and socialism – were here to stay and that it was necessary to reach some understanding with them. This was something the Church was ill-placed to do. The revolutions of 1848 would expose in a brutal fashion just how far the Church had yet to travel.

Pius IX and the Revolutions of 1848

In 1848, Europe was shaken by a series of revolutionary uprisings, from which only the peripheral areas of the Iberian peninsula, Britain, Scandinavia, Russia, Belgium, Poland and Ottoman Europe, together with Switzerland, were immune. This tumultuous year has been called many things: 'the Revolution of the intellectuals', 'the spring-time of the peoples', 'the last cry of the artisan'. Perhaps a more fitting epithet would be 'the unexpected year'. The liberal commentator Aléxis de Tocqueville displayed most prescience when, in January 1848, he warned his colleagues in the Chamber of Deputies that they were sleeping on a volcano. Few paid him any regard at the time. A series of extremely dangerous factors came together in an accidental conjuncture to vindicate his prophecy. The failure of the potato and cereal harvests of 1845–47 throughout much of Europe led inevitably to a hike in food prices, undermining the purchasing power of the urban artisans, and contributing to a collapse of the market for manufactured goods. Nor did it help that this coincided with a more general cyclical slump in business, part of an emerging pattern associated with the early stages of industrialisation, which was itself bitterly resented by the artisans as a threat to their jobs. Ironically, the worst of this was over by 1847, but against this backdrop of predominantly urban unrest, bourgeois elements sought to capitalise upon popular discontent to pursue their own nationalist and liberal agendas. Matters were compounded by the fact that the rulers of the day, Louis Philippe,

Frederick William IV and Ferdinand I, were weak, vacillatory men and did not readily heed their advisers who urged swift and draconian action which would undoubtedly have halted the insurrectionary movements in their tracks. To this list we may add Pius IX (1846–78), commonly known as Pio Nono, whose pontificate had started in more auspicious circumstances.

The character of Pius IX's pontificate was, to a large degree, determined by his immediate predecessor, Gregory XVI, who had fiercely repudiated liberal Catholicism and who had been hostile to the aspirations for Italian union, termed the Risorgimento. The new Pope was elected in a short Conclave in June 1846 whose heat and insanitary conditions were reminiscent of that of 1241 which had cost the life of one cardinal. Essentially, Pius was a compromise candidate between the arch-conservative Luigi Lambruschini and the 'progressive' Luigi Macara. Young (he was only fifty-four at the time of his accession), friendly, tolerant and outgoing, the former Bishop of Imola, Giovanni Maria Mastai-Ferretti, was known as a good administrator and was allegedly sympathetic towards the ideals of liberalism and nationalism. It was said that even his cat was a member of the Carbonari.

Although Pius IX does not deserve his later reputation of being a staunch reactionary, he was certainly no liberal. The notion that he was open-minded stemmed from a superficial reading of his behaviour prior to 1846: a readiness to entertain men of liberal views, his dislike of the Austrian presence in Italy, his reform initiatives in Imola, his willingness to embrace new technology, especially the railways, and his efforts to reduce the police apparatus within his own diocese. His first actions as Pope appeared to confirm these earlier impressions and secured an initial popularity among the people of Rome, even on the part of Mazzini. Pius IX initiated a commission to introduce railways into the Papal States; street lighting and public health measures were inaugurated; friendly meetings were conducted with Father Ventura, a close associate of Lamennais; extensive charitable works were set in train; restrictions on Jews were eased; the traditional amnesty granted to political prisoners was more extensive than in the past; tariff reform and agricultural innovation were championed; and some consideration was given to the dismissal of the Swiss Guard as they 'don't please, and they cost a lot'.[24] So far did Pius's reputation as the 'liberator pope' extend that fellow rulers in Europe believed that he would bring to a close the corruption and inefficiency that had for so long characterised the Papal States. Even in the USA, President James Polk sang Pio Nono's praises and recommended Congress to establish diplomatic relations with the Vatican. Almost alone, Metternich confessed to an extreme pessimism about the future if the Pope persisted with his liberal policies.

The real Pio Nono was very different. In private he did not disguise his abhorrence of Italian aspirations, remarking in a reference to the neo-Guelfs: 'A Pope ought not to throw himself into utopias. Will you believe it, there are people who even talk of an Italian federation with the Pope at its head? As if that were possible!'[25] His opening encyclical, *Qui pluribus* of November 1846, strangely unremarked at the time, harked back to the themes of *Mirari vos* and *Singulari nos* and looked ahead to the *Syllabus of Errors* in its outright

condemnation of all things liberal and any deviation from theological orthodoxy. He was a stickler for liturgical conformity. It was in the area of Church
discipline, however, that Pio Nono was at his most unreconstructed. He
rejected any lay involvement in the governance and administration of the
Church, lest this dilute the authority of the clergy.

Without realising the effect of his actions, and oblivious to the popular
mood both within the Papal States and elsewhere, Pio Nono had given rise
to hopes that he could never fulfil. Metternich caught his predicament precisely
when he compared him to a novice sorcerer who had conjured up spirits
outside his control. In effect, the Pope was sending out contradictory signals
which were being misinterpreted by liberals and conservatives alike. To both,
he seemed to be encouraging nationalist aspirations. In April 1847, he set out
plans for an advisory body of laymen to assist with the reform and government of the Papal States. In autumn that year, egged on by his adviser Cardinal
Bussi, he ventured the idea of some form of customs union between his own
territories and those of Tuscany and Piedmont-Sardinia, a scheme which was
approved by the King Charles Albert whom many believed would provide the
military muscle to oust the Austrians. In December, Pio Nono even threatened
Metternich with excommunication following the reinforcement of the Austrian
garrison at Ferrara, securing the withdrawal of these troops. Yet if Pio Nono
wanted Italy to be free of Austrian troops and to enjoy some degree of
economic cooperation, he was adamantly opposed to the overhaul of the
Papal States along constitutional lines, the implementation of a Mazzinian
reform programme and the more limited confederation envisaged by Gioberti
and his followers. Ultimately, his can only be described as a naive strategy
which displayed little awareness of diplomatic realities and popular sentiments
and which owed a great deal to the contradictory counsel the Pope was
receiving from his advisers, Cardinals Bussi and Gizzi.

Matters blew up in the Pope's face in late January 1848 when a separatist
revolt in Palermo forced Ferdinand, King of the Two Sicilies, to concede a
constitution. The example of revolution in France the following month was
all that it took to spark off revolution throughout the peninsula and farther
afield. Swept along by events, in March Pius introduced a measure of constitutional government in his own states, only to be horrified when he was
further pressed to expel the Society of Jesus. He was also urged to join with
Charles Albert of Piedmont-Sardinia who had recently launched his war
against the Austrians in northern Italy. Typically, Pio Nono issued contradictory
signals, allowing papal troops to head north but issuing orders that they were
not to engage the Austrians.

In an attempt to make his position clear once and for all, an emotional and
distraught pontiff uttered his famous declaration of 29 April. In this, he flatly
refused to wage war against co-religionaries in the shape of the Austrians. He
also dismissed the notion of a federal Italy under his leadership, encouraging
the Italian people to stay loyal to their natural rulers. This was not what
Italians wanted to hear, and the Pope's popularity took a nose-dive. Trying to
retain credibility, Rome responded by appointing Count Pellegrino Rossi, a

professor of constitutional law, as Prime Minister of the Papal States. It was all too late. The defeat of Charles Albert at Custozza in July, coupled with pontifical passivity, forced the revolution into a more radical mode. In November 1848, Rossi was assassinated, the papal palace was attacked, and the Pope himself was forced to flee to Neapolitan territory disguised as a simple priest. Rome was now the property of the radicals, Mazzini and Garibaldi. Together, they established a Roman Republic which specifically repudiated the authority of the pontiff and quickly adopted an anti-clerical stance: clergy were bullied and the property of the regulars was redistributed among the poor. The attack on the Church did not necessarily play well with the people of Rome; yet far more dangerous for the republic's survival was the attitude of Austria and France. In March 1849, at Novara, Habsburg forces decisively defeated Charles Albert who abdicated soon after. This prompted the new French ruler Louis-Napoleon Bonaparte, who was desirous to reach Rome before the Austrians, to respond to the Pope's appeals for assistance. So it was that French bayonets cleared the way for the 'liberal pope' to be restored to his capital, though Italian opinion had so turned against him that it was nine months before it was judged safe for him to re-enter Rome, his hair prematurely greyed following his experiences, by which time a fierce counter-revolutionary reaction had taken place. Nevertheless, while he had recovered his position without ultimately conceding any significant political reform, thereafter the acquisition of Rome was the prize held most dear by radical Italian nationalists. The omens were not good.

Given the ambiguity of Pio Nono's actions in the period 1846–49, it is small wonder that opinions about him have been divided. Few of the labels attaching to him – 'the liberal pope', 'the pope liberator' and 'the anti-national pope' – do him full justice. At heart, he was a simple and moderate man, whose love of the Italian people was unquestionably sincere, and someone who was prepared to countenance a measured degree of reform. Yet he was also unyielding in defence of papal and ecclesiastical prerogatives and was not prepared to sacrifice either at the altar of Italian nationalism. If Pio Nono had learned anything from his unhappy beginnings as Pope, it was the need to rearticulate those first principles which he had elaborated in *Qui pluribus*. He returned to these very themes in his address of April 1849 which once more foreshadowed the *Syllabus of Errors* and which was the precursor to placing on the *Index* the works of Rosmini, Gioberti and Ventura. For good measure, he condemned the *Statuto* (constitution) in Piedmont, the one tangible gain of the revolutions of 1848–49 in Italy, which circumscribed clerical controls over education.

If events in Italy in 1848 were traumatic for Pius IX, those in France were potentially much more serious; after all, this was the cradle of revolution and there was always the danger that when France sneezed the other states of Europe caught a cold. In truth, there was little danger of this revolution becoming infectious. It was predominantly an unexpected and Parisian affair, and the establishment of a republic was more or less a political expedient which came about because Louis Philippe's chosen successor, his grandson the Comte de Paris, was a ten-year-old child and was unacceptable to the revolutionaries. Initially, the Church was fearful of what might happen, but many of its anxieties proved misplaced. While the leadership of the revolution contained radical elements of the left who were committed to a republican and socialist programme, it also comprised former ministers of the July Monarchy and conservatives such as Thiers and Odilon Barrot, who were dedicated to the maintenance of law and order.

Certainly there was no intention of exporting the revolution, and Pio Nono's reputation as a liberal prevented an immediate anti-clerical backlash. There was apprehension, too, at the introduction of universal male suffrage, but this proved less damaging to the Church than anticipated. In the elections held in the early summer, the influence of radical *commissaires*, mobilised by Ledru-Rollin, the newly-installed Minister of the Interior, and the *instituteurs* (elementary school teachers) who had always resented their subservience to the clergy, was more than counter-balanced by a number of factors. The legacy of the revolution of 1789 meant that clerics were not unused to putting themselves forward for election; not just liberals such as Antoine Frédéric Ozanam, Lacordaire and the former priest Lamennais, but conservatives who in the event were more influential. Universal male suffrage had enfranchised a peasantry which was intrinsically conservative, and became even more so after the republic alienated any potential rural support by its introduction in March of a 45 *centimes* tax, designed to balance the budget, which fell disproportionately on peasant property. Notables used traditional patterns of deference to bolster the conservative vote. Nor was the Church averse to the open manipulation of electors, for it must be stressed that most clerics perceived the revolution and the republic as threats to morality, Christian discipline and social order. Above all, it was deeply troubled by the prominence of socialists such as Louis Blanc, Auguste Blanqui and Alexandre Martin Albert. So it was that the Bishop of Rennes sent out the following instructions to his parish priests, ordering them to explain the necessity of exercising their vote: 'They [parishioners] must concern themselves with one thing only, namely with choosing as their representatives men of recognised integrity who are frankly resolved to set up a republic in France that respects the sacred rights of religion, liberty, property and the family.'[26] Whereas in February many priests had been compelled to bless liberty trees, in April and May it was more common to see them leading their flocks to vote, usually for Legitimist or other right-wing candidates. The government *commissaire* in the Tarn noted the use of 'sermons from the pulpit, advice, homilies, commands, threats uttered in the homes and in the confessionals, pressure brought to bear on the electors' relations, harangues – some pronounced in public, some otherwise – slanders, lies about the republican candidates whom they represented as communists, terrorists and enemies of religion'.[27] The upshot was that the radicals and socialists secured a mere 100 seats out of 876, the majority being won by Orléanists, Legitimists and moderate republicans.

Whereas in Italy the revolutionary uprisings of 1848 became more radical with the passage of time, the reverse was the case in France, as the sting was taken out of the left-wing tail. The capacity of the revolution in France for extremism was vividly demonstrated on 15 May when a workers' demonstration in Paris stormed the Chamber of Deputies. This thoroughly alarmed conservatives and moderates, and, naturally, the Church. When a second demonstration erupted in June in protest at the closure of the national workshops which had hitherto provided some form of charitable relief, this was brutally suppressed by General Cavaignac, thus ending the hopes for a Social Republic. Although the republic continued for a further four years, as Lamennais himself observed it was but a republic in name. In November, a conservative-framed constitution was inaugurated and the following month the French voted on the first President of the Second Republic, their choices lying between Cavaignac, Ledru-Rollin, Lamartine and Louis-Napoleon Bonaparte. There was no obvious clerical candidate, but Louis-Napoleon attracted support from Catholics, both as a symbol of stability and because of his defence of Pius IX who had been forced to flee from Rome, and he won the election.

France's new President could not be described as a good Catholic, and it is difficult to label him at all, so ambivalent and shifting were his political and social views. Just as he had attempted two abortive coups in 1836 and 1840, he had been involved in an uprising against Gregory XVI. He appreciated, however, that in 1848 his route to power resided in the ballot box and in the courting of influential institutions, including the Church. Clerical support hardened as a result of his early actions as President. Abroad, he provided the military assistance which enabled Pius IX to regain his throne. At home, he showered favours upon the Church. Although the concordat and Organic Articles remained in force, relations between bishops and government were extremely cordial, and rarely did ministers interfere in communications between Rome and the episcopacy. The high point of the presidency for the Church was the Falloux Law of 1850, named after the highly devout Minister of Education, which enabled clerics to open their own secondary schools with minimum state interference, thus inaugurating a thirty-year period in which Catholic colleges flourished. The increasingly dictatorial methods of Louis-Napoleon also appealed to traditionalist Catholics, in particular the punitive legislation designed to restrict the activities of the so-called *Démoc-Socs* (Democratic Socialists), who had taken the radicalism of the June Days to the countryside with some electoral success. A supremely supple politician, Louis-Napoleon also took care to court in the Chamber the so-called 'Party of Order', a conservative bloc in which Catholics such as Montalambert were prominent; but, ultimately, he sought to emulate his uncle by bypassing the parliamentary procedure altogether, something which he accomplished by his *coup d'état* of 1851 and his proclamation of the Second Empire shortly afterwards.

A tiny number of acclaimed liberal Catholics, among them Frédéric Ozanam, the Sorbonne professor and founder of a lay association for the relief of poverty, and Bishop Dupanloup, the noted reforming Bishop of Orléans and ardent educationalist, together with a smattering of local clergy,

were dismayed at this usurpation of power. Yet clerical opinion overwhelmingly sided with the ultra-conservative Louis Veuillot, the Catholic convert
who transformed the newspaper *L'Univers* into the mouthpiece of reaction
during his period as editor. He declared unambiguously: 'There is only a choice
between Bonaparte as Emperor and a Socialist Republic.'[28] Montalambert, who
had enthusiastically welcomed the Falloux Law, urged all Catholics to vote
'Yes' in the plebiscite which the self-appointed Emperor used to legitimise his
assumption of power. The Catholic attitudes to the *coup d'état* were perhaps
best encapsulated by the pronouncement of Bishop Clausel de Montas, who
described it as 'the greatest miracle of God's benevolence known to history'.[29]
Soon after, a *Te Deum* was conducted by the Archbishop of Paris at Notre
Dame in thanksgiving for the *coup*. What Catholics could not have foretold
were two subsequent developments. Having cynically manipulated the Church
in support of his personal ambition, later in his regime Napoleon III would
not hesitate to pursue anti-clerical measures when it suited his purposes. In
so doing, he prefigured something of the institutionalised secularism that would
become part-and-parcel of the Third Republic. Moreover, his early benevolence
towards the Church and the reciprocal support lent by the episcopacy to the
dictator was something that both moderate and left-wing republicans could
not stomach. This gave rise to a trenchant secularism, which figured as one
of the (if not *the*) principal identifying characteristics of their cause. They
would not easily forgive or forget the Church's role when they were in power
in the 1880s.

  In contrast to the Italian and French examples, Catholics in the German
territories were generally more sympathetic to revolution, this for two reasons.
First, political change promised some relief from state interference in Church
matters, whether this was Josephinian controls in Austria or Hohenzollern
intolerance in Prussia. Second, it held out some prospect of a return to a
more united *Reichskirche*, such as had existed under the Holy Roman Empire,
although this did not necessarily mean that Catholics were fervent nationalists
and very few could be counted among the ranks of the radicals. Whereas in
France the clergy was fearful of independent popular action, within the
German Confederation there was much greater genuine cooperation between
laity and clergy, both of whom were quick to mobilise for political and
religious action. This initially manifested itself in the establishment of Catholic
associations such as that in Mainz created in March 1848 by Chaplain Heinrich
and members of the cathedral chapter, 'The Pious Association for Religious
Freedom'. As its name suggested, the *raison d'être* of this movement was the
defence of clerical freedoms, especially within schooling. Often adopting the
nomenclature *Piusvereine* out of respect for Pio Nono, another indicator of
how his 'liberal' reputation had extended, there were seven key associations
of this type with hundreds of affiliated branches by the autumn of 1848,
assembling for an impressive national conference in October. The corollary
to this flowering of Catholic activity was the proliferation of newspapers,
notably the *Deutsches Volksblatt* at Stuttgart and the *Rheinische Volkshalle* at
Cologne. Together, these newspapers and the fledgling associations cam-

paigned for the election of Catholic deputies to the self-appointed national assembly that was gathering at Frankfurt, subsequently deluging it with a flood of petitions on religious issues.

Some degree of coordination among Catholics from the different states was provided by Archbishop Geissel of Cologne, but it would be wrong to suggest that there existed a united Catholic party either inside or outside of the Frankfurt Assembly; there existed instead a loose confederation of like-minded clerical deputies, known as the 'Catholic Club'. Overwhelmingly dominated by middle-class liberals, the Assembly happily approved a series of measures designed to render the state neutral in religious matters while at the same time giving it an important role in matters which the Church regarded as its own domain, for instance civil marriage and public schooling. Nevertheless, in their desire to be seen as even-handed, the Frankfurt representatives allowed each denomination to run its own affairs. As in so much it did, or rather talked about doing, it ultimately mattered little what was agreed at Frankfurt. In both Austria and in Prussia, the monarchy began to reassert itself at the end of the year; first Ferdinand of Austria and then Frederick William of Prussia refused the crown of Germany, and in the summer of 1849 the Prussians felt confident enough to act militarily against the radicals in Saxony, Baden, the Rhine Palatinate and Württemberg who themselves had recently taken up arms to defend their hard-won constitutions against the expected conservative backlash. Within Habsburg lands, the Austrian military, combined with Russian troops, put a swift end to the hopes of the many minorities for national autonomy.

When the dust finally settled, the balance sheet of the German revolutions might have been a disappointing one for the radicals and many nationalists. Yet the Catholic Church could draw some crumbs of comfort. In traditionalist Bavaria, the old throne–altar alliance was reasserted, and in any case the revolution there had been principally supported by Protestants. Within Prussia, the conservative backlash, which especially targeted secular school teachers who had allegedly been behind much of the popular agitation, was not altogether displeasing to Catholics; nor was the Constitution of 1850. This put off civil marriage, something threatened by the Frankfurt Parliament, and recognised, in theory at least, the equality of religions. It was further stipulated that when establishing schools these should reflect the religious balance of the local population, although in practice Protestants benefited most. In Austria, where the issue of religion had taken second place to the overriding question of ethnic autonomy, there was a deliberate slackening of Josephinian controls as a means of cementing Catholic support for the regime as it proceeded with counter-revolution; the Church was permitted open contact with Rome, bishops were granted greater authority within their dioceses, and the right, known as the *placet*, which allowed governments to stop pontifical enactments automatically having an effect in their territory, was abolished. All this prefigured the Concordat of 1855. This was a truly astonishing document, designed to put an end to the century-old conflict between Church and state by reversing the Josephinianism of the latter. Although the clergy continued to be paid by the state and were still regarded as state employees, clerical influence over elementary schooling was substantially reinforced, ecclesiastical censorship reintroduced and, most surprisingly of all, the Church had its sequestrated properties restored or was indemnified. This concession proved a crippling financial burden for a state that was shortly to fight major wars with the French, Piedmontese and Prussians, and hardly encouraged liberals, whether Catholic or not, to look upon Austria as the natural leader in any unified Germany.

Within Austria itself, the association movement had made some progress, but it lacked the support of the bishops who, as we have seen, were well tutored in loyalty to the state. Nevertheless, this phenomenon of Catholic action had firmly implanted itself both here and elsewhere in the German Confederation and would constitute a valuable forum in resisting the militantly anti-Catholic Prussian state of the 1870s.

Conclusion: Restoration Reviewed

Surveying the years *circa* 1815 to 1850, it is possible to perceive that European Catholicism began to take on distinctive characteristics. We can already see that the papacy was moving towards a comprehensive rejection of all things modern and a retreat into a theological bunker. In so doing, it was encouraged by the widespread Ultramontanism which emerged among most conservative and some liberal Catholics, both lay and clerical. On the ground, there had been a resurgence of popular Catholicism to which the Church proved more accommodating than in the past. Catholics had begun to demonstrate a new-found fluency with techniques of mass mobilisation, electoral campaigning and propaganda which suggested that they had learned much from the traumas of the period 1789–1815. They had achieved some accommodation with the new political orders that emerged after 1815, although it must be stressed that in all countries it was the state that held the upper hand. Yet whether Catholicism fully faced up to the new challenges posed by the post-Napoleonic world, especially the rise, albeit uneven, of nationalism, remains doubtful. What is clear is that Catholicism within individual countries began to acquire distinctive national characteristics far more marked than in the eighteenth century. Inevitably, these characteristics contain a measure of stereotyping but within all stereotypes there is usually a smidgen of truth: English Catholics were high-minded while their Irish counterparts were catching up on developments elsewhere; within Belgium and the German Confederation, Catholicism had strong liberal overtones; in France, the faith was characterised by a plurality of attitudes; in Switzerland, it had taken on the features of a ghetto mentality; in Poland, it was a badge of identity and militancy; while in Italy, Spain and Portugal, the traditional Mediterranean features had come even more to the fore. Catholicism means universal but, in the second half of the nineteenth century, Rome experienced severe difficulties in keeping this disparate Church together.

CHAPTER FOUR

Catholicism Retuned,
1850–1914

IN the post-Napoleonic period, the Church had been preoccupied with the task of rebuilding: putting back institutions and structures that had been overwhelmed, reaching accommodations with secular rulers, and coming to terms with changes in patterns of lay religiosity. This process continued at least until the 1870s. Around that point, matters altered dramatically. While the Church still endeavoured to make good the losses of the earlier period, it also confronted a series of issues, previously bubbling beneath the surface, which now came to the fore: the emergence of nation-states in the cases of Italy and Germany, and later in the Balkans; the almost total loss of papal territorial sovereignty within the Italian peninsula; a broader erosion of the concept of papal worldly authority on a wider geographic scale; the eventual triumph of republicanism within France; the emergence of governments, purportedly neutral in religious affairs, but not slow to construct an institutionalised secularism far more corrosive than the Josephinianism and Erastianism of the past; truly dramatic social and economic changes, at least in northern and western Europe, that cried out for a response; the emergence of plurality within the political thinking of Catholics; and the growth of secularisation, represented not just by a rationalist opposition to revealed religion, but in an indifference on the part of the popular classes, whose spiritual needs were often supplanted by material pleasures.

It is all too easy to characterise the response of the Catholic Church to these challenges as ostrich-like, the assertion of fundamental and integralist religious beliefs which championed the traditional and fulminated against the modern. Pio Nono himself appears to embody this approach through the *Syllabus of Errors* of 1864, attached to the bull *Quanta Cura*, and the proclamation of infallibility of 1870. In truth, the Catholic answer was subtler, involving a retuning process in which all levels of the Church sought to find a solution to the modern world that was more than a mere assertion of old regime values. While the papacy might have grounded itself upon eternal theological and religious truths which helped to contribute to the growth of Ultramontanism, other Catholics, scattered throughout all layers of the Church and including members of the laity, ventured an understanding of the new social and economic environment. This often entailed a dismissal of the modern world, yet it nevertheless aspired to extricate the people from the supposed materialism and irreligion which enveloped them. The Church had always prided itself on its care of the poor and the spiritual nourishment offered to them, but never before had it been so preoccupied with their welfare. The previously flickering lights of liberal and social Catholicism now burned brightly in many of the European cities of the late nineteenth century. Nor did the Church forget men and women overseas. This was the great age of European imperialism, and religious orders were frequently at the fore-front of the so-called 'civilising mission' of European colonialism, even in respect of those states, such as France, which were avowedly secular at home.

This, then, was a period of retuning for European Catholicism, a time when it rejigged its appeal, nature and institutions in an attempt to deal with a strange new world that seemed to be in constant flux.

Ultramontanism and the Papacy

In chapters dealing with earlier epochs, the starting point was not the papacy, important though this was, as the Church then possessed a greater degree of collegiality; and some aspects of European Catholicism, such as lay religiosity, could be discussed largely without reference to the Pope. This was not the case in the second half of the nineteenth century when all roads led to Rome. Indeed, this period is characterised by the emergence of a fully-fledged Ultramontanism, the like of which had not been seen possibly since the era of Innocent III (1198–1216). It will be recalled that Ultramontanism literally meant 'over the mountain', a reference to the pontiff's privileged position as a source of universal authority. After 1848, the influence of Rome was more pervasive and more encompassing than ever before. In an age of 'isms' – nationalism, liberalism, socialism and Caesarism, represented by both Bona-partes – Ultramontanism also came to embody an ideology that took in liturgy, devotion, clerical discipline, theology and extended to the realm of politics, social action and culture. There was an irony in the pontiff's assertion of his authority at a time when monarchical absolutism was in retreat throughout much of Europe, even if autocracy persisted in Russia and the Ottoman Empire.

The reasons behind the flourishing of Ultramontanism have, to a degree, already been touched upon. It derived from a desire on the part of the lower clergy to escape the tyranny of the local episcopacy and from the wish of the hierarchy to escape the tutelage of the state. A smattering of liberal Catholics, led most famously by Lamennais, and those Polish and Swiss insurgents of 1830 and 1847, had even invoked the authority of the Pope to underpin their cause, although such men would subsequently have serious reservations about the way in which Ultramontanism evolved. As we have seen, it also fed on the institutional overhaul of the Church, linked in some instances with the establishment of concordats which made regular and routine contact with Rome much easier. Greater use was made of nuncios, who were encouraged to play an active role in the domestic life of national churches; the Curia accepted responsibility for the resolution of legal cases, even on trivial matters;

and pro-Roman candidates were favoured both at the level of the prelacy and lower down, even when they were men of moderate ability.

Within Rome itself, there was a new mood of combativeness and assertiveness which expressed itself in a readiness to aggregate power. This largely stemmed from a desire to enforce discipline within the Church, a discipline which had been notably lacking in the disparate and inchoate responses to 1848. Inspired by Jesuits within the Curia, this involved a repudiation of liberal Catholicism, which will be discussed later, as well as Febronian and Gallican concepts, and was most obviously manifested in the attempt to propagate theocratic teaching in the seminaries of Rome, notably that of the Gregoriana. Significantly, a number of national colleges were added to the older ones at Rome: the Belgian seminary in 1844; the French in 1853; the Beda seminary, for English speakers, of 1852; the Latin American Pius seminary in 1865; the North American seminary in 1859; and the Polish in 1866. During the same period, the mother houses of the regular orders were also encouraged to site themselves in Rome. Priests further took to wearing cassocks rather than frock-coats and breeches so as to distinguish themselves from the 'men of the age, infected with revolutionary principles'.[1]

None of this would have happened, however, had it not been for the Pope himself, and ultimately, without papal blessing Ultramontanism would never have blossomed in the way that it did. In several senses, the tone had been set by Gregory XVI who considered that the office of pontiff held sway over the civil power, and who had not hesitated to condemn any indiscipline within the Church whether it was the neo-Guelfs or the insurrectionary Poles, both of whom had ironically looked to Rome as a source of moral and spiritual support. As we have seen, his encyclicals *Mirari vos* and *Singulari nos* had already anticipated Pio Nono's pronouncements. Despite his reputation as a liberal, Pius IX continued in much the same vein, publishing the pessimistic *Qui pluribus* in 1846 and *Inter multiplices* of 1853, vigorously defending the reactionary Veuillot against the Gallican wrath of some of the French bishops.

Several factors combined to make Pius the natural champion of Ultramontanism. To begin with, he was theologically conservative and did not hesitate to assert his ascendancy in matters of dogma. This was vividly illustrated in his definition of the doctrine of Mary's Immaculate Conception as part of the Catholic faith in 1854, the dogma that the mother of Jesus was free of original sin, a matter of dispute since the Middle Ages. It was not surprising that the pontiff should have given the stamp of approval to the already flourishing cult of Marianism, but what was striking was that this was done on his authority alone. The subsequent appearance of the Virgin in an apparition at Lourdes four years later, announcing that 'I am the Immaculate Conception', served only to underpin the Pope's prescience and authority.[2] Sympathetic towards the emotive popular Catholicism of the mid-nineteenth century, the following year Pius promoted the cult of the Sacred Heart of Jesus, making this an official feast day of the clerical calendar and beatifying Marguerite-Marie Alacoque, the French seventeenth-century mystic and nun whose visions, created partly by eating cheese, had shaped its observances.

Additionally, Pius favoured a more general Romanisation of the liturgy, already noticeable in the 1830s, and reflected in the widespread use of the Roman missal in parishes throughout Europe. Its adoption was most enthusiastic in France, where it was in use by 1875, reflecting in part the energy of its champion, the Benedictine Dom Prosper Guéranger, and also the popular desire to replace the rather arid Jansenist rites of the eighteenth century.

In this swirl of saccharine devotion, the city of Rome blossomed as a centre of pilgrimage as never before. Much of the credit for this must go to Pius, but it also derived from the revived interest in Roman archaeology generally and the discoveries in the catacombs in particular. These were burial places, dating back to the Early Church, whose existence had been largely forgotten since the sixth century. Rediscovered in 1578, they were not excavated in any systematic way until the pontificates of Gregory XVI and Pius IX, the latter creating a Commission for Sacred Archaeology in 1852. Under the direction of the Jesuit Giuseppe Marchi and his protégé, Giovanni Battista De Rossi, 'Christian archaeology became Rome's very own science'.[3] This was at a time when, outside Germany, the intellectual clout of Catholicism was at a low ebb. De Rossi's writings provided the basis for a revival of interest in the history of early Christianity, and he himself always took a scrupulous scholarly approach towards his findings. Others, however, were inclined to read more into them than was justified by the facts. The catacombs became centres of pilgrimage, and parts of the bodies were removed and treated as saintly relics, a process assisted by the patronage of the popes themselves.

Most importantly, Rome's growth as a pilgrimage centre was inseparable from the personal popularity of Pius IX. He became a popular icon, the first Pope to have his picture widely displayed in Catholic households alongside plaster saints, a process facilitated by mass manufacturing techniques and the fact that Pius did not suffer from the physical deformities which had afflicted many of his predecessors. In large measure, Pius's appeal derived from his personality. While he might have mixed with intolerant and vituperative men, he himself was a genial, affable, snuff-taking individual, blessed with an easy manner and a good sense of humour, often playing practical jokes on his associates. His charisma communicated itself through a willingness to grant audiences to a wide range of personal visitors, whom he would entertain over a cup of tea, and pilgrims with whom he would regularly mingle. Although evidence remains impressionistic, several of these pilgrims, especially those from Spain and other especially devout areas, went to Rome in sympathy for the way in which Pius was being buffeted by the events of Italian unification (to be considered below), some no doubt worried that if they delayed their journey too long the eternal city would no longer be the centre of Catholicism. A few misguided souls even believed that if Cardinal Newman's Oxford Movement was to triumph, and to take the English back into the fold, then Britain might become the centre of the Catholic world just as it was the hub of economic and imperial activity.

Pius further contributed to the growth of Ultramontanism in that he was blessed with a long life, unlike so many of his forebears, the only Pope thus far to exceed the first apostle in years. Not only did this provide numerous opportunities for anniversaries and other celebrations, with Rome as their focus, it also enabled him to put his own men into post, thus creating a Church very much in his image, and the use of the very Italianate title 'Monsignor' only emphasised further their Roman sentiments. He appointed 122 cardinals, a greater number than any of his predecessors, several of whom would achieve a notoriety in their fight for Ultramontane principles. Apart from Manning, it is possible to cite Ledóchowski, the ambivalent leader of Polish resistance to the *Kulturkampf*; Gousset of Reims; Mathieu of Besançon; and Diepenbrock from Breslau. Together, these men constituted an Ultramontane party which included representatives throughout Europe: Cardinal Manning, Archbishop of Westminster, Louis Veuillot, editor of *L'Univers* between 1843 and his death in 1883 and Mgr George Talbot, the trusted, albeit mentally unstable, English confidant of Pio Nono. Like de Bonald and de Maistre some half a century earlier, the Ultramontane party's image of how the Church should be constituted was informed by a wide reading of history, but its interpretation of the past privileged the role of the pontiff above that of councils and other churchmen, and subordinated secular authority to papal direction. Moreover, it wielded an influence far greater than that of the early-nineteenth-century Romantics. Not only did Ultramontanes control influential sections of the press – for example, the Jesuit publication *Civiltà cattolica*, and *L'Univers* which Veuillot took into the reactionary camp – they were also well organised, exclusive and intolerant. As such, they readily indulged in the arts of black propaganda, not hesitating to impugn the character and motives of their opponents. Thus John Henry Newman, the famous English convert, was distrusted for his independent spirit and suspect theology, and was dismissed by Talbot as 'the most dangerous man in England', whose spirit was to be 'crushed'.[4]

It may appear paradoxical that Ultramontanism should have emerged victorious at a time when the Pope's temporal power was all but extinguished as a result of the unification of Italy, but it was precisely these events that shored up and consolidated the Ultramontane party. The build-up to unification has been extensively treated elsewhere and need not be rehearsed here. What should be stressed is that neither Cavour nor Napoleon III, when they met together in secret at Plombières in 1858, foresaw or wished for the disappearance of the Papal States. Both men, for different reasons, wanted the creation of a united Kingdom of Northern Italy comprising Piedmont-Sardinia and the territories of Lombardy and Venetia, both of which were under Austrian rule. Aware that the Pope would be unsettled by this re-arrangement, it was anticipated that he would be compensated with the presidency of a newly created Italian Confederation; in this regard, Napoleon III also hoped to win over Catholic opinion in France which he was bound to enrage by furthering Italian nationalism.

Nothing went to plan, events acquiring a dynamism of their own, leaving the papacy a hapless bystander, not least because its soldiers comprised Irish and Belgian volunteers who proved no match for the opposing forces. While

Napoleon III signed a truce with Austria in 1859, partly because he was so injured by Catholic criticism at home, the will of the Duchies of Parma and Modena to become part of the Piedmontese kingdom, the return to power of Cavour after a period out of office and the intervention of Garibaldi in the south eventuated in the creation of a Kingdom of Italy. Formally proclaimed in March 1861, this was ruled from the north, and included all of the peninsula bar Venetia, held by the Austrians, and Rome itself, protected by its French garrison which had been there since 1848. For many Romans, the stabilising effect of the French presence was no bad thing, for they had no wish to jeopardise the lucrative traffic in tourists; of the Papal States, only Bologna, always disaffected in its relationship with Rome, was delighted to slough off pontifical rule. There was no doubt, however, that the whole business dismayed Pius IX and the Catholic Church more generally. There was particular unease that the liberal constitution of Piedmont was now imposed willy-nilly through most of the peninsula, resulting in the confiscation of Church lands, the closure of monasteries and the secularisation of schooling. This was one of the many reasons why Catholics supported southern opposition to unification manifested in the so-called Brigand Wars of 1861–65. Even though Pius could take reassurance from the maintenance of the French garrison at Rome, which held off an attack from Garibaldi in 1867, and which was superior to the Irish volunteers whom he had correctly suspected of being prone to cheap Italian wine, Rome remained the ultimate prize of Italian nationalists, especially after Venetia became part of the kingdom following the Austro-Prussian war of 1866. So it was that Ultramontanes, faced with papal impotence in temporal matters, stressed the Pope's authority in the spiritual domain.

Since 1849 Ultramontanes, including Cardinal Pecci and the Jesuits associated with the *Civiltà cattolica*, had mooted the idea of some kind of statement which would both enhance papal authority and deal a body blow to liberalism. This notion surfaced again in 1859 when the city of Rome, and with it the pontiff's autonomy, seemed threatened by the wars of unification. A blueprint appeared from the pen of Bishop Gerbet, entitled *Instructions on the Errors of the Contemporary World*, which a commission adopted as the basis for review. This body laboured slowly and some hoped that its efforts would never see the light of day. Events conspired to force the issue. The application of Piedmontese religious legislation through most of the peninsula after 1861 led to alarmist conclusions that Ricasoli, Cavour's successor, wished to convert the Italian people to Protestantism. A second, and more important, episode was the international conference of liberal Catholics held at Malines in Belgium in 1863. This provided a platform for the movement's most articulate spokesman, Montalambert, to set out his agenda. Addressing an audience of over 3,000, he extolled the virtues of 'a free church in a free state', the same phrase that had been deployed by Cavour. To the delight of the many, and the disapproval of only a few, he argued that the Church in any particular country should no longer depend upon state power and financial wherewithal to sustain its activities. Catholics should especially dissociate themselves from reactionary regimes. Instead, they should be prepared to argue their case on equal terms with other denominations and those of no denomination at all. Toleration, even when this allowed error to exist, was preferable to intolerance. 'The bonfires lit by a Catholic hand horrify me just as much as the scaffolds on which Protestants have killed so many martyrs,' noted Montalambert.[5] Moreover, Catholics should not hesitate to involve themselves in the lives of the industrial classes. Such a message prompted Ultramontanes to demand that the Pope make an unequivocal stand, especially as Montalambert's words seemed to encourage others to speak out. That same year the influential German Professor Ignaz von Döllinger called for Catholic theologians to be allowed to follow the implications of their arguments without censure from episcopal authorities. And, finally, the actual timing of the long-promised papal pronunciation on pontifical authority was dictated by the renewed possibility of French withdrawal from Rome, something that had allegedly been discussed at a meeting between Napoleon III and the Italian government in September 1864. Yet again, Rome's physical independence seemed threatened, prompting an unambiguous statement of the pontiff's spiritual authority.

So it was that, in December 1864, the encyclical *Quanta cura* was published to which was appended the *Syllabus of Errors*, comprising eighty condemned propositions. The haste with which these were produced, under the pressure of events, was worthy of the speed with which Stalin drew up the first Five-Year Plan in the Soviet Union. Rather than working from first principles, the propositions had of necessity to be culled from a variety of existing encyclicals and pronouncements. This should have lessened their impact, and indeed there was much in the document with which the Catholic world was perfectly at ease. Proposition 5, which denounced the notion that Christ was a mythical figure – something recently argued in Ernst Renan's *Vie de Jésus* – was hardly contentious; nor was proposition 7 which affirmed the importance of revelation in conjunction with human reason. Later articles, especially 37 and 54, reasserted the primacy of the Pope over national churches, going on to denounce Gallicanism, materialism, Freemasonry and pantheism. It was the last group of statements (articles 77 to 80) which caused most astonishment. Herein, Pio Nono denied the freedom of non-Catholics to practise their religion and disavowed the call for the papacy 'to reconcile itself to progress, liberalism and recent civilisation'.

This final proposition, which was to cause so much furore, was in fact taken from the 1861 brief *Iamdudum cernimus* and referred explicitly to the Piedmontese constitution which had curtailed the freedoms of Church schools. This was not the context in which it was interpreted in 1864. Almost everywhere, it was seen as a wholesale rejection of liberal society and the modern world more generally. This was especially the case in Britain and the Netherlands. However much Catholics there attempted to persuade their compatriots that the Pope was not referring to the institutions of the British and Dutch states, the *Syllabus* appeared both absurd and offensive. Inevitably, there was a more chequered reaction in the Germanies. In Austria, where it will be recalled that a concordat had been signed in 1853 reversing much of the previous century's Josephinianism, the government was anxious lest it presaged clerical demands for yet further freedoms. Whereas the conservative theologians grouped around the University of Mainz applauded the rebuttal of atheism, their more liberal counterparts centred around Döllinger at Munich were mortified. It was in Italy and France that the *Syllabus* caused most reverberations. In the former it was banned throughout the peninsula and copies were burned in the streets of Naples; in the latter, it exacerbated the existing fissures within the Church. Recognising its potential to inflame the Ultramontane enthusiasms of their fellow prelates, and concerned by the rabid interpretation adopted by Veuillot's *L'Univers*, Bishops Darboy and Maret recommended that its publication should be prohibited, on the spurious grounds that it represented a condemnation of the imperial constitution. The government acquiesced in this point of view, especially since it was smarting from clerical criticism of its Mexican campaign, where an attempt to establish a Catholic empire under Maximilien was already running into trouble. Among liberal Catholics, Bishop Dupanloup used his very considerable skills as a polemicist to write a pamphlet, which went through thirty-six editions, nominally in defence of the *Syllabus*, but which actually sought to mitigate its worst effects and thus forestall an anti-clerical backlash. He argued that the *Syllabus* contained timeless and abstract truths but that these had always to be adapted to take account of contemporary circumstances. It was a masterly exercise in sleight-of-hand, a 'first-class verbal vanishing trick', as Montalambert famously referred to it, which earned Dupanloup the thanks of 636 bishops and ensured that liberal Catholicism, in France at least, received a stay of execution.

Just as the idea for the *Syllabus* had originated in the late 1840s, so too the notion of a general Church council had been mooted at the same time. The last such council had been held 300 years previously, at Trent, and there was an evident need to update Canon Law in the light of the social and other changes that had taken place in its aftermath. More importantly, a council was perceived as a means of reinforcing the Church and the papacy as a bulwark of the faith in an age of godlessness. A supplementary objective of the council, particularly dear to Pius, was the hope that such a body might bring to an end the schism that had long divided Rome from the Greek and Anglican faiths. Nevertheless, there was opposition, not least from within the Curia, and matters proceeded slowly. Outside events also caused delay, notably the Austro-Prussian War of 1866 and Garibaldi's incursion into the Papal States the following year. But on 29 June 1868, the bull *Aeterni patris* summoned the delegates to Rome, and the bull *Multiplices inter*, of 27 November 1869, indicated that the Pope himself intended to take a dominant part in the discussions. This was an early indicator that the question of papal infallibility, which had not initially been intended to figure prominently, was destined to be central. Conversely, the attempt to reconcile the differences between Catholicism and other Christian faiths was cack-handed from the outset, and an ecumenical opportunity was missed. Orthodox clergy were reminded that they needed to return to the faith in order to participate in the council;

Anglicans and other Protestants were told of their inevitable damnation as heretics; and while Pius offered to pay the expenses of bishops of the Eastern Rite who attended at Rome, he did not address an invitation directly to them, allowing this instead to be sent through intermediaries, thus emphasising their inferior status. In the event, 700 bishops, including sixty from the Eastern Rite and over 100 from America, did assemble for the First Vatican Council in December 1869, making it a truly international gathering, even though nearly three-quarters of the bureaucratic offices were occupied by Italians who also supplied the majority of the bishops. Meanwhile, freemasons, whose lodges Pius had earlier denounced as 'synagogues of Satan', assembled in Naples for a rival conference.

With the convoking of the Vatican Council, there was no avoiding the question of infallibility. In part, this was because the commissions charged with drawing up an agenda produced relatively little to discuss by way of pastoral endeavour or ecumenicalism. More critically, the dynamism of Ultra-montanism, and the weakness of papal temporal power, served to focus attention on the pontiff's spiritual authority, something which Pius himself had highlighted through the publication of the *Syllabus*. Accordingly, to have sidestepped this very issue would have been an impossibility, and the hard-line Ultramontanists were determined that papal jurisdiction should be defined in the most uncompromising of terms. Upon learning that a council was to be held, Archbishop Manning and Bishop Senestrey of Regensburg had vowed together 'to do all in our power to obtain the definition of papal infallibility'.[6] For their part, liberal Catholics feared that their very future within the Church was at stake and sought to mobilise opinion. Dupanloup called on Napoleon III to intervene; Döllinger rallied German and English public opinion. All this propaganda activity served to highlight yet again the extent of papal prerogatives.

Circumstances were not conducive to good debate. The participants assembled in the cavernous north transept of St Peter's where the acoustics were so poor that no one could be heard properly; eventually, proceedings were suspended for a month so that wooden partitions could be built to aid sound projection. Outside, the delegates were bombarded with polemical literature, some of which was based on leaked documents, for no one felt bound by the Pope's injunction to secrecy. It did not help matters that discussions were conducted in Latin, a language which representatives spoke with marked national accents and in which few were truly fluent, so inhibiting the cut and thrust of debate. Speakers more or less gave inaudible monologues, reflecting prepared positions which remained unaltered. Pius IX himself had intended to remain impartial, but was so angered by the liberal position, badly advanced by Montalambert and Dupanloup, that he came down on the side of the infallibilists who comprised the overwhelming majority. Few Catholics would have rejected out of hand the notion that the Pope could not err when teaching on matters of faith, yet the infallibilists pushed this position to extremes, urging that the Pope alone might make pronouncements which would then possess the force of declarations emanating from the whole

Church. Their opponents, represented by Maret and Dupanloup, together with many German and Austrian bishops, urged that such pronouncements needed the positive support of the entire Catholic community as expressed, for example, by a council or through the body of the bishops. A third grouping can also be identified, who have been labelled the 'inopportunists'. They simply thought that any discussion of infallibility was misplaced at that juncture, a time when many anti-clerical governments were on the warpath and the Church was itself divided on the issue; for them, any debate was likely to raise more problems than it would solve.

None of these groups was to be happy with the outcome. The inopportunists and anti-infallibilists could not withstand the pressure from Manning and others of his party to have the issue moved to the top of the agenda, yet the Archbishop and his men would not have it all their own way. The final decree, generally known from its first words as *Pastor aeternus*, was voted through on 18 July 1870 by 533 to 2, and even those two opposing votes may well have been mistakenly cast. Fifty-seven delegates had quit Rome the previous day to avoid voting against an issue to which the Pope had lent his personal backing. In essence, the dogmatic constitution revolved around two themes: the power and nature of the pontiff's primacy, and his infallible teaching office. It was the latter which grabbed the headlines and which provoked a flurry of debate, within both the Catholic and non-Catholic world, though the former was scarcely less significant in the long-term development of the Church.

The key wording in respect of papal primacy was thus:

> Hence we teach and declare that by the appointment of our Lord the Roman Church possesses a superiority of ordinary power over all other Churches, and that this power of jurisdiction of the Roman Pontiff, which is truly episcopal, is immediate; to which all, of whatever rite and dignity, both pastors and faithful, both individually and collectively, are bound, by their duty of hierarchical subordination and obedience, to submit not only in matters which belong to faith and morals, but also in those that appertain to the discipline and government of the Church throughout the world ... This is the teaching of Catholic truth, from which no-one can deviate without loss of faith and salvation.

Given the brusque manner in which other Christian bishops had been dealt with, the assertion of Roman primacy over all other Christian faiths was perhaps not surprising. Ecumenicalism for Rome meant a return to the true fold, and an admission of error; it did not involve any real compromise with Eastern Rite Catholics, Orthodox and Protestants. Second, the statement undercut centuries of debate within the Catholic Church about where authority was located. The papacy now claimed for itself disciplinary prerogatives over the bishops, stemming from Christ's original grant of authority to St Peter. This reflected Pius IX's own absolutist instincts which had already led to a steady erosion of episcopal autonomy. Henceforth, bishops would be regarded as mere lieutenants in the hierarchy of the Church, with the Pope as commander-in-chief. If the Pope had hoped that this uncompromising definition would be universally respected, he was to be sorely disabused; to this day, the parameters of papal and episcopal authority remain opaque, much depending on the willingness of an individual pontiff to assert his supremacy, as evidenced by the reign of John Paul II, for instance.

The second and better-known assertion, dealt with in chapter IV of *Pastor aeternus*, concerned the infallible teaching of the Roman pontiff. The key wording was as follows:

> That the Roman Pontiff, when he speaks *ex cathedra*, that is, when discharging the office of pastor and teacher of all Christians, by virtue of his supreme Apostolic authority, he defines a doctrine regarding faith or morals to be held by the universal Church, through the divine assistance promised to him in St Peter, is possessed of that infallibility with which the divine Redeemer willed that his Church should be endowed for defining doctrine regarding faith and morals.

This text was to be wildly misinterpreted, especially by those who had no love for the Church. It certainly claimed an authority for the pontiff when teaching on matters of faith and morals, which, like his disciplinary powers, derived from Christ's grant of authority to Peter. However, that authority was not limitless. First, the Pope was infallible only when speaking from his throne and addressing particular questions of doctrine and morality; he was not, for instance, infallible when speaking on matters of fact or politics, nor when he made a chance remark or intervened in a debate. Second, in a key phrase, his statements 'have authority from themselves, and not by virtue of the agreement of the Church'. This form of words was designed to rebut those who had argued that papal teachings were infallible only when they had been accepted by the whole Church, a position adopted in the Gallican Articles of 1682 and which was still defended by Maret. Uncompromising though this was, it did not go as far as the infallibilists wished, for this statement said nothing about how the Pope arrived at his definitions and did not preclude the possibility that he might consult other agencies. In the event, successive popes have been chary of explicitly invoking the doctrine of infallibility, only doing so on one occasion, in 1950, on the question of the Assumption.

Nor was it until the twentieth century that the First Vatican Council was formally brought to a close when, in 1962, high-ranking ecclesiastics once more assembled at Rome, this time to update the teaching, morality and discipline of the Church in the face of yet further recent social developments. The First Council was adjourned indefinitely, having completed only two out of fifty-one documents, because of the Franco-Prussian War of 1870, which necessitated the withdrawal of the French garrison in Rome to meet Bismarck's assault at Sedan. So it was that the frail Pius IX was confronted with repeating his flight of November 1848, but at the age of seventy-eight he had no appetite for an uncertain foreign venture and, like his unfortunate predecessor, Pius VI, wanted to die in Rome. The pontiff had hoped that some other friendly power would rush to fill the place vacated by the French, but in the event none was forthcoming; not even good Catholic states, including Bavaria, Spain or the new dual monarchy of Austria-Hungary, had the wherewithal, diplomatic *nous* or the stamina to take on a difficult and limitless commitment. Almost to the last, Pius believed that no regular army would dare attack the Holy City, but he had not reckoned with Victor Emmanuel, who calculated that if Rome was not incorporated into a united Italy then his own position as monarch would be uncertain. Accordingly, on 20 September 1870, the city was occupied by the King's troops, only to find that the Pope had locked himself into the Vatican. The following month, a plebiscite was held which endorsed the incorporation of Rome into a united Italy. It was at this point that Pius suspended the Vatican Council and, for good measure, excommunicated all those who had played a hand in the capture of the Holy City. Only such a sentence was thought appropriate, given the manner in which 1,500 years of papal temporal rule in Rome had been abruptly terminated. As Pius IX himself thundered, 'barrels of holy water would be needed to wash away the profanation of the Quirinal', the papal summer residence in which the King of Italy was installed.[7]

In practice, relations between the Vatican and the Kingdom of Italy would settle into a *modus vivendi*, but there was no hiding papal displeasure at the way in which anti-clerical legislation now ran rampant throughout the peninsula. The nature of Church–state relations will be discussed below, as will the ways in which other states, notably the German Empire, used the doctrine of infallibility as a stick with which to beat Catholics. Three other developments, however, must be noted at this juncture. The first was the emergence of the so-called 'Old Catholics'. Within Germany, some academics and theologians, as well as members of the middle classes, rejected the version of papal authority enunciated at the First Vatican Council, albeit reluctantly, a fact underscored by the refusal of the leading protester and pre-eminent theologian Döllinger formally to join the Old Catholic Church. Small numbers of Catholics in Switzerland and Austria also constituted 'Old Catholic' communities, achieving some semblance of unity when in 1889 they accepted the Declaration of Utrecht as the doctrinal basis of their sect, thus aligning themselves with the Church of Utrecht which had split from Rome in 1724 (see above). While this schism, involving several leading theologians, was a setback, and necessitated some administrative overhaul of the German bishoprics, the 'Old Catholic' movement was always an elitist phenomenon, and the vast majority of believers remained within the fold, sympathetic to the treatment suffered by Pius IX and offended by the propaganda campaign (*Kulturkampf*) which Bismarck launched against Catholicism.

A second group of believers who were positively alienated by the doctrine of infallibility were the Eastern Rite Catholics. Their diversity and independence had always been particularly irksome to Ultramontanes, for whom uniformity of liturgy and creed was as significant as unity of faith. Rome had repeatedly sought to undermine their autonomy, intervening in episcopal elections and synods, for example, and culminating in the issue of the bull *Reversurus* in 1867. This chastised churches of the Eastern Rite for their schismatic potential and revised their administrative structures. The reaction to this text was mixed, but generally hostile. The maladroit manner in which the

Eastern Rite bishops were then invited to the Vatican Council merely added insult to injury. It is small wonder that the Eastern Rite contingent was among those fifty-seven bishops who chose to leave Rome before the crucial vote was taken in 1870. It took the soothing overtures of Leo XIII (1878–1903), Pius's successor, who appreciated the value of the unique characteristics of the Churches of the Eastern Rite, to ameliorate relations between them and Rome.

The third immediate consequence of the doctrine of infallibility was to enfold the Catholic Church yet further in the cloak of conservative reaction. It was a millstone around the necks of liberal Catholics as they sought to come to terms with the forces of secularisation. Yet such an accommodation was of vital importance given that temporal rulers throughout Europe pos- sessed the upper hand in Church–state relations, and given that they were increasingly prepared to discriminate against Catholics in ways not witnessed since the French Revolution. It would be easy to blame Pius for putting the Church into an intellectual straitjacket which prevented it from responding to these challenges, yet it should be recalled that the Pope was merely echoing views of his predecessors, and was reacting to the wishes of an articulate and vociferous Ultramontane party which saw compromise of any sort as a weakness and a betrayal.

Identity and Nationalism: the Anti-Catholic Onslaught

In 1875, the English Jesuit Gerard Manley Hopkins was moved to return to his earlier passion for poetry following dramatic events in Germany. In one of his most moving poems, 'The Wreck of the *Deutschland*', he commemorated the death by drowning of five Franciscan nuns hounded out of their native Germany by Bismarck's *Kulturkampf*. The fate of these unfortunate sisters was unique, yet in large areas of Europe Catholics were coming under fire from the state, abetted by secular agencies. Although the rhythm of this persecution varied geographically, chronologically and in intensity during the period up to 1914, there was no doubt in the minds of churchmen that they were witnessing an onslaught reminiscent of those perpetrated by the French Revolution and the pagan emperors of Rome; they could not foresee what the twentieth century would bring in terms of religious persecution.

While there was a degree of hyperbole in such comparisons, something fundamental had indeed changed. At the beginning of the nineteenth century, it could no longer be assumed that there would be an established church and a state religion, yet there remained an assumption that the state would be broadly sympathetic towards, or at least tolerant of, Christianity. This was no longer true after the 1870s, principally because the nature of the state itself had altered.

In what senses was this true? The most obvious way was in the emergence of new polities on a scale unprecedented since 1815, which had the subsidiary effect of tilting the religious balance of power yet further to the Protestant camp. These new states comprised the Dual Monarchy of the Austro- Hungarian Empire in 1867, formed in the aftermath of Habsburg humiliation;

the North German Confederation, created in the same year, which gave way to the German Empire of 1871 under the domination of Prussia; the Liberal State in Italy of 1871; and the Third Republic within France, constitutionally consolidated in 1875. Given the strength of nationalism and the weakness of the Ottoman and Austro-Hungarian empires, there also remained the potential for the formation of yet more entities in the Balkans. Even Spain and Portugal dallied with anti-clerical regimes in the period up to 1914. What many of these new polities had in common, with the partial exception of the Austro-Hungarian possessions, was the wish of the state to establish an identity. This would satiate nationalist opinion, counter the threat of foreign encroachment, especially acute in the case of Germany which had alienated all of its neigh-bours in the process of unification, and inculcate a sense of loyalty among the populations thus transforming them from subjects into citizens who could be relied upon, above all, to bear arms when required.

Religion could comprise a significant element of identity, as it already did in well-established states such as the Scandinavian kingdoms and the Iberian monarchies. Protestantism was especially suited to play this role as it retained Gallican characteristics and possessed a willingness to adapt to modern circum-stances. In the hands of the late-nineteenth-century Tsars, even the Orthodox faith served as a rallying point. It was by no means impossible for Catholicism to make a similar contribution, as it did in the cases of Polish and Irish nationalism, but in the new political units of Italy, Germany and France it was now perceived by governments as a bar to a common identity, precisely because its loyalties transcended national boundaries. The development of Ultramontanism, culminating in the declaration of infallibility, had served only to sharpen perceptions of Catholicism as a transnational faith whose adherents owed primary allegiance to the Bishop of Rome rather than to the nation or the nation-state.

The other distinguishing feature of these new states, which impinged unfavourably on the Catholic Church, was that they all, to a greater or lesser degree, adopted mass politics through the use of near-universal male suffrage and representative institutions, leaving Russia and the Ottoman Empire as the only unreconstructed autocracies in Europe. Mass politics allowed oppor-tunities for a minority of individuals, principally middle-class liberals and radicals, to take up the reins of government, at both a local and national level, politicians who were frequently secular in outlook, having imbibed a heady mix of positivist, materialist, scientific and economic literature. These men were no friends of the Church, and a shared anti-clericalism often brought liberals and radicals together when they could not agree on other matters. In their eyes, Catholicism was a hindrance to economic progress and, in the aftermath of the *Syllabus of Errors*, was considered dangerous to those liberal and democratic ideals upon which they wished to build a new society. Most importantly, the Church had set itself implacably against the new political order in Italy, Germany and France. It was small wonder, then, that in these states governments would attack the Church in those walks of life where it was purportedly at its most influential, notably elementary schooling, the control of property and appointments, and in the shaping of the everyday habits and rituals of the population.

The remaining transformation in the nature of the state concerned the extent and character of its activities, in particular its relationship to the individual citizen. Governments, impelled by the need to cope with burgeoning industrialisation and its concomitant social problems, anxious to enhance economic efficiency, ever fearful of popular unrest, and alarmed by the founding of socialist parties and trade unions, increasingly involved themselves in measures of social welfare, economic regulation, medical care and education. In this process, the state frequently came into conflict with the Church which had hitherto enjoyed a pre-eminence in philanthropic and charitable initiatives and, in the guise of Social Catholicism, was making a very real contribution to an understanding of modern life. Even in under-industrialised states such as Spain, the Church still made great efforts in the realm of charity. For instance, in Bilbao an Institute of Guardian Angels was set up during the 1890s to look after those peasant women who had come to the city in search of work. Conceivably, then, Church and state might have worked together in the social domain, particularly as both had a vested interest in seeing off the challenge of socialism. All too often, however, the Church was at a disadvantage because of its continuing hostility to the political regimes, and the reluctance of ecclesiastical hierarchies to embrace the tenets of Social Catholicism.

Through the above developments, states became ever more secular in outlook and practice, a process that is especially associated with France, often described under the Third Republic as the anti-clerical state *par excellence*, but it was actually in the German Empire that the most dramatic events occurred. There had already been drama aplenty in the German states. In 1867 Protestant Prussia, impelled by Bismarckian diplomacy, economic prowess, popular nationalism and rivalry with the Habsburgs, formed the North German Con-federation, having defeated Austria the previous year. Effectively, Prussia had now achieved leadership inside Germany, excluding Austria and the southern states, notably Bavaria, whose Catholic populations were viewed as inimical to a sense of national belonging. It proved necessary, however, to incorporate the southern territories in 1871, in the aftermath of the Franco-Prussian War, because their allegiance could not be depended upon. Though the federal constitution of the new German Empire guaranteed Prussian hegemony, it was troubling to Berlin that over a third of the Reich's population were now Catholic. To those in the Rhineland and the Polish territories had been added co-religionaries in south Germany and, in lesser numbers, in the former French provinces of Alsace-Lorraine.

Bismarck, whose position as Chancellor was critical to the formation of policy, especially mistrusted these newcomers. Possessed of an individual piety, and a nominal Lutheran, he was sceptical of organised religion, above all of Catholicism, which he regarded as hopelessly reactionary, obscurantist and divisive. To a point, Bismarck was prepared to live with the diversity of denominations, but he suspected the Rhinelanders for their associations with

France, Bavarians for their separatist aspirations, and was wholly intolerant of the Poles who used Catholicism to assert their independence. As Trzecia-kowski notes, the convergence of religion and nationalism in Prussian Poland made for an explosive mixture.[8] At a time when Bismarck desired to protect the integrity of the German Empire from international aggression, Catholics thus constituted a fifth column.

Bismarck's prejudices were compounded by three episodes in 1870. The first was the proclamation of papal infallibility in October, which threatened the national integrity he was keen to foster in the aftermath of unification. For him, loyalty was owed to the Kaiser not to the Bishop of Rome. Second, the establishment of Catholic trade unions, which gathered together for their founding conference in 1870, raised further doubts about Catholic allegiances. Socialism was, of course, the other enemy akin to Catholicism in its trans-national appeal. It is no surprise that severely restrictive anti-socialist legislation went hand-in-hand with the *Kulturkampf* in a futile attempt to stem the growth of the Social Democratic Party (SPD). The final event was the creation in October of the Zentrum, a Catholic Centre Party. Drawing on a tradition of Catholic mobilisation, notably the so-called Katholikentage, or Congresses, which had met since 1848, the initial intention of this embryonic organisation was not to build a confessional body, but merely to send deputies to the new federal parliament in Berlin who would defend the interests of Catholics by asserting individual liberties more generally. Under the inspired leadership of the physically unprepossessing Ludwig Windthorst, the Zentrum won no fewer than fifty-eight seats in the first elections, proved a skilful player in the coalition politics of the Reichstag and enjoyed widespread Catholic approval, particularly among the lower classes.

This dismayed not just Bismarck but those bourgeois liberals who had supported unification and who regarded Protestantism as the only faith capable of protecting individual liberties and moving with the times. From their perspective, the new Germany was a product of Protestant initiative and resourcefulness, and this stood imperilled by the Catholic counter-culture, typically characterised as 'backward', 'stagnant' or a 'brake on civilisation'. In 1862, Daniel Schenkel, subsequently a founder of the Protestant Association, captured this mood perfectly, declaring, 'the entire cultural progress of peoples in our century is based on the foundation of religious, moral and intellectual freedom, and for that reason upon Protestantism'.[9] Such sentiments were echoed by a speaker at an assembly at Worms in 1868, held to commemorate Luther, who declared: 'We Protestants taking our stand on the Christian Spirit, on German patriotism and on civilization, reject all hierarchic claims intended to lead us back to Rome.'[10] So it was that the *Kulturkampf* was not merely the product of Bismarckian *realpolitik*, which aimed to appease enemies at abroad and persecute them at home, but reflected deep-rooted antagonisms which had been exacerbated by the process of unification.

The *Kulturkampf*, which took its name from an off-the-cuff remark by the free-thinking scientist, Rudolf Virchow, persisted throughout much of the 1870s. Virchow had coined the phrase to depict the struggle between two cultures, that of the modern and that of a regressive clericalism. Bismarck avoided the term, since, as we have seen, his aim was to test the loyalty of German Catholics, not to alienate them. It was, though, a very real struggle. As Owen Chadwick has remarked, it was one that operated on different levels.[11] In a sense, it involved a diplomatic war of words with Rome, which culminated in the recall of German diplomatic representation after Pius IX balked at Bismarck's nomination of Cardinal Hohenlohe as the Prussian ambassador; he happened to be a disciple of Döllinger and a private critic of infallibility. Another dimension was its attack upon Poles, the majority of whom were Catholic and were fiercely determined to raise their children in the Polish language. Trouble quickly brewed in Polish schools in Poznan and Silesia where teachers were reluctant to conduct classes in German, something which was banned by the Polish Archbishop, Ledóchowski. Ironically, Ledóchowski had been made Archbishop for Gniezno-Poznan at the request of the Prussian authorities, and he acted initially to remove the clergy from public life and nationalist agitation, forbidding them from participation in elections, for example, stopping the holding of patriotic demonstrations in churches and outlawing the singing of '*Boze coś Polske*' ('Father, You who have defended Poland') during services. But the closure of the seminary at Poznan and the compulsory use of German was too much for him and he felt obliged to protest. His consequent imprisonment in 1874 turned this lukewarm nationalist into a national hero. He languished in confinement for over twenty-four months before being turfed out of Germany, retreating to Rome. Pius IX, in an act of deliberate provocation, had conferred on him the purple the year previously. Ledóchowski would be joined in prison by other distinguished ecclesiastics, including Archbishop Melchers of Cologne and Bishop Martin of Paderborn, who had challenged the laws initiated by the new *Kulturminister*, Adalbert Falk, a Lutheran lawyer and skilled civil servant.

So began the major phase in the *Kulturkampf*, the so-called Falk Laws. In March 1872, all schools in Germany, whether public or private, were opened to scrutiny by state inspectors, whose ranks had been purged of Catholics. In 1873, the so-called May Laws stipulated that all clergy should possess a university degree, that the state had a right of veto over all clerical appointments, that papal discipline no longer extended over clerics and that seminaries were open to state supervision. Particularly galling was the introduction of civil marriage, always a cause of tension, and the Pulpit Law which left preachers open to prosecution and circumscribed the content of their sermons. A further tranche of legislation followed in 1875. This expelled all members of religious orders unless they were in charge of hospitals – the Jesuits had already been booted out of the new Germany – and legislation favouring the 'Old Catholics' was enacted, giving them the right to bury their dead in Catholic cemeteries, for instance. Pius IX responded by pronouncing the May Laws to be without effect, and one Catholic even took a potshot at Bismarck, but many clerics adopted a dignified stand of passive resistance which more often than not led to their imprisonment and loss of stipend. In 1875 alone, over 100 priests had been locked up or sent abroad. The final element of the

Kulturkampf was designed to make life difficult for the Zentrum, yet its electoral strength only burgeoned in the aftermath of the May Laws.

Thanks to the *Kulturkampf*, dioceses were left without bishops (a mere three were occupied at one point), and over 1,400 parishes, or around one-third of the total, were left without priests, but overall the campaign must be judged a failure. Despite their badgering by the government, the bishops, exemplified by the vigorous Archbishop Ketteler of Mainz, responded with dignity, firmness and shrewdness. Clergy and parishioners were bound more closely together as a result of the persecution, something which had not been the intention of the authorities. In an echo of the popular response to French dechristianisation in the 1790s, congregations gathered in the open air to celebrate mass, several members of religious orders abandoned the use of clerical dress but maintained their religious lifestyle, and pilgrimages enjoyed an unprecedented popularity, especially among women, implying a continued feminisation of religiosity. In the aftermath of the Napoleonic wars, a mere 36,000 people annually had visited the Marian shrine at Kevelaer close to Holland; in 1872, almost half a million attended. The shrine at Marpingen, the 'German Lourdes' as it was popularly known, attracted over 20,000 pilgrims in 1876. Alongside such pilgrimages was the spectacular growth of *Vereine*, local confraternities, cycling clubs, football teams and other societies which, at the turn of the century, included at least one-third of all Catholics, a figure that was even higher in the strongly devout areas of the Ruhr and the Rhineland. Equally impressive was the growth in support for the Zentrum. It has been calculated that in 1874 some 45 per cent of German Catholics (representing 56 per cent of the votes cast) were for the Centre Party which won ninety-one seats. The Zentrum would thus be critical in maintaining a Catholic political presence in Germany right up to 1914, no mean feat given the myriad of political parties that existed in Wilhelmine Germany. Although it lost votes to the SPD in working-class districts of Cologne and Düsseldorf, in 1907 once again the Centre Party garnered 45 per cent of all Catholic votes cast. To compound matters, the Bismarckian assault on the Church incurred not only domestic resistance, but opposition from abroad. Even Protestant states such as Britain, which had initially been enthusiastic about the legislation, expressed doubts, as did France which condemned the imprisonment of senior clerics.

Historians agree that, while Bismarck possessed uncanny political agility in so many of his foreign and domestic policies, his war on the Catholics was ill-judged and self-defeating, something which he himself eventually acknowledged, albeit not publicly. Eager to save face, by 1877 the Chancellor was looking for ways to tone down the legislation. His opportunity came the following year with the death of his venerable opponent, Pius IX, and the succession of Leo XIII, an ardent conservative but one who was nevertheless eager to build bridges, even hoping that Germany might assist him in recovering Rome. So it was that secret negotiations were conducted between Berlin and the Vatican in the period 1878–80. While these produced no instant tangible gains for the Church, in the next three years a series of discretionary measures were passed which took the sting out of the Falk legislation, culminating in the so-called Peace Laws of 1886 and 1887 which moderated the institutional secularism of the *Kulturkampf.* What remained of the ill-judged crusade was the state oversight of schools, civil marriage, the restrictions on critical sermons and the ban on the Jesuits who were not allowed to return until 1917, measures which the Church could live with. Theoretically, the state still possessed enormous jurisdiction over the Church, but given the unhappy experience of Bismarck, the mobilisation of the Zentrum, the skilful diplomacy of the episcopacy and, to a lesser extent, the watchful eye of the Vatican, Church–state relations achieved a *modus vivendi.* Bismarck's successors diluted the legislation still further, permitting the return of expelled orders, avoiding involvement in episcopal appointments; even Polish Catholics were granted concessions. Grateful for these temporising moves, the Zentrum itself became less oppositionist under the new leadership of Ernst Lieber. While there remained unease at the government's welfare legislation and its discrimination against trade unions which would cause division within the party, thus blunting its effectiveness in the Reichstag and resulting in an identity crisis, there was support for the expansionist naval policy of Wilhelm II enabling the group to slough off charges that it lacked patriotism.

Nevertheless, the long-term effects of the *Kulturkampf* were significant. A Catholic subculture had already begun to emerge following the introduction of universal suffrage in 1867, but it was crucially shaped by the struggles of the 1870s and 1880s. Not only had a confessional bloc come into being by 1873 which would endure until the Weimar Republic, but German Catholicism had also been democratised and laicised to a remarkable degree, through the spread and empowerment of lay forms of Catholic association. Bishops, harassed by the government, and cut off in some instances from their sees, had to cede authority to the lower clergy and to lay men and women. And papal authority, too, had been challenged by German Catholics, reflecting the confidence of those on the spot that they knew better how to handle the situation than did the pontiff, thus further enhancing the democratic roots of German Catholic organisation. Justifying his party's decision to ignore papal instructions on the Military Bill, Windthorst commented that 'the Centre Party subsists simply and solely on the confidence of the people ... it is required, therefore ... to heed the pulsebeat of the people'.[12]

The *Kulturkampf* was not merely a German phenomenon. Bismarck attempted to export his crusade to the Netherlands, Belgium, Luxembourg and Switzerland as part of an effort to surround his predominantly Protestant German Empire with sympathetic states who likewise viewed Catholicism as an enemy both within and without. This diplomatic *démarche* largely failed, both because the required ingredients were missing and because of the effective opposition put up by local churches. In Luxembourg, where Church affairs had been placed under the rule of an independent apostolic vicar in 1840, the late 1870s witnessed some half-hearted measures to regulate Catholic schools, but the refusal to implement Article 26 of the 1848 Constitution, which regulated the religious orders, meant that the Duchy, much to the chagrin of Bismarck, and later to the disappointment of republicans in France, became a refuge for exiled religious. In the Netherlands, there was an attempt to emulate French, rather than German anti-clerical legislation against schools, but this foundered thanks to the combined opposition of both Calvinists and Catholics, determined to maintain their parochial establishments. Similarly, in Belgium the campaign failed to ignite. Here, liberals, who took charge of government in 1878, viewed Catholicism as a threat to democratic gains and regarded the influence which the Church exercised in education as an obstacle to progress. So it was that the Belgian *Kulturkampf* resulted in the abolition of catechetical teaching in municipal schools, but this campaign quickly ran out of steam when, in 1884, Catholics won back political power. Thereafter, the rise of Belgian socialism, and with it the demand for universal suffrage, ensured that liberals and Catholics had much in common in resisting the left-wing threat.

It was in Switzerland that the *Kulturkampf* made greatest headway. Here, of course, the war of the Sonderbund had bequeathed a bitter religious legacy, and Protestants recoiled with horror at the declaration of infallibility and the consequent excommunication of Döllinger, and were prepared to provide a refuge for 'Old Catholics'. There were also those within Switzerland itself who were not prepared to accept infallibility and who formed the so-called Christ-katolische in 1873 comprising some 12,000 members. By and large, however, the Swiss Catholic Church accepted papal prerogatives, the Bishop of Basle using the weapon of excommunication against clerics who defied the encyclical *Quanta cura*. It was this assertion of Roman authority that prompted the Protestant cantons to press ahead with their long-cherished aim of a more centralised and efficient Switzerland which would, of necessity, undermine the autonomy and alleged obscurantism of the Catholic districts. As historians have emphasised, the scenes of religious conflict were to be most apparent in French-speaking areas, where religious orders were forcibly expelled; Bishop Lachat of Basle was run out of his diocese. Such episodes hardened yet further the religious divide within Switzerland, but the *Kulturkampf* ended before that in Germany. Just as in Bismarck's Reich, Catholics proved themselves to be extremely adaptable, importing French priests from the Jura to conduct ceremonies and, once again, Leo XIII showed himself to be an able conciliator, unwilling to provoke the dominant Protestant cantons in the manner of Pius IX. For their part, Swiss Protestants came to understand that they had initiated a campaign that could never truly succeed, and, given their liberal upbringing, they were never entirely comfortable at the rescinding of individual rights.

Across the Alps, in the newly united Italy, Bismarck likewise encouraged a *Kulturkampf*, not that the government there needed any outside urging. That said, immediately after the establishment of Rome as the new capital, the regime did not feel sufficiently confident to attack the Church openly, and was anxious lest any further harassing of Pius IX provoked foreign intervention. This concern led in 1871 to the Law of Guarantees, designed to place Church–state relations on a new and stable footing. This was, in many senses, a benevolent settlement, and one very similar to that offered by Cavour to Pius IX in 1861. The Pope, despite the loss of his temporal powers, was to be treated as a sovereign, retaining his own militia, postal and telegraphic services. Additionally, he was granted uninhibited use of the Vatican, the Lateran Palace and the Cancellaria, together with his summer retreat at Castel Gandolfo, although in none of these instances did he enjoy ownership. To maintain his comfortable lifestyle, the state agreed to pay him the sum of over 3 million *lira* per annum, free of taxation and in perpetuity. Although the *placet* and the *exequatur* were ended, Pius was recompensed. The state handed back to the Pope the control of episcopal appointments, some 237 in number, higher than in any other European country, although government still retained a right of veto. This had dual implications. On the one hand, it led to the appointment of men who were relatively well disposed towards the government. On the other, it meant that the Italian Church, hitherto extremely regionalised and local, began to take on a more national character and that, outside the peninsula, aspiring episcopal candidates were aware of the need to court the Pope's favours. In this way, the Law of Guarantees further facilitated the development of Ultramontanism.

Pius himself, however, was extremely disgruntled, and denounced the law in his encyclical of May 1871, *Ubi nos arcano*. This response imperilled the Vatican's finances, and was a rejection of the popular will as expressed in the overwhelming parliamentary support for the Law of Guarantees but, to the Vatican, accepting this legislation was tantamount to acknowledging what it still regarded as an illegal regime and placed the future of the Holy See in the hands of unstable party politics. In practice, Pius had little choice but to accept the provisions of the law and his early refusal served only to heighten anti-clerical feeling, both in government and at a popular level. St Peter's Square soon became a boxing ring for intermittent fights between papal supporters and radicals who, in 1872, provocatively placed a bust of Mazzini in the Capitol. Government chose a more legalistic path, imposing Piedmontese restrictive legislation on the activities of monks and nuns, sequestering religious houses which occupied one-fifth of land in Rome alone as well as conniving at local persecution of individual orders, such as the Poor Clares at the convent of Polla, where the municipality engineered a noisy and disruptive building programme adjacent to the house in the hope of hastening the deaths of the elderly sisters. In 1874, civil marriage was introduced in Rome and a divorce law was canvassed; in 1876, a bill similar to the German Pulpit Law was mooted which would have banned any political campaigning in sermons; and resentment festered over the Pope's continuing refusal to rescind his 1868 decree, *Non expedit*, forbidding Catholics to participate in political life. Much of this guerrilla warfare could have been avoided if the Vatican had accepted the Law of Guarantees at the outset. This might have persuaded governments, at least moderate ones, against pursuing the course they did. With the benefit of hindsight, Pius should have perceived that his spiritual authority no longer depended upon his temporal independence.

Although the fire of the *Kulturkampf* in Italy died down thanks in part to the deaths of both Pius IX and Victor Emmanuel II in 1878, up to 1915 friction was never far from the surface. Leo XIII still hankered after some partial restoration of the Papal States, and Rome itself became a symbolic battleground for European as well as Italian ideologues. Paradoxically, the capital became as much a pilgrimage centre for proselytising atheists and agnostics as for Catholics. In one of the best-known episodes, in 1889 the Radicals, supported by the national government, put up a statue of the Dominican Giordano Bruno, a leading figure of the Renaissance, whose unconventional views of Christianity had led to his execution at the stake, a commemoration that was attended by a crowd of 6,000 atheists drawn from throughout Europe. Leo was so personally offended that he contemplated quitting Rome altogether, a possibility that troubled the Crispi government. The occupancy of Rome would dog religious politics up to the First World War, and hampered any real chance of a reconciliation between the Pope and national government, despite the fact that both parties had a shared concern in combating the growth of socialism and radical politics. It was a fear of the left that led Pius X (1903–14) to relax the *Non expedit*, in the wake of the 1904 general strike, to ensure that Catholics voted for liberals and clerico-moderates as opposed to socialists, thus ensuring the hegemony of the liberals up to the outbreak of the First World War.

If in Italy the fires of a *Kulturkampf* never blew up into a full-scale inferno, the same was not true in France, where institutionalised secularism became more entrenched than anywhere else in Europe. Whereas the assaults on the Church elsewhere were sporadic, even in Germany, in France they were far more concerted, meaning that the religious question was never far below the surface of national politics before 1914. Broadly speaking, it is possible to identify two key phases in the French experience: the educational and social legislation of the 1880s and the anti-monastic laws of the early 1900s, which culminated in the separation of Church and state in 1905.

To comprehend the first episode, it is necessary to dwell on the political developments of the 1870s, when a Third Republic had been created out of the French defeat at Sedan. In its early phase, this new regime was dominated by monarchist deputies, Legitimist and Orléanist, who were eager for a restoration and who were keen to indulge the Church, which itself sided with the cause of royalism. There had been dismay at the civil unrest of the Paris Commune, in essence a patriotic response to the military defeat, infused with vague socialist and republican aspirations, which had proved unable to temper revolutionary excesses, including the shooting of Archbishop Darboy of Paris. For many Catholics, defeat at the hands of the Prussians and the emergence of the Commune were interpreted as divine punishment for national transgressions, particularly the maladroit foreign policy of Napoleon III, which had endangered the temporal power of the papacy, and the anti-clerical tone of the Second Empire's later educational legislation, which had been a far cry from the Falloux Law of 1850. The building of the Basilica of the Sacred Heart at Montmartre, overlooking Paris, was designed to seek God's forgiveness. The monarchists, however, were not to seize their chance. Internally divided, lacking credible contenders for the throne, and without any popular mandate, they lost the initiative and were too frightened to launch a *coup d'état* to fulfil their ambitions. So it was that the Republic was placed on a constitutional footing after 1875, and in the next four years republicans came to displace the monarchist majority in the lower house of the National Assembly.

These republicans, dominated by a group known as the Opportunists, were a far cry from the firebrands of the 1790s: they were moderate men, prudent with respect to government spending, keen on high tariffs and wary of radical social agendas. They were none the less imbued with a sense of Positivism (see below), a belief in state efficiency and the need to create a national identity, and eager to found political stability. In their eyes, the Catholic Church, with its obscurantist beliefs and its overtly royalist sympathies, was an obstacle to the attainment of these goals. It was in this context that, in 1880, the Opportunists reversed the so-called 'moral order' of the previous decade; in that year, Jesuits were expelled from France; in 1881, state elementary schooling was made free in a piece of legislation which clearly disadvantaged private Catholic schools since they were unable to compete financially; in 1882, the free-thinking Minister of Education, Jules Ferry, banned the teaching of the catechism in state-school premises; and, in 1886, the so-called *loi Goblet* prohibited religious orders from teaching in state schools, their places to be taken by a band of *instituteurs*, the notorious 'black hussars' of the Third Republic, who had been tutored in the severe and profoundly secular atmosphere of the training colleges known as *écoles normales*.

Accompanying this assault on Church influence within education, the Republic placed its own men in positions of civil authority, introduced liberal laws such as that making divorce easier, and gave the whole of government a profoundly secular tone. 'Marianne' became the symbol of the new regime, and in 1879 the blood-curdling 'Marseillaise' was adopted as the national anthem. The secular state organised lavish funerals to honour the republican dead – Louis Blanc, Léon Gambetta, Victor Hugo, Jules Ferry and many others – in events which were deliberately civic and non-religious in ritual. Whereas a minority of liberal Catholics, such as Albert de Mun and Jacques Piou, believed it was necessary for French Catholics to reconcile themselves with the Republic and work within it to control anti-clerical excesses, the majority of the hierarchy and priesthood still refused to acknowledge this new order as the legitimate government of France. They remained perplexed as to why their flock, especially the peasantry, voted republican at elections, failing to comprehend that they did so because in other areas of life the Republic was regarded as a moderate and temperate one, with its finger on the pulse of provincial France.

The Vatican was also dismayed at the turn of events and, astonishingly, was still hopeful that a French government might be persuaded to restore the Pope's temporal powers in Rome. Pius IX would never have reconciled himself to a republic, but his successor Leo XIII came to recognise in the course of the 1880s that one was here to stay, and although he would have preferred a restoration, he acknowledged this as wholly unrealistic. His new Secretary of State, the Sicilian Mariano Rampolla dell Taro, was of a like mind, and it may well be that this subtle change in the papal position communicated itself to the French episcopacy, at least to the maverick Archbishop of Algiers, Cardinal Lavigerie, who in 1890 proposed the famous toast in which he urged his dumbfounded audience of French naval officers to accept the constitution of the Republic. This instigated the so-called *Ralliement* of the 1890s, which attempted to engender more harmonious relations between Church and state. In 1892, Leo XIII did his bit by publishing the encyclical *Au milieu des sollicitudes*, directed specifically to French Catholics, urging them to make their peace with the republican regime.

The *Ralliement*, however, proved a failure. Whereas the Ultramontanes had been happy when the Pope's message coincided with their own prejudices, they were far less pleased when he spoke a different language. Catholic bishops were also afraid of offending what was known as 'Black France', the upper-class notables and wealthy bourgeoisie, who contributed much to the financial upkeep of the Church and whose patronage ensured that the pews were full on Sundays. Catholics of all backgrounds could not easily forget the battles they had fought in the 1880s, and were especially dismayed at the treatment of private schools. Once again, it was left to enlightened Catholics, such as de Mun, to defend the *Ralliement* and to carry the torch of Social Catholicism. Their task was not helped by the growing numbers of so-called 'Radical' politicians, men who saw themselves as the true disciples of the revolutionary tradition of 1789, and whose numbers swelled in the aftermath of the Boulanger Affair of 1889, when the ill-fated General, supported by a motley assortment from left and right, including Catholics, contemplated a *coup d'etat*. Ever keen to establish their position, the Radicals needed a cause around which they could coalesce, and anti-clericalism fitted that purpose.

The Radicals had their moment in the 1900s, in the aftermath of the Dreyfus Affair, the miscarriage of justice in which the unfortunate Captain Dreyfus, a Jew, was falsely accused of selling military secrets to the Germans. This opened the second phase of the French *Kulturkampf*. In the political fall-out, the whole of France seemed divided into two camps: Dreyfusards and anti-Dreyfusards. Among the latter were aligned all the forces of reaction, including the army and the Church, which was vituperative in its attacks on the Republic and indulged in a rabid anti-Semitism, some even going so far as to characterise the government as a Jewish–Masonic conspiracy. Fearful that the very survival of the regime was at stake, in 1899 the moderate Waldeck-Rousseau formed his Cabinet of Republican Defence, which oversaw the Law of Associations of 1901. This focused upon trade union rights, but the religious orders were caught up in its wake. The law decreed that all religious orders required state authorisation, including specific parliamentary approval. Not only were they an easy target, they represented the Church's most visible manifestation of obscurantism. The Assumptionists had bruited especially violent anti-Semitic sentiments.

Worse was to follow. In 1902, Waldeck-Rousseau's place as premier was usurped by Emile Combes, a provincial doctor and fervent anti-clerical who had turned his back on the priesthood, and who was keen to prosecute the assault on the Church with greater vigour. Backed by the Radical Party and their Radical-Socialist allies, he was able to introduce the 1904 bill which debarred the religious orders from any teaching whatsoever, a vindictive measure and one which even troubled the liberal consciences of many republicans, notably Clemenceau, whose battle-cry in the 1870s had been '*Cléricalisme: voilà l'ennemi*'. Combes was also engaged in a wider struggle, keen to use the concordat to intervene wherever possible in episcopal appointments. In 1904, France broke off diplomatic relations with the Vatican after a row erupted over the visit of President Loubet to Rome, when it emerged that the new Pope, Pius X, and his Secretary of State, Merry del Val, had been offended by the French delegation's decision not to attend upon His Holiness. In the furore that followed, and in the aftermath of the notorious *Affaire des fiches*, in which it became apparent that the War Minister, General André, was determining promotions in part according to files detailing officers' religious views kept by the Masonic Lodge of the Grand Orient, the clamour grew for the separation of Church and state, something which even Combes was reluctant to contemplate. Here, it is worth noting that the drive for parliamentary action leading to the Law of Separation was largely at the behest of socialists led by Jean Jaurès, who believed that this would resolve the Church–state question once and for all, and subsequently allow the government to take up the matter of workers' rights. The suspicion must thus remain that Combes and the Radicals were tempted to exploit the anti-clerical sentiments of the left as part of the game of parliamentary politics and to avoid grappling wholeheartedly with tricky contemporary social issues.

The Separation Law of December 1905 revoked the Napoleonic Concordat. In future, the state would no longer salary the clergy, and Church properties were to be sequestered by the government. These could be used by the Church, but only through religious organisations of lay people, the so-called *Associations Cultuelles*. This was an unwelcome Christmas present for Pius X, who denounced the law in his encyclicals *Vehementer* and *Gravissimo* of 1906. Herein lay a paradox. Whereas Leo XIII had encouraged a recalcitrant French clergy to reconcile themselves to the Republic, the French bishops now knew that they had little option but to live with the new legislative framework, and it was the Pope who was defying political realities. Both bishops and Pope understood, however, that the Separation Law was not uppermost in the minds of the French electorate. Although there had been some unpleasant demonstrations after the expulsion of the religious in 1904, especially in fervent areas such as Brittany where, as Caroline Ford has demonstrated, the assault was perceived as one on local tradition, and although there were some unseemly episodes over the registering of Church property in 1906, there was little else by the way of popular protest, certainly nothing to compare with the counter-revolutionary initiatives of the 1790s. In 1906, another parliament with a Radical majority was returned and, if anything, the Church in France suffered because of Pius X's obduracy. Not only did it now lose property to the tune of 500 million *francs*, but significant Catholic initiatives, such as the Action Libérale Populaire (ALP), an embryonic Christian Democratic Party led by Piou, and the Sillon (Furrow), the youth movement led by the charismatic Social Catholic Marc Sangnier, both of which urged a *modus vivendi* with the Republic, were thwarted by the Vatican's misguided attitudes.

Outside Germany, the Low Countries, Italy and France, a fully-fledged *Kulturkampf* never gained ground, largely because local conditions did not favour it. This is not to deny that Catholics were placed under pressure, but this represented either the continuation or the reassertion of earlier policies rather than the development of any new anti-Catholic assault. This was certainly the case in Austria, where there was a return to the Josephinian policies which had characterised the period up to 1856. The shattering defeat of Austria by Prussia in 1866 was blamed by some upon the Concordat of 1855, and even those members of the government who did not subscribe to this simplistic view were convinced that Austria needed a revived constitution. The basic law of 1867 reasserted Josephinian principles, which were consolidated by the three so-called Confessional Laws of 1868. These refused to privilege the position of any one faith over that of another, including Judaism; ended the Church's hegemony in education, although religious instruction still remained a part of the state-school timetable; and offered civil marriage as an option. In 1870, the concordat was unilaterally abrogated. There were subsequent attempts to introduce anti-clerical educational legislation akin to that elsewhere in Europe, and in 1878 a draft bill insisting upon civil marriage was introduced in the House of Representatives. Such initiatives were stymied, however, at least in the German-speaking territories, although in Hungary and the dependent territories such as Croatia during the 1890s obligatory civil marriage and the freedom of religion were passed into law.

The reasons why a more fully-fledged *Kulturkampf* failed to develop were essentially three-fold. First, the Austrian episcopacy, and with it large sections of the middle classes, regularly bruited their adherence to the Emperor, and indeed, in 1891, the bishops impressed upon the electorate the importance of such loyalty. Second, religious legislation always had to take second place to the more pressing questions of Bosnia and Herzegovina which threatened the very foundations of the empire itself. Finally, the court, particularly at the time of the Serbian crises in the early 1900s, welcomed the support of the Church and, alongside it, the sympathy of the Vatican which had been touched by offers from the imperial household to provide a refuge for the Pope outside Rome, even though Austria never offered to re-establish papal temporal power. In 1908, Franz Joseph celebrated his sixtieth year on the throne by reassuring the Church that he was a loyal son, 'grateful for the consolation it had offered in bad times and the guidance it had provided through all paths of life'. It was this gratitude which led the Austrian Emperors to indulge the Polish Catholics in Galicia, where religious faith was an icon of communal identity.

Such tolerance was not to be extended to Catholics within Russia. The rhythms and details of Tsarist religious policy varied, not least in response to the personality of the rulers and their trusted advisers, yet there was a continuity to be perceived in that all showed a concern with Russification and state-building which resulted in an ambitious and often disastrous foreign policy, witness the Crimean War (1854–56), the Polish Revolt (1863–64), the

Russo-Turkish war (1877) and the Sino-Japanese conflict (1905). The Orthodox Church, which commanded the allegiance of upwards of 70 per cent of the population, had been firmly under state control since the time of Peter the Great, its ruling synod dominated by a state-appointed director. In this situation, those outside Orthodoxy – Muslims, 11 per cent of the population; Catholics, 9 per cent, and Jews, 5 per cent – continued to be regarded with deep suspicion as obstacles to autocracy. After 1881, the year in which Alexander II was assassinated and succeeded by Alexander III, this drive towards Russification became more intense, culminating in the pogroms which were directed not just at the Jews but also at ethnic elements, including the Tartars, Ukrainians and Poles; in short, any group that displayed any kind of religious or cultural autonomy. This campaign was not merely a backlash following the murder of the Tsar, but originated from a concerted campaign in which bureaucrats, dignitaries of the Orthodox Church, Slavophils and military men, concerned with the security risks posed by minorities in the frontier lands, all came together. Whereas, in the past, non-Russians could gain acceptance through the demonstration of their fidelity to the crown, henceforth they were expected to display subservience and a preparedness to assimilate the traditions of Mother Russia.

This movement, which had the hallmarks of a crusade, persisted until 1917 and impinged on the Catholic Church in several key areas, representing a persecution more intense than anything witnessed previously, despite the proclamation of a toleration edict – honoured more in the breach than the observance – in the wake of the 1905 revolution. To begin with, the Tsar frequently disregarded Rome's diplomatic initiatives which usually revolved around clerical appointments. Although Alexander III consented to some papal nominees in 1881, within four years relations had deteriorated yet again. 'A midsummer night's dream' was how the Austro-Hungarian ambassador characterised the Vatican's attempts to establish a better working relationship with Moscow. Whereas Nicholas II applauded Leo XIII's denunciations of socialism, having these broadcast from the pulpits of Orthodox churches, the Tsars were not so indulgent of encyclicals and other pronouncements which were routinely suppressed. After 1910, direct contact between the Curia and the bishops was disallowed. Meanwhile, within the Ministry of the Interior, the Department of Foreign Cults closely monitored the activities of Catholics, and the state restricted the liberties of the Catholic clergy through the vehicle of the Roman Catholic Clerical College at St Petersburg which oversaw financing. The result was that many dioceses and parishes were deliberately kept vacant and underfunded as in the past. Shorn of any financial independence and short of clergy, there was little that could be done to resist demands for the Russian language to be employed in preaching and church services, and for Russian history and literature to be taught in seminaries.

The pressures on Catholics in Russian Poland were at their most intense as they constituted the majority of the population, some 6 million out of a total of 9.5 million, and were of course situated on the borderlands where the risks from a disaffected minority were held to be especially serious. After the failed Polish uprising of 1863–64, there were reprisals against bishops and priests, the building of new churches was closely circumscribed, the imposition of the Russian language was pushed through ruthlessly and the control of Catholic schools was ensured through a draconian penal system. To undermine the vigour of Catholic life, both the authorities and the Orthodox Church encouraged the schismatic Mariavite movement founded by Feliska Kozlowska, a female religious, dedicated to the Virgin Mary and concentrated around the town of Plock. Still active to this day, the Mariavites may have attained the support of up to 300,000 adherents in the years immediately prior to the First World War, and were known to occupy seventy parishes. So it was that, in the attempt to break Catholicism, Russia was paradoxically prepared to tolerate a religion rooted in the Polish subculture.

Of all the European states, the religious history of Britain perhaps displayed most singularities. Here, the state maintained an established Church – or more properly speaking churches.* Yet it did not seek to persecute Catholics and there was no parallel to the *Kulturkampf* found elsewhere, although popular hostility to Catholicism continued to be widespread among all social classes. Catholics, as well as dissenters more generally (Protestant Nonconformists comprising 44 per cent of Sunday worshippers in England and Wales in 1851 as against 51 per cent attending the established Church), benefited from the gradual relaxation of the strictures placed upon religious life which were part of a move from a confessional to a secular state, something facilitated in particular by the liberal Gladstone ministries. There was something of a paradox here in that Gladstone himself was a deeply religious man who began every day on his knees in prayer, and a high moral tone was expected of all those in public life – witness the fall of the Irish nationalist politician Charles Stewart Parnell in 1890 when the scandals of his private life hit the news sheets. This expectation coexisted with a pragmatic concern to divorce politics from religion in order to facilitate a harmonisation of society which would encompass the plurality of faiths, an especially marked characteristic of English spiritual life. Thus a series of measures were adopted, several of which stood to the benefit of Catholics: in 1850 the diocesan hierarchy was restored in England (1878 in Scotland); compulsory church rates were abandoned in 1869; Oxford and Cambridge were opened to non-Anglicans; 1858 saw the appointment of Catholic army chaplains to a permanent corps of

---

* The Church of Ireland and the Church in Wales were part of the Anglican communion headed by the Church of England, although autonomously governed until their disestablishment by Acts of Parliament in 1869 and 1914 respectively. The Act of Union of 1707 guaranteed the position of the Presbyterian Church of Scotland, which was quite distinct in terms of liturgy and government from the Church of England. Thereafter, British monarchs at their coronation effectively swore to preserve two different churches, both professing the 'true Protestant faith'. The Episcopal Church of Scotland, formed after 1690 to accommodate those who supported the presence of bishops in church government, was in communion with the Church of England, but was not a state church. For most of the eighteenth century the situation was even more bizarre. As Electors of Hanover, the British monarchs also ruled over a Lutheran state in Germany.

military clergy, as well as the issue of appropriate religious material to army recruits whose denominational affiliation began to be officially recorded; in 1870 the Anglican stranglehold over elementary schooling was loosened; and, in 1902, Catholic schools could at last become eligible for state funding so long as they adopted the prescribed syllabus.

Catholics still laboured under institutional discrimination, however, and continued to encounter widespread hostility, the origins of which remained diverse. There was anxiety at the sharp rise in the number of Catholics as Irish immigration intensified after the famine, swelling the overall Catholic population in England, Scotland and Wales to well over 2 million on the eve of the First World War. The fact that these new arrivals were poor, barely literate and concentrated in urban centres did little to assuage prejudice. At the same time, the older unobtrusive Catholicism led by elements of the landed gentry gave way to a more clerically dominated, triumphalist, Ultramontane and ritualist brand favoured by Manning and his acolytes. The charge of effetism, directed at upper-class converts, was not slow to follow. Cumulatively, these prejudices remained rooted in a set of attitudes which erected Protestantism as a part of the national identity and perceived Catholicism as essentially foreign and un-English, however much Catholics themselves were integrated into society. These instincts led Disraeli to pass the Public Worship Regulation Act of 1874 which clamped down on ritualistic practices in Anglican services, leading to the prosecution of some five clerics for contumacy, in particular for conducting the so-called 'mass in masquerade'.

Whereas Irish Catholics might have thought themselves subject to a British-inspired *Kulturkampf*, and historians have not always dissociated themselves from this point of view, in fact they suffered no new handicaps in addition to those which had existed for decades, and there was even some relaxation of Westminster's rule. In 1869, in a move which undoubtedly strengthened Catholicism, the Irish Church was disestablished, a recognition that a negligible proportion of the population supported the Anglican tradition; it should be remembered that the Protestant ascendancy comprised largely Presbyterians rather than Anglicans, many of them concentrated in Ulster, especially in the Lagan valley complex which housed the only industrialised area within the country. Too little reform, though, had been attempted to stave off a flowering of Irish nationalism in the second half of the nineteenth century. Propelled by the resentments and legacies of the famine, this manifested itself in several different guises: the Irish Republican Brotherhood, better known as the Fenians, who in the 1860s launched a campaign in the countryside against alien landlords; the National Land League of 1879–80, which campaigned against grasping landlords, and did not altogether relinquish the politics of terror; the Irish Home Rule Party, founded in 1880, to achieve representation in Westminster, upon whose votes in the House of Commons the Liberals would become increasingly dependent; and a cultural nationalism exemplified by the Gaelic League of 1893 which sought to proselytise the Irish language and traditions, and the literary renaissance pioneered by W. B. Yeats.

Inevitably, the Catholic Church became enmeshed in these moves for land reform and national autonomy, even more so when, in 1883, an emboldened Gladstone ventured the first Home Rule Bill. This project, revived on several occasions by the Liberals, foundered always on the rocks of Westminster politics where opponents, concentrated on the Conservative and Unionist benches, the latter party an offshoot of disaffected liberals led by Joseph Chamberlain, could play upon the fears of instability within the empire and the sacrifice of Protestants to the papacy. 'Home Rule is Rome Rule', declared the Unionists. Catholic political action now became centrally directed. Whereas in mid-century it had been diverse, with local clerics fiercely involved in all manner of politics, often to the disapproval of the episcopacy, after 1883 the hierarchy threw its weight behind the Irish parliamentary party. It signed a concordat with Parnell the following year which secured freedoms for Catholic education; and, in 1909, Asquith's Liberal government oversaw the dissolution of the Royal University of Ireland and the establishment of two universities, Queen's at Belfast and a national University of Ireland, with colleges in Dublin, Cork and Galway which were, to all intents and purposes, Catholic institutions. The controversies over education, land reform and Home Rule had focused Catholic political action and allied the Church to the cause of nationalism with a greater degree of coherence and vigour than ever before. Following the example set by Cardinal Cullen until his death in 1878, the hierarchy attempted to keep a tight, but sympathetic, control over the varied enthusiasms of the lower clergy, urging restraint and patience, a virtue much in need given that independence for the south would not be achieved until 1921. This local supervision compensated for the fact that papal policy towards Ireland was hampered by a misunderstanding of the local circumstances.

The other area within Europe where there was no sustained assault upon the Church was the Iberian peninsula. Within Spain, the constitutional monarchy of 1876–1923 was never fully accepted by the Church despite the fact that the constitution was extremely indulgent of clerical interests. Priests were to be subsidised by the state; education was placed exclusively in the hands of the Church; and archbishops were *ex officio* senators, thus playing a significant political role. Nevertheless, there was dismay that Article 11, while recognising Catholicism as the religion of the state, permitted the private practice of other cults. For traditionalists and integralists this was tantamount to national apostasy and they worked hard to have it revoked. These unreconstructed monarchists would never reconcile themselves to the parliamentary system despite the urging of Leo XIII who, in 1882, published an encyclical *Cum multa* which was designed to rally Catholics to the regime in much the same way as he would encourage the faithful in France to accept the Republic. In truth, the majority of Spain's Catholics were content since their interests were catered for by the Conservative Party and drew reassurance from the fact that the state remained extremely well disposed towards the Church. Matters changed at the turn of the century when the Liberals seized power in 1902. Convinced that Spain's recent loss of empire to the USA stemmed from the nation's failure to modernise, they attacked aspects of obscurantism, notably through the so-called Padlock Bill of 1910 aimed at constricting the number and influence of religious orders. This attack was, however, always blunted by the recognition that the government itself was incapable of replacing the Church in all of its educational and charitable endeavours; in any case, both Church and state had a vested interest in resisting the anarchism that flourished in parts of Spain at the turn of the century. In these circumstances, the Church failed to appreciate that the real dangers to Catholicism came not from liberalism but from a growing dechristianisation and the poor condition of the clergy, both of which remained untackled.

Within Portugal, too, there was limited tinkering with the Church apparatus before the proclamation of a republic in 1910. As we shall see in the following chapter, the new regime was ambitious in its attempts to secularise Portuguese society. Church and state were separated in a manner akin to the French settlement of 1905, religious instruction was taken out of schools, education was to be 'neutral in regard to religion', and public worship was restricted in the interests of order and security. Yet all this lasted for little more than a decade, as in 1926 a conservative *junta* overthrew the Republic and ushered in a traditionalist, authoritarian regime which sidled up to the Church.

As the example of the Iberian peninsula suggests, state encroachment into religious life was chequered and uneven throughout Europe. Yet everywhere the dynamics behind this infiltration were much the same, with the possible exception of autocratic Russia. The emergence of more liberal regimes, the onset of democratic, mass politics and the drive to create a sense of national identity, together with attempts to situate the individual in a new socio-economic context, all carried implications for churches of whatever denomination. Arguably, it was Catholicism that suffered most. Not every state had a *Kulturkampf*, but it seemed that the Church was intellectually opposed to modern values and, because of its transnational allegiances, the Catholic faith was apparently a more significant block to the creation of national awareness. In this regard, Protestant churches were more open to state influence as they were already organised on a national basis. Moreover, the Catholic faith embraced corporatist values which were inimical to the tenets of liberalism. Assaulted on all sides, it is small wonder that some Catholics believed a conspiracy was afoot to destroy their faith, a plot that could be traced back to the revolution of 1789 or, indeed, to the attacks of the Enlightenment writers of the eighteenth century. In truth, such an interpretation was fundamentally flawed. Secularisation, perceived most markedly after 1870, was not a linear process, but certainly it was one gathering in intensity as Europe underwent a fresh intellectual and cultural revolution.

The Catholic Intellectual World: Modernism versus Integralism

The last third of the nineteenth century witnessed a veritable renaissance in Catholic theological thinking, a movement known as modernism. While modernism needs to be understood within the context of the broader ideological ferment of this period, it was above all concerned with initiatives in biblical scholarship. As many commentators have stressed, Catholic endeavour involved a penetrating analysis of metaphysics and a move away from the sterile and narrowly-conceived scholasticism which increasingly dominated seminaries and universities. Catholic modernist writers were in no sense liberals or progressives, nor did they constitute a party with a discrete corpus of ideas and values. As the leading writer Alfred Loisy noted: 'There are as many modernisms as there are modernists.'[13] Rather, they were a collection of talented individuals, who drew their enthusiasm and stimulus from the intellectual and cultural effervescence of the contemporary world, notably advances in biblical scholarship often pioneered by Protestants. All shared an earnest desire to bring the practices and beliefs of their faith into harmony with the currents of contemporary thinking. As Loisy himself put it, they wished 'to adapt the Christian religion to the intellectual, moral and social needs of the present time'.[14] This was why they were labelled 'modernists', notably by the papacy which ultimately decided their fate. Ironically, it is debatable whether they would ever have emerged had it not been for the pontificate of Leo XIII. While he was attached to traditional teaching, the encyclical *Rerum novarum* (see below) tackling social issues had created such a mood of indulgence, that the Catholic 'modernists' were encouraged to put their heads above the parapet. It was precisely this adventurous, even foolhardy, behaviour that earned them the rebuke of the Church under the new Pope, Pius X. In 1907, he issued the decree *Lamentabili*, which denounced 'modernist' tendencies within the Church, thus stifling a fertile source of inspiration which would not be properly tapped until the 1960s. Moreover, the Church had missed an opportunity to grapple with, and provide answers to, the searching questions being posed by such radical thinkers as Marx, Darwin, Durkheim, Weber and others.

In the second third of the nineteenth century, biblical scholarship concerning the writing of the scriptures, archaeological evidence about the age of the earth, the discoveries of remains from the ancient world pioneered by Heinrich Schliemann and Darwinian theories of evolution forced a rethinking of the literalist interpretation of the Bible. This was a task spearheaded by such Protestant theologians as Auguste Sabatier and the outstanding patristic scholar, Adolf von Harnack, the Professor of Church History at Berlin. In a significant Catholic contribution, in 1892 the Dominicans founded the Ecole Biblique et archéologique française de Jérusalem. Paradoxically, this cutting-edge institution would seriously hinder subsequent scholarship into the Dead Sea Scrolls in the 1960s.

The Catholic contribution to this process was often inchoate, sometimes involving an acceptance and sometimes a rebuttal of recent discoveries. Yet the number of scholars and the range of their ideas is testimony to the vitality of modernism. Within England, the Cambridge historian Lord Acton acknowledged the new understanding of the drafting of the Old Testament. The Anglo-Irish Jesuit George Tyrrell, whose *Christianity at the Crossroads* was published posthumously in 1910, also accepted such findings, his opinions leading to his expulsion from the order and excommunication in 1909. Above all, Catholic modernists were located in France and Germany. Within the former, the historian Louis Duchesne, a professor at the prestigious Institut Catholique de Paris, proffered an interpretation of human history which excluded direct providential intervention while retaining a belief in an over-arching divine purpose for humankind. His pupil, Loisy, took these ideas a stage further, notably in his 1902 publication *The Gospel and the Church*, in which he suggested that not all of the scriptures were to be understood in a literal sense; rather, he advanced a teleological reading of history which emphasised an understanding of the Christian message through its ongoing development as well as its origins. For him, therefore, religious truths, as revealed in the Bible, stood in need of permanent revision and interpretation, a notion that went down well with some Catholics since it undercut the traditional Protestant stress on the authority of scripture alone, and em-phasised the significance of Church teaching and tradition.

Within Germany, it was notably the Tübingen school of biblical scholars who continued the tradition of unflinching and rigorous questioning personi-fied by Ignaz von Döllinger. Franz Kraus, an eminent archaeologist, cast doubt upon the veracity of relics from the early Church, including the Holy Nail at the cathedral of Trier, while Franz Xavier Funk challenged neo-scholastic thinking, especially the current fad for Thomism. In matters of Church discipline, Albert Ehrard and Hermann Schell championed the election of prelates, the end of priestly celibacy and the overhauling of seminary instruc-tion, to take into account recent theological and scientific developments. What should not be overlooked is that these trends had their echo across the Atlantic, in a movement that is known as 'Americanism', which shared many similarities with modernism. Here, Walter Elliot, the author of the contro-versial biography of Father Hecker, founder of the Paulists, and Cardinal Gibbons of Chicago, advocated that Catholic discipline and dogma should be adapted to meet contemporary exigencies. When Rome came to condemn modernism as heresy, it would not overlook the apparently dangerous develop-ments in America.

If Leo XIII had unwittingly created an environment in which modernist ideas could emerge, their establishment was always going to be an uphill struggle since the vogue within the Church establishment was for neo-Thomism, a philosophico-theological system based upon the writings of the thirteenth-century angelic doctor Thomas Aquinas, though whether he would have approved of the narrow interpretation of his ideas is debatable. This had been given an official imprimatur by the encyclical of 1879, *Aeterni patris*, and in 1880 Aquinas was declared to be patron of all Catholic universities. Often underestimated in its long-term implications, as the historian J. Gallagher notes, henceforth 'neo-Thomism became the theology of all the popes from Leo XIII to Pius XII'.[15] Its attraction stemmed from its ability to provide a supposedly timeless and coherent system for rebutting falsehood; in essence, it had all the answers. As the encyclical itself claimed, Aquinas 'still supplies an armoury of weapons which brings us certain victory in the conflict with falsehoods ever springing up in the course of years'. The result of this concentration upon neo-scholasticism was to focus attention on the writings of the early Fathers and the teaching of the popes to the neglect of scriptural studies and contemporary developments in archaeology and science, for example. By stressing the 'timelessness' of the theology, the neo-Thomists left no room for history as it was understood by the modernists, which involved an appreciation of the way in which eternal truths needed to be articulated within changing historical circumstances in the search for a lived-out faith; instead, neo-Thomism favoured historicism, which placed the writings of the past on a pedestal, beyond reproach and development. It was an intellectual outlook which permeated all branches of the Church, notably the seminaries. Mary Vincent relates how the institution at Ciudad Rodrigo in Spain had a rigid academic curriculum which neglected natural and social sciences together with biblical studies in favour of the scholastic catechism. Such a backward-looking approach ensured that within Spain at least modernism was kept at bay.

Modernism not only discovered that the Catholic intellectual world was inhospitable, it also encountered from 1903 to 1914 a far less indulgent Pope in the shape of Pius X. He was a man of a different stamp to his predecessor. Giuseppe Sarto, former Patriarch of Venice, sixty-eight years of age at his election, of humble origins, and a priest of unquestioned piety, wished above all to reinvigorate the religious life of the young: hence his emphasis on catechetical teaching and the reduction of the age of First Communion from eleven to seven. Such qualities would ensure his canonisation in 1954, the first Pope to be treated thus since Pius V in 1701. Such adulation could not, however, disguise the fact that he was an anti-intellectual who naturally gravitated to the supposed certainties of neo-Thomism. He looked upon modernism as a scourge and a betrayal of Catholic values, and he was not afraid to tackle it head on, in the process transforming a little-noticed intellectual current into a major crisis for the Church. Among many of his observations, he denounced modernists as 'enemies of the Church ... to say they are her worst enemies is not far from the truth ... their blows are the more sure because they know where to strike her'.[16] His paranoia was fed by the activities of Joseph Lemius, a Vatican theologian, who compiled dossiers on Church thinkers, and Umberto Benigni, head of the Department of Extraordinary Affairs, who was described by one contemporary as 'a strange character, and without scruples'.[17] Benigni sniffed out those of allegedly heretical tendencies, whether priest or prelate, deploying the techniques of a modern age with the zeal of a medieval inquisitor. So it was that Pius X presided over the emergence of what one insider later described as 'a secret espionage association outside and above the hierarchy, which spied on members of the hierarchy itself ... in short he approved, blessed and encouraged a sort of freemasonry within the Church'.[18]

Pius X was responsible for delivering a further body blow to modernism through the decree *Lamentabili* of 17 July 1907. This condemned sixty-five modernist propositions, culled from a variety of authors, most obviously Loisy who was cited in fifty of them. This was quickly augmented by the ninety-three-page encyclical *Pascendi* of 8 September that year which treated modernism as a fully developed theological system. Drafted by members of the Curia, Pius personally intervened to toughen up its stance, denouncing modernism as 'a compendium of all the heresies'.[19] Above all, this took issue with modernist theologians who perceived an allegorical message in the teachings of the Church, interpreting them in the context of their times, rather than accepting the unchanging validity of dogma. In response to modernist historians, *Pascendi* championed a providential reading of events. And against modernist reformers, the encyclical denounced any suggestions favouring decentralisation and the dilution of papal power and the more general acceptance of liberal democracy as the political path governments should follow. In this sense, *Pascendi* was not merely a diatribe against modernist theology but also against Americanism. It additionally represented a further affirmation of the supremacy of the pontiff and the centrist structure of the Church. As such, Pius X had established a hierarchical construct that would persist until the 1960s and which would permit little room for theological speculation, leaving the Church ill-placed to respond to several of the dramatic episodes of the twentieth century, most obviously the Holocaust.

The campaign initiated by Benigni and others now went into overdrive and came to be known as the 'Black Terror'. The *Index* was in a state of flux as new publications were constantly added. Liberal Catholic newspapers, among them the Roman paper *Nova et Vetera* and the French dailies *La Justice Sociale* and *La Vie Catholique*, were suppressed. No one was immune from suspicion. Teachers in seminaries had their letters opened, students were denounced on the basis of essays, even priests who rode bicycles were mistrusted for embracing modern technology. Some famous names came into the frame. In 1909, the priest Murri, who had earlier founded the Lega Democratica Nazionale, an embryonic Catholic party which aspired to reform both political and clerical institutions, was excommunicated. The youthful Angelo Roncalli, the future Pope John XXIII, was investigated for his remarks in a lecture at the seminary at Bergamo on the subject of faith and scientific research. What he had said was not especially controversial but he was careful to ensure that his teaching thereafter was impeccable to the point of blandness. Modernist sympathisers in France, a country which had earned the extreme displeasure of the papacy through the expulsion of the regulars and the Separation Law of 1905, fared little better. Attempts by Jacques Piou and Albert de Mun to launch a successful Christian Democratic party, in the shape of the ALP, were actively discouraged by Rome; and Marc Sangnier's flourishing Catholic youth movement, the Sillon, which campaigned for social justice, was condemned outright in 1910. That same year, ordinands and priests throughout Europe were obliged to swear the anti-modernist oath which demanded an unreserved and unquestioning obedience to all papal teaching, an oath still in existence today, albeit in a diluted form. To provide some kind of stiffening to the anti-modernist campaign, Benigni in 1909 had established the Sodalitium Pianum (The Pious Society) which erected an espionage network to spy on alleged modernisers throughout the Church. The death of Pius X, at the outbreak of the First World War, brought an end to the worst features of the campaign against modernism, although some unpleasantness persisted. In 1920, Benigni was busy producing a new publication titled *Antisémite*. When quizzed about the title the cardinal objected that he was not anti-Jewish; rather, he was against the Jewish–Masonic conspiracy which was afoot in the worlds of banking, Freemasonry and left-wing politics.

The effects of the anti-modernist campaign were catastrophic. Catholic biblical scholarship was strangled; a Pontifical Biblical Commission, first set up in 1901 by Leo XIII, was purged of any vaguely progressive representatives who were replaced by out-and-out doctrinal conservatives. As Alex Vidler observes, Catholics were compelled 'to maintain, or at least not to call in question, such opinions as the Mosaic authorship of the Pentateuch, the unity of the Book of Isaiah, the priority of St Matthew's Gospel, and the Pauline authorship of the Epistle to the Hebrews – opinions which had been abandoned by nearly all independent scholars'.[20] 'Obedience, not enquiry', observes another historian, 'became the badge of Catholic thought.'[21]

In this situation, it was the so-called 'integralist' Catholics who thrived in the decade before the First World War. As the Assumptionist journal *La Vigie* explained in December 1912: 'We are integral Roman Catholics which means that we prefer over everything and everybody not only traditional doctrine of the Church in regard to absolute truths, but also the directives of the pope in the area of pragmatic contingencies. The pope and the Church are one.' In sum, integralists advocated a 'package deal' which accepted everything taught by the pontiff without exception. Before long there existed a host of integralist publications. As Roger Aubert reminds us, these included the *Unità Cattolica* in Italy, *La Foi Catholique* and *L'Univers* in France, *Correspondance Catholique* in Belgium, *De Maasbode* in the Netherlands and the *Mysl Katolicka* in Poland.[22]

In light of the above, it might have been supposed that integralist Catholics were attracted to those new nationalistic and intensely xenophobic organisations that were beginning to spring up in many parts of Europe in the 1890s, supplanting the traditional conservative parties and movements which had hitherto dominated right-wing discourse. This process was only really true in France and, to a lesser extent, in Italy. In Germany, where extreme nationalist sentiments were expressed most vociferously by the Pan-German League, Catholics were largely left uninvolved since the League took Protestantism as its overriding identity and looked upon itself as the legatee of the *Kulturkampf*. The irony is that if the League had achieved its aim of a greater Germany, embracing most crucially the Austrians, then this would have been predominantly Catholic in its religious make-up. Undoubtedly, German Catholics were troubled by the unsteady international and political environment at the turn of the century, but most still remained loyal to traditional Catholic forms of organisation, notably the Centre Party; only a minority would subscribe to the Deutscher Vereinigung, a splinter organisation which disliked the Zentrum's supposed liberalisation. Across the Alps in Italy, there was likewise a flowering of militant and trenchant nationalist groups, and in this instance Catholics were attracted, at least after 1907. Apart from the clamp-down on modernism, which scuppered other forms of Catholic political and social action, extremists – congregated principally around Enrico Corradini and the Italian Nationalist Association – appreciated that their cause depended upon a wider reading of the peninsula's history, and so dropped their virulent anti-Romanism. Giovanni Papini caught the essence of the matter when he equated Catholicism with authority, domination, organisation, stability and security, a point of view which resonated with the clerical supporters of Pius X.

It was, though, in France that the extreme right, represented most ably by the Action Française, a neo-royalist organisation founded in 1899 by the ideologue Charles Maurras, had the greatest success in attracting Catholics to its cause. No doubt the popularity of the Action Française derived from the upheavals of the Dreyfus Affair when it appeared that many traditional French institutions, among them the army, Church and judiciary were under threat, but it also capitalised on the high calibre of its journalism, its innovatory methods of popular action and its successful distillation of many traditionalist values. Maurras had a particular admiration for the hierarchical structures of the Church and looked upon Catholicism primarily as a bastion of order in an ever-changing world. As he himself observed, 'The scriptures outside of the Church are poisonous', a sentiment shared by many integralist Catholics.[23]

While Catholics were not uniformly drawn to the emerging nationalist movements, in the aftermath of the condemnation of modernism many more were caught up in a growing mood of anti-Semitism. This was, of course, a Europe-wide phenomenon, not restricted to any particular class or religious denomination, born out of a variety of things: the pogroms in Russia which displaced thousands of refugees who settled in the west; a fear of the rapid social and technological changes that were overtaking society; economic downturns which fed the stereotype of the Jew as a grasping usurer living on the misery of others; the growth of Social Darwinism and pseudo-science practised and popularised by the likes of Edouard Drumont and Houston Stewart Chamberlain; and episodes such as the collapse of the Catholic Union Générale bank in 1882 and the Dreyfus Affair which were readily ascribed to Jewish conspiracies. This late-nineteenth-century anti-Semitism was novel in its biological racism, emphasising the supposed decadence and unassimilability of the Jewish stock which was regarded as alien, cosmopolitan and parasitical. Inevitably, this interlarded with the centuries-old anti-Judaism which was quintessentially religious in nature. This emanated from the belief that Jews were deicides for their murder of Christ. In the eyes of the Church, the obduracy of the Jews in refusing to acknowledge their 'crime' and embrace Christianity was further evidence of their guilt, as was their rootlessness and their alleged materialism.

So emerged, in integralist Catholic circles, a particularly unpleasant fusion of religious/cultural and biological anti-Semitism typified by the comment in the *Civiltà Cattolica* of 1897: 'The Jew remains always in every place immutably a Jew. His nationality is not in the soil where he is born, nor in the language that he speaks, but in his seed.'[24] As one commentator has observed: 'Catholic anti-Judaism had clearly mutated into full-blown antisemitism.'[25] In these circumstances, Jews were suspected of all kinds of evils, and were to be denied basic rights. The Papal States, like many other countries, had ensured this through the maintenance of a ghetto. While this might have disappeared with the unification of Italy, the modernist crisis now allowed the worst kinds of apologists for anti-Judaic sentiments to come to the fore. The Assumptionist newspaper *La Croix* thrived on anti-Semitism, achieving a circulation of 130,000 in 1889. At the time of the Dreyfus Affair, it peddled the notion that the rock of Gibraltar was secretly a telephone exchange manned by Jews and freemasons, operating with the connivance of the British government, to destroy Catholicism. In Italy itself, the *Civiltà cattolica* printed a series of articles in the 1880s and 1890s claiming that Jews were the guiding hand behind the establishment of modern liberal democracies, and were responsible for the killing of children, a revival of the medieval 'blood libel' that they took a child's blood for use in Passover rituals.

The corollary to the integralist campaign against the Jews was a renewed fear of freemasons. Freemasonry was, of course, a traditional bugbear of the Church and had been roundly condemned in the eighteenth century, notably in Clement XII's *In eminenti* of 1738. There was an established tendency on the part of Catholics, and the Curia in particular, to blame any misfortune on the evil doings of the lodges, the French Revolution being credited to a masonic and satanist conspiracy, for instance. It was almost inevitable, then, that, in the late nineteenth century, integralists would place the blame for the institutional attacks upon the Church, and the growth of secularisation more generally, upon this traditional enemy. The fact that several members of the French, Italian and Spanish governments of the 1880s and 1890s were indeed masons merely added grist to the mill. They were demonised as alien agents of irreligion whose objective was the elimination of Catholicism, the propagation of materialist values and the dissolution of morality. Leo XIII responded with his encyclical *Humanus genus* of April 1884 which urged the Catholic episcopacy to expunge the 'wicked pestilence', and to meet this most dangerous of challenges with the most vigorous counter-attack. On the ground, Catholics were not slow to respond to this clarion call. At Trent, a conference was organised in 1896 to rally the international Catholic community against the enemy. Within France especially, where Freemasonry was identified with the institutionalised and militant anti-clericalism of the Third Republic, there were a welter of integralist anti-masonic groups: La Croisade Franc-Catholique of 1884, La Ligue anti-Maçonnique of the same year, and the Maison de la Bonne Presse, an Assumptionist creation founded ten years later. It was, of course, within France that Léo Taxil, a former mason turned Catholic, perpetrated the hoax of the fictitious Diana Vaughan. It was alleged that, having become enmeshed in devil worship as part of her life as a mason, she had subsequently been forced into hiding to escape death at the hands of her former colleagues after her conversion to Catholicism. What this fraudulent story revealed was not just the association made by many Catholics between Freemasonry and satanism, but also the underlying paranoia which Church leaders as well as many ordinary Catholics had about the modern world.

Consistent with past behaviour, at the turn of the century the Church allied itself to the forces of reaction at a time when it needed vision and flexibility. As the Catholic poet and supporter of Dreyfus, Charles Péguy, noted in 1900, the world had changed more in the last three decades than at any time since the birth of Christ. The Church had not responded with sufficient vigour and clarity. This is not to deny that the practice of Catholicism continued to flourish, at least in certain areas of Europe, and among certain social groups in particular, but it is hard to resist the conclusion that the Church had left itself crippled and unable to combat a rising tide of secularisation which manifested itself in several different guises, not least of all in a broader intellectual challenge.

Secularisation

As Hugh McLeod reminds us, until the 1870s the term 'secularisation' was most frequently used to designate the transfer of ecclesiastical properties to lay ownership.[26] After this date, the word was deployed to describe a broader process whereby religion in general and Catholicism in particular was increasingly excluded from a range of human activities. This led several contemporary commentators to bemoan the decline of religion. In 1885, for example, Monsignor d'Hulst, rector at the Catholic Institute in Paris, bewailed the fact that the overwhelming crisis facing contemporary society was the weakening of religious ideas. Subsequently, a majority of historians and sociologists have accepted that this period was indeed one of secularisation, a process which was often conceived as a linear development following from the Enlightenment and French Revolution, and one which has continued unabated to this day. Only in the last thirty years have scholars such as Gérard Cholvy begun to challenge this orthodoxy, arguing that the period witnessed not so much a decline as a shift in patterns of religious belief, behaviour and expectation.[27] What does seem undeniable is that fundamental changes were occurring, though these depended on a series of variables: time, place, gender and circumstance. Inevitably, then, secularisation varied from country to country making it almost impossible to define its causation and to measure its extent. Contrary to what has traditionally been argued, Catholicism was not everywhere in retreat and nor was it suffering at the hands of an unremitting, long-term attack, regardless of what certain pessimistic churchmen might have feared. For the sake of clarity, we shall consider secularisation under three broad headings: the 'secularisation of the European mind', to borrow Owen Chadwick's famous phrase; the impact of social and economic upheaval; and the growing pluralism of religious practice, where mass pilgrimages coexisted with a material culture.[28]

The Realm of Ideas

The stock interpretation of secularisation is that it operated in the realm of ideas. That the closing decades of the late nineteenth century were a period of extraordinary artistic, cultural and philosophical endeavour cannot be disputed. This revolution in ideas was far more eclectic in its manifestations and more profound in its impact than any previous intellectual movement, including the Enlightenment, and as such raised a series of issues which the Church could not easily address. Whereas the Scientific Revolution of the seventeenth century had posed challenges to metaphysical thought, Catholic theologians had successfully managed to establish a synthesis which incorporated the Newtonian mechanistic universe within a divinely ordained structure. The Enlightenment writers of the pre-revolutionary era had equally attacked the Church, mocking its traditions, attacking its privileges and casting doubts on the truths of revealed religion. Yet such assaults had been blunted, not least of all by the limited diffusion of enlightened notions, the timidity of the *philosophes* themselves, their fear of overturning the social order and their acknowledgement of the essential utility of religion as a force for social stability. As R. R. Palmer long ago demonstrated, there was also a counterattack by the Catholic enlightenment.[29] By contrast, the intellectual ferment of the late nineteenth century was more challenging. Not only did it encompass all spheres of human endeavour, it had a much broader impact thanks to the growth of communications and expansion of the literate classes. Its other distinguishing feature, which set it apart notably from the Enlightenment, was the willingness to shock, a preparedness by artists and others to free themselves from the constraints of convention and provoke their audience of the respectable bourgeoisie. All in all, what was on offer from scientists, intellectuals, poets, historians, novelists and psychoanalysts was an interpretation of the origins, meaning and purpose of the world which owed nothing to providential intervention.

At root, this intellectual and cultural revolution drew upon science as its principal inspiration and muse. Science constituted the prism through which all human knowledge was mediated and proffered a means of understanding the world. Much of this unlimited and naive confidence in the ability of science to facilitate progress sprang from the ideas of Auguste Comte, a French mathematician and philosopher and one-time secretary of Saint-Simon, whose ideas he plagiarised. In the 1830s, he elaborated his *Course of Positive Philosophy*, widely regarded as the credo of what became known as Positivism. Herein, he expounded a tripartite division of history: the theological; the metaphysical; and the scientific or Positivist. In his view, human understanding had progressed over the ages. The Catholic, that is the theological, view of mankind, dependent on hierarchy and corporatist structures, had in the late eighteenth century been overtaken by the metaphysical which placed emphasis on the perfectibility of the human condition which would discover its most sophisticated expression in a new participatory political system. The French Revolution, he argued, was the product of these two ideologies clashing. He now articulated a new understanding of society which shunned any kind of metaphysical explanation. This Positivist outlook concerned itself uniquely with observable facts. Through the observation of the natural world, Comte argued, it was possible to formulate the laws which not only governed the natural sciences, but also the world of human affairs and human institutions. Because of an unhappy personal life, Comte in his later years came, paradoxically, to expound a religion of humanity which placed tremendous emphasis upon love and emotion: to all extents and purposes, Catholicism without Christianity. There thus emerged two divergent strands of thought among his followers after his death in 1856: those who emphasised the 'religious' aspects of his thought, and those who remained attached to his earlier Positivist approach, among them Victor Hugo, Emile Zola, Herbert Spencer, Jules Ferry, Emile Durkheim, Emile Littré and Max Weber. Many of these figures would reject particular elements of Comte's Positivist rationale, including his particular tripartite view of history, and would develop their own individual notions, yet all shared a vision of man as being part of Nature, not made in God's image, and rejected any system of ethics and morality founded upon religion, preferring instead to articulate a moral framework which was socially derived.

Aside from Comte, two other individuals whose thought gave rise to particular analyses of the human condition and whose ideologies posed fundamental challenges to religion demand particular attention: Charles Darwin and Karl Marx. While at first sight the focus of their interests may appear to be markedly different – Darwin was preoccupied with the organic world treated in his *Origin of the Species* (1859) and the *Descent of Man* (1871), and Marx was concerned with the economic determination of social class, notably in his *Communist Manifesto* (1848) and *Capital* (1867) – their work none the less shared a materialist philosophy. On the basis of their research, they proposed a set of scientific laws, incorporating evolution and conflict as the determinants of animal and human change, though there was a tension in Marx's case between evolution and revolution. When Darwin's ideas were given a social gloss as Social Darwinism, the similarities between the two men became even more apparent, one believing in the survival of the fittest and the other in the inevitable conflict between classes with a culmination in proletarian triumph. As Engels declared in 1883, at the graveside of his great friend and collaborator: 'Just as Darwin discovered the law of development of organic nature so Marx discovered the law of development of human history.'[30] This materialist exegesis cut a swathe through all religious explanations of the human condition. There was no room here for the soul, the exercise of free will, the redemption of mankind through Christ's suffering, or the literal interpretation of the Bible. If the here-and-now rather than the afterlife was the focus of both men's attention, even in the former the role of organised religion stood condemned as impeding that inevitable struggle which alone could contribute to evolution.

In their own ways, Marx and Darwin were suggesting that religion was a social construct, a notion that received its most sophisticated interpretation in the writings of the pioneering sociologists Emile Durkheim, Professor of Sociology at the universities of Bordeaux and the Sorbonne, and Max Weber, the lawyer, historian and Professor of Political Economy at the University of Freiburg. Neither neglected the significance of religion for the functioning of society. For Durkheim, it offered symbolic expression of communal structures; while Weber recognised the reality of religious belief as an influence upon men's actions. Yet, at the end of the day, both viewed religion, and ethics more generally, as a human artifice and, as such, limited in applicability to particular circumstances of time and place, and lacking universal validity. However, neither went as far as the German philosopher Friedrich Nietzsche, son of a Lutheran pastor in Saxony, who along with his rejection of religion also discarded materialism and science. Wholly contemptuous of the humility integral to Christianity which fettered the human will and was detrimental to the quality of life, and impatient of the constraints imposed by rationalism, Nietzsche declared in 1882 that God was 'dead'. By this he meant the demise of religion as a belief system, as a way of life and as a set of moral imperatives. Instead, he advanced a new concept of the individual, the so-called *Über-mensch* or 'superman', who would achieve autonomy and spiritual fulfilment through the unrestricted assertion of his will.

Collectively, these authors and others of their ilk are often loosely termed 'modernists' (though Nietzsche has also been hailed as post-modern), in that they were responding to a world in which, as Malcolm Bradbury has observed, the usual certainties had evaporated.[31] This was a very different brand of modernism to that which we noted earlier, when Catholic scholars had attempted to update theology and doctrine in the light of recent historical and archaeological findings. Any Catholic response to this secular modernism was, of course, gagged by the papacy, and it was left to essentially non-Catholic writers, such as the Jewish philosopher Henri Bergson, who came close to converting to Catholicism at the end of his life, and the Italian intellectual and so-called neo-idealist Benedetto Croce, to reassert the importance of faith and emotion and interpolate a rebuttal of the cold, deterministic and un-emotional world of Positivism and rationalism. That an opportunity was missed by Catholic scholars is evident in the more general rejection of Positivism resulting from the scientific discoveries of the *fin-de-siècle* which did much to undermine the premises on which Comte had articulated his Positivist philo-sophy. For example, the work on electrons by Ernest Rutherford and Niels Bohr, the research into X-rays and radiation by Konrad Röntgen, Henri Becquerel and Marie Curie, the theory of quantum physics elaborated by the Berlin scientist Max Planck, and the theories of relativity adumbrated by Albert Einstein revealed, in the words of Michael Biddiss, 'a strange new world ... characterised by a jerky unpredictability, utterly at odds with the traditional assumption that some regular pattern of continuity and determinacy must reign through all the causal relationships of nature'.[32] Science not only revealed the universe to be more chaotic than the Positivists had imagined, but no longer seemed capable of providing all the answers. These new discoveries offered the possibility of reconciling science and religion as Max Planck himself acknowledged in his *Religion und Naturwissenschaft*.

What was even more serious for the Catholic Church was the fact that, unlike Enlightenment writers, the intellectual heavyweights of the period were widely read by an increasingly literate public, underpinned by improvements in elementary and secondary schooling and a culture of self-improvement neatly summed up in the German term *Bildung*. For example, John William

Draper's book, *A History of the Conflict between Religion and Science*, which argued that a belief in God would be steadily undermined by successive scientific advances, was translated into eight European languages shortly after its initial publication in the USA in 1874. By contrast with the Counter-Reformation of the sixteenth century, when the Church had responded to the Protestant challenge in a more creative fashion, by seeking to educate the laity and provide them with wholesome literature while at the same time banning undesirable texts, the late-nineteenth-century papacy responded in a blinkered way. An excessive reliance was placed upon the *Index* as a way of preventing people from reading purportedly unwholesome literature. As we have already noted, it was not just intellectuals outside the Catholic world whose works were prohibited, but those within the faith who attempted some kind of synthesis and accommodation with modern developments who found themselves on the *Index*. Theological modernism was not allowed to take on secular modernism. The case of Hermann Schell, a German scholar who devoted much of his academic life to showing that Catholicism and progress were not antithetical, was not untypical. All his important books were banned, he himself was condemned, and his most able pupil was so disgusted at the treatment afforded his master that he converted to Protestantism.

Just as we noted with respect to the Enlightenment, it is far from easy to gauge the wider impact of this welter of scientific, materialist and Positivist ideas, not least because they were communicated through the written word. It is difficult to assess the impact of any reading matter upon its audience: reading is not necessarily believing, and for some the acquisition of a particular work was nothing more than a social accoutrement. While some literature with a materialist bias did undoubtedly reach a broader audience, for instance the works of Marx, the novels of Zola and the plays of Ibsen, it should be emphasised that most highbrow authors were still devoured predominantly by an educated elite.

It should be further stressed that popular literature, the heir to the *bibliothèque bleue* of the eighteenth century, still retained a substantial religious element, even if the proportion of it devoted to non-religious themes was growing. Cowboy stories, tales of empire, accounts of bandits such as the legendary Fantomas and those of pirates were produced in large numbers, together with almanacs, cookery books and a burgeoning literature of self-improvement sponsored by trade unions and workers' associations. All this sat alongside a solid corpus of Catholic literature recounting miracles, saints' lives, biblical stories, missionaries' adventures and admonitory tales. It is reckoned that one book in six published in Germany in 1851 dealt with theology and the figure remained at one in eight over twenty years later. St Theresa of Lisieux's *History of a Soul*, a collection of the Carmelite nun's memoirs supplemented by letters and jottings by her sister Agnès, first published in 1898, achieved sales of 700,000 by 1930, and was translated into no fewer than thirty-five languages. An abridged version managed an astonishing 2.5 million sales. The circulation figures of Catholic newspapers also rivalled that of a new 'yellow' press, the equivalent of today's tabloids, such as the *Daily Mail*, the *Petit Parisien* and the

Berliner Morgenpost. Within the German Empire, there were some 446 Catholic papers by 1912, one of which, the *Berliner Tageblatt,* had a quarter-of-a-million subscribers. Belgium could boast the *Bien Public* and Spain the *Siglo Futuro,* but few could rival the French daily *La Croix* which sold 700,000 copies in 1897. There were over 100 local versions in production, almost one for every diocese. Even in Prussian Poland, Catholics ensured that their voice was heard and that the Polish language was retained, even if it had been persecuted in schools. In 1874, the *Tygodnik Katolicki (Catholic Weekly),* was banned, but five years later it was replaced by the *Przegląd Kocielny (Ecclesiastical Review).* Perhaps the most influential of the Catholic newspapers was that initiated by Archbishop Stablewski in 1895, the *Przewodnik Katolicki* (the *Weekly Catholic Guide).* Unfortunately, much of the Catholic press, with the important exception of that in Germany, tended to be monochrome, deeply attached to traditionalist and integralist values. Liberal, progressive papers struggled to survive in the face of ecclesiastical disapproval.

Where such literature was less evident, and where anti-clericalism became particularly conspicuous, was among the new middle classes: doctors, lawyers, clerical officials and small businessmen. Not only were they influenced by the intellectual and cultural climate of the age, they also harboured a resentment against the traditional elites who often sidled up to the Church. Historians have demonstrated how doctors and school teachers were especially prominent in denouncing priests. Both groups mocked the obscurantist thinking of churchmen, but most critically they disliked the respected status in the community which clerics expected as their due. Ultimately, it was this social struggle rather than the intellectual one that did most to promote a popular anti-clericalism. The new middle classes were joined in their resentment of the Church by those peasants who had traditionally grumbled at the paying of tithes, surplice fees and the intrusiveness of the priest in the confessional and by those workers who saw the Church as the *porte-parole* of their employers. Although Catholicism made a very real effort to reach out to those living in a bleak urban landscape, the left was far better at organising among the proletariat, as we shall see shortly. Whereas anti-clericalism had once been the exclusive province of the lodge or *salon,* it was now commonplace in bars, the local *syndicat* or on the factory floor. Perhaps the one comfort for the Church was the fact that anti-clericalism was rare among women, partially because they were denied access to these outlets of sociability and forums of political action where criticism of the clergy was readily voiced.

The Social and Economic Challenge

If the Catholic response to the secularisation of the European mind was chequered, the Church articulated a more coherent and sustained rejoinder to the social and economic changes that were overtaking much of Europe at the close of the nineteenth century, although here again success in countering secularisation was only partial. The problems thrown up by industrial development had, of course, been the subject of debate since at least the 1830s, which witnessed the onset of industrialisation in much of northern Europe. With the exception of parts of the Iberian peninsula and the Austro-Hungarian Empire, industrialisation and urbanisation were entering a new phase by the last third of the nineteenth century. In 1910, London possessed a population of some 5 million, Paris boasted 3 million and Berlin 2 million. In Britain, there were more people living in the towns than the countryside by the 1850s; in the German Empire a comparable development took place by the 1870s, though in France the urban–rural balance would not have changed in favour of the former until 1929. Moreover, the nature of industrialisation itself had begun to change. While staple goods, such as iron and steel, remained important, technological change and the growth of international trade encouraged the emergence of so-called 'new' industries concerned primarily with chemicals, electricity and disposable goods; a new consumerism witnessed the establishment of the first department stores; and the world of work became more heterogeneous with job opportunities opening up in offices, shops, administration and government. Women in particular entered the job market in unprecedented numbers, employed as teachers, nurses, secretaries, shop assistants and minor clerks as well as continuing their traditional place as domestic servants.

Such momentous change threw up questions about the respective rights of the haves and the have-nots, the organisation of industrial society and the nature of worker representation. The corollary was the emergence of socialist parties and trade unions. Between 1864 and 1876, the first Workers' International had indicated the burgeoning strength of the left, but this organisation had been dominated by individuals, sectarian interests and ideological disputes. By the time of the Second International of 1889, in most countries there existed a national socialist party, the most influential being the German Social Democratic Party which commanded 1.5 million votes in the Reichstag elections of the following year gaining some thirty-five seats. Socialism might have made even greater advances had it not been so divided over the means by which to attain power. At the core of most workers' parties, except in Britain, was a division between those who favoured the ballot box as a means of obtaining change and those who countenanced change through violent means. The former, often referred to as the Revisionists, were notably championed by Eduard Bernstein; the latter, including luminaries such as Rosa Luxemburg and Georges Sorel, viewed trade union agitation as a way of securing political, rather than primarily economic, ends.

The Catholic response to these social and economic upheavals, which were grouped under the portmanteau term the 'Social Question', needs to be explored on several levels. To begin with, there were the initiatives of Leo XIII. He had been chivvied by Catholic social thinkers throughout Europe, who had been assembling at Freiburg every year since 1884. From here they urged the Curia to take cognisance of the rapidly changing economic environment and its implications for the welfare of the working class. In 1888, the so-called Union of Freiburg met with the Pope, a conference which resulted in the encyclical *Rerum novarum* of 1891. This opened with a conspectus of the many changes that had overtaken society in recent years: the proliferation of industry; the scientific discoveries; the changing relations between employee and employer; the growth of the working class; and the enormous disparities of wealth. Because of the overwhelming impact of these developments, it was appropriate that the Church should comment, and delineate the responsibilities of differing classes, in particular the relationship between capital and labour. While acknowledging that inequalities of wealth were inevitable, and reasserting the right to property, Leo XIII appreciated that the 'mass of the poor have no resources of their own to fall back upon', whereas the rich had 'many ways of shielding themselves'. In this situation, it was recognised that substantial numbers of workers had drifted towards socialism. But this was a dangerous remedy, for it was an ideology based on the notion of class conflict and flew in the face of the natural hierarchical and patriarchal bases of society. In its stead, the Pope urged that both the rich and the state itself were obliged to assist the poor, an endeavour which went beyond the mere distribution of alms. The state in particular was best placed to promote the public good by regulating working conditions, improving wages and avoiding strikes by addressing the underlying causes of dispute. The state should further permit working people to establish unions or associations. These would facilitate mutual aid, the promotion of Christian knowledge and the dissemination of moral values. Naturally enough, *Rerum novarum* anticipated that these unions would be Catholic in their orientation and, while acknowledging the right to strike, believed that this must be as a means of last resort.

The significance of *Rerum novarum* is not always easy to grasp. For many on the left, both inside and outside the Christian churches, Leo had not gone far enough, and indeed the encyclical's analysis of social conditions was not particularly sophisticated. Its true importance is perhaps best understood within the context of the Catholic intellectual world, where it quickly became known as the 'Magna Carta of Social Catholicism'. The championing of the right to strike, the duty of employers to offer a decent wage, the condemnation of unbridled capitalism alongside the denunciation of Marxism were bold statements. They helped to lay the foundations for the economic doctrine of corporatism which became popular in the 1920s and which sought to achieve a harmony between social groups by the rejection of individualistic liberalism and conflictual syndicalism. Whether Leo XIII truly deserved the soubriquet 'the liberal pope' as a result of *Rerum novarum* and subsequent pronouncements, including *Graves de communi re* of 1901 which advocated class reconciliation, remains questionable. He was undoubtedly a liberal in comparison to both his predecessor and successor yet, as we have already noted, doctrinally he was a conservative. Hence his championing of neo-Thomism and opposition to any diminution of papal authority. In part, his reputation as a liberal derived from his consensual manner as much as from any liberal instinct. Perhaps the real achievement of *Rerum novarum* was that it lent papal approbation and encouragement to Social Catholics who were already grappling with issues of poverty and deprivation, although even here Leo's proclamations did not go as far as many wished.

On the ground, Catholic social initiatives were many and varied. Not surprisingly they were most innovative in northern Europe where industrial-isation had made most headway; the Bishop of Segovia in Spain thought there was little point in even publishing *Rerum novarum*, arguing that 'neither workers, nor factories, nor by the mercy of God, the errors combated by the encyclical, abound in the city'.[33] In France, the initiatives included the *Cercles Catholiques d'ouvriers*, social study groups, set up in 1871 by Count Albert de Mun, which in 1906 could boast some 60,000 members, belonging to 418 workers' societies. It was de Mun's associate, Marc Sangnier who established the Sillon, an influential youth movement which encouraged discussion groups among Catholic bourgeois and workers, an initiative which was emulated by the Action populaire and the Semaines sociales. French Catholic youth move-ments came together under the aegis of the Association Catholique de la Jeunesse Française (ACJF) of 1910, while Christian trade unions were grouped under the Confédération française des travailleurs chrétiens (CFTC). Catholic industrialists also played their part, notably Léon Harmel who founded the CFTC cooperative association for shopkeepers and small businessmen, the Union Fraternelle du Commerce et de l'Industrie of 1889, and who attempted to introduce workers' councils, and health and saving schemes for his em-ployees at his factory in the Val-des-Bois near Reims. He was also one of the key organisers of workers' pilgrimages to Rome: 100 attended in 1885, 10,000 in 1889 and there may have been twice that number two years later, though on this occasion there were some unseemly scuffles with anti-clerical demon-strators. Across the border in Belgium, there were almost as many initiatives, among them the Aumôniers du travail of 1895, La ligue Démocratique Belge and the Catholic Workers' Movement of Father Rutten.

It was, though, in Germany that Social Catholics were most numerous and best organised, their activities reflecting the more progressive intellectual atmosphere that characterised German Catholicism. During the 1840s, Father Adolph Kolping had organised *Gesellenvereine*, societies of master craftsmen, which boasted 100,000 members by 1865. At that point, Emanuel Ketteler, Bishop of Mainz, was also encouraging Catholics to form their own trade associations. Faced with this massive expansion of lay trade unions, the Zentrum did its bit to provide leadership; and, in 1899, the first congress of the Christliche Gewerkvereine Deutschlands (CGD), the Christian Trade Unions of Germany, was held at Mainz. Christian Trade Unions now had a combined membership approaching 200,000. Further growth seemed likely but was hampered by the attitude of the Catholic hierarchy which remained suspicious of the right to strike, preferring instead the system pioneered by clerics, businessmen and nobles around Trier, the birthplace of Marx, which harked back to the guild system. Austrian Social Catholicism was also vibrant, inspired undoubtedly by the German example. Prominent among Social Catholics was Karl von Vogelsang, a Protestant convert from Mecklenburg, who edited the newspaper *Das Vaterland* in Vienna. He campaigned for the elimination of child labour, the introduction of welfare measures and the extension of the franchise to artisans and urged that the state should intervene where necessary to protect the little man. In Karl Leuger, Social Catholicism had another persuasive campaigner, and in his period as (a virulently anti-Semitic) Mayor of Vienna between 1897 and 1910 he initiated a series of major improvements to the city's infrastructure which demonstrated just what could be achieved by Catholic corporate action.

As already noted, within southern Europe, less industrialised than the north, Catholic initiatives were more piecemeal. In 1876, the Bishop of Cŏrdoba attempted to emulate the study circles of de Mun with the creation of the *Círculos Católicas Obreros*, yet these made little headway. When, in 1895, the Consejo Nacional de las Corporaciones Obrero-Católicas emerged as an umbrella for the workers' societies, it struggled to make its influence felt and had little political clout. Similarly, the development of Catholic trade unions and a rural cooperative movement struggled to get off the ground. In Italy, education lay at the heart of Catholic social endeavour, though other areas were addressed. Here, it is possible to cite the examples of the Sicilian priest Luigi Sturzo, a key figure in the Partito Popolare Italiano (Italian Popular Party, PPI), who established cooperative banks and parish councils in his native land; the initiatives of Giuseppe Toniolo, an academic at the University of Pisa, who similarly established workers' cooperatives in Lombardy and Venetia; and the various activities of the Opera dei congressi which distributed charity to the needy of the both the towns and the countryside.

Inevitably, Catholic social initiatives drew the scorn of the left, which believed that the Church was attempting to undermine the class-consciousness of the workers and restrain trade union activities, a charge not altogether wide of the mark. When Archbishop Ketteler encouraged his clergy to mobilise workers in the Rhineland, Marx famously remarked, 'The scoundrels are flirting with the workers' question whenever it seems appropriate.' In Belgium, the youthful architect Arthur Verhaegen had no compunction in entitling his grouping of Catholic workers' clubs as the Anti-Socialistische Werkliedenbond, (Anti-Socialist Workers' League). To be fair, there were a number of Catholics, predominantly young priests, who were genuinely radical in their approach to social questions and who deployed *Rerum novarum* as a springboard to promote their ends. What is striking about such men is that they were predominantly Christian Democrats: for instance the Abbé Jules Lemire, a deputy in the French Parliament, who rallied like-minded clerics at Reims in 1896 and at Bourges four years later; the Abbé Antoine Pottier, professor at the Liège seminary, who established the Union Démocratique Chrétienne; and the Italian priest Romalo Murri who, at the turn of the century organised workers' associations in central Italy and helped to found Azione Popolare, an embryonic Christian Democratic organisation.

What is telling is that none of these initiatives received the blessing of the episcopacy or the papacy, which made it clear that Catholics should toe the party line, and not allow the emergence of workers' associations outside clerical control. Pottier, Verhaegen, Sangnier, among others, all had their initiatives stymied in one way or another. Herein lay a conflict that bedevilled Social Catholicism for at least the first half of the twentieth century. Whereas

Christian Democrats embraced liberal democracy, and believed that this was the most effective machinery by which a just and tolerant society could be constructed, other Catholics who busied themselves with the Social Question adopted a more paternalistic approach, deriving their ideas from such theorists as Frédéric Le Play, Count de La Tour du Pin and von Vogelsang. They articulated an organicist conception of society which denied the importance of individual rights, arguing instead that man could achieve spiritual fulfilment and political identity only through membership of a wider community, for instance as a member of a Catholic association or trade union. This authoritarian and corporatist outlook, which was occasionally tainted by an unpleasant anti-Semitism identifying capitalism as Jewish in origin, was not that far removed from the integralism that was then finding favour in the Church. So it was that liberal and Social Catholicism sat awkwardly together, though on occasions the differences between them were more apparent than real.

Overall, it is difficult to calculate the success of Catholic initiatives in curbing the secularisation of the working classes. A quantitative assessment is of limited use. Impressive though the recruitment was to Catholic organisations, these never matched trade-union membership. Figures for Brussels, for example, reveal that in the period 1909 to 1913 the numbers of socialist unionists more than doubled from 8,000 to 18,000; Catholic unions recruited faster but, even so, totalled a mere 5,000 on the eve of the First World War. In qualitative terms, it is apparent that Catholic workers' associations were usually the inspiration of an elite; among the middle classes, only a few Catholics were prepared to involve themselves with the plight of the workers. The result was that these so-called workers' associations did not represent a natural outgrowth from the ranks of the employees themselves. In de Mun's words, they were, 'de l'extérieur'.[34] Nevertheless, detailed local studies of the Nord in France, Flanders, the Rhineland and Westphalia have illustrated how the Catholic workers' associations did much to combat the rising tide of left-wing political agitation. It is further apparent that the Church made a concerted and significant attempt to ameliorate the grim and unrelenting misery that characterised the lives of so many workers, for instance through the encouragement of sports, a process that was marked in France. Here, Catholics were eager to counter the organised games and outdoor activities that occupied a growing part of the school timetable. The Catholic Fédération Gymnastique et Sportif des Patronages de France, set up in 1898, claimed a membership of 180,000 on the eve of the First World War and presided over around 1,763 affiliated clubs. It is said that the Church encouraged the playing of soccer in France rather than rugby, because the latter was associated with the Protestant and anti-clerical south-west, though the main reason was that rugby was considered too violent. The Gaelic Athletics Association in Ireland was also important and attempted to stop Catholics playing 'Protestant sports'. Clearly, Catholic involvement reflected sectarian motives, but it pointed to an underlying loyalty on the part of many to the faith. This begs the wider question as to how far secularisation undermined popular religious beliefs and practice.

Popular Belief

It is widely assumed that the last quarter of the nineteenth century was a period characterised by a decline in popular observance, with burgeoning numbers of the laity forgoing the Catholic rites of passage, abstaining from attendance at mass and ignoring the moral prescriptions of the clergy. This supposed collapse in religiosity is usually attributed to a series of variables, most of them associated with the emergence of a modern world. These commonly include a process which sociologists have termed 'differentiation', whereby professionals (doctors, nurses, lawyers), state bureaucrats (mayors, local and national administrators, school teachers) took over the roles previously fulfilled by the priest, thus becoming rival foci of authority and generating anti-clerical squabbling. Another contributory factor was the growth of communications, the effect of which was two-fold. Secluded backwaters were opened up to outside influences which challenged traditional patterns of behaviour and thought. At the same time, this communications revolution facilitated migration to the dechristianised towns and cities and, together with agricultural innovations, ensured that the age-old cycle of harvest failure was ended, freeing people from the 'dearth, disease, devotion' syndrome which had helped to maintain a presence on the church pews. Urbanisation is the other factor frequently cited as key to the process of secularisation. Country people transplanted to the towns, it is said, lost their habits of religious observance, were seduced by the attractions of a burgeoning urban-centred leisure culture which offered them dance halls, theatres, cafés and the cinema, and found their religious needs were poorly provided for by a creaking parish structure which struggled to keep up with the urban sprawl. One can also point to the less tangible process of nation-building, achieved for example through conscription, which was much more effectively administered than hitherto, and the state elementary school system, which was generally free, obligatory and neutral in matters of religion.

Undoubtedly, these factors affected people's religious behaviour and outlook, but it is well-nigh impossible to produce empirical data to demonstrate the precise relationship between them and changing patterns of religious behaviour, this despite the fact that historians of the late nineteenth century have access to figures concerning religious practice, including attendance at Sunday mass, Easter communion and participation in the religious rites of passage, which are simply not available for earlier periods. Superficially, these statistics do suggest some measure of decline. But we should be very conscious of regional, class and gender variations, and note that these statistics tell us only about a certain type of religiosity, often termed 'official' or 'clerical', whereas 'popular' religion encompassed a far broader spectrum of activities, including pilgrimages, the cult of the saints, folkloric and superstitious practices, local festivals and private devotions, all of which are less easily quantifiable. Added to this is the perennial problem that mechanical observance of religious forms offers but limited insight into an individual's inner convictions. Indicators such as the observance of the Church's teachings on contraception and the level of illegitimate births may offer some help here, but frequently tell a contradictory story.

France has been most intensively studied, a tribute to the continuing influence of the pioneering endeavours of Gabriel Le Bras and Fernand Boulard,[35] the results being most usefully summarised in the synthesis of Gérard Cholvy and Yves-Marie Hilaire.[36] After the hiatus of the revolution, religious practice revived to reach a plateau in the period *circa* 1860–75 before declining steadily, albeit gradually, until 1905 when there was a recovery which endured until the outbreak of the First World War. However, regional variations were enormous. In the diocese of Nantes, the percentage of the population taking Easter communion (89 per cent) was actually greater in 1902 than it had been sixty years earlier; in Moulins, on the other hand, the decline was precipitate, from 94 per cent in 1805–16 to 43 per cent in 1904; while in dioceses which had long been characterised as dechristianised, such as Châlons and Paris, there was relatively little decline, but the percentage of communicants remained at a consistently low base, around 15–20 per cent of the eligible population. Overall, towns had below average levels of religious practice, although it remained the case that urban centres located in regions of low religious practice generally supported higher rates of observance than did the surrounding countryside.

Regional variation within France was expressed through the quality of religious life as well as through the extent of observance. The Midi, for instance, was characterised by a joyous, exuberant and public religiosity which intermingled the sacred and the profane, whereas Brittany had a more sombre and almost puritanical religiosity which focused upon death and the afterlife. There was an urban–rural dichotomy to be perceived in this respect, too. Townspeople frequently manifested a thoughtful and individual religious commitment contrasting with the naive, unthinking and conformist practice of the faith prevalent among so many of the inhabitants of the countryside. Nevertheless, it should be emphasised that though there had been some overall decline in piety, the map of religious observance in the late nineteenth century closely resembled that of a century earlier, and was not that dissimilar to that of the 1940s. The Catholic heartlands were, and would remain, Brittany, Normandy, the Massif Central and a belt of dioceses along the eastern frontier including the Franche-Comté. What were ominously described as 'missionary areas', where religious observance was in crisis, included the Paris basin, the Limousin and patches of industrialised northern France vividly portrayed in Zola's novel *Germinal*.

It is much more difficult to build up an overall picture of Catholic practice in Germany. The disparate nature of the political unit was still very prevalent even after unification in the late 1860s, and such statistical evidence as we have is locally based and largely concerns Protestants. Nevertheless, drawing largely on the work of Sperber and McLeod, three observations may be attempted.[37] First, it appears that in mid-century Catholic observance, particularly as demonstrated in figures on church attendance, the use of religious language in wills and ownership of religious books in the Rhineland and

Westphalia, bottomed out before rising again thereafter. The date of this revival is not altogether clear, being situated during the 1860s in Aachen and Münster, and during the 1870s in Cologne and Mainz. Second, it is manifest that the Catholic resurgence was everywhere related to, though not wholly explained by, the *Kulturkampf,* and reflected the tendency of Catholics to pull together when subjected to external attack. We have already seen how Polish Catholics rallied to their faith in Prussian Poland. This state discrimination ensured that levels of piety among German Catholics were much higher than among their counterparts in France, and also higher than among their Protestant rivals within Germany. Although the picture is not altogether clear, the forces of secularisation appear to have had greater impact on Protestants, and Catholics were more successful in retaining the loyalty of all social classes, notably the proletariat. The Church was able to see off many of the threats of secularisation. This was due to its willingness to countenance the 'Social Question', the development of the Centre Party, the adoption of popular practices, the reluctance to sidle up to Conservative political parties and the proximity of the Catholic clergy to their flock, both in terms of social origins and mental attitudes, although anti-clericalism could still rear its head in the working-class suburbs of Munich, for example. A final observation is that the Catholic strongholds in the south and west, most obviously Bavaria and the Rhineland, held firm, thus ensuring that the religious map of Germany remained remarkably constant up to the First World War. The 1870 acquisition from France of the highly devout Alsace (the more industrialised Lorraine could never make the same claim) did not alter this basic disposition.

Italy still awaits its Fernand Boulard, and we lack the same kind of detailed statistical measurements that are available for France. Impressionistic evidence usually contrasts the relatively devout Italian south with the more dechristianised north, a picture which is in need of nuance. While the more industrialised triangle formed by Genoa, Milan and Turin undoubtedly witnessed a decline in observance, in the surrounding countryside, especially in the uplands and Alpine districts, devotion was more solid. The Veneto also had a well deserved reputation for its Catholic loyalties; traditionally the most devout area of northern Italy, it would not be until the onset of industrialisation in the 1930s that matters changed here. Emilia-Romagna, a traditional bastion of anti-clericalism thanks to the onerous nature of papal government, was another area where the laity were conspicuous by their absence at Sunday mass.

Within Spain, William Callahan and Frances Lannon among others have identified several variables determining levels of practice, the former making the point that there was no 'single religious model applicable to all Spaniards in every region of the country'.[38] They have highlighted the geographical divide between a pious north and an impious south with the south-west being especially dechristianised and the north-east especially devout, although it is not possible to discern with clarity more subtle local differences. For example, the highest number of seminarians in 1854 were in Old Castile, León and Navarra, the lowest in Extremadura, Andalucia and La Mancha. Similarly, a mass petition campaign organised by the Church in 1869 on the issue of religious toleration, which secured 3 million signatures, revealed the north–south dichotomy with the bulk of support coming from the Catholic north. The Jesuit Francisco de Tarin, known for his missions of evangelisation between 1899 and 1906, painted a catastrophic picture of the south: 'It makes me sadder each time to see these towns; the indifference that reigns in them would not even be seen among the tribes of Africa.'[39] The experiences of the Redemptorist missionary Ramón Sarabía were identical. In Aznaga (Extremadura) only ten men and 200 women out of 18,000 inhabitants attended Sunday mass. On the other hand, he was enthusiastic about the devotion of the population in the north where 'traditional and honest Christianity' remained firm.[40]

One explanation of these patterns, which were becoming increasingly apparent in the nineteenth century, is the late, and relatively ineffectual, christianisation of the south as part of the *reconquista*. Another is the poor ecclesiastical organisation in the south whose paucity of parish clergy has already been noted. Undoubtedly, the social bias of religiosity also played a major part. Levels of practice were highest among property-owners and the well-to-do and lowest among the wage-earners and landless who were especially numerous in the south. For instance, in the province of Huelva the presence of large numbers of wage slaves, concentrated in the vast *latifundia* estates, resulted in massive social alienation and a concomitant rejection of Catholicism which was associated with the dominant elites.

A further feature of Spain's religiosity was the urban–rural dichotomy. Excepting regions in the south-west, observance generally held firm in the countryside, and many towns recalled a tale of decline. In the late 1850s, for instance, one priest from Barcelona noted that only around one in three of his flock attended for Easter communion; in the town of Logroño, almost 58 per cent of individuals stayed away from church at Easter by 1890, compared with only around 7 per cent three decades earlier, the decline being most precipitate after 1872; and in the parish of San José, in the manufacturing centre of Mataró, in 1900, less than half of those on the point of death received the last rites. Sarabía's experiences also pointed to a decline of the faith in towns, even in the pious north. The Bishop of Palau bemoaned the unwillingness of the laity to fulfil their paschal duties or to attend for Sunday mass. He at least appreciated the need for the Church to adapt its message to the burgeoning population of the urban centres, but the institution as a whole failed to keep up with the changing demographic patterns. In Madrid, for example, where the population almost doubled in the final four decades of the nineteenth century, not a single new parish was created. On the eve of the First World War, Barcelona and Madrid had the dubious honour of claiming the largest parishes in Europe. Moreover, the parish clergy, with some notable exceptions, was generally reluctant to serve in the overcrowded and squalid working-class districts of the cities.

If there were signs of serious religious decline on the Continent, it is rather paradoxical that Britain should have manifested the opposite trend. Here, of course, in the late eighteenth century, Catholics had been very much a minority, some 80,000 in England and 30,000 in Scotland, and had laboured under restrictive legislation, albeit fitfully enforced. Nevertheless, they had tended to congregate in peripheral areas, such as coastal Lancashire, the uplands of Northumberland and Yorkshire, and north-east Scotland, well away from the tentacles of central government, and often reliant on the patronage of the local dignitaries and priests. Matters changed significantly by the second half of the nineteenth century when the Catholic population of England and Wales has been estimated at 1,354,000 in 1887 and well over a third of a million in Scotland. The 1851 census revealed a total of 383,630 people attending Catholic services. This impressive upsurge not only reflected the massive surge of Irish immigration after the Act of Union and the famine, as well as the relaxation of government disabilities, but also indicated across the British Isles a greater confidence on the part of the Catholic Church which was prepared to go out and proselytise. It appears that it had some success, as did Nonconformists more generally, in winning converts from Anglicanism in areas where the Church of England was weak and poorly organised. This reinvigoration was most apparent in Ireland where Catholicism had always been a badge of identity and where it will be recalled there had been a 'devotional revolution'. In the 1870s, the better-trained and energetic clergy, produced by the earlier seminary reforms, went out of its way to stimulate religious fervour, resulting in higher attendance at mass, more and bigger churches and greater displays of public piety. Such features were especially prominent in the predominantly agricultural western counties where the faith had traditionally been weakest thanks to its isolation and distance from Dublin.

While statistics of communicants, mass attendants and partakers of the rites of passage portray a chequered picture of 'clerical' Catholicism for Europe overall, there is good evidence for a revitalisation of 'popular' Catholicism, though this is not to imply the two were mutually exclusive. Perhaps the most striking feature of this resurgence was the emergence of visionaries, new saints, pilgrimage sites and thaumaturgic centres, Marianism and ostentatious displays of popular piety. Among the first of the nineteenth-century visionaries was Sister Cathérine Labouré in Paris. After swallowing a piece of linen in 1830 which had belonged to St Vincent, she was visited by a vision of the Virgin, who also appeared to Charles X's Chief Minister Villèle on the eve of the revolution that year to reassure him that matters were going to be all right. A medal struck to commemorate the event two years later was associated with numerous cures, especially of cholera, and as a result this particular Marian cult achieved a nationwide status. In 1846, at La Salette, near Grenoble in the French Alps, two young children, Mélanie Calvat and Maximin Giraud, also witnessed an apparition of the Virgin, who this time had an admonitory message, warning of disaster if people did not mend their ways. La Salette was boosted by the endorsement of the influential Curé d'Ars who overcame his initial doubts about the validity of the sighting. Twelve years later Bernadette Soubirous, an illiterate teenage Pyrenean shepherdess, experienced some eighteen visions of a white light in a grotto near Lourdes, which soon announced itself as the 'Immaculate Conception', interpreted once again as the Virgin Mary. Lourdes quickly replaced La Salette as the chief place of pilgrimage. Organised by the Assumptionist fathers, it was visited by some half a million people annually by the turn of the century, many no doubt drawn by the healing waters of the spring which Bernadette had discovered on the site. Marian apparitions would persist in France throughout the century – there were nine significant instances in the 1870s, most famously at Portmain in 1871 at the time of the French defeat, and five in the following decade. They were also prevalent elsewhere: at Dolina in Austria in mid-century; at Ceretto in Italy in 1853; at Philippsdorf in Bohemia in 1866; at Marpingen in the Saarland in 1876; in the Bavarian village of Mettenbuch in 1877; at Knock in Ireland's County Mayo in 1879; and at Fatima in Portugal in 1917, to cite merely the best-known examples. And they have continued throughout the twentieth century, being concentrated in the inter-war years, the late 1940s and the 1980s, occurring as far afield as Germany, France, Italy, the Ukraine, Romania and beyond. Older types of vision, involving crucifixes, strange cloud formations and shepherds, for example, were still reported during the nineteenth century but they were largely eclipsed by the Marian apparitions. As David Blackbourn notes, the visions tended to become increasingly uniform in other respects: they generally involved women or children; the visionaries were almost always of low social status and marginal figures within their local community; and the Virgin had a message to impart, usually a warning of doom if people did not mend their ways.[41]

Complementing these visions was the creation of a raft of new saints, a practice fostered by Pius IX, who showed himself much readier to bestow canonisation than his predecessors, and who initiated the modern trend in granting recognition. So it was that, on taking office in 1846, he quickly canonised Paul of the Cross, the founder of the Passionists. Others were not slow in coming: Peter Claver, the so-called 'apostle of the Africans'; Pedro d'Arbues, a late-fifteenth-century inquisitor who was responsible for the deaths of some several thousand Jews and who met his end at the hands of one of his adversaries; and Marguerite-Marie Alacoque, beatified rather than being immediately turned into a saint. The same delay occurred in the case of Joan of Arc who was beatified in 1909, nearly 500 years after her death, and who was eventually canonised by Benedict XV in 1920. Bishop Dupanloup had launched the call for Joan's sainthood in the 1860s. In her were blended Ultramontane piety and nationalist symbolism, one of the reasons why the Republic embraced Marianne as its symbol. While the French left, notably at the time of the Popular Front, would embrace Joan as a symbol of nationhood, her sainthood appeared to be a triumph of right-wing values.

Among the new saints, perhaps the two most astonishing, though for very different reasons, were the Carmelite nun Theresa of Lisieux, and Philomena, supposedly an early Christian martyr. A victim of tuberculosis at the early age of twenty-four in 1897, Theresa was an unknown until the publication of her notebooks, heavily edited and added to by her sister and the members of her nunnery. As already noted, her *History of a Soul* sold on an astonishing scale, and she was canonised in 1923, a speed record in the recognition of sainthood. Meanwhile, the cult of St Philomena had all but disappeared. Her story began in 1802 with the discovery in the catacombs of Rome of the bones of a young girl, together with an inscription and a supposed phial of blood. The remains were interpreted as those of an early Christian martyr, though nothing else was known about her. St Philomena's full story was subsequently revealed in the visions of a Neapolitan nun according to which the girl had come to a gruesome end for refusing the advances of the Emperor Diocletian. Pius IX established a mass for her day, and this was subsequently made a feast for the whole Church by Pius X. Archaeological advances put an end to her fame by questioning the dating of the remains and the manner of her death, although it was not until 1961 that she was removed from the Calendar of Saints.

In addition to the list of individuals who received formal recognition as saints, there was a plethora of local figures who appeared in no Church manual yet who nevertheless were accorded a saintly reputation and popularly venerated, enjoying a regional reputation which was often based on the curative powers of a shrine, image or grotto. The revived cult of the saints was also supported by the fondness for relics. When the remains of Christ's seamless robe were put on display at Trier in 1844, only the fourth such showing since 1585, they attracted 1,050,833 pilgrims in seven weeks. The supply of relics had burgeoned since the opening up of the catacombs under Rome, though the papacy grew embarrassed at the trade and Leo XIII put a stop to it in 1881. Kissing the remains of a saint was believed to provide some safeguard against misfortune, at the very least, and relics were also held to have curative powers. St Philomena's bones, for instance, first began to attain some local fame when they produced healings of the sick as they were being transported to the village shrine at Mugnano near Naples.

The marbling texture of this type of devotion was a Marianism which reached its peak at the close of the century. The cult of Mary was, of course, not new, but it now reached unprecedented heights and novel forms, thanks in part to the patronage of the papacy, notably through the introduction to the litany in 1883 of the entreaty *Regina Sacratissimi Rosarii* dedicated to the Blessed Virgin, although something of this personality cult was restrained by the 1891 encyclical *Octobri mensi*, which laid out the daily rosary for the month of October. In 1907, Pius X approved the Festival of the Appearance of the Virgin for the entire Catholic world, and encouragement was given to Marian confraternities, always excepting the wayward Polish clerical society of Mariavites. Hilda Graeff cites a wide range of new orders devoted to the Virgin, among them the Society of Missionaries of Mary (1853), the Prêtres de Sainte Marie (1851) and the Little Companions of Mary, established at Nottingham in 1877.[42] Marian congresses were also popular; those held at Livorno, Turin and Lyon complemented the eucharistic celebrations which had become popular at the same time. A burgeoning art and literature was also devoted to the Virgin, and the month of May was set aside in her honour. The narrator in Proust's *Swann's Way* recalls how the altar in his local church was decked out in almond-smelling hawthorns, replete with white buds, and how the family made a special effort to attend services on a Saturday evening when the sins of the young were forthrightly condemned. The month of May further honoured St Joseph who, in 1870, had become the patron of the whole Church. The encyclical *Quamquam plures* of 1889 promoted Joseph as an example of a good husband, father and, above all, worker, a source of comfort for those in 'modest circumstances', though this cult never attained the same degree of support as that of Mary. Under Pius XII, the feast day of St Joseph was located on 1 May deliberately to antagonise the left.

While there is irony in that such displays of devotion could take place at a time of supposed secularisation, there is an even greater paradox in that they flourished at a moment when rationalism, a belief in progress and the invincibility of science were the hallmarks of intellectual life. Inevitably the *cognoscenti*, among them the novelist Zola who wrote critically of Lourdes, condemned the visionaries as charlatans and the cures as hoaxes; but such doubting Thomases were not to put off the faithful. If anything, they strengthened the rectitude of the pilgrims and the clergy. Contemporaries and some subsequent historians have indeed argued that such examples of religiosity were indications of faith. This was reason enough for the papacy and the bishops to encourage them, even if the clergy were not prepared to validate the original vision or the actual historical events. That said, there were some local cults, visionaries and claims for sainthood which the upper echelons of the Church were not prepared to entertain and approve, either because they were manifestly absurd or because they were dangerous.

It should also be noted that the Church was not averse to taking advantage of the developments of commercialisation, modern science and industrialisation to sponsor these forms of worship. For example, 'modern' techniques of fund-raising were used to sponsor the building of the Sacré Coeur in Montmartre. In order to bring in small investors, donors were given cards of the Sacred Heart on which they ticked off squares each time they set aside ten *centimes*; pieces of the church (individual stones and pillars) were 'sold' and purchasers could personalise these in some manner, say by the addition of initials; other benefactors could have a personal prayer inscribed on parchment, sealed into glass tubes and placed in specially-cut chambers in the wall. In this way, the value of popular donations came to exceed the traditional bequests from wealthy individuals and corporations, substantial though these were. Paray-le-Monial, the site where the seventeenth-century nun Marguerite-Marie Alacoque had visions of Jesus in which he promised blessings to those who venerated his heart, took off as a mass pilgrimage site in the nineteenth century thanks partly to improved means of communication: group rates were offered for train travel and lodgings. Similarly, Lourdes would never have become a popular place of pilgrimage without the railway, and full use was made of newspapers, electric lighting for the display of relics and the illumination of grottoes. The Authentification Bureau at Lourdes was an additional method of deploying science in the service of the Church; doctors vetted each of the miracles and maintained a detailed statistical record of all claims. Mass pilgrimage elided into organised leisure trade and a veritable tourist industry soon attached itself to towns such as Lisieux, Marpingen and elsewhere where the overriding concerns were commercial rather than spiritual. Hoteliers, restaurateurs, café-owners and the hawkers of knick-knacks all had a vested interest in maintaining the popularity of the site and no interest whatsoever in undermining its credibility. Techniques of mass production allowed for the sale and distribution of countless numbers of religious arte-facts. Plaster saints abounded, as did crucifixes, their presence helping to create what Susan O'Brien has called a distinctive 'Catholic space' in houses and some schools and factories.[43] Around one billion medals of La Salette were struck in France alone, and the cult of the Sacred Heart flourished as emblems of the heart were produced in their millions. In a very real sense, then, one may talk about the commodification of Catholicism during the nineteenth century.

Whether or not a given cult or pilgrimage site took off depended a good deal on chance, for instance whether there was a local bishop prepared to offer support. The success of Lourdes, for example, very much relied on the diocesan bishop as well as the patronage of the French imperial court which overrode the objection of the local priest and prefect. Clerical attitudes towards the new cults also need to be seen in the wider context of a Church attempting to recover its hold over the masses in the aftermath of the revolutionary and Napoleonic decades. In this respect, it is further significant that such displays of piety abounded at times when national churches were under considerable strain: the shrine at Marpingen flourished during the *Kulturkampf*; Lourdes thrived spectacularly in the aftermath of defeat and civil war in 1870–71 and at the moment when the Republic converted to anti-clericalism; Knock co-incided with the decisive phase of the Irish land war; and Fatima appeared when the Portuguese regime became allegedly anti-Christian. Within Spain, Philomena was dubbed the saint of the Carlists by their liberal opponents. It is in this context that we can note the tendency of Marian apparitions to come in waves, coinciding with times of serious emergency.

Local circumstances further played a part, notably in the case of La Salette which coincided with a cholera epidemic. The most successful shrines and places of worship were indeed those which boasted miraculous powers and curative properties. Another common aspect of this piety was the predom-inance of young girls, often poor and untutored like Joan of Arc herself. Theirs was a simple, trusting, sentimental and naive faith which correlated with the trend within Catholicism towards a more unthinking, unintellectual and mawkish religiosity. To recall the words of Ralph Gibson, there was a shift in emphasis from an eighteenth-century 'God of Fear' to a 'God of Love'.[44] It is surely significant that the earlier visions spoke in admonitory terms, warning of the punishment that would inevitably follow if people did not mend their ways, whereas the later ones brought words of comfort and consolation.

For some commentators, this style of religion, typically dubbed 'saccharine' and expressed at its most maudlin in its Mariological manifestations and in the effeminate Saint-Sulpice Christ of the Sacred Heart Devotion, accounts for the propensity of women to practise the faith in far greater numbers than men. Of the ongoing feminisation of religion during the nineteenth century there can be little doubt. Women were more numerous as members of confraternities and regular orders, statistically women appear to have attended Sunday services more routinely than their husbands, and women were more conspicuous in the confessional box. As one parish priest in 1850s Barcelona observed, women predominated at Easter communion. In the diocese of Moulins, in 1904, 17.9 per cent of men, compared to 48 per cent of women, attended mass for that year. The detailed studies on Lourdes by Ruth Harris and on Marpingen by David Blackbourn have again revealed that women outnumbered men as pilgrims, and were vastly overrepresented in the statistics of those who experienced cures.[45] This was a reversal of the late Middle Ages when men had claimed the majority of miracle recoveries. And women did a good deal to shape the material culture of nineteenth-century Catholicism. Their skills as embroiderers, seamstresses, flower arrangers, laundresses and cleaners were constantly called upon as altars and side chapels were cleaned and decorated with linen, drapery and floral displays and as houses were similarly tricked out. In this way they made a marked contribution to the formation of a distinctive 'Catholic space' in homes and churches.

So much for feminisation, yet whether it can be subsequently deduced that women were inherently more susceptible to this kind of Ultramontane piety remains questionable. Such a conclusion betrays a persistence of nineteenth-century anti-clerical and chauvinistic attitudes which believed that women were somehow mentally inferior and physiologically weaker, prone to irrational beliefs and easily suborned by the machinations of the clergy. Recent scholarship has moved away from this somewhat sterile debate but has not necessarily solved the riddle.[46] There may well have been a series of factors at work. Men, as we already noted, were put off the confessional by the intrusion of the priest into their private lives and were alienated by the clerical suppression of the festive elements of popular religiosity, and by clerical domination of confraternities. Men also had outlets for sociability outside the Church and, with the growth of suffrage, trade unions and political parties, they were increasingly engaged in the political process often combining this with an anti-clericalism. Another suggestion is that women discovered a form of empowerment through their attendance at pilgrimages and their participation in forms of popular piety. While the male hierarchy of the Church still severely restricted a woman's sphere to that of wife, mother and model of virtue, within the confraternities, pilgrimages and Marian devotions, all of which were under nominal clerical supervision, women secured a freedom, authority and an independence of spirituality which was otherwise denied them.

A further explanation for the appeal of Catholicism to women, recently advanced by Olwen Hufton, was the solace it offered for specifically female problems in the here and now.[47] A Marian girdle placed on a woman's stomach eased the pain of childbirth. In the Massif Central scrapings of stone from a statue of the Virgin Mary were made into an elixir which assisted conception;

and dotted throughout France and Italy were miracle-working shrines for those who believed themselves to be barren. In Burgundy, *sanctuaires à répit* existed where 'stillborn' infants were resuscitated just long enough to receive the sacrament of baptism so as to save them from a perpetual limbo existence. St Rita of Cascia was the unofficial patron saint of battered wives. As has been stressed, such 'remedies' reflected specifically feminine concerns which could not be addressed by the medicine or science of contemporary nineteenth-century society.

Overall it is difficult to escape the conclusion that the late nineteenth century was one of enormous upheaval in all walks of life and that many of the changes, whether in the realm of intellectual life, the growth of industrialisation, demographic shifts, the rise of the nation-state and the consolidation of institutionalised laicism, could prove deleterious to Catholicism. Yet it did not follow that any of these things necessarily resulted in secularisation. Much depended on how the Church responded. Where it addressed social issues and displayed an empathy for popular concerns, it was successful in retaining the loyalty of its flock. Where popular belief and practice remained attuned to the needs and fears of ordinary people, religion again continued to enjoy a vitality. Where the Church harnessed the forces of progress such as the newspaper and railways in its service, it likewise rode out the storm. Most importantly, the Church could still draw upon what may be best termed a 'raw allegiance', perhaps strongest in those predominantly Catholic countries. So it was that this period may be characterised at one and the same time as 'an age of unbelief' and 'an age of belief'. The other irony is that, as religion was allegedly in retreat in Europe, it was on the march in the rest of the world.

Catholicism Overseas

The Catholic Church had always taken a keen interest in the overseas activities of the European powers, most obviously in the sixteenth century with the discoveries of the New World by the Spanish and Portuguese.[48] Among the missionary orders who quickly involved themselves in proselytising and conversion, the Jesuits had a particularly honourable reputation in seeking to protect the indigenous peoples from the frequently rapacious and cruel regimes that white settlers imposed. By the late eighteenth century, these missionary activities were in some disarray: there was little coordination of their efforts; there was controversy over the extent to which local cultural forms should be integrated into Christianity; and the number of volunteers coming forward to serve in overseas orders was declining. It is often said that the scale of missionary work is symptomatic of the general health of a particular Church and, in this respect, the problems of European Catholicism clearly hampered ecclesiastical endeavours in Latin America and South-East Asia. The onset of the revolutionary and Napoleonic decades dealt a further blow even though Bonaparte permitted the re-establishment of the three French missionary orders – the Fathers of the Holy Spirit, the Lazarists and the Fathers of the

Faith – recognising their value in consolidating the outreach of his empire. So it was that the Church was badly placed to meet the challenges posed by the period from 1860 to 1914, known by historians as the 'New Age of Imperialism', when European powers asserted a far more effective control and influence over a greater percentage of the globe's surface than at any previous epoch, especially in Africa and South-East Asia. Among the colonising powers, Protestant Britain was pre-eminent, closely followed by Russia; Germany was a late entrant into the race. Among Catholic powers, France was the key player, even if its empire could not quite rival that of Britain; Italy played only a minor part while Spain and Portugal, once at the forefront of overseas expansion, had run out of steam; Spain even lost lands such as Cuba and the Philippines to the USA.

The reasons behind this 'New Imperialism' have been intensely debated by historians in recent years, and here is not the place to review the arguments, except to say that the Catholic Church played only a small part in facilitating colonial expansion. Broadly speaking, this role may be subsumed under three headings. The first, and indeed traditional method, was the dispatch of missionaries to uncharted territories in order to spread the word, and a process which enabled individual churchmen to claim a particular area for their country. So it was that, in 1878, Cardinal Lavigerie, the French Bishop of Algiers, authorised a dozen members of the Missionary Congregation of White Fathers, which he himself had established in Carthage, to set up mission centres in Equatorial Africa, enabling him to claim these lands for France, thus heading off rival claims by the British and the Dutch. Second, it was often the case that missionaries ran into trouble with the native populations, necessitating their rescue by their national governments which were often looking for a pretext to involve themselves in such a way. For instance, it was the death of two missionaries in 1897 in China which provided the Germans with an excuse to occupy Kiaochow and secure the support of the Centre Party in parliament to pursue further imperial ambitions. Third, religious rivalry played its part in facilitating colonialism. In the 1840s, the veteran German missionary, the Protestant Johann Ludwig Krapf, ventured into East Africa precisely with the intention of preventing this region falling under the sway of Islam or Roman Catholicism.

Gauging the success of the Church's overseas activities depends heavily on what criteria are deployed. If it is judged in terms of the growth in the number of missionary orders, then clearly there was achievement. Reflecting the recuperation of the regular orders in Europe, there was a welter of new foundations, among them the Oblates of the Blessed Virgin Mary Immaculate (1816), the Marists (1817), the Silesians (1859), the Schute Fathers (1862), Fathers of the Holy Spirit (1848), the Lyon Society of African Missions (1856) and the Mill Hill Fathers (1866), a secular society of Dutch and British priests based in north London.

If success is to be judged rather in terms of the involvement of the indigenous population as priests and acolytes, then the story is less rosy. A report of 1862 on the situation in India, where the issue of caste often interfered, revealed that six vicariates had not a single indigenous priest and six others had no seminary for training them. In China, by 1890, there were 369 native priests compared to 639 foreign missionaries. This situation was healthier than in Japan where Christianity had until recently been proscribed. Here, the first ordinations occurred in 1883; yet on the eve of the First World War, there were a mere thirty-three native priests. Within Africa, where the tradition of early marriage flew in the face of the vow of celibacy, it was similarly difficult to win recruits, leading to the conclusion that somehow Africans were not natural leaders. If we compare Catholic efforts with those of the Protestant churches, then clearly there was a lot of catching up to be done, and it should be remembered that the principal colonising country, Britain, was itself Protestant. Throughout the globe, Catholic missionaries arrived late in the day and their activities were often circumscribed by a number of factors, including the blessing of the mother country. The Australian government, which controlled Papua New Guinea, allotted different denominations separate areas within which to proselytise, confining the Catholics to a narrow southern strip of the island. The Church did best in colonies belonging to nominally Catholic states, most obviously in those lands attached to France. Whereas the Third Republic was happy to circumscribe clerical activities at home, it valued missionary orders as standard-bearers of French civilisation. '*Cléricalisme, voilà l'ennemi*' might have been the battle-cry at home, but republicans acknowledged that anti-clericalism 'was not for export'.

The measurement of success which the missionaries themselves valued most highly was the number of converts. In this respect the picture was chequered, but not unimpressive overall. In Indo-China (including Cambodia, Laos and Tonking), it has been calculated that the Catholics comprised over 7 per cent of the population at around 1.5 million souls; in the rest of South-East Asia, gains were not so impressive. In 1890, there were about half a million Catholics in China, a small fraction of the overall population, but more numerous than the Protestant converts, a situation replicated in parts of India where the inspired leadership of Constante Lievens, a Flemish Jesuit, had secured the conversion of thousands of former Lutherans as well as Hindus and so-called pagans. Within Africa, the Church, along with all other denominations, developed settlements, known as *chrétientés*, which gathered together young children, freed slaves and otherwise nomadic tribesmen so that they could be isolated from the unregenerate world outside. These could be formidable establishments, especially as they often provided a better standard of living than was otherwise available. Two such enclaves run by the Premonstratensians catered for 1,600 orphans in 1905, and the Jesuits at Kisantu sometimes had authority over 1,000 inhabitants. Particularly successful was the Roman Catholic settlement at Marianhill in the Natal, which emulated medieval monastic life. Additional to the *chrétientés* were the so-called *ferme-chapelles,* a kind of half-way house between total isolation and absorption by the local community. These permitted some limited interchange between members of the *ferme* and their non-Christian neighbours, including the exchange of goods, handicrafts, mixed farming and even marriage.

One important variable in determining the number of conversions was indigenous culture, particularly pre-existing religious beliefs. Least success was achieved in those areas where there was already a well developed religious structure such as Shinto, Confucianism and Islam, or where the local tradition and class structures did not blend easily with Catholicism. Little headway was made in the deserts and mountains of North Africa where Islam held sway. In Latin America, the mainly creole male elites, descendants of early European settlers, thought that the Church had an important role in maintaining the social order and bringing salvation to Indians, blacks and those of mixed race, but they found it difficult to acknowledge that the clergy had anything to offer to themselves, and regarded their own spiritual health as a private matter. At the same time, the traditional pre-conquest Indian religions had focused upon the worship of goddesses, and this predisposed the masses to embrace the Virgin and female saints as their own. So it was that religion tended to become female-centred, this contrasting sharply with the *machismo*, or cult of manliness, that predominated in the secular world. Such a dichotomy helped to give Catholicism in Latin America some of its particular characteristics. In India, the rituals of the faith often overlapped with those of Hinduism, for example the use of bells, incense and chanting, which made for more converts, especially when missionaries, Lutherans included, embraced the local caste system. Conversely, other Hindus were alienated by the sanguine imagery of Christianity and the notion that an innocent should have died to atone for sins of mankind, all of which was foreign to the Hindu way of thinking. Everywhere, however, the spread of Catholicism, and for that matter Protestantism, was hampered by the paternalist approach of missionaries. Although they paid lip-service to the eventual establishment of a self-generating and locally organised Church, in practice this was always seen as something well in the future, and there was a profound reluctance both to induct indigenous people into the priesthood and to grant them any real measure of responsibility.

Although the papacy, in particular Gregory XVI and Pius IX, praised the missionary activity of the Church, recognising that this bolstered their faltering prestige within Europe, imperialism was to create a series of difficulties for Rome, in particular by raising the issue of temporal authority. This had been a source of contention ever since the Portuguese and Spanish conquests of the sixteenth century, but had been resolved by the balance of power within the colonies themselves which, to all extents and purposes, were governed by Madrid or Lisbon. Rome had little or no say. In the nineteenth century, the issue was reopened, at least in the case of Latin America, by the growth of Ultramontanism and the granting of autonomy within former Spanish and Portuguese territories: Brazil acquired its independence in 1822 and much of Spanish America followed suit in the next two years. Although many churchmen were uncomfortable with the new regimes which emerged within the Americas, they did not automatically accept the jurisdiction of Rome over their affairs. This dilemma was perhaps best expressed in the writings of the Peruvian priest Francisco de Paula González Vigil, a staunch advocate of democratic and liberal principles who, in the 1830s, began his mammoth eight-volume treatise asserting the independence of national governments, and criticising the growing authoritarianism of Rome which he saw as inimical to the spirit of early Christianity. Typically, Pius IX never bothered to read his endeavours, merely consigning the writings of Vigil to the *Index*. Other priests, however, continued to assert their autonomy, notably José Antonio Martínez in New Mexico. That a schism was avoided in the Americas may be attributed to the growing political instability which overtook the continent, leading many priests to the conclusion that what was needed was a revitalisation of authority, order and discipline, qualities best provided by the Church, which itself possessed a traditional and hierarchical structure. Within Mexico, in particular, during the civil wars of the 1850s, the Church engaged in a rearguard action against the anti-clericalism of the liberals, an anti-clericalism that was soon to spread into much of Central America, albeit resisted in Colombia.

Schism did, however, afflict the Church in India thanks to the persistence of the *Padroado* which granted the Portuguese crown the sole right to appoint bishops in the dioceses of Goa, Crangamore, Cochin and Mylapore. On many occasions, these sees had been left vacant, and the existence of a rival jurisdiction meant that many orders had shifted their allegiance from Rome to Lisbon whenever it suited their interests. To rectify matters, in 1838, Gregory XVI introduced the bull *Multa praeclare* which abolished the dioceses of Crangamore, Cochin and Mylapore, and reduced that of Goa to those small patches of land which were still under Portuguese rule. At the same time, Rome appointed vicars apostolic for the remainder of India. This initiative did not go down well, especially as diplomatic relations did not exist between Rome and Portugal at that point. Within India itself, the Portuguese clergy refused to acknowledge papal authority and rejected the bull as a forgery. The conflict rumbled on throughout the century, inflamed by the actions of Silva Torres whom the Pope appointed to the archbishopric of Goa in 1843 in an attempt to reconcile the Portuguese. Torres soon went native, more or less creating a separate Goanese Church through the ordination of several hundred new priests. Through a concordat of 1886 concluded with the Portuguese government, Leo XIII was able to reassert papal control over India by the creation of new ecclesiastical provinces, yet Goa still retained much of its autonomy and many clerical institutions elsewhere still possessed *Padroado* privileges.

Significantly, it would not be until the close of the nineteenth century that Rome would agree to indigenous bishops in India, pointing to the overall purpose of the Church's missionary activity which was not only to propagate the word but also to teach the natives the superior values of European traditions. This had, of course, included the slave trade, although in fairness we need to note that it was Muslim Arab merchants who had done much to keep this alive against the wishes of an increasing number of European governments, most notably Britain which outlawed the trade in 1807, declaring it an 'act of piracy' some sixteen years later. Holland was not slow to follow suit. To his credit, Gregory denounced the trade in his bull *In supremo* of

1839, but Catholic states were much slower than their Protestant counterparts to take limiting action. Portugal wavered for some time, introducing a series of piecemeal measures, whereas France did not go the whole hog, abolishing slavery throughout its colonies only in 1863. All manner of injustices were perpetrated by the Europeans overseas, among them the apartheid partially facilitated by the Dutch Reformed Church in South Africa, but few rivalled the crimes of Leopold II of Belgium who governed the supposedly independent Congo Free State as a personal fiefdom, and where the Church could have spoken much more loudly in protest.

In the course of the twentieth century, it would be the growing numbers of Catholics in overseas lands, notably in Latin America and the Philippines, that would compensate for the declining percentage of adherents in Europe, nominal though many of these overseas converts were. This support did, however, come at a price. Not only would it prove difficult to exert discipline over these non-European lands, but they would also develop a disconcerting variety of liberal theologies which ran counter to the orthodoxy of Rome.

Conclusion: a Church in the Pope's Image

In its own way, the period under consideration was as momentous as the turning point that was the French revolutionary and Napoleonic epoch. The Catholic poet Péguy was surely right when he claimed that the world in the late nineteenth century had changed more in three decades than at any time in the preceding 1,500 years. The Church, with its weight of tradition, its intricate institutional structures which were already strained after the upheavals of the 1790s, and the natural conservative instinct of its leadership, inevitably struggled to keep in touch with the new order of things, and it was not wholly unsuccessful. Whereas Catholic innovatory scholarship in the shape of modernism was suffocated at birth, with the result that old-fashioned attitudes remained intact, and whereas there was no real engagement with the intellectual heavyweights of the day, Catholicism as a faith had remained integral to many people's lives, and had found ways to come to terms with the forces of industrialisation, urbanisation and anti-clericalism in its many guises. It will no longer suffice to describe this era as one of irreligion, for, as we have seen, the process of secularisation was extremely complex and belief was not uprooted; indeed, in many instances it was strengthened. There is no doubt, however, that the balance of power between Church and state in individual countries, whether Catholic or not, had tilted irrevocably in favour of the latter.

The overriding feature of this period was the accumulation of power on the part of the papacy, a paradoxical situation given the spread of liberal democracy within so much of the rest of Europe. As Timothy McCarthy has commented, the Church *qua* institution, and above all as manifested by the papal office, was the dominant image of the Church as a whole.[49] In itself, the growth of pontifical power was not necessarily a bad thing, as it lent Catholicism greater cohesion than it had previously possessed, but in the twentieth century, much would now depend on the personal qualities of individual pontiffs, and their ability to accommodate the many enthusiasms and initiatives of the lower clergy and laity who sought to explore the possibilities of liberal and social Catholicism and, indeed, of fascism within the context of two world wars.

CHAPTER FIVE

Catholicism and Reaction, 1914–45

THE period between 1914 and 1945 was one of hope and disappointment for the European Catholic Church. There was dismay that the great powers indulged in two world wars, both of which the Vatican considered wholly futile. The resulting horrors of war were equally deplored although, in this respect, the papacy appeared to value some categories of humankind more highly than others. At the same time, the fighting seemed to give rise to new dangers, notably an international balance of power that, with the emergence of the USA, was tilted yet further towards the Protestant world. An even greater peril was perceived to come from communism. In much the same way as the 1789 Revolution in France had been attributed to satanic inspiration, so too the Bolshevik achievement of 1917 was seen as the work of the devil, who was now in a position to spread materialism and atheism throughout the globe. The Church never denounced fascist dictatorships with the same vehemence, and national churches and the Vatican often drew comfort from the traditionalist regimes which were being built in Spain, Portugal, Austria and elsewhere. Even within Nazi Germany, Catholic criticisms were muted. This was partly thanks to the reluctance of the papacy to do battle with temporal powers, preferring instead to engage with governments in the negotiation of concordats which, on paper at least, gave the Church significant advantages. For, as already stated, this was also a period of great hope. The papacy was pleased that its own power continued to rise unabated. Even though Ultramontanism had firmly established itself, successive popes toiled hard to enhance their position yet further, for instance through Benedict XV's overhaul of Canon Law and through the Curia's insistence that only a disciplined body of believers, under the firm direction of the Vatican, was capable of seeing off modern-day challenges. Within the laity and local clergy, indiscipline still operated, yet paradoxically war offered an opportunity for the reassertion of hierarchical control. War additionally enabled the Church to show off what it did best, that is to assist the needy and less fortunate. This Catholicism did with vigour and skill, except in the case of the Jews. The Holocaust posed a series of formidable questions of conscience which simply could not be ducked. It is to the credit of many rank-and-file Catholics that they actively resisted Hitlerian persecution. It is to the papacy's eternal discredit that this racial war was not tackled head on.

The First World War and its Aftermath

It was symptomatic of the declining temporal and international power of the papacy in the nineteenth century that the Church had little role in resisting the outbreak of fighting in 1914, a hapless bystander as the great powers entered a murderous war from which there seemed no escape. Historians have ever since tried to make sense of this terrible onslaught and have proffered a series of reasons for its origins: the secretive diplomacy of the great powers which bred mistrust and division; the arms race which had witnessed Russia and Germany in particular add to their already considerable arsenals; the rigidity of military planning which guaranteed a war in both east and west; the race for empire which fostered imperial and capitalist rivalry; the attempt to resolve domestic difficulties by resort to an aggressive, jingoistic foreign policy; and even the cultural 'mood of 1914' which was so xenophobic and aggressive that a bellicose public was prepared to countenance the resort to arms. It is agreed, however, that religious animosities played no significant part in the march to the Marne; the age of religious war, within Europe at least, was well and truly over. This did not stop the papacy, in the shape of Benedict XV, from putting forward its own explanation as to why war had occurred. In his encyclical *Ad beatissimi* of 1 November 1914, he cited a pervasive moral decay which manifested itself in selfishness, disregard for authority, divisive class struggles and materialism, an analysis not so different from that offered by communists who saw war as the outgrowth of bourgeois greed.

If there was any way in which Catholicism contributed to the outbreak of the war, it was through the signature of a concordat with Serbia on 24 June 1914, a mere four days before the assassination of Archduke Franz Ferdinand at Sarajevo. What this did was to remove Austria-Hungary's protectorate rights over Catholics living in this troublesome Balkan state. It is easy to see why both the Catholic and Serbian negotiators felt that they had come to a satisfactory agreement. The former achieved the ability to make episcopal appointments, something formerly the prerogative of the Habsburg emperor, and gained much greater central control over the local church. Moreover, the concordat offered the possibility of proselytising among the Orthodox and Islamic peoples of the Balkans. For the Serbs, the gains were no less welcome. The concordat was an emphatic rejection of Austrian cultural and political hegemony and an assertion of Slavic nationalism. Additionally, by showing how well disposed the Orthodox Serb government was to Catholicism, the agreement might well pave the way for the development of a greater Serbia which would incorporate Catholics from Croatia who had hitherto been suspicious of Belgrade's intentions. In the event, the concordatory negotiations were disastrous within the wider context of byzantine Balkan politics. Austrians felt slighted, the influential newspaper *Die Zeit* leading with the headline, 'New Defeat'. Nor did Istanbul wish to see any strengthening of Serbian nationalism or Catholic expansion. So it was that the concordat contributed to the ground-swell of anti-Serbian sentiment which encouraged Austria-Hungary to overplay its hand in the July crisis of 1914, making a series of harsh and provocative demands of the Serbs.

The Vatican's Serbian *démarche* in 1914 was ill-timed to say the least, but the Church was fortunate in that, only four weeks after the outbreak of war, the Conclave of cardinals elected Giacomo Paolo Battista Della Chiesa, the fifty-nine-year-old Genoese aristocrat, as Benedict XV (1914–22), a man whose long experience as a papal diplomat stood him in good stead for the trying years to come. Known in Spain as the 'Curate of the Two Pesetas' thanks to his charitable initiatives while posted to Madrid, in Italy he was referred to as 'Piccoletto' (the tiny one) – there were no robes sufficiently small to accommodate his diminutive frame when he became pope. He also suffered from a limp, with one shoulder higher than the other. He had received his cardinal's hat only three months earlier, being out of favour because of his association with Cardinal Rampolla whom Pius X had dismissed in the wake of the separation of Church and state in France. Benedict had his revenge by immediately sacking Rafael Merry del Val, the Spanish-Irish Secretary of State, whose influence had confined Della Chiesa to relative obscurity. 'We forgive but we cannot forget,' quipped the new Pope. He was, though, less flippant about the war itself which he regarded as wholly futile and an affront to Christian conscience.

Shrewdly, Benedict decided to adopt a position of steadfast neutrality throughout the war, even though both the allies and the Central Powers constantly sought to bring him into their camp for his propaganda value and to boost morale. All sides sent representatives to the Vatican, including Britain which had not previously maintained an accredited representative for some three centuries. Papal neutrality did not prevent accusations of bias. Within France and Belgium particularly, Benedict was sometimes referred to as the 'Boche' Pope because of his condemnation of the allied blockade of Germany and his suggestions that peace should be made without reparations, a proposal that did not find much favour with countries whose lands were the scene of constant devastation. He further incurred the displeasure of the allies when, in 1915, he condemned Italy's intervention in the war. If we are to believe Ernest Hemingway's semi-autobiographical *A Farewell to Arms*, anti-clerical Italian officers thought the Pope was in the pocket of the Austrians. Claims of bias also emanated from the Central Powers who labelled him the *Französen-papst*. Although they were permitted to retain delegations at the Vatican, warmongers among their number were quickly expelled. In 1917, the Kaiser was further enraged when Benedict denounced the sinking of the *Lusitania*. Nevertheless, just like London and Paris, Berlin and Vienna never relinquished the hope that Rome would bless their own cause. To facilitate this, the Germans attempted to attract Benedict with a promise to end the 'Roman question' by granting the Pope temporal sovereignty over an independent territory. As an astute diplomat, Benedict had indeed contemplated this possibility, but for the overriding sake of his neutrality he decided that this was an issue which must wait for a peacetime solution. It was a wise decision, given the furore that would have resulted. In 1915, Italy had already persuaded the allies that they should not become involved in any dealings with the Vatican lest these were used as a cloak to disguise the recovery of Rome.

As a corollary to his policy of neutrality, Benedict pursued one of charity, the massive statue in Islamic Istanbul erected in his honour in 1921 a lasting testimony to his support of the needy while an envoy in the Ottoman Empire. Making full use of Rome's authority, and pulling all the Ultramontane strings, the resources of the Church were directed towards the repatriation of prisoners, the location of missing persons, the search for news of the dead, the facilitation of postal traffic and the supply of food and medicines to civilians and prisoners-of-war. Over 65,000 prisoners were returned to their families; many of those who remained in confinement received packages, decorated with the papal insignia, containing chocolate, biscuits, American cigarettes, soap, cocoa, tea and sugar. Bishops whose dioceses included a prisoner-of war camp were instructed to deploy priests with relevant language skills to tend to the spiritual welfare of the inmates and to facilitate contact with the outside world. The Vatican spent over 82 million *lire* on its relief work, leaving its coffers denuded of funds. It was a precedent which would not be repeated with the outbreak of the Second World War when Pius XII was far more parsimonious, albeit just as keen to maintain his neutrality. There was a rich irony here, as Pacelli, the future Pius XII, was in charge of organising the Church's relief effort during the years 1914–18. Pacelli might also have learned from Benedict's letters to Sultan Mehmed V deploring the Turkish massacre of Armenians. Much more could undoubtedly have been done to halt this genocide of a million people, but at least Rome brought about some slowdown in the killings, guaranteeing that Armenian orphans were provided with safe havens. During the Second World War, when faced with genocide on an even more massive scale, papal condemnation needed to be far more explicit.

Generalised denunciations of the war from the papacy were plentiful. On 7 February 1915, Benedict urged the peoples of Europe to pray for peace, a request that was subsequently directed to Catholics worldwide in the following months. Equally laudable were Benedict's unstinting efforts to assemble the representatives of the great powers around the negotiating table. As part of these endeavours, in April 1917 he dispatched Pacelli to Munich, the newly-appointed nuncio ensuring that he had plenty of food supplies with him so that his delicate constitution was not upset by the ersatz fare on offer in wartime Germany. In May, Pacelli went to Bavaria to meet King Ludwig III, and in June had an audience with the Kaiser himself, on both occasions urging acceptance of peace proposals which were formulated in more concrete fashion in a letter which Benedict addressed to the belligerents in August. While continuing to champion papal neutrality, these suggestions included the following: arms reduction; the institution of supra-national bodies of arbitration; freedom of the seas; the restoration of Belgian independence; and a general restitution of the territorial *status quo ante* subject to some renegotiations, especially over Alsace-Lorraine. For some historians, these proposals helped Woodrow Wilson shape his Fourteen Points, although whether this overly irenic president needed such inspiration is a matter of doubt.

Unlike some of his earlier interventions, Benedict's letter of August 1917 was met with popular acclaim on both sides of the divide, though in practice it was disregarded. Not only was this a reflection of the Pope's lack of international clout, sadly it also reflected the belief, astonishingly retained by both the allies and the Central Powers, that the war was still winnable. Most importantly, the initiative failed because of the suspicions which the Vatican still aroused. Germany merely interpreted Benedict as the *porte parole* of the allies, especially after the dismissal of the Reich's Chancellor, Bethmann Hollweg, whose presence had restrained the hard-liners. Britain and the USA likewise saw the Vatican as a catspaw of Germany, and felt that the Wilhemstrasse could not be trusted in any circumstances. Britain especially was concerned about the question of reparations and restoration of territory, as were Italy and France, the latter insisting that Germany should bear the shame of war guilt. In the case of France, matters were not helped by the fact that no diplomatic relations were maintained with the Vatican, giving rise to all kinds of paranoia that the Pope was in the pocket of the enemy. For Benedict's part, he had perhaps miscalculated when earlier in the war he had established contact with prominent French Jews as intermediaries of peace, reflecting the unfortunate notion that the Paris government was dominated by Jewish interests.

Benedict was prescient in his appeal to the peace-makers when they eventually assembled in Paris after the Armistice of 11 November 1918, calling upon them to address both the material and moral damage done by the war and to act in a spirit of reconciliation rather than one of revenge. Unfortunately, such injunctions carried little weight with the 'Big Three', even President Wilson, whose claim for the moral high ground was always tenuous. As Clemenceau noted, he had never known anyone talk so much like Jesus Christ but behave like Lloyd George. (Incidentally, Christ had also made an appearance at the Congress of Vienna when the mystic Alexander I, dining with his companion Madame de Krüdener and Metternich, had insisted on laying a fourth place at the table for the Son of God.) The papacy was excluded from the main decision-making process – the allies had agreed in the Treaty of London in 1915 to omit both the Vatican and Italy from any peace talks – and merely sent Cardinal Gasparri as a mediator to be used as required and to look after the interests of Catholic missions in German colonies which were about to be divided up among the allies. The Italians' fear was, of course, that the Vatican would raise the 'Roman question', although this in fact was not addressed. Benedict might not have approved of Clemenceau's blasphemous characterisation of Wilson, nor would he have concurred with the draconian French objectives apropos Germany, but would have agreed with the French Prime Minister that this was an armistice and not a peace. He bemoaned the dissection of both Austria and Germany, recognising that this was a recipe for instability within central Europe and was concerned that, in the case of the former, this marked the demise of the last great Catholic power. Indeed, the new world order of 1919 was distinctly Protestant in its make-up, especially with the emergence of the USA as the real beneficiary of the war. That said, Benedict was disheartened that the Republican-dominated Senate in Washington refused to sign up to the newly-formed League of Nations, an institution in which he invested much hope for the future, especially with respect to its attempts to secure disarmament. For instance, the first Arms Conference in 1921 received a papal blessing. Overall, then, Benedict emerged from the First World War saddened at the pointless loss of life and the inadequacies of the peace settlement but with his personal reputation for even-handedness and altruism enhanced, even though he had been unable to secure acceptance of his own proposals.

Benedict's diplomatic prowess was also put to the test by the other great issue that troubled the Church during the First World War, that is the modernist crisis. In this area, his position was more ambiguous. On the one hand, he appeared to hark back to the approach adopted by Leo XIII in that he dismantled much of the machinery set up to root out supposed dissent and unorthodox theology. He further removed the ban on Catholic participation in political life within Italy, opening the way for the Partito Popolare Italiano (PPI), a newly-formed Catholic party headed by the radical cleric Don Luigi Sturzo. Among other purportedly 'liberal' initiatives, he lifted the bar on heads of Catholic states visiting Rome, thus opening up the possibility of a compromise on the 'Roman question'; he favoured the extension of the franchise to women in Italy; he encouraged Catholics to join trade unions; and he even telegraphed Lenin to plead for religious toleration and an end to the persecution of the Orthodox. On the other hand, he oversaw the introduction of the Code of Canon Law in 1917, a project begun some thirteen years earlier under Pius X. No mere compilation of existing legislation, the Code restructured and clarified existing materials. In so doing, it imposed upon the Church a new centralist, hierarchical and even authoritarian vision that stressed the primacy of the papacy at the apex of the pyramidal structure, and reinforced the disciplinary and other powers of his lieutenants in the episcopacy. The Code was universally applicable without recognising local variation or leaving room for local discussion; for instance, particularist stipulations on the contracting of marriage in Germany and Hungary were now standardised. In matters of theology, ecumenicalism was actively circumscribed, issues of doctrinal orthodoxy were settled by the Holy Office, the teaching role of the Holy See was reaffirmed, and new censorship regulations, much stricter than anything seen since the Inquisition, were implemented. Small wonder the Code has been widely interpreted as the high-water mark of Ultramontanism and the shoring up of papal absolutism, a process aided by the sole right of the pontiff to nominate bishops, via Canon 329.2.

If the effect of the Canon Law was to consolidate the lines of command between Rome and local churches, the effects of the First World War more generally were to create a greater sense of national loyalty among Catholics, at least in the belligerent states. Admittedly, there was some opposition to the outbreak of the fighting: for instance, in Germany in 1914 Matthias Erzberger, a leading deputy within the Zentrum, urged a negotiated settlement and obtained the support of most of his party, while in Italy in 1915 the radical journal *Coenoburm* advocated a pacifist line; and here, a majority of bishops opted for their country's neutrality, as had other groups of citizens, notably the socialist parties. Everywhere, as the fighting took a grip, Catholics fell in behind the war effort. Within France, there was a Union Sacrée, a temporary burying of the hatchet between clericals and anti-clericals, which saw a suspension of some of the most aggressive anti-clerical legislation of recent years and the introduction into the Cabinet of a small number of Catholics, notably Denys Cochin who became Minister for Blockades. Within Belgium, where Catholics had long been assimilated into the political process, the violation of the country's cherished neutrality, enshrined in the Treaty of London of 1832, meant that Catholic politicians had little compunction in serving alongside their socialist and liberal counterparts. Cardinal Mercier of Mechelen, the Primate of Belgium, emerged as the principal spokesman for the interests of Belgian citizens of all religious faiths through his courageous and uncompromising denunciations of German brutality. Within Italy, despite earlier doubts over the maintenance of neutrality, the eventual entry into the war was generally endorsed by the hierarchy, and elements of the laity and lower clergy quickly saw how this involvement would facilitate their more general involvement in the political processes. Sturzo's PPI of 1919 was the most obvious example of this. Similarly, Catholics within Germany saw the war as a chance to slough off those accusations of disloyalty which had been bandied about ever since the *Kulturkampf*. Within the Zentrum itself, early opposition to the conflict quickly gave way to general support which healed, albeit temporarily, the long-standing fissures between the aristocratic and middle-class leadership and its *Mittelstand* supporters. It was perhaps only within Austria that the war proved most centrifugal in its effects, hardening the divisions between the socialists and the Christian Social Party.

As the fighting ground on, and casualties mounted, Catholics throughout Europe began to entertain reservations about its conduct, although in this regard they were clearly not alone and rarely did such doubts lead to outright opposition to the war effort. It was in Belgium, which suffered so terribly from the ravages of trench warfare, and where Catholics were accustomed to supporting and playing a part in government, that such wavering was least apparent. Across the border in France, leading clerics such as Cardinal Baudrillart of the Institut Catholique de Paris might have been indefatigable in their distribution of anti-German propaganda, but there was resentment at the way in which the Union Sacrée quickly evaporated both within parliament and in public life. If the war was to be fought in this manner, then at least the Church should reap some material rewards. In Germany, too, protests mounted. The Zentrum and the SPD discovered a common cause in their repeated criticisms of the General Staff, although this association with the left played badly with the centre's supporters. It would prove doubly unfortunate for the Zentrum that its leader, Erzberger, was obliged to sign the Armistice, thus reopening the charge of disloyalty and permitting extremists, under the Weimar Republic, to allege that the party had colluded in the 'stab in the back'.

The abortive revolution in Germany in 1918–19 was widely condemned by

Catholics, as it augured the march of Bolshevism which had already taken a hold in Russia a year earlier. For several reasons, this fear of communism would not relent until the dissolution of the Soviet Empire in 1991. To begin with, Bolshevism was ideologically incompatible with Christianity since it spread a message based on class conflict, materialism and atheism. As historians have observed, it was, in many senses, a kind of religion in itself. This is why the Soviets emulated those French dechristianisers of the 1790s, articulating their own festivals and iconography. The Bolsheviks quickly proclaimed the religious neutrality of the Soviet Union; a Union of the Militant Godless was created in 1921 to promote atheism; the red star supplanted the crucifix in public buildings; baptisms gave way to the process of Octobering whereby children were named after revolutionary events and leaders; and Electric Day replaced Elijah Day in the calendar. Additionally, Bolshevism actively persecuted faiths of all kinds, singling out the Orthodox Church for its links with Tsardom. Such persecution would have been even fiercer had it not been for Orthodoxy's traditional deference to state hierarchy. It was Catholicism that was the real religious enemy, even though the numbers of Catholics within Russia had decreased from 15 to 1.6 million thanks to the territorial rearrangements of 1919, notably the setting up of an independent Poland and of the Baltic states. As in Bismarck's Germany, this hostility stemmed from the international nature of Catholicism and the fact that the Pope exercised a high degree of centralised authority.

While Bismarck's *Kulturkampf* did not shirk from active persecution, it did not stoop to murder and torture. Within Bolshevik Russia, members of the Catholic episcopacy were expelled, shot or imprisoned, the Vicar-General of the diocese of Mohilev coming to a particularly unpleasant end, his ears being cut off in a relentless torture that led to his death. To make up the shortfall of priests in the USSR, in 1925 Pius XI (1922–39), who himself had bitter memories of the Soviet–Polish war of 1919–20, established a Commission for Russia, designed to train students for service inside these hostile lands. A French Jesuit was dispatched thence, and succeeded in ordaining six bishops, but within a short period they endured the same fate as their predecessors. Catholic religious life thus largely ceased to exist in public, and in 1930 the Vatican organised an expiatory mass for Russia which more or less signalled the end of its attempts to evangelise the Soviet Union. Nor was there any real effort to assist Eastern Rite Catholics. While Rome was appalled at the handling of other Christians, it did not regard this as the moment to promote ecumenical unity. In his encyclical *Mortalium animos* of 1928, Pius XI simply expected the full submission of other denominations to Rome. Such discipline was seen as vital in countering the international threat of Soviet Russia. This naturally remained the Vatican's greatest worry. Would the USSR attempt to export world revolution through the Comintern (Third International), a fear seemingly justified by the emergence of communist parties throughout Europe? Anxieties reached a highpoint in the 1930s with what the Vatican termed the 'red triangle', formed by the USSR, Republican Spain and revolutionary Mexico. There followed a series of encyclicals – *Bona sana* (1920), *Miserentissimus redemptor*

(1928), *Caritate Christi compulsi* (1932) and, most significantly, *Divini redemptoris* (1937) – all of which condemned communism, in much stronger terms than papal condemnations of Nazism. As we shall see, Pius XI kept his distance from Hitler, yet none the less believed that the Nazi leader was preferable to Stalin.

Paradoxically, the emergence of a clear-cut enemy in the shape of communism strengthened the position of the Church overall, at a time when its influence could easily have declined. While war had undoubtedly divided Christian consciences, and while it shifted the international balance of power yet further away from a Catholic standpoint, the future looked healthier than it had for many years. The papacy, which had gained a not undeserved reputation for intransigence and doctrinaire rigidity under Pius X, had proven itself compassionate and diplomatic, its overriding concern a cessation of hostilities. Through Benedict, it had recovered several diplomatic links which would facilitate reconciliation with a number of hitherto mistrustful states, most notably France and Italy, in the 1920s. There were twice as many diplomatic representatives at the Vatican in 1918 as there had been in 1914. More generally, the Church had displayed its charitable side to best advantage, ironic given the way in which state bureaucracies had been previously usurping Catholic enterprises. In this manner, the Church displayed its finest qualities, the bringing of relief directly to those in need without concern for issues of class, politics and rights. The conflict had further seen Catholics emerge on to the political stage in much greater numbers than before, a process that was subsequently enhanced by the extension of the franchise in 1918–19, a reward to many of the peoples of Europe, including women, for the sufferings they had endured. Catholics, even among the hierarchy, knew that they had to take advantage of this process if they were not to be left behind. The new territorial arrangements on the Continent posed another opportunity, as in the new states of Poland, Lithuania, Hungary, Romania, Czechoslovakia and Albania the governments were keen to work with the Church in establishing political stability; and where the majority of the population was Orthodox there was no desire to alienate Catholics by marginalising them. Only in the Soviet Union was the persecution of religion officially sanctioned and, as we have seen, this victimisation only hardened Catholic unity elsewhere.

Catholics and Dictators

If the Catholic position on communist totalitarianism was straightforward, it was anything but when confronted with fascist and right-wing dictatorships. There were a good many of these. Despite the high-minded intentions of the victorious powers at Paris, who had looked towards the creation of a new European order based on the principles of national self-determination and liberal democracy, country after country succumbed to the authoritarian temptation: Italy (1922), Spain (1923), Poland (1926), Portugal (1926), Yugoslavia (1929) and, most famously, Germany in 1933, closely followed by Austria the year after, and eventually Hungary under Gyula Gömbös. Given the uneasy relationship that many Catholics, particularly within the Church hierarchy, had previously enjoyed with democratic regimes, this trend posed both fascination and fresh dangers. On the one hand, there was the possibility of alienating large swathes of the population by becoming enmeshed with governments whose values were inimical to Christian beliefs; and the views of fascist regimes with respect to the supremacy of the state and the education of the young threatened the situation of the Church. On the other hand, these regimes often seemed to promise untold benefits, and ultimately the allure proved too great. To be sure, on many occasions there was little the Church could do to reverse or resist the march to authoritarianism, which was often a product of specific national circumstances, especially in the former states of the Austro-Hungarian Empire, yet all too often clerics appeared satisfied with the results, in particular the emphasis placed upon corporatism and traditional values, the rejection of communism, socialism and capitalism, and the stress on the Church as a key building block of national culture and identity. Indeed, in the minds of many Catholic intellectuals, this move away from liberalism was another indicator of the revived strength of the faith.

To a point, the Church's close association with dictatorship was facilitated by a change in leadership, in that the untimely death of Benedict XV in January 1922 robbed the Church of a principled and diplomatic leader. His surprising replacement was Ambrogio Damiano Achille Ratti, whose chief prowess lay in his skills as a linguist, as a librarian and as a distinguished scholar of medieval palaeography, and who took the name Pius XI in honour of Pio Nono in whose reign he had been born. Like his forebear, he possessed a genial demeanour but, as the trials of office mounted, he developed a fiery and unpredictable temper. Unlike Pius IX, he was not an integralist, yet he had no real love of the masses and deeply mistrusted liberal democracy which, at least in the Italian instance, he considered the fountainhead of political instability. Soon adept at ordering his charges around, he scornfully paraded the gifts sent to him by an admiring public. As will be seen, much of his energy was put into curtailing the activities of Catholic political parties; trust instead was placed in the burgeoning social and youth movements which operated under the broad umbrella of Catholic Action (see below). In the Pope's eyes, these were malleable and highly effective in maintaining Catholic rights and influence. And, of course, the new Pope was fiercely anti-communist. When posted to Warsaw as papal nuncio in 1919, he was scarred by the experience of the bitter war which the Poles fought against the Bolsheviks. This, then, was the new Catholic leader who faced the 'Europe of the dictators'. Authoritarian in instinct, largely unsympathetic to the intrinsic values of liberal democracy and lacking any worldliness, it is no surprise that he saw merits in the regimes of Mussolini, Primo de Rivera and Salazar, especially when they came offering the Church tangible gains which would be safeguarded in the legal framework of concordats. For Pius, concordats were everything, reflecting his naive trust in the written word and the integrity of international guarantees. More were signed in his pontificate than at any previous stage in the modern era.

Events in Italy highlighted the inner tensions that existed within the Catholic world with respect to the Church's attitudes towards political parties, liberal democracy and dictatorship. This was partly because of the success of the PPI. The newly-formed party performed well in the 1919 general elections, gaining over 20 per cent of the votes overall, a proportion that was significantly higher in traditional practising areas such as Venetia and Lombardy; and the fissiparous nature of Italian politics ensured that the party's inclusion was essential to the formation of every government between 1919 and 1922. The six Cabinets that governed during this period always contained at least a brace of PPI ministers. Such success did not necessarily please the new Pope. In the words of Cardinal Gasparri, the PPI was merely 'the least bad of all the parties'.[1] Not only did this remark reflect a generic mistrust of parliamentarianism, it was based on a suspicion of radical elements within the party who gave ready credence to the rumours peddled by Mussolini's fascists that Don Sturzo was planning a Cabinet of the extreme left. Such accusations were easy to spread, as the PPI was undoubtedly a 'broad church' encompassing men clearly on the political left and their counterparts on the right. The party's political platform of proportional representation, female suffrage, decentralisation, endorsement of Catholic trade-union rights and the advocacy of collective security also played badly with the pontiff, as it smacked of 1890s Christian Democracy. Most importantly, the PPI offered no solution to the long-standing 'Roman question'. The 1919 manifesto contained no reference to this whatsoever, a lacuna which was particularly galling as the Vatican had only countenanced an Italian Catholic political party in the expectation that it would deliver on the issue.

This provided an opening for Mussolini and his ever-pliable Fascist Party which had initially adopted a decidedly anti-clerical position in 1919. In that year, he declared: 'There is only one possible revision of the Law of Guarantees and that is its abolition, followed by a firm invitation to His Holiness to quit Rome.'[2] By 1922, this had been abandoned as Mussolini looked to broaden his appeal to the middle classes, promising a restoration of political order and firm government, pledges that also played well with the papacy. 'Fascism neither practises nor preaches anticlericalism.'[3] Although Vatican officials believed that fascism would be only a transient phenomenon, perhaps enduring for two decades, it offered a release from the popular democracy that had allegedly failed Italy and augured an end to the PPI itself. Above all, Mussolini hinted at a solution to the 'Roman question', and this led the papacy increasingly to favour the fascists. When Mussolini executed his theatrical 'March on Rome' in October 1922, Pius was definitely of the opinion that the *duce* was the best hope for the future.

Fascism, in the Italian instance, was always an awkward mesh of radicalism and tradition, and the Catholic Church was undoubtedly one of those long-standing institutions that served as a prop to Mussolini's regime. The 1920s thus came to be characterised by a series of *quid pro quo* measures. Mussolini quickly granted the Church a series of favours: freemasons were expelled from the Fascist Party; masonry was banned in higher education; the crucifix was reinstated in public buildings; the Gentile educational legislation of 1923 restored religious instruction in state elementary schools; and Catholic schools were placed on an equal financial footing with their public counterparts. In return, the Vatican made life difficult for the PPI. Sturzo was instructed to stand down as party leader, and the Pope permitted the establishment of the Unione Nazionale (UN), a loose gathering of pro-fascist Catholics, a move which inevitably dissipated PPI energies. The party was already beginning to fall apart. Indeed, it was the defection of fourteen party members that allowed Mussolini to do away with proportional representation through the Acerbo Law, without which his regime would have been stillborn. With the dissolution of parliament and the announcement of new elections in 1924, the entire PPI contingent in the Senate crossed the floor into the fascist camp. To make matters worse, former PPI deputies stood on behalf of Mussolini, and several Catholic newspapers backed his cause.

Moreover, Catholic support was critical in enabling Mussolini to overcome the scandal that broke out in 1924 over the murder of the socialist Matteotti, which again threw the whole fascist project into doubt. Despite some misgivings over fascist behaviour, the Vatican banned the PPI from entering any coalition government with the socialists, which would have excluded Mussolini entirely. In this manner, Catholic political inaction opened the way for his dictatorship. Within the next two years, the PPI had been dissolved, together with the Catholic trade union confederation, and the majority of Catholic news titles were also outlawed. Wider circumstances further conspired to undermine Catholic autonomy. For instance, the devaluation of the *lira* in 1926 had dire consequences for Catholic banks, newspapers, peasant leagues and cooperatives. By the close of the decade, only two Catholic political groups subsisted, the clerico-fascist Nazi Unioneonale (NU) and Centro Nazionale Italiano (CNI). Both wholeheartedly supported the regime, thus facilitating the passage of fascist legislation in parliament. This was of little concern to the Pope, who took satisfaction in achieving his aim of reasserting control over the political activities of his flock, directing it increasingly towards Catholic Action which had been reorganised in 1923 to ensure stricter ecclesiastical direction. Although there was some disquiet at the fascist trajectory pursued by Mussolini, especially in 1938 when, in an attempt to please Hitler, the Racial Laws were introduced, this unease never amounted to very much. Early Catholic anti-fascist initiatives, notably the Allianza Nazionale of Lauro De Bosis and the Movimento Guelfo D'Azione of Piero Malvestiti, were short-lived, and were quickly suppressed at the start of the 1930s. Thereafter, what dissident Catholic activity there was, came from individuals rather than having an institutional basis, making the regime's task that much easier.

The essential backdrop to these machinations was the papacy's concern to regularise Church–state relations, something that was achieved in the 1929 Lateran Accords. This agreement gave the Church the following: the Pope was granted his own independent state in the form of the Vatican City, together with the summer residence of Castel Gandolfo and the Lateran; within the Vatican City, only 108.7 acres in size and with a permanent population of 500, the Pope had his own post office, police force, troops, radio station and, eventually, a newspaper, *L'Osservatore Romano*, all indicators of his independence and ability to talk to the outside world; diplomats were accredited to the Holy See and the Pope had the right to appoint representatives to foreign powers, although the Vatican had to promise not to become involved in conflicts of a temporal nature, unless the participants requested such intervention as a 'mission of peace', thus circumscribing something of papal authority; Canon Law was placed on a par with the law of the Italian state; Catholic doctrine was to become a part of both the elementary and secondary state-school timetable; the validity of Catholic marriages was recognised; the place of the crucifix in public buildings was assured; and Pius received 1,750,000,000 *lira* in compensation for the loss of the Papal States, most of which was paid in government stock, thus giving the papacy a significant interest in the good health of the regime.

For the papacy, the concordat was a vindication of the policies adopted towards Mussolini throughout the 1920s. 'Italy has been given back to God, and God to Italy,' proclaimed *L'Osservatore Romano*. Not only had the concordat brought to a resolution the 'Roman question', it had laid to rest the complicating factor of a Catholic party which impeded direct negotiations with the state. The Lateran Accords thus quashed any residual notions of 'a free church in a free state'. At the same time, protection was offered against the atheistic forces of Freemasonry and communism. Other Catholics were less sure, although they were all urged to show their approval by voting positively in the plebiscite. Giovanni Battista Montini, later elected Pope as Paul VI, subsequently argued that the deal yielded little real reward. Elements within Catholic Action, whose future had been assured by Article 43 which granted the movement the dubious privilege of being the only non-fascist organisation in the state Mussolini was building, were also uncertain about the future, foreseeing the difficulty of holding the Italian leader to his word. Their fears were justified. Within two years, the *duce* was angling for the creation of a single youth organisation, thus absorbing the Catholic scout movement, the graduate association, the Movimento Laureati, and other student bodies belonging to the Federazione Universitari Cattolici Italiani. The Pope's response was the 1930 encyclical *Rappresentanti in terra* which asserted the importance of Christian teaching in daily life, a clear criticism of Mussolini's policies. This was followed the next year by *Non abbiamo bisogno*, berating the fascist regime for its persecution of Catholic Action which had been monitoring the government's lax observance of the Lateran pacts. It also included a broader assault on the importance which fascists attached to the state. Such protests did not stop the fascist juggernaut which dissolved nearly all the Catholic youth organisations, leaving Catholic Action as a rump. As John Pollard notes, the papacy pursued a policy of '*sauve qui peut*' and there was a reluctance to condemn fascism outright, either in Italy or elsewhere. Pius XI still believed Mussolini was most suited to govern Italy; the Pope was merely asserting something of the Church's independence, which in itself was hardly novel.[4] For the remainder of the decade, Church and state within Italy remained wary of each other but closely linked.

Spain was the next country to succumb to the temptation of dictatorship when General Primo de Rivera seized power in a military *coup* of 13 September 1923, and once again Catholicism was inextricably linked with the support of authoritarianism. The reasons for this lay more in Spain's peculiar historical development than with any more general mutual compatibility between fascism and Catholicism. Towards the end of the nineteenth century, the languid pace of social and economic development within the peninsula had not given rise to a new, noisy, nationalist right as was evidenced elsewhere in *fin-de-siècle* Europe. This torpor nevertheless predisposed the country to embrace an authoritarianism which, under Franco, evolved into a 'categoric fascism', a process in which the Church was deeply implicated.[5]

Mary Vincent has most succinctly explained why this was so.[6] First, she writes, Spanish Catholicism remained wedded to a nostalgic and integralist view of society in which the monarchy was the chosen form of government and agriculture was the basis of economic organisation. The rejection of liberal and centralising reforms inherent in this vision went back to the Napoleonic experience when the French Emperor had sought to impose his vision of a modern state upon the Iberian peninsula. Ever since, Spanish politics had been characterised by a tension between Catholicism and liberalism (see Chapter 2). Second, continues Vincent, Spanish socio-religious structures were influential in the welcoming of authoritarianism. It will be recalled from an earlier chapter how the Church in Spain had been slow to acknowledge the issues thrown up by industrialisation and urbanisation, limited though these twin phenomena were. Catholic trade unions had struggled to survive; the only real success was the Basque Workers' Solidarity, founded in 1911, which in truth garnered support because of its appeal to Basque nationalism as opposed to its championing of the proletariat. Social Catholicism was most successful in the countryside through the National Catholic Agrarian Confederation (CNCA) which had been set up in 1917. This had oversight of a raft of savings banks, cooperatives, friendly societies and insurance schemes, located mainly in northern and eastern Spain. Accordingly, the working classes of large urban centres such as Bilbao and Barcelona felt alienated from the Church as did the rural inhabitants of the extensive *latifundia* in the south; while the middle class and rural small-holders in the Basque regions, in the flat lands of Castile, Navarra and the old kingdom of Aragon, looked to Catholicism as a bulwark against socialism and the liberal tentacles of national government at Madrid. As the highly influential Catholic writer Marcelino Menéndez y Pelayo proclaimed in the 1880s, the Church in Spain had transformed 'a crowd of assembled people' into a great nation, underpinned by its spirituality and love of God, only for the whole edifice to be challenged by outside influences.[7]

In this environment, the one attempt to establish a Catholic political party before 1923 was going to be a struggle. While it had long been a hope of prominent Spanish Catholics, especially those clustered in the influential lay organisation the National Catholic Association of Propagandists, that the faithful could be combined into one movement, it is doubtful whether the

People's Social Party (PSP), which came together as a centre for debate in 1919 and transformed itself into a political party in 1922, was what it had envisaged. This party was similar to the Italian PPI in that it drew together a wide spectrum of supporters, including leading Social Catholics such as Aznar and Arbeleya, together with Carlists, and set out to be aconfessional. Its commitment to liberal democracy was certainly important for the later emergence of a Christian Democratic party under Franco, but it was precisely this which alienated integralist Catholics, ensuring that the PSP never really broke the mould, merely imitating the Catholic associations of the past. The PSP enjoyed only limited popular support, and its fate was sealed with the coup of 1923, but unlike the PPI this particular Catholic experiment in pluralist politics was not open to the charge of colluding in the rise of dictatorship. Instead, Primo had relied upon promises to end government corruption and social disorder.

His authoritarian regime, based on the military, was widely welcomed in Catholic circles as a break from the turbulent and uncertain politics of the past, and the corruption and moral decadence which had produced the humiliating defeat of the Spanish army at Anual in Morocco in 1921, the first time a European army had been routed by indigenous tribesmen. Lacking any real ideological vision, the General himself was quick to reciprocate the support offered by traditional Spanish institutions, especially the monarchy and the Church. One army chaplain, quoted by Frances Lannon, spoke for many traditionalists when he proclaimed that Primo was an Atlas 'holding the family, the monarchy and the church on his shoulders';[8] while a Catholic journal enthused 'all Catholic Spain is praying for the success of the honourable generals who in their holy zeal for the nation and religion have expressed their intention to save our people'.[9] So it was that bishops were given seats in the National Assembly; parliamentary legislation reflected Catholic Canon Law; education was, to all extents and purposes, handed over to the clergy; the school syllabus was infused with Catholic teaching; corporatism was officially sanctioned although never actually practised; and Catholics featured prominently in his Patriotic Union (UP); indeed, practice of the faith was a prerequisite of membership for this quasi-fascist political party, its motto being 'Fatherland, religion and monarchy'. Historians have since discussed whether *Primoderiverismo* was a form of fascism and whether the UP prefigured the Falange, yet most agree that the General failed to breathe any real life into his regime, losing the instinctive support of both Alfonso XIII and the army.[10] Primo's centralising impulses also alienated regional support in Catalan and Basque territories, where Catholics themselves felt they could no longer support the government. This explains why dictatorship was brushed aside so easily in April 1931, despite the protests of leading churchmen such as Bishop Múgica who declared that to vote for the republicans was a mortal sin. The overwhelming majority of Spaniards supported the installation of the Second Republic.

In that year, few Spanish Catholics questioned the easy demise of Primo's regime, failing to spot the connection between the ritual strengths of their faith, expressed in pilgrimages, processions and symbols, and the declining nature of religious practice that typified several areas of the country and which undermined support for a regime that was expressly Catholic in complexion. They soon became convinced, however, that they confronted a dangerous and aggressive regime in the shape of the new Republic, their certainty strengthened by the repeated appearances of the Virgin Mary in the little village of Ezkioga. As Lannon relates, Count Rodríguez Sampedro, the president of Catholic Action, did not wait around to see what might happen. In unconscious imitation of Louis XVI's brother the Count of Artois who quit France on 14 July 1789, he left Spain the day the Republic was declared.[11]

To be sure, the regime was instinctively anti-clerical, and unprepared to compromise. Ministers quickly indulged in anti-Catholic rhetoric; a fresh constitution was inaugurated which reversed many of the gains made under Primo; Spain received its first divorce law; cemeteries were secularised; the Jesuits were expelled; secular ideologues such as Miguel Unamuno were trumpeted; and real efforts were made to dislodge the extensive influence which the Church possessed within schooling, both at the primary and secondary levels; and, for the first time in the nation's history, Church and state were separated. As early as May 1931, there was widespread violence against the clergy and churches in Madrid, a violence that quickly spread to other cities, and which conservatives soon attributed to Soviet Bolshevism, the force thought to be running national government. In this situation, as Mary Vincent has convincingly shown in the case of Salamanca, Catholics who had initially voted for moderate republicans quickly came to disavow the Republic as the legitimate government of Spain.[12] While Salamanca was not especially devout, it bitterly resented the intrusion of state anti-clericalism, in the same away that, as Caroline Ford has demonstrated, Brittany resented the secular assault of the early 1900s.[13]

Nationally, Catholics who continued to adhere to the Republic were largely the survivors of the PSP and the Basque Nationalist Party, the Partido Nacionalista Vaco (PNV). The remainder of the faithful gravitated towards the Acción Popular (AP), acknowledged to be the first truly national Catholic party in Spain, which drew support from the CNCA, numerous other Catholic rural associations and Catholic women's groups, quick to turn their enfranchisement against the Republic which, paradoxically, had granted them the vote. The AP, alongside numerous other Catholic initiatives, joined the Confederation of Autonomous Right-Wing Groups (CEDA) which achieved handsome successes at the polls in 1933, becoming the largest single party in the Cortes. What should be stressed is that neither the AP nor CEDA were fully reconciled to the Republic, and tolerated it only out of a respect for legitimacy. CEDA, under the leadership of José Maria Gil Robles, was never instinctively republican or Christian democrat, but set its heart on a reversal of institutionalised secularism, the defence of clerical property, the implementation of Catholic corporatist principles, championed by Gimenéz Fernández, and the rejection of the socialist party which was regarded as the agent of Moscow. Its youth movement, in particular, bore an uncanny resemblance to the fascism that was developing under the deeply xenophobic and extremist movement of the Falange. When, in February 1936, the left-wing parties of the Popular Front won convincingly in the elections, and anti-clericals were given prominent posts in Cabinet, Catholics found it difficult to resist the temptation of aligning with the extreme right, taking to the streets, precipitating public disorder and lending support to the military in its uprising of July that year.

Catholics readily endorsed the nationalist cause fronted by the exceedingly devout General Franco, who was welcomed as the saviour capable of rescuing his country and the faith from the perils of atheistic communism. The exception was the Basque PNV. Founded in 1893, this advocated a Catholic nationalism not dissimilar to that espoused by the Spanish Church, and was especially popular in areas of high practice and where the Basque language was used. Yet PNV members became mistrustful of the prelacy because of its opposition to separatism: one bishop had banned the use of Basque names in baptism; another had welcomed the prohibition of catechism class in the regional language. The PNV now recognised the dangers for its own cause in the centralist policies espoused by the *Caudillo*, just as it had opposed the centralist instincts of Primo. A small number of Catholic intellectuals, both within and outside Spain, also questioned the validity of the nationalist cause. Elsewhere, there were no such doubts, especially after republican violence in the summer of 1936 left dead thirteen bishops, over 4,000 priests and 2,600 religious, all of whom were revered as martyrs in a civil war which became treated as a religious crusade. Indeed, there was even a welcome for the cataclysmic confrontation between Catholicism and the forces of evil which many churchmen, heirs to the conspiracy theories inspired by the experiences of Napoleonic invasion, regarded as inevitable. In the words of Bishop Gomá, this was a veritable war between two civilisations: Catholic Spain and Marxist anti-Spain. Catholics conveniently overlooked the atrocities committed in the nationalist name, most famously at Guernica, as they lined up to endorse Franco's campaign. Catholic youths volunteered enthusiastically for the militias, girls devoted themselves to war work, bishops spoke of the new society that would emerge out of this struggle between good and evil. Not surprisingly, Franco's triumphant entry into Madrid in April 1939 was greeted by the ringing of church bells and singing of *Te Deums*, the *Caudillo* himself being consecrated by the Cardinal Primate. Despite earlier misgivings about Franco's German connections and Hitler's involvement in Spain, the Vatican under the new Pope Pius XII (1939–58) also came to praise the new Spanish leader as a bulwark against communism.

In the event, the new society that Franco built meant an end to independent Catholic political initiatives since he dissolved all the nationalist groupings, including the Falangists and Carlists as well as Catholic bodies, into his Partido Unica (PU) of 1937. This, though, was welcomed by Catholics. Hitherto reluctant participants in party politics, they were now well represented in the new regime. During the Second World War, no fewer than eleven members of the Catholic Association of Propagandists were given Cabinet posts;

Catholicism was, as under Primo, an essential prerequisite of state service; and Catholic organisations such as Pax Romana and Opus Dei were given privileged treatment, working towards the rehabilitation of Spain in the international community, something cemented through the concordat of 1953. By this stage, Spanish Catholics, with some honourable exceptions, had what they wanted, not a fascist nation but one based on corporative, authoritarian and traditionalist values. The downside was that the Church was almost entirely reliant on the sanctuary provided by the state, and Catholics within Spain were isolated from progressive religious trends found elsewhere.

Portugal was similar to Spain in that the history of Catholicism was fundamentally influenced by the unique circumstances of the country's history and geography, and this background explains why the Church readily embraced the dictatorship of Salazar.[14] During the nineteenth century, Catholicism had repeatedly been on the back foot. It had failed to stem the slippage from the faith which occurred particularly among the landless labouring classes of southern Portugal; it had no answer to the secularist attitudes of the middle classes; and it had failed to develop any vigorous movements of social action; it had essentially acquiesced in the state's encroachment on its jurisdiction and activities; and it had tied itself in particular to the monarchist cause which was looking increasingly forlorn at the turn of the century, proof that the Church had not learned the lesson of its disastrous espousal of the reactionary Miguelistas during the 1832–34 upheavals. Portuguese Catholicism was therefore ill-placed to meet the aggressive secularist challenge posed by the Republic which emerged out of the 1910 revolution. To be fair, most sections of society were not unhappy to see the back of a monarchy which had proved both corrupt and wholly inept, but any latent Catholic support for the new regime rapidly evaporated as its lower-middle-class urban leadership embarked on a series of violently anti-clerical measures, attacking the Church as the most prominent symbol of the old regime. In a series of sweeping decrees of 1911, some of which were influenced by the French example, almost every aspect of Catholic life came under fire: Church property was nationalised; seminaries were shut down, those which remained open being placed under government control; Faculties of Theology, notably that at the University of Coimbra, the jewel in the admittedly lacklustre crown of intellectual Catholicism, were closed; state censorship of ecclesiastical pronouncements was imposed; the Jesuits and foreign orders were expelled; and, in an attempt to expunge religious sentiment from daily life, holy days were terminated, as were processions and bell-ringing. All this culminated in the enforced exile of most of the episcopacy and the cessation of diplomatic relations with the Vatican in 1913.

Just as in Spain, where anti-clerical attacks had stimulated a reaction, so too in Portugal the breadth and severity of these measures aroused Catholics to action, most notably in the more pious regions of the north. Significantly, this response was led by the laity rather than the clergy, another sign perhaps of the enfeeblement of the institutional Church. In 1917, the Centro Católico Portuguesa (CCP), a political party, was established which did well in elections through its support of Catholic interests; yet, as several historians have suggested, its impact was always limited by the fact that the vote was denied to the illiterate and to women, people who would almost certainly have proffered their allegiance, and more importantly by its moderation at a time when the most fervent of the faithful wanted to see the abolition of the Republic. Five years earlier a more fertile source of Catholic activity had emerged, the Centro Academica da Democraçia Cristão (CADC), an association of Catholic intellectuals based at Coimbra, who rallied to the slogan 'Piety, study, action'. Despite the plaudits of sympathetic writers, this was not an embryonic Christian democrat movement but one devoted to the restoration of integralist values, its leading spokesmen being Manuel Gonçalves Cerejeira (1888–1977), a young priest and writer, and António de Oliveira Salazar (1889–1970), an economics lecturer. CADC members became prominent in the military dictatorship that, in 1926, toppled a republic which had proved even more ineffectual and crony-ridden than the preceding monarchy. In the new regime, it was the ultra-pious Salazar who emerged as Minister of Finance in 1928 and Prime Minister in 1932.

While Salazar unquestionably borrowed ideas for his *Estado Novo* from Mussolini, it is again the parallels with Spain that are most immediately apparent. There was to be personal dictatorship, a single party in the shape of the Uniaco Nacional (UN), a corporatist economy and an extremely regressive constitution, all the hallmarks not so much of fascism but of a authoritarian conservatism. In this new order, the Church was lavished with praise, constant reference was made to Portugal's religious past, Catholic values were inserted at the forefront of education, the Virgin who made an appearance at Fatima in 1917 was appropriated by the regime as its symbol, while Salazar himself regularly referred to papal encyclicals and the Holy Fathers as his ideological inspiration. Yet there was only so far Salazar was prepared to go, and Catholics were so in hock to the regime and, outside the CADC, so badly organised that there was little they could do but accept the situation. Some attempt was made by Cerejeira, who became the Archbishop of Lisbon in 1929, to assert the autonomy of the Church through the instigation in 1933 of the Acção Católico Português (ACP), the first flowering of Catholic Action in Portugal. Yet this disappointingly proved no real match for the official youth movement, the Moçidade Portuguesa (MP). Perhaps more worryingly for the Church, the 1930s were a missed opportunity to reclaim secularised territories for the faith and, despite its trenchant anti-communism, it made few attempts to curb the growing power of the underground Communist Party in the south of Portugal. When, in 1940, a concordat was at last signed between Church and state, this demonstrated the extent to which the latter possessed the upper hand. Although the Church remained tax-exempt and received some fiscal support from government, properties seized in 1910–11 were not restored, Salazar enjoyed a formidable role in the nomination and appointment of prelates, religious teaching in schools remained a voluntary option and civil marriage and divorce were retained.

Austria was also similar to the models of Spain and Portugal in that here, too, Catholicism played a significant part in the dismantling of liberal demo-cracy, but was likewise accorded a marginalised position within the new state, although in this instance Catholics were far more vociferous in complaining about their denuded status. Though Austria was over 90 per cent Catholic, there was no monolithic Catholic political bloc in the inter-war years. Thus in the 1930 elections, the Social Democrats received 41 per cent of the vote and the Christian Social Party nearly 38 per cent. That said, there is evidence that a majority of practising Catholics backed the Christian Social Party and the numerous and influential Catholic journals and newspapers were supportive of it and its diminutive leader, Engelbert Dollfuss. He made a particular play for the religious vote. Strongly influenced by the corporatist ideals of *Quadragesimo anno* of 1931, he declared: 'The day of the capitalist-liberal economic order is past ... We demand a social, Christian, German Austria on a corporative basis and under strong authoritarian leadership.'[15] This is what he attempted to implement the following year when a new constitution was introduced on 1 May, closely resembling Salazar's experiment in Portugal. Dislike of the sup-posed instability of Austrian parliamentarianism, coupled with a profound hatred of the left in the shape of the Social Democrats, also led churchmen, particularly the lower clergy, to rally to Dollfuss. The Austrian bishops were an additional pillar of support, although inwardly they were highly concerned about the threat posed to the autonomy of Catholic lay organisations by the increasing power of the state, as expressed through its bureaucracy, police and army. There were 219 such associations by 1938 with over one million members, mainly grouped under the umbrella bodies of Catholic Action and the People's League of Austrian Catholics. The papacy further rallied strongly to the Dollfuss regime, when he became Chancellor in 1932, not only because of its unashamed Catholic bias, but also because it provided an obstacle to Nazi Germany, a regime which deeply unsettled Pius XI, as we shall see. Moreover, the Vatican hoped for a successful outcome to negotiations for a concordat which would eventuate in the signing of a draft in 1933.

The main opposition to the regime sprang from the Austrian Nazis. This hostility was based not so much on Dollfuss's religious policies, but because of his rejection of an *Anschluss* while Hitler was Chancellor and his more general revulsion at Nazism. In the view of Dollfuss, it was Austria which now embraced the true German ideal, precisely through its Catholic culture, whereas the Hitler regime, with its paganism and racism, had betrayed this. It was, of course, the Austrian Nazis who assassinated Dollfuss during their terrorist campaign of 1934, leading to the authoritarian regime of Kurt von Schusch-nigg. He was quick both to curtail the influence of the Nazis and to embrace Catholicism as his muse, but once again the Church was suspicious of his intentions, fearing for the autonomy of its youth movement. In clerical eyes, the regime resembled not so much a fascist template as a return to the kind of Josephinian centralism that had marked the Habsburgs in the eighteenth and nineteenth centuries. They would soon have to confront a far more threatening state power when Hitler engineered his takeover of Austria in 1938.

Further east, the picture was more chequered but a number of themes present themselves, notably the attraction which authoritarianism had for Catholics (and, it may be noted in passing, for members of the Orthodox faith whose concern for ritual, its mystical bent and its sublimation of the individual provided a bridge to fascism). While it had been hoped that liberal democracy would flourish in the states created out of the Paris Peace Conference, this was not to be: Poland became a quasi-dictatorship under General Pilsudski (1925); Lithuania similarly succumbed to the coup of Antonas Smetona (1926); Yugoslavia, under King Alexander, became first authoritarian and then semi-fascist after his assassination in 1934; and in Hungary a conservative regime led by the Calvinist regent Admiral Horthy (a landlocked state ruled by a sea lord with an absentee king) gave way to something more sinister under the premiership of Gyula Gömbös in the 1930s. Historians have since stressed how the successor states of the Austro-Hungarian Empire were especially susceptible to authoritarianism thanks to the need of the new regimes, which had been former opponents of the Habsburgs, to defend themselves from the claims of ethnic minorities. Only Czechoslovakia remained immune from the authoritarian temptation, thanks partly to the political finesse of Tomáš Masaryk and its relatively prosperous economy, although even here it should be stressed that the state apparatus was dominated by Czechs largely to the exclusion of the Slovaks.

In all these states, the history of Catholicism was bound up with national identity, in that governments either employed the Church as an agent of reconstruction or challenged its influence as a bar to the formation of a new polity, the overall picture being complicated by the existence of ethnic–religious rivalry. In the former instance, it was where Catholics were the majority: in Poland, they comprised 75 per cent of the total population of 27.1 million in 1921; in Lithuania they amounted to 74 per cent of the much smaller overall population of 2.3 million; and in Hungary they formed 66 per cent of the 7.6 million inhabitants. Here, Pilsudski, Smetona and Horthy, all of whom can best be described as secular nationalists, maintained a separation between Church and state, something enshrined in the Polish Concordat of 1925 and that concluded with Lithuania in 1927, yet at the same time they allotted a considerable role to Catholicism in public life, recognising the strength of the faith as an underpinning of national unity. As in Spain and Portugal, Catholics colluded in this process, although there were undoubtedly tensions with the state, for example over the status of the diocese of Vilnius which was contested by Poland and Lithuania. Nevertheless, these arguments did not threaten the *rapprochement* between the governmental authorities and the ecclesiastical hierarchy. The result was that Catholicism thrived; the religious press burgeoned; the number of clergy, both secular and religious, expanded; pilgrimages, religious associations and congresses became commonplace; and the Catholic Action organisations recorded impressive membership. In Poland, they enjoyed nearly one million supporters on the eve of the Second World War; in Lithuania, many of the young gravitated towards the secondary-school movement, Ateitis (The Future). Christian democracy hardly figured in any of these examples – rather, a corporatist and distinctly right-wing Catholicism held sway – and it is small surprise that a number of Catholics were attracted to the many fascist groupings that proliferated in eastern Europe. Among the most prominent of these was the Arrow Cross of Ferenc Szálasi in Hungary which proved a constant thorn in the flesh of the Horthy regime. A devout Catholic, Szálasi sought to outbid Horthy in his supposed embrace of Christian principles allied to Hungarian nationalism. 'Hungarian national socialism is inseparable and indivisible from the teaching of Christ,' declared the movement's manifesto.[16] He thus evolved a concept of 'Hungarism' which aspired to the creation of a Carpathian-Danubian Great Fatherland in which all citizens would be members of one of the three religious traditions: Catholic, Protestant or Orthodox. In this bizarre mix of ethno-religious prejudices, infused with an open admiration of National Socialism, Judaism would have no place. Church leaders might have had little time for the Nazi version of National Socialism, but they did not seem to perceive the dangers inherent in the heady mix of Hungarian nationalism and Christian principles. Although the Vatican condemned the ideology of the Hungarist movement in 1938, local Church leaders did not give this much publicity, with the result that Catholics continued to join its ranks, and support for both the Szálasi and the Horthy regimes thus persisted.

The two places where Catholics discovered themselves to be a minority, and potentially a brake on the forging of national identity, were Czechoslovakia and Yugoslavia. As a result of the 1919 treaties, the mainly Catholic Slovaks (70 per cent) were governed by a predominantly Czech and anti-clerical administration, whose Slovak elements moreover were mainly Protestant. This government sequestrated Church property, secularised elementary schools, discriminated against priests and abolished Catholic festivals. In 1925, the Lutheran Czechs, disproportionately represented in government, forced the papal nuncio to withdraw from the celebrations honouring Jan Huss. In this situation, Catholics asserted their identity in the largest Slovakian party the Hlinka Slovenská l'Udová Stranka (HSLS), the Slovak People's Party, led by Father Andrej Hlinka, which forged intimate links with the Catholic Church, something reflected in the party's refrain, 'One God, one people, one party'. Another, more openly scurrilous, refrain was, 'Slovakia for the Slovaks, Palestine for the Jews, the Danube for the Czechs'.[17] In 1927, HSLS was able to secure some concessions, including the Vatican's right to nominate to sees, a promise of state funding for clerics and concessions in the domain of education, in return for an end to the Church's hostility towards Prague. Yet tensions remained.

If Catholicism and ethnicity walked hand-in-hand in Czechoslovakia, the same was true in Yugoslavia where Croatian Catholics resented the dominance of the Orthodox Serbs who manned the government desks in Belgrade. All manner of Croatian nationalist groups emerged, notably the Hrvatska Seljacka Stranka (HSS), the Croatian Peasants' Party, under the direction of the Radic brothers, and the terrorist/fascist Ustaše-Hrvatska Revolucionarna Organizaciga (UHRO), generally known as the Ustaše, the Insurgency-Croatian

Revolutionary Organisation of Dr Ante Pavelic. His febrile imagination gave birth to a type of extreme nationalism which combined peasant life with Catholic values, portraying Croatia as a bulwark against an unregenerate outside world comprising Greek Orthodox, Russian communists and Jews. Some of the ideals of the Ustaše were also to be found in the Catholic Action movements which were carefully nurtured by Archbishop Antun Bauer of Zagreb and his youthful successor Alojzije Stepinac who, in 1946, was imprisoned for his tolerance of such militant Catholic bodies as the Hrvatski Katolicki Pokret (HKP), the Croatian Catholic movement, and the Krizari (Crusaders), another association of Catholic angry young men.

It was the triumph of National Socialism in Germany and the outbreak of Hitler's war that gave the Ustaše their opportunity, thus highlighting more generally the ambivalent relationship between Catholicism and Nazism. It is often claimed by Catholic historians that the Church in Germany was an increasingly strident critic of the Nazi state. Admittedly, these protests could be fierce, yet they should not obscure the role which Catholicism, or more particularly Rome and the leadership of the Centre Party, inadvertently played in Hitler's rise to power, and the mutual benefits which Church and state drew from their association after 1933. To understand why Catholics were not more forceful in resisting the growth of Nazism, it is necessary to reflect on their experience under Bismarck when they had learned to protect their interests while, at the same time, voicing their support of the German state. In this context, it is worth noting that three-quarters of the German bishops had been born during or before the *Kulturkampf*. It is also necessary to reflect on their experience of the Weimar Republic, a time of missed opportunities. During this period, Catholics had comprised a sizeable presence in the population, some 32.5 per cent, and had contributed to an impressive revitalisation of spiritual life, once again fronted by the youth movements of Catholic Action, skilfully led by Quickborn and his newspaper *Die Schildgenossen*. There also seemed to be a desire to play a leading part in the new liberal democracy of Weimar, exemplified by the involvement of Christian democratic trade unionists in the creation of the Deutscher Gewerkschaftsbund (DGB), the German Trade Union Federation, in 1919. Influential Centre Party politicians, for instance Mathias Erzberger and Adam Stegerwald, also played a vital part in the establishment of the Weimar constitution which itself guaranteed Church rights: Church and state were recognised to have shared interests, and were thus not separated; churches were acknowledged in public law to be corporate institutions; they were empowered to collect income; religious orders were given a free hand in their activities; and priests were allowed into public buildings to tend to the faithful. Such privileges were further strengthened through the signing of concordats with Bavaria in 1924, Prussia in 1929 and Baden in 1932, although an agreement with Weimar itself proved unobtainable.

In truth, Catholics in Germany were badly placed to confront the trials ahead. The unhappy experience of the 1918–19 revolution led many to shy away from national politics. Whereas Catholic Action might have rejuvenated spiritual feelings, this too had resulted in a distancing from the political scene.

Not that Catholics were especially enamoured of Weimar. Rural Catholic peasants in the south and west detested price capping on agricultural products and came to resent what they saw as unnecessary deflationary policies that operated in the interests of the towns. There was also a fragmentation of Catholic politics, local issues often being viewed as more pressing than national ones, a feeling fostered by the general ennui engendered by coalition politics in which the socialist SPD seemed ever present. In reality, the Centre Party was omnipresent in government, and initially benefited from the extension of the franchise to women in 1919 when it garnered 62.8 per cent of the Catholic vote. This figure would drop by some 16 per cent by 1930, reflecting the more general difficulties of the Centre Party whose *raison d'être* to some degree had been removed once the persecution of the *Kulturkampf* was a distant memory. Tensions existed as to whether the party should shake off its confessional origins and aspire to become a broader-based movement. It did not help matters that Catholics now had rival parties to vote for, in the shape of the rightist Bayerische Volkspartei (BVP), the Bavarian People's Party, which split from the Centre Party out of resentment at the burgeoning influence of the Christian trade unions on policy, as well as the German National People's Party (Deutschnationale Volkspartei – DNVP) which, towards the close of Weimar, was scoring 6–8 per cent of the Catholic vote. Zentrum support was further fragmented by the Christian Social Party of Vitus Heller. So it was that the polarisation of politics under Weimar made it increasingly difficult for the Centre Party, which had always been a broad church, to reconcile the divergent social and economic interests of its constituent parts.

Unquestionably, the Nazi Party had some appeal to Catholics, in its denunciations of Weimar pluralism, in its espousal of traditional values such as hard work and the domestication of women, in its demands for a restoration of order and an attack on the communist menace in the form of the KPD (Kommunistische Partei Deutschland), the other party to have benefited sharply from the depression of 1929–32. Despite the initial Bavarian focal point of the National Socialists (Nationalsozialistische Deutsche Arbeitpartei – NSDAP), it should be stressed that it was Protestant Germany that soon came to vote most enthusiastically for the party. While some Catholics in the Silesian towns of Liegnitz and Breslau lent their support, as did peasants in the countryside of the Palatinate, such examples were the exception which proved the rule. The episcopacy also did its bit to combat an ideology which was deemed irrevocably pagan. In Mainz, Nazis were debarred from receiving the sacraments and the Bavarian bishops railed against the anti-clericalism that was perceived to be at the heart of Nazi educational policy. In Paderborn and Cologne, the prelates declared Catholicism and National Socialism to be wholly incongruent. The Fulda Episcopal Conference, which represented all but eight of the twenty-five bishops, stated in 1931 that National Socialism 'actually stands in the most pointed contradiction to the fundamental truths of Christianity and with the organisation of the Catholic Church created by Christ'. Additionally, the Catholic press, which comprised around 400 newspapers, was not slow to denounce the perils of voting Nazi. The prominent journalist Walter Dirks declared in 1931 that Nazi ideology 'stood in blatant, explicit contrast to the Catholic Church'.[18]

Given this opposition, it was unfortunate that the Centre Party should have been the unwitting facilitator of Hitler's rise to power, partly because of the intervention of the papacy, which hindered its freedom of manoeuvre in the difficult game of coalition politics. Fearful of the constant threat from the left and ever mistrustful of allowing Catholics to play a political role, Pius XI and his Secretary of State, Pacelli, were prepared to ditch the Centre Party in return for a concordat from Hitler who, in January 1933, had been invited to become Chancellor with the veteran Zentrum politician von Papen as his deputy. Despite widescale intimidation from the Nazi stormtroopers, the Centre Party fought a brave campaign against the NSDAP in the March elections, securing almost 14 per cent of the vote, but that same month its deputies capitulated, passing the Enabling Act which terminated democracy in Germany and sealed the fate of political parties, including their own.

Why was this? Part of the answer lies in the fact that the Centre Party, through its experiences of pluralistic politics, was used to doing deals and working alongside political partners who were not to its taste. This argument can take us only so far, however, as many of the party's supporters had grave reservations about Hitler. For example, the devout Brüning, a previous Chancellor and veteran Zentrum stalwart, declared the Enabling Act to be 'the most monstrous resolution ever demanded of a parliament'.[19] What they shared with many of the other conservative elements within Germany was an underestimation of Hitler's cunning and ambition, and a belief that he would continue to work within legal restraints as he had done thus far. Hitler was additionally perceived as the most effective obstacle to Red revolution, a role he highlighted through his exploitation of the Reichstag fire. For his part, Hitler was mindful of the resistance manifested during the *Kulturkampf* and was resentful of the organising abilities of the Catholic Church. He thus feared potential opposition from the Catholic quarter, even though he had obtained the backing of the BVP. This fear led him to make all kinds of extravagant promises to gain Catholic backing for the Enabling Act, such as a continuing role for the faithful in shaping education and public law, guaranteed rights of confession, and other more general political pledges including the independence of the Reich's President and judiciary which were of particular concern to the Zentrum. Few actually believed him but, in the event, they placed party unity above their scruples, a move facilitated by Ludwig Kaas, a priest and the party's leader, who was hand-in-glove with Pacelli in the desire for the concordat. This underestimation of Nazi designs and the onus on unity probably forestalled any alliance with the SPD which would have thwarted Hitler's plans. In this way, the Centre Party played a similar role to the hapless PPI in Italy in legitimising the fascist acquisition of power, although it should be stressed that blame should also be shared with the German left, notably the communists who refused to do any deals with the socialists. At the end of the day, only the SPD voted against the Enabling Act which was passed by 441 votes to 94.

Now that Hitler was legitimately in place, it became ever more difficult for Christians, socialists, trade unionists and others to oppose his subsequent dismantling of the Weimar state, the process of *Gleichschaltung*, which involved the dissolution of all political parties save for the NSDAP, the replacement of trade unions by government-run bodies, the suppression of local state administration and extinction of civil liberties. Catholics were particularly badly placed to resist these moves, not just because of the demise of the Centre Party, but also thanks to the continued eagerness of the papacy to secure a concordat. It was Vatican pressure which obliged the Bishops' Conference of 28 March 1933 to express its loyalty to the new regime, although a handful of bishops went further by sending personal birthday greetings to the Führer. The bishops' statement was subsequently portrayed by the Nazis as an endorsement of their regime, provoking bewilderment among the faithful. Potential Catholic resistance was splintered yet further by the ratification of the long-awaited concordat in September 1933. Comprising thirty-four articles, the accords apparently granted the Church major concessions: freedom of worship; uninterrupted communication between Rome and the German episcopacy; the right of German bishops to publish pastoral letters unhindered; state funding of Catholic pupils both in elementary and the secondary systems; and government provision of confessional schools where these did not already exist. As a *quid pro quo*, the Church acquiesced in the demise of the Centre Party and Catholic trade unions, and barred clergy from participating in politics, the infamous 'depoliticisation' clause.

Only a handful of Catholics, principally those right-wing extremists associated with the Cross and Eagle movement led by von Papen, were wholly trusting of the deal, hoping in part that it might stymie any hopes the Nazis had of erecting a state church which was likely to be Protestant in complexion. Others were quickly disabused of any lingering trust they placed in Hitler's ability to keep his word. Within five days of the concordat's signing, a sterilisation law was introduced. Bishops soon discovered they did not have free access to Rome, and often found themselves the targets of black propaganda. One leading archbishop was smeared with the accusation that he maintained a Jewish mistress; the Vatican was denounced as a Jewish banking house; religious services were closely monitored; 'suspect' priests were watched; religious orders were accused of all manner of unusual sexual practices; and there were high-profile prosecutions, the so-called 'morality trials', of purportedly homosexual clerics. Most seriously, the Nazis implemented the *Karitasverband* by which they reneged on all their promises to respect the independence of Catholic schools, which were transformed into non-confessional ones, while Catholic lay organisations were abolished, and the SS murdered Erick Klauserer and Adalbert Probst, leaders respectively of Catholic Action in Berlin and the Catholic Sports Organisation. Meanwhile, the Hitler Youth went from strength to strength, boasting some 4 million members in 1935. Membership was, however, denied to those who also belonged to Church youth groups, not that they would have found the atmosphere especially congenial. The anti-clerical nature of the Hitler Youth was vividly expressed in one of its songs which caused offence among more moderate elements in the party:

> Swift they say a Pater Noster
> Priest and monk and pious nun.
> Swifter then with jealous purpose
> Smuggling currency they run.[20]

On the eve of war, hundreds of priests languished in concentration camps. All this formed part of the Nazi attempt to intimidate opponents into submission

Like so much of Nazi legislation, there was no clear pattern to the persecution of religion. Yet, by 1937, the attacks had reached such an intensity that Pius XI felt compelled to speak out, publishing his encyclical *Mit brennender Sorge* ('With Burning Concern'), smuggled into the country and read from the pulpits on Palm Sunday that year. This denounced breaches of the concordat and took issue with Nazi racial ideology. The following year, the Vatican bemoaned the *Anschluss* with Austria, something it had previously favoured but which was now viewed as a further body-blow to the international strength of Catholicism. Papal pronouncements undoubtedly had an impact within Germany, deeply annoying Hitler himself, and gave succour to those brave individuals who dared speak out. Such was the case of Father Lichtenberg, the Provost of Berlin, who led his congregation in silent prayer in protest at the attacks on Jewish properties in November 1938, the so-called *Kristallnacht*, when incidentally the episcopal palaces at Munich and Vienna were also desecrated.

Historians are generally agreed that the Catholic Church, alongside the army, was the only real remaining focal point of potential opposition to Nazism after 1933. Yet the ability of the faithful to resist had been seriously compromised. While Rome did eventually speak out, it was too little too late. Through its earlier insistence on the concordat, always a feeble defence against totalitarianism, through its neutering of the episcopacy, through its disapproval of Catholic political action in the shape of the Centre Party, and through its preference for Nazism over communism, the Vatican disadvantaged German Catholics in their stand against fascism. The German Church, however, cannot shrug off all blame. It had too easily acquiesced in the Enabling Act, and its voice of criticism was often muted or directed at particular issues such as euthanasia. It also continued to be duped by Hitler who, when it suited him, reined in his henchmen. For instance, in the build-up to war in 1939 he curtailed the open policy of exterminating the mentally ill. The unfortunate habit of German Catholics, picked up during the *Kulturkampf*, to protest but at the same time to affirm their loyalty to the nation and its lawful government, withdrawing into their own religious sphere and waiting for better days to come, had stood them in poor stead when confronted by the monstrous regime that was Nazism. As Martin Conway has suggested, it may not be too strong to speak of a *modus vivendi* existing between the Church and Nazism during the 1930s.[21]

With the exception of the Soviet Union, where the enemy was clear-cut, the overall Catholic response to the emerging dictators was thus an undistinguished one. Apart from an honourable minority, Catholics from the Vatican downwards were lured by the fact that some at least of the dictators were professing Catholics, by the adoption of corporatist polices which owed much to thinkers like Le Play, by the authoritarian espousal of traditional values, by the explicit rejection of communism and by the willingness of authoritarian regimes to sign concordats which promised much even if they delivered little. In this environment, Catholics too easily relinquished individual liberties and were restrained in their criticisms of secular authority. The same temptations would also bedevil those co-religionaries who lived in the dwindling number of Europe's liberal democracies. Why they did not ultimately succumb is the question to which we must now turn.

Catholics and the Liberal Democracies

When looking at the liberal democracies – in the Netherlands, Belgium, France, Britain and the newly independent state of Ireland – it is not difficult to uncover Catholics who possessed rabid right-wing sympathies. Yet this should not necessarily give rise to the belief that there was some intrinsic urge within European Catholics that led them to support dictatorships, albeit the corporatist solutions of Salazar and Franco rather than the racial model offered by Hitler. It should also be remembered that in those states that succumbed to authoritarian regimes there was widescale instability which made people on all points of the political and religious spectrum look to extreme solutions. To be sure, the liberal democracies were not without their own share of problems, yet these were contained within the political framework largely because a majority of people, Catholics included, believed that the existing structures were their best safeguard of stability. In the case of Belgium and Netherlands, this process has been termed 'pillarisation', a process whereby social and religious groups rallied to their own organisations yet used these for the common good as well as for their own interests.[22] Such was the function of the unitary Catholic party which existed in this part of north-western Europe. Even within France, where there was no mainstream Catholic political party, the faithful largely reconciled themselves to the institution of a republic even though they still harboured hopes of changing its details. In Britain, too, Catholics were generally able to resist the fascist temptation, as they were in Ireland, although here a strident anti-democratic voice was undoubtedly an element of political life in the 1930s. Finally, it is worth noting that in each of the liberal states, most of which (Britain and Ireland excepted) already had a vibrant tradition of Christian democracy, it was easier for Catholic liberals to make their voices heard, since they never experienced the same kind of state restrictions on their activities imposed elsewhere; and, additionally, the perils of fascism during the 1930s were evidenced in newspaper and radio reports for those who chose to regard them, though most still considered the communist alternative the principal danger. It was precisely this plurality of politics that produced a pluralist response on the part of Catholics to the problems of the inter-war years.

Within the Netherlands, it was the very expansion of liberal democracy at the close of the First World War that brought Catholics into mainstream political life and secured their adherence to the state. When, in the 1880s, Herman Schaepman toyed with the notion of a unitary Catholic party, an idea revived by Willem Nolens in the 1900s, their efforts were discouraged by the episcopacy which held on to anti-modernist views, regarding any such institution as an acknowledgement of the legitimacy of parliamentary politics. The prelates preferred instead to rely upon a gathering of Catholic deputies to defend the Church's interests, especially with regard to education. After confessional schools were given parity with state establishments in 1918, this particular cause was no longer so vital. Moreover, the war effected a radical extension of the suffrage to include all men in 1917 and all women two years later, with the further proviso that voting was compulsory. This situation forced a dramatic rethinking of the Catholic position, particularly as the socialists were quick to mobilise their vote, threatening to siphon off working-class support which had already been canvassed by dissident Catholic organisations, notably the left-leaning Michaelists. To prevent such a haemorrhaging, the Rooms Katholieke Staats Partij (RKSP), the Roman Catholic State Party, which had existed in embryonic form since 1898, was relaunched in 1926 and was almost continuously represented in government up to 1940. Having performed a *volte-face*, the Dutch episcopacy now consistently supported Catholic involvement in politics exclusively through this new creation whose message was both virulently anti-socialist and corporatist, but at the same time pro-democratic. Historians have since argued that the phenomenon of pillarisation prevented the rank-and-file from wholeheartedly engaging in day-to-day politics, often expending their energies in the enormously varied social organisations of the Church (see below), but at least it helped fend off the extreme right-wing challenge. Additionally, the bishops in 1935 forthrightly debarred the faithful from membership of the Nationaal Socialistische Beweging (NSB), a Nazi imitator, after the party had gained over 7 per cent of the vote, backing up their order with a threat to withhold the sacraments to its adherents. During the Spanish Civil War, a handful of crypto-fascist Catholics, predominantly students and journalists, created the Zwart Front, but this never achieved representation in parliament and would have to wait until the Nazi occupation before it exercised any real influence.

The case of Belgium, explored most incisively by Martin Conway, provides both profound differences and striking parallels to the Dutch experience.[23] Unlike the Netherlands, the faithful had long possessed their own unitary political body in the shape of the Catholic Party, created to resist the anti-clerical onslaught of the 1870s and an extremely successful player in pluralist politics thereafter. In every election between 1884 and 1914, it secured an overall preponderance of seats in parliament, enabling the party to monopolise government, further the interests of the bourgeoisie and expand the many educational and social initiatives of the Church. In 1918, however, the introduction of universal manhood suffrage threatened this privileged position, just as it gave a boost to the creation of a clerical party in the Netherlands.

In future, the Catholic Party would have to compete with the Liberals and Socialists on a different electoral playing field, and could no longer look forward to guaranteed victories at the polls. Cohabitation with these rivals in cabinet thus became the norm. Moreover, historians argue that the legacy of wartime, in particular the shared experiences of the trenches and resistance to German autocracy, gave rise to a greater democratisation of politics. Within the Catholic Party, this was reflected in the desire of the working-class Christian democrats and Flemish elements to question the continuing pre-eminence of the overwhelming middle-class francophone leadership. Always a broad church of interests, many of which had fought to assert their autonomy, in 1921 the Catholic Party reconstituted itself to become the Union Catholique Belge/Katholiek Verbond van België (UCB), the Catholic Union Party. Fragmentation beckoned, especially with the creation of a Flemish grouping within parliament, the Katholieke Vlaamse Kamergroep (KVK), the Flemish Catholic Parliamentary Group of Frans Van Cauwelaert and the decision of Prosper Poullet, a leading UCB Christian Democrat, to enter into a coalition government with the socialist Parti Ouvrier Belge (POB) in 1925–26, the first governmental alliance featuring Marxists and Christian Democrats.

As Martin Conway has again argued, fragmentation was avoided because of two factors.[24] The first was the succession of Cardinal Van Roey as Primate of Belgium in place of Cardinal Mercier. Though sharing many of the conservative instincts of his predecessor, Van Roey did much to facilitate the continuing vigour of Catholic social and educational activities, thus providing the laity with a strong supporting network, and declared the UCB to be the only authorised outlet for Catholic political expression. Second, maintains Conway, Belgian parliamentary politics lost something of their bitterness in the inter-war years. While liberals, socialists and Catholics asserted their independence, an identity reinforced by their own educational, welfare and social systems, within the Chamber they often found themselves in agreement with one another, thus contributing to the process of pillarisation.

As in the Netherlands, it was the support of the ecclesiastical hierarchy for the Catholic Party and the phenomenon of pillarisation that dissuaded a majority of Belgian Catholics from seeking alternative political outlets, not all of which were necessarily extreme. One such was the left-wing Flemish Christian Democratic organisation, the Algemeen Christelijk Wekersverbon (ACW), which contemplated running its own election candidates as well as schism from the UCB, something which was ultimately avoided, largely because its supporters still valued the support networks offered by the Catholic community. A more serious threat was posed by the Vlaams Nationaal Verbond (VNV), the Flemish National Union of 1933, initially a *pot-pourri* of all manner of political ideologies, but which later evolved as a Catholic, right-wing nationalist movement, strongly attracted to authoritarian values. Its formation reflected the long-standing fault-line within Belgium between Walloon and Flemish populations, and has been compared to the Catholic nationalist bodies in Croatia and Slovakia. Predominantly youthful in its support, it eroded the electoral support for the UCB which responded by establishing a local party apparatus, the Katholieke Vlaamse Volkspartij (KVV), the Flemish Catholic People's Party, which did enough to draw the sting out of the tail of Flemish nationalism.

A final challenge was situated in the French-speaking areas of Belgium and fed on the economic dislocation of the early 1930s which affected both peasants and the middle classes. Here, especially among the young and student groups, congregated in the Association Catholique de la Jeunesse Belge (ACJB), the Association of Belgian Catholic Youth movements, there grew an admiration for the regimes of Salazar and Dollfuss, as well as an enthusiasm for the writings of the French neo-royalist polemicist Charles Maurras. Often viewed as a generational revolt, this yearning found its most concrete expression in the Rexist movement of Léon Degrelle, the name coming from the Christus Rex publishing house situated in Louvain and owned by the ACJB. The dynamic Degrelle, impatient with traditional Catholic solutions, articulated a formulaic blend of authoritarian and nationalist ideas which he publicised in his own widely-distributed journals. Like all proto-fascists, his aim was to achieve sufficient political momentum to propel himself into power, and for a time he appeared to be building up a head of steam. In 1935, at Courtrai, he directly challenged the UCB leadership in a dramatic *coup de théatre*, and in the following year his party won twenty-one seats in parliament.

The upward trajectory was unsustainable: Degrelle's imitative 'March on Brussels' in October 1936 was risible, and when he stood as a by-election candidate, challenging the Prime Minister Paul Van Zeeland the following year, he was a conspicuous failure. His inability to overturn democracy must undoubtedly be credited to the capacity of the Belgian government to stand up for itself and to his failure to win converts outside a narrow geographical area, but credit is also due once again to Cardinal Van Roey who roundly condemned the Rexist phenomenon, and to the unwillingness of senior Catholic politicians to back Degrelle's programme. His moment, like that of Catholic fascists in the Netherlands, arrived with the *Wehrmacht*, by which time Degrelle himself had largely relinquished his spirituality for a crude Nazism.

It might be thought that Catholics in France would have succumbed most readily to the temptations of the far right, given their long-standing antipathy towards the Republic. It will be recalled, from the previous chapter, that at the height of the Dreyfus Affair many had gravitated towards the royalist, deeply xenophobic and anti-Semitic Action Française (AF) of Charles Maurras, ignoring the injunctions of Leo XIII to make their peace with the Republic. Catholics unquestionably continued to be strongly represented in the ranks of the right during the inter-war years, not so much in the AF, which suffered a decline in its fortunes thanks to the emergence of rival right-wing leagues of the 1920s, but in the Fédération Républicaine, which drew together the conservative republican forces in the Chamber of Deputies, and the Fédération Nationale Catholique (FNC), the National Catholic Federation. Created in 1924 in an attempt to head off the anti-clericalism of Herriot's newly-elected Cartel des Gauches, as James McMillan has illustrated, the character of this organisation largely mirrored that of its president, General de Castelnau.[25] Deeply aristocratic, exceedingly devout and a trenchant patriot who had fought in both the Franco-Prussian and First World War in which he had lost three of his twelve children, he aimed to restore France to its rightful place as the 'eldest daughter of the Church' so that the values of discipline, order, obedience, respect and family would reign supreme. To this end, de Castelnau envisaged the FNC not so much as a political party – something of which he heartily disapproved – but as a pressure group through which to promote issues such as religion in schools, large families, anti-Bolshevism and anti-masonry. It subsequently held festivals and large rallies, and published its own newspaper, the *Action Catholique de France*, later renamed *La France Catholique*. Just as in Belgium and the Low Countries, where traditionalist Catholics would have to wait for national military defeat before they had their opportunity, so too would de Castelnau's reactionary vision depend upon the establishment of Pétain's authoritarian regime, the Marshal himself being a close associate of the General though, as we shall see, his government was not as pro-clerical as is sometimes alleged.

As historians have begun to suggest, what is truly significant about inter-war France is that the automatic connection between Catholicism and the right was irrevocably broken, and a plethora of Catholic movements and organisations evolved which belonged either in the centre, or indeed on the left of the political spectrum.[26] Why was this so? Part of the answer lies in the so-called second *ralliement* of the 1920s. As Harry W. Paul has shown, this emerged out of the desire of successive French governments to mend fences with the Church, most notably in the immediate aftermath of the First World War when Catholics, like their co-religionaries elsewhere in Europe, had proven their loyalty to the national cause.[27] In 1920, when diplomatic relations were reopened with Rome, it was agreed that the newly acquired provinces of Alsace and Lorraine should remain immune from the laic laws, government officials attended the canonisation of Joan of Arc, and much of the financial detritus of the 1905 Separation Law was tidied up. Admittedly, this *rapprochement* between Church and state did not run very deep and did not preclude the reappearance of anti-clerical governments, most famously Herriot's ministry of 1924, which threatened to reinvigorate the *lois laïcs*, extending these to Alsace and Lorraine. Yet no other administration thought seriously of reactivating this legislation, not even Léon Blum's Popular Front of 1936 which hoped to conciliate Catholics, nor the radical administration fronted by Edouard Daladier in 1938, which passed family legislation reflecting clerical concerns.

Aside from the improvement in Church–state relations, credit must also be extended to the papacy for curtailing the right-wing instincts of French Catholicism. In 1926, exasperated by the AF's agnosticism rather than its racism, Pius XI forbade clergy from membership. In 1932, the bellicose and Germanophobic tone of the FNC, which ran counter to the values of collective security promoted by the Foreign Minister, Aristide Briand, led the Pope to make known his displeasure at that organisation's activities. In any event, Catholics had a large number of extremist organisations to choose from, among them Francois Coty's La Solidarité Française, Pierre Taittinger's Jeunesses Patriotes and Georges Valois' Faisceau, but none of these, with the exception of Colonel de la Rocque's Croix de Feu, admittedly the most influential of all the leagues, placed religion high among their priorities. Finally, it is clear that French Catholics in the 1930s were less concerned with politics than they were with the problem of dechristianisation. It was in France that the father of modern religious sociology, Gabriel Le Bras, and his acolyte, Fernand Boulard, conducted pioneering studies, which reinforced fears that sections of the nation were becoming *pays de mission*.[28]

In this situation, French Catholics gravitated not so much to the extremes of politics, but to the centre-right, to Christian democracy and to Social Catholicism, building on the legacies of Marc Sangnier, Albert de Mun and the *abbés démocrates* of the 1890s. The Silloniste tradition of Christian democracy was to be reinvigorated by the establishment of Marc Sangnier's Jeune République (JR) in 1919, a party dedicated to pacifism, reconciliation with Germany, disarmament and a radical restructuring of society. Five years later, there emerged the Parti Démocrate Populaire (PDP), the Popular Democratic Party, once again proffering a brand of Christian democracy, perhaps best situated on the centre-right, and dedicated to the promotion of the family, social welfare schemes, the provision of cheap housing and Christian trade unionism. While both parties could agree upon their opposition to the extreme right, in the shape of the AF, they could agree on little else: in the eyes of the JR, the PDP was merely another version of the ill-fated ALP of Jacques Piou; in the view of the PDP, the JR was too left-leaning.

Such disagreements, together with the disapproval of the papacy and the traditional reluctance of the French electorate to vote for a confessional party, a fact illustrated by the paltry numbers of deputies securing seats in parliament, ensured that inter-war France would not see the emergence of a Catholic party akin to that found in Germany, Belgium and elsewhere. Rather, Catholic energies were articulated through a wide range of newspapers and journals. Among them were the Dominican *La Vie Intellectuelle*, which urged Catholics to abandon Maurrasian ideals; *Sept*, another Dominican-inspired publication which, in its brief life between 1934 and 1937, achieved a weekly circulation of 100,000, urging the faithful to support the Popular Front and condemning the French right's support for Franco; *Esprit*, the periodical of the personalist philosopher Emmanuel Mounier, created in 1939, which advocated a 'third way' in politics between the polarities of left and right, although on closer inspection his ideas owed more to the right than to the left; *La Terre Nouvelle*, founded in 1935, which published articles by Protestants, Catholics and socialists and which earned the censure of the archdiocese of Paris; *La Vie Catholique*, which strongly supported Pius XI's outlawing of the AF; and *L'Aube* of 1932, the most influential voice of French Christian democracy, despite its relatively small circulation. In the words of the British commentator Alexander Werth, *L'Aube* was '*the* organ of liberal Catholicism'.[29]

Alongside this burgeoning and highly energising Catholic press, there stood

a wide variety of Social Catholic movements, most importantly the Confédération Française des Travailleurs Chrétiens (CFTC) which enjoyed an all-
time high in its membership at the close of the 1930s, and the Jeunesse
Ouvrière Chrétiennne (JOC), originally set up in Belgium in 1925 but quickly
imitated in France, and which gave rise to such other youth movements as
the Jeunesse Etudiante Chrétienne (JEC) and the Jeunesse Agricole Chrétienne
(JAC). While the latter was distinctly right-wing in its advocacy of corporatist
values, all of these initiatives sought to bridge class divides and promote
discussion about a more equal society, organising discussion groups and prayer
meetings. This was also the aim of the Nouvelle Equipes Françaises (NEF),
created in 1938 by the eminent Christian Francisque Gay, which endeavoured
to build consensus around the centre ground, establishing some 150 groups
on the eve of the Second World War. It is highly significant that many of the
early resisters, most famously Edmond Michelet, were drawn from the NEF
network, illustrating the diversity, vibrancy and commitment to liberal democratic values that had overtaken French Catholicism by this stage.

By contrast with France, Britain could never boast the same richness, variety
and depth of Catholic political action, for the simple reason that Catholics
remained a minority, even though their numbers were swollen by the arrival
of a new intake of Irish immigrants following the growing reluctance of the
USA to provide a haven for European settlers. This was reflected in the
growth of Catholic churches and chapels from 1,380 in 1918 to 1,883 in 1945
as well as by the near-doubling in the number of priests to *circa* 8,000 in the
same period. It is calculated that there were some 3 million Catholics in
Britain by 1945 in comparison to nearly 2 million in 1918. As in the past,
prejudice against Catholics was not far below the surface, despite the fact that
they had proved their loyalty in the First World War. Such eccentric organisations as the Council for Investigation of Vatican Influence and Censorship
(CIVIC) continued to retail the notion that Catholics were a breed apart,
committed in the final analysis not to the state but to Rome. Indeed, full
integration was not achieved during the inter-war years, signified by the fact
that they were popularly referred to as 'left-footers', 'papists' or 'paddies'; the
suggestion in George Orwell's little-known novel, *A Clergyman's Daughter*,
published in 1935, that a prominent Catholic family was teaching its pet parrot
phrases in Latin was a reflection of surviving prejudice.[30] As perceived outsiders, there was a strong suspicion that Catholics would succumb to the
continental influence of fascism, and once again it is not difficult to find
examples. Prominent Catholic intellectuals in the 1920s, such as G. K. Chesterton and Hilaire Belloc, were anti-Semites and known admirers of Mussolini.
When, in 1926, the *duce* survived an assassination attempt a *Te Deum* was
celebrated in St Peter's, Liverpool. Across the Pennines, Mosley's British Union
of Fascists (BUF) recruited so strongly among Catholics in Leeds that he was
known locally as the 'Pope'. The Spanish Civil War illustrated yet further how
Catholic intellectuals, among them Douglas Jerrold and John Strachey Barnes,
were drawn to the right, and Cardinal Hinsley himself cherished a signed
photograph of Franco which he kept on his desk throughout the Second

World War. Yet, once again, Catholics generally resisted the fascist temptation and political activity was characterised by its plurality and concern for social issues above political ones.

Testimony to this is the absence of any specifically Catholic party. There were many reasons for this. Aside from the apprehension it would have created with the papacy, British Catholics lacked the financial wherewithal to establish such a body; the British electorate mirrored that of France in its mistrust of confessional parties; any such party would, in any case, have further stigmatised British Catholics as outsiders; and the hierarchy considered that the interests of the faithful were best achieved through pressure groups which had already proved their worth in securing advantages for clerical schools. It had been the supposed threat to these establishments, posed by the 1906 Birrell Education Bill, that had led to the creation of the highly influential Catholic Federations, organised on a diocesan basis. Moreover, Catholics were well catered for in the mainstream political parties. Catholic political life has often been characterised as being divided on ethnic grounds, yet in truth it was organised on class lines, the well-to-do lending their support to the Conservative Party, while the working class owed allegiance to the Liberal and Labour Parties. Support for the latter was a real concern to the episcopacy in the early 1920s, an aspect of the Church's more general opposition to socialism. The problem was circumvented by Cardinal Bourne who, in 1924, proclaimed that the Labour Party 'has nothing in common with the socialists of the Continent',[31] thus allowing the laity to both join and vote for it, although Bourne was merely excusing a reality which was that many Catholic workers were natural Labour supporters.

This did not stop the Church in Britain from seeking to offer its own avenues for social action, and it is fair to say the 1931 encyclical *Quadragesimo anno* was enthusiastically received. Among the initiatives, Tom Buchanan lists the following: the Distributist League, founded in 1926, which sought to proffer an alternative to modern capitalism and socialism while arguing for a dispersal of property; the Catholic Social Guild (CSG), originally set up in 1909 and the brainchild of the enthusiastic Jesuit Father Charles Plater (also founder of the Catholic Workers' College, now Plater College in Oxford), which promoted an academic interest in a range of social and political issues through its 4,000-odd local study circles; the Catholic Women's League (CWL) of 1906, and its offshoots such as the Union of Catholic Mothers and the Junior League, which were chiefly concerned with the improvement of women's social conditions; the Catholic Women's Suffrage Society (CWSS) of 1911 which was more militant in its championing of women's causes; and the National Confederation of Catholic Trade Unionists (NCCTU), the work of Thomas Burns, although this 1912 creation scarcely survived the ending of the First World War; the Catholic Guilds, which operated within trade unions during the 1930s; and the Catenian Association of the same decade which aimed to bring together Catholic businessmen.[32] As Buchanan continues, what these various institutions had in common was a concern to lift the social question out of party politics. Perhaps the only Catholic body in Britain which unashamedly embraced politics was the People and Freedom Group set up, significantly, by the exiled PPI leader, Don Sturzo, on his arrival in London in 1924.

The one part of Britain where Catholics were overtly involved in politics was, of course, Northern Ireland which had emerged out of the Anglo-Irish Treaty of 1921. Here, Catholics were not only a minority, at just over a third of the population, but were also subject to open discrimination. For instance, some 5,000 Catholic workers were sacked from the Belfast shipyards (1920–22), churches were often vandalised and church-goers were attacked. Moreover, they lived under a parliament at Stormont dominated by hard-line Protestant Unionists, although they did have their own representation in the form of the constitutional Nationalists and the republican sympathisers of Sinn Féin. Moreover, because the fault-lines in Irish politics ran along religious/national lines, there was no possibility of Catholics avoiding political engagement of some kind. This, though, did not lead to the establishment of a separate and distinct confessional party. When, in 1928, such an idea was mooted through the National League, it never achieved any momentum. The Republicans, organised through the Irish Republican Army (IRA), opposed any movement which might dissipate the wider support for a united Ireland; Catholic opinion was in any case split on whether to accept or reject partition; and, above all, the Catholic Church, which exercised a predominant influence over political activity, was opposed to the formation of any unitary party, fearing the loss of its own influence and the unpredictability of what it might bring. So it was that the episcopacy endeavoured to funnel the laity's energies into Catholic Action.

At first sight, it is perhaps surprising that no separate Catholic political party should have emerged south of the border in the Irish Free State which received its constitution in 1922. Here, Catholics comprised the overwhelming majority of the population; and politics were suffused with nationalist and Catholic sentiment. The absence of such a party was due, first, to the opposition of the well-organised Church hierarchy, which had a preponderant and continuing effect upon political life; and second, to the fact that the state was never at any stage an enemy of religion; rather the opposite, for its leaders of every political hue were staunch Catholics and endowed the faith with a range of benefits and protections. There were especially close links between the Church hierarchy and William Cosgrave's Cumann na nGaedheal party which held power after the establishment of the Irish Free State, though it kept at arm's length those militants congregated in Sinn Féin and the IRA whose deployment of violence as a political weapon had been mythologised after the Easter Rising of 1916. When Éamonn de Valera's more intransigent nationalist party, Fianna Fáil, formed in 1926, came to power in the 1932 elections, there were mixed reactions. The Vatican at first feared the launch of an anti-clerical campaign, whereas some integralist Catholics within Ireland looked to the devout de Valera, whose piety had been inculcated through his education by the Christian Brothers and the Holy Ghost Fathers, to establish a confessional state. That was the hope, for example, of the influential Father

Edward Cahill, founder of the League for Catholic Social Action (An Ríogh-acht) and author of *The Framework of a Christian State*, completed in 1932.

In the event, neither the fears of the one nor the hopes of the other came to pass, for while the pragmatic de Valera was keen to support Catholicism, he was at the same time concerned to avoid the extremism both of left-wing nationalists and of right-wing Catholics. He was thus happy to develop close working relations with the Irish episcopacy, which for its part hastened to assure the new government of its support. The fruits of this *entente* came in the 1937 constitution which de Valera piloted through, and which was strongly influenced by Catholicism. For instance, the preamble reaffirmed the Catholic character of the Irish nation; Article 41 pledged the state to preserve the institution of marriage and not to permit any legislation for divorce; the same article followed an essentially Catholic social line in ascribing women a prepon-derant role within the home; Article 44 acknowledged the special position of the Church as 'the guardian of the Faith professed by the great majority of its citizens'; and the upper House of the Seanad (Senate), which contained representatives from the professions and interest groups, was organised along the corporatist lines advocated by many Catholics, though this probably had more to do with de Valera's concern to extend Fianna Fáil's patronage network in the Oireachtas (Parliament) than any desire to implement Catholic social teaching.

These religious provisions in the constitution did not go far enough for some Catholics who continued to campaign for a repeal of Article 44 and its replacement with a more explicit profession of faith, though Ireland never advanced further down this road towards the establishment of a confessional state. The strength of feeling on this issue should not surprise us, for there had always been a strong authoritarian, integralist sentiment among Catholics, expressed most notably in the Blueshirt movement. Founded by General Eoin O'Duffy, a former commander of the IRA in Monaghan and Commissioner of Police who had been sacked by de Valera in the wake of his 1932 election victory, the movement drew upon the idealist aspirations of the young and spoke in vague terms of a renewal of society and economy on the lines of Degrelle's Rexists and Mussolini's fascist party. In August 1933, the Blueshirts (now named the National Guard) fused with Cumann na nGeadheal and the National Centre Party eventually to form Fine Gael, with O'Duffy as its president. In that same year, the effervescent General opted for a showdown with de Valera by staging a march to Dublin, clearly hoping to emulate Mussolini's victory parade in Rome. The event was a fiasco, and the following year O'Duffy was squeezed out of the leadership by Cosgrave, to the delight and with the connivance of the Church hierarchy. Cosgrave took Fine Gael back towards democracy, thus helping Ireland avoid the fascist temptation. Two years later, at the time of the Spanish Civil War, right-wing Catholic opinion rallied to Franco's cause, and the Irish Christian Front was formed under the leadership of Patrick Belton. As well as supplying Nationalist troops with medical aid, the movement called, albeit in vague terms, for the inauguration of a Catholic social and political order within Ireland, an ambition which earned it the praise of the Vatican. Yet the Front met with no more success than O'Duffy's Blueshirts. There were widespread suspicions that the two movements were one and the same; moreover, Irish prelates entertained several doubts about the Front. Not only were they troubled by allegations of financial irregularities, they also questioned the wisdom of endorsing Belton's demand for a fundamental Catholic Law. Eventually, these anxieties translated themselves into outright opposition, thus sounding the death knell for the Front.

In Ireland, as was overwhelmingly the case elsewhere among the other surviving liberal democracies, Catholic political action was characterised by diversity. Within this general European context, some Catholics undoubtedly gravitated towards a fascist trajectory, yet their numbers were not as great as is sometimes imagined, and their influence was constrained by a series of generic factors: the fetters imposed by the ecclesiastical hierarchy; rival traditions of Christian democracy; the role of unitary Catholic parties, at least in Belgium and Holland; and the instinctive allegiance of the faithful to the existing political set-ups, a loyalty reinforced by the experiences of the First World War. It was one of the distinguishing features of fascist movements that they recruited from among those who felt most alienated in society and those who considered that their sacrifices within the war in particular had not been recognised by the state. Catholics in the surviving liberal democracies did not share this degree of disaffection, and it was significant that they all lived in states which had been victorious in the 1914–18 conflict. Even if they were not necessarily enamoured of their post-war governments, they did not feel threatened in the manner of the past. Moreover, with the exception of Czechoslovakia, it seemed that the liberal democracies had grown tired of anti-clericalism, and even France only occasionally flirted with fresh anti-Catholic legislation, enabling Catholics there to break emphatically with the right-wing tradition. Paradoxically, it would take the military victories of the overtly pagan Nazi Empire to provide extreme right-wing Catholics with their opportunity, although it is difficult to believe that these opportunities would have survived an overall German military victory. As we shall see, Catholics were prominent in the resistance to Nazism in occupied Europe, reflecting another trait of political Catholicism of the inter-war years, that is a willingness to challenge authority, especially in the shape of the ecclesiastical hierarchy. Only in Protestant Britain and especially devout Ireland was this trend less apparent. Yet to explain why this questioning habit was to take root, it is necessary to move away from the political sphere and look more closely at the manifold attempts of the Church to combat secularisation, when even Catholics in authoritarian states posed questions about the rightness of unblinking obedience.

Catholics and Belief during the Inter-war Years

Amid the dramatic political upheavals of the 1920s and 1930s, and the agonising choices that these posed for Catholics, it is easy to forget that members of the Church continued to forge a spiritual life, and that this underwent both change and revival during this period. The overwhelming feature of this renewed devotion was the greater participation of the laity, something encouraged by the papacy itself. The impetus for this involvement was various. At one level, it reflected more general developments within theology. With the otiose and self-destructive debates over the modernist crisis largely contained, if not fully resolved, Catholic theologians dared to articulate a less academic and more personal organic faith, which recognised the value of involving the laity in the liturgy and study of the scriptures, although admittedly such trends caused disquiet within conservative circles and would not really achieve fruition until the Second Vatican Council.

Greater lay involvement was also spurred by a growing awareness of the extent of secularisation. To a degree, this had been curbed by the experience of the First World War which was a sharp reminder to everyone of their mortality. Following a Committee of Inquiry upon the army and religion, it was concluded that 'the men who had been in the trenches had experienced an awakening of the primitive religious convictions – God, prayer, immortality'.[33] Pews were thus full again and, if anything, Catholic congregations were larger than their Protestant counterparts. In this regard, there is some evidence to suggest that the Catholic tradition of prayers for the dead and anniversary masses accommodated the religious sensibilities of those who had lost loved ones and fended off the temptation of spiritualism which seemed especially prevalent in Protestant England. The graphic scene recounted in Robert Graves's famous war memoirs *Goodbye to All That*, in which he is woken in the middle of the night by Siegfried Sassoon's mother attempting to get in touch with one of her dead sons by means of spiritualism, is but one testimony to this phenomenon.[34] The Church could also draw reassurance from the fact that the war had not disturbed traditional popular practices, something evidenced in both the belligerent and non-belligerent states. In the town of Salamanca, women on their wedding day still presented eggs to the convents in the hope that the sisters' prayers would ensure good weather. There was, though, plenty of anecdotal evidence to suggest that, in the 1920s and 1930s, secularisation had become a real problem. In 1936, the noted Spanish Redemptorist preacher and mission leader Sarabia concluded, on the basis of his wide experience, that 'many have already lost the faith'.[35] When, shortly before the Civil War, the Archbishop of Seville wrote to his parish priests urging them to create committees of adult, practising Catholics to aid the Church in the fight against dechristianisation, to a man his clergy replied that such pious individuals simply did not exist. Catholic observers noted that among the working-class districts of Barcelona, Bilbao, Madrid and Valencia men lived their lives without any knowledge of Catholic doctrine and without participating in the Church's rituals. Worryingly, the Church was soon in possession of statistical evidence to illustrate a drop in observance, thanks largely to the pioneering studies of the French religious sociologist Gabriel Le Bras. Inspired by Le Bras' techniques, and troubled by the lack of faith he witnessed daily in the streets of Paris, the little-known priest Abbé Godin published, in 1943, his *France. Pays de mission?*, a book whose findings so troubled

Cardinal Suhard that he could not sleep for two successive nights. The findings for France were echoed by the Madrid-based Jesuit Francisco Peiró who, in 1936, published his *El problema religioso-social en España* which revealed that less than 7 per cent of his 80,000 parishioners bothered with Sunday mass, a mere 6 per cent fulfilled the paschal obligation, 20 per cent married in civil ceremonies, 25 per cent of children were not baptised, and 40 per cent could not recite the Lord's Prayer. 'The working masses, in their great majority, are no longer Catholic,' he concluded.[36]

Such concerns went right to the very top of the Church. In his 1925 encyclical *Quas primas*, Pius XI declared: 'The plague of our age is the so-called laicism, with its errors and godless aims.' Significantly, he also highlighted the role which the faithful could play in combating this danger. Hitherto, Catholics had 'neither that social position nor that influence which those really should have who hold high the torch of truth ... but if only the faithful understand that they must fight under the standard of Christ the King with courage and perseverance, then they will strive with apostolic zeal to lead the alienated and ignorant souls back to the Lord.' In part, this recognition of the role of the laity was an acknowledgement that an undermanned clergy could not cope on its own. In no sense did the Vatican envisage greater lay participation resulting in a dilution of ecclesiastical authority. It was simply another means of harnessing the flock and directing its energies, especially away from the political arena. This sentiment is perhaps best expressed in Pius XI's description of Catholic Action which he termed 'the organised participation of the laity in the hierarchical apostolate of the Church, transcending party politics'.[37] As already hinted, the problem was that not all lay Catholics were prepared to play the unassuming and meek roles attributed to them by the Church leadership.

It was in the practice of the faith itself that greater lay involvement was immediately apparent. This was facilitated most obviously by Catholic Action. Several popes had deployed this term in the past, yet it was Pius XI who gave it shape and form. His deep concern with the issues of capitalism, socialism, communism and the apparent atomisation of society implied by the growth of governmental authority and the concomitant decline of intermediate bodies capable of resisting this had been signalled in the 1931 encyclical *Quadragesimo anno*, published to mark the fortieth anniversary of *Rerum novarum*. He thus looked to Catholic Action as a means for promoting an organicist society, characterised by a plenitude of subsidiary groupings of the faithful. In the words of the pontiff himself, the aim of these organisations was 'of advancing the Kingdom of our Lord Jesus Christ and thereby communicating to human society the highest of all goods ... of spreading everywhere the principles of the Christian faith and of Christian doctrine, defending them energetically, and giving effect to them in private and in public life'.

Originally created in Italy, where Catholic Action endured an uncomfortable existence within Mussolini's regime, it quickly spread elsewhere. The Acção Católico Português was formed in 1933, for instance. In Spain, the Foment de Catalunya was established in 1916 by Father Buixô to distribute religious books and pamphlets. Yet Catholic Action was never especially instrumental in the less industrialised nations of the Iberian peninsula and Ireland. Despite worthy initiatives, Frances Lannon observes that all too often Catholic Action in Spain was 'little more than a ritual lament that things were as they were, and an institutional aspiration that they should be different'.[38] 'Words and gestures were', she writes, 'in place of purposeful organization.'[39] As Mary Vincent adds, there was no shortage of leaders in Spain, but a dearth of people to lead![40] Instead, Catholic Action enjoyed greatest success in countries such as Poland and Hungary, where the regimes were strongly sympathetic to its overall aims and where the episcopacy was very supportive. It also did well in the liberal democracies of France, Belgium and the Netherlands where it was not considered a threat to rival youth organisations (the arrival of Hitler more or less finished off the movement in Germany), and where economic conditions lent themselves to the remedies offered by Catholic militants who sought to cultivate support among specific occupations, such as the workers, students and peasants. Always avoiding the term 'class', which smacked of Marxist polemics, Catholic Action preferred instead to work within different social *milieux*, ensuring that re-evangelisation was carried out by people belonging to the same social grouping as their clientele.

Although the nature of Catholic Action varied widely from country to country, it is perhaps the model of the JOC (Jeunesse Ouvrière Chrètienne) that best illustrates the overall aims of the phenomenon. Initially founded in Belgium in 1925 by the priest Joseph Cardijn, an admirer of the British scouting movement who had also closely studied British trade unions, it was transplanted to France two years later by Father Georges Guérin in the working-class Parisian suburb of Clichy. Although the JOC originated in youth groups belonging to the ACJF and ACJB, it quickly established its own identity. The guiding ethos was that the proletariat should be reorientated towards Catholicism not so much by the priesthood but by elements of the working class itself. 'For them, by them, among them', was the JOC's battle-cry. So it was that militants established workers' study circles in which they discussed the problems of the age and their own difficulties in particular. These were to be overcome by the operation of the precept articulated by Cardijn: 'see, judge, act'. In this sense, the JOC claimed that it was primarily concerned with an apostolic mission, yet there is no doubting the fact that it also sought to steer the working class away from socialist and communist organisations. This was done through pamphlets, mass rallies, retreats, the Semaines Sociales Catholiques in which workers addressed their spiritual and temporal problems, and the cultivation of elites who would spread the word – in essence, the type of mass politics being cultivated by both communists and fascists at the same time. For instance, a huge *Jociste* conference was conducted in Paris in July 1937, by which time the movement within France boasted some 20,000 members. Many of these gravitated to the Ligue Ouvrière Chrétienne (LOC), established in France in 1935, which defined itself as 'a school, service and representative body', but whose chief purpose was still the bringing of Catholicism to the workers. This never achieved the sophistication of the

Mouvement Ouvrier Chrétien (MOC) in Belgium, which oversaw trade unions and social welfare schemes, even though in 1941 the LOC became the Mouvement Populaire des Familles (MPF), deploying the family unit as a means of proselytising among the 'masses'. Inevitably, *Jocistes* were strongly mistrusted by conservatives, who labelled them 'Red Christians'; and there is indeed evidence to indicate that Catholic Action members often strayed from the strict supervision of their prelates, especially in their criticisms of Franco and support for the Blum experiment. For instance, Jacques Maritain, one of the inspirational figures of the movement in France who drew on neo-Thomist humanistic philosophy to justify the reinsertion of spirituality into the life of the popular classes, was outspoken in his disapproval of the Spanish Civil War.

Under the aegis of Catholic Action, all manner of lay involvement in the practice of Catholicism was encouraged, a surefire sign of the vitality and renewed purpose of the Church. One manifestation of this was the liturgical movement which had originated in the Benedictine monastery of Maredous in Belgium where a people's missal had been authored with the intention of making the Church's message more immediate and familiar to parishioners. This development was not without its critics who feared that it might give rise to mysticism and schism within the clergy let alone the laity, but at the turn of the century Pius X had recognised the benefits to be had in the 'active participation of the faithful in the sacred mysteries and the public and solemn prayer of the Church',[41] and was thus prepared to tolerate and even encourage moves, especially marked in Belgium and Germany, to provide commentaries on liturgical texts and the use of new types of music in services. European-wide attempts were further made to invigorate catechetical teaching, making catechisms more accessible to the young, although it was not until after the Second World War that these reforms truly bore fruit. The Vatican and Catholic Action were further keen to involve the faithful in the so-called 'Spiritual Exercises Movement', that is the development of retreats and training centres in which predominantly young people had the opportunity to study the scriptures and liturgy and to recite prayers. The Jesuits had traditionally been at the forefront of such activities, and in 1936 delivered some 16,000 courses to nearly three-quarters of a million students, but their efforts were soon reinforced by the activities of other orders.

Such innovation was not to the neglect of traditional forms of nineteenth-century worship in the shape of eucharistic piety, dedication to the Sacred Heart of Jesus and Marian devotion, all of which flourished in the inter-war years. Concern about the eucharist was, of course, nothing new. Well before the Council of Trent, Nicolas de Clamanges, a noted fifteenth-century reformer, had lamented that

> Often [the laity] only hear part of the mass and leave before the priest's permission. Many parishioners are content to enter the church and dampen their forehead with holy water. Others judge it satisfactory to genuflect before the Virgin. There are many who believe they have done well enough if they

have kissed the image of a saint on the wall. Those who have seen the body of Christ during the elevation judge that the Christ has satisfied their obligation and regard it as a great sacrifice [to have stayed so long].[42]

Similar complaints emanated from the Archbishop of Toulouse in 1619 who bemoaned 'the great and extraordinary irreverences that are daily committed ... even (which we can only say with horror) when the very August sacrament and sacrifice is raised at the altar'.[43] To judge from Mary Vincent's account of 1930s Salamanca, not much had changed in the intervening years, although such behaviour at mass was traditionally a part of Mediterranean culture. It was a wish to enhance the dignity and significance of the eucharist that had led Pius X in 1905 to instruct Catholics to receive communion 'frequently and even daily', and he had accordingly relaxed the age requirement to seven for First Communion and exempted the sick from fasting requirements. During the 1920s, such injunctions were augmented by the staging of eucharistic celebrations. In 1930, some 1,000 gathered in Salamanca to celebrate the feast of St Anthony. This was not anywhere near as impressive as the one million Catholics who gathered at Phoenix Park in Dublin in 1932 for a Eucharistic Congress, although it should be stressed that such events, especially in Spain, attracted the pious and the better-off above all.

The cult of the Sacred Heart was also reworked and deployed in an attempt to staunch the haemorrhaging of men in particular from the Church. Through the encyclical *Miserentissimus redemptor* of 1928, Pius XI invested the feast of the Sacred Heart with renewed importance, and four years later recommended its veneration as a certain means of demonstrating piety. Marian observances also multiplied, thanks to the Virgin's appearance at Fatima in 1917, and later at Beauraing and Banneux in Belgium in 1932–33. As Mary Vincent argues, whereas the Sacred Heart symbolised the crusade against secularisation, Marian devotion was a means by which women could make good the sins of Eve.[44] To do this, they were required to be obedient to God's will and to that of their husbands, and to be modest in their dress and conduct. Within France, young girls were directed to the Children of Mary, a league which supervised dress codes, habits and morals, an institution which spread to Spain and later England. In Spain, Catholicism was astonishingly prurient, although the call of the archbishops in 1926 for girls to desist from wearing short skirts was a ubiquitous one. Existing alongside the Children of Mary in Ireland was the Association of Our Lady of Mercy, founded by Frank Duff in 1921 and renamed the Legion of Mary four years later, which provided strictly supervised accommodation for young women. The Militia of the Immaculate Conception was set up in Germany by the Polish Franciscan Maximilian Kolbe in 1917. Pleased at such initiatives, in 1937 the Pope issued the encyclical *Ingravescentibus malis* commending the regular use of the rosary which was viewed as a powerful prophylactic against both fascism and communism.

The continuing adulation of the Virgin Mary reflected a growing worry of the Church in the inter-war years about sexual laxity. Of course, this had always been a traditional concern; and the late nineteenth century witnessed a greater willingness on the part of the clergy to raise the issue in the confessional. Yet in the aftermath of the First World War it seemed that the forces of secularisation – the development of professional sports, mixed bathing, coeducational schools, the growth of the cinema and commercial advertising – had brought sex into the public domain in an unprecedented fashion. In this situation, official Catholic teaching on sex did not change. It was still regarded as part of 'the inferior life' led by most Catholic laity as opposed to priests and religious, and was something to be practised only in a monogamous marriage as a means of producing children.[45] Yet there was now a shrill note of prurience in the clergy's attempts to curb the laity's behaviour, especially that of women who remained more outwardly pious than men. Hence the frequent calls to wear suitable dress, to refrain from blouses with short sleeves, so that women were the 'eternal feminine', the expression of the Virgin's values, as opposed to those of Eve. Yet the extent to which the laity obeyed such calls remains ambiguous, especially in peasant societies which, with the exception of Ireland, were generally open about sexual matters. Reading Gabriel Chevalier's contemporary novel about 1930s Beaujolais, *Clochemerle*, it seems little had changed since the eighteenth century.[46] Chastity, at least among men, was regarded as an overrated virtue and even the priest had no problem in condoning 'shotgun weddings' as these were proof of a couple's fertility, suggesting that not all the clergy were enthused by the campaign for morality taken up by the prelates and militant lay movements.

Women's inferiority to men was further stressed in the patriarchal structures of the many secular bodies which flourished in the inter-war years. Apart from Catholic Action, there were the so-called 'Secular Institutes', first recognised by Leo XIII in the constitution *Conditae a Christo* in December 1900, and then more formally by Pius XII (1939–58), whose *Provida mater ecclesia* of 1947 acknowledged them as 'a third state of perfection'. These bodies built upon the legacy of the nineteenth-century congregations in that they were associations of lay men and women who pledged themselves, sometimes through the swearing of vows, to live out to the highest degree the apostolic injunctions contained in the scriptures. Members might dedicate themselves full-time to the religious life or they might continue in their chosen professions, serving as models of all that was best in Catholicism. Unlike the congregations, many of the Institutes had an academic bent and not all displayed the same concern with charitable and social work. Prominent among them were the Prêtres du Prado, a community of exclusively French clerics, founded in the late nineteenth century by Father Chevrier, whose members were initially pledged to bring the gospel to the poorest elements of society, subsequently working among the youth and urban working class. Within Germany, the best-known Institute was the multifaceted Schönstatt Werk, founded in 1914 by Father Josef Kentenich, comprising various branches of lay men, women and clergy who were chiefly concerned with education and charity. After 1933, they expanded to South America, Australia and the USA, partly as a result of the arrival of the Nazi regime, though the Schönstatt Marian Sisters, with their unobtrusive lifestyle and everyday clothes, were able to persist with their ministry throughout the decade, emerging after 1949 as the largest female secular grouping in West Germany.

Perhaps the best known of the Institutes is that originally founded at Madrid in 1928 by the young cleric José María Escrivá de Balaguer as the Sociedad Sacerdotal de la Santa Cruz y Opus Dei. Always shrouded in secrecy, and characterised by a high degree of internal discipline, almost military in its nature, it was not until the aftermath of the Spanish Civil War that the existence of Opus Dei became widely known. Members were equipped with copies of *El Camino* ('The Way'), authored by Escrivá, more or less a Maoist 'little red book', containing the moral precepts and maxims of the movement. One such was the celebration of celibacy. 'Marriage is for the foot soldiers, not for the general staff of Christ,' announced another of its textbooks.[47] The aim of Opus Dei was to infiltrate universities, colleges, the professions and the higher reaches of business and to orchestrate a cadre of adherents who would emerge as leaders in their respective fields, dedicated to the spread of piety and obedience. The integralist *Opusdeístas* were suffused with a naive and at times sentimental faith, and shunned any kind of theological critique, instead preferring assertion to constructive debate. Supplanting the National Catholic Association of Propagandists as the principal forum for the dissemination of Catholic propaganda, they were indulged by Franco and were quick to reciprocate his regard, providing a substantial number of leading figures in his regime. Membership itself operated on several levels, with separate branches for laity and clerics, but all maintained a veil of secrecy about their operations which subsequently led to suspicion about their activities which occasionally had a masonic and Jesuitical air.

The evolution of Secular Institutes and greater lay involvement in the practice of Catholicism should not disguise the fact that during the inter-war years the Church still relied heavily on traditional structures, notably the regular orders. Inevitably, the massive growth in the number of religious, congregations and confraternities witnessed during the nineteenth century could not be maintained. This was especially true of women's orders. The beginning of the twentieth century had witnessed a flowering of alternative opportunities for women. Those who wished to contribute to society could be satiated by the office, schoolroom and even by some of the professions, including medicine and academe which were beginning to open their doors, although this is not to disguise the fact that within Europe male chauvinism still ruled triumphant, and was reinforced by the distinctly traditionalist image of women shared by the Nazis and Italian fascists. Nevertheless, with the exception of Nazi Germany which curtailed recruitment, the numbers belonging to religious orders continued to rise in the 1920s and 1930s, especially in traditionally devout countries and in those areas where the Church was keen to make up lost ground. In Spain, it is calculated that there were 11,000 male regulars in 1914 and some 31,000 by 1972; the number of female religious had risen from 35,000 in 1925 to 91,000 in 1965. Britain, one of those countries where the Church was especially keen to establish a presence, likewise experienced a renaissance. It is known that in 1850 there were no more than ten male orders, whose ranks maintained a paltry 263 priests. A century later, seventy orders were operating, boasting some 2,360 priests. Aside from traditional orders such as the Jesuits and Oratorians, more recently founded religious such as the Passionists also established themselves in the United Kingdom. Here, the progress of the women's orders was remarkable since there was no conventual experience on which to build, given that they had only been allowed to operate since the mid-nineteenth century. Further afield, the 1920s and 1930s saw the emergence of some wholly new communities, among them the Little Brothers of Jesus, the Little Sisters of Jesus, the Brothers of the Virgin of the Poor and the Little Brothers of the Gospel, who often drew on the life of the Christian explorer Charles de Foucauld as their inspiration. Turning away, as he had done, from the pleasures of the material world, and living in small communities, they preached the gospel to the very poor, especially in the deserts of North Africa.

Within Europe, too, regulars were increasingly involved in preaching. Perhaps the secret of their survival was the ability to reinvent themselves, much as the women's communities had done from the late seventeenth century onwards. The onus was less on a contemplative existence than on going out into the community to complement the work of seculars, to oversee the many lay Catholic organisations and to take charge of Catholic schools. Mary Vincent reports how, in Salamanca, nuns belonging to the ten closed convents in the city regularly went out to conduct good works in the community.[48] The contribution of the regulars also remained vital in the realm of education, even in France where the anti-clerical legislation of the early 1900s had actively discriminated against teaching orders. In the event, the restrictive laws were never truly implemented and were often circumvented by ingenious monks and nuns who took to wearing civilian dress. In 1937, they taught at least 47 per cent of pupils in Church secondary schools and some 15 per cent in primary schools. To make up the deficit, the Church had begun to employ an increasing number of exclusively lay personnel who resented the influence of the regulars, especially their willingness to accept low wages which encouraged a miserly episcopate to keep salaries low.

As to the seculars, the picture is more chequered. Although some regions saw a notable rise in their numbers, in others they stagnated or were in decline. Once again, it tended to be in those areas where the Church was attempting to reinvigorate itself that figures were healthiest. In Poland, there was a 43 per cent increase in the three decades after 1920; in Lithuania, the numbers rose by 50 per cent in the 1930s; in Britain, there was also an increase, albeit from a relatively low base of just under 4,000 in 1914, to 5,100 in 1966. Interestingly, in traditionally pious lands, always excepting Poland, the picture was not so rosy. Spain oversaw a decline from 34,000 in 1914 to 24,000 fifty years later, and to make matters worse the seculars were poorly distributed with respect to the needs of parishioners. At the Pontifical Seminary in Salamanca, there were some 345 graduates in 1928–29, but a mere 134 in 1935–36, although the climate of civil war was not necessarily the best time to be thinking about a seminary education. Not surprisingly, we are best informed about the situation in France, the focus of the pioneering studies of Fernand Boulard.[49] In absolute terms, there was a decline in the number of diocesan clergy from 54,800 in 1913 to 46,980 in 1929 and 42,487 in 1948. In proportional terms, this meant that there was one priest for every 832 inhabitants in 1913, a ratio of 1:960 in 1929 and 1:1,029 in 1950. What Boulard has designated as the ordinations quota, that is to say the number of ordinands for every 10,000 males aged between twenty-five and twenty-nine, also displayed a worrying trend, showing a marked drop between 1934 and 1938. On the eve of the Second World War, there was a shrill note of panic in the *Semaines Religieuses*, the weekly diocesan newsletters, which often published the local shortfall, drawing attention to the growing age of the priesthood and bemoaning the fact that secularisation had choked off the supply of pious adolescents entering the seminaries. It was in this situation, both in France and the Iberian peninsula, that the regulars were deployed to serve in parishes, supplementing the work of the seculars. Northern Spain regularly witnessed Capuchin Friars undertaking preaching duties and performing services. This may be one factor explaining why, in contrast to the nineteenth century, male religious tend to be more conspicuous than their female counterparts who were prevented by their gender from fulfilling the sacerdotal duties and were deemed unsuitable for the oft-times dangerous work of proselytising in rough working-class districts.

If the low number of seculars was giving rise to concern, this did not dent the self-confidence that was an overriding feature of inter-war Catholicism, which may be finally observed in the proliferation of local, national and international agencies concerned with charity and in the willingness of the Church to embrace new methods of mass communication. Charitable enterprises had, of course, always been at the heart of the Church's endeavours, but the experience of the First World War in particular pointed to the need for more systematic cooperation transcending state boundaries. As early as 1903, the way ahead had been indicated by Austria which had established a national charity association, an initiative that was copied by Switzerland in 1920, Hungary in 1931, Belgium in 1938, Ireland in 1941 and Spain in 1942, leaving France as the odd one out. On the international front, a permanent body was set up in 1928 with papal blessing, the Caritas Catholica, to coordinate the disparate local efforts of assistance and to emphasise the fundamentally religious aspects of their work. Inter-war charities were also distinguished by the sheer range of activities and concerns. The poor, the sick and the orphans, traditional foci of attention, were not neglected, but now refugees, demobilised soldiers, the unemployed, subsistence producers, female workers, young adolescent girls and alcoholics were also incorporated in the Catholic vision. To cater for these unfortunates, self-help groups, friendly societies, insurance schemes, kindergartens, funerary clubs, employment exchange offices and cooperative banks became commonplace. For example, Catholic peasant leagues multiplied among the sharecropping sections of peasant society in northern Italy, although admittedly Italian Catholicism had always boasted a strong tradition of mutual aid. Spain likewise oversaw a flowering of peasant syndicates, and in 1917 the National Catholic Agrarian Confederation (CNCA) was founded to monitor their energies. Within Germany, the Nazi seizure of power spelt an end to the autonomy of many Catholic assistance schemes, including the suppression in 1938 of the influential Institute for Charity Science at the University of Freiburg, which since 1925 had pioneered the academic study of charity. Yet this did not stop the Church from pursuing its own endeavours and providing much-needed support to those vulnerable groups in society, notably the handicapped and the mentally unwell, whom the Hitler state wished to eliminate.

The Church was slower in getting to grips with twentieth-century innovations in the field of what the Vatican termed in 1963 'instruments of social communication': newspapers, radio, cinema and, later, television. This hesitancy contrasted with the precedent of the Counter-Reformation of the sixteenth and seventeenth centuries when it had rapidly adopted the printed word, education and the visual arts as means to halt the spread of Protestantism and to put across its message. The twentieth-century Church did at least maintain a commitment to the printed word. The Catholic press was, of course, already well established and continued to thrive before 1939. The exception was in those totalitarian states, most obviously Germany, which ruthlessly controlled the free expression of ideas. Especially noteworthy were Catholic intellectual journals, frequently centred upon Catholic universities such as Coimbra, Louvain, Fulda, Nijmegen, Lublin and Kaunas in Lithuania. Although circulation was not always large, these reviews had a disproportionate influence on debate. In the Netherlands alone, twenty-two of the seventy-nine daily newspapers were Catholic by 1937. Such titles saw their purpose in life as both spreading Christian precepts and countering what was termed the 'colourless press' which had replaced the so-called 'bad press' of the liberals and socialists as the principal danger to morality. The 'colourless press', which emerged in the late nineteenth century, earned its name precisely because it had no clear partisan or ideological axe to grind. The Church knew where it was with socialists and liberal titles, but was wrongfooted by newspapers which relied on advertising as well as subscriptions and which concentrated on the dissemination of information rather than opinions. To counter this, the Church inaugurated its own news agencies, the first of these appearing in 1879, the German Centrums-Parlaments-Correspondenz (CPC). There followed the Catholic International Press Agency, founded at Freiburg in 1917, and within twenty years similar bodies existed in sixteen European countries. In addition to acquiring its own newspaper in the shape of *L'Osservatore Romano*, the Vatican in 1927 developed the International Fides Service which acted as a semi-official conduit of information, though its significance declined in the wake of the Second Vatican Council. Three years later, Pius XI oversaw the creation of his own radio station, Vatican Radio, complementing local initiatives, for instance the Katholieke Radio Omroep which operated in the Netherlands after 1925. From the 1930s, Italians could thus listen to religious services on their wirelesses although, disturbingly for the Church, state radio also broadcast football matches and American jazz.

It was extremely debatable, however, whether the Vatican was fully alive to the possible benefits of new technology, most obviously the cinema, although it was not slow in seeing the potential dangers. Picture-going had emerged in Paris in 1895, thanks to the Lumière brothers, and it was their Italian agents who were responsible for a short film depicting Leo XIII in 1896. The first true film to be shown at the Vatican was in 1913 and, much to the delight of Pius X, depicted the restoration of the bell tower at the Piazza San Marco. The Church could also take some comfort in that many of the early experiments in movies dealt respectfully with religious themes, notably *Procession de Lourdes* (1897), *Jeanne d'Arc* (1900) and *Quo Vadis* (1902). Before long, there were even religious film companies whose purpose was to proselytise, although their efforts never matched those of the Catholic press. These efforts included the Photographic Society at Mönchen-Gladbach set up in 1910, the Leo Film Production Company established at Munich in 1927, and the Eidophon Firm of Berlin. All of these were financial failures, and may well have dissuaded the Church from pursuing this line further.

It was inevitable that innovations in cinema would cause concern at the height of the modernist crisis, and in 1912 the Consistorial Congregation banned the practice of showing films within churches. Papal pronouncements were not slow in following, Pius XI declaring in 1936 that 'today there is no medium more powerful than the motion picture for bringing influence to bear on the masses'. By that stage, he had already issued three encyclicals dealing, either implicitly or explicitly, with the issue: *Divini illius magistri* of 1929, *Casti connubii* in 1930 and, most importantly, *Vigilanti cura* of 1936. This last pronouncement tackled head on the question of morality in a medium which, for a long time, had been viewed as transient and rather superficial. Heaping praise on the American Legion of Decency founded three years earlier to combat the alleged moral turpitude of Hollywood, and building on the work of the Office Catholique Internationale du Cinéma (OCIC) set up at the Hague in 1928, this encyclical promised a regular review of films suitable for viewing by the faithful. The same task was also executed at a local level by such publications as *Le Fascinateur* in France and production societies which loaned out suitable celluloid viewing. Within Spain, Catholic newspapers took it upon themselves to publish licences for films, announcements which were then pinned on church noticeboards. A 'white' notice meant that a film was suitable for viewing, a 'red' one signified that parishioners should stay away as 'certain danger existed'. Among films earmarked as especially corrupting for Spanish youth were those produced by Glenn Ford and those starring Rita Hayworth. What ordinary people made of all this remains unclear. For the most part, Hollywood films were dreadfully coy about sex; traditional peasant society was remarkably open.

The divergent and fluctuating fortunes of inter-war Catholic initiatives precludes any easy summary of the practice of Catholicism in the period 1918–40. For some, it remained a 'private faith', this to the dismay of many priests who stressed the communal and social elements of ritual. It is further apparent that, for many, being a Catholic was only one factor in their identity which was also informed by class, ethnicity and schooling. For instance, Irish immigrants in England deployed their religious allegiance as one token among several in forging an identity. One thing, however, is clear; the renewed self-confidence of Catholics led them to express their faith in a far more open, and sometimes aggressively triumphalist, manner which went some way towards recovering the confidence lost in the late nineteenth century when it seemed to the more despondent that the forces of secularisation were unstoppable. The First World War had laid down the underpinnings for this renewed vigour; the Second World War would severely fracture this process.

The Second World War

When, in March 1939, Eugenio Maria Giuseppe Giovanni Pacelli was enthroned as Pope Pius XII (1939–58), his successor, the future John XXIII (1958–63), was heard to mutter that the difficulties confronting the Church at that time were enough to turn one's hair white. There is no question that the next six years would pose agonising choices for Catholics. Yet, as Martin Conway has stressed, there was 'no such thing as a common Catholic experience of the war'.[50] The faithful, he observes, were to be found on all sides: within the Axis powers of Germany and Italy; within those territories overrun by German forces; and within the Grand Alliance itself (USSR, USA and Great Britain), although here, of course, they were numerically a minority. Nor was it necessarily the case that all Catholics were directly affected by the fighting. While we commonly think of the Second World War as being a 'total war' in the sense that it impinged on the lives of both civilians and those on the front, people clung on to their work-a-day habits and endeavoured to get on with their lives as best they could. It was principally in Poland, where the Germans attempted to destroy all vestiges of national culture, that this was impossible from the very outset. Elsewhere, most obviously in Croatia and Slovakia, where the Germans seemingly offered the possibility of a new national autonomy, and in France, where defeat promised the opportunity to reverse the institutionalised secularism of the Third Republic, the war appeared to augur a new elevated status for Catholics.

In none of these instances did the Church hierarchy appreciate that complete Nazi victory would mean an unbearable future for the faith. To many Catholics throughout Europe, Soviet communism remained the principal enemy, not German Nazism. It was only in the later stages of the war, roughly from 1942 onwards, that reality sank in and Catholics were forced to confront their predicament, and it was only then that they truly began to wake up to the horrors of the Holocaust. A small number chose resistance; even fewer would throw in their lot wholeheartedly with the Nazis, some opting for those unsavoury volunteer units which served alongside Axis troops on the eastern front, others persecuting their own peoples as well as Jews and resisters. Like most civilians, the majority of Catholics kept their heads down and hoped to escape attention. Lucky were those who lived in the purportedly neutral countries of Switzerland, Ireland, Spain and Portugal, though even here the long-term ramifications of the war ultimately made themselves felt. In many regards, these countries would not undergo what might potentially have been a 'liberating experience', an opportunity to build on shared wartime experiences, to break out of a narrow mind-set and embrace unconventional ideas, although ultimately the war would enhance the conservative instincts of the Church overall, just as much as it facilitated a new openness. In this context, facile notions that the Second World War paved the way for the Second Vatican Council will not do.

The future John XXIII had good reason to be worried, and it was unfortunate that in 1939 the Church had a novice Pope who, unlike Benedict XV in 1914, was ill-suited for the trying times ahead. It might have helped the new Pope if the so-called 'lost' encyclical (*Humani generis unitas*), dealing robustly with Nazi racial policy, which Pius XI had commissioned in 1938 and to which Pacelli almost certainly contributed, had been published. In the event, Pius XI died before it could be delivered and his successor ensured that it was subsequently buried in the Vatican Archives, whence it has only recently been unearthed by Belgian scholars. While its words still pandered to traditional Catholic prejudices about Jews, particularly their role as deicides and materialists, historians are agreed that it would at least have made clear the Vatican's reservations about overtly anti-Semitic policies. Pius XII was anything but clear. Like his predecessor, he was a traditionalist, a believer in hierarchy, a staunch anti-communist and a sceptic with regard to liberal values. He was even more of an intellectual, fluent in seven languages and, reflecting the time he had spent as papal nuncio to Germany during the 1920s, preferred to speak German to his household. It was this love of all things German, together with his Italian ancestry, that ensured allied suspicion about his sympathies and which has subsequently led historians to speculate whether this, above all else, made him reluctant to condemn outright the atrocities perpetrated by Hitler's Reich. The truth was far more complex. Pius was a deeply thoughtful man but, unlike his predecessor, he lacked any pastoral pedigree and was completely without the popular touch. As the French ambassador to the Vatican, Charles-Roux, put it: 'To a robust Milanese mountaineer succeeded a Roman bourgeois, more passive in temperament. A diplomat took the place of a student.'[51] His whole training was indeed that of a diplomat, and he exhibited the excessive caution and wariness of confrontation that characterised this profession. He thus preferred private initiatives to public gestures. Conscious of the majesty of his office – every evening he descended to the crypt to pray alongside the graves of his predecessors – he was wary of any action which might jeopardise this. As a consequence, subtlety, reserve and behind-the-scenes manoeuvres were to characterise his wartime role, confusing the faithful and sending out mixed messages to the ecclesiastical hierarchies of Europe, who were left rudderless and thrown back upon their own resources. That many bishops, notably in Belgium and Holland, were publicly outspoken in their denunciations of Nazism are indications that the silence of Pius XII was ill-judged. He should have trusted his humanitarian instincts. Speaking out did not necessarily make things worse.

Just as in 1914, Catholicism in 1939 had no part to play in the outbreak of war; indeed, the Church sought above all to maintain peace and assert its own neutrality. These concerns were immediately apparent on Pius XII's accession. Seasoned Vatican observers quickly noted a warmer tone in papal dialogue with Germany. *L'Osservatore Romano* and Vatican Radio were forbidden to indulge in polemics against the Nazis. One of Pacelli's immediate initiatives was to call a meeting of the German cardinals to whom he made known a letter he was planning to address to Hitler, in which he stressed his love for the German people; by contrast, before his death, Pius XI had been composing a letter announcing the withdrawal of the papal nuncio from Berlin. Small wonder, then, that there was no condemnation of the German occupation of Prague that March, although this was a clear violation of the Munich agreements. The indefatigable Charles-Roux pressured Pius to make clear that, should Europe go to war, then the responsibility lay at the door of Germany. Still the Pope asserted his neutrality, while appearing indulgent of Hitler's increasingly belligerent behaviour. He was an appeaser to the very end, developing in summer 1939 a series of peace initiatives whereby, to the astonishment of the British and French, he exerted pressure on the beleaguered Poles to make yet more concessions to the Reich. On the very day that war was declared, the pontiff urged the Germans and Poles to avoid any action which might inflame matters, placing the liberal democracies on a par with the fascist dictatorships. The recent work by José Sánchez, which in so many respects is indulgent of the Pope, nevertheless reminds us of the deafening silence of the Vatican in the case of Poland throughout the war.[52]

With the outbreak of war, Pius XII continued to protest that, as Vicar of the Prince of Peace, it was incumbent upon him to maintain neutrality. This was evident in his first encyclical, *Summi pontificatus*, of October 1939, devoted to the responsibilities of government, in which his condemnation of state absolutism, if such it could be called, was equally applicable to Stalinist Russia as it was to Nazi Germany. Unbeknown to the papacy and the rest of the world, the two had in August signed a pact which contained a secret protocol agreeing to divide up Catholic Poland. Behind the scenes, Vatican officials attempted to mollify outraged French and British diplomats, who had recently been joined by President Roosevelt's personal representative, Myron Taylor, by assuring them that Pius's failure to condemn German aggression was designed to save the Poles from yet worse suffering. It was a worrying portent for the future. This persistence with peace efforts was even more bizarre, given that Pius XII recognised that European stability could never endure while Hitler was alive. It was, then, with considerable interest that he learned in November 1939 of a plot hatched by senior German generals and officials, including General Beck, to assassinate the Führer. Hiding his activities from even his closest advisers, he liaised between the plotters and the allied powers, notably the British representative, Francis d'Arcy Osborne. This was a truly astonishing move. Had news of the Pope's involvement been leaked, it would have incurred terrible reprisals in Germany and would have effectively meant the end of the Lateran Accords with Mussolini. In the event, the wariness of the British and French and Pius's moral reservations about political killing, despite his personal loathing of Hitler, ensured that this particular project came to naught. Instead, Pius contented himself with criticism of Nazi misdeeds and refused to be duped by Ribbentrop, who came visiting in March 1940 with a purported peace plan which was clearly nothing more than a propaganda blind, immediately appreciating its unacceptability to the allies. So it was that up to the invasion of Holland, Belgium and Luxembourg on 10 May 1940, the Vatican's peace feelers and policy of neutrality earned nothing but the mistrust of both sides and resulted in naught. This was of little comfort to the governments of Belgium, Holland, Luxembourg and France, which had all fallen by June 1940, and to whom Pius addressed his sympathy, still failing to attach war guilt to Germany. When an opportunistic Mussolini decided that this was the moment when Italy could, at long last, enter the fray, the Vatican was again silent. *L'Osservatore Romano* merely published the Italian declaration of war without editorial judgement.

As the dust of the western campaign settled in June 1940, Catholics shared the common belief that Nazi hegemony was unassailable: few believed that Britain would last for long, the USA was neutral and the USSR was tied to Germany by the non-aggression pact. In this situation, it is not surprising that both Catholic clergy and laity hastened to make the best of things, and were in many respects well placed to do this. As the historian Bill Halls has noted, whereas state bureaucracies crumbled under the weight of German armour, clerical structures emerged more or less intact, thus giving them a greater prominence in national affairs.[53] Indeed, the changed situation offered possibilities for a resurgence of Catholic influence. Within the Netherlands, Dutch Catholics flocked to the newly-established Nederlandse Unie, a purportedly secular movement but one which was avowedly corporatist and anti-democratic in outlook. Because it also took Dutch patriots under its wing, in 1941 it was outlawed by the Nazis who favoured the crypto-fascist NSB. This garnered little Catholic support. Within Belgium, the episcopacy stood side by side with King Leopold III, who, unlike Queen Wilhelmina of the Netherlands, had refused to retreat into exile. National defeat was explained in terms of moral decadence and presaged the urgent need for reform. This explains why lay Catholics, particularly those belonging to the Flemish nationalist VNV and Degrelle's Rexists, quickly articulated a corporatist and authoritarian blueprint for Belgium and readily assisted the Germans. Even within Britain, which was not subject to the jackboot, the collapse of the liberal democracies gave rise to hopes, entertained in certain Catholic quarters, that Europe would see the emergence of a Latin Catholic bloc, comprising Italy, France, Spain and Portugal, an idea which was quickly quashed by Cardinal Hinsley, who was at pains to stress the loyalty of British Catholics to the anti-Nazi cause, and who was feted by the *Daily Mail* in 1943 as 'the greatest English cardinal since Wolsey'.[54] Similar restraint was much needed in France, Croatia and Slovakia, as it was here that Catholics were most impetuous in the rush to exploit national humiliation for their own particular ends.

Catholic willingness to take advantage of German military advances was first witnessed in the new state of Slovakia which had emerged out of the dissolution of Czechoslovakia in March 1939. The new regime was headed by the Slovak People's Party (HSLS), formed by Andrej Hlinka and whose leader was now the Catholic priest, Dr Jozef Tiso. Thanks to his influence, Slovakia quickly came to resemble a theocracy: the bases of national education were founded on papal teaching, army officers were obliged to attend religious services, a corporatist economy began to evolve, and members of the clergy were prominent in all layers of the state bureaucracy. While Tiso's state would retain something of its Catholic character to the very end, this was diluted in 1941 when the government, under the increasing influence of the proto-fascists Alexander Mach and Vojtech Tuka, sought to Nazify the country, agreeing in June to join with the *Wehrmacht* in its ill-fated invasion of the USSR. As the demands of total war began to take their toll, Tiso's regime came to depend increasingly on the paramilitary Hlinka Guard, formed in 1938, and the support of Hitler himself, who paradoxically preferred the clerical Tiso over Mach and Tuka, recognising that this kind of clerical conservative was more reliable than troublesome fascist militants. When dissent finally broke out, it primarily emerged within liberal, communist and military circles, prompting Germany to occupy the whole of the state in 1945.

    Croatia was also to become a Nazi puppet state, although this could not necessarily have been foreseen in April 1941 when Hitler's invasion of Yugoslavia resulted in the creation of a purportedly independent Croat state under the leadership of Ante Pavelic and his Ustaše fascists. Glorying in the moment, Pavelic speedily asserted the Catholic nature of his regime. As in Slovakia, clerics were appointed to numerous government positions; Freemasonry was outlawed; Catholic schools were promoted and Serb ones were closed down; contraception was banned; laws against blasphemy were tightened; and the new constitution of 1942 augured the creation of a corporatist economy based on 'chambers of professional association'. The same constitution also asserted the distinct nature of Croatians as a race apart, and herein lay the most troubling aspect of the Ustaše regime. When the state had first emerged, it comprised not only Croatia but Bosnia, Herzegovina and most of Dalmatia. This meant that out of a total population of 6.7 million, over half of whom were both Croat and Catholic, there were some 2.2 million Orthodox Serbs, 0.75 million Muslims, 70,000 Protestants and 45,000 Jews. As John Cornwell has noted, neither the Protestants nor the Muslims troubled the Ustaše, yet the Orthodox and the Jews were perceived as a threat to the purity of the Croatian stock.[55] Racial legislation was not slow to emerge. The Cyrillic script deployed by the Serbs was outlawed; Jews were barred from marrying Aryans; they were segregated and stringent racial definitions of Jewishness were laid down; and as early as 1941 the first convoy of Jews left Zagreb for the Danica concentration camp. To be fair, not all Catholics, notably Archbishop Stepinac, were necessarily sympathetic to these overtly racial measures, and the prelate kept a certain distance from the regime, though unquestionably he could have done more to halt the march towards genocide.

    Not all members of the clergy, however, showed such reserve, recognising that the persecution of the Serbs and Jews afforded a wonderful opportunity for forced conversion. When, in July 1941, the Croatian Ministry of Justice made it known that the state was no longer prepared to acknowledge Orthodox converts to Rome, Catholics made little protest and were actively involved in the enforced deportations and mass exterminations that followed. It is well documented that clerics, in particular a number of Franciscans, actively took part in these murders which resulted in the deaths of 250,000 Serbs in some twenty-four concentration camps, the most infamous being that at Jasenova. Controversy has since arisen over how much Pius XII was aware of these atrocities. It appears that the Vatican probably knew little about their origin, but it was obvious from the very start that the Ustaše had a deeply odious ethno-religious ideology and owed their ascendancy not to 'a heroic rising by the people of God' as was proclaimed, but to the triumph of Hitler and Mussolini. This did not stop Pius XII from personally meeting Pavelic, whom he valued as a bulwark against communism. Once again, the pontiff had failed to see the logical outcome of collaboration with a fascist regime, and although the Vatican was perhaps better informed about events in Croatia than anywhere else in Europe outside Italy, it never did enough to dissociate itself from the regime, which it indulged to the bitter end. The excuse often used elsewhere to justify papal silence, that it would have brought about retribution, has no validity in this Catholic state. It is, then, little surprise that the Vatican has since attempted to gloss over and cover up this most painful and distasteful episode in Catholic history.

Within France, Hitler's most important victim in 1940 and the most significant Catholic power to fall into his grasp, there was an ambivalent reaction to defeat on the part of the faithful. On one level, there was dismay at the speed and the overwhelming nature of the German victory. The Church was in no doubt that the root cause of the catastrophe lay in a moral malaise. Several leading prelates attributed disaster to national apostasy, and theologians writing in *La Croix* asked whether the events of June 1940 were not God's way of punishing France for past misdemeanours, in particular the institutionalised secularism of the Third Republic, a question also posed by purportedly liberal Catholics such as Emmanuel Mounier. Members of the new government assembling in the little spa town of Vichy which, under the terms of the armistice concluded with Germany, governed the unoccupied southern third of France, joined in this chorus of recriminations. General Weygand, the new Minister for Defence, piped 'France has been vanquished because for half a century it has expelled God from the classroom'.[56]

On another level, there was hope for the future. The new authoritarian regime that centred around the octogenarian leader Marshal Pétain promised a return to traditional values and seemed to offer an opportunity to reverse the tide of secularisation that had purportedly overtaken France, through the much vaunted National Revolution, whose watchwords were *travail, famille, patrie*. In truth, Vichy was far less clerical, even in these early days, than is sometimes imagined. Pétain himself had no spiritual needs and viewed religion of any type, with the important exception of Judaism, merely as a bulwark of social stability. Deeply fervent Catholics were always a minority at Vichy: Raphaël Alibert, the first Minister of Justice; Jacques Chevalier, an academic who briefly served at Education; Xavier Vallat, a veterans' leader who became Vichy's first Commissioner of Jewish Affairs; Pierre Caziot, who served at Agriculture; and finally Philippe Henriot, who in 1944 took charge of Propaganda. The influence of such ministers was always countered by more formidable players who were expressly anti-clerical, notably Pierre Laval and Admiral Darlan, who were Pétain's right-hand men. As Maurice Larkin has further stressed, Catholic influence at Vichy waned after 1940, and the *Catholiques avant tout* generally occupied lesser posts, notably in youth and educational affairs.[57] This meant that government policies designed to help the Church, for instance financial palliatives to Catholic schools, the purging of the state educational system of republican bias, the lifting of the teaching ban on religious orders, and initial experiments with a corporate economy, came early in the day; after 1941, little that Vichy did was directly designed to please Catholic opinion.

The drying up of pro-clerical measures, and in particular the failure to negotiate a concordat to replace the Separation Law of 1905, came as a bitter disappointment to most Catholics, but there is no denying their initial enthusiasm for the regime. This was especially true of an ageing episcopacy which had lived through the anti-clerical battles of the Third Republic, and which was headed by a series of cardinals who lacked political nous, most famously Cardinal Suhard at Paris, whose primary concern was to reverse the decline in levels of religious observance. It was generally the custom of the Church to acknowledge a *de facto* government, and in August 1940 a number of bishops incautiously described Vichy as the *pouvoir légitime*. In 1941, the Assembly of Cardinals and Archbishops, which had earlier labelled Vichy as such, rearticulated its statement of support, merely describing it as the *pouvoir établi*, an indication that the episcopacy had at last realised the dangers of associating itself with civil authority. Later Vichy actions, in particular the stepping-up of measures against the Jews and forced deportation of labour to Germany, led certain brave prelates, among them Archbishop Saliège of Toulouse and Monsignor Théas, Bishop of Montauban, to speak out. The overwhelming majority were far more reticent, and never broke completely with the regime. As Bill Halls has argued, this continuing support may be explained not just in terms of their distaste for the Third Republic, but by their admiration for Pétain, by the failure of both the French cardinals and the Vatican to provide emphatic direction, by their tardiness to wake up to the horrors being perpetrated against Jews, and by fear.[58] Social upheaval was always a paramount concern and there was a constant worry that this would be unleashed: by the neo-fascist sympathisers of Paris, by the Germans themselves, by General de Gaulle, by the internal Resistance which was considered merely a front for communist designs, and by the allies whose bombing of France was, on occasion, equated to 'acts of terrorism'.

Within other ranks of the clergy there was growing disquiet. Although evidence remains impressionistic, it appears that a younger clergy, especially those who had not fallen under Pétain's spell during the First World War and who lived in German-occupied territories, were less enamoured of the regime. Among male religious, the Dominicans and Jesuits, who had toyed with progressive ideas in the 1930s, were especially cautious about endorsing the Marshal. The eminent Jesuit, Father Dillard quipped: 'The Vichy enterprise was a magnificent adventure to be resisted.'[59] Prominent lay Catholics were also sceptical. The leader of the Christian Democrat PDP, Auguste Champetier de Ribes, was one of those few deputies who voted against investing Pétain with plenary powers in July 1940. Even Mounier, who had established a leadership school at Uriage to train the elites of the new *état français*, soon lost patience with the regime, and as we shall see, Christian Democrats, trade unionists and the young activists of Action Catholique, including many *Jocistes*, followed suit. Unease at the collaborationist policies being pursued with Germany, the intensification of measures against Jews and other minorities, the inability of Vichy to alleviate material conditions, and the growing anti-clericalism of the regime, drove many of these into the ranks of the Resistance. Perhaps the only Catholics to remain loyal to the regime to the very end were those middle-class *notables* who had readily filled positions within Vichy's local bureaucracies and its veterans' association, La Légion Française des Combattants.

Trends within France were repeated elsewhere, and for similar reasons. In this regard, historians have stressed that the invasion of the Soviet Union in June 1941 played little part in changing Catholic attitudes. While Operation Barbarossa offered additional reason for some within Italy and Germany to support their dictatorial governments, the majority of the faithful were untouched as they had long been conditioned to think of Bolshevism as the enemy in their midst. Signs of growing Catholic dissatisfaction were evident throughout Nazi-dominated Europe in 1941. Within Belgium, the steady growth of the VNV and Rexist movements alienated Catholic opinion, which soon repented its earlier dalliance with extremism, moving to rediscover and reinvigorate those Christian Democrat values which had been evident in the 1930s. Even Cardinal van Roey, not one to rock the boat unnecessarily, used his pastoral letters to indict German crimes. In the Netherlands, the German condemnation of the NU provided the cue for greater vocal opposition to the occupier, especially since it was now the NSB which ruled supreme. Dutch Catholics did not easily forget that this movement had been condemned in no uncertain terms by the episcopacy in the previous decade, and here too Catholics gravitated towards resistance. So it was that the general realisation in 1941 that the war had not ended drove the faithful in many regions of Europe to appreciate that German hegemony was not necessarily here to stay.

In this situation it is not difficult to understand why so few outwardly chose the path of political collaboration. The exceptions were, of course, those belonging to the Hlinka Guard in Slovakia and the Ustaše in Croatia, whose fortunes were inextricably linked with those of the Axis armies, and it is no surprise that Slovaks and Croats would later fight alongside the SS and the *Wehrmacht* on the eastern front and help crush internal resistance. We have also seen how Catholic support for the Rexist and NSB programmes was extremely limited. Similarly, within France, outright Catholic collaborators were a distinct minority. Prominent lay collaborators numbered Marcel Bucard, founder of the Franciste and the eminent novelist Alphonse de Châteaubriand who, in September 1940, established the cultural body Groupe collaboration. Among leading clerics we may cite Canon Polimann, a deputy from the Meuse, Cardinal Baudrillart, the infirm rector of the Institut Catholique at Paris, and Mgr Feltin, the Archbishop of Bordeaux. It was Bordeaux rather than Paris that became the principal centre of Catholic collaboration in France, partly because of the indulgence displayed by Feltin himself, and the influence of the regional Catholic daily, *La Liberté du Sud-Ouest*, which loaned out its presses to Catholic militants. Inevitably, some Catholics, most famously the self-styled 'Monsignor' Mayol de Lupé, rallied round the Légion des Volontaires français contre le Bolshevisme, the organisation established by the leading collaborator Jacques Doriot with the aim of organising recruits to fight on the eastern front. A small number of Catholics were also to be found in the ranks of Vichy's paramilitary police force, the Milice, founded in 1943 to root out resisters and deserters from compulsory work service in Germany. The best known of these is Paul Touvier, an ACJF militant from the Rhône, who was involved in the murder of Victor Basch, the founder of the League of the Rights of Man, and in the summary shooting of seven Jews at Rillieux-le-Pape. Thanks to the help supplied by fundamentalist religious orders, and by officials in the archbishop's palace at Lyon, Touvier was able to escape justice and was pardoned by President Pompidou in 1972, only to be indicted and convicted for crimes against humanity in the 1990s, an act which carries no statute of limitations. What marks out these collaborationists, not just in France but throughout Europe, was their diversity. What they had in common was their dependency on the German cause, their political naivety, their hatred of communism, their racial prejudices, and their fear of social disorder. Little of this owed anything to their Catholic values.

If Catholics were a minority within collaborationist movements, and were motivated by a range of factors, the same was true of Catholic resisters. Crudely speaking, historians have identified three broad categories of Catholic opposition to Nazism.[60] The first may be best described as patriotic in inspiration and expression. This was evidenced in the pages of the Belgian newspaper *La Libre Belgique* and the existence of the Armée Secrète. Across the border in France, the best example of this type of Catholic patriotic opposition would be Défense de la France, founded in the cellars of the Sorbonne by the students Philippe Viannay and Robert Salmon. It was in Poland, however, where the Germans had from the outset been at pains to dismantle any vestiges of national culture, that this fusion between patriotic resistance and Catholicism was most marked. Here, the Church was more or less dissolved by the Nazis and the clergy was decimated. At the start of 1941, there were no longer any functioning churches or chapels in the diocese of Poznan-Gneizen, where approximately one-tenth of the clergy had been murdered and the remainder interned in concentration camps. In 1945, the roll-call of clerics killed by the Nazis included four bishops, 1,996 priests, 103 male religious and 238 nuns, while a further 5,000 or so had been consigned to concentration camps. It was in opposition to this kind of brutalisation that Polish Catholics rallied to such organisations as the Armia Krajowa. Common to resisters in Poland, France and Belgium was an intrinsic conservatism and distaste for the left, and all undoubtedly subscribed to the principle of freedom of religion; yet it is important to stress that they were not so much inspired by some distant political vision as by a desire to secure the immediate destruction of the Nazi war machine.

Given the proliferation of Christian Democrat groups, especially in northern Europe, in the 1930s, it is no wonder that the second broad category of Catholic resistance highlighted by historians is political in complexion. Within Belgium, it is possible to identify several groups who were later to come together to found the Social Christian Party in 1945. These comprised the Aalast organisation, a gathering of conservative politicians fronted by Baron Romain Moyersoen, the ex-leader of Catholics in the Senate; the so-called Herbert faction, headed by the prominent industrialist Tony Herbert, who drew together members of Catholic Action from Flanders; and the Catholic workers' group, centred on the Algemeen Christelijk Werkersverbond, a Catholic Action organisation based in Flanders. Christian Democrats were similarly prominent in the Netherlands, both Protestants and Catholics coming together in 1944 to form a Committee for Inter-Ecclesiastical Consultation, which quickly set up subsidiary organisations to distribute foodstuffs and discuss post-war plans for renewal.

It was, though, within France that Christian Democrats were most in evidence. It is generally acknowledged that the very first resister on metropolitan soil was Edmund Michelet who transformed the NEF study circles into a resistance network. It was former PDP members Georges Bidault and François de Menthon who were responsible in November 1940 for the publication of the newspaper *Liberté*. The following year, de Menthon worked alongside the army officer Henri Frenay to launch the clandestine movement Combat, which became one of the key resistance organisations in the unoccupied zone. A Catholic presence may also be identified in the other resistance movements and activities in both the principal zones. In northern France, CFTC militants were prominent in the miners' strikes of 1941; in southern France, *Témoignage Chrétien*, the brainchild of two Jesuit priests, Fathers Chaillet and Fessard, became the principal voice of opposition, and was widely read by both *Jocistes* and *Jecistes*. And it should not be forgotten that French Christian Democrat sympathisers contributed to the resistance overseas. In Britain, René Pleven, a former head of the ACJF, and Maurice Schumann, onetime editor of *L'Aube*, were early recruits for de Gaulle, while the writers François Mauriac, Georges Bernanos and Jacques Maritain, all based in the Americas, also targeted their sights on Vichy. Yet again, it is difficult to perceive any common thread running through this resistance other than a belief that Christian conscience dictated a rejection of Nazism in all its guises, most particularly its repugnant racism.

The remaining element of Catholic resistance commonly identified is that of pastoral and humanitarian inspiration. This might have included what historians have also termed 'passive resistance', that is the eschewing of violence for more discreet acts of defiance, ranging from a refusal to serve German soldiers in shops, retailing anti-Nazi jokes, listening to the BBC and assisting those labelled as undesirables by the Nazis. Some Catholic apologists have gone as far as to suggest that the very acts of attending church and receiving communion constituted acts of resistance: maybe so in the case of Poland, but surely this is an exaggeration in the instances of France, Belgium and the Netherlands where German interference was at best intermittent and unsustained. By and large, the Nazi authorities were happy to leave people to continue their day-to-day habits so long as these did not disturb social order or hamper the war effort. Where Catholics were most closely involved in pastoral and humanitarian resistance was in protecting Jews and others who were subject to the policies of genocide. Even Cardinal Gerlier of Lyon, so purblind in his admiration for Pétain and mealy-mouthed in his criticisms of the Vichy government, ordered monks and nuns in his diocese to hide Jewish children and was not afraid to alert the Marshal to the appalling conditions of Jews who were held in the nearby concentration camp of Gers. At Utrecht, Monsignor Johannes de Jong was far more explicit in his attempts to derail the regular deportations. In Hungary, during the 'occupation' by Germany of its ally in 1944–45, Catholics joined the Resistance Front with the blessing of the Primate and priests helped to distribute anti-Nazi literature as well as attempting to frustrate deportation of the Jews.

It was perhaps in Germany, where it was inevitably most difficult to express dissent and facilitate military opposition, despite the fact that the priest Alfred Delp was implicated in the July 1944 bomb plot, that such humanitarian efforts were the only real method by which Catholics could make their opposition to Nazism known. It is generally acknowledged that the Nazis encountered the greatest obstacles in Catholic Bavaria and other strongly practising areas. For instance, an order from the Bavarian department of education banning the display of crucifixes and Christian prayers in schools was met by a so-called 'mothers' revolt', in which thousands of women protested, leading to a withdrawal of the decree. Elsewhere, Catholics threatened to withhold their taxes. What is striking is that the contribution of the ecclesiastical leadership to such humanitarian protests was often muted, and focused on policies of compulsory eugenics, including the killing or sterilisation of the handicapped and mentally ill as opposed to the Jewish pogroms. Acclimatised by the *Kulturkampf* to a tradition of quiet protest, Cardinal Bertran worked behind the scenes to stop the incessant persecutions, leaving it to others, most famously Bishop von Galen of Münster, to speak out. The latter published three sermons against euthanasia in 1941. Thousands assembled at the cathedral in a vigil to support his stand. It was partly thanks to such protests, together with the use of forged death certificates, that there was a temporary reduction in the euthanasia processes, at least as centrally organised, although they carried on in piecemeal fashion. While clergy of all ranks worked to shelter individual

Jews, and an aid bureau was set up after *Kristallnacht* specifically to help Catholic Jews and their families, there was never any consolidated and open opposition on the part of the episcopacy to the Holocaust and the question remains as to how much more might have been done to halt the programme.

However honourable and robust Catholic resistance to Nazism may have been, it must be remembered that ultimately Catholic resisters were thinly spread among the faithful, just as Catholic collaborators were also a distinct minority. For the most part, rank-and-file Catholics throughout occupied Europe adopted a 'heads-down' attitude for much of the war, in common with the population in general. This raises the broader question as to whether Catholic resistance would have been more vocal, vehement, robust and co-herent had the papacy offered a much stronger lead in its condemnation of Nazism, in particular through an outright condemnation of the persecution of the Jews. After all, this posed, as John Cornwell has elegantly put it, 'an unprecedented test of the Christian faith, a religion based on the concept of *agape*, the love that accords each individual, irrespective of difference, equal respect as a child of God'.[61] The suffering of the Jews, so well documented by historians and others, resulting in the deaths of some 6 million, remains almost as difficult to grasp for contemporaries today as it was for people at the time. Genocide on this scale was wholly unprecedented. In this respect, the Pope was as much at a disadvantage as anyone else. The difference was that, as Cornwell reminds us, Pius XII was regarded as the Vicar of Christ on earth by the faithful, and accordingly he 'carried unique obligations on his individual shoulders'.[62]

Herein lies part of the reason why the role of the papacy in the Holocaust remains so controversial. In the immediate aftermath of the war, this contro-versy was sidestepped by most of the key players. Whereas the Vatican and many Catholic apologists stressed the charitable initiatives displayed towards the Jews, the allies (whose own role in failing to prevent the Holocaust was certainly an ambivalent one) preferred to portray Pius XII as an infirm and feeble figure whose lack of temporal power rendered him largely impotent in the face of the unfolding tragedy. Many Jews, too, were so overwhelmed by the tragedy that had befallen their people that they looked no further than the obvious culprits. Additionally, Jews were wary of reactivating traditional anti-Semitism, and depended on the Church hierarchy to reclaim those children who had been protected in Catholic schools and religious houses during the war. It was not until 1963 that the role of the Vatican in this appalling business received wide public attention, thanks to the production of Rolf Hochhuth's play, *The Representative*, subsequently translated into more than twenty languages and recently adapted into the film *Amen*. The drama portrayed Pacelli as a pusillanimous and anti-Semitic figure unwilling to raise a finger to help the Jews, especially those in Rome. The subsequent furore could not be ignored by the Vatican and a team of Jesuit scholars was commissioned to publish all the documents concerning the role of the Holy See during the Second World War.[63] This eleven-volume compilation did not altogether dampen the debate; it was fuelled further by the release of individual state archives from the 1970s onwards which often presented a very different picture. Recent discoveries within the Vatican's own papers, notably those uncovered by Cornwell himself and by Susan Zuccotti, have only served to keep the issue alive, and ensure that Pacelli remains an embarrassment to the Church at a time when moves are afoot to canonise him.[64]

The role of the Vatican, and of the Pope in particular, is not easy to resolve even with the benefit of hindsight. Yet in one respect at least Pius XII may be absolved, in that he was in no sense a sympathiser with the brand of biological racial prejudice espoused by Hitler and his acolytes. He did, however, share in the long-standing Catholic culture of anti-Semitism which viewed Jews as deicides and the authors of their own not wholly undeserved record of misfortunes, a cultural anti-Semitism which influenced several right-wing dictatorships of the time, notably those of Pétain, Franco and Salazar. Pius XII was quite happy to keep company with Catholic anti-Semites; one of his closest advisers was the Dominican neo-Thomist theologian Garrigou-Lagrange, who allegedly reassured Léon Bérard, Vichy's ambassador to the Vatican, that His Holiness was comfortable with the anti-Jewish measures adopted by the Marshal's regime. Moreover, there is sizeable evidence stemming from Pacelli's time at Munich that the Pope himself was not without prejudice against the Jews, a bigotry which owed much to his reading of the international situation. Like the Nazis themselves, he was firmly of the opinion that there existed a mutual compatibility between Judaism and Bolshevism, and that left to their own devices these two forces would combine to destroy the edifice of Christianity. Beginning from this standpoint, it was always going to be difficult for Pacelli to make his opposition to Hitlerian persecution plain.

It might reasonably be asked what Pius XII knew of the treatment of the Jews, and how far he remained aware of their fate, an argument which has been applied to other leaders of the time, including Pétain, whom we now know to have been fully apprised of the horrors being perpetrated in the east by the Catholic and Protestant dignitaries with whom he liked to dine. Doubts will always remain about how fully the Pope primed himself about what was going on, and there can be little doubt that news of the killings was spread in a piecemeal fashion, particularly in regard to events in 1940–41 before the Holocaust had assumed a systematic character. Yet, after the conclusion of the Wannsee Conference in January 1942, when the remaining bureaucratic details of genocide were tidied up, the evidence on the ground made it difficult *not* to know what was happening across Europe. In March of that year, Pius received via his nuncio in Berne a lengthy document compiled by the World Jewish Congress and Swiss Jews chronicling the atrocities being perpetrated in Slovakia, Croatia, Hungary and Vichy France, all countries where it was believed the Pope could exert some restraining influence. In August, Archbishop Sheptycki notified the Vatican from Lvov that over 100,000 Jews had been killed in the Ukraine alone. Other reports were not slow to follow, both the British and American representatives at the Vatican, Osborne and Tittman, bringing these to the Pope's notice, the former even going to the length of providing a daily digest of the commentaries which were appearing in the allied press. In September 1942, the USA despatched Myron Taylor as a special envoy to the Vatican whose task was to urge Pius to issue an unequivocal denunciation of German barbarities. He brought yet further distressing news of Nazi atrocities and, on 18 December of that year, Pius XII was presented with evidential documentation compiled by the allies. It is sometimes claimed that the Vatican needed time to compile its own dossiers before speaking out, but we now know that the Church's files were replete in this respect. If it was the case that ultimately the Pope chose not to digest fully this information, then the indictment of his pontificate must be all the stronger.

Pius XII's apologists spring to his aid by asserting that he did indeed speak out against the persecution of the Jews, citing the numerous Vatican statements condemning totalitarianism. They further stress that when individual churchmen protested, for instance those outspoken prelates in Holland and Belgium, they were acting as the *porte-parole* of the Holy See. Most play is made of the now infamous Christmas Eve broadcast of 1942, something on which the Pope and his advisers had been working for a good while, and which tackled the broad theme of the rights of man. This commenced with a lament for the way in which the state had become too powerful in its ability to ride roughshod over individual liberties, a process credited to recent economic developments which were themselves driven by the profit motive. (In this regard, it is interesting to note that earlier in 1941, Pius had failed to endorse openly Marshal Pétain's *Principles of the Community*, an exposition of National Revolution beliefs designed to supplant the 1789 Declaration of the Rights of Man and the Citizen, because it did not allocate sufficient protection to the individual). Bemoaning the current state of society, the Christmas address went on to rehash a series of arid corporatist dictums, making no distinction between the different economic systems that were practised by the capitalist and communist states respectively. Only at the end of this turgid litany of complaints did the Pope comment on the horrors and pointlessness of war, which was credited to 'an unbridled lust for profit and power', a remark which, many historians have pointed out, could have been levelled at both the Axis and the allies. After the war, Pius asserted that his pronouncement had been far from equivocal, drawing attention in particular to this sentence which purported to be an explicit reference to Nazi abominations. Men of goodwill should bring society back under the rule of God, a duty they owed to 'the hundreds of thousands of innocent people put to death or doomed to slow extinction, sometimes merely because of their race or their descent'.[65] Yet however this statement is regarded, it does not amount to very much, especially given the enormity of the crimes being perpetrated; even Mussolini observed that it was nothing more than a speech of platitudes, which might well have been made by the priest of his native village. It is difficult, then, to avoid Cornwell's conclusion that 'the chasm between the enormity of the liquidation of the Jewish people, and this form of evasive words, is shocking'.[66] As Cornwell continues, Pius might have been referring to any of the war victims, carefully avoiding at all points the words 'Jew' and 'Nazi', and speaking in terms of 'hundreds of thousands' rather than the 'millions' who faced extinction. It is now known that at least one million Jews had been killed by the end of 1941 alone.[67]

Pius XII's apologists have further argued that if he had spoken out against the deportation of Jews and others, this would have only have made matters worse: the Germans would have been incensed and even more determined to execute their policies against the Jews, and they might even have seized the Pope himself in the manner of Napoleon, thus destroying the Vatican's independence. Reprisals might even have been extended to include Catholic clergy and laity. In this regard, the example often cited is that of the Dutch Jews in 1942. In Holland, a combined protest on the part of Catholic and Protestant clergy prompted the Nazis to exempt pre-1941 Jewish converts to Christianity from deportation. While this satisfied certain clergymen, the Catholic Archbishop of Utrecht was not mollified, and authored an outright condemnation of Nazi policy which was read out from the pulpits. This, it is argued, so angered the Germans that they corralled all Catholic-Jewish converts they could lay hands on, most notoriously the Jewish Carmelite intellectual, Edith Stein. Knowledge of all this purportedly dissuaded Pius XII from making his own intervention. According to his housekeeper, Sister Pasqualina, giving evidence to the recent tribunal charged with scrutinising the beatification of Pius XII, the Pope observed: 'If the letter of the [Dutch] bishops has cost the lives of 40,000 persons, my own protest ... could cost the lives of 200,000 Jews. I cannot take such a great responsibility.'[68] Whether this statement is factually accurate is another matter. More to the point, it is exceedingly dubious whether the Dutch prelates' protest actually resulted in additional deaths, and it has been speculated that Pius deliberately exaggerated the number of deportees to justify his silence. It has since been calculated that in occupied Holland there were a mere ninety-two converts from Judaism to Catholicism, and statistics indicate that by mid-September 1942 the overall total of deportations had reached only 20,588.

The French case was slightly different, but again offers no evidence that a stronger line on the part of the prelates would have worsened the situation of either Catholics or Jews. Admittedly, ecclesiastical protests in France were extremely muted. It was not until August 1942, a month after the infamous Vél d'Hiv round-ups in Paris when 1,400 foreign-born Jews were herded together for deportation, that Archbishop Saliège of Toulouse and Bishop Théas of Montauban became the first prelates to speak out openly. Such protests proved nothing more than a minor irritant to the Germans who simply pressed ahead with their policies, the main obstacle to their designs paradoxically being the squalid bargaining of Vichy's Chief Minister, Pierre Laval, who was ready to hand over foreign-born Jews in return for the protection of French ones. Thanks to the work of Michael Marrus and Robert Paxton, it is known that only one-half of the prelates in unoccupied France, and none at all in the occupied zone, made open statements condemning Nazi deportations, and one is left wondering whether this timorous episcopacy would have been more emboldened had Pius XII himself given a lead.[69] As historians have pointed out, a broadcast on Vatican Radio, an unequivocal statement in *L'Osservatore Romano*, an exhortation to the bishops to publicise the Pope's displeasure, would have revealed to the world the grim fate that awaited Jewish deportees when they arrived at the railway termini of Auschwitz and elsewhere. Because the magnitude of the horror was so difficult to comprehend, because the Pope was neutral in the war itself, because he was Christ's Vicar on Earth, such an action would have carried far more weight than the publicity distributed by the allies, which could easily be dismissed as mere propaganda.

The arguments for the Pope to make an emphatic stand against the Final Solution were made even more compelling by events in the summer of 1943. The Allied invasion of Sicily in July prompted the collapse of the Mussolini regime, something which the Vatican privately welcomed. Subsequently, the appointment of the caretaker government of Marshal Badoglio provoked a German advance from the north of the peninsula and the ensuing occupation of Rome on 10 September. Badoglio and Victor Emmanuel III rushed to meet the allies in the south of the peninsula, but Pius decided to remain in the Eternal City, even though this compromised his independence. Among the occupying German forces were members of the SS who were keen to implement the same policies they had recently executed in France and elsewhere. At the end of the month, the Jews of Rome, some 8,000 in number and congregated in the 2,000-year-old ghetto, were presented with a stark choice: pay a ransom of fifty kilograms of gold or face deportation. After a slow start, the citizens of Rome, both Israelite and Gentile, proffered jewellery, coins, ingots and ornaments to make good the amount. Contrary to what is sometimes claimed, such objects did not include hastily melted-down Vatican vessels; rather the Pope, when approached by Jewish leaders, made known that he was prepared to countenance a loan, not a gift, something which ultimately he was not called upon to provide.

This mealy-mouthed show of generosity boded ill for what was to follow when, in October, the Germans ordered the round-up of Jews for transport to Mauthausen and Auschwitz. Papal protests were notable by their absence. Although Pius instructed Mgr Hudal, the rector of Santa Maria dell'Aniama, to complain to the German commander, it was left to Maglione, the Secretary of State, to make his own protests. Paradoxically, the deportations were slowed down by the intervention of the German ambassador to the Vatican, Ernst von Weizsäcker, a diplomat of the old school, who had little truck with SS ambitions. He reported to Berlin that Pius XII had gone out of his way so far not to make difficulties for the Germans but the ambassador exaggerated the extent of potential papal protests to make Berlin think again, even though such protests never materialised. That Hitler took such possible papal protestations seriously is confirmed by the fact that he contemplated a plan to take Pius hostage. To be fair, the Pope was not wholly inactive in the face of German barbarism. He reputedly ordered the opening of nearby religious houses which gave sanctuary to some 5,000 Jews, though his personal role in this gesture has lately been questioned. Pius did not, however, take any action over the plight of the 1,000 or so individuals who were herded together like cattle in the Collegio Militare before transhipment to certain death. He was more preoccupied with the possibility that partisans (by which he understood communist resisters), might use the occasion to launch guerrilla attacks. In another strange inversion of priorities, in January 1944 he urged that the allies should not include any coloured troops in the garrison ear-marked for duties in Rome after the German withdrawal.

As the Final Solution reached its grim conclusion with the murder of over 400,000 Hungarian Jews in March 1944 – an occasion when the Pope at least authorised his representatives to make their open displeasure known and provided letters of accreditation which saved the lives of many thousands in Budapest, although once again it was local Catholics acting on their own initiative that did most to stem the killing – the Vatican became increasingly obsessed with the communist menace which was now perceived as the principal threat to Christian civilisation. In this regard, Pius XII was quicker to speak out, urging the allies to make a just peace, a sharp contrast to the reticence he had displayed towards Nazism. That he had never explicitly condemned the Holocaust must stand to his eternal discredit. His initiatives to save individual Jews were unquestionably praiseworthy, and there is no doubting his personal detestation of Hitlerian racial policy, yet his silence amounted to an abandonment of moral direction on a frightening scale. As Osborne commented at the time, 'he does not see that his silence is highly damning to the Holy See'.[70] Here was an issue of such overriding moral imperative that no considerations of neutrality or diplomatic niceties could justify avoidance of a clear and unambiguous statement. Ultimately, the absence of such a pronouncement must be credited to the fear of communism, the failure to wake up to the enormity of the crimes being committed, an over-concern for the issue of neutrality stemming from a preference for diplomacy over moral pronouncements, a natural reticence, and a predisposition to a traditional anti-Semitism which clouded his judgement. Pacelli was heir to a long-standing Catholic anti-Judaism which still enjoyed a respectability in the 1930s, a decade when the early signs of Nazi racial intentions had already discredited what was, in any case, a tawdry moral position.

Pius XII's broader concern with the spiritual development of the Church, which perhaps obscured his humanitarian instincts, may also explain his hesitancy about protesting against the Holocaust. There is no doubt that he himself was devout to the point of asceticism: he spurned any of life's little luxuries such as coffee and heating; workers in the Vatican gardens had to hide whenever he appeared so as not to disturb his solitude; and he routinely cleansed his hands with antiseptic oils in an attempt to ward off contagion. Above all, he wanted to be remembered as a great Pope, and that meant making a lasting contribution to the religious life of the Church, not just rebuilding a bit of Rome or excavating the Crypt of Saint Peter's, though he did that too. Even during the war, he began to release encyclicals, numbering forty by the end of his pontificate, which he hoped would have an enduring effect in this regard. *Mystici corporis*, in 1943, articulated an organic template for the Church as the body of believers, albeit with the Pope firmly at the head. *Divino afflante* of the same year rejected the anti-modernist campaign which had been so damaging to Catholic theology and pointed towards the Bible as a varied source of inspiration rather than of fundamentalist truth. And in *Mediator dei* of 1947, the pontiff looked to greater lay participation in the liturgy as a way of renewing Catholicism. In each of these pronouncements, Pius tapped into the intellectual trends being pioneered particularly by the French Jesuit Henri de Lubac and the Dominican Yves Congar, although he was reluctant to embrace wholeheartedly de Lubac's ecumenicalism and questioning of ecclesiastical hierarchy. A series of practical reforms followed in the 1950s, including the establishment of evening masses, the removal of some of the more stringent requirements on communicants (the obligation to fast from midnight before taking communion was lifted, for instance), and a reform of the emotive Holy Week services. The vestiges of his conservatism, however, were demonstrated in his condemnation of the worker-priest movement in France which had originally been designed to provide spiritual sustenance to those deported to German factories and which later became a crucible for testing lay participation.

He was, above all, a powerful patron of the Marian cult, viewing this as a bulwark against the corrosive influences of communism and atheism. It will be recalled that in 1942 he had consecrated mankind to the Immaculate Heart of Mary and eight years later he enunciated *ex cathedra* the landmark doctrine of the Assumption of the Virgin Mary into Heaven. He further sponsored the cult of Our Lady of Fatima, which had a mystical significance for him, not least because he had been elevated to the position of bishop on the same day in 1917 as the first apparition. He took very seriously the messages which the vision had passed on concerning the dangers of communism, the potential for world destruction if God's will was ignored and the need for the faithful to seek Mary's intervention to maintain global peace. The famous Third Secret of Fatima, which had been confided to Pius by the last surviving seer in 1944, allegedly giving the date of the Third World War or perhaps the end of the papacy itself, was kept locked up in his desk drawer with instructions to be opened in 1960 by his successor. On retrieving the message, John XXIII would ponder it without expression, before consigning it to the Vatican Archives.

That Pius XII is now being seriously considered for canonisation is due less to his wartime record than to his initiatives in the area of Catholic religious life. Yet, even in this regard, his record does not bear wholly favourable scrutiny. For example, it is doubtful whether he was fully committed to the increased lay participation and freedom of theological speculation announced in his early pronouncements. Subsequent encyclicals went back on earlier initiatives. *Humani generis* of 1950 warned of the dangers of relativism inherent in liberal theological debate, and condemned any close association with non-Catholics, an allusion to the bond which many of the faithful had struck up with their religious 'adversaries' during the course of the war. Leading theologians, including Congar, were silenced, and Catholics were enjoined to take up arms against communism to the inevitable neglect of pastoral initiatives. In this respect, Pius XII is perhaps better seen as a successor to Pius X than as a precursor to John XXIII.

There were undoubtedly changes in religious practice to be perceived. Yet if these owed something to Pius's early initiatives, they owed much more to the impact of the war. This was especially true with respect to the upturn in levels of religious observance. Throughout Europe churches were full again; prayers were commonplace; pilgrimage sites, for instance that at Le Puy, flourished; in a somewhat mechanistic display of piety, scapulas and amulets were carried to shield the wearer from injury; personal devotion was more ostentatious, the crucifix being displayed in homes and carried by soldiers and civilians alike; and processions regained a new fashionability, most notably the statue of Notre-Dame de Boulogne which travelled from village to village in France, often coming to rest at the local war memorial where followers prayed for the return of prisoners-of-war. Some of this religious devotion was self-interested in the extreme, perhaps excusable and readily comprehensible given the dangers which were part-and-parcel of wartime life, whether on the home or fighting fronts. The use of religion as a means of protection and solace echoed trends in the First World War and harked back to the older tradition of 'dearth, disease, devotion' characteristic of the eighteenth and nineteenth centuries. The Cardinal Archbishop of Mechelen was sufficiently concerned at the self-absorbed nature of such practices that he reminded his flock to pray for others as well as themselves. Yet it is clear that the reinvigoration of Catholic practice was not simply a result of superstition and fear, but owed much to the greater prominence which the institution of the Church enjoyed in daily life. Whereas state structures had often been dislodged, the rituals and presence of the Church and clergy provided continuity in an uncertain world, its ceremonies and festivals offering opportunities for sociability, and its doctrine pointing towards some hope for a better future.

Some of the levels of wartime Catholicism inevitably slipped with the close of the war, as did part of the understanding which had developed between Christians and non-Christians and between Christians of different denominations as a result of their shared sufferings and experiences within the Resistance. For a brief while, in 1944–45, Catholics and communists, at least within France and Belgium, discovered a common set of values as they strove to build a New Jerusalem. The so-called Christian Progressives in France made a point of taking out Communist Party membership. As will be seen, it was the emergence of the Cold War that would wreck this fragile *rapprochement* and call into question initiatives such as the worker-priest movement which had originated in France when Cardinal Suhard had despatched *curés*, dressed in lay attire, to attend to the spiritual needs of those conscripted for compulsory work service in France. The Cold War would also prompt the newly-created Christian Democratic parties to travel in a rightwards direction. These had initially flourished out of the shared experience of Resistance: in France, the Mouvement Républicain Populaire (MRP) founded in January 1944; the Union Démocratique Belge (UDB) created at Liège in 1945; and the

Democrazia Cristiana (DC) in Italy. The evolution of these initiatives will be discussed in the next chapter, but it should be noted here that they did not necessarily reflect a shift in the power structures inherent in the Catholic laity. Although workers and left-wing Catholics were more prominent in the *après guerre*, thanks especially to the discrediting of nationalism in the form of fascism, the majority of adherents still stemmed from the middle classes and the peasantry, both of them intrinsically conservative in outlook and desirous to have political representation which accorded with their own social and political values.

Conclusion: Change and Continuity

The historical concepts of change and continuity often appear terribly hackneyed since most periods display such characteristics, but the terms appear especially relevant for inter-war Catholicism though it is the notion of continuity that dominates. This is most obviously true in the case of the papacy. With the triumph of Ultramontanism in the late nineteenth century, successive popes were quick to use their new-found authority to emphasise further both their theological and hierarchical supremacy. Papal encyclicals adopted a loftier tone – there were over 180 of them in the period 1878–1962 – and they played a defining role in doctrinal matters especially. The pontiff also readily intervened in the affairs of national churches. Here there lies a paradox, in that the prestige of the Holy See was at a high point when its moral leadership, thanks to the failure of Pius XII to respond to the Holocaust, was highly questionable. At the same time, the Catholic Church within Europe remained defiantly self-contained, unwilling to tolerate dissent within its own ranks and unprepared, by and large, to forge links with other faiths. This process was unwittingly facilitated by the continued growth of social organisations, the initiatives of Catholic Action, insurance societies and confessional trade unions. Within this world, there was undoubtedly dissent and a desire to enter into dialogue with Christians and non-Christians, but this was clamped down on by a hierarchy which sought dogmatic conformity and which was wedded to a traditional view that 'error had no rights'. That this imposed conformity often revolved around an organicist and corporatist vision of society, at odds with the principles of liberal democracy, was of little concern. Having undergone the trials of the late nineteenth century, Catholicism still perceived itself as under threat, helping to explain why episcopal hierarchies at least were so willing to prostrate themselves in front of the authoritarian regimes headed by Salazar, Franco and Pétain. In this regard, both the bishops and Rome were fortunate in that they could still draw upon deep reserves of religious enthusiasm among the laity. Here again, Catholicism was picking up on the trends of the nineteenth century, when the rank-and-file had enthusiastically embraced the 'God of Love' as opposed to the 'God of Fear'. The experience of the two world wars exacerbated this trend, as the faithful were uncomfortably reminded of their mortality.

The Church of 1945 was, then, not so dissimilar from the one which had emerged at the end of the First World War, but to believe that there had been no change whatsoever would be misguided. During the inter-war years and, thanks to the shared experience of Resistance, Christian Democracy in particular had acquired a legitimacy and a confidence which it had hitherto lacked. It was unforeseen that the radicalism of this movement would be diluted by the Cold War, the growth of secularisation and the watchful eye of the papacy. Real change in the direction of the Church would come in the 1960s. The reasons for this are the subject of the next chapter.

CHAPTER SIX

Catholicism Revised:
1945–2002

IF elements of the Catholic hierarchy and laity were tempted by extreme right-wing politics during the inter-war years, albeit the stale traditionalist and corporatist conservatism of Salazar, Franco and Pétain rather than the 'radicalism' of Nazism and Italian fascism, in the post-war world there seemed little alternative but for the Church to throw its weight behind liberal democracy. While Catholics continued to enjoy a closeted existence in Spain and Portugal, these surviving dictatorships were more or less ostracised by the remainder of the West. Moreover, the Soviet takeover of most of Eastern Europe and the onset of the Cold War gave the Church even less option but to seek salvation behind the liberal democratic cloak which the USA wished to throw over the 'free' world. In this situation, it appeared that free-thinking Catholics would, at last, have their chance, and indeed, Christian Democratic parties, predominantly Catholic in inspiration, flourished in most Western democracies. They were propelled by the general revulsion against extreme nationalism, the moves towards European integration and the desire to construct a new style of politics built on consensus rather than opposition. Doctrinally, too, Catholicism seemed to be marching in a liberal direction, a step epitomised in the enthronement of John XXIII and the summoning of the Second Vatican Council in 1962. Unlike previous councils, notably that of 1870, the intention was not to erect a Berlin Wall around the faith, preventing the more skilled and able laity and clergy from escaping, but to inaugurate a continuous process of internal debate, renewal and evangelisation. The Council was intended less as an event than as the initiation of a process. Admittedly, some of its conclusions and legacy came as a disappointment to liberals, yet they could still draw hope from this promise of constant and continued discourse.

In the event, things did not proceed in the way that many, both conservative and liberal, hoped and feared. The 1960s witnessed a truly seismic shift in cultural, moral and social values, which inaugurated a more corrosive secularisation than had been witnessed in the past. Whereas previously it had been easy to pinpoint anti-clericals, free-thinkers and the debilitating influences of industrialisation and urbanisation, the secularisation of the 1960s was diffuse and all-pervading and correspondingly difficult to contend with. Governments themselves were likewise troubled by changes in attitudes, not least because they threatened existing social and political structures. Yet, in the eyes of many

Catholics, governments appeared to collude in the very process of dechristian-isation, in particular by facilitating much greater freedoms in the areas of sexual morality: contraception, the provision of divorce, the availability of abortion and the gradual, albeit hesitant, acceptance of homosexuality. The one ray of hope for the Church in this bleak landscape was the collapse of the materialistic and atheistic culture of communism, in which Catholics played a major part, especially in Poland. The truth was, however, that Catholics were still extremely divided as to how to respond to yet another major change in the international balance of power. Already confused by the many options opened up by Vatican II, some still hankered after greater liberalism, while others, most notably the new Polish Pope, John Paul II, interpreted the collapse of communism as a vindication of the hard-line, and some might say reaction-ary, policies he had been pursuing since his inauguration in 1978. Towards the end of his pontificate, the questions about the future of Catholicism remained no more resolved than they were at the termination of the Council in 1965 or at the close of the Second World War in 1945.

Catholics and Cold War: Eastern Europe

Previous post-war settlements of 1815, 1871 and 1919 had all marked a shift in the religious balance of Europe away from Catholicism. In 1945 the picture was even bleaker. Not only had an avowedly atheistic state in the shape of the Soviet Union helped to win the war, it had also won the peace, emerging alongside the USA as one of the two superpowers around which global politics would henceforth revolve. Within central and eastern Europe, it enjoyed an unrivalled and unprecedented hegemony. It is calculated that in 1945 it directly accrued territory more or less equivalent in size to the Iberian peninsula, lands which often included substantial numbers of Catholics as well as Ortho-dox, Protestants and others. As Chadwick relates, some 3 million Catholics were inherited from the former Baltic states; nearly one million from the Carpathians; maybe a similar number from Bessarabia, Moldavia and Bukovina; and others from those bits of Poland and East Prussia which the USSR now claimed for itself.[1] Nor was there any hurry to release the 2 million German prisoners-of-war, many of whom were Catholic, and who were dragooned into Soviet industries to make good the labour shortage resulting from the war. Additionally, between 1945 and 1948, those states bordering the USSR quickly allied to the Soviet camp, usually thanks to *coups* executed on the part of local communist parties ably assisted by Moscow. Eventually coming together in the Warsaw Pact of 1955, these states comprised: Poland, pre-dominantly Catholic; Czechoslovakia and Hungary, both containing sizeable numbers of Catholics; and Bulgaria and Romania where Catholics were a minority. As Chadwick again remarks, it was little consolation to the Church that the formal division of Germany into East and West in 1949 meant that, for the first time since Napoleon's destruction of the Holy Roman Empire in 1806, a German state, apart from Austria, contained more Catholics than Protestants, its capital based at Bonn in the deeply fervent Catholic Rhineland.[2]

Ever since 1864, when Pius IX had declared that communism was no better than the hateful Protestant Bible Societies, the Church had been well aware of the dangers inherent in Marxist ideology, and by the twentieth century it could deploy a plethora of theological and intellectual refutations. Catholicism naturally rejected communism's atheistic ideal, founded as it claimed to be on an empirical, scientific reading of history. Further, Catholicism's fundamental belief in the existence of the supernatural and in a transcendental Being was clearly at odds with communism's materialist interpretation of life in which the economy was the determinant of social structures. It was, of course, this onus on economics that gave rise to the Marxist notion of class conflict which was also rejected by a faith which stood for natural hierarchies and the peaceful reconciliation of differences, and which regarded corporatism as the answer to the ills of industrial society. Despite Christ's insistence upon the futility of material wealth and the well-established tradition of monastic poverty, the Church believed wholeheartedly in the inviolability of private property, something which communists rejected, as a safeguard of social order. Ultimately, Catholicism, certainly as it was expressed in the integralist guise influential at the time of the Bolshevik Revolution, stood for a hierarchical society wholly incompatible with the social egalitarianism espoused, at least in theory, by communism.

Given the absolute incompatibility of the two ideologies, it was always going to be difficult for the Church in the post-war period to hold to its customary policy of acknowledging *de facto* governments, a dilemma exacerbated by the strength of communism in the Vatican's backyard, Italy. As in France, the communists' heavy involvement in esistance had greatly strengthened their popularity and patriotic credentials. To make matters worse, the leader of the Italian Communist Party, Palmiro Togliatti, appeared set upon pursuing a democratic path to power, despite the fact that communists were behind the assassination of some fifty-two priests in the period 1944–46. In the event, the communist threat within Italy was contained thanks to the power of the Christian Democrats (to be considered below), the strenuous attempts of Church organisations such as Catholic Action to stymie communist support and the enormous financial support lent by the USA to the Vatican and Catholic trade unions to promote anti-Marxist propaganda. Such 'lounge crooners' as Frank Sinatra and Bing Crosby sang on Italian radio with the political cadenza that voting communist meant the end of freedom. These *démarches* ensured that, in 1948, the Christian Democrats emerged with 48.5 per cent of the overall vote against the 31 per cent for the Socialist/Communist Popular Front alliance, thus inaugurating a long period of Catholic hegemony in national politics. Yet the fear of communism, and the tension between communists and Catholics, encapsulated in the tales of the 'little world of Dom Camillo', persisted. This led Pius XII to take a bolder step, which was to have reverberations far beyond the Italian peninsula. On 2 July 1949, the Pope published a decree making it unlawful for Catholics to belong to a communist party. Catholics were further debarred from writing or even reading articles favouring communism, and priests were instructed to withhold the sacraments from any Catholic who was a party member or publicist. Admittedly, a Catholic could still be a communist sympathiser, but the message was clear; and it was interpreted in Eastern Europe as evidence, if any more was needed, that religion was an enemy of the communist ideal. It did not go unnoticed that the Vatican had condemned communism in far more outspoken terms than it had fascism. Only as the Cold War began to take on an air of permanence did the Vatican move to an effective policy of détente, which often disgusted those believers who had struggled against the atheistic ideal. Battlers such as Gyorgy Bulanyi, a Hungarian priest who denounced compulsory military conscription and was muzzled both by his native episcopacy and by the Vatican. Even in Poland, where the Church was inextricably caught up in the opposition to communism, the prelacy frequently intervened to keep protest within bounds; for instance, it was the Primate of Poland who smoothed things over after the violent strikes of 1970.

It would be a mistake to regard the 1949 decree and the early Vatican anticommunist rhetoric as the only catalyst for the intensification of the antireligious measures in the USSR and Eastern Europe which occurred around this period. This was a time when pro-Soviet regimes had consolidated their grip on power and when the Cold War globally was beginning to freeze over, a development signalled by the Berlin airlift and formal division of the two Germanys. Communist regimes also feared the centrifugal, disintegrative force of unfettered nationalism and, recognising that nationalism and religion were closely intertwined, moved easily to a policy of religious persecution. Typical of what Eric Hobsbawm has termed the 'monochromatic' texture of communist government, the new structures introduced to regulate the Churches were remarkably similar.[3] Everywhere, departments of state were created, their names reminiscent of the Nazi apparatus created to oversee the Protestant denominations. As often cited, these comprised: the Council for Religious Affairs in the USSR; the Ministry for Religious Affairs in Poland; the Secretariat of State for Church Affairs in East Germany; the State Office for Church Affairs in Czechoslovakia; the State Church Office in Hungary; the Department of Cults in Romania; and a specialist section of the Foreign Office in Bulgaria. This development was naturally fuelled by communist opposition to religion *per se*, but some form of regulation was always going to be a necessity given the fact that ecclesiastical property was henceforth owned by the state in the name of the people. In truth, this was not altogether a new development. The Tsarist state had long involved itself in matters of the Orthodox ministry, with the result that the Orthodox Church complied fairly readily with this new bureaucratic intrusion, as did the Lutheran sects in East Germany where there existed a similar tradition of compliance dating back to the Hohenzollerns. It was in Protestant areas of Czechoslovakia that there was greatest defiance. Yet it was Catholics who had most to fear, especially given the hierarchical nature of their Church, its reliance on the Vatican and the near indispensability of bishops in the exercise of the faith. To the horror of Pius XII, those precious concordats he had laboriously secured were unceremoniously dumped. This did not prevent the communist autocracies from insisting upon the right to approve bishops, which inevitably created friction. The fact that the state only accepted men who were independent of the Holy See, and who were willing to accommodate the Marxist line without alienating the priesthood by becoming mere sycophants, meant that the choice of candidates acceptable to both the Communist Party and the Vatican was limited. When candidates could not be found, the state was perfectly prepared to see dioceses remain vacant. Where Catholics were in a majority, notably Poland, Croatia and Slovenia, empty sees were rare and compromise candidates could usually be recruited. Where Catholics were less numerous, in areas such as Slovakia and Hungary, the situation was pretty grim, worsened by discrimination against individual prelates.

While such discrimination was very real, it should be stressed that the many Stalinist departments overseeing religious matters never sought to deploy the ample state apparatus of repression to eliminate the Churches altogether. As Chadwick has demonstrated, the worst cases of persecution were to be found in Albania in respect of Catholics of the Eastern Rite, and in the show trials of individual bishops.[4] Albania, of course, did not fall within the Soviet orbit and was, in any case, predominantly Islamic, the remainder of the population being Orthodox (17.1 per cent) and Catholic (10.1 per cent), mainly concentrated in the north. It was, though, governed by communists after 1945, led by the bigoted dictator Enver Hoxha. Catholics were tainted by their earlier support for fascist Italy, but it was the need to promote unity by destroying a long-standing religious pluralism that truly sealed their fate. In the event, religious practice subsisted and even flourished, but only after several prominent prelates had been imprisoned or shot, churches closed down and Catholics compelled to join a national Church which had no contact with the Vatican. Uniquely in Eastern Europe, the Albanian constitutions of 1967 and 1976 denied individuals the right to practise their religious faith in private, although again it is debatable how successful such a proscription really was. Active persecution of religion was eventually moderated when, in the early 1990s, the government sought to forge links with Catholic and Muslim Albanians living in neighbouring Serbia.

Catholics of the Eastern Rite fared little better. They were concentrated in the Ukraine (4.5 million), Romania (just under one million), eastern Czecho-slovakia (300,000), Hungary (250,000), Poland (200,000) and Bulgaria (10,000). Everywhere, they were resented by the communist regimes for their links with the Vatican; in the Ukraine, they came under particularly heavy fire as they served as the focus for national identity. In the tide of persecution, which involved the closure of churches, the imprisonment of clergy and the holding of state-sponsored synods which voted for reunion with Orthodoxy, members of the Eastern Rite were forced to live a clandestine religious existence, often attending either Catholic or Orthodox services without reveal-ing their true loyalties. There was some sympathy for their plight on the part of Catholics themselves, and they made good propaganda material for the Vatican in its campaign against the atheism of Moscow, yet they were unable to count on the support of the Orthodox Church whose leaders were not altogether displeased to see the harassment of this nonconformist element and welcomed recruits from the Eastern Rite fraternity, however dubious their allegiance.

There remained the persecution and show trials of prominent Church leaders. There were several of these, for instance the Czech Cardinal Beran, the Polish Cardinal Wyszyński and Archbishop Matulionis in Lithuania, who, in unconscious imitation of the socialist Ledru Rollin, paid the price for his faith by spending his ministry either in prison or in hiding, as one of the so-called 'bishops of the catacombs'. It is, though, the sufferings of Father Jozef Tiso in Slovakia, Archbishop Stepinac in Yugoslavia and Cardinal József Mindszenty in Hungary that are best remembered. This is principally because their trials had, as Chadwick notes, a resonance throughout Europe and the USA.[5] It will be recalled from the previous chapter that Tiso had led the Slovak People's Party and, through Hitler's dismemberment of Czechoslovakia, became head of the new Slovak Republic, rapidly turning this into a theocracy while resisting some of the worst excesses of Nazism. There was no denying, however, that he had presided over a shabby state which clung on to power through the Hlinka guard, an obnoxious body responsible for all manner of atrocities; and in 1944 he invited the *Wehrmacht* to help suppress an uprising designed to link up with the advancing Red Army, subsequently using a church ceremony of thanksgiving to pin medals on the chests of SS officers. He may not have ranked among the most odious of Hitler's sympathisers, yet he had committed that unpardonable offence of employing Nazi military successes to pursue his own ends. It was largely because of the need for vengeance that he was hanged by the Czechoslovakian state in April 1947, his death transforming him into an unlikely martyr, principally because he was a convenient icon for Catholics to wave at the communist regime.

Stepinac likewise suffered for the highly ambivalent and reprehensible role he had played during the war when he had been Archbishop of Zagreb and effective Primate of the puppet state of Croatia set up by the Nazis. Even today, his actions and personality give rise to searching questions which are difficult to answer, not least of all because his own official diary and other key documents from the diocesan archives at Zagreb remain unavailable to scholars. While he had kept a distance from Pavelic, and had disapproved of the imitative racist measures which had led to the massacres of Jews and Serbs, atrocities often committed by Franciscan friars, he had seen the hand of Providence behind the German establishment of an independent Croatia. This made it easy to hang a charge of collaboration on him after the end of the war, and the Tito regime sentenced him to sixteen years' forced labour, of which he served seven, eking out the remainder of his life under house arrest. His unbending defiance of the communists made him, like Tiso, a martyr figure, his fate being deplored both by the Vatican and the USA in particular.

It was Mindszenty – he had courageously changed his name from the German-sounding Pehm to a Magyarised form in 1941 – who had the most justifiable claims for martyrdom, both because of his appalling treatment at the hands of the Russians and his unsympathetic handling by the Vatican. An unrelenting critic of Nazism, he was no less outspoken in his condemnation of Marxism, having being a hostage of the communists during the Hungarian revolution of 1919. Recognising this voice of defiance, in 1945 Pius XII appointed him Primate of all Hungary, whereupon Mindszenty resumed his criticisms of communism, leading to his arrest in 1948 on trumped-up charges of collaborating with the Nazi occupier. After a travesty of a three-day trial the following year, which was roundly denounced by the United Nations and in which a physically and mentally tortured Mindszenty admitted all the charges, he was sentenced to life imprisonment. Released in 1956, at the time of the Hungarian rising, in unconscious imitation of the Pope as prisoner in the Vatican, he soon found himself immured in the American embassy at Budapest where he stayed for the next fifteen years. His presence there served as an embarrassment to the communists and to the papacy which would have liked him to resign his see as a first step to improving Church–state relations. The Pope also wanted to prevent him publishing his memoirs, which he wrote during his twilight years in Vienna, lest these too upset relations with the Eastern bloc.[6] No doubt the Vatican was also aware that Mindszenty's sharp intellect and wit might be directed at the pusillanimous diplomacy adopted by the papacy towards Moscow.

Although treatment of all Churches remained brutal right up to the dissolution of the communist regimes in the late 1980s, it was generally appreciated, especially after the downfall of Khrushchev in 1964, that outright violence could well prove counter-productive. Perhaps the best example of this stems not from the Soviet bloc but from Yugoslavia. In 1981, a group of teenagers at Medjugorje in Herzegovina claimed to have witnessed a vision of the Virgin Mary. The sighting was taken less than seriously by the local bishop, whose investigative commission soon proved the fallacy of the claims, but the attempts by the police to seal off the location of the vision and the imprisonment of some of its publicists only boosted the site's popular appeal. Over the next six years, it is calculated that the shrine was visited by at least 8 million pilgrims. To prevent such displays of dissent, most of the Eastern-bloc countries adopted more refined means to curb the influence of the Church, often appropriating techniques used previously by democratic regimes such as the French Third Republic and the Portuguese Republic of 1910–26.

Schooling was crucial. Religious education was banned altogether, or permitted on school premises only outside normal teaching hours in the cases of Hungary and Czechoslovakia; teachers known to hold religious beliefs lost their jobs, a policy which proved to be more effective at the level of colleges and universities than in elementary schools; and those who proffered or attended voluntary religious education, whether this meant assembling for prayers or the recital of the catechism in the house of a priest or a neighbour, were denied educational and job opportunities as well as access to state benefits. Where the communist regimes went further than the secularising liberal democracies was in the positive propagation of atheism. Within schools, courses in scientific materialism were obligatory, and were designed to show that religion was not merely irrelevant for an understanding of the world, but was detrimental in its effects on human conduct. Aside from education, the regimes further offered atheist alternatives to the religious rites of passage. Recognising eventually the need for some ritual splendour to mark these occasions, notably that of marriage, special wedding services were designed in the Soviet Union to supplement the drab civil ceremonies. Atheist funerals were also commonplace, providing an opportunity to evoke memories of the anti-fascist struggle by making explicit reference to the war dead. The need to substitute some kind of state rituals for those of the Church was further apparent in the establishment of New Year and May Day festivals and, most famously, in the *Jugendweihe* in East Germany whereby children of confirmation age took a vow of loyalty to socialism, a practice that became well-nigh universal if only because of peer pressure. Outside the GDR, however, it appears that these atheistic ceremonies were less popular, and in Poland the historical weight of Catholic tradition was so great that the regime scarcely thought it worth the effort to stage them.

Finally, communism made life uncomfortable and unwelcoming for both secular and regular clerics who were always unsure how far they should compromise their spiritual roles in carrying out their religious duties. The regulars, who existed in considerable numbers in Poland and Yugoslavia particularly, were easy to target since all property was owned by the state, and religious houses thus had no independent economic support. In Czechoslovakia, the wearing of religious habits and the communal life were strictly forbidden although, strangely, in East Germany monks and nuns were left alone, maybe because they performed welfare and charitable functions which the state could ill afford to lose. In many senses, the communists were relearning the lessons of the enlightened despots of the late eighteenth century. The Eastern-bloc countries sought to neuter the influence of the seculars by encouraging them to join priests' associations whose role was to preach loyalty to the regime and, incidentally, to foment division between the upper and lower clergy. In Poland, for instance, the government-sponsored Stowarczyszemie PAX created a body of 'patriotic' priests to argue that there was no necessary dichotomy between communism and Catholicism, and to sow confusion among the clergy. Ironically, PAX helped to get Western Catholic literature published in Poland. Thanks to the high levels of state intervention in ecclesiastical affairs, it was the so-called 'patriotic' priests who could look forward to prominent positions in the Church hierarchy.

Assessing the effects of the anti-God campaign in the Eastern bloc is fraught with all manner of difficulties. As with the dechristianising campaign of the French Revolution, the most successful aspect appears to have been the attack on the fabric of churches of all denominations and their personnel. Everywhere, religious buildings were closed and turned over to other uses, or allowed to fall into disrepair. For instance, the church of St John at Vilnius, built in 1387, was initially used as a newsprint warehouse for the local communist publication, before it was rented out to a Belorussian film company which specialised in military movies, letting off live ammunition and grenades in the building. Few establishments were built to make up the shortfall. The process was especially pronounced in Hungary where, between 1945 and 1950, the Catholic Church lost almost all its property, including 3,344 schools, most of its printing presses and 705 convents. Personnel also suffered. There were insufficient new recruits; the average age of the clergy rose sharply; and severe restrictions were placed on clerics' ability to perform public ceremonies. In Lithuania in 1940, there had been 1,451 priests of all types; there were 869 in 1965; and 772 in 1974. That same year, there were only nine priests aged in their twenties. Poland was the exception: it is calculated that in 1974 there were some seventy-seven bishops, and an astonishing 4,200 ordinands presenting themselves for the ministry. Surveys undertaken in 1964 and 1966 revealed that between 72.5 and 81 per cent of town dwellers and between 82.8 and 91 per cent of rural inhabitants professed to be believers.

With the exception of Poland, levels of practice underwent a slump, a trend keenly monitored by communist sociologists who were interested to know just how far state atheism had percolated throughout society. Within Czechoslovakia, the state-funded Institute of Scientific Atheism uncovered that 36 per cent of the population deemed themselves 'religious', an identity most commonly adopted by Catholics, and that rural workers, pensioners and women were most observant. Similar patterns were uncovered in Hungary where again religious practice thrived in rural areas, and among the older sections of society, while nearly two-thirds of young people chose to spurn church weddings. In Yugoslavia, where the institutional structures of the Catholic Church displayed remarkable resilience, nearly half the population in the 1960s professed either to be atheist or simply indifferent to religion, the highest figure in Europe, but it should be stressed that such responses may well have reflected a prudence in the face of questioning by state officials rather than a genuine statement of attitude.

How much emphasis should be placed on these inquiries is open to doubt as the evidence they provide is extremely fragmentary, and gives little indication about the quality of religious observance. What is certain is that religious practice did decline, albeit with marked regional and national variations, Poland always being the area where Catholicism held firmest. As many historians have pointed out, this decline mirrored that in Western democracies, casting considerable doubts on the effectiveness of state-sponsored atheism which often displayed a crassness worthy of those pioneer French dechristianisers of the 1790s. R. F. Leslie, for instance, notes: 'Much more significant than the deliberate efforts of the Party were the long-term social consequences of industrialisation and urbanisation.'[7] On close inspection, trends in East and West display marked similarities, suggesting that the forces of secularisation possessed a symmetry everywhere in Europe.

Catholics and Cold War: Western Europe

Although in Western Europe there was also state involvement in religious affairs, this was of a different order to that in the Eastern bloc. In Spain and Portugal, the Second World War seemed to have changed little, since the survival of the dictatorships of Salazar and Franco ensured that the marriage between authoritarianism and Catholicism continued. With the dismantling of these regimes in the 1970s, Iberian Catholics had to confront the brave new world of liberal democracy. Given the Church's pre-1940 relationship with parliamentarianism, there were good grounds for anxiety. How would Catholics fare in such a pluralistic society? In the event, they did well, and the situation within the Iberian peninsula has slowly come to resemble that found in Italy, France, Belgium, Holland, Austria and West Germany. Here, Christian Democracy enjoyed notable success in promoting Catholic values and in protecting the Church from a repetition of nineteenth-century state anti-clericalism, although Catholics still had to deal with the popular anti-clericalism which emerged as part of a 'New Secularism'. On the periphery of Europe, there remained Great Britain and Ireland, doggedly distinct in so many ways. In the former, both toleration and a growing indifference towards religion guaranteed the assimilation of Catholics into the political mainstream. Paradoxically, from the 1960s onwards the province of Northern Ireland displayed many of the trappings of seventeenth-century sectarianism. The Republic of Ireland itself was fortunate to escape much of this strife but, as a predominantly Catholic state, it discovered that its remoteness from mainland Europe could not isolate it from the currents of change.

The Iberian Peninsula

Because Spain had studiously avoided entering the Second World War, the right-wing dictatorship of Franco survived, unlike those of his friends Hitler and Mussolini, and as a result the close relationship between Church and state, which had been established before 1939, continued. While this meant that Catholic political parties, together with all other political groupings, were subsumed within the Francoist movement, this mattered little as the majority of Catholics had more or less the regime they desired, and they enthusiastically worked to make up the losses of the recent civil war. As Bishop Tarancón observed: 'The prelates – and the vast majority of priests, religious and practising Catholics – were profoundly convinced that Franco's regime ... was like the Church's secular arm.'[8] Franco also had good reason to indulge the Church, as in the immediate post-war period he was anxious, in the words of John Hooper, 'to present a non-fascist face to the world'.[9] At home, divorce was made illegal, the sale of contraceptives was outlawed (although, confusingly, their manufacture was legal), the catechism was made obligatory in both public and private schools (primary and secondary), and Catholics were exceedingly well represented in the civil bureaucracy. On the international scene, the regime sought respectability by hosting, in 1945, the conference of the International Catholic Organisation, Pax Romana. Further, a number of so-called Catholic Propagandists, most famously Joaquín Ruíz Giménez, busily cultivated links with the wider Catholic community, even engaging in dialogue with Christian Democratic parties in Europe. Pleased at the manner in which Franco had accommodated the Church within Spain, and glad to have another ally in the Cold War, the Vatican subsequently allowed Franco considerable say in the appointment of bishops. This cosy, triangular relationship between Church, state and the Vatican culminated in the Concordat of 1953, which signalled an end to Spain's diplomatic isolation. Immediately after the war, the United Nations had called for the imposition of sanctions in response to Franco's support for the Axis powers.

Grateful for Church support in sloughing off Spain's international pariah status, Franco thus went much further than many Catholics had expected. The concordat provided the following: Church immunity from taxation; generous state subsidies for the construction and repair of church buildings; the right of bishops to request the censorship of 'undesirable' printed material; the ability of Catholic newspapers and radio stations to operate freely; the guaranteed place of the catechism within schools; the option for the Church to open its own universities; the immunity of priests from criminal charges without consent from the bishop, and a similar immunity for prelates; immune legal status for religious buildings; and the precedence of Church marriages over civil ones. Small wonder that Spain was trumpeted as 'the spiritual reserve of the West'.

The concordat was the cue for Spanish Catholics to indulge in a new *reconquista*, aimed this time at communists, freemasons and Jews rather than the Moors, though it continued to embody the notion that to be Spanish was to be Catholic. Enduring until the 1960s, this campaign took on many dimensions. At one level, it comprised mass pilgrimages, such as that to El Ferrol del Caudillo, Franco's natal village; on another, it involved the promotion of maternal values, and stressed the centrality of the mother at the heart of the Catholic family. Most importantly, it involved the suffusion of education at all levels with the values of Catholicism. The stranglehold on elementary and secondary education has already been noted; now this was extended to higher education. 'Suspect' professors, that is those believed to harbour republican sympathies, were dismissed; the Propagandists were elevated to influential positions over the heads of their rivals; and undergraduates were obliged to attend courses in religious instruction. It was, of course, in higher education that Opus Dei, the *Obra* or 'work of God' as it was known in Spain, was particularly influential. José Martín, an intimate of the movement's founder, was Minister for Education for a decade; its members comprised around one-quarter of the professoriate by the start of the 1950s; and since the 1960s it has operated its own university near to Pamplona, a business school at Barcelona and a college of administration at San Sebastián, whose elite graduates have infiltrated the worlds of academe, industry, commerce and the bureaucracy to a remarkable extent.

The first fissures in this close, suffocating relationship between Church and state opened up as a result of the Second Vatican Council of 1962–65 (see below), which proved extremely painful for a Church which, in Audrey Brassloff's phrase, was 'corseted in political and social terms' by its alliance with Franco.[10] The liberal spirit emanating from the Council, and actively propagated by Pope John XXIII, embraced every aspect of life from liturgy through relations with other faiths to the claims of the poor, and struck a chord with those in Spain who perceived an increasing dichotomy between the stated Christian ideals of the regime and what it actually delivered in terms of social justice. Particularly affected were those Catholics, both lay and clerical, who had been active in the attempt to reach out to the de-christianised and traditionally anti-clerical working classes of the larger cities, and who had operated under the umbrella of various societies set up in the 1940s and 1950s: the Hermandades Obreras de Acción Católica (HOAC), the Juventud Obrera Católica, Vanguardias Obreras Juveniles (VOJ), and the Vanguardias Obreras Sociales (VOS). These organisations were acutely aware of the ways in which Franco's regime had not managed to halt a drift away from the faith. A 1957 HOAC study of 15,491 industrial workers revealed that 86.1 per cent were Catholic in rites of passage, 89.6 per cent described themselves as anti-clerical, 41.3 per cent claimed to be anti-religious, 54.7 per cent said they were 'completely uninterested in religion', 28.5 per cent were 'Easter-duty Catholics', 23.2 per cent were 'occasional mass attenders', 7.6 per cent went to mass on Sunday, and a mere 2.9 per cent were members of Church organisations.

Contact with the underprivileged urban poor, whose numbers were swelled by a rural exodus in the 1950s, brought about a growing awareness of the social divisions upon which the Francoist regime rested, and resulted in the appearance of 'red priests' who took advantage of the privileged position of the clergy in respect of the law to stage workers' meetings and sit-ins in their churches, and to rally striking workers with fiery oratory and impassioned pamphlets. In 1972, the appointment of Mgr Iniesta to the working-class diocese of Vallecas (a suburb of Madrid) even added a bishop to the ranks of the *curas rojos*. Yet, more significant than the opposition to Franco's regime from the 'red priests' – for they were few in number – was the more general disaffection felt by younger members of the clergy, who comprised a disproportionate percentage of the Church's workforce by the early 1960s. Inspired by the emphasis upon individual rights embodied in *Gaudium et spes* (see below), they were disconcerted by the regime's blatant disregard for liberties. It was this anxiety, coupled with the refreshing liberal spirit of Vatican II that led Joaquín Ruiz Giménez in 1963 to found the Cuadernos Para el Diálogo, whose purpose was to promote discourse between Catholics and the rest of society, including Marxists. In a 1966 episode known as the *Caputxinada,* 130 priests undertaking a dignified protest in Barcelona against recent police brutality concerning students were themselves subject to rough handling and verbal abuse.

Finally, some of the emerging Catholic antipathy to the Franco regime drew on Spanish regionalism. In the traditionally pious Basque area and in Catalonia there had long been widespread support among laity and clergy alike for some kind of particularist privileges; this had led these two regions to side with the Republicans in the Civil War and to continue to call for separation after the General's victory. Subsequently, Franco's repressive measures alienated many Catholics, especially in the Basque country, and created support for a militant nationalist movement. Nearly 340 Basque priests signed a protest letter to the government in 1960; the separatist group ETA had its origins in Catholic youth groups of the area; Basque clergy sheltered its activists; and in Catalonia the Benedictine abbey at Montserrat enjoyed a long-standing and well-deserved reputation as a centre of militancy. In 1968–69, regional terrorism was so endemic that a state of emergency was declared, and the 1953 Concordat was amended so as to permit the imprisonment of clergy who were held at a gaol in Zamora.

So long as Franco lived, there were no concessions. Most importantly, he refused to yield his control over episcopal appointments, even though Vatican II called for the separation of Church and state, including the removal of government influence over clerical appointments. Nor did the Church hierarchy wish to relinquish its influence over education and public morality and, most critically, feared the loss of state finance. It was the General's death in 1975, and the transformation of Spain into a constitutional monarchy under the inspired leadership of King Juan Carlos, that heralded profound changes in Church–state affairs, and in the wider place of Catholicism within national life. This was unquestionably a painful experience for the hierarchy as a whole, but, as Brassloff has revealed, the wider body of the Church was accepting of democracy.[11] Several reasons account for this. There was no wish to relive the Civil War of the 1930s; younger clerics had already acquired an honourable reputation for defending individual rights; even the hierarchy had consented to the granting of sanctuary to the regime's opponents; and Paul VI (1963–78) was instrumental in urging Catholics to accept the reality of the situation.

The move to democracy heralded a shift in the relationship between Church and state, and in 1979 the so-called Partial Agreements augmented the 1953 Concordat. In essence, these recognised the legal status of the Church within society, especially its right to exercise its apostolic mission, and sanctioned canonical marriage; religious education in schools was available on tap for those parents who wished it for their children; Catholic chaplains were established within the armed forces; and there was some guarantee of state funding for the Church. A provision was included enabling taxpayers to opt out of contributing to the Church, but this in practice meant little since the state made up the difference. One person who was unhappy at the deal was the new Pope, John Paul II, who could not understand why such a powerful Catholic nation had permitted such a liberal settlement. With the start of his pontificate, the conservatives in the Spanish hierarchy were brought back into prominence. This trend was typified by the appointment of Cardinal Suquía, an affiliate of Opus Dei, who succeeded the emollient Tarancón as Archbishop of Madrid in 1983 and who served as president of the immensely influential Bishops' Conference for six years from 1987. His criticisms of Spanish society as 'sick', his condemnation of the use of condoms in the campaign to eradicate AIDS and his diatribe against democracy harked back to an earlier age. His words nevertheless struck a chord with many ordinary Catholics – including Women's Catholic Action – who, as Mary Vincent has remarked, hesitated to look beyond the certainties of the past.[12]

The persistence of conservative attitudes within Spanish Catholicism was also reflected in the political arena. At the switchover from dictatorship to democracy in 1977, high-ranking ecclesiastics agreed that it would be unwise to found a political party which contained either the words Christian or Catholic in its title as this would potentially compromise its future, just as in the 1900s Albert de Mun and Jacques Piou had attempted to avoid such associations when founding the Action Libérale Populaire. In any case, Spanish Catholics were so fragmented that they could not pursue any single trajectory. Some stood under the banner of the Alianze Popular (AP), said to comprise the 'left overs' of the Franco regime, while others gravitated to the Unión de Centro Democrático (UCD). The split in the vote helped to open the way for a long period of socialist party hegemony, although it should be stressed that the left could call upon a tremendous groundswell of public sympathy, which it took care not to alienate by passing anti-clerical legislation. Unlike in the 1930s, the left now recognised and respected the religious bases of Spanish life. Whether the conservative Partido Popolar, which eventually broke the socialist grip on power, can be truly described as Christian Democrat, remains a moot point.

Events in Spain were largely reproduced in its smaller neighbour, Portugal. Here, too, dictatorship persisted under Salazar with the result that Catholics were divided between a traditionalist majority and a much smaller progressive grouping. The former, strongly influenced by Opus Dei which had spread from Spain in the immediate post-war years, clung to the gains which the Church had apparently made through the 1940 Concordat. Although not nearly as generous as in Spain, these were considerable. On the one hand, some measure of state secularism was preserved: religious teaching was not compulsory; civil marriage and divorce survived; ecclesiastical property seized in 1910 stayed in state hands; and nominees to bishoprics were vetted by the government. On the other hand, the Church was exempt from taxation, received a government subsidy, and generally benefited from the regime's wish to dress itself in a cloak of Christian ideals.

As in Spain, it was the younger generation, both lay and clerical, that showed most disenchantment with the stultifying authoritarianism of Salazar. Their voices were heard in a series of congresses staged by Catholic Action which focused upon the need of the Church to reorientate its approach so as to bring alive the Christian message and to address social problems. In 1959, a bizarre episode, known as the Cathedral Plot, was uncovered which aimed to remove Salazar and involved a sizeable number of progressive Catholics including Manuel Serra, a youth leader, together with around 300 youthful activists from the Juventud Operaria Catolica and the Juventude Universitaria Catolica. Yet the progressive wing was always stymied by its lack of organisation, and the fact that the Church hierarchy remained resolute supporters of the regime. The only member of the prelacy who defied the conformist stance, Ferreira Gomes, the Bishop of Oporto, was forced into a ten-year exile between 1959 and 1969. Such stifling of debate, however, proved counterproductive in the long-term. When political revolution came in 1974 and

Portugal took unsteady steps towards democracy, the frailties in the organisational strength of the Church became apparent. In the critical period 1974–76, the Church found itself largely ignored, although individual priests were significant in rallying their flock to stave off the communist menace. As in Spain in 1975, a critical opportunity was lost for the emergence of a healthy Christian Democratic party. Since then, moderate centrists have dominated, ensuring the marginalisation of both far right and far left.

The West European Model: Belgium, Holland, West Germany, Italy, Austria and France

Outside the Iberian peninsula, Church and state did not share the same suffocating embrace. The relationship was instead both relaxed and distant. In part, this easing of tension resulted from the superior powers of the state. While governments emerged exhausted from the Second World War, under the impetus of the Marshall Plan they soon recuperated, and took on a far more interventionist role. At the same time, the success of liberal democracy, underpinned by American money and arms, together with the fear of the Soviets, ensured that they could count upon the loyalty of their citizens. Catholics, often mobilised through the forces of Christian Democracy, were now largely reconciled to the parliamentary model and saw little point in rocking the boat. After two centuries of struggle, the state was now supreme.

For its part, the Church has had little choice but to accept its role as the junior partner, even though it fought tooth and nail over certain moral issues, and managed a shrewd rearguard action in defence of existing institutional arrangements. In France, the Separation Law of 1905 remained intact, but in Italy, Germany and Austria renegotiation of Church–state relations was unavoidable. In Italy, the 1929 Lateran Accords were called into question as a creation of the discredited Mussolini regime. In the event, their advantages outweighed their shortcomings, with the result that they were left largely intact until the 1970s and 1980s. In 1984, the Vatican, acknowledging the extent of secularisation within the peninsula, eventually agreed a revised text with Prime Minister Craxi. This recognised that although Italy was no longer a Catholic state, 'the principles of Catholicism were a part of the historic inheritance of the Italian people', which came close to saying the same thing. The Vatican City would no longer be designated a 'sacred city', something which had allowed the Church to ban books, plays and films. In West Germany, the bishops hoped that the 1933 Concordat could be preserved, despite the manner in which Hitler had abused it. A ruling from the Supreme Court in 1957 subsequently recognised the continuing validity of the settlement, but opened the possibility for the provincial states (*Länder*) to reject certain of its tenets, in particular with regard to schooling. Across the border in Austria, the status of the 1933 Concordat was also disputed, and ultimately a series of individual accords were made similar to those concluded with German states such as Lower Saxony in 1965 and Rhineland-Westphalia in 1973. These dealt with the most vexatious problem, that of state funding, which was largely retained. In Switzerland, where the system of cantonal independence was long established, a series of bilateral arrangements was made which tweaked the Church–state relationship, marking a trend towards religious pluralism in a country which had been deeply riven by religious antagonisms. In 1972, for example, the long-standing prohibition on the establishment of new dioceses was lifted, the ban on Jesuits and new convents going the following year. In several regards, Switzerland exemplified the general picture of Church–state relations in Western Europe: less state interference, and a general acceptance of religious plurality. The Swiss none the less continue to be distinctive in the extent of democratisation within the Church. This led to some clashes with the Holy See, most notably in 1988 when the reactionary Bishop Wolfgang Haas was appointed to the bishopric of Chur, much to the fury of local clergy and laity.

It was above all in the fields of education and personal morality that there was a continuing struggle between Church and state. The latter will be dealt with below, but some mention must be made at this juncture of schooling. In this area, Church teaching had changed little since 1929 when Pius XI had proclaimed in the encyclical *Divini illius magistri* that 'Religion shall be the foundation and crown of all teaching'. This meant that the Church was eager for religious instruction to be dispensed throughout all sectors of schooling, both primary and secondary, private and public, and that its own denominational schools should be eligible for state subsidies, if only to relieve the burden on Catholic parents who had to find the fees (for such establishments were generally fee-paying), when they were already contributing to state schools through general taxation. In Italy, the Church had mixed fortunes. The revision to the Lateran Accords in 1989 permitted religious education in state schools, but gave parents the prerogative to withdraw their children if they so chose. The Church was further given the right to vet both teachers of religion and the curriculum they delivered, something which intellectuals have since hotly contested. In West Germany, matters were decided at the local level, successfully containing any anti-clerical outbursts.

It was in Belgium and France that the Church–state battle over education was fiercest. A settlement was reached in the former in 1958, when government underwrote the rapid development of its own schools while, at the same time, providing safeguards for the survival of Catholic ones. A similar compromise was reached in France, that traditional clerical–anti-clerical battleground, the following year when Prime Minister Michel Debré used the distraction of the Algerian crisis to push through legislation permitting some limited funding of private teachers and the upkeep of private schools. The dominance of the right and centre right in French politics thereafter ensured that the schools question remained off the agenda. It was the election of the socialists in 1981, and their plans to withdraw financial subventions to private secondary schools, that caused the issue to flare again. In 1984, thousands of parents protested in the streets of Paris. While these demonstrations have often been interpreted as a religious manifestation, it is fair to say that they were principally an attempt on the part of the middle classes to cling on to state assistance. The bishops more or less accepted the changes, and it was the Gaullists under Chirac who presented the issues as a defence of religious freedoms, essentially in an attempt to attack the Mitterrand regime. Paradoxically, in recent years, it has been elements of the French right, hitherto champions of Church rights, who have called for the strict imposition of the laws governing religious neutrality in state schools, principally as a means to campaign against Islamic influence, for instance trying to ban the wearing of the *fa* or headscarf in the classroom.

Another explanation as to why Church and state have entered calmer waters lies in the post-war strength of Christian Democratic parties. These have not only shaped national politics, but have promoted moves towards European integration which in itself has helped to advance the values of assimilation and religious tolerance. Indeed, Christian Democratic parties have long been pivotal in the workings of the European Parliament, reflecting their strength at a national level. Within West Germany, the Christliche Demokratische Union (CDU)/Christliche Soziale Union (CSU), under the skilful leadership of Konrad Adenauer, was in power continuously during the period 1949–69, and it was not until 1972 that the rival socialists won more votes at the polls. In 1982–83, in the so-called *Wende* (turning point) the Christian Democrats, in alliance with the Freie Demokratische Partei (FDP), entered a second phase of political dominance, this time under the watchful eye of Helmut Kohl, a dominance that was not broken until the Socialist/Green coalition of the 1990s. Within Italy, the Democrazia Cristiana (DC), ably led by De Gasperi until his death in 1954, enjoyed a similar supremacy. It regularly won over 40 per cent of the national vote and held power, either on its own or as a coalition partner, for much of the post-war period, as well as usually providing the premier, the first break in tradition coming with the republican Giovanni Spadolini in the 1980s. In the following decade, the DC disintegrated thanks to party corruption, and underwent a number of transformations, the political vacuum eventually being filled by Berlusconi's centre-right Forza Italia. Within Belgium, the Parti Social Chrétien (PSC) and Christelijke Volkspartij (CVP), operating in the Walloon and Flemish provinces respectively, maintained their own organisational structures but operated as a joint group in national politics, securing an overall majority in the Chamber of Deputies in 1950. By the start of the 1970s, the PSC and CVP had split, and their share of their vote declined, yet they have continued to play a key role in both national and regional affairs, a situation repeated in Holland. Here, the phenomenon of 'pillarisation' prevented the emergence of a single Christian Democratic party in the immediate post-war years, yet the social and economic turbulence of the late 1960s witnessed a realignment within Dutch politics and the amalgamation of the three confessional parties, one Catholic and two Protestant, which in 1976 formed the Christen Democratisch Appel (CDA). In France, Christian Democracy was represented by the Mouvement Républicain Populaire (MRP) which figured in twenty-two out of the twenty-six governments of the Fourth Republic. Under the Fifth Republic, Christian Democracy underwent a terminal decline largely because the MRP had been pushed aside by the Gaullists and because most of the specific issues affecting Catholics had been largely resolved.

In the early 1970s, Christian Democratic parties underwent mixed fortunes throughout much of Europe. The reasons behind this relative decline are addressed below but were generally the obverse of those which had contributed to their earlier popularity. To begin with, they had benefited both from the discrediting of the fascist right, which was associated with the horrors of the Holocaust, and the compromising role which several conservative politicians had played during the occupation of Europe. In contrast to those other bourgeois parties that emerged in 1945, Christian Democrats seemed to offer a new way forward, often embracing ambitious schemes for renewal, even though in practice membership often comprised unreconstructed right-wing elements: the *Machine à Ramasser les Pétainistes* was the satirists' nickname for the MRP in France. In Italy, the DC comprised such men as Amintore Fanfani, a Milanese lawyer who had actively supported fascist legislation in the 1930s; in West Germany, the CDU figured former Nazis such as Kurt Kiesinger. The fact that Christian Democrats saw themselves as belonging to movements rather than parties also facilitated their rise. They offered consensus rather than the polarisation which characterised both the years 1939–45 and the subsequent Cold War. A message of hope for the future, combined with a political platform based on traditional religious moral values, played especially well with the female electorate which, in the case of France at least, was voting for the first time. During the 1949 elections in West Germany, 52 per cent of all women voted for the CDU as opposed to 37 per cent of men.

It was a message that additionally appealed to the Vatican which urged Catholics to vote Christian Democrat as a safeguard against the rise of communism, viewed as the principal danger in the late 1940s. Bishops echoed the papal endorsement but, unlike in pre-war years, they were less inclined, as well as less able, to intervene in the detailed running and policy-making of the parties, thus enabling these to develop a life and momentum of their own. In certain instances, notably France where the hierarchy was devalued because of its wartime record, the bishops were exceedingly wary of putting their heads above the political parapets. While they were prepared to exert their authority within their own domain, for instance colluding with the Vatican in the suppression of the worker-priests and the silencing of such theologians as Yves Congar, they were less keen to meddle with the MRP. This was perhaps a wise move. Alongside the communists, the MRP was the most forthright critic of the prelacy, demanding in 1945 the removal of several prominent clerics, including the Archbishop of Bordeaux, for having 'collaborated'. Free of episcopal fetters, the Christian Democrat parties of the late 1940s were not truly 'confessional' in nature. While standing on the same moral ground as their pre-war antecedents, they wholeheartedly embraced the tenets of liberal democracy, happily accepted the strictures of pluralist politics, retained a marked independence of the institutional Church, and developed wide-ranging policy statements which went beyond religious concerns.

Because of their adoption of broad attitudes as opposed to the advocacy

of specific policies, it is not always easy to discern what the Christian Democrats actually stood for. The national context is a further complication since
all espoused particular objectives which had regard to local circumstances.
For example, in Belgium the PSC/CVP was much agitated by what position
it should adopt towards the return of King Leopold whose wartime record
was not without blemish. In Germany, the CDU was primarily concerned
with the task of national reconstruction, in particular through the advocacy
of a social market. These differences notwithstanding, it is still possible to
offer some broad definition of post-war Christian Democracy. As in the pre-
1939 period, it was part of that elusive quest for a third way in politics which
avoided the pitfalls of capitalist individualism on the one hand and socialist
collectivism on the other although, as in the 1930s, there is little doubt which
of these twin evils Christian Democrats considered the greater. Perhaps
the best summary of post-1945 Christian Democracy is that provided by
R. E. M. Irving.[13] First, he writes, it was devoted to the promotion of Christian
values, especially in relation to individual rights. Second, there was no doubting
its commitment to the principle of democracy, something which had not
necessarily been clearcut in the case of pre-war confessional parties. And,
finally, it was dedicated to 'integration in the dual sense of a commitment to
class reconciliation through the concept of the broadbased *Volkspartei* and to
transnational reconciliation, manifested especially through the strong Christian
Democratic commitment to European integration'.[14] Vague though such concepts sound, they none the less ran through the party programmes of the
1950s and 1960s, providing a series of unifying themes in an otherwise
fragmented political discourse. European integration, an espousal of welfarism,
support for capitalism, a rejection of extremes, a moderate conservatism –
these became the characteristics of nearly all Christian Democratic parties. In
this way, they performed an important role in reconciling Catholics with liberal
democracy and integrating them into the political mainstream.

Irving has similarly outlined the reasons for the reversal of Christian
Democratic fortunes from the early 1970s onwards, reasons which were
inextricably bound up with their initial success. First, the fear of communism,
while still real, was no longer all-pervasive. Although the Korean War, the
crushing of the Hungarian uprising of 1956, the building of the Berlin Wall,
the Cuban missile crisis and revelations about Stalinist atrocities were vivid
reminders of communist aggression, the Cold War brought a stability to
international relations, and people simply adjusted to this. With the tarnishing
of the far left, socialist parties made themselves more acceptable to the
electorate by abandoning unreconstructed Marxism, embracing the social
market and generally moving to occupy the centre ground. It was factors such
as these which undermined CDU support in Germany and contributed to the
revival of SPD fortunes. As Irving continues, a secularisation of Western
culture in the 1960s further chipped away at the support of Christian
Democracy, for the Church found that it could no longer influence the
electorate in the manner of the past. When, in 1972, the hierarchy in Germany
attempted to mobilise votes to oppose abortion, it was widely ignored; two

years later, Italian voters went against the advice of their bishops who had resolutely opposed new legislation on divorce. In these circumstances, where a growing number of people believed that moral matters in particular were a matter for individual conscience, the association of Christian Democrat parties with the Church could prove a handicap. Despite their very best efforts, Christian Democratic parties were never entirely successful in shaking off their confessional appearance. This image played awkwardly with an electorate that was undergoing profound changes other than secularisation. Increasingly youthful, wealthy, urban-based and liberal in its moral views, the electorate was often frustrated with conventional parties, and looked towards new forms of political and cultural discourse. Once the parties of the future, by the 1970s the Christian Democratic parties were perceived as the parties of the establishment and of the past, rooted in their bourgeois and peasant strongholds. It has not helped that in recent years Christian Democrat parties in Italy and Germany especially have become enmeshed in corruption. Commentators frequently cite the example of the Victor Emmanuel Hospital of Catania, a town in Sicily, which has not only provided 'jobs for the boys' but also a ready core of voters in the shape of the patients whose numbers were swelled at elections. Nor has it helped that the Second Vatican Council unintentionally weakened Christian Democracy by enfeebling many of the institutions which had hitherto given support to Catholics, including trade unions, working men's associations and Catholic Action.

Whereas in Western Europe Christian Democracy has struggled of late, the collapse of communism in the East gave it a new lease of life. It has done especially well in the Czech Republic; and it is also striking that nearly 75 per cent of former East Germans initially cast their vote for the CDU. The depth of support may perhaps best be explained by the fact that Christian Democrats had been closely associated with opposition to communist dictatorships while maintaining their independence of the Church, thus avoiding the damaging label of confessionalism. In this regard, it is significant that in the Catholic stronghold of Poland, no Christian Democratic party of note has emerged, partially because the Church hierarchy had maintained relatively amicable relations with the communist regime, restraining the more radical instincts of Solidarity, and has not yet fully accepted liberal democracy, preferring instead to trust its own organisations. There are strong parallels here with Spain's adjustment to liberalism. Here, too, the hierarchy's collusion with dictatorship initially thwarted Christian Democratic initiatives.

Whatever the fortunes of individual Christian Democrat parties, and whatever the future may hold for them – and they do seem to have one – there is no denying that the post-war period has witnessed a seachange in the nature of Catholic political action. Gone are the days when Catholic parties were essentially confessional, with a mission to defend clerical interests, tied to the apron strings of the prelacy, and with a patronising sense of their own moral rectitude and obligations to the popular classes. Two other fundamental changes are also apparent. First, as Martin Conway has emphasised, the Catholic laity no longer perceive any necessary or natural link between their faith and loyalty to a particular political party.[15] This has happened partly because of the emergence of new issues to do with ethnicity, ecology, the Third World and nuclear power, for instance, which are of concern to Catholics (and Christians more generally) because of their strong 'ethical' content, but which have not been appropriated by any particular party and are not even tied to the political left or right. Second, the Church as an institution has largely withdrawn from direct involvement in party politics. While this may have enabled it to devote more time and energy to spiritual and social issues, it has certainly not spelled the end of its political role, rather it has merely developed other mechanisms for exerting influence, usually over moral issues such as contraception, divorce, abortion, pornography, genetics and sexually transmitted diseases. This has involved an extension of the traditional role of the pulpit. If the parish clergy rarely use Sunday homilies to instruct their flock on which way to vote, they are none the less accustomed to mobilising them as part of wider programmes: signing petitions, letter writing, subsidising national campaigns and pressure groups.

Britain and Ireland

It remains to consider the way in which Catholics in the British Isles responded to such changes. The Irish Free State, which became a republic by virtue of the Republic of Ireland Act of 1949, has often been perceived as standing outside mainstream European trends. In that an overwhelming majority of the population were Catholic and in that the Church exerted a profound influence on all aspects of life, it apparently had most in common with the situation in the Iberian peninsula. Such a view does less than justice to the situation. While none of the three major political parties, Fianna Fáil, Fine Gael and Labour, styled itself Christian Democrat, all shared a very similar social and political outlook with their continental counterparts, and within the European Parliament the Irish delegates naturally gravitated to the same benches as the Christian Democrats.

The lack of a specific Christian Democrat party is not surprising. As we have noted earlier, the fact that politics in Southern Ireland were suffused with religion, the overwhelming numerical dominance of Catholics in the population and the benign attitude of the state towards Catholicism largely removed the need for one. Moreover, Éamon de Valera's skill in seeing off the challenge from the extremes of both left and right positioned the three main parties in the centre. This is not to say that frustrated elements from among the faithful did not seek to organise themselves within specifically confessional parties. The most important of these was Maria Duce (Under Mary's Leadership), the brainchild of Father Denis Fahey in 1954, which sought 'to vindicate the Social Rights of Christ the King'. Corporatist and integralist in outlook, the movement aimed at the *de facto* establishment of a confessional state. Yet it made little headway. With the exception of Archbishop John McQuaid, the Irish episcopacy, as in the 1930s, was wary of its extremist stance, and did nothing to encourage it. Nor did the fact that the movement had the word '*Duce*' in its title help its cause. Largely confined to Dublin, and with its supporters drawn from a restricted elite of intellectuals, Maria Duce busied itself with picketing theatres and cinemas and denouncing communist subversion. Its membership declined in the 1950s, the mantle of integralist Irish Catholicism passing to other fringe groups such as the Legion of Mary and Muintir na Tíre, which campaigned on moral issues and directed their fire against consensual politics epitomised by the former Taoiseach (Premier) Garret Fitzgerald and President, Mary Robinson.

If this marginalisation of confessional groups and the willingness of Catholics to adopt the centrist political parties as vehicles for the expression of their views is typical of European politics as a whole, so too is the indirect role played by the Church. There was no desire to reopen a debate on Article 44 of the constitution which acknowledged the special role of the Roman Church as 'guardian of the Faith professed by the great majority of [the state's] citizens', and the hierarchy has thus been content to intervene on specific issues, rather than push for the establishment of a confessional state. Among the most significant of these was the clash over the Mother and Child Bill of April 1951 which aimed to provide free post-natal care to mothers and children up to the age of sixteen, a proposal which the Church opposed on the grounds that it undercut parents' right to care for their own children and would leave the young open to non-Catholic teaching about sex. In a remarkable display of Church influence, ecclesiastical pressure forced the sacking of Noel Browne, the Minister of Health who was piloting the bill, after he was abandoned by his colleagues in the coalition cabinet. A second clash came shortly afterwards in 1954 over secondary education. Yet, on the whole, Church–state relations have been harmonious, even though in the period after the Second Vatican Council the Church has found its influence curbed by an increasing secularisation, again something common to the rest of Europe.

Across the border in Northern Ireland, religious divisions proved more fractious than anywhere in Europe outside the Balkans, where ethnicity further embittered religious differences. Here, Catholics had long laboured under a range of disabilities: the Ulster Unionists dominated the parliament at Stormont; the rigging of constituency boundaries, together with suffrage restrictions, nullified the Catholic vote; work opportunities were frequently denied Catholics who also came off second best in the distribution of council houses and welfare benefits; the Royal Ulster Constabulary, if not formally organised along sectarian lines, was nevertheless overwhelmingly Protestant in membership; and anti-Catholic sentiment abounded, feeding off the mythology of an all-powerful Church in the South. The creation of an independent Republic of Ireland in 1949, the weight of this discrimination and the rise of civil rights movements in both the USA and mainland Europe subsequently gave rise to Catholic protest in the 1960s. This was articulated initially through the Campaign for Social Justice, created at Dungannon in 1964, which eventuated in the establishment of the Northern Ireland Civil Rights Association (NICRA) in 1967. Catholic demands for equality were further expressed by the Republican Labour and Nationalist parties, together with the IRA which split in 1971 into the Officials and Provisionals, the latter espousing violence in pursuit of their aims.

By this stage, politics in Northern Ireland had already taken to the streets, despite the implementation of some measures by Premier O'Neill designed to head off Catholic agitation. In 1969, the British government was forced to send in troops who were initially welcomed by Catholics as protectors against Unionist extremism, a sentiment that did not last for long. In 1970, the Home Secretary, Reginald Maudling, introduced internment without trial which merely exacerbated the situation: the Catholic population was alienated; relations between London and Dublin, which was deeply concerned with the fate of co-religionaries in the north, deteriorated; and moderate bipartisanship evaporated. With hindsight, there was almost an inevitability about events on 30 January 1972 when a civil rights march in the Catholic Bogside area of Londonderry resulted in the deaths of thirteen civilians. 'Bloody Sunday', as it became known, presaged a long period of depressing violence – in that year alone, there were 467 violent deaths in Ulster with more than 10,000 shootings – and political disintegration on the part of both Catholics and Protestants. Despite the efforts of clergy on all sides to halt the bloodshed, it has only recently been arrested, albeit partially, by the 1985 Anglo-Irish Agreement between premiers Margaret Thatcher and Charles Haughey and, more recently, by the Good Friday Agreement of 1998 signed by Tony Blair and Bertie Ahern. The latter arrangement has led to some integration of former extremists into the political mainstream, although the future still remains uncertain. Northern Ireland's recent history has thus been one of religious bigotry and concomitant social and political exclusion, played out in the wider context of a struggle for national independence, with the admixture of violence contributing still further to a legacy of mistrust and misunderstanding.

If religious antagonism deepened in Northern Ireland, in mainland Britain it has dwindled, at least in respect to Catholics. Admittedly, some anachronistic legislative restrictions still remain in force. As *The Spectator* magazine observed in 1980, it is curious that the monarch can wed a Jew, Hindu, Muslim, atheist or devil-worshipper but not a Roman Catholic, a state of affairs that Cardinal Cormac Murphy-O'Connor, the Archbishop of Westminster, wishes to have changed.[16] Yet Catholics now possess equal treatment, and have been quick to mobilise against any potential discrimination, successfully lobbying in the 1950s to raise the state grant, allocated by the 1944 Education Act, for the building of new schools from 50 to 75 per cent. Prominent in this campaign were the Catholic Parents' and Electors' Associations. These remained firmly under the tutelage of the Church hierarchy which was generally suspicious of any autonomous lay movements which might revive religious bigotry, generally preferring to deal directly with government or go through pliable and conservative bodies, most notably the Catholic Union of Great Britain. Additionally, Catholics could continue to count on the mainstream political parties which have maintained a non-sectarian position. Hesitantly, other elements of the establishment, most notably the Church of England, have also moved to an integrationist position, the Archbishop of Canterbury welcoming John Paul II to Britain in 1982, the first ever visit of a reigning Pope to England. Joint services were suggested by the Anglicans but received with embarrassment by the Catholics. Moreover, Catholics had proven their loyalty in the Second World War, resisting the fascist temptation, and the British state saw no reason to antagonise them, especially as they constituted such a powerful community. Pockets of anti-Catholic sentiment still persist – there were protests when the mass was televised for the first time in 1954 – yet these are largely confined to remote areas, notably in the northern peripheries of Britain, such as Skye and the Western Isles where fringe groups such as the militantly Protestant Scottish Reformation Society still operate. Indeed, British Catholicism, in common with other denominations, has been challenged by secular attitudes rather than specifically anti-Catholic ones.

Against this background, the number of Catholics continued to grow, fuelled above all by Irish immigration – a quarter of a million people arrived in Britain in the war years, a further 100,000 between 1945 and 1950 – as well as by immigrants from Eastern Europe. To these must be added a substantial body of converts, though their number is not easy to quantify. The result was that, according to *Social Trends*, Church membership stood at 2,530,000 in 1975, outstripping that of the Church of England. Recently, as with all Christian churches, it has undergone decline, although it is worth noting that even in the 1950s less than 10 per cent of the overall population were regular in their Sunday observance.

The influx of immigrants from overseas and converts who joined the so-called 'old Catholics', heirs to the recusant tradition, has produced a 'hybrid' Catholic community in Britain, as Tom Buchanan terms it, which permits no easy social or political categorisation, but one which has still integrated well.[17] This historical evolution has ensured that Catholics have not sought separate political representation, and their many organisations have continued to fragment. As a result, they have largely shed those characteristics of a 'fortress faith' which continued to set them apart from their fellow citizens right down to the 1960s, a process assisted by the liberalising tendencies of the Second Vatican Council. As elsewhere in Europe, the Catholic Church has often intervened in matters of morality, and Basil Hume was arguably the first Archbishop of Westminster to have real status on the national stage, yet both laity and clergy have preferred to expend their energies on charitable work, especially in the Third World.

The position of the Church within Britain, always excepting Northern Ireland, has come to resemble that of Europe more generally, although this is not to deny the significant differences that continue to exist within and between individual states. Church and state are no longer locked in conflict, for reasons particular to the post-war period. As we have seen, the state is now unquestionably supreme in its administrative apparatus. Thanks to the triumph of liberal democracy in Western Europe, religion is regarded as a matter of private conscience. Secularisation and simple indifference have further taken the sting out of religious debate. All these are things which

Christian Democrats have more or less come to terms with, even if individual Catholics might hanker after authoritarian solutions, and elements within the clergy are unsettled by living in a pluralistic environment. What is undeniable is that the Church itself encouraged an acceptance of pluralism through the Second Vatican Council which had reverberations, not all of which had been anticipated, and not all of which have faded away.

The Second Vatican Council

In 1923, Pius XI, wishing to draw a line under the savage upheavals of the First World War and to reassert the spiritual values of mankind, had toyed with the idea of a great council. When he asked to see the archives of the 1870 assembly, the request was not easily met until the papers were found in an understairs cupboard, stuffed into cardboard boxes. After the Second World War, as Western Europe gravitated towards a religious pluralism, Pius XII also gave thought to the possibility of a council to conclude the work initially undertaken at the assembly in 1870 which had never been officially closed. Such an initiative would enable the Pope to leave his indelible stamp on the Church. This would be an institution which left no doors open for ecumenicalism, one which denounced communism in uncompromising terms, and one which exalted the cult of Mary. It was not to be. In the 1950s, Pius XII's health, something which had always been a preoccupation for the hypochondriac Pope, took a genuine turn for the worse. This deterioration was not reversed by frequent resort to quack nostrums, one of which – the use of chromic acid to cure a weakening of the gums, but more appropriately used in the tanning industry – left him with incurable hiccups. Isolated from Vatican officials, but surrounded by his carers, most infamously Sister Pasqualina and Dr Galeazzi-Lisi, who brought in the Swiss practitioner Paul Niehans to inject cells from monkey and lamb foetuses, he surrounded himself with books, believing that he had become the oracle on any given subject, even intending to give a lecture to boiler-workers. His death in October 1958 was a release for an increasingly tortured soul.

The advent of a new pope guaranteed the calling of the council which Pacelli had longed for, yet this proved to be a very different occasion to that envisaged by Pius and the conservatives who dominated the Vatican's corridors of power. Not having assembled for a considerable period of time, the grey-templed cardinals, most of whom were in their seventies and eighties, were in disagreement as to whom to elevate, and settled, in the best traditions of Vatican elections, on the rotund Angelo Giuseppe Roncalli, the seventy-six-year-old Patriarch of Venice, who was thought to have little time to live, so enabling them to think more about a successor. On adopting the title John XXIII, he joked that more popes had taken the name 'John' than any other name, perhaps an acknowledgement of his short life-expectancy. In truth, he took the name because it was that of his father. (He was nicknamed 'Johnny Walker' as a result of his nocturnal visits to Rome's poorer areas.) There had been a John XXIII before, from 1410 to 1415 at the time of the Great Schism, but his legal status had been disputed, just as today there are several claimants to the title of heavyweight champion of the world. Heavyweight John certainly was, registering around 16 stone on the scales; he struggled to fit into his new robes, quipping that 'everyone wants me to be Pope except the tailors'.[18] He was heavyweight too in his personality which reflected his upbringing. Of humble origins, he had pursued a diplomat's career, serving in Bulgaria, Turkey, Greece and, most notably, in France where, in 1945, he had to withstand the bludgeoning of General de Gaulle who was insistent on the removal of some thirty-three high-ranking clerics for their collaboration with both the Germans and with Pétain. In this capacity as envoy, he displayed those human qualities which marked his pontificate: warmth, generosity, forgiveness, tolerance and human understanding. Not since Pius IX had there been such a genial occupant of the papal throne, and it is scarcely surprising that his hero and the subject of his doctoral thesis was the sixteenth-century Archbishop of Milan, Carlo Borromeo, who was likewise known for his affability and popularity. Unlike Pius XII, John did not live in ascetic isolation, and his good humour was always close at hand. When asked how many people worked at the Vatican, he quipped 'about half of them'. This engaging demeanour could not hide the fact, however, that doctrinally he was a cautious man, and had willingly obeyed the commands of Pius XII, most notably bringing about the end of the worker-priest movement in France. What lifted him above an otiose and knee-jerk conservatism was his desire that the Church should engage more with the world and not pretend that things it disliked were simply not happening. As early as 1957, he had used the expression *aggiornamento* at a synod in Venice, a confusing term in Italian which can mean both to update and to delay. It rapidly became apparent that John deployed it in the former sense, to express his wish that the Church, while remaining true to its core principles, should adapt so as to bring about inner renewal and a full engagement with the world.

Given this spirit of *aggiornamento*, it was John who pressed ahead with the idea of a council, overcoming a rearguard action on the part of conservatives who sought initially to block its summoning and hijack the agenda. It is said that Spanish bishops, with the exception of Mgr Lacoma, the auxiliary Bishop of Tarragona, wanted it to be a continuation of Vatican I. The most intransigent conservatives were to be found in the Curia, however. Recognising his own limitations in the face of this entrenched opposition, John brought in Cardinal Montini, whose chief merits, apart from his sympathy with *aggiornamento*, were his deep knowledge of Vatican politics and ability to outmanoeuvre the wreckers. John was also fortunate in that he could call upon the goodwill of Catholic intellectuals who had long sought such a forum in order to bring doctrine into line with the modern world. The years between 1959, when the idea of a council was first announced, and 1962, when it finally assembled, were thus awash with Catholic literature debating its purpose: the Bishop of Paderborn's *Ecumenical Council of the Church* cogently articulated the case for greater lay participation and an adaptation of the Christian message to make it relevant for the times; Hans Küng's *Council, Reform and Renewal* was an impassioned plea for the urgency of reform (his 1974 publication *On Being a Christian* remains one of the classic reworkings of the Christian doctrines); Cardinal Alfrink of Utrecht called for greater local autonomy within the Church; while other significant contributions were made by Yves Congar and the immensely influential Jesuit Karl Rahner, both forced into silence during the pontificate of Pius XII. Moreover, the concerns of these theologians and prelates were widely shared by ordinary Catholics who experienced the religious pluralism and engagement with politics which were a *de facto* reality in the post-war period, even if they were unable to express their longings in the language of the theological college. There was, then, a groundswell of opinion for change within the Catholic world which naturally responded to Pope John's call for *aggiornamento*.

The Council was the twenty-first and the largest and most representative in Church history. Among the 2,540 delegates entitled to vote there were men from all parts of the world: Europe's contingent of 1,041 constituted the largest single bloc, but they did not enjoy the predominance of earlier occasions and could easily be outvoted by some combination of the 956 bishops from America, the 279 from Africa and the 300 or so from Asia; while the traditionally powerful Italian grouping made up less than 20 per cent of the delegates. In practice, the delegates quickly polarised along 'progressive' and 'traditionalist' lines, the former principally comprising bishops from North America, Western and central Europe and Africa, outnumbering the conservatives who were centred upon the Italian delegates. 'Universality' was further guaranteed by the presence of laymen and representatives from other faiths as observers. While the Orthodox and Eastern Rite Churches, no doubt recalling the high-handed manner in which they had been treated in 1870, were wary of attending, Protestant denominations had fewer scruples. The Church of England, for instance, sent three emissaries while the Lutheran Reformed World Union, the Evangelical Church of Germany and the Ecumenical Assembly of Geneva all dispatched high-profile individuals to watch over events. Admittedly these non-Catholics could not vote but their very presence, and amended procedures, ensured that their views were factored in. Such cooperation was welcome given the fact that the Council became a source of attraction for much of the world's media: some 1,000 members of press, radio and TV corps reported on proceedings. Far less conspicuous at the Council were women. As Thomas Rausch reminds us, it was only when Cardinal Suenens remarked on their absence that a token twenty-two were eventually added as 'auditors', hardly sufficient given the range and significance of gender issues that were to be addressed.[19] Apparently, one nun was advised to attend only sessions relevant to women, something she courageously refused to do.

When, on 11 October 1962, the Pope was led through the ornate bronze doors into St Peter's, he quickly set the accommodating tone for the opening session by stepping down off the *sedia gestatoria* and walking through the assembled throng of representatives, a gesture typical of a man who favoured a Renaissance-style hat to the traditional white skullcap of his immediate predecessors, irritated that this flimsy piece of cloth could not safely be fastened to his thinning pate. Communication with the outside world, the need to build bridges and not to erect barriers, the desire to make the faith relevant to the laity – these emerged as the themes of his opening address, *Gaudet mater ecclesiae*. In this, he elaborated on his earlier declarations which had notably attempted to bring about an improvement in relations with communist Russia. In truth, John XXIII had few specific ideas about what the Council should do and was painfully aware he might not live to see its conclusion; he would, in fact, die the following year. Yet this early commitment to *aggiornamento* outfoxed conservative prelates who, in the preparatory commissions, had deliberately drawn up copious documentation designed to enshrine the spirit of the *Syllabus of Errors* and forestall any acceptance of modernism. During the ensuing sessions, four in total, the last finishing on 8 December 1965, the whole apparatus of the modern Church came under the spotlight. It was often a painful process. Traditionalists might have been outwitted, yet they were determined to have their two-penny worth.

Conservatives were especially troubled by the mood of the Council which seemed to differ profoundly from that of earlier assemblies. As Louis de Vaucelles has noted, these meetings had their own characteristics, which tell us much about the epochs in which they were held.[20] The fifteenth-century councils, culminating in that held at Basle in 1431–39, had to do with the reordering of the Catholic world, dealing not just with heresy but the papacy and the internal governance of the Church. Trent (1545–63) was an explicit response to the Reformation, establishing markers between Catholics and Protestants. Both Basle and Trent thus dealt with interpretations of the faith within what remained a Christian world. On the other hand, Vatican I in 1870 was an exercise in trench-digging, an attempt to establish the Church as a fortress against an unregenerate and irreligious outside world. Vatican II was conceived less as an event than as the initiation of a process which would harmonise the Church and the political and social environment. It was, in the words of Karl Rahner, 'the beginning of the beginning'.[21] Whether the Council has fulfilled this aspiration is a matter to which we will return.

Broadly speaking, it is possible to distinguish two categories of statement emanating from the Council: the first were decrees tackling particular issues; the second were the central documents, *Lumen gentium* and *Gaudium et spes*, which dealt with broader themes relating to the organisation of the Church itself.[22] Among the former, the most controversial was that approving the use of a non-Latin liturgy, thus breaking with a centuries-old tradition which had been endorsed at Trent. It was a move bitterly resisted by conservatives who argued that Latin, despite having fallen out of common usage, still bound people of different nations together; additionally, they fretted that the vernacular would take away the mystique of the mass. The debates further revealed a gulf not just between traditionalist and progressives, but a generational one between the aged and the young and a geographical divide between the old and the new worlds. Bishops from the so-called mission lands pressed hard for a radical revision. Duschak from the Philippines argued that the mass should be stripped of all its historical Western-European accretions and that it should be available on an inter-faith basis so that it became truly a *missa orbis*. This was asking too much and, in the event, the Council approved the adaptation of the Divine Office for local circumstances, dropped the celebration of numerous saints' days so as to make the liturgical cycle more Christocentric, and established Easter as a set date in the calendar. Inter-faith relations were not jettisoned altogether, however, and the Decree on Ecumenism strove for unity among all Christian believers. It was merely a pity that the paperwork drawn up by the preparatory commissions was couched in language that was bound to offend those Eastern Rite and Orthodox representatives who now felt that their earlier reservations about attending had been justified.

Along similar lines, the Decree on Revelation indicated that tradition was to be important in the interpretation of the Bible, but could not in itself be regarded as another source of revelation, thus moving some way to healing the breach opened with Protestants who had stressed the exclusive significance of the scriptures. Here, it is worth recalling that at Trent the teachings of the early Fathers and the Church had been placed on a par with the Bible. In another effort to build ecumenical bridges, the Decree on Other Religions rejected the notion on which traditional Catholic anti-Semitism had been premised, that the Jews were deicides deserving of ongoing punishment; and the liturgy of the paschal mass itself was purged of its offensive references to the 'perfidious Jews'. This caused some unease on the part of bishops from Arab states who feared such statements might be seen as support for the state of Israel. Significantly, however, the Church did not confront the ambivalent role it had played in the Holocaust, even though Rolf Hochhuth's play *The Representative* had first been staged in 1963. The other decree of particular note, that on Religious Liberty, accepting that everyone possessed the prerogative to practise their chosen faith, was an advance on the mere toleration which Catholics had hitherto extended to other denominations, and significantly included non-Christian ones. This had an especial appeal to Catholics in the Eastern bloc, who struggled under a welter of official and unofficial restrictions, but also signalled the fact that the Church accepted the laity could engage wholeheartedly in democratic politics.

The spirit of the above decrees was reflected in the longest of the texts, *Gaudium et spes* ('Joy and Hope') of 1965, which aimed to establish 'a fundamental new definition of the relation of the Church to the world'. This again signalled a step forward in that it urged Catholicism to take stock of social, economic and political change, to assert the continuing validity of its principles while at the same time attuning these to the needs and tempers of the contemporary epoch; and it shied away from a rejection of the modern world as wholly unregenerate and the Church as the sole arbiter of truth. This was admirable, and well merited the acclaim with which it was greeted among Catholics. The problem was that it was too abstract and glibly optimistic about the degree to which the world would change in conformity to the Church, and underestimated the extent to which secular values might seep into religious life. Article 58 trumpeted the value of all human cultures, always excepting communism which had been excommunicated in 1949, but had little explicit guidance on how these might be incorporated, and there was no proper comprehension of the nature and basis of modern atheistic philosophy. It was particularly unfortunate that key issues which would come to dominate lay–clerical relations in the ensuing decades, most notably contraception and clerical celibacy, as well as the Church's attitudes towards conflict, were ignored or not properly addressed. While having many laudable ideas about the reconciling of differences among states, Pope John's successor, Paul VI, came out against contraception, and at the last moment prohibited debate on celibacy (see below).

Lumen gentium ('Light of the World'), the product of the third session in 1964, was possibly the landmark declaration to emanate from the Council, tackling as it did the fundamental issue of the source and location of authority within the Church, something which had been critical in the formation of ecclesiastical structures going right back to early Christianity. This document effectively defined the Church as 'the people of God', and implicitly positioned sovereignty in the whole body of believers. As a result, the laity could expect to play a much more active role at all levels of the Church's organisation; the bishops would be co-equals with the pontiff; and there would be a concomitant reduction in papal power. In its potential ramifications, *Lumen gentium* was as far-reaching as the Declaration of the Rights of Man and the Citizen of 1789 which identified the people, not the monarch, as the source of sovereignty, and in large measure the document was intended to bring the Church up-to-date with the world that emerged out of the 1790s: the growth of Ultra-montanism had been a potent indicator of how reluctant Rome was to surrender any of its temporal and spiritual powers. The defect was that *Lumen gentium*, like *Gaudium et spes*, was aspirational in character and failed to set out any precise mechanisms whereby its vision for the future might be implemented. Significantly, it entailed no revision of the 1917 edition of Canon Law which had sapped the vitality and independence of the bishops, synods and laity. Nor was there any additional reform of the Curia which might also have curbed the centralising instincts of the Vatican. There was thus no mechanism to ensure that succeeding popes honoured the spirit of *Lumen gentium*.

Assessing the overall radicalism of the Second Vatican Council is, then, a highly problematic business, and like Trent it may well be that the full effects will not manifest themselves until the passage of many decades. Judged in the social and cultural context of the 1960s, a decade when so many conventions were torn up and wholly rewritten, the Council might have appeared as a regressive affair, obsessed with matters that had little to do with everyday life, despite John XXIII's preoccupation with relevance. This, after all, was a time of pervasive secularism and growing individual liberties, at least within the Western world, and it is not difficult to believe that several of the debates, for instance that on the College of Bishops' right of co-rule, conducted in Latin and arcane legalistic language, must have seemed anachronistic. Judged by the standards of the Church itself, however, it was a truly epoch-making event, the most comprehensive and far-reaching occasion since Trent. This was something recognised by progressive and conservative Catholics alike, the former happy that their voices were at last being heard, the latter fearful that forces unleashed by the Enlightenment would now destroy the very fabric they held so dear. Yet both sides were left unsatisfied. Intransigents were unhappy about the breaches that had been made in the Church's defences built up since the Reformation. The use of the vernacular, the spirit of ecumenicalism, the apparent dilution of hierarchical structures, the relativism engendered by the recognition of other faiths were most unwelcome. If the progressives rejoiced at the thaw in the glacial hold which had frozen over so much of religious life, they were disappointed that the issues of contraception, priestly celibacy, the amelioration of poverty and the continuing Eurocentric concerns of the Church had not been properly explored. As to the rank-and-file clergy and laity, as Eamon Duffy remarks, the majority appear to have looked on the Second Vatican Council as a highly confusing affair, giving rise to all manner of novel directives which they were enjoined to follow.[23] John O'Malley notes: 'Never before had so many and such sudden changes been legislated ... never before had such a radical adjustment of viewpoint been expected of [the laity].'[24]

The implementation of these decisions was always going to be a delicate and difficult matter, especially given the cumbersome hierarchy of the Church and its naturally conservative instincts which seemed increasingly at odds with a society undergoing rapid social and cultural change. This would have been true regardless of the personality of the Pope himself. It is likely that even John XXIII would have run into opposition over the implementation of its decisions. Yet, in view of his warm and compassionate nature, it is probable that he would have at least elicited sympathy and support among both clergy and laity. With good reason he is remembered as the most loved Pope in recent history, and not just among Catholics, and has recently been made a saint. His successor, Giovanni Battista Montini, elected as Paul VI on 21 June 1963, was in many senses far more sophisticated than his peasant-born predecessor, having spent much of his life in the Secretariat of State where he learned all the tricks of Vatican policy, yet he lacked a popular touch, and was not inspired with any sort of radicalism. On coming to power, one of his first intentions was to bring the Council to a close as soon as possible and to thwart any overly liberal measures, such as the debate over clerical celibacy to which he quickly put a stop. This caution, coupled with procrastination, was to mark his reign. His hope, to please everyone and offend no one, was always an impossible ambition, resulting in a strange balancing act in which progressive measures were countered by conservative ones.

In one area at least Paul VI seemed to capture the spirit of the Second Vatican Council. This was in his attempts to reach out to other faiths, something facilitated in a practical sense by his willingness to board international airlines and to travel the world, the first Pope to do so. He journeyed as a pilgrim to Israel and to Fatima in Portugal; he addressed the United Nations in 1965, delivering a powerful message which caught the *Zeitgeist* of the Vietnam anti-war movement, proclaiming 'no more war, war never again'; he donated his episcopal ring to the Anglican Archbishop of Canterbury, Michael

Ramsay, who visited Rome the following year; and he even kissed the foot of the emissary of the Patriarch of Constantinople, thus diluting some of the centuries-old animosity that had existed between East and West. Not for nothing was he called the 'pilgrim Pope'. Most famously, he attempted to enter some kind of dialogue with communist regimes in order to improve the conditions of Christians in the Eastern bloc. This was not a new policy. John XXIII had already dispensed with the Cold War rhetoric of Pius XII, developing warm relations with Khrushchev, securing the release of the Eastern Rite dissident Slipyj, and denouncing the dangers of nuclear war in *Pacem in terris*. Paul VI went further. Although it was US pressure which forced the Hungarian Mindszenty to leave its embassy in Budapest, an act which the prelate deeply resented, Paul connived at this so as to open a way to more fruitful relations with the East, something he further attempted by declaring Mindszenty's see at Esztergom vacant in 1973. As part of further attempts to cultivate a policy of *Ostpolitik*, in 1968 the Vatican arbitrated as a peace-broker in negotiations between the USA and North Vietnam, talks held at Paris, and in 1972 the Holy See attended the Helsinki peace conference as a fully-fledged participant, the first occasion since the Congress of Vienna that Rome had enjoyed such international recognition. Paul's representative, Cardinal Casaroli, subsequently built on this *démarche* by travelling to Moscow and Cuba, and intervening in the escalating violence in Northern Ireland.

Complementing these measures were attempts to move the Church forward by continuing the process of *aggiornamento*, while at the same time ensuring that a balance was maintained between progressives and traditionalists. The Curia was reformed; the College of Cardinals was enlarged to include 138 members by 1976, drawn from all five continents, thus ending the Italian hegemony within elections; and the rules were amended to restrict the right of those over eighty years of age to partake in Curial business; a Synod of Bishops was established, a clear manifestation of the Pope's commitment to the principle of episcopal collegiality; and the 1967 encyclical *Populorum progressio* showed a heightened awareness of the dangers, both for individuals and for the developing world, of unrestrained capitalism, calling as it did upon the West to devote more of its resources to overseas aid. Unlike Pius XII, Paul VI had little hesitancy in speaking out over human rights issues, clearly exemplified in his forthright denunciation of genocide in Biafra. His emboldened attitude towards the Third World made him a hero among those who were articulating a liberation theology, although he himself was not keen to develop this.

The emphasis on the mass in the vernacular was further welcomed although it went down badly with traditionalists, most famously Archbishop Marcel Lefebvre, the former Bishop of Tulle in France and latterly Archbishop of Dakar in West Africa. The fact that this see had been a Pétainist stronghold throughout the war may help to explain why Lefebvre was so opposed to alterations in the liturgy, a reluctance to countenance change which stood in marked contrast to the attitude of other bishops from non-European sees. His disillusion went deeper than the question of language. He denounced wholesale the reforms of the Second Vatican Council which he likened to a 'new Protestantism'; he condemned Paul VI himself as a 'modernist'; and in 1974 founded his own seminary at Ecône in Switzerland to form a body of pastors in the traditional manner. He was provocative to the bitter end, despite excommunication in 1988, celebrating mass in Rome, founding a seminary in France and a chapel at Glasgow, together with a nunnery in Belgium, while associating himself with the Francoists in Spain and the Front National in France. In 1982, he openly speculated that the short-lived John Paul I had been murdered by liberals in the Vatican. He condemned John Paul II as an apostate following the Pope's visit to a synagogue, deplored the fact that in 1981 the new Archbishop of Paris was of Jewish origin, and made a series of increasingly outlandish statements both in public and in private. For instance, he declared of the post-1960s Catholicism, 'the Church authorities and the clergy are suffering from AIDS, that condition characterised by a lack of immunity to disease'.[25] His appeal, while it should not be overstated, still managed to tap into that substantial body of Catholics, especially in France, who hankered after the security of the old ways and whose politics were encapsulated in the anti-Semitic and anti-Islamic slogans of Jean Marie Le Pen. Yet, at his death in 1991, it was manifest that Lefebvre was a figure from the past rather than a sign for the future.

Other conservatives were far more sophisticated in their resistance to the Second Vatican Council. Represented in associations such as Una Voce, Opus Sacerdotale, Credo, Silenziosi della Chiesa, Familles de France and the Associations Familiales Catholiques, as well as the usual suspects in the shape of Opus Dei and members of the episcopacy such as Bishop Graber of Regensburg, they have argued that the decisions of the Council were primarily concerned with pastoral matters and, as such, possessed no dogmatic value and could therefore be rejected. Others have taken elements from the texts issued by the Council and have distorted their sense. They have thus managed to read into these documents a vindication of their pre-conciliar attitudes.

It was over sexual matters that the fissures within the Church would be most clearly revealed. The almost Jesuitical and profoundly pragmatic philosophy which underpinned *Gaudium et spes* had elevated the role of individual conscience as the key to determining matters of moral standing, giving hope to liberals that this spirit would prevail when the Church came to pronounce on contraception, as inevitably it would, given the wish to engage with the wider world. Both John and Paul were uneasy about the Council discussing this matter, and a commission comprising doctors, married couples, theologians and scientists was charged with reporting back. Paul was not pleased with its recommendations, which urged the Church to update its teaching so as to permit some limited form of artificial contraception among married couples who already had children. Having considered the findings, largely in isolation, he found that he could not take this particular step. He felt contraception would encourage marital infidelity and promiscuity, as well as defying the procreative function of marriage. Instead, *Humanae vitae* of July 1968 upheld conservative teaching. While acknowledging the importance of healthy sexual relations within the framework of a marriage, this document reaffirmed the Church's opposition to any form of physical or chemical means of contraception; only the rhythm method was approved. Naturally, abortion also remained a taboo.

Such attitudes went down badly among non-Catholic and secular commentators in the Western world. The influential magazine *New Scientist* published the shortest editorial in its history in August 1968 announcing, 'Bigotry, pedantry and fanaticism can kill, maim and agonise those upon whom they are visited just as surely as bombs, pogroms and the gas chamber. Pope Paul has now gently joined the company of tyrants, but the damage he has done may well outclass and outlast that of all earlier oppressors.'[26] Within the Catholic world itself, conservatives were reassured, liberals angered and many Catholic families nonplussed, although for some it became a source of sardonic humour, captured in the novels of David Lodge. The Jesuits mounted a challenge to the encyclical, as did prelates in the Third World, concerned above all with the potentially devastating demographic effects on poverty of Paul's teaching.

Paul VI burst into tears of rage at this challenge but refused to alter his position. Through *Humanae vitae* he had hoped to seal off a particular source of Catholic disquiet. He had only succeeded in making it worse, something he himself bitterly regretted. For the next ten years, he made no further pronouncements, retreating into a slough of despond, with the result that the impetus for further change was left floundering. In the words of Peter Hebblethwaite: 'He was entering a period of dark night, of depression, of deep agonising over his stewardship.'[27] In unconscious imitation of the Habsburg Emperor Joseph II, who had penned a particularly gloomy epitaph, Paul himself reflected: 'What is my state of mind? Am I Hamlet or Don Quixote? On the left? On the right? I don't feel I have been properly understood.' To his credit, he never allowed himself to become the Prince of Denmark, nor did he tilt at any windmills. If he was honest with himself, he was on the right, at least in Catholic politics, a man of conservative instincts who was unfortunate enough to live at a time when the Church as a whole was advancing slowly in its journey of *aggiornamento*.

To be fair, any pope would have been taxed to the limit during this period, and Paul was one of the few with the ability to bring the Council to a successful conclusion. From what can be surmised, his immediate successor John Paul I (26 August–28 September 1978) would also have struggled. Although of cheerful countenance, he lacked worldliness and was soon of another world, being found dead of a heart attack only a month into his job. Because there was no post-mortem, rumours quickly sprang up that he had been assassinated before he could expose corruption in Vatican finances, claims publicised in the 1984 book by David Yallop, *In God's Name*. The allegations were based on circumstantial evidence. As John Cornwell has argued, perhaps the real crime was the failure on the part of the Vatican to provide adequate medical attention during John Paul I's brief tenure of office and the Curia's subsequent inept handling of the matter.[28] This only contributed to the image of an institution under siege, and gave ammunition to the conspiracy theorists. If the Church was saved from inquisitive Italian prosecutors, its structures and beliefs would be more severely tested by the new secularisation of the late twentieth century.

The Challenge of a New Secularisation

The secularisation of the past forty years has often been interpreted as the continuation of a long-term trend, reaching back to the Enlightenment and which subsequently developed in a linear fashion. This was the pattern predicted by those pioneering sociologists who first theorised about the decline of religion, most notably Auguste Comte, Emile Durkheim and Max Weber. In unconscious agreement, nineteenth-century Catholic thinkers concurred that it had been the previous century which had witnessed the opening shots of what would become a sustained salvo against organised religion in general and Catholicism in particular. In point of fact, secularisation has not been an uninterrupted feature of the modern period, something recognised by religious sociologists writing in the 1930s, especially the Catholic authors Gabriel Le Bras and Canon Boulard. As we ourselves have seen, Catholicism has displayed not so much decline as remarkable resilience and adaptability in the face of extraordinary social, economic and political challenges, well illustrated by the rise of Lourdes as a centre of pilgrimage at a time when modern medicine, science and industrial progress augured a different future. Recent studies, focusing on the gender dichotomies within religion, have further signalled the importance of women in maintaining the practice of the faith, a two-way process involving the feminisation of piety and pietisation of femininity. Such reinvigorative mechanisms enabled Catholicism to weather what, in other spheres, proved to be major turning points, most obviously the experience of 'total war'. Clearly, this is not to suggest that nothing altered: the loss of papal temporal authority is one example among several. Nevertheless, the enduring nature of Catholicism highlights the most striking feature of the post-1945 world, namely the onset of a decline which appeared wholly downwards and irreversible. As a result, some analysts have spoken about the emergence of a post-Christian and post-Catholic world, at least in Western Europe after the 1960s. The paradox is that, outside Europe, religions of all types have flourished, in the Third World, in the pluralist USA and the Muslim sphere.

What changes in the post-1945 world, or more especially in the period from the 1960s, were significant for Catholic belief and practice? Perhaps the most dramatic shift has been the revolution in communications, with the evolution of television, radio, the explosion of print, digital technology, computers and the worldwide web, a revolution which dwarfs in its scope and consequences the printing developments of the late fifteenth and sixteenth centuries. One upshot has been to make Europe a smaller place, a trend further facilitated by the moves within the fifteen member-states of the European Union towards greater integration, something recently signalled by the introduction of the single currency, the euro. Accompanying these developments has been massive cultural change, evidenced in popular music, dress, leisure pursuits, tourism and sexual freedoms, a cultural upheaval propelled by the post-war baby boom, the growth in prosperity and the expansion of higher education. This has all too often served to undermine traditional hierarchies, institutions and established patterns of thought, which have been further challenged by the outgrowth of new forms of political action, spanning the spectrum from pressure groups on the environment, the women's movement, campaigns for homosexual equality and alterations to the economic structures which disadvantage both social groups and the Third World. Those most impatient at the rates of change have resorted to terrorism, recognising that their aims, whether for a united Ireland or a new society in the case of the Red Brigades, would not be fulfilled by the type of demonstrations that had been witnessed in 1968 or by working with liberal democrats who retained a faith in gradualism despite the onset of numerous problems. These difficulties have included the economic transition to a post-industrial world which has seen the rise of oligopolies and the proliferation of societal ills, among them unemployment, divorce, AIDS, drug abuse, pollution, urban degeneration and rural collapse.

In this context, the Church can at least take some comfort in the fact that Catholicism remains the most numerous faith in Europe, although its strength worldwide is now predominantly in the Third World. In 1900, around 77 per cent of Catholics were to be found in Europe and North America and 23 per cent elsewhere; in 1990, 70 per cent lived in the Third World and only 30 per cent in Europe and North America. Figures for 1998 suggest that 62.9 per cent of the population of the Americas, both North and South, was Catholic, 41.4 per cent of the population of Europe, 14.9 per cent of Africa, 27.5 per cent of Oceania and a mere 3 per cent of Asia.

Behind the overall picture, there were striking regional and generational variations, not least of all within Europe itself. According to the European Values Systems Study (EVSS) of 1981–82, which surveyed a large number of Western states, France presents some of the most telling of these. Among the post-1968 generation, a staggering 45 per cent indicated that they adhered to no religion, a percentage also matched in the Netherlands where the old Catholic structures which had once been all-embracing were giving way to a new society. At the other extreme, in those states such as Ireland and Italy where Catholicism was part of the national identity the overwhelming majority of all age groups, well over 90 per cent in the case of the latter and reaching 98 per cent in the case of the former, still professed allegiance to religion, most obviously Catholicism. The same pattern was uncovered in Spain: 99 per cent of the Spanish respondents to a survey by the Fundacioñ Santa María, conducted during the 1970s, declared their continuing allegiance to the Church of Rome. Within the Protestant world, the knowledge that Catholics outnumbered practising Anglicans in England has been tempered by the prophecies of the Bishop of Hexham and Newcastle who, in 1998, commented that, if current trends persisted, within three decades his own diocese would possess no Catholics whatsoever.

Even though a majority within Europe have continued to express a residual allegiance to the Church, many no longer practise their faith. Looking first at attendance at mass, even in that most Catholic of countries, Spain, monthly observance fell from 53 per cent of the population in 1981 to 43 per cent a decade later. Traditional regional differences, first plotted by the pioneering sociologist Duocastella, remained, with levels of practice highest in the Basque country and Old Castile, and lowest in the south. Figures for 1990 revealed a particular link with poverty and backwardness, with attendance holding up best in deprived rural Castile and La Mancha, and falling most markedly in urban centres, notably those of Catalonia. In Italy, figures are less reliable and harder to come by as they are collated by the local clergy. Nevertheless, 'regular' Sunday observance slumped dramatically from almost 70 per cent of the population in the mid-1950s to a mere 48 per cent in 1968, and has collapsed still further in the contemporary era. Once more, regional disparities were huge. One example would be that of Tuscany where, in the 1960s, over 60 per cent of the adults in the province of Lucca regularly attended mass compared to less than 10 per cent in Florence and Pisa. A sharper fall can be observed in Holland where national figures reveal that, whereas two-thirds of Catholics went to church on Sunday in 1966, less than one-third did so a decade later, and attendance has continued to fall by over 1 percentage point a year, such that by the end of the 1980s three-quarters of those who called themselves Catholic avoided celebrating the eucharist. In contiguous Belgium, the decline in weekend mass observance was not quite as pronounced and the downward trend set in slightly later, but has been marked nevertheless, from around 45 per cent of all Catholics in 1964 to under 23 per cent in 1985. Regionally, the rate of decline has been more or less uniform in Brussels and most of Belgium, the situation in Flanders has been marginally healthier. In France, we know that adult attendance at mass, on a weekly basis, tumbled from approximately one-quarter of the population at the start of the 1960s to under 15 per cent by 1970, and stood at 10 per cent by the close of the 1980s. Figures for monthly confession display an even more marked fall, standing at only 1 per cent of adult French Catholics in the 1980s compared to around 20 per cent thirty years earlier. Most worryingly for the Church, these trends have infected areas which were traditionally pious. Yves Lambert's delightful study *Dieu change en Bretagne*, published in 1985 and centred on the small western town of Limerzel, notes a precipitate fall-off in all aspects of Catholic observance, apart from the rites of passage, in the period since the 1950s.[29] And in England, figures for weekly attendance at mass dropped by around one-quarter between *circa* 1950 and the late 1980s. It is estimated that in the contemporary UK, less than one-quarter of Catholics regularly attend mass.

Figures for the rites of passage suggest the emergence of the 'occasional conformist', that is to say one who no longer regularly attends services on a Sunday though still, for the most part, adheres to the sacraments of baptism, marriage and burial. In France, the number of infant baptisms held relatively stable during the 1950s and 1960s, standing at 91.7 per cent of all births in

1958 and 82.7 per cent in 1968, yet by 1984 the percentage had fallen to 66 per cent and tailed off still further to 58.1 per cent in 1993. Today in France, it is believed that only around half the new-born population is baptised in the first year of life. To be fair, there has some been some rise in baptisms of those aged between seven and twelve, and of adults, but this has been nowhere near enough to compensate for the decrease in infant baptism. The picture in the Netherlands is broadly similar, falling by 0.8 percentage points annually between the 1960s and 1980s, with the result that by 1984 approximately one-third of children born to Catholics were baptised. In Belgium, the decline has been nowhere near as steep: 93.6 per cent of all live babies born to Catholic parents received that sacrament in the 1960s, and 78.6 per cent in 1985.

Marriage patterns, too, have confirmed the emergence of the *pratiquant saisonnier*. We can take as examples the two countries most generally identified with high levels of religious observance, Italy and Spain. In the former, civil marriages accounted for about 4 per cent of all ceremonies in the period *circa* 1945 to 1970, when they began to rise, almost doubling during the 1970s and increasing still further to 14.2 per cent by 1985. Regional diversity was considerable, with Liguria reaching 25 per cent compared to less than 6 per cent in Apulia. In Spain, with the passing of Franco, matrimonial law was brought into line with much of the rest of Europe so as to permit purely civil ceremonies. These proved exceedingly popular: nationwide, 16 per cent of all marriages were of this kind by 1986 and, in some districts, the proportion reached well over 60 per cent. In Belgium, 86.1 per cent of Catholics still opted for a religious ceremony in the 1960s compared with just less than 70 per cent in 1985, a drop of 16 per cent. A much more pronounced fall is to be perceived, over a similar period, in neighbouring Netherlands from 41 per cent to 24.5 per cent. A survey in France in 1986 displayed that only 51 per cent of the respondents sought a clerical service. The other trend within marriage, also to be noted here, has been the growth of non-endogamous unions, something the Church has always felt uncomfortable with, despite the growth of ecumenicalism. In England, before 1960, less than a third of Catholics were in mixed marriages and around one-in-eight went through a civil, but no religious, ceremony. By the close of the 1970s, two-thirds of Catholics married outside the faith, and over one-third sought no canonical blessing. Mixed marriages have also proved popular on the Continent. By the mid-1980s, one in three of all ceremonies celebrated within the Catholic Church in West Germany involved a non-Catholic. The proportion in East Germany was over half, and similar statistics can be confirmed for Holland and many of the Swiss cantons.

The remaining ritual to be mentioned here is that of burial. In this area, the occasional conformist has been reluctant to take too many chances or the relatives have taken the decision for the bereaved. What is worth noting is the rise of cremations as against interment. Although cremation was authorised by the Vatican in 1963, the Church still preferred burial, something reiterated as recently as 1990. But as a study of Belgium published in 1998 revealed, 50 per cent of Catholics in Brussels opted for cremation, and 30 per cent nationwide. Perhaps even more revealing is that, in both instances of burial and cremation, the survey uncovered a changing role for the priest. He no longer occupied centre-stage in the ceremony, but was marginalised in favour of friends and relatives, one inference being that the deceased was treated primarily as a member of a kinship group rather than as a member of the Church.

That other proxy indicator of religious vitality, clerical recruitment, has manifested a similar downturn. Globally the *Statistical Yearbook of the Church*, which has provided figures on an annual basis since 1971, has shown that the total of Catholic priests has fallen from around 425,000 to approximately 399,400 in the period *circa* 1970 to 1985. What makes this figure more disturbing for the Church is that there has been a sharp demographic increase over the same period and there has been a greying of the clergy. Everywhere within Europe, there now exists a shortage of vocations; even in Poland where the fight against communism and the election of a co-national as pontiff initially allowed it to buck the trend, numbers are beginning to fall. Ireland, too, has begun to lose its claim to immutability. While there is one priest to every 647 believers compared to a European average of 1:1,200, statistics show that there were some 750 vocations in 1970, falling to 91 in 1991. During the same period, actual ordinations dropped from 259 to 43. The Netherlands, again, have illustrated the most rapid downturn. The total number of priests being ordained in 1967 fell to under 200 and, by the 1980s, an average of only 22 ordinations a year were taking place. Within France, too, a crisis in recruitment has seen the number of secular clerics drop from around 40,000 in the mid-1960s to just 27,000 in the mid-1980s. In the year 1984, a paltry 13 priests were ordained. Belgium has likewise struggled to enlist ordinands. The number of ordinations since the 1980s has been only 20–25 per cent of that of 1965, and equally significant is the fact that a mere half of those entering seminaries went on to take orders. In southern Europe, we know that, during the 1960s, priestly ordinations in Italy fell by some 20 per cent. In Spain, the number of seminarists dropped from 9,000 in the 1950s to only a little over 1,500 in the 1970s, though there was some rise to approximately 2,000 by 1992. Once again, there were extraordinary regional varieties: there were fewer than 200 ordinations in Catalonia in the decade leading up to 1995. Across the border in Portugal, where there were some forty seminaries, the total of students tumbled from some 7,000 in 1952 to just under 5,000 by 1968, with little sign of the trend being reversed.

This European-wide crisis of recruitment has meant that it is now common for several parishes to be served by a single priest so that Sunday worship is held only perhaps once per month in the local church, and the priest, instead of being a central, resident figure in the parish, is a visitor. In 2001, it was estimated that between 30 and 50 per cent of parishes had no permanent priest. Such is the case Yves Lambert describes in Brittany. The situation would be far worse if the Church had not succeeded in deploying its manpower to cover the gaps, national churches being only too happy to employ

priests from other countries. Additionally, the resort to deacons, first introduced in 1968, who may recite part of the scriptures, lead prayers and
distribute previously consecrated hosts, and most of whom (90 per cent) are
married, has staved off disaster. Presently, there are some 1,000 in France
alone. Yet the episcopacy has not been comfortable with the use of the
deacons whose status remains ambiguous: most deacons would wish to enter
the priesthood but are prevented from doing this because of their married
status, a state of affairs whereby the wife automatically becomes an impedi-
ment. Should the woman die, the widower may not become a priest without
dispensation, nor may he remarry. For these reasons, several bishops have
ceased to ordain deacons altogether.

   The issue of celibacy has most frequently been cited as the reason why
vocations have tumbled, putting off prospective ordinands and leading others
to abandon their vocation. Celibacy has only ever been a matter of Church
discipline and has no scriptural basis: indeed, all the evidence suggests that
the apostles themselves were married men. Introduced as a custom into the
western Church in the course of the eleventh-century reforms of Leo IX
(1049–54) and Gregory VII (1073–85), celibacy was not properly enforced
until the high tide of the Counter-Reformation. During the French Revolution,
some of the most rabid dechristianisers insisted that clerics should marry as
proof of the abandonment of their vocation, an indication that clerical
celibacy had emerged as a defining characteristic of the priesthood. Perversely,
married priests became associated, particularly in the minds of the hierarchy,
with those who had capitulated. Yet there is plenty of anecdotal evidence to
suggest that in the rural Mediterranean world it was not unusual for a priest
to have sexual relations with his 'housekeeper', and that such liaisons were
not regarded as scandalous by the laity. Quite the reverse. In Chevalier's
Clochemerle, in the Spain described in Gerald Brenan's *South from Granada* and
in the southern Italy so acutely observed in Carlo Levi's *Christ Stopped at Eboli*,
all areas where Catholicism revolved around the communal celebration of
festivals and where the sacerdotal functions of the Church were secondary,
priests who did not have a heterosexual sex life were regarded as distinctly
odd.

   From the mid-twentieth century onwards, the Church hierarchy became far
less indulgent of such frailty, perhaps a reflection of the way in which the
conservative instincts of the Vatican were beginning to seep through the
whole of the Church. It was not a popular policy among parish clergy and
this, coupled with the declining numbers of clerics, led to widespread expectations of a relaxation in the Church's rule at the Second Vatican Council. Yet,
in October 1965, Paul VI withdrew the matter from discussion, and two years
later issued the encyclical *Sacerdotalis caelibatus* which reasserted traditional
teaching in tough language, describing celibacy as 'a heavy and sweet burden'
and a 'total gift'. This papal fiat caused a haemorrhaging of the priesthood,
a trend especially marked in Spain, France and Holland. During Paul's pontificate, 32,357 priests requested laicisation and all but 1,033 were granted. It is
said that the Pope went through each application individually. In 1978, when

John Paul II refused abruptly to sanction any more clerical departures, one-in-twelve on the waiting list was a Spaniard, perhaps not surprising given that one survey of the diocese of Santiago de Compostela, a bastion of Catholic practice, discovered that nearly a quarter of priests believed chastity to be an unrealistic expectation and 'behaved accordingly'.[30] Within certain parts of Europe, the celibacy debate left a bitter aftertaste. The Dutch Church, in particular, which had voted to end celibacy in 1969, has remained divided over the question, a division made worse by the parachuting of ultra-conservative bishops into newly vacant dioceses. Within Switzerland there was astonishment in June 1995 when Hansjörg Vogel, the prelate of Basle, announced his resignation because of his 'relationship with a woman' which had ended in pregnancy.[31] While it is well documented that many priests do not observe the teaching on celibacy – one recent survey of priests in Germany and the USA suggested that only 10 per cent observed complete chastity – others have struggled to adhere to the rule. John Cornwell quotes one Irish priest speaking at a renewal weekend in Dublin: 'Well, we all get by, fathers, don't we, on the three excesses: an excess of whisky, an excess of golf, and an excess of masturbation.'[32] This disillusionment is exacerbated by the fact that probably a majority of lay Catholics are happy to accept married priests. To cite one instance among many, 69 per cent of French Catholics in the 1980s indicated that they had no fundamental objections, with only 22 per cent opposed.

It would, however, be a mistake to attribute this flight from the priesthood merely to the issue of celibacy. Testimony from those who have relinquished their vocation suggests that many felt a sense of isolation, something which can only get worse as their numbers decrease and as Catholic social organisations crumble. They also considered themselves poorly supported by the hierarchy, and ill-prepared for the challenge of pastoral work by their seminary training which continued to privilege their sacerdotal and leadership role in the parish, something at odds with Vatican II's stress upon the clergy as servants of the people. In 1967, the Bishop of Bilbao received a letter from the spiritual directors of the seminary at Derio demanding that the syllabus be overhauled so as to attune clerical training to the pressures of modern living. That little has changed since may be gleaned from the telling observation in Cornwell's conspectus of contemporary Catholicism, *Breaking Faith*, in which he writes: 'Diocesan priests, in particular, live in virtual solitude many miles from brother priests. Educated in seminaries, which are still modelled on cloistral monasteries, their priestly formation has taken pace in the exclusively male companionship of an enclosed institution.'[33] Other clerics have complained of frustration at their inability to discuss openly with their parishioners sensitive topics and the episcopal enforcement of a party line on issues such as contraception, married clergy, the ordination of women and homosexuality. Finally, societal changes have worked to the clergy's detriment by undermining their status. During the nineteenth century, priest and teacher had often been in competition with one another, but since the 1960s the increasing professionalisation of society has left the clergy trailing in the wake of doctors, lawyers, psychiatrists, pyschoanalysts, teachers, social workers and other members of the caring professions, and lacking that social esteem which was once theirs by virtue of their office and which is increasingly attached to middle-class professionals. Some observers in Italy have explained the decrease in recruitment by reference to the unwillingness of rural families to reserve a son for the clerical vocation since this is no longer seen as enhancing social status.

The decline in the seculars has been more than matched by the fall in the figures for regulars. While accurate figures are hard to obtain, not least because of problems over definition as to who counts as a monk or a nun, the problems of recruitment and defections are all too visible. It is widely stated that, by 1979, there was no country, either in Europe or in the wider world, including those traditional Catholic heartlands of Poland and Ireland, which was self-sustaining in respect of admissions to nunneries. In Ireland, the congregations have witnessed a 31 per cent decline since 1970, a 40 per cent decline in brothers and a 25 per cent decline in sisters. In Spain, where the contemplative orders were above all concentrated, there were some 79,000 sisters in 1982, a figure that had fallen to 55,000 by 1992; and there was a concomitant rise in the average age of females. To take another example, that of Belgium, we know that there was actually a steady increase in the totals of nuns up to 1947, followed by a slippage until 1960, and a much sharper tail-off thereafter. Among other countries for the period 1983–98, the fall in the number of women religious is as follows: France 78,996 to 51,311; Germany 62,200 to 41,257; Britain 12,236 to 8,856; and Italy 143,997 to 112,958. The knock-on effects were not insignificant: Catholic schools were deprived of teachers; orphanages of carers; charities of workers. In sum, the decline in nuns reduced the effectiveness of one of the Church's 'agencies of socialisation'.

Among the male religious, recruitment held up best among the traditional orders of the Franciscans and Jesuits, although in the latter case membership had dwindled to 29,436 by 1974. Some of the lesser-known orders have diminished almost to the point of extinction. Traditional Spain, always characterised as priest-ridden, again exemplified the seriousness of the trend with the numbers down from 30,000 in 1982 to 18,000 in 1992, the issue of celibacy once again being credited with the sharp decreases. Even more than the seculars, the regulars have been marginalised by the emergence of the 'caring professions', an area they formerly made their own. Changes in societal structure have affected the women's orders particularly. The growth of career opportunities for women, feminism and sexual liberation have removed several of the imperatives that previously led women to take vows. So too have developments in the medical sphere which have dramatically reduced the risks of childbirth, the fear of which may formerly have driven some women to the religious life. Incidentally, the practice in Ireland of putting mothers of illegitimate children into nunneries to act as servants to the sisters, a practice common until the 1960s, remains a stain on the Church's reputation as do the Magdalene laundries where unmarried mothers were effectively sentenced to slave labour.

Declining levels of religious observance, a decreasing resort to the use of the rites of passage, falls in the numbers of clerics – these are conventional indicators of modern-day secularisation, all the more troubling in that they indicate sharper rates of decline than have been witnessed at any other previous epoch. Eighteenth-century France, for instance, might have seen a crisis of clerical recruitment but nothing on the scale evidenced in the 1960s and 1970s. What has made matters worse for the Church has been the emergence of what some historians have recently characterised as 'pick-and-mix' or 'cafeteria Catholicism', in which the laity has rejected clerical authority, preferring to follow the dictates of individual conscience rather than adhere to Church teaching. We can see this in a number of spheres, most obviously contraception. It will be recalled that, in 1968, *Humanae vitae* reaffirmed the notion that the primary function of marriage and the sexual act was procreation, and that any deliberate intervention by physical or chemical means to impede this was *intrinsice inhonestum*, 'intrinsically dishonest'. Coming at a time of demographic change, unprecedented prosperity among the young, higher levels of education, the development of the oral contraceptive pill and the breakdown of traditional moral and cultural norms, this was always going to be an unpopular measure and one difficult to police. Not that this was a wholly new issue. The studies by Sevregand reveal the agonies already endured by couples in the 1920s who wanted to adhere to the Church's teaching on sexual matters but found this conflicted with the debilitation caused to mothers' health by a sequence of unwanted pregnancies and the economic vicissitudes caused by having too many mouths in the family to feed.[34]

In the event, most Catholics paid little heed to the 1968 pronouncement, something of which the clergy was only too aware. In France, bishops counselled clerics not to adopt too hard a line in the confessional on contraception for fear that parishioners would abandon the Church altogether. In pluralist Britain, where the official Catholic stance was a fertile source of humour for satirists, the faithful likewise saw this as a matter of individual conscience. In a survey conducted in London and Preston, in the mid-1970s, it was nigh on impossible to identify ordinary Catholics who unambiguously supported the Church's teaching. One respondent remarked, 'it's up to me, not the Church ... if I want to (use contraceptives). I just go ahead and do it.'[35] Another replied, 'the rules have been made by celibates for celibates'.[36] Here, as elsewhere in Europe, people questioned the ability of chaste seminary-trained males, with little appreciation of advances in psychological medicine, to understand or to grapple with the realities of married life and the pressures of modern living.

In other areas of personal morality, notably with regard to sex before marriage, the laity has also made up its own mind. As for illegitimacy, the figures are notoriously difficult to interpret. Levels have certainly risen in Catholic countries, though they remain low compared to other states. For example, in Spain they stood at 4–8 per cent of live births in the 1980s and 6 per cent in Italy, compared to 36 per cent in Denmark and 25 per cent in the United Kingdom. Nevertheless, it is unclear how far this reduced rate of growth is due to adherence to Catholic teaching or reflects cultural norms which allow young people to remain in the family home until marriage. More certain are the results obtained from opinion polls conducted in Germany and Poland. In 1993, nearly two-thirds of Catholic Poles rejected official teaching on contraception and pre-marital sex. Another reliable study for 1990s Germany revealed that four-fifths of Catholics opposed the ban on sex before marriage.

As to abortion, rates have been relatively high despite the fact that successive popes since Pius XII have equated abortion with the actual murder of a child, something reiterated in John Paul II's statement of 1981. Few members of the hierarchy have gone as far as Cardinal Meissner, the Archbishop of Cologne, who likened the morning-after pill to Zyklon B, the infamous poison used by the Nazis in their death camps. It is calculated that in Italy, in the wake of the 1978 law liberalising abortion, there were 30 abortions per 1,000 live births during the 1980s, but this was as nothing compared to Spain where a report from the High Court in 1974 suggested a staggering annual total of 300,000 which, if correct, would be the equivalent of 40 per cent of all live births. Belgium and Ireland are the only two Western European countries to resist the tide towards relaxation, the Belgian parliament passing a law in 1990 permitting abortion only in the first twelve weeks of pregnancy, legislation which the Catholic King of the Belgians could not bring himself to sign. He abdicated for two days to permit the passage of the bill and save his conscience, retaking his throne immediately thereafter. In Ireland, abortion laws continue to be the strictest in Europe and, since a referendum of 1983, form part of the constitution. The upshot has been a steady stream of women undergoing operations in British clinics where abortion-on-demand was legalised in 1967. The Irish example points more generally to the Catholic attitude to abortion. Outside those feminist groups who have equated the right to abortion with the right to take charge of their reproductive processes, and apart from those Catholic militants who have espoused the anti-abortion cause and who have been so prominent in groups such as the Society for the Protection of the Unborn Child, lay people of all denominations, and of none, feel uncomfortable over the issue. Yet, as the above evidence suggests, the ban on contraception has only exacerbated the resort to abortion, ensuring that Catholic states have some of the highest rates in Europe.

On the issue of divorce, the Church has also found it difficult to hold the line, despite repeated pronouncements upholding the permanence of marriage. While there has been some sympathy for the pressures which couples have to endure in the modern age, it is still the case that, in a consummated marriage of two Catholics, the right of communion is denied to one of the partners should he or she divorce and remarry, the reasoning being that the divorced and remarried couple are imperfect symbols of Christian love and are effectively living 'in sin'. John Paul II reiterated this position in his 1981 *Familaris consortio*. Such intransigence has created problems on several fronts. First, it has been out of step with the increased liberalisation of marriage laws throughout Europe, leaving Malta and Ireland as the countries with the most restrictive provisions for divorce. Second, the Church's stance has been at odds with Catholic lay opinion. In England, a survey of Catholics conducted in the 1970s uncovered that two-thirds of the sample believed that they should have the right to divorce, and figures derived from the Office of Population Censuses and Survey reveal that Catholics are just as likely to divorce as other denominations. Admittedly, this has to be put in the context of a state where divorce rates are among the highest in Europe. The European Union (EU) reported in June 2001 that 2.7 Britons in every thousand get divorced annually in comparison to an EU average of 1.8 per thousand, a proportion greater than in Italy (0.6) and in Spain (0.8). However, cross-national illustrations are always difficult, not least because the figures reflect individual socio-economic circumstances. In the case of Spain, for example, where the death of Franco led to some liberalisation of matrimonial law, the failure of the legal system to enforce maintenance payments has meant that many women have preferred separation to divorce; otherwise, it is hard not to believe that divorce rates would be much as elsewhere in Europe. And, finally, Church teaching has raised unfinished theological issues. If the divorced and remarried are 'sinful' and thus to be denied the eucharist, who, in a Church which adheres to the doctrine of original sin, may be admitted to communion?

One particularly serious result of the Church's hard-line teaching on moral issues has been the alienation of its core supporters in the shape of women. As has been demonstrated, the support of women had often proved a comfort to the Church both during the dark times of the French Revolution and the assault of Positivism when they, above all, remained assiduous in their attendance and religious observance and, in a sense, kept Catholicism alive. This was more than the Church deserved given the manner in which it looked upon women. The statements on contraception and other moral matters merely reaffirmed the clericalised male culture of the hierarchy and its innate fear of the 'second sex'. To be fair, John XXIII in his *Pacem in terris* spoke with great feeling, noting that 'since women are becoming ever more conscious of their human dignity, they will not tolerate being treated as mere material instruments, but demand rights befitting a human person in both domestic and public life'. Yet in practice virtually nothing has been done to implement this enlightened view. Vatican teaching has continued to restrict women to the role of mothering since it denies them the possibility of combining family life and wider social functions, thereby perpetuating the traditional Catholic bifurcation of women into those who marry and raise children and those who remain virginal and take up vows. As in the past, women are defined and constrained by their reproductive capacity, something wholly unacceptable in the context of the movement for sexual equality and feminism broadly defined. This is not to say that women have given up on the Church altogether. They still provide the bedrock for such organisations as the St Vincent de Paul Society, the Union of Catholic Mothers and the Catholic Women's League and, more recently, they have been drawn into initiatives such as the catechetic movement. There have also been liberal Catholic feminists, among them Schüllser Fiorenza and Anne Carr, who have questioned the male dominance and patriarchal language of the Church. Yet such bodies and individuals are mostly on the fringe, and have been rivalled by pressure groups campaigning for gay rights, child-care and abortion on demand. Unlike in the eighteenth and nineteenth centuries, women in the twentieth acquired alternative forms of sociability outside religion. As already noted, those looking for a life of adventure, for responsibility and to serve society are no longer restricted to religious orders or congregations. Additionally, women who choose not to marry can make their own way in society, and no longer need the support systems offered by an order or a congregation. The fact that the Church still defines women through their reproductive role simply adds insult to injury, and has prevented any proper debate on their ordination despite the fact that repeated opinion polls have revealed communities which would accept women priests. Merely to take one example, 61 per cent of French Catholics surveyed in the 1980s confirmed that they would be happy to see the ordination of women. Although the Anglican Communion has gone down this path, the debate within the Catholic Church has been largely stifled, notwithstanding the crisis over vocations.

That other great matter of individual conscience, homosexuality, has also raised problems about equal rights and human dignity. This issue was side-stepped by the Second Vatican Council, perhaps not surprisingly given that in the 1960s even liberal secular states were only just coming to terms with the matter. It was not until 1967 that sexual relations between two consenting males, above the age of twenty-one, were accepted as lawful in England and Wales. Only as campaigns for homosexual equality have mounted in Europe has the Church felt compelled to enter the debate. In 1975, the Congregation for the Doctrine of the Faith issued its *Personae humanae*, condemning any sexual behaviour which was outside marriage and which did not place pro-creation as its chief purpose. In subsequent pronouncements, the Vatican and individual bishops have attempted to blend traditional objections to engaging in homosexual genital activities with an acknowledgement that an orientation towards homosexuality is not in itself a moral failing or a sin. What has undermined the Church's position are the continuing revelations that the clergy itself contains a disproportionate number of homosexuals, both practising and non-practising, compared to the population as a whole. The much respected American author Father Donald Cozzens, Rector and Professor of Theology at St Mary's Seminary in Cleveland, Ohio, suggests in his *The Changing Face of the Priesthood* that 'approximately half of American priests and seminarians are homosexually oriented ... the percentage appears to be highest among priests under 40'.[37] Recently, the journalist Marco Politi uncovered a 'gay network' among Italian priests, detailed in his book *La Confessione*; while in Spain the respected national newspaper *El Pais* disclosed a minor scandal at the Benedictine community of Montserrat, where two abbots were forced to resign after the discovery of homosexual practices. The Church has also found it impossible to turn a blind eye to the social discrimination experienced by gays. This led Catholic activist groups, notably in Holland, England and the USA, to campaign for the inclusion of homo-sexuals in the Christian community. The high incidence of AIDS among the gay community has further forced the Church to reconsider its position. In 1986, the Congregation for the Doctrine of the Faith published its *The Pastoral Care of Homosexual Persons* which called for an end to discrimination, yet still labelled homosexuality as an 'objective disorder'. This may well have proved counter-productive, giving ammunition to traditionalist clergy. Cardinal Winning's recent campaign in Scotland against the jettisoning of the infamous Section 28, prohibiting the portrayal of same-sex relations as 'normal', is only one example among many where prelates have discriminated against gays. Ultimately, the Church is again caught in a theological snare. So long as it denounces all sexual practices – masturbation, contraception and homosexuality – that are not focused on a reproductive purpose, it can never condone practising gay relationships.

If the faithful have often reached their own decisions about moral matters, there is also growing evidence to suggest that they have become more selective about what they believe, a further trend in cafeteria Catholicism. On one level, this has meant a rejection of core beliefs. A 1978 survey of Catholics in England revealed that nearly 13 per cent did not believe in heaven, life-after-death or the devil. Up to 25 per cent did not believe in hell, and even more than this adhered to the notion of reincarnation. Europe-wide evidence also indicates a declining acceptance of doctrines of the Virgin birth; and, partially in response to the popularisation of science, even the Vatican has acknowledged that 'evolution is more than a theory'. What is perhaps more serious is that, in the wake of the Second Vatican Council's reforms, the laity has been confused about what it should believe or practise. Before the 1960s, there were a series of specifically Catholic prayers and devotions. This distinct culture included regular mass attendance, the observation of holy days, monthly confession, private prayers, the stations of the cross and abstinence from meat on Fridays. In an attempt to project a new confidence and to respond to the modern world, Vatican II did much to undo these certainties, embracing the vernacular, permitting greater lay participation in the mass, abolishing obligatory Friday abstinence, facilitating personal prayers and championing biblical study. These initiatives were not always well received. Apart from outright defiance by Archbishop Lefebvre, there were many instances of lay Catholics hankering after the Latin liturgy. In Lambert's Limerzel, parishioners did not take kindly to the extra participation required by new forms of mass; they disliked giving up time which could be spent in leisure pursuits, and attempts to adjust the time of services and to introduce penitential masses, providing a general absolution for the congregation in lieu of confession, have struggled to take root. Aware of these traditionalist instincts, John Paul II, who was himself intrinsically conservative, has offered some reassurance in his *Ecclesia dei* of 1988, allowing the regular celebration of the Tridentine Latin rite. With such contradictory signals, it is not surprising that many Catholics are confused as to what they should believe and do.

It would be wrong to present too bleak a picture with respect to popular belief and practice. There have undeniably been some bright spots. Catholic revival has sometimes been focused upon Marian apparitions, such as those at San Sebastian de Garabandal where the Virgin passed on the message that many of the clergy were 'on the road to perdition and are taking many souls with them'.[38] Similar warnings have been proffered by the Virgin at Melleray, Inchigeela and Bessbrook in Ireland; at San Damiano and Schio in Italy; and, most famously, at Medjugorje in Yugoslavia where, in 1981, the Marian messages were less doom-laden and instead supported the progressive ideals associated with Vatican II. Yet, on the whole, the revival sparked by these apparitions has been transient, and there has been nothing to compare with Lourdes in the nineteenth century, or Fatima earlier in the twentieth. More significant have been a large number of initiatives, often ecumenical in nature, which have sought to recharge religious vitality and address the needs and aspirations of the laity. These have included national synods, which have elaborated and developed the texts produced by Vatican II, the most important of these being held in the Netherlands, West Germany and Switzerland in the early 1970s. In Austria, it proved impossible to organise a national synod but thanks to the Archbishop of Vienna some cross-diocesan dialogue did take place, though the conservatism of the bishops and the apathy of the laity undermined these efforts. We may also cite a wide range of local projects, comprising the establishment of Bible and prayer groups, pastoral teams, the establishment of inter-faith dialogue, new types of worship (borrowing techniques from other cultures and religions), and new catechetical teaching. Additionally, some Catholics have organised a push for change in the area of environmental practice, relations with the Third World and the campaign against nuclear weapons, most famously Mgr Bruce Kent who headed the British-based Campaign for Nuclear Disarmament and who eventually left the priesthood to marry.

Was this enough to compensate for the slippage which we identified earlier? The answer is no, and not simply because these initiatives have failed to compensate for the massive decline in gregarious conformity. Nor may it be argued that the Church is leaner and fitter thanks to the shedding of nominal Catholics, leaving behind a residue of activists. Progressives and militants are deeply divided over the kinds of Catholicism which they espouse; and the Church hierarchy which, by and large, continued to adopt a Romanised, traditionalist, patriarchal and clericalised outlook remains at odds with the Gallican, lay and relaxed tendencies of much of the Church on the ground. The answer must also be a resounding 'no' since, over the last four decades, there has been a collapse in Catholic identity. This has operated at two levels. First, that distinctive Catholic culture, best expressed through pillarisation in the Netherlands and elsewhere through the multiplicity of Catholic social and youth endeavours, has largely disappeared. Whereas Catholic Action in Spain numbered one million supporters in 1966, six years later this had dropped off to 100,000. Many people now define themselves primarily through secular forms, for instance as trade unionists or members of professional bodies. Only secondarily are they Catholics. On another level, western European society has ceased to be defined within a religious paradigm. It is notable that the societal influence of religion, which Karel Dobbelaere identified as central to the issue of secularisation, has been in decline.[39] As we ourselves have seen, state legislatures have paid scant regard to the protests of Church leaders and lay Catholics in the liberalisation of laws on divorce, the availability of contraception, abortion, homosexual rights, to which list may be added pornography. The case of Ireland is perhaps the exception which proves the rule.

Indifference, individual conscience and indiscipline: these are the hallmarks of much of post-conciliar Catholicism. These trends are not only damaging to the faith, but are deeply harmful to papal authority. The moral issues of the 1960s brought into sharp relief the very issue of infallibility. It will be remembered that, in 1870, the intention of the First Vatican Council was that the pontiff should only be infallible when he spoke *ex cathedra* over fundamental matters of conscience, not on Church discipline. In the case of *Humanae vitae*, the Pope was not speaking thus, yet there was an attempt to present the teaching as if His Holiness had spoken formally on a question of ethics. In practice, the encyclical was simply ignored, raising profound doubts about the very bases of Rome's status: was the Pope truly infallible; and should the papacy occupy such a pre-eminent position in the constitution of the Church? The response of the Holy See to these dilemmas has not been to engage in debate, but to withdraw into a ghettoised mentality. When Hans Küng queried infallibility in the wake of *Humanae vitae*, Paul VI sneered: 'The smoke of Satan has entered God's temple in order to spoil and wither the fruits of the Vatican Council.'[40] This process of ghettoisation may be better explained by an examination of John Paul II, who has been described as a reincarnation of his conservative predecessors Pius IX and Pius XII.

John Paul II: 'A Living Cult'

The elevation of the first non-Italian Pope since 1522, when Hadrian VI of Utrecht (1522–23) took the throne, was not a straightforward matter. The Conclave which gathered in October 1978 to choose a successor to John Paul I was still smarting from the aftermath of Vatican II, and was split between those who favoured Giuseppe Siri, the conservative candidate, and Giovanni Benelli, the liberal option. It was not until the eighth vote that they settled, albeit by a huge majority of 103 votes out of 109, upon the compromise choice of Cardinal Karol Wojtyla, Archbishop of Cracow, a man little known outside clerical circles. At fifty-eight years of age he was the youngest Pope since Pius IX, and had led a colourful life before taking up the priesthood. The son of a retired military man, Wojtyla attended state schools, dabbled with acting, worked as a labourer in a quarry and a factory, dated a girlfriend and enjoyed a range of sports, including football, skiing and mountaineering, before entering the local university at Cracow where his education was cut short by the Nazi occupation of Poland. It was during these dark moments that he discovered a calling to the priesthood for which he trained in secret. After a two-year visit to Rome, where he received a doctorate in theology, he returned to Poland and was made auxiliary Bishop of Cracow in 1958, at the comparatively young age of thirty-eight, assuming the mantle of archbishop five years later. His appointment coincided with the Second Vatican Council, where he was an important player behind the scenes, some crediting him for example with the pastoral constitution *On the Church in the Modern World* which dealt with issues of family life. Having taught philosophy earlier in his career, he had an abiding interest in ethical matters and read widely in the whole gamut of contemporary philosophical works. He was thus well placed to take a view on such affairs.

Although not well known outside the ecclesiastical *milieu*, and not initially well received within the Italian Church for not being Italian, he was enthusiastically embraced by the rest of the world, not least because of his refreshing change of style, his upright morality and his easy handling of the media which ensured him a good press: less than a week after his election, he took the unprecedented step of inviting over 2,000 journalists into the Vatican for a press conference. There soon developed a cult of John Paul II, not altogether dissimilar from that associated with Pius IX, stimulated by his willingness to travel, something which Pio Nono had not done. The peripatetic nature of his pontificate was marked out within the first couple of years by visits to Mexico, Poland and the USA. His willingness to meet the crowds was not without danger, however, and on 13 May 1981 in Rome itself he was the victim of an attempted assassination by Mehemet Ali Agca who shot him in the stomach, right arm and hand. The Pope's survival, which he attributed to providential intervention, and his forgiveness of the would-be assassin at a meeting in 1984 added to his appeal. It was not long before he was touring once again, averaging four overseas visits per annum, albeit now protected in a specially constructed 'popemobile' with bulletproof glass. In his hagiographical account of John Paul II published in 2001, George Weigel recorded that during his pontificate His Holiness had travelled some 670,000 miles, more or less the distance three times over between the earth and the moon.[41]

Beyond style, this was a man of substance. In terms of devotion, he was a curious mixture of Tridentine and post-Vatican II attitudes. On one level, he retained an affection for ritual, visiting shrines at Fatima, Knock and Guadaloupe; he revived the cult of the Sacred Heart; and he retained a trust in routine divine intervention in the here-and-now. On another plane, he embraced a Christian humanism which chimed in well with some of the more liberal ambitions of the contemporary Church. Doctrinally, however, he was a conservative, an aspect of his character which would become increasingly prominent over time when he openly mixed with such men as Max Scheler, the conservative Catholic anthropologist. On sexual ethics, he was uncompromising: a staunch advocate of *Humanae vitae*, a firm opponent of abortion, a strong believer in clerical celibacy and an opponent of the ordination of women. In his eyes, Mary is the model for women, and he himself had the motto '*Totus tuus*' ('I am completely yours, O Mary') emblazoned on his robes. He has spoken of sexual activity outside marriage and of contraception as a 'culture of death'. Politically, he mixed populism with authoritarianism. He was a believer in hierarchy, including the sharp division between laity and clergy and he upheld papal authority within ecclesiastical structures, voicing fierce criticism of Western liberalism which he feared had permeated sections of the Church. Naturally enough, being a Catholic Pole, he was even more fiercely anti-communist; it was his defiance of General Jaruzelski that contributed further to his personal stature.

It was in the East European world, even in the Protestant areas of Hungary, East Germany and Czechoslovakia, that his nationality and message of religious freedom offered real hope for greater individual liberties. Such aspirations were especially vigorous in Poland where Lech Walesa had created the illegal Solidarity movement. This drew together some 10 million trade unionists, with close support from the lower Catholic clergy who saw an opportunity of sloughing off atheistic rule. As in the past, the hierarchy retained a certain deference for the communist regime. In 1979, after his first visit to Poland as Pope had brought thousands out on to the streets, John Paul II indicated to Walesa that he approved of his undertaking. In the following year, he intervened with the Soviet leader, Brezhnev, to warn him against military intervention, thus helping to bring about the Polish government's official recognition of Solidarity's existence. Subsequent financial and moral support from Rome helped Solidarity survive the declaration of martial law in 1981, the fresh banning of the movement a year later, and the murder of the leading Catholic priest Father Popieuszko.

In this way, both the Vatican and the Church helped to pave the way for Poland's eventual release from communism, though their efforts need to be set in the broader context of Cold War politics in the 1980s: the anti-Red rhetoric of President Ronald Reagan on the one hand, and the reforming zeal of President Gorbachev after 1985 on the other. The Soviet leader's policies of *perestroika* and *glasnost*, fuelled by an urgent desire to modernise the ailing Soviet and East European economies and to meet some of the nationalist and democratic protest movements which were springing up in imitation of Solidarity, albeit without its Catholic bias, resulted in a gradual relaxation of the restraints which had hitherto suffocated religious freedoms. In 1988, an invitation was extended to John Paul II to attend the celebration of 1,000 years of Christianity in the Ukraine, an invitation which was turned down only when the Pope was told he could not visit his co-religionaries in Lithuania. He none the less dispatched an envoy of cardinals, and in 1989 Gorbachev made a point of meeting the Pope while on a state visit to Rome, reassuring him that a law granting religious freedom was in the offing. More than that. Over the next year, communist Europe fell apart. As quickly as the regimes disappeared, the old state apparatus controlling clerical affairs vanished, although the problems associated with the reconstruction of a Church, not dissimilar to those experienced after 1815 in France and following the *Kulturkampf* in Germany, did not. How to redistribute former state property sequestered from the Church? How to appoint priests and bishops? How to re-educate whole generations deprived of religious instruction? How to re-establish lapsed habits of observance? These issues were difficult enough to resolve in Poland, where Solidarity more or less became the Catholic ruling party, and in Lithuania, where Catholics were eager to assert themselves, but proved even thornier in the cases where Protestants, Eastern Rite Catholics and Orthodox were the majority, as in Hungary, the Ukraine and Romania. After all, the Orthodox Church had been given privileged status by the former Soviet-backed regimes, something which it was not altogether pleased to have set aside. At least these areas escaped the violence which accompanied the collapse of communism in Yugoslavia, and the concomitant disintegration of the state. Whereas Croatia and Slovenia were predominantly Catholic, Serbia was overwhelmingly Orthodox, and took it upon itself to protect its national identity by a policy of ethnic cleansing which it soon exported to Muslim-dominated Bosnia-Herzegovina. This time it was the Orthodox Serbs, rather than the Catholic Croats, who were perpetrating genocide. Aghast at what was happening, the Vatican could do little else but support the intervention of the United Nations, which was slow in coming.

Events in former Yugoslavia notwithstanding, John Paul II drew hope from the example of Eastern Europe. First, the successful defiance of Marxism provided an opportunity to rein in those so-called liberation theologians, mainly operating in South America, whom he believed had allowed their Christian principles to be compromised by their association with socialist ethics and who had supported the violent overthrow of right-wing dictatorships. John Paul II was no supporter of dictatorship, whether of the left or the right: his language in respect of General Pinochet of Chile was as uncompromising as it was with regard to communist regimes. Yet he would not subscribe to clerical involvement in politics, although it might be objected that he had supported precisely that in Poland. Whatever the case, he could not condone the use of force; he even had scruples about the violent toppling of such unreconstructed tyrants such as Ceausescu. Second, Eastern Europe seemed to proffer both a wake-up call and an opportunity for the West. In 1991, shortly after the fall of the Berlin Wall, he called a synod of bishops from East and West, at which he propounded his ideas for European re-evangelisation. That same year, he commemorated the centenary of Leo XIII's *Rerum novarum* with his own *Centisimus annus* in which he warned that the failure of communism should not blind the liberal democracies to their own deficiencies, especially in regard to their consumerism, social inequality, materialist philosophy and excessive zeal for individualism. It was, though, their policies on moral ethics with which he took most issue. Prosperity had been the mother of lax morality. In 1994, he sided with the Islamic states at the UN-sponsored conference on population and development, held at Cairo, denouncing any form of artificial contraception. The next year, he issued *Evangelium vitae*, which reaffirmed his long-standing opposition to contraception, abortion, euthanasia and capital punishment.

The death penalty aside, John Paul II's doctrinal conservatism was reflective of his authoritarian instincts in regard to the Church itself. This was a Pope trained in the hands-on school of management. Radical thinking among the Jesuits was to be constrained by the appointment in 1981 of the semi-blind eighty-year-old Father Paolo Dezza, as 'personal delegate of the supreme pontiff to the Society of Jesus', a portfolio with no historical precedent.

Conservatism, as opposed to being Italian, now became the *sine qua non* of appointments to the College of Cardinals. Free-thinking and innovative theologians, among them Father Charles Curran, Archbishop Raymond Hunthausen and the Sri Lankan priest Tissa Balasuriya were silenced. In 1998, the English nun Sister Lavinia Byrne who regularly broadcast on the BBC's *Thought for the Day* slot claimed that she had been bullied out of her order because of her book *Woman at the Altar* in which she had seemingly condoned contraception. The German theologian Father Bernard Häring described his ordeal in front of the Congregation for the Doctrine of the Faith as more offensive than those audiences he had endured with the Nazi courts. Elsewhere, Thomistic teaching in seminaries was encouraged at the expense of progressive theology as manifested in the work of Edward Schillebeeckx who saw Vatican II as an opportunity to rebuild Church teaching, taking into account developments of modern science. The other voice which Rome attempted to silence was that of the pre-eminent Professor of Divinity at the University of Tübingen, Hans Küng, who had been central in the operation of the Vatican Council. His efforts to overturn such encyclicals as *Humanae vitae* provoked a censure in 1979 that prevented him from lecturing as a Catholic theologian, although the university countered this by appointing him to a personal chair of ecumenical theology.

The abrupt handling of these individuals contrasted markedly with the relative leniency with which Lefebvre was treated: sustained efforts at accommodation were attempted, only to be rejected by the irascible Archbishop. His case may be further juxtaposed with that of the outspoken Bishop of Evreux, Jacques Gaillot. Through his advocacy of the use of condoms in the fight against AIDS, his championing of the ordination of married men and women, and his support for left-wing causes, he flouted every one of John Paul II's prohibitions. His dismissal in 1995 was no surprise. To the Vatican's chagrin, thousands gathered in his support and the congregation for his last mass numbered 30,000. He was subsequently granted the diocese of Partenia in Algeria, essentially a strip of desert, but paradoxically a place of enormous symbolism as it had traditionally been a place of exile for the Latin Church and was where Gaillot himself had served during his National Service.

As well as dealing in high-handed fashion with liberal theologians and bishops, John Paul II ensured that the grip of the Congregation for the Doctrine of the Faith, the retitled Holy Office of Inquisition, was tightened under the leadership of the Austrian Cardinal Joseph Ratzinger. Himself a distinguished theologian, the Cardinal's liberal attitudes had been completely overturned by what he saw of secular developments after Vatican II, and he thus became the guardian of an old-fashioned doctrinal orthodoxy. Whereas the Council had spoken of the need for constant reinterpretation, debate and engagement, Ratzinger and John Paul II expected complete obedience once the head of the Church had spoken. Perhaps the most glaring example was the *Ordinatio sacerdotalis* of 1985 which declared that the issue of ordination of women was 'now closed'. Significantly, although this was an apostolic letter, and thus not an *ex cathedra* statement, it contained the phrase 'this judgement is to be definitively held by all the Church's faithful', a phraseology which led Ratzinger to claim infallibility for the utterance. That same year, an Extraordinary Synod of Bishops met at Rome, endorsing a commitment to the principles of Vatican II. Yet, in their conclusions, they re-emphasised elements of Church life which the Pope felt had been underplayed in the Council: the importance of hierarchy; the dangers of 'democratic tendencies'; and the adoption of a pessimistic view of the world in which hunger, oppression, violence and injustice continued to multiply, with none of the hopeful indicators of renewal that had been highlighted in John XXIII's *Gaudium et spes* and *Pacem in terris*. As a consequence, the synod subtly but significantly modified the tenor of the Council's principles. It is small wonder that, in 1989, 400 Catholic theologians responded to such smoke and mirrors by signing the so-called Cologne Declaration which protested at the way in which John Paul II was stifling initiative and debate within the Church. Starting within Austria, a largely lay movement known as 'We are Church' has arisen, perhaps totalling half-a-million members worldwide, which asserts that Catholicism is theirs and not Rome's. Rome, however, remains set in its ways. The *Universal Catechism of the Catholic Church*, produced by the Congregation for the Doctrine of the Faith in 1990 and approved in 1992, was insistent on the doctrine of papal infallibility and cold in its language towards other faiths.

Theological intransigence and papal absolutism, reminiscent of the nineteenth century, have been coupled with an inability of the Church to put its own house in order. The controversy surrounding allegedly dubious Vatican finances continues to this day, and the death in London of the banker Roberto Calvi found dangling beneath Blackfriars Bridge in 1982 remains a mystery despite two inquiries by Scotland Yard. More recently and more significantly, we can point to the unwillingness to recognise and correct the harm done by paedophile priests. The extent of this problem remains uncertain, and it may have been exaggerated by a sensationalist media, but its existence cannot be doubted. In the early 1990s, Cardinal Groer of Austria was charged with criminal sexual misconduct. That same decade, the Irish Father Brendan Smyth was given a twelve-year gaol sentence for seventy-four sexual assaults. Disturbingly, the Church authorities had been aware of his behaviour since 1969. Even more disturbing, such behaviour continued, thanks to the patriarchal and hierarchical culture of not washing dirty cassocks in public. In 1999, Father Sean Fortune, another Irish priest, committed suicide shortly before he was due to be tried on twenty-nine charges of sexual assault. In 2002, Dr Brendan Comiskey, Bishop of Ferns, was forced to stand down because of his failure to deal with the problem. In the period 1980–98, no fewer than thirty-eight separate cases of priestly misconduct have come before the court in Ireland. October 2000 saw the Norman priest, René Bissey, sentenced to eighteen years on eleven counts of assault on young boys; that same month, Father Joe Jordan was sent down for eight years for preying on young boys in Cardiff. Within the USA, the problem has been of a greater magnitude, highlighted by the goings-on of Father Paul Shanley, a maverick priest, who worked among Boston's homeless and advocated 'man–boy' love, and has been exacerbated by the unwillingness of Bernard Law, Archbishop of Boston, perhaps the most important diocese in America, to take effective sanctions. Only in 2002, as a result of this particular scandal, did the Vatican allude to the issue, and then in the most circumlocutory fashion, when John Paul II's Maundy Thursday letter referred to 'the most grievous forms of the mystery of evil at work in the world'.[42] That same year, American cardinals were summoned to Rome for a crisis meeting, although its deliberations were largely kept private. Compensatory pay-outs to victims of child abuse, thought to run into millions of dollars, may force the Church to be more candid. The saddening upshot of this squalid business is the loss of trust in the clergy and the shadow of suspicion which has fallen on many.

In another area, too, the acknowledgement of the Church's relationship to the Holocaust, John Paul II's record is not without blemish. Reflecting his interest in the Jewish religion, his upbringing among Jews in Poland, his friendship with Jerzy Kluger, and his intimate knowledge of Auschwitz, which he himself described as the 'most meaningful symbol of the Holocaust', he declared that 'anti-Semitism is a great sin against humanity'.[43] And he was the first Pope to attend the synagogue at Rome, an experience which he described as 'truly exceptional'. In 1993, he established diplomatic relations with Israel, and in 2001 he also acknowledged, albeit in guarded language, something of the failings of the Church to act sooner over the fate of the Jews. Such gestures reflected his more general interest in ecumenicalism. He has met the leaders of the Orthodox, Eastern Rite and Anglican communions; dialogue with the World Council of Churches has been intensified, something simply thrown out of court when first mooted in 1948 and 1955; and ecumenical services, including Muslims, Hindus, Shamans and Jews, have taken place. It is unfortunate that these gestures of reconciliation and inter-faith dialogue have been undermined by his policy towards beatification and sainthood. Reflecting his conservative instincts, in 1992 he beatified Escriva de Balaguer, the founder of Opus Dei, and he has moved towards the beatification of Isabella of Spain, the hammer of Islam and Jews, as well as canonising the more worthy Pius IX and John XXIII. Support for 'Saint' Pius XII, along with the canonisation in 1985 of Edith Stein, the Jewish Carmelite convert, whose order provocatively maintains a shrine close to the scene of her death in Auschwitz, can only be considered ill-judged. As Küng has suggested: 'What is the use of pompous confessions of guilt if the pope excludes his pre-decessors, himself and "the Church" and does not follow them up with acts of repentance and reform.'[44] Indeed, the failure of the Vatican to be open over its role in the Holocaust has encouraged national churches to adopt a similarly covert attitude. For example, in the 1980s French public opinion was shocked at revelations that the Church had protected war criminals such as Paul Touvier and had been reluctant to open up its archives to state prosecutors, despite Archbishop Lustiger summoning the Rémond Commission charged with getting to the bottom of the matter.

Given the manner in which John Paul II has centred power in himself, it is tempting to blame some of these shortcomings on his failing health, were it not for the fact that his instincts had been clearly revealed in his early years when he displayed a vigour, energy and enthusiasm, qualities which were only momentarily dented by the assassination attempt which left him *hors de combat* for five months. For some observers, his reign has vindicated Cardinal Newman's quip, originally made with respect to Pius IX, that it does no good for a pope to live for more than twenty years as he then becomes a god. It is thus difficult to come to any balanced judgement about the longer-term significance of his period of office, but some attempt may be hazarded.

Conclusion

The relationship between Vatican II, John Paul II's pontificate and the type of Catholicism which has emerged at the beginning of the third millennium remains paradoxical. On the one hand, the Pope continuously affirms his attachment both to the words and the spirit of the Council. On the other hand, so much of what he has done appears to fly in the face of this. It may be that the key to understanding his attitudes and actions lies, above all, in his identity and experiences as a Pole, something evidenced by the number of references he makes to his early upbringing in his 1998 book *Crossing the Threshold of Hope*, which itself was based on a televison interview, the first time ever a Pope had been questioned in this way. For him, the environment of Polish Catholicism as an oppressed religion, attacked both by the Nazis and the communists, was crucially formative, and served as a prism, refracting the strategies elucidated by Vatican II. In his opinion, religious liberty was not so much part and parcel of a wholesale ecumenicalism but was more a defensive position against the powers of atheism, all too often sponsored by the state. He accepted the Church as a community of believers, but considered that lay involvement in the running of Catholicism had to be tempered by the need for discipline, lest divisions within the ranks were exploited by the Church's enemies. He adopted a similar position apropos the need for clerical subordination to Church authority. He was, of course, no more sanguine about the future of the West than of the communist East, since both were founded on versions of materialism, and he therefore stressed the primacy of original sin and the active presence of evil within the world, his resolute pessimism putting him at odds with the optimism of others, notably John XXIII, the Council itself and post-conciliar progressives in France and the Netherlands in particular. Even his attitudes towards women bear the imprint of his Polish upbringing, as Hebblethwaite has plausibly suggested. *Mulieris dignitatem*, which prohibited the ordination of women, at least threw out archaic notions that sexual promiscuity was the result of Eve's initial fall from grace.[45] No longer did Eve equate with evil. Yet it is arguable that the Pope spoke more out of Polish gallantry and romanticism than through a wholehearted engagement with women's issues. The uncompromising stance of the Church on such associated issues as contraception, divorce and, to a lesser degree, abortion has remained a millstone around its neck, alienating so much of world opinion.

The continuing treatment of women as the second sex remains a black spot of the modern-day Church, illustrating the inability of the upper echelons of the Church to abandon altogether their defensive and insular thinking. The Jewish ghetto in Rome might have gone, but the Vatican itself remains immured in a ghetto of its own making. It is, then, not difficult to understand why the Church faces an uncertain future. But there is nothing new here. If the pluralist, interactive and reformist impulses of the Second Vatican Council have not come to full fruition, in the grand scheme of things the two-and-a-half decades of John Paul II's pontificate are as nothing. It seems unlikely that the next Conclave will opt for a Pope in the same mould. Who knows what fresh vistas would open up with the election of a Third World candidate? When all is said and done, Catholicism may be conditioned by the papacy, but is not altogether constrained by it.

CHAPTER SEVEN

Conclusion: Catholicism Reviewed

FEW institutions, if any, can rival the Catholic Church in terms of its longevity, complexity of structure, depth of support, cultural impact and breadth of influence. As Hans Küng has observed, the Church was truly global before the concept of globalisation was invented.[1] We should not, of course, imagine that because of its claim to purvey unchanging truths it remained immutable itself: as a lived-out faith, Catholicism of necessity has responded to, and been altered by, changes in the social, cultural and political *milieux* of which it forms a part. It is, however, the combination of universality, venerability and intricacy of its institutional structures and practices which renders it suitable for study over the long term, for only then is it possible to plot transformation and continuity, and to differentiate between tectonic shifts and mere fads. What might have appeared to contemporaries as significant has not always turned out thus, while seemingly innocuous trends have acquired longer-term import. Although the present study adopts a chronological compass of a mere 250 years, and a geographical sweep limited to Europe, even within this restricted scope it is still possible to identify structural movements, nuances in the practice of the faith, and adaptations to a changing world. Because of this ability to remain current, there is much in Küng's view that the history of the Catholic Church has been a 'success story'.[2] Yet the process of adjustment has not been an easy one, and there are those who would argue that its recent record is one of decline and increasing irrelevance, especially when placed alongside the previous 1,700 years which, despite ups and downs, saw the establishment of Catholicism as the dominant religion in the civilised world with a concomitant political and social authority.

At the outset, it is worth noting that the map of Catholicism, with which this study began, has changed little in outline over the period in question. We would still consider Spain, Portugal and Italy in the south, Ireland in the west and Poland in the east as the bastions of Catholic piety and influence. Germany, Belgium and Austria retain a commitment with some pockets of particular strength. The one major change is that of France. Aptly known as the daughter of the Church in the eighteenth century, it has moved farthest down the road of secularisation. Even more striking is the fact that within countries, regional patterns of observance have, by and large, stayed astonishingly stable. In France, site of the most extensive sociological research, the *carte Boulard* for the 1950s reveals a picture familiar to the historian of the 1850s and the 1750s. Brittany, Normandy, the south-west and pockets of the north continue to be strongholds whereas the Paris basin, pre-eminently, continues to enjoy its well-merited soubriquet as a *pays de mission*.

Yet if, in outline, the frontiers of Catholicity are enduring, levels of practice have everywhere gone down. Not that this is a trend specific to the Roman religion; it is a feature to be found in Orthodoxy, Protestantism and Judaism which, if anything, have suffered more. It is in this context that Callum Brown has recently posited 'the death of Christian Britain'.[3] Only evangelical Christians and the Islamic faith appear so far to have bucked the trend, at least in recent decades, not just within Britain but across the Continent. The reasons for the decline will be reviewed later, but it should be stressed, at this juncture, that the fall in levels of practice has been neither continuous nor linear; the graph shows plenty of peaks and troughs, often conditioned by dramatic, external events as well as by more slow-moving socio-economic trends. The picture is further complicated by the fact that apparently similar contingent circumstances might produce quite different results. For instance, there can be little doubt that, in the long perspective, the French dechristianising campaign of 1793–94, and the experience of the revolution more generally, contributed powerfully to a long-term decline, whereas in Germany Bismarckian persecution had exactly the reverse effect to that intended, stimulating Catholic piety and organisation.

If the heartlands of practice have remained largely unaltered, albeit witnessing a lessening in levels of fervour, political power has very definitely seeped away from the Catholic world. Already by the eighteenth century, the collapse of Catholic Spain as the world's superpower presaged a longer-term shift, speeded up by the French revolutionary and Napoleonic wars. At every key juncture in international affairs, the Catholic world was eclipsed as the balance of power was readjusted. In 1815, Protestant Britain and Orthodox Russia were the key beneficiaries, and although the Habsburg Empire, centred on Austria, appeared set to maintain its dominance, with hindsight it can be seen how the Congress of Vienna inadvertently laid the basis for the rise of Prussia. Moreover, France could no longer be relied upon automatically to espouse the Catholic cause, something witnessed under Napoleon III whose erratic foreign policy was often determined by domestic variables.

The year 1870 saw not only the end of the house of Bonaparte but a further tilting of influence away from the Catholic camp through the creation of the German Empire, dominated by Protestant Prussia, the emergence of anti-clerical governments in France and Italy, and the additional waning of Habsburg Austria. It was a powerful testimony to the collapse of Catholic political power in the international domain that, in 1870, the Pope could find no state ready to ride to his rescue. Post-war, 1919 might have offered the Church the occasion to make up lost ground in former parts of the Habsburg Empire, but the Paris peace settlements confirmed the status of the USA, Japan, Britain, France as the great powers together with the USSR and Germany, although the latter were of course eclipsed in comparison to their pre-war status. After the Second World War, 1945 brought further anxieties to the Church with the establishment of the USA and the USSR as super-powers. It was of little comfort that the USA lent its support to religious and political freedoms in Western Europe when the Soviet Empire had gobbled up more or less all of the East. While the sudden collapse of communist authority in 1989–91 was interpreted as an omen by John Paul II, it remains to be seen what long-term impact some fifty years of sustained atheistic schooling and acculturation more generally will bring. Meanwhile, as western Europe gravitates towards greater integration around a Franco-German-British axis, the economic and political shortcomings of southern Catholic Europe may well be thrown into yet sharper focus.

In all European countries, regardless of religious complexion, the state has sloughed off notions of partnership with the Church, the possible exception being Ireland where successive governments have made a point of consulting religious leaders when devising policy. Even post-communist Poland is in-creasingly negligent of the Church voice in the conduct of public affairs. Things were very different in the eighteenth century when Church and state enjoyed a symbiotic relationship, so close that we may properly speak of confessional states in which government support for a single, established Church extended through protection for its doctrines, exclusive civil rights for its members and financial support for its institutions. In return, the Church preached submission to the temporal authority, undertook extensive charitable and educational work and functioned in some measure as a state bureaucracy and mouthpiece. Unquestionably, there were nuances in this overall picture. The Church in France, for instance, had achieved a significant independence from an otherwise powerful royal authority, and in Poland royal frailties permitted clerical supremacy. Everywhere, however, the trend was towards a more Erastian set-up, in which the state enjoyed the upper hand. What remained comforting for Catholicism was that nowhere did the state express an ideological hostility towards the spiritual and religious claims of the dom-inant religion, even if the temporal powers of the clergy were clipped. The so-called enlightened absolutism or despotism of the late eighteenth century merely continued this trend, as the emphasis was always on making government more efficient. It is true that certain rulers might have expressed some doubts, at least in court circles, about the claims of revealed religion, wanting to present themselves as being in the vanguard of European intellectual life, but they, like the *philosophes* more generally, championed religion for its social utility.

As in many other areas of human endeavour, it was the French Revolution which made the first breach in the otherwise sympathetic relationship between Church and state, and even this had not been anticipated in 1789, but emerged out of the particular circumstances of the ensuing decade, most obviously the resort to war in 1792 and the perceived shortcomings of the Constitutional Church. The subsequent attempt to extinguish Catholicism altogether and to substitute a state religion, the Cult of the Supreme Being, proved a disastrous experiment, and thereafter no government until the twentieth century attempted such a dramatic stratagem. Nevertheless, the manner in which

Napoleon dealt with the Church, through the inauguration of the concordat and the associated Organic Articles, which shackled the Church and more or less turned it into a department of state, revealed what might be achieved by a determined and forceful ruler.

Despite some disappointment with the French Concordat, which the Restoration monarchy was happy to leave in place, the papacy also saw such legal agreements as being the best way of safeguarding its own position and that of local churches. In the eyes of Rome, the very act of signing such a legally binding agreement was an implicit acknowledgement on the part of the state of the pontiff's authority; and what Rome delegated, it might in different circumstances be able to take back. There thus followed a plethora of accords during the first half of the nineteenth century in which the state offered some limited protection to the doctrines of the Catholic Church while permitting a degree of religious toleration. At the same time, the state accrued extensive control over such things as clerical appointments and exercised a degree of *de facto* control by dint of fiscal subsidies. While such arrangements reassured the papacy, other Catholics, most obviously Lamennais, were less sanguine. They viewed with alarm this move from what René Rémond terms 'a sacral state', combining government and religion, to a 'concordatory regime', in which the state did not necessarily support a single religion but still liked to interfere in clerical matters.[4] It was this concern which led Lamennais in particular to relinquish his earlier Ultramontanism and to champion the notion of 'a free church in a free state'. This standpoint was both logical and farsighted, recognising as it did that there could be no half-way house between the confessional state and complete state neutrality in matters of religion.

Lamennais' fears were confirmed in the aftermath of the Wars of Unification of the 1860s. In the newly united states of Germany and Italy, in the defeated France, and even momentarily in Spain and Portugal, Catholicism came under assault. The reasons were much the same everywhere, although the intensity of the attack varied according to local circumstances. In all these instances, there was resentment at the growth of Ultramontanism, epitomised in the declaration of papal infallibility. As we have seen, as state power grew, Catholics increasingly looked to Rome as a counter-weight. Such supra-national loyalties were always going to be anathema at a time when states were attempting to create a sense of belonging among their diverse populations. Nationhood, citizenship and social harmony were the concerns of the new regimes that ruled after 1870, and the Church had to be brought into line if these were to be attained.

It is thus possible to see why, in the late nineteenth century, the battle-grounds between Church and state were in areas such as marriage, education and appointments within the government bureaucracy. Civil marriage was a *sine qua non* of a modern state which refused to allow the definition of citizens to be at the behest of the Church; a patriotic and utilitarian elementary schooling was vital for national efficiency and the formation of responsible, 'right-thinking' individuals who would not abuse their democratic rights, limited though these were; and ecclesiastics could no longer be permitted to teach or administer if a state was to build for the future. That future, fuelled by industrial take-off, was bright on the one hand, but also brought with it, on the other, social problems on a scale which could no longer be left for private, philanthropic bodies to deal with, most notably the Church. The state, albeit hesitantly, accepted some responsibility for welfare, and increasingly took on this role in order to see off the socialist challenge which, after the initial anti-clerical assault, became enemy number one. While the mass politics of the late nineteenth century might have brought to the fore new men, influenced by Positivism, they were not radical in the sense that they sought fundamental social change, and often attempted to offset the left-wing challenge by coalescing in the cause of anti-clericalism.

It is against this nineteenth-century background that we can better understand the lure of twentieth-century right-wing dictatorships for many Catholics, since such authoritarian models involved a rejection of liberal anti-clericalism and individualism. The pro-clerical and traditionalist regimes that emerged in Italy, Hungary, Spain, Portugal, Poland, Yugoslavia, Austria and eventually in Vichy France augured a return to the moral certainties of the past, and promised a favoured position for the Church in the state. There was a fresh round of concordats, not so dissimilar in their essentials from those of a century earlier. These agreements were happily conceded by the dictators. Imbued with hierarchical, corporatist and patriarchal values, which superficially at least resembled Catholic teaching, they wished to have the Church on side in order to underpin their own authority. They also saw how the Church could infuse a sense of national identity, especially where Catholics formed a majority of the population, act as an agent of government propaganda and neutralise any potential opposition. For its part, the Church sought a restoration of its place in national society, access to state schools, the security of its own youth movements, a say in government policy and some measure of financial support.

Yet it was always going to be an unequal relationship. In Portugal and Spain, the Church more or less subjugated its identity, whereas in Italy the joy at the Lateran Accords was quickly overtaken by concern at the high-handed manner in which Mussolini flouted these arrangements. Nowhere was the policy more ruinous than in Germany where the 1933 Concordat helped legitimise the rise of Nazism at the cost of the Church's independence, marked most clearly by the collapse of the Zentrum and the Catholic trade unions and the muzzling of the clergy. It was one thing doing business with nineteenth-century monarchs, who actually possessed a residual respect for the Church and who were to a greater or lesser degree believers, but quite another signing concordats with Mussolini and Hitler who were wholly unscrupulous and irreligious. For them, religion was merely one of a number of pieces on a chessboard to be shuffled in pursuit of their one-party state, and should they have won the war the gains which the Church made in Croatia and Slovakia would have struggled to survive. Although the Vatican might not have appreciated it, the Church was better placed in those surviving liberal democracies such as France, Belgium, Ireland, the Netherlands, and indeed Protestant Britain, where it was allowed to function as part of a pluralist society, something which it did with outstanding success in the Low Countries where it was fundamental to the process of 'pillarisation'.

The aftermath of the Second World War ushered in a new phase in Church–state relations. In Eastern Europe, the communist takeover inaugurated a systematic assault not witnessed since the 1870s in Germany and the 1790s in France. Although this varied in intensity, and although it is not clear that the objective was the complete eradication of Christianity, this attack was none the less more dangerous because it was prosecuted with all the power available to totalitarian regimes. Within Western Europe, the experience of the Cold War, coupled with the uncomfortable dalliance with dictatorship, meant that the Church had little option but to accept a pluralist religious settlement. In certain places this was guaranteed by concordats, but in most instances these were not necessary. The state did not feel threatened by institutional religion and, though far from indifferent to matters of faith, was happy to accord Catholics considerable latitude. The passions engendered by the anti-clericalism and state-building of the nineteenth century had spent themselves, and the state was secure in the knowledge that it was supreme, even in Ireland and Spain. The Church could, in no sense, match the state in its range of activities; religious affiliation no longer posed a threat to national identity (though Northern Ireland, certainly from the standpoint of Ulstermen, remains a more complicated instance); the growth of secularisation, albeit uneven in its effects, undermined the standing of the Church; and the decline of specifically Catholic social and political organisations meant that the Church could not present itself as an alternative power-base to the state. In this situation, there was no need to revisit the battle-grounds of the past, and, apart from occasional jousting over such issues as divorce and abortion, Church–state relations in Western Europe have been largely harmonious.

Despite the presence of John Paul II to inveigh against the perils of unlimited freedom, this acceptance of liberal democracy is a reminder that the political history of Catholicism should not be written as a history of the right. That the Church has often sided with conservative forces – monarchism, Romanticism, Ultramontanism, anti-modernism, traditionalism and even fascism – cannot be doubted, and this is a trend especially marked in Catholic heartlands such as Spain. (Not for nothing did George Orwell comment that nationalist offensives in the Spanish Civil War were always prefaced by the ringing of church bells.)[5] Nor is this trend in any way surprising. Under the old regime, throne and altar were bound together, and the revolutionary experience, so frightening in its intensity, merely confirmed the predilection for social stability believed to be best ensured by monarchical regimes. Throughout the nineteenth century, Catholics were not unusual in believing that legitimate monarchs were a safeguard against destabilising ideologies and a repeat of the revolutionary experience. Yet if this was the dominant trend within Catholicism, the fear that the Church was suffocating under state tutelage gave rise to a liberal tradition, articulated notably by Montalambert, Lamennais and Lacordaire, which championed new forms of political and social action: greater participation of the laity in the everyday affairs of the

Church; the engagement of Catholics in the political life of the nation through the ballot box, petitions and the media; and the establishment of democratic and collegial principles throughout all levels of the Church.

Despite unpropitious circumstances, these ideals took deepest root in the Netherlands, Belgium and France. In the case of the Low Countries, this was hardly surprising given the long-standing tradition of political toleration and free thought. In the case of France, a vibrant fecundity of political options deriving from the revolution meant that Catholics were already familiar with novel forms of popular mobilisation. The first murmurings of industrialisation in these areas, and in the newly united Germany, also necessitated a bolder approach, and it is significant that Social Catholicism began to evolve alongside its liberal counterpart. Tellingly, it was again these countries which first experimented with Catholic political parties, most famously and successfully the Zentrum in Germany and the UCB in Belgium. None of these initiatives would have an easy ride. Apart from the legacy of the 1848 revolutions and the *Syllabus of Errors*, they also had to contend with the fall-out from the condemnation of modernism. This eclectic movement represented a brave attempt to come to terms with the stunning archaeological, scientific and cultural advances of the last third of the century, and was not necessarily liberal or even political in its implications. The wholesale condemnation of modernism further enhanced the reputation of the Church for reaction, and ensured the suppression of such movements as the Sillon. Small wonder that many Catholics in the inter-war period saw integralist movements and right-wing dictatorships as the best safeguard for the future.

As intimated above, the outcome of the Second World War created the environment in which liberal Catholicism could breathe more easily, most especially in the shape of Christian Democracy. In Italy, West Germany, France, Belgium, Austria and Holland, Christian Democratic parties all succeeded in achieving government representation, and for largely the same reasons: the devaluation of extreme right-wing politics; the shadow of the Holocaust; the untainted reputation of party members; the shared experience of the Resistance; the unwillingness of ecclesiastical hierarchies, tarred by their association with dictatorship, to throw their weight around; the vogue for European integration; and the promise of a new style of politics which emphasised consensus, hope and traditional values. Whether the Christian Democrats were truly 'liberal', especially when placed alongside their secular equivalents, is a matter for debate. Their stand on such issues as abortion, divorce and contraception can hardly be described in this fashion. What is incontrovertible is their commitment to democracy and the key role which they played in bringing Catholics into mainstream political life.

That participation endures, but the link between Catholicism and any particular party or political stance has largely been broken since the 1960s. This was when a variety of factors undermined the place of religion more generally within politics: the fading appeal of the Christian Democrats; the emergence of new forms of political discourse; the disintegration of Catholic Action and other social movements; and the coming-of-age of a fresh generation of voters with no experience of the Second World War who were largely secular in outlook. As an institution, the Church has also contributed to this process, by withdrawing largely from the hurly-burly of politics in the belief that its interests are best served by speaking out on particular issues rather than trying to drill the faithful into loyal soldiers of any particular party. The only Catholics who still wish to exert such discipline are to be found in authoritarian bodies such as Le Pen's Front National and Haider's Freedom Party which are, by nature, disciplinarian in their instincts if not always in their behaviour.

Social Catholicism has been riddled with as many ambiguities as political Catholicism, something again best explained by the adoption of a long-term perspective. The Church had always taken its mission to care for the less fortunate with the utmost seriousness, and old regime governments had been only too willing to leave the care of the sick, orphans, prostitutes, former soldiers and the aged to specialist Catholic agencies. By the late eighteenth and early nineteenth centuries, women's congregations were even teaching industrial skills, including lace-making, to young women who would otherwise have been unemployed. Impressive though these efforts were, the resources at the Church's disposal simply did not permit it to cope with the massive social and economic problems of pre-industrial Europe. The industrial Europe of the mid-nineteenth century posed challenges which were even greater. No longer could governments stand idly by, and the 1870s witnessed a steady drip of welfare legislation, if only to counter the beast of socialism which had arisen alongside technological change. Handicapped by the regressive thinking of Pius IX, obsessed with the Roman question, denuded of resources and readying itself to fight anti-clerical governments, the Church was painfully slow to mobilise in face of the Social Question, and such initiatives as there were tended to be concentrated in the Low Countries, France and Germany, and to emanate from well-meaning individuals such as Ketteler, Harmel and de Mun. *Rerum novarum* of 1891 was Rome's belated ideological response to a rapidly changing world, and has provided the enduring context in which Catholics have approached social issues ever since. On the one hand, the encyclical rejected the class conflict of Marxism and the militancy of trade unions, a line accepted by the majority of Catholics, the exception being some *Jocistes* in the 1930s and those Catholic activists who made common cause with their communist allies in the Resistance. On the other hand, it denounced the unbridled egoism of capitalism, something recently repeated by John Paul II, although it might be objected that the Church has condemned the left using far more strident terms than it has ever applied to the advocates of the free-market economy.

Ever since *Rerum novarum*, Social Catholicism has attempted to steer a middle way between the extremes of capitalism and socialism, yet it has never been certain what this third path should involve. What has undermined the search has been a struggle at the very heart of Social Catholicism. On the one hand there are those paternalists who, in line with Le Play and La Tour du Pin, have argued that man can find fulfilment only through membership of organic communities such as a Christian organisation overseen by the clergy; on the other hand there are those liberal-minded Catholics, successors to the *abbés démocrates*, who are prepared to leave their co-religionaries to their own devices. More recently, the disparate activities of the Church have struggled to compete with state welfarism which swelled in scale after 1945. By that date, the Church was also shifting its priorities to combating the perils of secularisation which were now seen as the greater threat, even though it was increasingly acknowledged that social problems were often at the heart of dechristianisation. The Second Vatican Council was, in large measure, designed to reverse the secularisation process by emphasising evangelisation but, by being insufficiently precise as to how this might be achieved, it inadvertently contributed to the decline of Catholic social organisations whose vigour was already being sapped by a growing religious indifference.

The decline in levels of piety, at least as traditionally measured, has led many commentators to regard the period under discussion as one of unabated secularisation. If secularisation is to be understood as a decline in the social significance of religion, then this trend may be detected in most spheres of human activity: the intellectual world is no longer dominated by religious concepts, and theology has been marginalised as an area of academic inquiry; politics have come to revolve largely around the secular; popular culture has witnessed the replacement of saints' days with secular leisure pursuits; artistic life, after the grandeur of the baroque, has largely ceased to play to a religious audience, and musicians, writers, sculptors and painters long ago gave up on the Church as the prime source of patronage; and the mental world inhabited by the individual, whether Catholic or non-believer, has less and less room for the workings of Providence. None of these developments has, however, been linear, irreversible, congruent or geographically uniform. Indeed, establishing the chronology of secularisation is no easy matter. The traditional perspective accords great importance to the Enlightenment as the start of this process, for the *philosophes* were cogent and noisy critics of the defects of revealed religion. Others would place emphasis on mid-nineteenth-century industrialisation and the concomitant shift from a predominantly agricultural and hierarchical world to a city-landscape of modernism, democracy and wealth. Historians of ideas have often preferred to locate the real beginnings of secularisation in the Belle Epoque when there was a veritable revolution in European thought, drawing on such materialist ideologies as Positivism, Marxism and Darwinism, and when governments themselves were eager to undermine the standing of the Church in civil society.

There is some validity in the above interpretations, though all need careful nuancing. In the case of the Enlightenment, it should be recalled that the principal attack was against the Church's doctrinal apparatus, its abuse of privilege and its parasitical nature. The *philosophes* themselves, however, were overwhelmingly deist, rather than atheist; their message may have permeated the salons, but went little further; and they themselves were enormously supportive of religion as a social cement. Likewise, industrialisation and secularisation were not covalent: industrialisation, and the associated phenomena of urbanisation and wealth-creation *might* but did not *necessarily* result in a decline in levels of piety and the marginalisation of religious values. The upheavals of the modern age led many to find refuge in religion; peasant migrants to the cities could just as easily use their faith as a prop to support their adaptation to city life as have it eroded by the urban environment; and novel technologies, including railways and methods of mass production, facilitated a new kind of faith, permitting the take-off of mass pilgrimages and the production of religious bric-à-brac, for instance. Theories of continuous secularisation also tend to neglect the religious response which, despite the shortcomings of Social Catholicism, attempted with some success to steer people away from a purely materialist existence. The challenge posed at the end of the nineteenth century by progressive values and state-sponsored laicism was undeniably real but, as we have seen, the diffusion of ideas was still socially restricted (reading was not necessarily believing) and the persistence of traditional forms of worship survived state persecution.

This study has demonstrated that, from Catholicism's point of view, and probably with respect to Christianity more generally, twentieth-century developments have had the greater impact, although undeniably drawing on earlier trends. Modern secularisation has resulted not so much from the experience of 'total war' or the growth of purely materialistic ideologies in the shape of communism and fascism, but from the broader social and cultural revolution which overtook Europe after the 1960s. The rhythm, pace and manner of this have varied between countries, but in all the liberal democracies it has manifested certain common characteristics: the growing professionalisation of society; an underlying prosperity; the material security underpinned by state welfarism; the post-war baby boom; the decline in patterns of deference; the experimentation with new forms of political and artistic discourse; greater educational opportunities; and the evolution, in particular, of the feminist movement which has transformed women's understanding of themselves and their place in society, and which eroded some of Catholicism's core support. Much of what the nineteenth-century Positivists had claimed for science as an essentially progressive activity now seemed to have become a reality as a man was landed on the moon, new drugs appeared almost daily and computerisation altered the workplace. It is arguable, however, that the advances of science over the twentieth century have increased, rather than decreased, the mysteries of the universe, both on the microscopic and macroscopic levels, something which Positivism had not envisaged. As both Catholics and others have pointed out, we now know much more about the scale of what we do not know, rather than what we do. This presents a nice opportunity for believers to reassert the relevance of their faith. So too does the growing awareness of an ecological crisis which highlights the difference between seeking to dominate Nature, as Positivists had sought to do, and acting responsibly towards it, a theme on which the scriptures have much to say.

This very rapid, amorphous and eclectic secularisation has not necessarily destroyed a belief in God, but it has pushed back the frontiers of religious influence and created a body of believers, many of whom adopt a pick-and-mix attitude towards their faith, and whose allegiance to their Church is piecemeal. Although some conservatives have bemoaned this drift to so-called 'cafeteria Catholicism', this could as easily be interpreted as a sign of continuing vitality, another example of the elasticity of a faith which has a long tradition not just of accommodating political, social and economic changes, but which has also adapted to satisfy people's emotional needs, hopes, fears and aspirations. There has always been a tension between what some have termed 'official' and 'popular' religion. The eighteenth-century clergy struggled to raise the quality of belief and practice, through the inculcation of greater knowledge of fundamental doctrines and the eradication of superstitious and abusive practices. The nineteenth-century clergy had perforce to be more accepting of certain 'popular' practices, lest the faithful succumbed to the secularising trends unleashed by the French Revolution and abandoned the Church altogether. This has often been characterised as a move away from a 'God of Fear' to a 'God of Love', expressed in the adoption of Liguorian principles in respect of confession and absolution, involving a less austere, intrusive and unwelcoming approach than previously. This new approach also manifested itself in the adoption of popularly recognised saints, the adulation of Mary, the growth of pilgrimages and the proliferation of religious artefacts. It has been characterised as a 'saccharine' faith, with a particular appeal to women. Whether this description is really valid must be a matter of dispute, as must the implicit suggestion that women are more susceptible to such blandishments. What is indisputable, however, is that women were conspicuous by their high levels of religious observance and their membership of the religious orders and congregations which remained the backbone of the Church's charitable and social endeavours and which offered women a challenging, adventurous and rewarding career. Nor should we imagine that the threat of hell-fire and damnation disappeared altogether from the rhetoric of the clergy and from the popular imagination, at least in certain geographical areas. Philippe Guignet's study of clerical sermons reveals that preachers in early-nineteenth-century Cambrésis continued to frighten parishioners with descriptions of 'prisons of flames' reserved for those who died impenitent;[6] while the sermon which James Joyce has Stephen Dedalus recounting in *Portrait of the Artist as a Young Man* is a reminder of how seventeenth-century concepts of hell, punishment and damnation remained current some three hundred years later.

Twentieth-century Catholicism perhaps lacks the same kind of identity, but one possible descriptor is of 'A God afar', by which is meant the emergence, in recent decades, of a belief in a fundamentally benign Creator God, but one who does not intervene in routine fashion in the workings of the natural world, and who may be worshipped in a variety of ways or, indeed, in none at all. What does seem clear is that since the initiatives of Catholic Action in the 1930s, there have been moves to encourage much greater lay involvement in Church affairs, something which was given official blessing by the Second Vatican Council, although one unintended result of this has been that people are no longer quite so sure of their obligations towards the Church. An additional corollary to this trend has been a privatisation of religion, assisted by the breakdown of social and legal obligations to outward conformity.

Such developments in popular piety reflect a changing role for the priest in the parish. No longer is he always the dominant figure in the sacral process, not least of all because of the shortage of clergy which has, of necessity, brought the laity into greater prominence. Paradoxically, the marginalisation of the parish priest, a process whose origins may be traced back to the French Revolution, has been mirrored by an enhanced role for the pontiff. This could not have been foreseen before 1789. At that stage, the papacy appeared obsessed with labyrinthine Italian politics, was socially and economically ill-placed to influence the decisions of the great powers, was theologically at sea (although this should not be taken to imply that it has now come safely into harbour), and exerted little practical influence in the day-to-day ordering of the national churches. The French Revolution initiated the rise of Ultra-montanism, and subsequently local churches in the nineteenth century looked to the counter-weight of Rome for guidance and leadership in their conflict with state power. Several other factors also came into play: a rejection of liberal Catholicism; the growth of the city of Rome as a pilgrimage centre; the conservative instincts of Gregory XVI; the length of Pius IX's pontificate and his personal popularity; and the unforeseen outcome to Italian unification which left the Pope a prisoner in the Vatican, something that paradoxically boosted papal prestige. The declaration of papal infallibility was a product of the drive towards Ultramontanism, and although infallibility was quite narrowly defined, it nevertheless created an impression of supremacy and encouraged Catholics to look to Rome, while at the same time encouraging anti-clericals to attack Rome.

The accretion and pretension of power might not, perhaps, have mattered so much in an earlier period, but it was unfortunate in the twentieth century. In an 'age of extremes', when Rome could have provided moral guidance, all too often the incumbents of Peter's throne were found wanting, most notably Pius XII, whose pusillanimous response to the Holocaust left a wound which has yet to heal. The inability of successive pontiffs to relinquish their purported authority, in defiance of the spirit of the Second Vatican Council, has created a situation where they are out of step with public opinion. This would not matter so much if they were not also out of step with so many ordinary Catholics. Despite the personal charisma and media skills of John Paul II, the papacy still appears wedded to an otiose vision of Catholicism: Eurocentric, male-dominated, hierarchical, and doctrinally absolute. Some see this as providing strength, stability and direction. Yet a history of the past 250 years suggests otherwise. Unless there is a profound change of attitude and a significant readjustment in the relationship between the Vatican and the rest of the Church, then the diversity within unity which has always been the underlying strength of the Church and a feature of its universality may well give way to a Church that claims to be universal but is in truth hidebound and merely monolithic.

Notes

Introduction

1. See J. Delumeau, *Catholicism between Luther and Voltaire* (Cambridge, 1977) and E. Le Roy Ladurie, *Montaillou. Cathars and Catholics in a French Village, 1294–1324* (London, 1980).
2. H. Daniel-Rops, *The History of the Church of Christ*, Vol. 7 (London, 1964), p. 2.
3. See the Bibliographical Essay for a more detailed analysis of the literature.
4. H. Jedin and J. Dolan (eds), *History of the Church*, 10 vols (London, 1965–81).
5. F. Fehér, *The French Revolution and the Birth of Modernity* (Los Angeles, 1990), p. 177.

1. Catholicism in Retrenchment

1. J. McManners, *The French Revolution and the Church* (London, 1969), p. 105.
2. The notion of a 'fortress faith' is a common theme in the historiography of Catholicism in Britain, but see especially M. Hornsby-Smith, *Roman Catholic Beliefs in England. Customary Catholicism and Transformations of Religious Authority* (Cambridge, 1991) together with his *Roman Catholics in England. Studies in Social Structure since the Second World War* (Oxford, 1987).
3. Quoted in A. Latreille, *L'Eglise Catholique et l révolution française*, Vol. 3 (Paris, 1946), p. 45.
4. Much of what follows on individual countries is taken from W. J. Callahan and D. Higgs (eds), *Church in Society in Catholic Europe of the Eighteenth Century* (Cambridge, 1979).
5. Quoted in H. Jedin and J. Dolan (eds), *History of the Church*, Vol. 6 (London, 1981), p. 171.
6. Quoted in W. J. Callahan, *Church, Politics and Society in Spain, 1750–1874* (Cambridge, MA, 1984), p. 5.
7. Quoted in H. Daniel-Rops, *The History of the Church of Christ*, Vol. 7 (London, 1964), p. 234.
8. Quoted in D. Holmes and B. W. Bickers, *A Short History of the Catholic Church* (London, 2001), p. 178.
9. Quoted in L. von Pastor, *The History of the Popes from the Late Middle Ages*, 40 vols (London, 1923–53), Vol. 33, p. 301.
10. E. E. Y. Hales, *Revolution and the Papacy, 1769–1846* (London, 1960), p. 32.
11. Daniel-Rops, *History of the Church of Christ*, Vol. 7, p. 216.
12. Quoted in Hales, *Revolution and Papacy*, p. 36.
13. Jedin and Dolan (eds), *History of the Church*, Vol. 7, p. 216.
14. Quoted in Daniel-Rops, *History of the Church of Christ*, Vol. 7, p. 238.
15. Quoted in Callahan, *Church, Politics and Society*, p. 10.
16. Ibid., p. 15.
17. See D. Julia, 'Le Prêtre au XVIIIe siècle. La théologie et les institutions', *Recherches*

de Sciences Religieuses, 58 (1970), 521–34, and D. Julia and W. Frijhoff, 'The French Priest in Modern Times', *Concilium*, 7 (1969), 66–71.

18. Quoted in Daniel-Rops, *History of the Church of Christ*, Vol. 7, p. 225.

19. Ibid., p. 227.

20. Ibid., p. 38.

21. The original phrase is that of Max Weber, 'Entzauberung der Welt', in his *The Protestant Ethic in the Spirit of Capitalism* (New York, 1958), p. 105. See too R. W. Scribner, 'The Reformation, Popular Magic and the "Disenchantment of the World"', *Journal of Interdisciplinary History*, 23 (1993), 475–94, and K. Thomas, *Religion and the Decline of Magic* (London, 1971), pp. 27–89.

22. Quoted in A. Lugarde et al. (eds), *Encyclopédie. Extraits* (Paris, 1967), p. 120.

23. Quoted in R. Trappes-Lomax, 'Archbishop Blackburne's Visitation Returns of York', *Publications of the Catholic Record Society*, 32 (1932), 384.

24. See M. Elliott, *The Catholics of Ulster* (London, 2000).

25. Quoted in P. Gay, *Voltaire's Politics. The Poet as Realist* (Princeton, 1959), p. 265.

26. Ibid.

27. See most especially F. Dostoyevsky, *Crime and Punishment*. Also see J. M. Byrne, *Glory, Jest and Riddle. Religious Thought in the Enlightenment* (London, 1996), p. 125.

28. See his essay in *Dictionary of the History of Ideas* (New York, 1973), pp. 100–12, reprinted in H. Hardy (ed.), *Against the Current. Essays in the History of Ideas* (New York, 1980).

29. Quoted in E. Preclin and E. Jarry, *Les Luttes politiques et doctrinales aux XVIIe et XVIIIe siècles* (Paris, 1956), Vol. 19 of A. Fliche and V. Martin, *Histoire de l'Eglise*, 26 vols (Paris, 1946–64), p. 736 (authors' translation).

30. G. Le Bras, 'Statistique et histoire religieuse. Pour un examen détaillé et pour une explication historique de l'état de catholicisme dans les diverse régions de France', *Revue d'histoire de l'Eglise de France*, 17 (1931), 425–49; reprinted in his *Etudes de sociologie religieuse*, 2 vols (Paris, 1955–56).

31. Quoted in R. Po-Chia Hsia, *The World of Catholic Renewal, 1540–1770* (Cambridge, 1998), p. 53.

32. See M. Vovelle, *Piété baroque et déchristianisation en Provence, 1750–1820* (Paris, 1973).

33. P. Chaunu, *La Mort à Paris, XVI, XVII et XVIII siècles* (Paris, 1978).

34. See D. Gentilcore, '"Adapt Yourselves to the People's Capabilities". Missionary Strategies, Methods and Impact in the Kingdom of Naples, 1600–1800', *Journal of Ecclesiastical History*, 45 (1994), 269–96.

35. See the essays in S. J. Brown and D. W. Miller (eds), *Piety and Power in Ireland, 1760–1960. Essays in Honour of Emmet Larkin* (Belfast, 2000).

2. Catholicism in Revolution

1. Quoted in J. M. Roberts and R. C. Cobb (eds), *French Revolution Documents*, Vol. 1 (Oxford, 1966), pp. 171–4.

2. See R. Rémond, *Religion and Society in Modern Europe* (Oxford, 1999).

3. Quoted in N. Aston, *Religion and Revolution in France, 1780–1804* (Basingstoke, 2000), p. 144. Camus went on to argue that 'we are a National Convention, we have the power to change religion'. Quoted in D. C. Miller, 'A.-G. Camus and the Civil Constitution of the Clergy', *Catholic Historical Review*, 76, (1990), 448, n.8.

4. Quoted in M. J. Mavidal et al. (eds), *Archives parlementaires de 1781 à 1860*, première série (Paris, 1879–1990), Vol. 16, pp. 408–9, 535.

5. Contained in Roberts and Cobb (eds), *French Revolution Documents*, Vol. 1, p. 187.

6. T. Tackett, *Becoming a Revolutionary. The Deputies of the French National Assembly* (Princeton, 1996), pp. 71–2.

7. T. Tackett, *Religion, Revolution and Regional Culture in Eighteenth-Century France. The Ecclesiastical Oath of 1791* (Princeton, 1986), see esp. the map on p. 53 and compare this with maps of religious practice in the nineteenth and twentieth centuries, conveniently reproduced in R. Gibson, *A Social History of French Catholicism, 789–1914* (London, 1989), pp. 171–2.

8. Quoted in A. Aulard (ed.), *Recueil des actes du comité de salut public avec la correspondance officielle des représentants-en-mission et le registre du conseil exécutif provisoire*, 26 vols (Paris, 1888–1923), Vol. 10, p. 561.

9. Archives Départementales du Doubs, L244, letter of 11 October 1793, and L213, order of 28 September 1793.

10. Quoted in G. Cubitt, 'God, Man and Satan. Strands in Counter-Revolutionary Thought among French Catholics', in F. Tallett and N. Atkin (eds), *Catholicism in Britain and France since 1789* (London, 1996), p. 136.

11. Quoted in P. Gueniffey, 'Robespierre', in F. Furet and M. Ozouf (eds), *Dictionnaire critique de la révolution française* (Paris, 1988), p. 328.

12. Quoted in C. B. McNamara, *The Hébertists. A Study of a French Revolutionary 'Faction' in the Reign of Terror, 1793–1794* (London, 1979), p. 244.

13. Quoted in S. Desan, *The Revival of Religion during the French Revolution* (Michigan, 1988), p. 281.

14. Quoted in S. Desan, *Reclaiming the Sacred. Lay Religion and Popular Politics in Revolutionary France* (Ithaca, 1990), p. 204.

15. *Le Figaro*, 16 August 1989.

16. K. Carpenter, *Refugees of the French Revolution. Emigrés in London, 1789–1802* (Basingstoke, 1999).

17. Quoted in G. Williams and J. Ramsden, *Ruling Britannia. A Political History of Britain, 1688–1988* (London, 1990), p. 161.

18. Quoted in E. R. Norman, *The English Catholic Church in the Nineteenth Century* (Oxford, 1984), p. 21.

19. Quoted in E. Duffy, *Saints and Sinners. A History of the Popes* (Yale, 1997), p. 202.

20. Quoted in E. E. Y. Hales, *Revolution and the Papacy, 1769–1846* (London, 1960), p. 116.

21. Quoted in Duffy, *Saints and Sinners*, p. 203.

22. Taken from D. G. Wright, *Napoleon and Europe* (London, 1979), p. 102.

23. Quoted in M. Vaughan and M. S. Archer, *Educational Change and Social Conflict in England and France, 1789–1848* (Cambridge, 1971), p. 184.

24. Quoted in O. Chadwick, *The Popes and the European Revolution* (Oxford, 1981), p. 484.

25. Quoted in Duffy, *Saints and Sinners*, p. 206.

26. See F. J. Coppa (ed.), *Controversial Concordats. The Vatican's Relations with Napoleon, Mussolini and Hitler* (Washington, 1999).

27. Quoted in Hales, *Revolution and the Papacy*, p. 117.

28. Quoted in M. Rey, *Le Diocèse de Besançon et de Sainte-Cloud* (Paris, 1977), p. 155.

29. Quoted in W. J. Callahan, *Church, Politics and Society in Spain, 1750–1874* (Cambridge, MA, 1984), p. 163.

30. See M. Broers, 'The War against God. Napoleon, Pope Pius VII and the People of Italy, 1800–1814', *The Historian*, 69 (2001), 16–21.

31. Quoted in M. Broers, *The Politics of Religion in Napoleonic Italy. The War against God, 1801–1814* (London, 2002), p. 31.

32. Quoted in A. Dansette, *A Religious History of Modern France*, Vol. 1 (London, 1961), p. 152.

33. Duffy, *Saints and Sinners*, p. 213.

3. Catholicism Restored

1. N. Davies, *God's Playground. A History of Poland*, 2 vols (London, 1981).

2. J. Steinberg, *Why Switzerland?* (Cambridge, 1995), p. 217.

3. E. Duffy, *Saints and Sinners. A History of the Popes* (Yale, 1997), p. 215.

4. D. Hempton, *Religion and Political Culture in Britain and Ireland from the Glorious Revolution to the Decline of Empire* (Cambridge, 1996), p. 81.

5. M. Rowe, 'The Napoleonic Legacy and the Politics of Reform in Restoration Prussia', in D. Laven and L. Riall (eds), *Napoleon's Legacy. Problems of Government in Restoration Europe* (Oxford, 2000), p. 139.

6. Quoted in H. Jedin and J. Dolan (eds), *History of the Church*, Vol. 7 (London, 1981), p. 289.

7. Contained in E. E. Y. Hales, *Revolution and the Papacy, 1769–1846* (London, 1960), pp. 257–8.

8. O. Chadwick, *The Popes and the European Revolution* (Oxford, 1981), p. 569.

9. H. Daniel-Rops, *The History of the Church of Christ*, Vol. 8 (London, 1965), p. 181.

10. J. N. D. Kelly, *The Oxford Dictionary of the Popes* (Oxford, 1986), p. 307.

11. R. Carr, *Spain, 1808–1975* (Oxford, 1982), p. 146.

12. Quoted in J. D. Holmes, *The Triumph of the Holy See. A Short History of the Papacy in the Nineteenth Century* (London, 1978), p. 71.

13. Quoted in ibid., p. 172.

14. Quoted in A. R. Vidler, *Prophecy and Papacy. A Study of Lamennais, the Church and the Revolution* (London, 1954), pp. 184–220.

15. Quoted in Holmes, *Triumph of the Holy See*, p. 98.

16. Quoted in R. Gibson, *A Social History of French Catholicism, 1789–1914* (London, 1989), p. 57.

17. F. Lannon, *Privilege, Persecution and Prophecy. The Catholic Church in Spain, 1875–1975* (Oxford, 1987), p. 63.

18. Quoted in Gibson, *Social History*, p. 168.

19. Ibid., p. 71.

20. Quoted in D. Laven, *Venice and Venetia under the Habsburgs, 1815–1835* (Oxford, 2002), p. 169. See, too, B. Bertoli, 'La Chiesa Veneziana nel clima della restaurazione', in G. Andolfo et al. (eds), *La Chiesa Veneziana Dal Tramonto Della Serenissima al 1848* (Venice, 1986).

21. E. Larkin, 'The Devotional Revolution in Ireland 1850–75', *American Historical Review*, 77 (1972), 625–52. See also his *The Roman Catholic Church and the Home Rule Question in Ireland, 1870–1874* (Dublin, 1990), and his *Historical Dimensions of Irish Catholicism* (New York, 1976).

22. See, for example, F. Mather, 'Georgian Churchmanship Reconciled. Some Variations in Anglican Public Worship, 1714–1830', *Journal of Eccesiastical History*, 36 (1985), 255–83.

23. Quoted in A. D. Gilbert, *Religion and Society in Industrial England. Church, Chapel and Society, 1740–1914* (London, 1976), p. 174.

24. Quoted in O. Chadwick, *A History of the Popes, 1830–1914* (Oxford, 1998), p. 66.

25. Ibid.

26. Quoted in R. Price (ed.), *1848 in France* (London, 1975), p. 92.

27. Ibid., p. 93.

28. Quoted in Jedin and Dolan (eds), *History of the Church*, Vol. 8, p. 68.

29. Ibid.

4. Catholicism Retuned

1. Quoted in J. D. Holmes, *The Triumph of the Holy See. A Short History of the Papacy in the Nineteenth Century* (London, 1978), p. 134.

2. See especially R. Harris, *Lourdes. Body and Spirit in the Secular Age* (London, 1999).

3. H. Jedin and J. Dolan (eds), *History of the Church*, Vol. 8 (London, 1981), p. 229.

4. Quoted in E. Duffy, *Saints and Sinners. A History of the Popes* (Yale, 1997), pp. 228–9.

5. Quoted in M. Ward, *William George Ward and the Catholic Revival* (London, 1969), pp. 158–9.

6. Quoted in O. Chadwick, *A History of the Popes, 1830–1914* (Oxford, 1998), p. 186.

7. Quoted in T. G. McCarthy, *The Catholic Tradition. Before and After Vatican II, 1878–1993* (Chicago, 1994), p. 3.

8. L. Trzeciakowski, *The Kulturkampf in Prussian Poland* (New York, 1990), pp. 3, 13ff.

9. Quoted in H. McLeod, *Secularisation in Western Europe, 1848–1914* (Basingstoke, 2000), pp. 104–5.

10. Quoted in Holmes, *Triumph of the Holy See*, p. 175.

11. Chadwick, *History of the Popes*, p. 254 *et seq.*

12. Quoted in M. L. Anderson, 'The Kulturkampf and the Course of German History', in *Central European History*, 19 (1986), 112, n. 78.

13. Quoted in B. M. G. Reardon (ed.), *Roman Catholic Modernism* (London, 1970), p. 10.

14. See A. Loisy, *The Gospel and the Church* (London, 1903). *My Duel with the Vatican* (New York, 1968), first published 1924, presents his side of the story.

15. J. Gallagher, *Times Past, Time Future. An Historical Study of Catholic Moral Theology* (New York, 1990), p. 49.

16. Quoted in Duffy, *Saints and Sinners*, p. 249.

17. M. Baigent and R. Leigh, *The Inquisition* (London, 2000), p. 216.

18. Quoted in Chadwick, *History of the Popes*, p. 357.

19. G. Daly, *Transcendence and Immanence. A Study in Catholic Modernism and Integralism* (Oxford, 1980), p. 51. See too Reardon (ed.), *Roman Catholic Modernism*.

20. A. R. Vidler, *The Modernist Movement in the Roman Catholic Church* (Cambridge, 1934), p. 95.

21. Duffy, *Saints and Sinners*, p. 251.

22. Jedin and Dolan (eds), *History of the Church*, Vol. 9, pp. 468–9.

23. See E. Weber, *Action Française* (Stanford, 1961), *passim*.

24. Quoted in R. Wistrich, 'Unpardonable', *Times Literary Supplement*, 1 March 2002, pp. 6–7.

25. Ibid.

26. McLeod, *Secularisation in Western Europe*, p. 1.

27. G. Cholvy, *La Religion en France de la fin du XVIIIe à nos jours* (Paris, 1991), pp. 189 ff.

28. O. Chadwick, *The Secularisation of the European Mind in the Nineteenth Century* (Cambridge, 1975).

29. R. R. Palmer, *Catholics and Unbelievers in Eighteenth-Century France* (Princeton, 1939).

30. M. D. Biddiss, *The Age of the Masses* (London, 1979), p. 112.

31. See M. Bradbury and J. M. McFarlaine, 'The Name and Nature of Modernism', in M. Bradbury and J. M. McFarlaine (eds), *Modernism, 1890–1930* (London, 1976), pp. 19–55.

32. M. D. Biddiss, 'Intellectual and Cultural Revolution, 1890–1914', in P. Hayes (ed.), *Themes in Modern European History, 1890–1945* (London, 1992), p. 87.

33. W. J. Callahan, 'An Organisational and Pastoral Failure. Urbanisation, Industrialisation and Religion in Spain, 1850–1930', in H. McLeod (ed.), *European Religion in the Age of Great Cities, 1830–1930* (London, 1995), p. 45.

34. J. McMillan, 'France', in T. Buchanan and M. Conway (eds), *Political Catholicism in Europe, 1918–1965* (Oxford, 1996), pp. 34–68.

35. G. Le Bras, 'Statistique et histoire religieuse. Pour un examen détaillé et pour une explication historique de l'état de catholicisme dans les diverse régions de France', *Revue d'histoire de l'Eglise de France*, 17 (1931), 425–49, reprinted in his *Etudes de sociologie religieuse*, 2 vols (Paris, 1955–56) and F. Boulard, *An Introduction to Religious Sociology* (London, 1960).

36. G. Cholvy and Y.-M. Hilaire, *Histoire religieuse de la France contemporaine*, 3 vols (Toulouse, 1985–86).

37. McLeod, *Secularisation in Western Europe*, and J. Sperber, 'Roman Catholic Religious Identity in Rhineland-Westphalia, 1800–1870', *Social History*, 7 (1982), 305–18, and his *Popular Catholicism in Nineteenth-Century Germany* (Princeton, 1984). See most recently E. Yonke, 'The Problem of the Middle Class in German Catholic History. The Nineteenth-Century Rhineland Revisited', *Catholic Historical Review*, 88 (2002), 263–80.

38. W. J. Callahan, *The Catholic Church in Spain, 1875–1998* (Washington, 2000), p. 273. See also his *Church, Politics and Society in Spain, 1750–1874* (Cambridge, MA, 1984) and F. Lannon, *Privilege, Persecution and Prophecy. The Catholic Church in Spain, 1875–1975* (Oxford, 1987), especially pp. 12–13.

39. Quoted in W. J. Callahan, 'Was Spain Catholic?', *Revista Canadiense de Estudios Hispanicos* (1984), p. 166.

40. Ibid.

41. D. Blackbourn, *Marpingen. Apparitions of the Virgin Mary in Bismarckian Germany* (Oxford, 1993), pp. 17–42.

42. H. Graeff, *Mary. A History of Doctrine and Devotion* (London, 1994), p. 126.

43. S. O'Brien, 'Making Catholic Spaces. Women, Décor and Devotion in the English Catholic Church, 1840–1900', in D. Wood (ed.), *Studies in Church History* (Oxford, 1995) pp. 449–75.

44. R. Gibson, 'Hellfire and Damnation in Nineteenth-Century France', *Catholic Historical Review*, 74 (1988), 383–402.

45. Harris, *Lourdes*, and Blackbourn, *Marpingen*.

46. J. McMillan, 'Religion and Gender in Modern France. Some Reflections', in F. Tallett and N. Atkin (eds), *Religion, Society and Politics in France since 1789* (London, 1991), pp. 55–66.

47. O. Hufton, 'What is Religious History Now?', in D. Cannadine (ed.), *What is History Now?* (London, 2002), pp. 57–79, and her *The Prospect before Her. A History of Women in Western Europe, 1500–1800* (London, 1995).

48. For much that follows here, see chs 12–14 in J. McManners (ed.), *The Oxford Illustrated History of Christianity* (Oxford, 1990).

49. McCarthy, *The Catholic Tradition*.

5. Catholicism and Reaction

1. Quoted in J. Pollard, *The Vatican and Italian Fascism, 1929–1932* (Oxford, 1985), p. 21.

2. Ibid., p. 22.

3. Ibid.

4. Ibid., pp. 103–32.

5. S. Payne, *A History of Fascism, 1914–45* (London, 1995), pp. 252–67.

6. M. Vincent, *Catholicism in the Second Spanish Republic* (Oxford, 1986).

7. Quoted in F. Lannon, *Privilege, Persecution and Prophecy. The Catholic Church in Spain, 1875–1975* (Oxford, 1987), p. 37.

8. Ibid., p. 175.

9. W. J. Callahan, 'Was Spain Catholic?', *Revista Canadiense de Estudios Hispanicos* (1984), p. 175.

10. See S. Ben-Ami, *Fascism from Above. The Dictatorship of Primo de Rivera, 1920–1930* (Oxford, 1983).

11. Lannon, *Privilege, Persecution and Prophecy*, p. 180.

12. Vincent, *Catholicism in the Second Spanish Republic*, pp. 1–3.

13. See C. Ford, *Creating the Nation in Provincial France. Religion and Political Identity* (Princeton, 1993).

14. For much of what follows, see T. Gallagher, 'Portugal', in T. Buchanan and M. Conway (eds), *Political Catholicism in Europe, 1918–1965* (Oxford, 1996), pp. 129–55. This collection of essays, and its bibliographical suggestions, is indispensable for inter-war Catholicism and we are indebted to its findings.

15. Quoted in M. Conway, *Catholic Politics in Europe, 1918–1945* (London, 1997), p. 60.

16. Quoted in L. Laszlo, 'Hungary. From Cooperation to Resistance, 1919–1945', in R. J. Wolff and K. J. Hoensch (eds), *Catholics, the State and the European Radical Right, 1919–1945* (Boulder, 1987), p. 126.

17. See K. J. Hoensch, 'Slovakia. "One God, One People, One Party". The Development, Aim and Failure of Political Catholicism', in Wolff and Hoensch (eds), *Catholics, the State and the European Radical Right*, pp. 158–81.

18. Quoted in Z. Zeendal, 'Germany. The Catholic Church and the Nazi Regime, 1933–45', in Wolff and Hoensch (eds), *Catholics, the State and the European Radical Right*, p. 96.

19. Quoted in ibid.

20. Quoted in J. S. Conway, *The Nazi Persecution of the Churches, 1933–45* (London, 1964), p. 126.

21. Conway, *Catholic Politics in Europe, 1918–1945*, pp. 51–2.

22. See especially H. Post, *Pillarisation. An Analysis of Dutch and Belgian Society* (Gower, 1989).

23. See M. Conway, 'Belgium', in Buchanan and Conway (eds), *Political Catholicism in Europe*, pp. 187–218.

24. Ibid.

25. J. F. McMillan, 'Catholicism and Nationalism in France. The Case of the Fédération Nationale Catholique, 1924–39', in F. Tallett and N. Atkin (eds), *Catholicism in Britain and France since 1789* (London, 1996), pp. 151–63.

26. J. F. McMillan, 'France', in Buchanan and Conway (eds), *Political Catholicism in Europe*, pp. 34–68.

27. See H. W. Paul, *The Second Ralliement* (Washington, 1967).

28. G. Le Bras, 'Statistique et histoire religieuse. Pour un examen détaillé et pour une explication historique de l'état de catholicisme dans les diverse régions de France', *Revue d'histoire de l'Eglise de France*, 17 (1931), 425–49, reprinted in his *Etudes de sociologie religieuse*, 2 vols (Paris, 1955) and F. Boulard, *An Introduction to Religious Sociology* (London, 1960).

29. A. Werth, *Twilight of France* (London, 1942), p. 216.

30. G. Orwell, *A Clergyman's Daughter* (London, 1935).

31. Quoted in T. Buchanan, 'Great Britain', in Buchanan and Conway (eds), *Political Catholicism in Europe*, p. 264.

32. Ibid., p. 266.

33. D. S. Cairns (ed.), *The Army and* Religion (London, 1919), p. 9, also quoted in H. McLeod, *Religion and the People of Western Europe, 1789–1970* (Oxford, 1981), p. 94, and the report, *The Army and Religion. An Enquiry and its Bearing upon the Religious Life of the Nation* (London, 1919).

34. R. Graves, *Goodbye to All That* (London, 1960), pp. 241–2. See too J. Stuart Roberts, *Siegfried Sassoon, 1886–1967* (London, 1999), p. 235.

35. Quoted in Callahan, 'Was Spain Catholic?', p. 161.

36. Ibid.

37. *Non abbiamo bisogno* (1931). The phrasing had previously been employed informally by the Pope. See H. Jedin and J. Dolan (eds), *History of the Church*, Vol. 10 (London, 1981), p. 307.

38. Lannon, *Privilege, Persecution and Prophecy*, p. 148.

39. Ibid., p. 149.

40. Vincent, *Catholicism in the Second Spanish Republic*, p. 120.

41. Quoted in Jedin and Dolan (eds), *History of the Church*, Vol. 10, p. 300.

42. From P. Adam, *La Vie paroissiale en France au XVII siècle* (Paris, 1964), p. 250. See too C. M. Bellitto, *Nicolas de Clamanges. Spirituality, Personal Reform and Pastoral Renewal on the Eve of the Reformation* (Washington, 2001).

43. R. A. Schneider, *The Ceremonial City. Toulouse Observed, 1738–1780* (Princeton, 1995), p. 175.

44. Vincent, *Catholicism in the Second Spanish Republic*, p. 102.

45. Lannon, *Privilege, Persecution and Prophecy*, p. 52.

46. G. Chevalier, *Clochemerle* (Paris, 1933).

47. Lannon, *Privilege, Persecution and Prophecy*, p. 52.

48. Vincent, *Catholicism in the Second Spanish Republic*, p. 37.

49. Boulard, *Introduction to Religious Sociology*.

50. Conway, *Catholic Politics in Europe*, p. 79.

51. J. Cornwell, *Hitler's Pope. The Secret Life of Pius XII* (London, 1999), p. 208.

52. J. M. Sánchez, *Pius XII and the Holocaust* (Washington, 2001).

53. W. D. Halls, 'Catholicism under Vichy', in H. R. Kedward and R. Austin (eds), *Vichy France and the Resistance. Culture and Ideology* (London, 1985), p. 133.

54. Quoted in S. Mews, 'The Sword of the Spirit. A Catholic Crusade of 1940', in W. J. Shiels (ed.), *Studies in Church History* (Oxford, 1985), p. 410.

55. Cornwell, *Hitler's Pope*, pp. 241–77.

56. Quoted in J. Duquesne, *Les Catholiques français sous l'occupation* (Paris, 1966). See too M. Ferro, *Pétain* (Paris, 1987), pp. 125–6.

57. M. Larkin, *Religion, Politics and Preferment in France since 1890. La Belle Epoque and its Legacy* (Cambridge, 1995), p. 175.

58. W. D. Halls, *Christianity, Society and Politics in Vichy France* (Oxford, 1995), p. 83.

59. Quoted in ibid., p. 49.

60. Conway, *Catholic Politics in Europe*, pp. 87 ff.

61. Cornwell, *Hitler's Pope*, p. 280.

62. Ibid., p. 297.

63. P. Blet et al. (eds), *Actes et documents du Saint Siège relatif à la seconde guerre mondiale*, 11 vols (Vatican City, 1965–82).

64. S. Zucotti, *Under his Very Windows. The Vatican and the Holocaust in Italy* (Yale, 2001).

65. Cornwell, *Hitler's Pope*, p. 292.

66. Ibid., p. 293.

67. Ibid.

68. Quoted in ibid., p. 287.

69. M. Marrus and R. O. Paxton, *Vichy France and the Jews* (New York, 1981), p. 273.

70. O. Chadwick, 'The Pope and the Jews in 1942', in Shiels (ed.), *Studies in Church History*, p. 467.

6. Catholicism Revised

1. O. Chadwick, *The Christian Church in the Cold War* (London, 1992), p. 5.

2. Ibid.

3. E. Hobsbawm, *Age of Extremes. The Short Twentieth Century, 1914–1991* (London, 1994), p. 238.

4. Chadwick, *The Christian Church*, pp. 46 ff, 60–72.

5. Ibid.

6. J. Mindszenty, *Memoirs*, trans. R. and C. Winston (London, 1974).

7. R. F. Leslie et al. (eds), *The History of Poland since 1863* (Cambridge, 1980), p. 330.

8. Quoted in A. Brassloff, *Religion and Politics in Spain. The Spanish Church in Transition, 1962–1996* (London, 1998), p. 6.

9. J. Hooper, *The New Spaniards* (London, 1995), p. 129.

10. Brassloff, *Religion and Politics in Spain*, pp. 6–24.

11. Ibid.

12. M. Vincent, 'Spain', in T. Buchanan and M. Conway (eds), *Political Catholicism in Europe, 1918–1965* (Oxford, 1996), pp. 97–128.

13. R. E. M. Irving, *The Christian Democratic Parties of Western Europe* (London, 1979).

14. Ibid., pp. xviii–xix and *passim*.

15. M. Conway, *Catholic Politics in Europe, 1918–1945* (London, 1997), p. 97. See also the introduction in S. Berger (ed.), *Religion in West European Politics* (London, 1982), pp. 1–7.

16. Quoted in D. Samuel, *Pope or Gospel? The Crisis of Faith in the Protestant Churches* (London, 1982), pp. 79–80.

17. T. Buchanan, 'Great Britain', in Buchanan and Conway (eds), *Political Catholicism in Europe*, pp. 248–74.

18. Quoted in T. G. McCarthy, *The Catholic Tradition. Before and After Vatican II, 1878–1993* (Chicago, 1994), p. 15.

19. T. Rausch, *Catholicism at the Dawn of the Third Milennium* (Kansas, 1995), p. 279.

20. L. de Vaucelles, 'The Changing Social Contexts of Postconciliar Catholicism', in G. Alberigo et al. (eds), *The Reception of Vatican II* (Washington, DC, 1987), p. 44.

21. See his 'Towards a Fundamental Theological Interpretation of Vatican Council II', *Theological Studies*, 40 (1979), 716–27.

22. See W. M. Abbott, *The Documents of Vatican II* (London, 1966).

23. E. Duffy, *Saints and Sinners. A History of the Popes* (Yale, 1997), p. 275.

24. J. O'Malley, *Tradition and Transition. Historical Perspectives on Vatican II* (Willmington, 1989), p. 17.

25. Quoted in W. Smith, 'The Church', in S. Perry (ed.), *Aspects of Contemporary France* (London, 1997), p. 159.

26. Quoted in the *Guardian*, 26 February 2002.

27. P. Hebblethwaite, 'Paul VI', in A. Hastings (ed.), *Modern Catholicism. Vatican II and After* (London, 1991), p. 48.

28. J. Cornwell, *Thief in the Night. The Death of John Paul I* (London, 1990). See too D. Yallop, *In God's Name* (London, 1984).

29. Y. Lambert, *Dieu change en Bretagne* (Paris, 1985).

30. Quoted in Hooper, *The New Spaniards*, p. 135.

31. J. Steinberg, *Why Switzerland?* (Cambridge, 1995), pp. 223–4.

32. J. Cornwell, *Breaking Faith. The Pope, the People and the Fate of Catholicism* (London, 2001), p. 157.

33. Ibid.

34. See M. Sevregand, *La Mort en toute lettre* (Paris, 1995) and her *Les Enfants du bon dieu* (Paris, 1995)

35. Quoted in M. Hornsby-Smith, *Roman Catholic Beliefs in England. Customary Catholicism and Transformations of Religious Authority* (Cambridge, 1991), p. 170.

36. Ibid., p. 175.

37. D. Cozzens, *The Changing Face of the Priesthood. A Reflection on the Priest's Crisis of Soul* (Collegeville, 2000).

38. See J. Cornwell, *Powers of Darkness. Powers of Light. Travels in Search of the Miraculous and the Demonic* (London, 1991), pp. 125–45.

39. K. Dobbelaere, *Secularisation. A Multi-Dimensional Concept* (London, 1981).

40. See the papers in *Theological Studies*, 39 (1978) and the article in the *National Catholic Reporter*, 31 July 1998, for a sense of the controversy over the encyclical.

41. Quoted in Cornwell, *Breaking Faith*, p. 1.

42. Quoted in the *Guardian*, 25 March 2002.

43. John Paul II, *Crossing the Threshold of Hope* (London, 1994).

44. H. Küng, *The Catholic Church. A Short History* (London, 2001), p. 206.

45. P. Hebblethwaite, *Introducing John Paul II. The Populist Pope* (London, 1982).

7. Conclusion

1. H. Küng, *The Catholic Church. A Short History* (London, 2001), p. 4.

2. Ibid.

3. C. G. Brown, *The Death of Christian Britain. Understanding Secularisation, 1800–2000* (London, 2001).

4. R. Rémond, *Religion and Society in Modern Europe* (Oxford, 1999).

5. G. Orwell, *Hommage to Catalonia* (London, 1989 Penguin), p. 49.

6. P. Guignet, 'Pour une thématique de la predication populaire. Observations sur quelques sermonnaires de cures du Cambrésis au début du XIXème siècle', in Y.-M. Hilaire, *La Religion populaire. Aspects du christianisme populaire* (Lille, 1981), pp. 81–109.

Bibliographical Essay

The following is intended as an introductory guide, privileging books and articles in English, though works in other languages have been cited where these are the best available. We have also tried to give some indication where the author is *parti-pris*, something which is not uncommon in religious history.

General Histories

There is no single volume covering the history of Catholicism from the eighteenth century to the present, one of the reasons for writing this particular book. Perhaps the closest is R. Rémond, *Religion and Society in Modern Europe* (Oxford, 1999), although this suffers from being Francocentric and adopts an overly thematic approach which hampers any real grasp of events. H. McLeod, *Religion and the People of Western Europe, 1789–1970* (Oxford, 1981) is also impressionistic, but is extremely clear in the presentation of the key subjects. A brilliant conspectus is offered in H. Küng, *The Catholic Church. A Short History* (London, 2001), though it should be noted that the coverage of the modern period is necessarily brief and not surprisingly, given the author's treatment at the hands of the Vatican, the tone is polemical. A further single volume is J. McManners (ed.), *The Oxford Illustrated History of Christianity* (Oxford, 1990) which has particularly good coverage of the non-European world but, as the title suggests, Catholicism is only one aspect of the coverage. Also partial in its scope is G. Davis and D. Hervieu-Léger, *Identités religieuses en Europe* (Paris, 1996).

There are, however, as befits the breadth of the topic, several multi-volume histories of Catholicism. One older work but still useful on institutions is that of A. Fliche and V. Martin, *Histoire de l'Eglise depuis les origines jusqu'à nos jours*, 26 vols (Paris, 1946–64); vols 18–21 is especially pertinent. Another mammoth undertaking is the ten-volume *History of the Church* (London, 1965–81) edited by H. Jedin and J. Dolan, originally published in German, of which the last six volumes are relevant here. This has not translated terribly well and the intricacies of theological debate in particular are not always easy to follow, but it is a mine of information and insights. K. V. Latourette, *A History of the Expansion of Christianity*, 7 vols (New York, 1970–71), is useful albeit lightweight at times. Now beginning to show signs of age is the Pelican History of the Church, of which volumes 5 to 7 by G. R. Cragg, *The Church and the Age of Reason, 1648–1789* (London, 1960), A. R. Vidler, *The Church in an Age of Revolution, 1789 to the Present Day* (London, 1961) and S. Neill, *Christian Missions* (London,

1964/1984) are especially useful. Also long in the tooth is H. Daniel-Rops, *The History of the Church of Christ* (London, 1964–65), vols 7–9, which is also polemical and Francocentric. In French, there are the outstanding volumes edited by J.-M. Mayeur, C. Pietri, A. Vauchez and M. Venard, *Histoire générale du christianisme des origines à nos jours* (Paris, 1990–), vols 10 to 12 of which cover our period; we still await the concluding section on the contemporary world. We should not forget the *New Catholic Encyclopaedia* (New York, 1967) and E. A. Livingstone (ed.), *Oxford Dictionary of the Christian Church* (Oxford, 1997), both of which contain invaluable entries on specific aspects. R. Aubert (ed.), *Dictionnaire d'histoire et de géographie ecclésiastique* (Paris, 1912–), of which 28 volumes have appeared (covering the letters A–J), is outstanding.

While single volumes tackling the whole of the period are thin on the ground, shorter eras are better served. A good overview of the Catholic world of the old regime is provided in W. J. Callahan and D. Higgs (eds), *Church and Society in Catholic Europe of the Eighteenth Century* (Cambridge, 1979), drawing together essays on individual countries, and which was invaluable for the writing of the present volume. J. Delumeau, *Catholicism between Luther and Voltaire* (London, 1977) is helpful for background, and his approach has informed much subsequent historiography. The excellent W. R. Ward, *Christianity during the Old Regime* (Cambridge, 1999) is principally concerned with Protestantism, while R. Po-Chia Hsia, *The World of Catholic Renewal, 1540–1770* (Cambridge, 1998) is the best overview of the Catholic faith after the Reformation. This latter text may be usefully supplemented by R. Bireley, *The Refashioning of Catholicism, 1450–1700* (Basingstoke, 1999), L. Châtellier, *Europe of the Devout* (Cambridge, 1989) and F. Heyer, *The Catholic Church from 1648 to 1870* (London, 1969). Though the latter is marred by some factual errors, it has the virtue of brevity.

The revolutionary period is best approached through O. Chadwick, *The Popes and European Revolution* (Oxford, 1981) which is broader than its title suggests. E. E. Y. Hales, *Revolution and the Papacy, 1769–1846* (London, 1960) is still worth consulting, although the emphasis is very much on the Napoleonic period, as is S. K. Latourette, *Christianity in a Revolutionary Age*, 5 vols (New York, 1971). All these, especially Chadwick, provide coverage of the early part of the Restoration period. D. Laven and L. Riall (eds), *Napoleon's Legacy. Problems of Government in Restoration Europe* (Oxford, 2000) has some useful treatment of religious matters, as does R. D. Gildea's brilliant overview of the nineteenth century, *Barricades and Borders. Europe 1800–1914* (Oxford, 1987). H. McLeod (ed.), *European Religion in the Age of Great Cities, 1830–1930* (London, 1995) provides further coverage of the century, albeit from a particular standpoint, as does M. Schmidt and G. Schwaiger, *Kirchen und Liberalismus im XIX Jahrhundert* (Göttingen, 1976). Another title, whose scope is wider than might be imagined, is O. Chadwick, *A History of the Popes, 1830–1914* (Oxford, 1998).

On the twentieth century, by far the best study of politics, and once again an invaluable source for this particular work, is T. Buchanan and M. Conway (eds), *Political Catholicism in Europe, 1918–1965* (Oxford, 1996) which can be usefully supplemented by M. Conway, *Catholic Politics in Europe, 1918–1945* (London, 1997) and S. Berger (ed.), *Religion in West European Politics* (London, 1982). Another study broader than its title suggests is J.-M. Mayeur, *Des partis catholiques à la démocratie chrétienne* (Paris, 1980). A. Hastings has edited an outstanding collection of essays on the post-1945 period, *Modern Catholicism. Vatican II and After* (London, 1981). O. Chadwick, *The Christian Church in the Cold War* (London, 1992) completes the Pelican History of the Church (vol. 8), while T. G. McCarthy, *The Catholic Tradition. Before and after Vatican II, 1878–1993* (Chicago, 1994) is a helpful introduction to some of the key themes, with the emphasis on the later period. Inevitably, there are a mass of studies on contemporary Catholicism, among which may be cited J. F. Eagan, *Restoration and Renewal. The Church in the Third Millennium* (Kansas, 1995), T. P. Rausch, *Catholicism at the Dawn of the Third Millennium* (Minnesota, 1996) and R. P. McBrien, *Report on the Church. Catholicism after Vatican II* (New York, 1992). H. Mol (ed.), *Western Religion. A Country by Country Sociological Enquiry* (The Hague, 1972) contains a mass of factual information, although some of this now needs updating.

The Papacy

There is no shortage of histories of the papacy, many of which offer more general insights into the Church. Standing out from the crowd is E. Duffy, *Saints and Sinners. A History of the Popes* (Yale, 1997), which deals with complex topics with great learning and a lightness of touch. Also valuable are F. Coppa, *The Modern Papacy since 1789* (London, 2000) and A. D. Wright, *The Early Modern Papacy. From the Council of Trent to the French Revolution, 1564–1789* (London, 2000), the first volumes to appear so far in the Longman History of the Papacy; P. Prodi, *The Papal Prince: One Body and Two Souls. The Papal Monarchy in Early Modern Europe* (Cambridge, 1987); E. E. Y. Hales, *Revolution and Papacy* (Notre Dame, 1966); J. D. Holmes, *The Triumph of the Holy See. A Short History of the Papacy in the Nineteenth Century* (London, 1978), and his *The Papacy in the Modern World, 1914–1978* (London, 1986); and Y.-M. Hilaire (ed.), *Histoire de la papauté. 2000 ans de mission et de tribulations* (Paris, 1996). The two best reference works are J. N. D. Kelly, *The Oxford Dictionary of the Popes* (Oxford, 1986), now superseded by P. Levillain, *Dictionnaire historique de la papauté* (Paris, 1994). The standard work on the papacy, particularly helpful for details of pontiffs who have not generated biographical studies, is the multi-volume L. von Pastor, *The History of the Popes from the Late Middle Ages*, 40 vols (Nendeln, Kraus reprint, 1968–69).

On the eighteenth-century papacy generally, a good starting point is H. Gross, *Rome in the Age of Enlightenment. The Post-Tridentine Syndrome and the Ancien Régime* (Cambridge, 1990). There are a number of inferior biographies of eighteenth-century popes which compare badly with J. Leflon, *Pie VII. Les abbayes bénédictines et la papauté* (Paris, 1958) and M. M. O'Dwyer, *The Papacy in the Age of Napoleon and the Restoration. Pius VII, 1800–1823* (New York, 1985). It is understandable why so little is written about the brief reign of Pius VIII, but it is odd that Gregory XVI is still awaiting a good biography, as are Leo XII and Benedict XIV. Pius IX has inevitably attracted a good deal of attention. Among the most rewarding studies, we may cite E. E. Y. Hales, *Pio Nono. A Study in European Politics and Religion in the Nineteenth Century* (London, 1954), F. J. Coppa, *Pope Pius IX. Crusader in a Secular Age* (Boston, 1979) and the three-volume work by G. Martina, *Pio Nono* (Rome, 1974–90). Leo XIII is another pope awaiting a good biography, yet some insights are provided in L. P. Wallace, *Leo XIII and the Rise of Socialism* (Durham, NC, 1966) and the tome edited by E. T. Gargan, *Leo XIII and the Modern World* (New York, 1961). Pius X has attracted the usual hagiographers, perhaps the best study being G. Romanato, *Pio X. La Vita di pape Sarto* (Milan, 1992). Thanks to his involvement in the First World War, Benedict XV has received ample attention in the form of H. E. G. Rope, *Benedict XV. The Pope of Peace* (London, 1941), W. H. Peters, *The Life of Benedict XV* (Milwaukee, 1959) and most recently J. F. Pollard, *The Unknown Pope. Benedict XV (1914–1922) and the Pursuit of Peace* (London, 1999).

A. Rhodes, *The Vatican in the Age of the Dictators, 1922–1945* (London, 1973) constitutes an introduction to the controversial reigns of Pius XI and Pius XII, as does C. Falconi's less than reverential *The Popes in the Twentieth Century* (London, 1967). See, too, the important essays in P. C. Pollard and J. F. Kent (eds), *Papal Diplomacy in the Modern Age* (Westport, 1994). Pius XI is best approached through M. Agostino, *Le Pape Pie XI et l'opinion publique* (Rome, 1990); P. Hughes, *Pope Pius XI* (London, 1937) remains useful, despite its age and laudatory tone. A whole library of biographies could be put together for Pius XII, but useful starting points include J. Cornwell's splendid *Hitler's Pope. The Secret History of Pius XII* (London, 1999), S. Zuccotti's unforgiving *Under his Very Windows. The Vatican and the Holocaust in Italy* (Yale, 2001), C. Falconi's scathing *The Silence of Pius XII* (London, 1970) and J. M. Sánchez's judicious *Pius XII and the Holocaust* (Washington, 2001). O. Chadwick, 'Weizsäcker, the Vatican and the Jews of Rome', *Journal of Ecclesiastical History*, 28 (1977), 179–99, deals with the German occupation of the Holy City. A defence of Pius XII is mounted by R. J. Rychlak, *Hitler, the War and the Pope* (Huntingdon, 2000). J. Chélini, *L'Eglise sous Pie XII. La Tourmente, 1939–1945* (Paris, 1983) is also worth consulting, as is G. Miccoli, *I Dilemmi e I Silenzi di Pio XII* (Milan, 2000). M. F. Feldkamp, *Pius XII und Deutschland* (Göttingen, 2000) plays down the role of the Vatican in the collapse of the Centre Party. John XXIII has likewise been the subject of numerous scholarly studies. Notable are those by P. Hebblethwaite, *John XXIII. Pope of the Council* (London, 1984), E. E. Y. Hales, *Pope John and his Revolution* (London, 1965) and B. R. Bonno, *Pope John XXIII. An Astute Pastoral Leader* (New York, 1979). Hebblethwaite again has written the best study of John's successor, *Paul VI. The First Modern Pope* (London, 1993), and the same author has written on *The Year of the Three Popes* (London, 1978). J. Cornwell, *Thief in the Night. The Death of John Paul I* (London, 1990) is the most balanced account of his death. Conspiracy theorists can turn to D. Yallop, *In God's Name* (London, 1984) and G. Thomas and M. Morgan-Witts, *Pontiff* (London, 1983), not to mention the film *Godfather III*!

As befits one of the most influential popes of the twentieth century, John Paul II has received extensive coverage. See, in particular, M. Walsh, *John Paul II. A Biography* (London, 1994), J. M. McDermott (ed.), *The Thought of John Paul II. A Collection of Essays and Studies* (Rome, 1993), T. Szulc, *Pope John II* (New York, 1995), D. Willey, *God's Politician. John Paul II at the Vatican* (London, 1992), P. Hebblethwaite, *In the Vatican* (Oxford, 1987), together with his earlier *Introducing John Paul II. The Populist Pope* (London, 1982) and G. Blazynski, *John Paul II. A Man from Kraków* (London, 1979). B. Hoose (ed.), *Authority in the Roman Catholic Church. Theory and Practice* (Aldershot, 2002) looks not just at the papacy but at the exercise of authority more generally, both in the past and in a contemporary setting.

Individual Countries

FRANCE   Among individual countries, it is France that has been most studied, reflecting its significance as the birthplace of modern religious sociology, although strikingly some key studies are in English. G. Cholvy and Y.-M. Hilaire provide a conspectus in the three-volume *Histoire religieuse de la France contemporaine* (Toulouse, 1985–88), A. Dansette does something similar in his, *A Religious History of Modern France*, 2 vols (London, 1961), and many socio-religious approaches are embraced in F. Lebrun (ed.), *Histoire des catholiques en France du XVe siècle à nos jours* (Toulouse, 1980) and J. Le Goff and R. Rémond, *Histoire de la France religieuse* (Paris, 1988–92). A. Latreille, *Histoire du catholicisme en France*, 3 vols (Paris, 1957), is now beginning to show signs of age. F. Tallett and N. Atkin (eds), *Religion, Society and Politics in France since 1789* (London, 1991) displays something of the concerns of Anglophone historians, as does their *Catholicism in Britain and France since 1789* (London, 1996). K. Chadwick (ed.), *Catholicism, Politics and Society in Twentieth-Century France* (Liverpool, 2000) is a similar collection, albeit featuring French contributions.

On the pre-1789 period, see J. McManners, *Church and Society in Eighteenth-Century France*, 2 vols (Oxford, 1998); his *French Ecclesiastical Society under the Ancien Regime. A Study of Angers in the Eighteenth Century* (Manchester, 1960); J. Quéniart, *Les hommes, l'église et Dieu dans la France du XVIIIe siècle* (Paris, 1978); T. Tackett, *Priest and Parish in Eighteenth-Century France. A Social and Political Study of the Curés in a Diocese of Dauphiné, 1750–1791* (Princeton, 1977); L. Châtellier, *Tradition chrétien et renouveau catholique dans le cadre de l'ancien dicocèse de Strasbourg, 1650–1770* (Paris, 1981); P. T. Hoffman, *Church and Community in the Diocese of Lyon, 1500–1789* (New Haven, 1984); and D. Van Kley, *The Religious Origins of the French Revolution. From Calvin to the Civil Constitution, 1560–1791* (New Haven, 1996). The series of diocesan histories published by Beauchesne, which are especially good for the early modern period, unfortunately seems to have died a death.

Still useful for the revolutionary years is P. de la Gorce, *Histoire religieuse de la révolution française*, 5 vols (Paris, 1902–23), and A. Latreille, *L'église catholique et la révolution française*, 2 vols (Paris, 1946–50). More accessible introductions may be found in J. McManners, *The French Revolution and the Church* (London,

1969) and N. Aston, *Religion and Revolution in France, 1780–1804* (Basingstoke, 2000). The definitive study on the clerical oath is T. Tackett, *Religion, Revolution and Regional Culture in Eighteenth-Century France. The Ecclesiastical Oath of 1791* (Princeton, 1986). Dechristianisation is tackled in M. Vovelle, *The Revolution against the Church. From Reason to the Supreme Being* (Oxford, 1991) and S. Desan, *Reclaiming the Sacred. Lay Religion and Popular Politics in Revolutionary France* (Cornell, 1990). For Napoleon, there is no single treatment of religious policy, but this is broached in E. E. Y. Hales, *Napoleon and the Pope* (London, 1962).

The nineteenth century is brilliantly covered in R. Gibson, *A Social History of French Catholicism, 1789–1914* (London, 1989), while C. S. Phillips, *The Church in France, 1848–1907* (London, 1936) considers the political side. For an outstanding local study, see G. Cholvy, *Religion et société au XIXe siècle. Le diocèse de Montpellier* (Lille, 1973). T. Zeldin (ed.), *Conflicts in French Society* (London, 1970) is good on the Second Empire, whereas the Third Republic is brilliantly assessed in J. McManners, *Church and State in France, 1870–1914* (London, 1972), M. Larkin, *Church and State after the Dreyfus Affair. The Separation Issue in France* (London, 1974), his *Religion, Politics and Preferment in France since 1890. La Belle Epoque and its Legacy* (Cambridge, 1995), and J.- M. Mayeur, *La Séparation de l'église et de l'état* (Paris, 1991). A. Ben-Amos, *Funerals, Politics and Memory in Modern France, 1789–1996* (Oxford, 2000) is good on the construction of the nation and what this meant for the Church. There is but one key study on the First World War, J. Fontana, *Les Catholiques français pendant la grande guerre* (Paris, 1990).

The interwar years are tackled by H. W. Paul, *The Second Ralliement* (Washington, 1967) which describes the upturn in Church–state relations, while R. Rémond, *Les Catholiques, le communisme et les crises* (Paris, 1960) describes the dilemmas posed by the 1930s. A. Dansette, *Le Destin du catholicisme français* (Paris, 1957) is an uneven account of the mid-century. W. D. Halls, *Politics, Society and Christianity in Vichy France* (Oxford, 1995) is by far the best entry into the murky world of the Occupation, although this may be read alongside R. Bédarida, *La vie quotidienne des catholiques sous Vichy* (Paris, 1999), J. Duquesne, *Les Catholiques français sous l'occupation* (Paris, 1986) and M. Cointet, *L'Église sous Vichy* (Paris, 1998). W. Bosworth, *Catholicism and Crisis in Modern France. French Catholic Groups at the Threshold of the Fifth Republic* (Princeton, 1962) has stood the test of time. A more recent interpretation is provided by J.-M. Donegani, *La Liberté de choisir. Pluralisme religieux et pluralisme politique dans le catholicisme français contemporain* (Paris, 1993) and D. Hervieu-Léger, *Vers un nouveau christianisme?* (Paris, 1986). See, too, the synoptic essay by M. Larkin in M. S. Alexander (ed.), *French History since Napoleon* (London, 1999). See also the *Dictionnaire du monde religieux dans la France contemporaine* (Paris, 1992)

SPAIN AND PORTUGAL   An introductory overview of Spain, that other great bastion of Catholic sentiment, is provided in S. G. Payne, *Spanish Catholicism. An Historical Review* (Madison, 1984), which begins its journey in the Middle Ages. There is much to be gleaned on the eighteenth century from A. Domínguez Ortiz, *La sociedad español en el siglo XVIII* (Madrid, 1955) and his *Sociedad en el siglo XVIII español* (Madrid, 1976), and in W. J. Callahan, 'The

Spanish Church', in Higgs and Callahan (eds), *Church and Society*, cited above. C. C. Noël, 'The Clerical Confrontation with the Enlightenment in Spain', in *European Studies Review*, 5 (1975), 103–22, is good on reform and the Bourbon monarchy. The nineteenth and twentieth centuries are more comprehensively tackled in W. J. Callahan's two superb volumes, *Church, Politics and Society in Spain, 1750–1874* (Cambridge, MA, 1984) and *The Catholic Church in Spain, 1875–1998* (Washington, 2000) and in F. Lannon, *Privilege, Persecution and Prophecy. The Catholic Church in Spain, 1875–1975* (Oxford, 1987). The reaction of the Church to the revolution is well set out in W. J. Callahan, 'The Origins of the Conservative Church in Spain, 1793–1823', in *European Studies Review*, 10 (1980), 199–233, and this theme is carried on in N. Rosenblatt, 'Church and State in Spain. A Study of Moderate-Liberal Politics in 1845', *Catholic Historical Review*, 62 (1976), 589–603. In Spanish, outstanding works are those by J. Andrés-Gallego, *Pensamiento y acción social de la Iglesia en España* (Madrid, 1984), which tackles the social side, and his two-volume *La Iglesia en la España contemporánea, 1800–1999* (Madrid, 1999), co-authored with A. M. Pazos. V. Cárcel Ortí, *Historia de la Iglesia de Valencia*, 2 vols (Valencia, 1986), compares well with the classic French diocesan studies. On the twentieth century, see A. Vidal Baraquer, *Iglesia y Estato durante la Segunda Republica española, 1913–1936*, 2 vols (Montserrat, 1971). A splendid introduction to Spain's first experimentation with dictatorship is S. Ben-Ami, *Fascism from Above. The Dictatorship of Primo de Rivera, 1920–1930* (Oxford, 1983). On the Second Republic, the key work in English is M. Vincent, *Catholicism in the Second Spanish Republic. Religion and Politics in Salamanca, 1930–1936* (Oxford, 1996) which provides a superb analysis of the province of Salamanca. She has also contributed a good introductory chapter in Buchanan and Conway (eds), *Political Catholicism*, already cited. G. Hermet, *Los católicos en la España franquista*, 2 vols (Madrid, 1985), covers the years when the Spanish Church was cut off from European influences. A superb chapter on Catholicism after Franco may be found in J. Hooper, *The New Spaniards* (London, 1995). Yet the key study is A. Brassloff, *Religion and Politics in Spain: The Spanish Church in Transition, 1962–1986* (London, 1998).

Works on Portugal, in English, are hardly overflowing, and the chapter in Buchanan and Conway (eds), *Political Catholicism*, by Tom Gallagher is the best entry point. His *Portugal. A Twentieth Century Interpretation* (Manchester, 1983) is also worth consulting. F. de Almeida, *Historia da Igreja en Portugal*, 4 vols (Porto-Lisbon, 1970), is the standard work in Portuguese. For the republican assault on the Church, see D. L. Wheeler, *Republican Portugal. A Political History, 1910–1926* (London, 1978).

ITALY   In English, the principal study on Italy is A.-C. Jemolo, *Church and State in Italy, 1850–1950* (Oxford, 1960) which deals briefly with material covered in greater depth in his works in Italian, although much general information may also be gleaned from M. Clark, *Modern Italy, 1871–1982* (London, 1983), P. Ginsborg, *A History of Contemporary Italy. Society and Politics, 1943–1988* (London, 1988) and C. Seton-Watson, *Italy from Liberalism to Fascism* (London, 1967). The standard works on the Church are in Italian, and even then they are thin on the ground. These include G. de Rosa, *Il movimento cattolico in Italia. Dalla restaurazione all'età Giolittana* (Rome, 1970). Among the many general works on unification, see L. Riall, *The Italian Risorgimento. State, Society and National Unification* (London, 1994). For events in the late 1860s, see N. Blakiston, *The Roman Question* (London, 1962). On the twentieth century, J. Pollard, *The Vatican and Italian Fascism, 1929–1932* (Oxford, 1985) tackles the signing of the Lateran Accords while M. E. De Franciscis, *Italy and the Vatican. The 1984 Concordat between Church and State* (New York, 1989) updates the story. R. A. Webster, *The Cross and the Fasces. Christian Democracy and Fascism in Italy* (Stanford, 1960) explores the uncomfortable relationship between Italian Catholics and Mussolini's regime, as do the essays by John Pollard in M. Blinkhorn (ed.), *Fascists and Conservatives. The Radical Right and the Establishment in Twentieth-Century Europe* (London, 1990) and L. Rope and R. Samuel (eds), *Disciplines of Faith. Studies in Religion, Politics and Patriarchy* (London, 1987). It is further worth consulting the contributions in R. J. Wolff and J. K. J. Hoensch (eds), *Catholics, the State and the European Radical Right, 1919–1945* (Boulder, 1987). A concise introduction to the post-war years is provided in G. Poggi, 'The Church in Italian Politics, 1945–1950', in S. J. Woolf (ed.), *The Rebirth of Italy, 1943–1950* (London, 1972). Recent squabbles in Italy's religious history are examined in D. Kertzer, *Comrades and Christians. Religion and Political Struggle in Communist Italy* (Cambridge, 1980), J. M. Molony, *The Emergence of Political Catholicism in Italy* (London, 1977) and R. Leonardi and R. Wertman, *Christian Democracy in Italy. The Politics of Dominance* (Basingstoke, 1989).

AUSTRIA AND EASTERN EUROPE The mass of material on the Church in Austria contained in general studies compensates to some degree for the absence of an anglophone study of the topic. See especially R. A. Kann, *A History of the Habsburg Empire, 1526–1918* (Berkeley, 1974), C. A. Macartney, *The Habsburg Empire, 1780–1918* (London, 1969). In German, see A. Wandruska and P. Urbanitsch, *Die Konfessionen. Die Habsburgermonarchie*, 4 vols (Vienna, 1985), J. Wodka, *Kirche in Österreich* (Vienna, 1959), and E. Weinzierl (ed.), *Kirche in Österreich, 1918–1965*, 2 vols (Vienna, 1965). P. Vrankić, *Religion und Politik in Bosnien und der Herzegovina, 1878–1918* (Paderborn, 1998) deals with Church–state relations, but is heavy going. Josephinianism is neatly discussed in T. C. W. Blanning, *Joseph II* (London, 1994), E. Wangermann, *The Austrian Achievement, 1700–1800* (London, 1973) and P. G. M. Dickson, 'Joseph II's Reshaping of the Austrian Church', *Historical Journal*, 36 (1993), 89–114; the nineteenth century is well covered in vols 8 and 9 of Jedin, *History of the Church*; A. Diamant, *Austrian Catholics and the First Republic* (Princeton, 1960) discusses the post-war years; the chapter by E. Weinzierl in Wolff and Hoensch (eds), *Catholics, the State and the European Radical Right*, considers the Dollfuss episode; while R. Luza, 'Nazi Control of the Austrian Catholic Church, 1939–1941', *Catholic Historical Review*, 63 (1977), 537–72, examines the post-*Anschluss* period. The chapter in Mol (ed.), *Western Religion*, now in need of updating, still repays visiting.

The available literature in English on Eastern Europe more generally is limited and of uneven quality, the emphasis naturally lying with the post-1945 persecution of religion. On Lithuania, see M. Bourdeaux, *Land of Crosses* (Chulmleigh, 1979) and V. Stanley Vardys, *The Catholic Church, Dissent and Nationality in Soviet Lithuania* (New York, 1978); on Yugoslavia, see S. Alexander, *Church and State in Yugoslavia since 1945* (Cambridge, 1979) and his 'Religion and National Identity in Yugoslavia', in S. Mews (ed.), *Studies in Church History* (Oxford, 1982), pp. 591–607 which contains a lot of basic factual information, while R. Patee, *The Case of Cardinal Stepinac* (Milwaukee, 1953) is useful on the unfortunate prelate; on Czechoslovakia, see L. Nemec, *Church and State in Czechoslovakia* (New York, 1955); on Hungary, see E. Andras and J. Movel, *Church in Transition. Hungary's Catholic Church from 1945 to 1962* (Vienna, 1983) and L. Laszlo, 'Fighting Evil with Weapons of the Spirit. The Christian Churches in Wartime Hungary', *Hungarian Studies Review*, 10 (1983), 125–44; on Estonia see V. Salo, 'The Catholic Church in Estonia, 1918–2001', *Catholic Historical Review*, 88 (2002), 281–92; and, for the region as a whole, see B. R. Bociurkiw and J. W. Strong (eds), *Religion and Atheism in Eastern Europe* (London, 1975) and the essay by K. Gabriel and F.-X. Kaufman in T. M. Gannon (ed.), *World Catholicism in Transition* (New York, 1988). Chadwick, *The Christian Church in the Cold War*, is especially strong on Eastern Europe, while H. Stehle, *Eastern Politics of the Vatican, 1917–1979* (Athens, OH, 1981) tackles the phenomenon of papal *Ostpolitik*. On the persecution of earlier years, see Y. Jelinek, *The Parish Republic. Hlinka's Slovak People's Party, 1939–1945* (New York, 1976) and J. R. Felak, *'At the Price of the Republic.' Hlinka's Slovak People's Party, 1929–1938* (Pittsburgh, 1994). There are very useful essays on Croatia, Hungary and Slovakia in Hoensch and Wolff (eds), *Catholics, the State and the European Radical Right*, cited earlier.

POLAND   The standard work in English by N. Davies, *God's Playground. A History of Poland*, 2 vols (London, 1981), is a helpful entry point, though the sections on religion are not the strongest elements of the book. R. F. Leslie et al. (eds), *The History of Poland since 1863* (Cambridge, 1980) is also worth consulting. Easily the most useful summary is J. Kloczowski, *A History of Polish Christianity*, 2 vols (Cambridge, 2000). This may be supplemented with G. Castellan, *'Dieu garde la Pologne!' Histoire du catholicisme polonais, 1795–1980* (Paris, 1981). J. Kalik, 'Attitudes towards the Jews and Catholic Identity in Eighteenth-Century Poland', in M. Crăciun, O. Ghitta and G. Murdoch (eds), *Confessional Identity in East-Central Europe* (Aldershot, 2002), pp. 181–93, deals with the impact of Enlightenment ideas. On the late nineteenth century, see most importantly L. Trzeciakowski, *The Kulturkampf in Prussian Poland* (New York, 1990). On the inter-war years, A. Polonksy, *Politics in Independent Poland, 1921–1939* (Oxford, 1932) is helpful on religion, as is N. Pease, 'The "Unpardonable Insult". The Wavel Incident of 1937 and Church–State Relations in Poland', *Catholic Historical Review* 77 (1991), 422–36. On the breakdown of communism, see A. Kemp-Welch (ed.), *The Birth of Solidarity* (Basingstoke, 1991); R. Boyes and J. Moody, *The Priest Who Had to Die. The Tragedy of Father Jerzy Popieluszko* (London, 1986) and M. Pomian-Srzednicki, *Religious Change in Contemporary Poland. Secularisation and Politics* (London, 1982).

RUSSIA AND THE SOVIET UNION Being a minority, Catholics do not figure prominently in studies on Russia and there is no standard study of them in either the Tsarist or Soviet period. Individuals and groups, notably the Jesuits, have received some journal treatment, and there is a good synthesis in English by C. L. Zugger, *The Forgotten. Catholics of the Soviet Empire from Lenin through Stalin* (New York, 2001). Valuable information may also be found in all of the following: G. T. Hosking, *Church, Nation and State in Russia and Ukraine* (London, 1991), primarily concerned with the Orthodox; P. Ramet (ed.), *Eastern Christianity and Politics in the Twentieth Century* (Durham, NC, 1988); M. Spinka, *The Church in Soviet Russia* (New York, 1956); I. Wlasovsky, *Outline of the History of the Ukrainian Church* (New York, 1956); M. Bourdeaux, *Religious Minorities in the Soviet Union* (London, 1984); and T. Beeson, *Discretion and Valour. Religious Conditions in Russia and Eastern Europe* (London, 1982).

GERMANY In contrast to Russia, there is a glut of literature on Catholicism in the Germanys, although this inevitably concentrates on the *Kulturkampf* and the Nazi persecution of the Churches. A good starting point is T. Nipperdey, *Deutsche Geschichte, 1806–1918*, 2 vols (Munich, 1983–90), which deals with both Protestants and Catholics. Jedin's *History of the Church* also constitutes a good introduction, as the focus throughout is almost always on Germany. An excellent review of the more general literature is provided in M. L. Anderson, 'Piety and Politics: Recent Work on German Catholicism', *Journal of Modern History*, 63 (1991), 681–716. Church and state also figure in M. Raeff, *The Well-Ordered Police State. Social and Institutional Change through Law in the Germanys and Russia, 1600–1800* (New Haven, 1983) and in J. Sperber's wide-ranging analysis, *Popular Catholicism in Nineteenth Century Germany* (Princeton, 1984). There is some comparative material in D. Mangenest and W. Merle (eds), *France-Allemagne. Eglises et Société du Concile Vatican II à nos jours* (Paris, 1988).

Among the mass of literature on the *Kulturkampf*, see M. L. Anderson, *Windthorst. A Political Biography* (Oxford, 1981); his 'The Kulturkampf and the Course of German History', *Central European History*, 19 (1986), 82–115; D. Blackbourn, 'Progress and Piety. Liberals, Catholics and the State in Bismarck's Germany', and his 'Catholics and Politics in Imperial Germany: The Centre Party and its Constituency', both in D. Blackbourn (ed.), *Populists and Patricians. Essays in Modern German History* (London, 1987); M. Lambertini, 'State, Church and the Politics of School Reform during the Kulturkampf', *Central European History*, 19 (1986), 63–81; and H. Walser Smith, *German Nationalism and Religious Conflict. Culture, Ideology, Politics, 1870–1914* (Princeton, 1995). Perhaps the best summary is R. J. Ross, *The Failure of Bismarck's Kulturkampf. Catholicism and State Power in Imperial Germany, 1871–1887* (Washington, 1998), together with his article in the *Journal of Modern History*, 56 (1984), 456–82.

To understand the Catholic subculture which developed during the late nineteenth century, see the useful collection in O. Blaschke and F.-M. Kuhlemann (eds), *Religion in Kaiserreich. Milieu, Mentalitäten, Krisen* (Gütersloh, 1996), together with the penetrating analysis provided in H. McLeod, 'Building the Catholic Ghetto. Catholic Organisations, 1870–1914', *Studies in Church History*,

23 (1986), 411–44, Sperber, *Popular Catholicism* cited above, his 'Roman Catholic Religious Identity in Rhineland-Westphalia, 1800–1870', *Social History*, 7 (1982), 305–18 and, most recently, E. Yonke, 'The Problem of the Middle Class in German Catholic History. The Nineteenth-Century Rhineland Revisited', *Catholic Historical Review*, 88 (2002), 263–80. On Catholic politics in Imperial Germany, see D. Blackbourn, *Class, Religion and Local Politics in Wilhelmine Germany: The Centre Party in Württemberg before 1914* (London, 1980) which should be read alongside E. L. Evans, *The German Centre Party, 1870–1933* (Carbondale and Edwardsville, 1981) and R. J. Ross, *Beleaguered Tower. The Dilemma of Political Catholicism in Wilhelmine Germany* (Notre Dame, 1976). See, too, M. L. Anderson, 'The Limits of Secularisation. On the Problem of the Catholic Revival in Nineteenth-Century Germany', *Historical Journal*, 38 (1993), 647–70 and the helpful essays in R. J. Evans (ed.), *Society and Politics in Wilhelmine Germany* (London, 1978).

Among the very few studies on religion during the 1914–18 crisis, see A. J. Hoover, *God, Germany and Britain in the Great War. A Study in Clerical Nationalism* (New York, 1989), although Protestants dominate. On the Second World War, it is difficult to know when to stop. J. S. Conway, *The Nazi Persecution of the Churches, 1933–45* (London, 1968) is now slightly dated in parts. See also G. Lewy, *The Catholic Church and Nazi Germany* (London, 1964), although this is not indulgent of the Church. See too E. C. Helmreich, *The German Churches under Hitler. Background, Struggle and Epilogue* (Detroit, 1979), R. P. Ericksen (ed.), *German Churches and the Holocaust* (Minneapolis, 1999), P. Matheson (ed.), *The Third Reich and the Christian Churches* (Edinburgh, 1981), K. Scholder, *The Churches and the Third Reich*, 2 vols (London, 1987–88), N. Stoltzfus, *Resistance of the Heart. Intermarriage and the Rosenstrasse Protest in Nazi Germany* (London, 1996), and G. C. Zahn, *German Catholics and Hitler's War. A Study in Social Control* (South Bend, 1989). S. R. Haynes, 'Who Needs Enemies? Jews and Judaism in Anti-Nazi Religious Discourse', *Church History. Studies in Christianity and Culture*, 71 (2002), 341–67 is a recent useful offering on attitudes towards Jews and has useful bibliographical pointers to works in English.

Religion in West Germany is handled in F. Spotts, *The Churches and Politics in Germany* (Middletown, 1977) while R. W. Solberg looks over the Berlin Wall in *God and Caesar in East Germany* (New York, 1961). The survival of Catholicism in the GDR is covered in W. Tischner, *Katholische Kirche in der SBZ/DDR, 1945–51* (Paderborn, 2001).

SWITZERLAND Accounts of the religious divide in the land of Calvin may be briefly summarised: J. Steinberg, *Why Switzerland?* (Cambridge, 1995); R. Pfister, *Kirchengeschichte der Schweiz*, 3 vols (Zurich, 1984); and P. Stadlerr, *Der Kulturkampf in der Schweiz* (Frauenfeld, 1984).

THE NETHERLANDS Thanks to the mobilising capacity of Catholics in the Low Countries, there is a mass of interpretative literature which is best approached after reading the contextual history by E. H. Kossmann, *The Low*

Countries, 1780–1940 (Oxford, 1978). Various aspects of Dutch Catholicism are discussed in A. Lijphart, *The Politics of Accommodation. Pluralism and Democracy in the Netherlands* (Berkeley, 1968), H. Bakvis, *Catholic Power in the Netherlands* (Kingston, 1981), P. Brachin and L. J. Rogier, *Histoire du Catholicisme Hollandais depuis le XVIème siècle* (Paris, 1974), H. Post, *Pillarisation. An Analysis of Dutch and Belgian Society* (Gower, 1989), M. Wintle, *Pillars of Piety: Religion in the Netherlands in the Nineteenth Century, 1813–1901* (Hull, 1987), and J. A. Coleman, *The Evolution of Dutch Catholicism, 1958–1974* (Berkeley, 1978).

BELGIUM   On Belgium see R. Obert, *150 ans de vie des églises* (Brussels, 1980), C. Stikwerda, *A House Divided. Catholics, Socialists and Flemish Nationalists in Nineteenth Century Belgium* (Lanham, 1997), L. Voyé, J. Rémy and J. Billiet (eds), *La Belgique et ses dieux. Eglises, mouvements religieux et laïques* (Louvain-la-Neuve, 1985) and the many things by Martin Conway, including 'Building the Christian City: Catholics and Politics in Interwar Francophone Belgium', *Past and Present*, 127 (1990), 117–51 and his *Collaboration in Belgium. Léon Degrelle and the Rexist Movement* (Newhaven, 1993). On pillarisation in both Belgium and the Netherlands see especially the works of K. Dobbelaere, conveniently listed in R. Laermans, B. Wilson and J. Billiet (eds), *Secularisation and Social Integration. Papers in Honour of Karel Dobbelaere* (Leuven, 1998), pp. 321–38, notably his 'Secularisation, Pillarisation, Religious Involvement and Religious Change in the Low Countries', in Gannon, *World Catholicism in Transition*, pp. 80–115 and M. Thung et al., 'Dutch Pillarisation on the Move? Political Destabilisation and Religious Change', in S. Berger (ed.), *Religion in West European Politics* (London, 1982), pp. 127–48.

GREAT BRITAIN   Surprisingly, there is no single-volume coverage of the period other than E. R. Norman, *Roman Catholicism in England from the Elizabethan Settlement to the Second Vatican Council* (Oxford, 1985). A conspectus may be built up by reference to the following: J. Bossy, *The English Catholic Community, 1570–1850* (London, 1975), D. Mathew, *Catholicism in England* (London, 1948), G. A. Beck (ed.), *The English Catholics, 1850–1950* (London, 1950), and the other important work by E. R. Norman, *The English Catholic Church in the Nineteenth Century* (Oxford, 1984). Both O. Chadwick, *The Victorian Church*, 2 vols (London, 1972) and A. Hastings, *A History of English Christianity, 1920–1990* (London, 1990) have much to say about Catholicism. L. Colley, *Britons. Forging the Nation* (London, 1994) has some interesting ideas on religious identity.

On the arguments and aftermath of Catholic emancipation, see J. Wolffe, *The Protestant Crusade in Great Britain, 1829–1860* (Oxford, 1991), W. Hinde, *Catholic Emancipation. A Shake to Men's Minds* (Oxford, 1992) and D. Quinn, *Patronage and Piety. The Politics of English Roman Catholicism, 1850–1900* (Basingstoke, 1993), and R. W. Linker, 'The English Roman Catholics and Emancipation. The Politics of Persuasion', *Journal of Ecclesiastical History*, 27 (1976), 151–80. On early British resentment towards Catholicism see E. R. Norman, *Anti-Catholicism in Victorian England* (London, 1968), F. H. Wallis, *Popular Anti-Catholicism in Mid-Victorian Britain* (Lewiston, 1993), W. L. Arnstein, *Protestant versus Catholic in*

Mid-Victorian England (Columbia, 1982) and D. G. Paz, *Popular Anti-Catholicism in Mid-Victorian England* (Stanford, 1992). On the Irish influence on English Catholicism, see D. A. Kerr, *Peel, Priests and Politics. Robert Peel's Administration in Ireland, 1841–46* (Oxford, 1982), J. Cumming and P. Burns (eds), *The Church Now. An Enquiry into the Present State of the Church in Britain and Ireland* (Dublin, 1980), S. Fielding, *Class and Ethnicity. Irish Catholics in England, 1880–1939* (Buckingham, 1993) and R. Swift and S. Gilley (eds), *The Irish in the Victorian City* (London, 1985). Local studies on Catholic communities include J. Hickey, *Urban Catholics. Urban Catholicism in England and Wales from 1829 to the Present Day* (London, 1967), T. Gallagher, *Glasgow, the Uneasy Peace: Religious Tension in Modern Scotland* (Manchester, 1987), M. Hornsby-Smith, *Roman Catholics in England. Studies in Social Structure since the Second World War* (Oxford, 1987). On the nature of Catholic practice, see M. Heimann, *Catholic Devotion in Victorian England* (Oxford, 1995) and M. Hornsby-Smith, *Roman Catholic Beliefs in England. Customary Catholicism and Transformations of Religious Authority* (Cambridge, 1991). On intellectual life and especially the impact of the Oxford Movement, see D. J. Holmes, *More Roman than Rome. English Catholicism in the Nineteenth Century* (London, 1978). For the impact of traditionalist ideas, see J. P. Corrin, *G. K. Chesterton and H. Belloc. The Battle against Modernity* (Athens, OH, 1981) and R. Griffiths, *Fellow Travellers of the Right* (Oxford, 1983). The experience of the Second World War is best approached through T. Molloney, *Westminster, Whitehall and the Vatican. The Role of Cardinal Hinsley, 1939–43* (London, 1985). O. Chadwick, *Britain and the Vatican in the Second World War* (Cambridge, 1986) considers the diplomacy of the period. The recent life of British Catholics is touched upon in C. G. Brown, *The Death of Christian Britain. Understanding Secularisation, 1800–2000* (London, 2001) and G. Davie, *Religion in Britain since 1945. Believing without Belonging* (Oxford, 1994).

IRELAND   The best overview is to be found in D. Hempton, *Religion and Political Culture in Britain and Ireland. From the Glorious Revolution to the Decline of Empire* (Cambridge, 1996) which usefully reviews the historiography. This has largely superseded S. Connolly, *Religion and Society in Nineteenth-Century Ireland* (Dundalk, 1985). Also worth consulting are E. R. Norman, *The Catholic Church and Ireland in the Age of Rebellion, 1859–1873* (London, 1965), E. Larkin, *The Roman Catholic Church and the Home Rule Question in Ireland, 1870–1874* (Dublin, 1990), his *Historical Dimensions of Irish Catholicism* (New York, 1976), D. Miller, *Church, State and Nation in Ireland, 1898–1921* (Dublin, 1973), D. Keenan, *The Catholic Church in Nineteenth-Century Ireland. A Sociological Study* (Dublin, 1983) which deals mainly with Dublin, J. M. Whyte, *Church and State in Modern Ireland, 1923–1979* (Dublin, 1980) and J. O'Shea, *Priests, Politics and Society in Post-Famine Ireland. A Study of County Tipperary, 1850–1891* (Dublin, 1983). S. J. Brown and D. W. Miller (eds), *Piety and Power in Ireland, 1760–1960. Essays in Honour of Emmet Larkin* (Belfast, 2000) has some very fine pieces, notably the introduction which discusses the concept of a devotional revolution and the chapter by Miller on levels of attendance at mass.

On Northern Ireland in particular, see M. Elliott, *The Catholics of Ulster*

(London, 2000), O. P. Rafferty, *Catholicism in Ulster, 1603–1983* (London, 1994), J. H. Whyte, *Interpreting Northern Ireland* (Oxford, 1990), F. O'Connor, *In Search of a State. Catholics in Northern Ireland* (Belfast, 1993) and M. Irvine, *Northern Ireland. Faith and Faction* (London, 1991).

Themes

CLERGY   There is no single study of the secular clergy in this period, and such material as exists is local or national in scope and restricted in its chronological treatment. Much has been written about the contemporary crisis in the priesthood, notably D. Rice, *Shattered Vows. Exodus from the Priesthood* (London, 1990), while the numbers of priests may be monitored by recourse to the *Statistical Yearbook of the Church* (Rome, 1971–).

Many of the general books cited on the religious history of the period contain insights and information on the seculars. Chadwick, *The Popes and European Revolution* and his *A History of the Popes, 1830–1914*, both cited above, contain useful material. O. L. Arnal, *Priests in Working-Class Blue. The History of the Worker-Priests, 1943–1954* (New York, 1986) takes a trans-national perspective. T. Schulte-Umburg, *Profession und Charisma. Herkunft und Ausbildung des Kleurus im Bistum Münster, 1776–1940* (Paderborn, 1999) is a heavyweight study of Münster, a bastion of Catholicism in northern Germany. W. D. Bowman, *Priest and Parish in Vienna, 1780–1880* (Leiden, 1999) is a solid, archivally-based study. It is France, though, that has been disproportionately investigated, and the approaches adopted by religious historians of this country would repay replication elsewhere. B. Plongeron, *La vie quotidenne du clergé français au XVIIIe siècle* (Paris, 1974) remains a useful starting point for France, now supplemented by T. Tackett, 'The Social History of the Diocesan Clergy in Eighteenth-Century France', in R. M. Golden (ed.), *Church, State and Society under the Bourbon Kings of France* (Lawrence, KS, 1982), his 'Ecclesiastical Structures and Clerical Geography on the Eve of the French Revolution', *French Historical Studies*, 11 (1980), 352–70, *Priest and Parish in Eighteenth-Century Century France* and his *Religion, Revolution and Regional Culture*. See also McManners, *Church and Society in Eighteenth-Century France* and N. Aston, *The End of an Elite. The French Bishops and the Coming of the Revolution, 1786–1790* (Oxford, 1992). On nineteenth-century France, a wonderful series of vignettes are presented in B. Singer, *Village Notables in Nineteenth-Century France. Priests, Mayors and Schoolmasters* (Albany, 1983). See also the magisterial P. Boutry, *Prêtres et paroisses au pays du curé d'Ars* (Paris, 1986) and P. Pierrard, *La Vie quotidienne du prêtre français au XIXe siècle, 1801–1905* (Paris, 1986) and J. Faury, *Cléricalisme et anticléricalisme dans le Tarn, 1848–1900* (Toulouse, 1980).

Literature on the regular clergy is also uneven. There exist numerous studies of individual orders, but these are of varying quality and are often hagiographical. On Britain, P. F. Anson, *The Religious Orders and Congregations of Great Britain and Ireland* (Worcester, 1949) is more or less a listing of foundations. The influx of French orders into Britain at the time of the Revolution is deftly handled in A. Bellanger, *The French Ecclesiastical Exiles in England, 1789–*

1815 (London, 1986). S. O'Brien, 'Lay Sisters and Good Mothers: Working-Class Women in English Convents, 1840–1910', in W. J. Shiels and D. Wood, (eds), *Studies in Church History*, (Oxford, 1990), pp. 453–65, and her *'Terra Incognita*. The Nun in Nineteenth-Century England', *Past and Present*, 121 (1988), 110–40 both provide an insight into the religious life. On their counterparts across the Irish Sea, C. Clear, *Nuns in Nineteenth-Century Ireland* (Dublin, 1988) is well worth consulting.

M. Libert, *Vie quotidienne des couvents féminins de Bruxelles au siècle des lumières, 1764–1787* (Brussels, 1999) draws conclusions from some limited examples which have a wider significance. L. Scaraffia and G. Zarri (eds), *Women and the Faith. Catholic Religious Life in Italy from Late Antiquity to the Present* (Cambridge, MA, 1999) includes essays on the regulars, as does G. Zarri, *Recinti. Donne, clausura e matrimonio nella prima età moderna* (Bologna, 2000).

As in the case of the seculars, most has been written on France and concentrates on the pre-1914 period. Much basic information can be gleaned from R. Aubert (ed.), *Dictionnaire d'histoire et de géographie ecclésiastique* (Paris, 1912–) and Abbé Migne, *Dictionnaire des ordres religieux*, 3 vols (Paris, 1947–48). J. Burnichon, *La Compagnie de Jésus en France. Histoire d'un siècle, 1814–1914*, 4 vols (Paris, 1914–22), remains the standard work on the Jesuits, with G. Cubitt, *The Jesuit Myth. Conspiracy Theory and Politics in Nineteenth Century France* (Oxford, 1993) providing insights into attitudes towards the order. Women's orders and congregations have been the focus of much attention as befits the most dynamic area of Catholic life. The fundamental work, though not easy-going, is C. Langlois, *Le Catholicisme au féminine. Les congrégations françaises à supérieure générale au XIX siècle* (Paris, 1984). More approachable are C. Jones, 'The Filles de la Charité in hospitals', *Actes du Colloque Internationale d'Etudes Vincentiennes, Paris, 25–26 September 1981* (Rome, 1983), his *The Charitable Imperative. Hospitals and Nursing in Ancien Regime and Revolutionary France* (London, 1989), O. Hufton and F. Tallett, 'Communities of Women, the Religious Life and Public Service in Eighteenth Century France', in M. J. Boxer and J. H. Quataert (eds), *Connecting Spheres. European Women in a Globalizing World, 1500 to the Present* (Oxford, 2000), pp. 93–103, and M. Vacher, *Des Regulières dans le siècle. Les soeurs de Saint Joseph du Père Médaille aux XVIIe et XVIIIe siècles* (Clermont Ferrand, 1991). There is a good deal on the nursing orders in P. Guillaume, *Médecins, église et foi, XIXe–XXe siècles* (Paris, 1990).

BELIEF AND PRACTICE Fundamental to an understanding of the long-term process of Christianisation in the West is J. Delumeau, *Catholicism between Luther and Voltaire* (Cambridge, 1977). E. Le Roy Ladurie, *Montaillou. Cathars and Catholics in a French Village, 1294–1324* (London, 1980) reveals the lack of basic religious knowledge in this Pyrenean village. The obvious starting point on practice are the statistical inquiries conducted at various times into the regularity of mass attendance and take-up of the rites of passage, many building on the suggestions of G. Le Bras, *Etudes de Sociologie Religieuse*, 2 vols (Paris, 1955–56), and F. Boulard, *An Introduction to Religious Sociology* (London, 1960). As ever, these are especially rich on France. See F. Boulard et al. (eds),

Matériaux pour l'histoire religieuse du peuple français, XIXe–XXe siècles (Paris, 1982–), F. Boulard and J. Rémy, *Pratique religieuse urbaine et régions culturelles* (Paris, 1968) and G. Cholvy and Y.-M. Hilaire, *Histoire religieuse de la France contemporaine*, 2 vols (Toulouse, 1985–86). Nobody has really replicated this thoroughgoing approach elsewhere, though we are well supplied with statistical information for the contemporary period, contained in general texts on individual polities and in Mol, *Western Religion*, already cited, while the results of the European Values Study are provided in S. Harding et al., *Contrasting Values in Western Europe* (London, 1986) and M. Abraham et al., *Values and Social Change in Britain* (London, 1985).

Useful insights, which range beyond mass attendance and which uncover the links between official and popular religion, include L. Châtellier, *The Religion of the Poor. Rural Missions in Europe and the Formation of Modern Catholicism, c. 1500–1800* (Cambridge, 1997), his *Europe of the Devout. The Catholic Reformation and the Formation of a New Society* (Cambridge, 1989); T. A. Kselman, *Death and the Afterlife in Modern France* (Princeton, 1993), his *Miracles and Prophecies in Nineteenth-Century France* (New Brunswick, 1983); and J. Devlin, *The Superstitious Mind. French Peasants and the Supernatural in the Nineteenth Century* (New Haven, 1987). See also Y. -M. Hilaire, *La Religion populaire. Aspects du christianisme populaire* (Lille, 1981). The activity of missioners is splendidly tackled in D. Gentilcore, '"Adapt Yourselves to the People's Capabilities". Missionary Strategies, Methods and Impact in the Kingdom of Naples, 1600–1800', *Journal of Ecclesiastical History*, 45 (1994), 269–96, and L. Perouas, *P. Fr. Hacquet. Mémoire des missions des Montfortains dans l'Ouest, 1740–1779* (Fontenay-le-Comte, 1964). Local studies often have much to say about practice. See especially R. A. Schneider, *The Ceremonial City. Toulouse Observed, 1738–1780* (Princeton, 1995), and the two books by W. A. Christian, *Moving Crucifixes in Modern Spain* (Princeton, 1992) and *Person and God in a Spanish Valley* (Cambridge, MA, 1972). The provocatively titled 'Was Spain Catholic?' by W. J. Callahan in *Revista Canadiense de Estudios Hispanicos* (1984), 159–82, pulls together the scanty information on religious practice and attitudes from the eighteenth century onwards. The ground-breaking study of religious attitudes, based upon the exploitation of Provençal wills, is M. Vovelle, *Piété baroque et déchristianisation en Provence, 1750–1820* (Paris, 1973). It has inspired a number of investigations, notably that of P. Chaunu, *La Mort à Paris, XVI, XVII et XVIII siècles* (Paris, 1978). S. K. Cohn, *Death and Property in Siena, 1205–1800. Strategies for the Afterlife* (Baltimore, 1988) does not fully confirm Vovelle's conclusions in an Italian context. For a good study of attitudes to the hereafter in an earlier period see C. Eire, *From Madrid to Purgatory. The Art and Craft of Dying in Sixteenth-Century Spain* (Cambridge, 1995). E. Larkin, 'The Devotional Revolution in Ireland, 1850–75', *American Historical Review*, 77 (1972), 625–52 is a key starting point for changes in Irish religious practice.

On particular aspects of devotion, Marianism is tackled in M. P. Carroll, *The Cult of the Virgin Mary. Psychological Origins* (Princeton, 1986), R. Masson, *La Salette ou les larmes de Marie* (Paris, 1992), M. Warner, *Alone of her Sex. The Myth and Cult of the Virgin Mary* (London, 1976) and H. Graef, *Mary. A History of Doctrine and Devotion* (London, 1994), although the latter is very dated. R. Jonas, *France and the Cult of the Sacred Heart. An Epic Tale for Modern Times* (Berkeley, 2000) links the cult of the Sacred Heart to the conservative political culture of France. C. Savart, 'A la recherche de l'art dit de Saint-Sulpice', *Revue d'Histoire de la Spiritualité*, 52 (1976), 265–83, analyses the art associated with the cult. Pilgrimages are brilliantly treated in P. Boutry and M. Cinquin, *Deux Pélerinages au XIX siècle. Ars et Paray-le-Monial* (Paris, 1980), D. Blackbourn, *Marpingen. Apparitions of the Virgin Mary in Bismarckian Germany* (Oxford, 1993), R. Harris, *Lourdes. Body and Spirit in the Secular Age* (London, 1999). The two latter authors have contributed useful essays to J. Devlin and R. Fanning (eds), *Religion and Rebellion* (Dublin, 1997), which also has interesting material on Ireland. B. Cousin, *Le Miracle et le quotidien. Les ex voto provençaux. Images d'une société* (Aix-en-Provence, 1983) is a penetrating study based on church architecture. On festivals, see B. Stambolis, *Religiönse Festkultur. Tradition und Neuformierung Katholische Frömmigkeit im 19. Und 20. Jahrhundert* (Paderborn, 2000). On saints, see G. T. W. Ahlgren, *Theresa of Avila and the Politics of Sanctity* (Ithaca, 1996) and M. Warner, *Joan of Arc* (London, 1984). Festivals are also dealt with by B. Plongeron, 'Le procès de la fête à la fin de l'ancien régime', in B. Plongeron and R. Parret, *Le Christianisme populaire. Les dossiers de l'histoire* (Paris, 1976) which also contains other essays on aspects of popular religion. On the sacrament of the confession, and concepts of the divine, see J. Delumeau, *Sin and Fear. The Emergence of a Western Guilt Culture* (New York, 1990), his edited collection, *Alphonse de Liguori, pasteur et docteur* (Paris, 1987), T. Rey-Mermet, *Le Saint du siècle des lumières. Alfonso de Liguori* (Paris, 1987) and R. Gibson, 'Hellfire and Damnation in Nineteenth-Century France', *Catholic Historical Review*, 74 (1988), 383–402. F. M. Jones, *Alphonsus de Liguori. The Saint of Bourbon Naples, 1696–1787* (Dublin, 1992) is also good on this key figure. M. Walsh (ed.), *A Dictionary of Devotions* (London, 1993) is helpful on Catholic observances.

On the gender dimension of religion, see B. G. Smith, *Ladies of the Leisure Class. The Bourgeoises of Northern France in the Nineteenth Century* (Princeton, 1981); the key article by O. Hufton, 'Women in Revolution, 1789–96', *Past and Present*, 53 (1971), 90–108, her 'The Reconstruction of a Church, 1796–1801', in G. Lewis and C. Lucas (eds), *Beyond the Terror. Essays in French Regional and Social History, 1794–1815* (Cambridge, 1983); S. Desan, *Reclaiming the Sacred. Lay Religion and Popular Politics in Revolutionary France* (Ithaca, 1990); C. Langlois, *Le Catholicisme au féminin. Les congrégations françaises à supérieure générale au XIXe siècle* (Paris, 1984); J. Delumeau, *La Religion de ma mère* (Paris, 1992); G. Duby and M. Perrot (eds), *A History of Women in the West*, 3 vols (Cambridge, MA, 1993); and L. Scarrafia and G. Zarri (eds), *Women and Faith* (Cambridge, MA, 1999). On the representation of women, see the important essays in C. W. Atkinson (eds), *Immaculate and Powerful. The Female in Sacred Image and Social Reality* (Boston, 1985). C. M. Prelinger, *Charity, Challenge and Change. Religious Dimensions of the Mid-Nineteenth Century Women's Movement* (New York, 1987) and S. Paletschek, *Frauen und Dissens. Frauen im Deutschkatholizismus und in den Freien Gemeinden* (Göttingen, 1990) both deal with Germany in the nineteenth century. A

European perspective is offered in C. Ford, 'Religion and Popular Culture in Modern Europe', *Journal of Modern History*, 65 (1993), 152–75. Something of women's religious attitudes is revealed in a study of their diaries in P. Lejeune, *Le Moi des demoiselles. Enquête sur le journal de jeune fille* (Paris, 1993). There is fascinating analysis of the advice proffered by a priest who acted as an agony aunt for a Catholic periodical in M. Sevregand, *La Mort en toute lettre* (Paris, 1995) and *Les enfants du Bon Dieu* (Paris, 1995). On bourgeois male religiosity, see P. Seeley, 'O Sainte Mère. Liberalism and the Socialisation of Catholic Men in Nineteenth-Century France', *Journal of Modern History*, 70 (1998), 862–92.

The process of secularisation is best approached through H. McLeod, *Secularisation in Western Europe, 1848–1914* (Basingstoke, 2000), while the sociological perspective is set out in E. K. Dobbelaere, *Secularisation. A Multi-Dimensional Concept* (London, 1981), S. Bruce (ed.), *Religion and Modernisation. Sociologists and Historians Debate the Secularisation Thesis* (Oxford, 1992), E. Barker et al. (eds), *Secularisation, Rationalism and Sectarianism. Essays in Honour of Bryan R. Wilson* (Oxford, 1993) and R. Laermans et al. (eds), *Secularisation and Social Integration. Papers in Honor of K. Dobbelaere* (Leuven, 1998). There are useful essays by K. Dobbelaere, M. Hornsby-Smith and C. Davies in B. Wilson (ed.), *Religion. Contemporary Issues. The All Souls Seminars in the Sociology of Religion* (London, 1992) touching on the theme of secularisation. Cultural change, which had a role to play in the process, is dealt with in C. Sowerwine, *France since 1870. Culture, Politics and Society* (Basingstoke, 2001) which privileges the place of gender, as does S. Weiner, *Enfants Terribles. Youth and Femininity in the Mass Media in France, 1945–1968* (Baltimore, 2001). An influential cultural analysis is K. Ross, *Fast Cars, Clean Bodies. Decolonisation and the Reordering of French Culture* (Cambridge, 1994). For Britain, see Brown, *The Death of Christian Britain*, cited above. A number of 'readings' from Durkheim, Weber and Marx, together with reprints of articles on the sociology of religion, are to be found in S. Bruce (ed.), *The Sociology of Religion*, Vol. 1 (Aldershot, 1995).

THE VATICAN COUNCILS On the first Vatican Council, the best starting point is C. Butler, *The Vatican Council* (London, 1962). A. B. Hasler, *How the Pope became Infallible. Pius IX and the Politics of Persuasion* (New York, 1981) is an unfavourable interpretation. See, too, the essays in A. Hastings (ed.), *Bishops and Writers* (Wheathampstead, 1977) for some perspective on Ultramontanism. There is much wider literature on the Second Vatican Council. Hastings (ed.), *Modern Catholicism*, already cited, is a good starting point on Vatican II although the essays are generally of a liberal Catholic standpoint. This may be usefully supplemented by R. Latourelle, *Vatican II. Assessments and Perspectives*, 3 vols (New York, 1988); A. Stacpoole (ed.), *Vatican II by Those Who were There* (London, 1986); T. M. Gannon, *World Catholicism in Transition* (New York, 1988), which has especially good essays on France, the Low Countries and Eastern Europe; G. Alberigo et al. (eds), *The Reception of Vatican II* (Washington, 1987), which deals thematically with the impact of the council; R. P. McBrien, *Report on the Church. Catholicism after Vatican II* (San Francisco, 1992), which chronicles an individual theologian's thoughts on the process of change; and the monumental study by G. Alberigo and J. A. Komanchak, *History of Vatican II* (Maryknoll and Leuven, 1995), the first five volumes of which have now appeared. J. F. Eagan, *Restoration and Renewal. The Church in the Third Millennium* (Kansas City, 1995) brings the story up to date.

THE WORLD OF IDEAS The best introduction to the eighteenth-century context is D. Outram, *The Enlightenment* (Cambridge, 1995), which possesses a very helpful list of further reading. Alongside the useful older scholarship, such as P. Gay, *The Enlightenment*, 2 vols (New York, 1973), P. Hazard, *The European Mind, 1680–1715* (Cleveland, 1963, first published in 1935), E. Cassirer, *The Philosophy of the Enlightenment* (Princeton, 1951) and N. Hampson, *The Enlightenment* (Harmondsworth, 1968), see more recent works which move the debate outside the narrowly defined history of ideas, including M. Jacob, *Living the Enlightenment. Freemasonry and Politics in Eighteenth-Century Europe* (Oxford, 1991), her *The Radical Enlightenment. Pantheists, Freemasons and Republicans* (London, 1981), R. Porter, *The Creation of the Modern World. The Untold Story of the British Enlightenment* (New York, 2000), J. G. A. Pocock, *Barbarism and Religion* (Cambridge, 1999), D. Gordon, *Citizens without Sovereignty. Equality and Sociability in French Thought, 1670–1789* (Princeton, 1994), D. Goodman, *The Republic of Letters. A Cultural History of the French Enlightenment* (New York, 1994) and R. Porter and M. Teich (eds), *The Enlightenment in National Context* (London, 1981). J. Israel's encyclopaedic *Radical Enlightenment. Philosophy and the Making of Modernity, 1650–1750* (Oxford, 2001) reorientates the Enlightenment both towards the seventeenth century and to the Low Countries and Bernard Spinoza in particular, but adopts a traditional 'men and ideas' approach. The Catholic response, first identified by R. R. Palmer, *Catholics and Unbelievers in Eighteenth-Century France* (Princeton, 1939) has been amplified in J. Byrne, *Glory, Jest and Riddle. Religious Thought in the Enlightenment* (London, 1996) and D. M. McMahon, *Enemies of the Enlightenment and the Making of Modernity* (Oxford, 2001) but could still do with further treatment. The Jansenist quarrel may be approached through the succinct offering by W. O. Doyle, *Jansenism* (Basingstoke, 2000) as well as D. Van Kley, *The Jansenists and the Expulsion of the Jesuits from France, 1757–1765* (New Haven, 1975) and his *The Religious Origins of the French Revolution. From Calvin to the Civil Constitution, 1560–1791* (New Haven, 1996). The origins of Ultramontanism are considered in B. Reardon, *Liberalism and Tradition. Aspects of Catholic Theology in Nineteenth-Century France* (Cambridge, 1975). A. R. Vidler, *Prophecy and Papacy. A Study of Lamennais, the Church and Revolution* (London, 1954) has stood the test of time. The intellectual assault on Catholicism is discussed in O. Chadwick, *The Secularisation of the European Mind in the Nineteenth Century* (Cambridge, 1975). In this regard, M. D. Biddiss, *The Age of the Masses* (London, 1979), H. Stuart Hughes, *Consciousness and Society* (London, 1964), J. W. Burrow, *The Crisis of Reason. European Thought, 1848–1914* (New Haven, 2000) and M. Bradbury and J. M. McFarlaine (eds), *Modernism, 1890–1930* (London, 1987) all handle the transformation in ideas. Catholic modernism has been recently treated in D. Jodock (ed.), *Catholicism Contending with Modernity. Roman Catholic Modernism and Anti-Modernism in Historical Context*

(Cambridge, 2000). B. M. G. Reardon, *Roman Catholic Modernism* (London, 1970), A. R. Vidler, *The Modernist Movement in the Roman Catholic Church* (London, 1934) and G. Daly, *Transcendence and Immanence. A Study of Catholic Modernism and Integralism* (Oxford, 1980) all repay visiting.

Catholic theological developments in the twentieth century are set out in Jedin, *History of the Church*, Vol. 10, and the many works on Vatican II already cited. See, too, A. Nichols, *The Shape of Catholic Theology* (Edinburgh, 1991), J. Gallagher, *Times Past. Time Future. An Historical Study of Catholic Moral Theology* (New York, 1990), T. P. Rausch, *The Roots of Catholic Tradition* (Wilmington, 1998) and A. Nichols, *From Newman to Congar. The Idea of Doctrinal Development from the Victorians to the Second Vatican Council* (Edinburgh, 1990). A good entry into the work of the hugely influential theologian Karl Rahner, the author of over 4,000 titles, is H. Vorgrimler, *Understanding Karl Rahner. An Introduction to his Life and Thought* (London, 1986). On the recent crises over liberal theologians, see H. Häring, *Hans Küng. Breaking Through: The Work and Legacy* (New York, 1998). M. Baigent and R. Leigh, *The Inquisition* (London, 2000) provides an extremely critical appraisal of how the Congregation of the Office for the Doctrine of the Faith has operated in recent years. The views of its head can be found in J. Ratzinger and V. Messori, *Ratzinger Report. An Exclusive Interview on the State of the Catholic Church* (San Francisco, 1985).

CATHOLICS, POLITICS AND THE 'SOCIAL QUESTION' There is no sustained analysis of Catholics and politics during this period. It is dealt with episodically in the literature cited earlier on individual countries. M. Conway, *Catholic Politics in Europe, 1918–1945* (London, 1997) picks up on themes dealt with in his collection edited with T. Buchanan, *Political Catholicism*, already cited, and contains an excellent bibliography. Some mention must be made of the allure of far-right politics, tackled in Wolff and Hoensch, *Catholics, the State and the European Radical Right*, mentioned above. O. Arnal, *Ambivalent Alliance. The Catholic Church and the Action Française, 1899–1939* (Pittsburgh, 1985), provides a national context. On Christian Democracy, the best starting point remains R. E. M. Irving, *The Christian Democratic Parties of Western Europe* (London, 1979) which amplifies his *Christian Democracy in France* (London, 1973), and is better than M. Fogarty, *Christian Democracy in Western Europe, 1820–1953* (London, 1957). There exist scores of histories on individual Christian Democratic parties and it would be otiose to list them all here, though N. D. Cary, *The Path to Christian Democracy. German Catholics and the Party System from Windthorst to Adenauer* (Cambridge, MA, 1996) is worth singling out, not least of all for the breadth of its approach.

A conspectus on Social Catholicism is P. Misner, *Social Catholicism in Europe. From the Onset of Industrialisation to the First World War* (New York, 1991). A. R. Vidler, *A Century of Social Catholicism* (London, 1964) is helpful in places, while P. Furlong and D. Curtis (eds), *The Church Faces the Modern World. Rerum Novarum and its Impact* (Hull, 1994) contains some uneven essays. On individual countries, P. Joye and R. Lewin, *L'Eglise et le mouvement ouvrier en Belgique* (Brussels, 1967) tackle the Low Countries, R. Rollet, *L'Action sociale des catholiques en France, 1871–1901*, 2 vols (Paris, 1958), remains fundamental, while G. Cholvy, *Histoire des organisations et mouvements chrétiens de jeunesse en France, XIX–XX siècles* (Paris, 1999) tackles the youth aspect of the problem. J. Andrés-Gallego, *Pensiamento y acción social de la Iglesia en España* (Madrid, 1984) and D. B. Gómez, *Democracia y Cristianismo en la España de la Restauración, 1875–1931* (Madrid, 1987) consider the Iberian peninsula. G. Rainer-Horn and E. Gerard (eds), *Left Catholicism, 1939–1955. Catholics and Society in Western Europe at the Point of Liberation* (Leuven, 2001) explores the alliance between the left and Social Catholics that existed at the moment of Liberation in 1945.

CATHOLICISM OVERSEAS   In addition to J. Spence, *The Memory Palace of Matteo Ricci* (New York, 1984), on relations with early modern China, an excellent entry into the influence of Catholicism outside of Europe may be found in McManners (ed.), *The Oxford Illustrated History of Christianity*, and Neill, *History of the Christian Missions*, both cited above.

Documents

For an introduction to unpublished sources, see O. Chadwick, *Catholicism and History. The Opening of the Vatican Archives* (Cambridge, 1978). Too many published sources exist to be listed here, yet certain collections do deserve mention, although these tend to present the institutional version of Catholicism. A. Freemantle (ed.), *The Papal Encyclicals in their Historical Context* (New York, 1956) is a helpful selection of the key texts in translation. The definitive guide is M. C. Carlen (ed.), *Papal Pronouncements. A Guide, 1740–1978* (Ann Arbor, 1990), which provides an abstract of every document. For the official listing of all papal pronouncements, and major statements from Vatican departments, see *Acta Apostolicae Sedis* (Rome, 1909–). Reardon, *Roman Catholic Modernism*, cited earlier, contains some useful texts from Loisy and other Modernists. On the Second World War, see P. Blet et al. (eds), *Actes et documents du Saint Siège relatif à la seconde guerre mondiale*, 11 vols (Vatican City, 1965–82). The text of three key concordats is contained in F. J. Coppa (ed.), *Controversial Concordats. The Vatican's Relations with Napoleon, Mussolini and Hitler* (Washington, 1999). The Second Vatican Council has produced a welter of materials. Most importantly, see A. Flannery (ed.), *Vatican Council II. The Conciliar and Post-Conciliar Documents* (New York, 1975) and his *Vatican Council II. More Post-Conciliar Documents* (New York, 1983). More compact is W. M. Abbott, *The Documents of Vatican II* (London, 1966). On the history of facts and figures, see the *Statistical Yearbook of the Church* (Rome, 1971–), while the publications of the European Values System constitute a useful insight into public perceptions and habits. Finally, the Catholic press, most obviously *L'Osservatore Romano* in Italy (which has an English-language weekly version), *La Croix* in France and the *Catholic Herald* and *The Tablet* in Britain provide a running commentary on Catholic life.

Index